Contemporary Cultural Anthropology

Fifth Edition

MICHAEL C. HOWARD

SIMON FRASER UNIVERSITY

HarperCollins*College*Publishers

Acquisitions Editor: Alan McClare
Developmental Editor: Philip Herbst
Project Coordination and Text Design: Thompson Steele Production Services
Cover Design: Linda Wade
Cover Photo: Kevin Shafer/Tony Stone
Photo Researcher: Carol Parden
Electronic Production Manager: Eric Jorgensen
Manufacturing Manager: Hilda Koparanian
Electronic Page Makeup: Interactive Composition Corporation
Printer and Binder: RR Donnelley & Sons Company
Cover Printer: New England Book Components
Insert Printer: The Lehigh Press, Inc.

For permission to use copyrighted material, grateful acknowledgment is made to the copyright holders on pp.551–554, which are hereby made part of this copyright page.

Front Cover: No society today is isolated from the modern world. These Huli children of Papua New Guinea are learning about the Polaroid camera.

Contemporary Cultural Anthropology, Fifth Edition

Library of Congress Cataloging-in-Publication Data

Howard, Michael C.
     Contemporary cultural anthropology / Michael C. Howard.–5th ed.
          p. cm.
     Includes bibliographical references and index.
     ISBN 0-673-52373-X
     1. Ethnology.   I. Title
GN316.H68   1995
306--dc20   95-21460
                                                                CIP

95 96 97 98 9 8 7 6 5 4 3 2 1

Contents

APPLIED ANTHROPOLOGY PORTFOLIO
The Changing Face of Irian Jaya

CHAPTER 7   < SOCIALIZATION >   140

CHAPTER 8   < KINSHIP AND DESCENT >   166

CHAPTER 9   < SEX, MARRIAGE, AND THE FAMILY >   190

CHAPTER 10   < ETHNICITY AND SOCIAL STRATIFICATION >   234

CHAPTER 11   < POLITICS AND POLITICAL ORGANIZATION >   264

CHAPTER 14   < ARTISTIC EXPRESSION >   334

FOCUS ON ANTHROPOLOGISTS ESSAYS

Since it was first published in 1983, *Contemporary Cultural Anthropology* has provided a large number of students with a comprehensive, coherent and readable introduction to cultural anthropology within a framework for understanding the evolving modern world system. Each new edition has sought to ensure that the material provided is as up-to-date as possible, reflecting changes in anthropology and within the world at large. This fifth edition contains a great deal of new material. The organization, format, some pedagogy, and much of the illustration program have also been modified to improve the overall presentation of the field of cultural anthropology to the student.

General Overview of the Text

Contemporary Cultural Anthropology explores the rich complexities of human life and culture with a focused treatment that effectively communicates the depth and breadth of the discipline of cultural anthropology. Moreover, the text strives throughout to illustrate the relevance of the perspective of cultural anthropology and the work of anthropologists in the modern world.

The text examines cultures from an ecological perspective that view humans as creative beings who seek to adapt to a multifaceted environment. Thus a dynamic ecology is presented that shows humans trying to overcome the problems they face in adapting to their ever-changing surroundings.

I have carefully chosen ethnographic examples from a wide range of cultures that effectively illustrate the points raised. A few peoples are also covered in more depth throughout the text to provide students with a more holistic view of culture.

Understanding the culture of any people today requires attention to how they fit into the modern world system. I have emphasized that all societies are part of an evolving world order and have examined the different ways and degrees to which they are incorporated. I have then sought to show how the nature of this integration influences various aspects of people's lives.

In keeping with the perspective that human culture is constantly evolving, the topics of change and acculturation are integrated throughout the text, rather than treated in a separate chapter. I have also sought to integrate the subject of gender broadly into the text, rather than isolating it in a separate chapter, in a way that shows how gender is interrelated with the various aspects of culture.

New to the Fifth Edition

Important content and organizational changes in the fifth edition include:

➤ An entirely new chapter on art which explores artistic expression in small-scale and large-scale societies and the globalization of artistic expression.

➤ Treatment of the history of anthropology and anthropological theories, which now includes a section on the comparative method, has been placed in an appendix rather than being treated as a separate chapter. The chapter on socialization now follows the chapter on society, introducing students to the basic process of becoming a part of society before the discussions of kinship and family.

➤ Among the new features in the Culture and Communication chapter is a section on communication and technology that examines this topic both historically and within the context of the modern world. I have also added to this chapter a discussion of issues surrounding the setting of language standards.

➤ The chapter on subsistence patterns presents extensive material on how the Mlabri foragers are adapting to the demands of the encroaching world system. A map showing the current distribution of foraging peoples in the world has also been added.

➤ Chapter 9, Sex, Marriage, and the Family, contains a substantial new section on homosexual behavior. There is also a much expanded section on prostitution that includes an extensive discussion about prostitution in Thailand today.

➤ Among the changes made in Chapter 10, Ethnicity and Social Stratification, is a new section on international tribes that looks at ethnic groups that operate globally within the world system. There is also a new section on ethnicity and religion.

➤ The Law and Conflict chapter includes a substantially revised discussion about revolutions.

➤ In Chapter 13, Religious Belief, Behavior, and Symbolism, I have expanded coverage of the role of religion in the modern world and added a new section on religion and the environmental movement.

➤ The final chapter, Anthropology and Modern World Development, has new sections on the impact of tourism and on sustainable development.

Overall the fifth edition places even greater emphasis on adaptation to the modern world system, contemporary human problems, and applied anthropology.

There have also been changes regarding the original Focus on Anthropologists essays:

➤ Throughout the book the essays have been integrated with chapter text to better illustrate concepts discussed within chapters.

➤ The most popular essays have been retained and revised. Hans Dagmar's essay on his work among the Rabi Islanders in particular has been substantially updated.

➤ There are three new essays. The first is Kinship, Land Rights, and Aboriginal Culture in Australia, by David Trigger in Chapter 8. The second is an essay in the new art chapter on my research among the carvers of Northern Irian Jaya. Finally, Otome Hutheesing has written an essay on AIDS among the Lisu of Northern Thailand for the chapter on illness and curing .

➤ In addition, the new color portfolio, placed near the beginning of the text as an extension and illustration of some of the important points of Chapter 1, treats applied anthropology in Irian Jaya. This portfolio draws attention to the important role of applied anthropology and provides current case study material concerning the adaptation of people to the modern world system.

Special Features

Contemporary Cultural Anthropology contains a number of special features to assist the student and instructor. These include:

➤ *Focus on Anthropologists* is a general title for 14 original essays, each offering a vivid account by a practicing anthropologist in a specific subfield. Since their inception in the first edition, these essays have proven extremely popular with students as a means of conveying to them a better understanding of the work of anthropologists.

➤ The Applied Anthropology Portfolio: *The Changing Face of Irian Jaya* includes an essay focusing on the work of the author in conjunction with Indonesian anthropologists, as well as a series of color plates relating to this work.

➤ Each chapter begins with a "What to Look for" list—a convenient preview of the chapter for students.

➤ At the end of each chapter there is a concise summary of the chapter contents and a glossary of *key terms*, another new feature, to help the student review chapter material. There is also a carefully selected list of *suggested readings*.

➤ *Key terms* also appear in boldface type in the text with definitions immediately following.

➤ A *bibliography* of works cited in the text provides the student with additional resources, many of which have been updated.

➤ Both a *name index* and a *subject index* are included.

➤ An *instructor's manual* has been prepared to accompany the text. It includes suggestions for using the text, annotated film suggestions, learning objectives, and individual and class projects for each chapter. A test bank in the manual provides over 700 test items: 40 to 50 multiple-choice questions and 5 to 10 essay questions for each chapter.

‹ ACKNOWLEDGMENTS ›

Once again, I would like to thank my wife, Linda, for her tolerance and my development editor, Phil Herbst, for his hard work and insights.

I am also grateful to the following reviewers who commented on various stages of the manuscript. They include:

Peter Aschoff, University of Mississippi; Bradley A. Blake, New Mexico State University-Las Cruces; Jan Bruckner, Indiana University School of Medicine; James Garber, Southwest Texas State University; Katie Goodell, Normandale Community College; Ronald S. Himes, San Diego State University; Ruth Krulfeld, George Washington University; Joan Laxson, Pine Manor College; Frances Risher, California State Polytechnic University; John A. Ross, Eastern Washington University; Richard Scaglion, University of Pittsburgh; Maria Lydia Spinelli, University of Massachusetts-Amherst.

Michael C. Howard

About the Author

Michael C. Howard received his A.B. degree in 1971 from the University of Southern California and his M.A. degree in 1973 from Memorial University in Newfoundland. Work for his M.A. included fieldwork with the Maya of southern Belize. He then moved to Perth, Western Australia, where he began research on urban-dwelling Aborigines and Aboriginal politics under the supervision of anthropologist Ronald Berndt. He was awarded his Ph.D. from the University of Western Australia in 1977.

Dr. Howard returned to the United States in 1976 to teach at California Polytechnic State University, where he began work on the first edition of *Contemporary Cultural Anthropology*. In 1978, Howard began teaching at the University of Houston. In addition to working on applied projects in the Houston area, he continued to pursue his research interests in Australia and also resumed work in Central America. He examined change taking place in Belize and became involved in debates surrounding U.S. involvement in Central America.

In 1981, Dr. Howard went to Fiji to teach at the University of the South Pacific. In Fiji, he became involved with a workers' education project for the South Pacific, undertaken by the International Labour Organisation; served as a consultant on worker participation at Fiji's international airport; and carried out research on a variety of political, economic, and labor-related topics in Fiji, Vanuatu, the Solomon Islands, Nauru, and Kiribati. He also developed a close relationship with the Transnational Corporations Research Project at the University of Sydney, conducted research in India on labor and transnational corporations, and began conducting research in the Philippines.

Howard's association with Fiji's labor movement took a dramatic turn in early 1987 when the head of the Fiji Labour Party, for whom Howard served as a personal advisor, became prime minister. Four weeks after the prime minister assumed office, the government was overthrown by a military coup, and a short time later, Howard, whose freedom in Fiji was at risk, left for Australia. There he took a teaching position at the University of New South Wales and lobbied on behalf of the overthrown government of Fiji.

Dr. Howard moved to Vancouver, British Columbia, in 1988. There he taught first at the University of British Columbia and then at Simon Fraser University, where he is currently a professor with the Department of Sociology and Anthropology. While maintaining his interest in the South Pacific, he has, since coming to Canada, increasingly focused his attention Southeast Asia. He has continued to work in the Philippines, but most of his work has been in Indonesia and Thailand, with his research focusing on mining, environmental issues, ethnic relations, and material culture. Through Simon Fraser University, he has also directed field schools for Canadian students in Thailand and worked with a Canadian aid project in eastern Indonesia.

In addition to *Contemporary Cultural Anthropology*, Michael C. Howard has written five other books and coauthored one. He has also edited five books and coedited four. Dr. Howard's other anthropology textbook, coauthored with Janet Dunaif-Hattis, is *Anthropology: Understanding Human Adaptation*, published by HarperCollins.

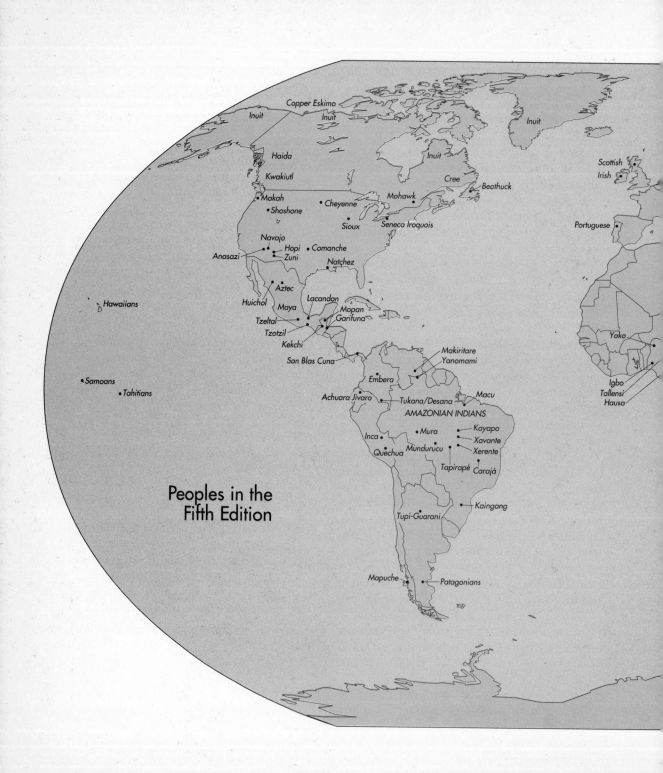

Copper Eskimo

Inuit

Inuit

Inuit

Inuit

Haida

Kwakiutl

Cree

Beothuck

Scottish
Irish

Makah
Shoshone

Cheyenne

Mohawk

Sioux

Seneca Iroquois

Portuguese

Navajo
Hopi
Zuni

Comanche

Anasazi

Natchez

Aztec

Huichol

Maya

Lacandon

Hawaiians

Tzeltal

Mopan
Garifuna

Yako

Tzotzil

Kekchi

San Blas Cuna

Makiritare
Yanomami

Igbo

Embera

Tallensi
Hausa

Samoans

Achuara Jivaro

Tahitians

Tukana/Desana

Macu

AMAZONIAN INDIANS

Inca

Mura

Kayapo

Xavante

Quechua

Mundurucu

Xerente

Tapirapé

Carajá

Tupi-Guarani

Kaingang

**Peoples in the
Fifth Edition**

Mapuche

Patagonians

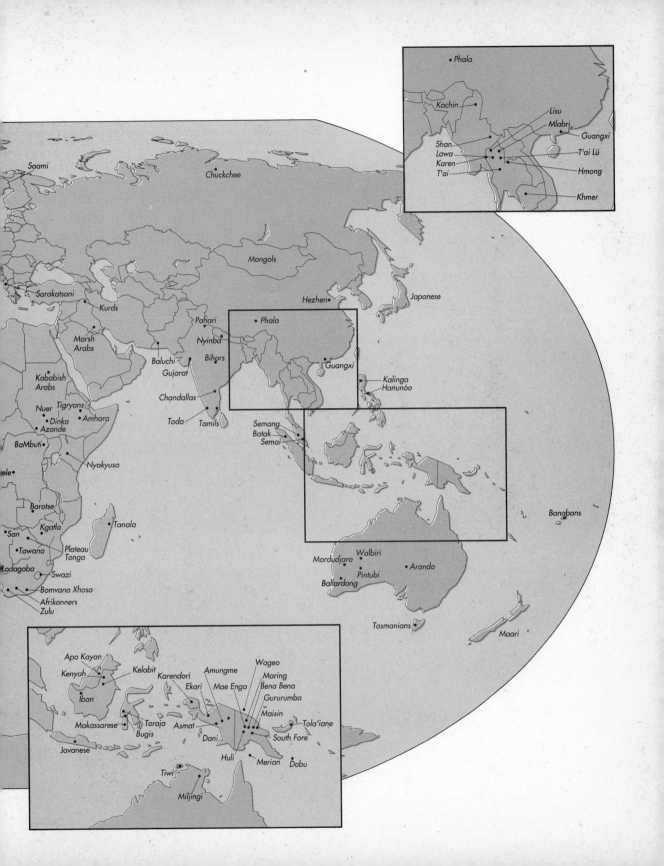

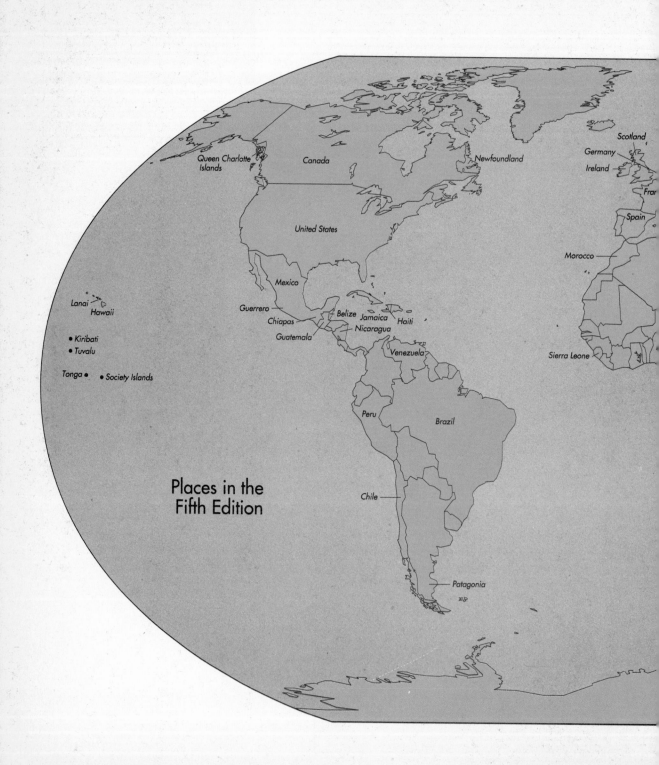

Places in the
Fifth Edition

Queen Charlotte
Islands

Canada

Newfoundland

Scotland

Germany

Ireland

Fran

Spain

United States

Morocco

Mexico

Lanai
Hawaii

Guerrero

Belize

Jamaica

Haiti

Chiapas

Nicaragua

Kiribati

Guatemala

Tuvalu

Venezuela

Sierra Leone

Tonga

Society Islands

Peru

Brazil

Chile

Patagonia

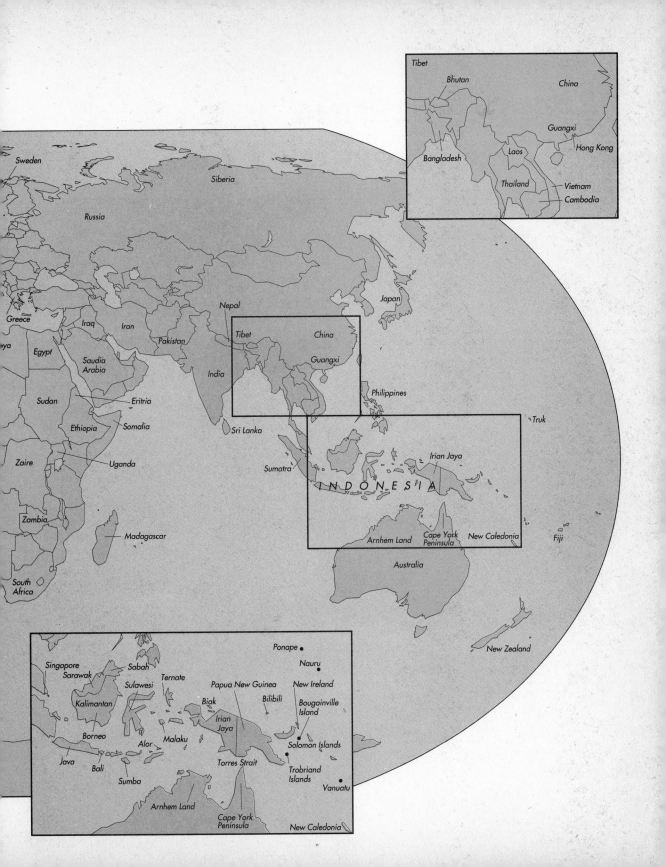

1 > INTRODUCING ANTHROPOLOGY

Humans are an incredibly diverse group of animals. We come in so many different colors, shapes, and sizes; speak so many mutually incomprehensible languages; exhibit so many distinct mannerisms; and hold so many contrary ideas

WHAT TO LOOK FOR

➤ The five main themes that unify the field of anthropology

➤ How an adaptive strategy serves humans to survive in their environment

➤ How ethnocentrism impedes our understanding of other cultures

➤ The general aims of the major subdivisions of anthropology—biological anthropology, archaeology, linguistic anthropology, and sociocultural anthropology

➤ How the insights of anthropology can be applied toward solving the human problems that arise as societies throughout the world become more interrelated (See also the Applied Anthropology Portfolio, "The Changing Face of Irian Jaya.")

that it is sometimes hard to believe that we are all part of the same species. Yet we are, in fact, unified by a common biological heritage; moreover, we do have a great deal in common with one another.

Anthropology, the scientific study of humanity, seeks to explain how and why people are both similar and different through examination of our biological and cultural past and comparative study of existing human societies. Anthropology's ultimate goal is to develop an integrated picture of humankind—a goal that encompasses an almost infinite number of questions about all aspects of our existence. We ask, for example: What makes us human? Why do some groups of people tend to be tall and lanky while others tend to be short and stocky? Why do some people practice agriculture while others forage, that is, hunt and gather food, for a living? Why do some societies abhor homosexual practices and forbid them whereas others accept or even encourage them in certain cir-

cumstances? Why do some religions believe in reincarnation of the spirit while others reject such beliefs as superstition? Anthropologists find all things human fascinating and worthy of study.

◄ ANTHROPOLOGICAL THEMES ►

Because of its broad scope, anthropology is divided into subdisciplines, each with its own set of specialists. In this text, we are primarily interested in those subdisciplines that study the cultural and social aspects of human existence—those aspects involving the shared ways people organize their social behavior and thought in relation to the environment (we will define *culture* and *society* more explicitly later in the chapter). However, all of anthropology is unified by certain overarching themes, including universalism, holism, integration, adaptation, and cultural relativism. These themes distinguish anthropolgy

〰〰〰〰〰

Many indigenous peoples today face the imminent disappearance of their way of life as Western industrial society spreads to their regions of the world. Some peoples have been violently forced into this new system; others have had more choice. This Yanomami girl of the Amazonian rain forest is flying to Caracas, Venezuela, to work as a wage-earning household maid.

from other fields that study human life, such as history, psychology, or sociology.

Universalism

A fundamental principle of modern anthropology is that of human **universalism:** all peoples are fully and equally human. Whether San, Navajo, Arab, or British royalty, we are all one species. No group of people is "closer to the ape," and none is more highly evolved than any other. Since we are all equally human, anthropologists are as interested in the BaMbuti (Pygmies) and Australian Aborigines as they are in people living in the industrial societies of North America and Western Europe. No human group is too small, too large, too remote, too ancient, or too unusual to merit an anthropologist's attention. *All* human beings—the living and the dead, the familiar and the exotic—are the subject of anthropological studies. All people tell us something important about the human condition, about what it means to survive by culture, a social inheritance, and still be a part of the animal kingdom. All people tell us something about the potentialities and limitations of the human species.

Holism

Economists study systems of production, exchange, and consumption. Political scientists study the bases of social order and conflict, and the distribution and dynamics of power and authority. Other scholars select other facets of human life for intensive study. Anthropologists, on the other hand, seek to comprehend *all* aspects of the human condition. In addition to gaining insight into a society's economy and political organization, anthropologists want to know about its religion, its rules of marriage and etiquette, its language, its technology, its art, its child-rearing practices, and its physical environment. They are also interested in a society's past as well as its present. This concept of **holism,** in which human existence is viewed as a multifaceted whole, also recognizes the biological as well as the cultural aspects of human existence. Thus, anthropologists are interested in the physical characteristics of peoples past and present. This multifaceted concern is based on the desire to understand the *whole* of the human condition.

Integration and the World System

Integration emphasizes how the various aspects of cultural life function together. It is not enough to study the politics, art, religion, kinship, or economics of, say, the Navajo. The anthropologist views these aspects of life as interwoven threads that form a social whole. They are also recognized as integral parts of the larger physical and social environment within which the Navajo live—the arid lands of the American Southwest and U.S. society. To fully comprehend any belief or practice, we must view it within the context of the society of which it is a part and within the context of the broad environmental factors shaping that society.

Many anthropological studies have focused on small, relatively isolated societies, such as those of the Australian Aborigines or the indigenous societies of South America's Amazon, where social integration is readily apparent. These **small-scale societies** are characterized by localized social interaction and localized exploitation of environmental resources. In these societies, kinship, politics, work, and other aspects of social life are all closely interrelated, and links to the environment are fairly direct. More than in the past, contemporary anthropology studies aspects of **large-scale societies,** which are much less localized in orientation and much more dependent on extensive and highly specialized interchanges of goods, ideas, and people. In such societies, social and environmental integration is less apparent and is different from integration in small-scale societies, but such integration exists nonetheless—an urban-dweller in Toronto or Paris, too, is an integral part of a larger social fabric and his or her life is greatly influenced by environmental considerations.

In recent years we have also become more aware of the extent to which all societies are an integrated part of a larger **world system:** a social and economic structure encompassing the entire world. Individual societies are interdependent, and their internal characteristics must be understood in relation to this broader global system, the underpinnings of which are to be found in international trade (see Shannon 1989: 20–21; Wallerstein 1979: 5). Thus, for example, in seeking to understand modern small-scale societies such as those found in New Guinea or the Amazon, it is not enough to study the local history and observe the local environment. These societies are also influenced by the global tourist industry, the global commodities market, international companies, telecommunications, and the strategic concerns of foreign powers— all of which are themselves parts of an integrated world system. The Yanomami girl of the Amazonian rain forest, seen in the photo at the

opening of the chapter going with a Venezuelan pilot to Caracas to work as a maid in a wage-earning household, represents one of the consequences of her people being incorporated into the world system.

The world system concept is used in many important ways in anthropology. For example, anthropologists are interested in how modern communications technology is integrating many formerly isolated societies into the wider world. They are interested in the effects on societies of industrialization attuned to the global market— changing values, undermining many traditional forms of social organization, and replacing old forms of work with new ones. Many village economies today are thoroughly integrated into a global economy that provides them with goods, establishes the prices of what they produce, and influences their economic goals and tastes. Local indigenous groups commonly seek international support in their struggle to improve their lives and many have linked themselves with similar peoples around the world

This Huli tribesman of Papua New Guinea hiked to nine thousand feet to help clear landing space for a helicopter bringing supplies to oil wells where no roads exist. The characteristics of societies such as this tribesman's must be understood in relation to the broader global system that encroaches on their ways of life.

through international organizations of indigenous peoples. The study of ethnicity also requires attention to the world system. Some ethnic groups, such as Jews and Anglo-Americans, have created extensive global networks that have served them in achieving prominence in world commerce. These and other ways in which modern cultures are part of the world system will be explored throughout the chapters that follow.

Adaptation

Humans, like other animals, are influenced by their surroundings, or **environment.** This includes the *physical environment*—the climate, rainfall patterns, terrain, and so forth; the *biotic environment*—all the plant and animal life in a given area; and the *social environment*—interaction with other members of our species. A coastal Californian's environment would include the beaches, the almost desertlike terrain and climate, the animals that have survived or thrived with human occupation, pockets of fog in some places, and the mixture of humanity that has been drawn to the region.

The study of the relationship between organisms and their physical, biotic, and social environments is called **ecology.** A major concern of anthropology, and one that strongly applies ecology, is the study of how humans and their environment are interrelated—the study of human adaptation. As a process, **adaptation** can be broadly defined as the means by which individuals or populations react to environmental conditions in order to maintain themselves and survive. The term also is used to refer to the end product of adaptation as a process—a particular behavior, social system, or physical structure. This is what is meant by *an* adaptation.

How an organism, species, or society is adapted to its environment reflects its **adaptive strategy:** the set of solutions consciously or unconsciously applied by members of a population to contend with basic environmental or biological problems (Dobzansky 1974). These problems include securing food, protecting themselves from the elements, and finding mates. Humans adopt certain adaptive strategies in exploiting their environment, relying primarily on three aspects of culture: technology, social organization, and values and beliefs. *Exploitation* in its most basic sense means to turn to economic account, or to utilize. It is common to think of exploitation in terms of minerals, plants, and animals. But other human beings—for example, laborers or slaves—may serve as resources within the environment as well.

Because of its concrete results, the role of *technology*—the skills and knowledge by which people make things or extract resources—constitutes the most obvious part of an adaptive strategy. The traditional adaptive strategy of the native peoples of the Arctic, for example, included an array of technical means for meeting their subsistence needs and for achieving a reasonable degree of comfort. They used spears, harpoons, hooks, and traps to catch and kill animals. To move across the sea and land, they built boats and sleds and made snowshoes. To protect themselves from the elements, they produced an array of clothes made from animal skins and built dwellings of ice and skins. All these activities required knowledge of local resources and technical skills passed down over the generations.

The ways people organize themselves socially are an equally important part of their adaptive strategy. A particularly significant social dimension of the adaptive strategy is the **division of labor**—the technical and social manner in which work is organized in a society. Australian Aboriginal foragers divided their labor primarily according to gender: Males hunted large animals and females gathered plants. In modern industrial societies, the division of labor is much more complex, involving highly specialized activities that reflect a very different adaptive strategy.

The third cultural component of an adaptive strategy is composed of a people's *values and be-*

Ethnocentrism may be a positive force in giving people a sense of well-being, as shown in the ethnic parade. Many times, however, ethnocentrism fosters bigotry and discrimination. In the photo on the right, Turkish migrants are protesting German destruction of a Turkish home in Germany.

liefs. To many hunters, being able to recite the correct prayers is as important in hunting as knowing how to set a trap or stalk an animal. How individuals interact with the environment is conditioned by their society's belief system and the values it promotes to guide actions. The religious beliefs of Australian Aborigines stress harmonious relations with the environment. Through myth and ritual, these beliefs link humans with their natural environment, space people across the landscape, and promote the well-being of plant and animal resources.

Human adaptation has its biological side as well. In fact, the biological and cultural aspects of our adaptation evolved together, so that humans truly have a *biocultural* adaptation, one that depends on closely tied biological and cultural means of contending with environmental pressures. Our unique biological history and physical makeup—especially the human brain—make possible the cultural aspects of our adaptive strategy. In turn, aspects of our contemporary cultural adaptations, such as medical care and agriculture, have influenced human biological evolution by relieving environmental stresses. Then too, environmental pollution and overcrowding have served to create biological stresses for the human species.

Cultural Relativism

In addition to its scientific goals, anthropology also seeks to promote understanding of people who are culturally different. The most important factor inhibiting the understanding of other people is **ethnocentrism**—judging the behavior and beliefs of others in terms of one's own cultural values and traditions. Why don't they eat what we eat, dress as we dress, and act as we do? At its most extreme, ethnocentrism is *cultural chauvinism*—the attitude that one's own customs and beliefs are automatically and unquestionably superior to those of others.

To a degree, ethnocentrism is a characteristic of all human societies. Every person learns from earliest childhood how to think and act. A thorough indoctrination in the values of one's own culture is a lifelong process. The basic values and standards of our culture are continuously reinforced in religious ceremonies, in school, on television, at sporting events, and at parties. Wherever we go, we are tutored in what is considered to be true, real, just, desirable, and important from the perspective of the particular social group of which we are a part. Such built-in ethnocentrism can serve as a positive force by giving people a sense of pride, well-being, and security. This is the aim of many consciousness-raising movements among ethnic minorities such as the native peoples of the United States and Canada. But ethnocentrism has its negative side as well. Extreme ethnocentrism lies at the heart of bigotry and discrimination. The denial of human rights is commonly based on the notion that those being oppressed are "backward," "primitive," or in some other way inferior.

Ethnocentrism does not promote understanding. To truly understand others, one must apply the concept of **cultural relativism**—that is, judging and interpreting the behavior and beliefs of others in terms of *their* traditions and experience. What is "right" for one group of people is not necessarily "right" for another. Such contrasting views can be seen, for example, in

beliefs about the killing and eating of animals. Many Westerners view the Hindu custom of not eating cattle as silly and wasteful; at the same time, they abhor the Chinese practice of eating dogs. On the other hand, many Hindus view Westerners' slaughter of cows as barbaric, and many Chinese react to the Westerners' refusal to eat dog meat with bewilderment and humor.

Cultural relativism does not mean that we should approve or accept without criticism anything a particular people does or thinks. Few, if any, anthropologists today would tolerate slavery, racism, or the abuse of women and children, nor would many people wish to be victimized in these ways. Rather, cultural relativism means evaluating cultural patterns within the context of the history, environment, and social circumstances of the people. The harsh treatment of the Kurds, tribal peoples living in the Middle East, by Iraqis and Turks, for example, must be understood in light of the region's history and social and economic considerations, but knowledge of this context does not imply that one should approve of such treatment. Such considerations are at the heart of efforts through the United Nations to arrive at universal standards of human rights. Similarly, an understanding of the economic, educational, and social class backgrounds of member of hate groups such as the Ku Klux Klan or the Neo-Nazis may throw light on their racist views and behavior without in any way suggesting that such racism is to be accepted.

◄ ANTHROPLOGY AS A SCIENCE ►

Anthropology is linked with other disciplines in both the humanities and the social sciences, and today many anthropologists perceive themselves as working in the humanities. Nevertheless, the discipline has developed as and remains primarily a social science. As a science, anthropology involves systematically observing and classifying facts and establishing verifiable laws. While es-

∧∧∧∧∧

The Inuit are closely bound to the natural environment. Their short, stocky build is a biological adaptation for retaining body heat in a cold, harsh climate. Inuit cultural adaptations include clothing and equipment designed to contend with the special

tablishing such laws in anthropology remains a goal for many, for the most part we must be satisfied with **theories**—general principles offered to explain observed facts—which are subject to alteration as a result of research which tests them or generates new theories. Anthropology is guided by the same general principles that influence all sciences. These principles include the use of the scientific method, acknowledgment of differing viewpoints within a given science, and changes in paradigms, or major ideas, that dominate scientific thought.

The Scientific Method

The *scientific method* is a precise way of designing and conducting research. It consists of three basic steps: (1) *establishing a hypothesis, a* statement that something observed is caused by a particular set of factors; (2) *determining ways to test the hypothesis,* incorporating them in a research design; and (3) *testing the hypothesis* through research and further observations. To these one might add further steps that entail repeating the

study and revising one's hypothesis in light of initial and subsequent findings.

Different Viewpoints

Ideally, science strives to establish verifiable laws that govern phenomena. In a practical sense, however, scientists can usually only approach a deeper understanding of "what is real." The search for scientific understanding is a long and difficult process made up of many small steps. Often a number of scientists will concurrently investigate the same problem. These scientists may hold conflicting viewpoints, or theories, that reflect different approaches to interpreting the same information. This may sound discouraging, but without its controversies, a science would surely stagnate. With continued research, scientists eventually separate viewpoints that are sound from those that are not, thereby advancing scientific understanding.

As with other sciences, anthropology includes many differences of opinion. Controversies abound over such issues as the exact course of human biological evolution, explanations of the origin of agriculture, and the origins and implications of the incest taboo. For example, while some anthropologists view the material base (which includes, for example, our technology and the things we are able to produce) as the most important determining factor of cultural patterns, others stress the role of ideas and symbols and their relative independence from material considerations. Such differences are exemplified in the contrast between the materialist theories of Leslie White and Julian Steward and the cognitive or symbolic theories of Claude Lévi-Strauss and Clifford Geertz discussed in the appendix. Also like other sciences, anthropology occasionally changes through the introduction of major new intellectual viewpoints, or paradigms. A good example of a paradigm is nineteenth-century English naturalist Charles Darwin's theory of biological evolution. Darwin's theory of evolution initiated a new approach to the study of life, offering important insights and raising new questions. It introduced new ways of thinking about human society as well.

◄ THE FIELDS OF ANTHROPOLOGY ►

Although the discipline of anthropology strives to create a holistic and systematic picture of humanity, no single individual can possibly command a detailed understanding of every aspect of the lives of all peoples past and present. Consequently, specialization in anthropology is practical. Most anthropologists select one or two aspects of the human condition for intensive study, but remain interested in relating their own specialized findings to what researchers are doing in other areas. The major subdivisions of anthropology are (1) biological (or physical) anthropology, (2) archaeology, (3) linguistic anthropology, and (4) sociocultural anthropology.

Biological Anthropology

Many anthropologists focus on the biological aspects of humankind. The various types of **biological anthropology** fall within two major categories: evolutionary studies and studies of the biological diversity of modern human populations.

Evolutionary studies seek to discover how and why humans evolved, including the ways in which biological evolution has acted to shape the living world. Some biological anthropologists study *fossils,* the preserved remains or traces of long-dead animals and plants. By looking at the ancient fossil remains of humans and related species, biological anthropologists can tell us when our ancestors began walking upright or the stage of evolution at which the human brain attained modern proportions. Biological anthropologists work with other specialists, such as geologists and archaeologists, to help complete the picture of our early ancestors and their evolution.

Humans belong to the order of mammal known as the *primates*, which also includes monkeys, apes, and prosimians. Thus, another way of exploring human evolution is through *primatology,* the study of the primates other than humans. The nonhuman primates are, in a biological and evolutionary sense, humankind's closest living relatives. Primatological research helps us to understand what we share with other animals, what makes us part of the natural world, and what makes us unique. Studies of these nonhuman primates also help anthropologists interpret the fossil record of evolution.

While some primatologists focus on primate biology, others investigate the social behavior of primates such as chimpanzees, gorillas, and baboons. Their studies help us to reconstruct the behavior of our early ancestors. For example, Jane Goodall (1964) found that wild chimpanzees consistently make and use crude tools. Many biological anthropologists therefore concluded that tool-using is much more ancient

Fieldwork conducted by some biological anthropologists focuses on human evolution. Fossil-hunter Mary Leakey starts to uncover a prehuman fossil skull as her Dalmatians, Sally and Victoria, keep her company.

than was previously believed. Even though significant differences exist in the degree to which the skill is expressed, tool-using is clearly a behavior found among both chimpanzees and humans. Might, then, it also have been a characteristic of their common ancestor?

Other biological anthropologists investigate the *biological diversity* of modern populations. This field is closely tied to evolutionary studies, since biological diversity is the result of evolution. These anthropologists seek to describe patterns of human diversity and to explain why the differences exist. Since researchers of contemporary human populations deal with living specimens, they can study such visible characteristics as skin color and hair texture. They can also examine traits that are all but invisible, such as blood type and genetic makeup. It is therefore possible to explore the relationship between the biological configuration of a local population and its environment. For example, many scientists contend that some groups of

people tend to be tall and lanky in warm climates while others are short and stocky where it is cold; these characteristics are thus seen as evolved adaptive responses to climatic factors, since body form affects the conservation or radiation of body heat. Students of human biological diversity also seek to explain how biological differences develop within individuals.

Archaeology

Archaeology is the study of the cultural past through the material remains left by people. *Classical archaeologists,* who study the ancient civilizations of Europe and the Near East, are closely associated with art historians and specialists in religious studies. *Anthropological archaeologists,* on the other hand, are anthropologists of earlier cultures who attempt to answer the kinds of questions that concern all anthropologists. Anthropological archaeologists take an integrated approach by placing cultural remains

Some biological anthropologists like Cynthia Beall conduct fieldwork to gather data on the biological diversity of contemporary human populations. Beall is studying Tibetan nomadic pastoralists, whose lifestyle depends on herding yak, sheep, and goats. Her major interest is understanding these people's adaptation to high altitudes.

within a broad context: How did the society and its environment interact? How and why did these people and their culture evolve? Contemporary anthropological archaeologists are most concerned with explaining cultural processes rather than describing and classifying past societies. In other words, they try to understand the general principles that govern the form and development of human cultures. For example, some anthropological archaeologists are interested in general principles that determined the origin of agriculture—a revolutionary event that occurred in different parts of the world at different times. One theory is that agriculture originated as a cultural adaptation in response to population pressure. When populations became too large to be supported by the naturally occurring resources, the need for a stable food source triggered the origin of agriculture (Boserup 1981).

Many anthropological archaeologists study societies that did not leave written records. Their field is known as *prehistoric archaeology*. Besides using material remains to reconstruct prehistoric ways of life, prehistoric archaeologists also study contemporary peoples whose lifestyles are comparable to those of past societies. For most of our existence, we humans have lived by hunting and gathering wild foods—that is, by foraging. Thus, by studying present-day foragers, prehistoric archaeologists can gain insights into the ways in which our foraging ancestors lived—insights about their methods of hunting, their distribution across the land, and their religious beliefs.

By contrast, the field of *historical archaeology* concentrates on societies with written records, as does classical archaeology, although historical archaeologists work within the general framework of anthropology. While many past societies have left written records of their activities, these records are never a complete reflection of the peoples' lives. Historical archaeologists are proficient at extracting from the incomplete material remains of these societies every possible clue about these peoples' daily lives. Archaeological excavations in California, for example, have yielded much information about the daily operation of old Spanish missions. These mission sites are helping us to learn more about early contact between Native Americans and Europeans.

Linguistic Anthropology

The ideas and modes of behavior that constitute culture are transmitted largely by a complex system of symbols that includes language. While all organisms have some ways of communicating, and some animals, such as porpoises and chimpanzees, have highly developed means of communicating, humans have evolved a unique and extremely complex system. Without it, human culture as we know it would be impossible. The field of **linguistic anthropology** focuses on this

Student labor is an important source of labor in the excavation of archaeological sites. Both high school and college students provided the workforce for the excavation of the Koster Site, a prehistoric Native American site in southern Illinois.

aspect of human life. It is, in turn, divided into a number of subfields.

Descriptive linguistics deals with how languages are constructed and how the various parts (sounds and grammar) are interrelated to form coherent systems of communication. *Historical linguistics* concerns the evolution of language—how languages grow and change. *Sociolinguistics* studies the relationship between language and social factors, such as class, ethnicity, age, and gender. For example, speech usage in a society often varies between men and women. Finally, a topic of interest to many anthropological linguists is *language and culture,* which examines the ways that language affects how we think and,

conversely, how our beliefs and values influence our linguistic patterns.

Sociocultural Anthropology

Sociocultural anthropology is the study of the social, symbolic, and material lives of contemporary and recent historical human societies. Whereas biological anthropology concentrates on the study of the biological basis of the human condition, sociocultural anthropology is concerned with the social and cultural inheritance of humankind. While sociocultural anthropology and archaeology overlap in some ways, especially in their focus on culture and their concern with the history of societies, they have many important differences. The most obvious difference is that sociocultural anthropology focuses on societies that can be studied directly, while archaeologists study extinct societies that cannot be directly observed.

The concept of culture, important to anthropology as a whole, is central to the field of sociocultural anthropology. It is also perhaps the most important defining characteristic of what it means to be human. Culture, as used by anthropologists, means much more than opera, poetry, paintings, ballet, and other artistic endeavors. **Culture** is the customary, learned manner in which human groups organize their behavior and thought in relation to their environment. Defined in this manner, culture has two principal aspects: behavioral and cognitive. The *behavioral* component refers to how people act, and especially interact, with one another. In child-rearing, for example, parents and children interact in a fairly patterned fashion. *Cognition* involves how people perceive, classify, and interpret their world. For example, the views parents have about how they should act, how their children should act, and what significance parenthood carries in the scheme of things are cognitive elements of a culture.

Most of what goes into making up culture is a result of **learning:** modifying behavior in response to experience within an environment. Learning is practically universal among organisms. However, no other organism has a greater capacity for learning, or depends more on learned behavior for its survival, than a human. While the survival of most other organisms is safeguarded somewhat by instincts, humans rely heavily on culture, socially shared learned behavior, for their survival. People must learn how to live in a particular social and physical setting, with instincts playing but a minimal role. Think of the chances for survival most urban-dwelling Westerners would have if suddenly stranded in a tropical rain forest or an arid desert. Without the help of someone who had learned how to

live in that setting, the urbanite would probably perish.

As the term implies, sociocultural anthropology is concerned with human society in addition to culture. Culture is not created in a vacuum or by isolated individuals; rather, it is the creation of humans interacting in groups. Through such social interactions, humans learn how to act and how to think in ways that are shared by others. We humans are social animals, with a biological makeup that predisposes us to form groups. Since the beginning of human evolution, our survival has been a cooperative enterprise. Thus, culture is a group effort and is socially shared. Those who share particular cultural perceptions and modes of behavior belong to a **society**—a group defined by the patterns of interaction of its members. It is through their common experience as members of a society that humans create shared cultural attributes. This is not a one-way process, for human society depends on culture. Neither exists apart from the other.

Sociocultural anthropology is delineated by differing theoretical traditions and by more precise forms of specialization that may focus, for example, on politics, economics, or kinship. By far the largest branch of sociocultural anthropology is **ethnology**—the systematic, comparative study of patterns and processes in living and recent cultures.

Sociocultural anthropology is built on a body of recorded material that describes the vast array of human beliefs, practices, and achievements. This process of describing individual cultures—largely through direct interaction with the people concerned, or fieldwork—is called **ethnography.** The amount of ethnographic information available on all human cultures is far too vast to be studied in depth by a single individual. Therefore, most sociocultural anthropologists specialize in the ethnography of one or two geographical areas, such as sub-Saharan Africa, the Amazon Basin, or a culture of drug abuse in an American city. A sociocultural anthropologist usually does

Sociocultural anthropologist Homa Hoodfar (right), with a friend, conducted her fieldwork in an urban setting—Cairo, Egypt. The in-depth immersion of the field-worker in a culture, observing and participating in a people's way of life, is one of the hallmarks of sociocultural anthropology.

in-depth fieldwork among one or two groups in the area, living among them and observing and participating in their life. For purposes of comparison and background, the anthropologist will also be informed about other peoples in the region. This in-depth immersion in a culture is one of the hallmarks of sociocultural anthropology.

An increasingly respected and growing specialty within anthropology is **applied anthropology,** which uses anthropological knowledge to produce a sociocultural condition with the goal of improving the lives of certain people. Anthropology in the United States first emerged as a profession in no small part because the government had to learn to understand and govern Native Americans being subdued and moved to reservations. Although anthropologists first applied their special knowledge in such a colonial setting, over the years the field has broadened its scope and shed that unfortunate association. Anthropology has contributed, for example, to the reform of immigration policy, the development of public policy toward drug abuse, the

implementation of culturally sensitive education programs, and the control of disease and development of adequate health care. It also has helped international businesses interact with counterparts in very different cultures.

Aware of the dilemma that may arise when they advise on changes which may not be embraced by those who are affected, applied anthropologists try to be sympathetic to the people's point of view and may side with their stated interests. As advocates, anthropologists may be called upon to support an indigenous people whose way of life is threatened with destruction or whose land is being appropriated when the larger society perceives them as standing in the way of development. Advocacy may involve enhancing a people's power of self-determination or assisting them to negotiate effectively to protect their land or other interests. One anthropologist, James Spradley (1970) took an advocacy approach in his pioneering study of the homeless in Seattle, Washington. By providing information to Seattle newspapers regarding how the police and courts deprived the homeless of the rights accorded other citizens, he helped a group of homeless people to gain more control over their lives.

The Applied Anthropology Portfolio, "The Changing Face of Irian Jaya," looks at applied anthropologists' interests in a region where many people had not encountered the outside world until recently in this century. In this once relatively isolated area of Indonesia, where the pace of economic development is now increasing rapidly, the indigenous people face a number of practical problems in adaptation. Irian Jaya is now coming to terms with the modern world, and anthropologists are using their special knowledge and expertise in assisting them in this process.

◄ ANTHROPOLOGY AND THE ► CONTEMPORARY WORLD

Today we face a world that is changing faster than ever before. It is also a world that, despite a great deal of human progress, is beset by a multitude of serious problems. Anthropology is at the forefront in the search for solutions to problems of rapid change, social upheaval, environmental degradation, and inequities in the allocation of resources for different ethnic groups, social classes, nations, and sexes. With its commitment to the principle of holism, anthropology is the field best suited to promote understanding of the human condition in its many forms and contexts. Its emphasis on integration is especially suited for coming to terms with the world system. In the face of change, crisis and uncertainty, we need, more than ever, to understand where we came from, what we are, what we have the potential to become, and how we depend on others in the global community. By studying our evolution and comparing the ways we have adapted to an array of environments, anthropologists can contribute a great deal toward gaining this understanding. Furthermore, anthropology's long-standing concern with promoting the notions of universalism and cultural relativism give it an important role in a world overrun with communal and racial intolerance, hatred, and violence.

In the chapters that follow, the reader will see how anthropology is attuned to all of contemporary life. We will explore, for example,

The approach of anthropology, especially its emphasis on the integration of society, is well suited for shedding light on the modern world system. Here Barbie dolls, a product of a U.S. manufacturer, are being made in China, linking Asia with the rest of the world.

not only the rapid disappearance of isolated small-scale societies such as those in Irian Jaya, but also the conditions of modern urban life; we will look at the situation of peoples in the developing world and how their problems are tied to the world as a whole; and we will seek answers to why different societies regard and treat illness so differently. We will see how anthropologists can further our understanding of what makes us human, while simultaneously helping us to appreciate all our differences.

SUMMARY

Anthropology, the scientific study of humanity, seeks to develop a whole, integrated picture of humankind. By studying all things human, anthropologists examine how and why people are both different and similar.

Because of its broad scope, anthropology is separated into subdisciplines that are linked by unifying themes. Universalism is the fundamental principle that all peoples are fully and equally human. Holism dictates that all aspects of the human condition must be understood. Through the theme of integration, anthropologists recognize that the various aspects of cultural existence are interrelated; in fact, as the world system concept informs us, all the world's societies are interrelated. Another anthropological focus is the study of adaptation—how humans have evolved biological and cultural adaptations to contend with environmental conditions. Cultural relativism—judging and interpreting the behavior and beliefs of others in terms of their traditions and experiences—provides a means of counteracting ethnocentrism, judging the behavior and beliefs of others in terms of one's own cultural values and traditions.

Though related to both the humanities and social sciences, anthropology is primarily a science. As a science anthropology is concerned with systematically observing and classifying facts and explaining processes. The scientific method consists of three basic steps: establishing hypotheses, determining ways to test the hypotheses, and, finally, testing them. Another aspect of anthropology as a science is the realization that the search for scientific understanding is a long and arduous process consisting of many small steps; consequently, anthropology encompasses a wide range of viewpoints and opinions.

Anthropology is divided into four subdisciplines. Biological anthropology focuses on the biological aspects of humankind. The various types of biological anthropology fall into two major categories: evolutionary studies and studies of the biological diversity of modern human populations. Archaeology is the study of the cultural past through the material remains left by people. Linguistic anthropology focuses on how humans communicate and transmit culture, particularly through language.

Sociocultural anthropology is the study of the social, symbolic, and material lives of contemporary and recent historical human societies. The concept of culture—the customary, learned manner in which human groups organize their behavior and thought in relation to their environment—is central to sociocultural anthropology, as is its focus on human society. Divided by differing theoretical traditions and by many specializations, the largest branch of sociocultural anthropology is ethnology, the systematic comparative study of patterns and processes in living and recent cultures. Applied anthropology uses the knowledge of anthropologists to produce desired sociocultural conditions.

KEY TERMS

Adaptation As a process, the means by which individuals or populations react to environmental conditions, physical and social, to maintain themselves and survive. As an end product, a particular behavior, social system, or physical structure that allows populations to survive.

Adaptive strategy   The set of solutions, such as those having to do with securing food, consciously or unconsciously applied by members of a population to contend with basic environmental or biological problems.

Anthropology   The scientific study of humanity that seeks to explain how and why people are both similar and different through examination of our biological and cultural past and comparative study of existing human societies.

Archaeology   The study of the cultural past through the material remains left by people.

Biological anthropology   The branch of anthropology that deals with the biological aspects of humankind, particularly from the standpoint of evolution and the biological diversity of human populations.

Culture   The customary learned manner in which human groups organize their behavior and thought in relation to their environment.

Cultural relativism   Judging and interpreting the behavior and beliefs of others in terms of their traditions and experiences. (Contrast with *ethnocentrism.*)

Division of labor   The technical and social manner in which work is organized in a society.

Ecology   The study of the relationship between organisms and their physical, biotic, and social environments.

Environment   The physical, biotic, and social surroundings.

Ethnocentrism   Judging the behavior and beliefs of others in terms of one's own cultural values and traditions. (Contrast with *cultural relativism.*)

Ethnography   The process of describing individual cultures, largely through direct interaction with the people concerned, or fieldwork.

Ethnology   The systematic, comparative study of patterns and processes in living and recent cultures.

Holism   The anthropological concept by which human existence is viewed as a multifaceted whole, including both the biological and the cultural aspects.

Integration   The anthropological principle that emphasizes how the various aspects of cultural life function together.

Large-scale societies   Societies that are characterized by a high degree of social complexity and dependence on extensive and highly specialized interchanges of goods, ideas, and people.

Learning   Modification of behavior in response to experience within an environment; culture depends on the great human capacity for learning.

Linguistic anthropology   The branch of anthropology that studies language and its relation to culture.

Science   A kind of study that systematically observes and classifies facts and establishes verifiable laws.

Small-scale societies   Societies that are characterized by localized social interaction and localized exploitation of environmental resources.

Society   A group defined by the patterns of interaction of its members.

Sociocultural anthropology   The study of the social, symbolic, and material lives of contemporary and historical human societies.

Theory   A general principle offered to explain observed facts and which is subject to alteration as a result of research designed to test or generate new theories.

Universalism   The anthropological principle that all peoples are fully and equally human.

World system A social and economic structure encompassing the entire world. In the world system, individual societies are interdependent, and their internal characteristics must be understood in terms of the broader global system.

SUGGESTED READINGS

Anthropology is not only an important part of the quest for answers to human problems, it is an exciting, multifaceted field of study. The following readings are designed to introduce the beginning student to some interesting and well-written studies in sociocultural anthropology from different parts of the world:

Bestor, Theodore C. 1989. *Neighborhood Tokyo.* Stanford, CA: Stanford University Press.

Bowen, Elenore Smith. 1964. *Return to Laughter.* New York: Doubleday/Anchor. (Africa)

Ehlers, Tracy Bachrach. 1990. *Silent Looms.* Boulder, CO: Westview. (Guatemala)

Fernea, Elizabeth. 1969. *Guests of the Sheik.* New York: Doubleday/Anchor. (Middle East)

Goldstein, Melvyn C., and Cynthia M. Beall. 1990 *Nomads of Western Tibet.* Berkeley: University of California Press.

Liebow, Elliot. 1967. *Tally's Corner.* Boston: Little, Brown. (United States)

Read, Kenneth. 1980. *The High Valley.* New York: Columbia University Press. (Papua New Guinea)

Ruesch, Hans. 1950. *Top of the World.* New York: Harper & Row. (Arctic North America)

Siskind, Janet. 1973. *To Hunt in the Morning.* New York: Oxford University Press. (South America)

Thomas, Elizabeth Marshall. 1959. *The Harmless People.* New York: Vintage. (Southern Africa)

Tonkinson, Robert. 1978. *The Mardudjara Aborigines.* New York: Holt, Rinehart and Winston. (Australia)

Turnbull, Colin. 1962. *The Forest People.* New York: Doubleday/Anchor (Central Africa)

Wikan, Unni. 1980. *Life Among the Poor in Cairo.* London: Tavistock. (Egypt)

Wilson, Carter. 1974. *Crazy February.* Berkeley: University of California Press. (Southern Mexico)

THE CHANGING FACE OF IRIAN JAYA

Irian Jaya, Indonesia's easternmost province occupying the western portion of the island of New Guinea (see the accompanying map), is one of the least developed places on earth. It is also one of the most marginal parts of the modern world system. In recent years, however, the pace of economic development has increased rapidly, accompanied by dramatic social change and greater integration into the world system.

The people living in Irian Jaya exhibit a great deal of cultural diversity. Over 260 languages are spoken by different groups of approximately one million indigenous people whose cultures evolved over thousands of years in relative isolation from the rest of the world. In addition, there are many migrants from other parts of Indonesia of different cultural backgrounds who speak other languages. Binding this diverse group of people together is the Indonesian language, today spoken by a majority of the population and used in various government institutions and programs.

Among the changes that the people of Irian Jaya have had to face are the controversial efforts by the Indonesian government to integrate the province into the nation. The initial incorporation of Irian Jaya into Indonesia in the early 1960s, after it was wrested from Dutch colonial rule, spawned an independence movement that persists today in a few isolated pockets. Government programs to sponsor and encourage migration from other parts of the country to what is perceived to be an underpopulated province have also been controversial and have created numerous social problems. Moreover, exploitation of resources such as timber, minerals, and ocean resources by outside interests have often caused environmental problems and led to conflict with local people.

Faced with the strains of such a rapidly changing and diverse region, the Indonesian government has turned increasingly to social scientists for solutions to existing problems and for ways to avoid future ones. Sociocultural anthropologists in particular have been able to contribute the special insights and methods of their field toward understanding and managing the problems that arise as these people attempt to deal with the impact of the outside world. The anthropology department of the province's Cenderawasih University has been singled out for promotion among departments in recognition of its potential for helping intercultural understanding and providing guidance in the course of socioeconomic change.

From the outset, professional anthropology in Irian Jaya has combined a desire to record the region's diverse cultures with a desire to apply its knowledge to the adaptational problems of the indigenous peoples. While the area was under Dutch colonial rule, Governor J. van Baal helped give anthropology a central role in assisting local populations faced with rapid incorporation into the modern world system. A Bureau of Native Affairs was established in 1951 to carry out research and to serve as an advisory body to the governor on the process of adaptation. Much of the anthropological research conducted over the next decade was done either by bureau anthropologists or by other anthropologists in cooperation with the bureau. One of the best-known studies to English-speakers dating from this period is Leopold Pospisil's work about the Ekari (at that time known as Kapauku), which focuses on their economy and legal practices (Pospisil 1958, 1963).

American anthropological research in Irian Jaya began in 1961 with the Harvard Peabody Expedition. Fieldwork was conducted among the Dani of the high interior Baliem valley, at the time still extremely isolated from the outside world. The research among the Dani highlighted traditional warfare, as shown in *Dead Birds*, a 1963 film, which is still shown to anthropology students throughout North America (see Gardner and Heider 1969). Anthropologist Karl Heider also published an important ethnography of the Dani (Heider 1970). International attention was focused on the expedition when Michael Rockefeller, son of then New York Governor Nelson Rockefeller, who worked on the filming of *Dead Birds*, disappeared while on a visit to the Asmat on the southern coast. The mystery surrounding his disappearance continues to spark debate.

Throughout the remainder of the 1960s and 1970s, very little anthropological research was conducted in Irian Jaya, largely because of unsettled conditions surrounding the transfer of authority from the Netherlands to Indonesia and violence arising from the separatist movement. In 1978, however, an anthropology department was opened at the province's newly founded Cenderawasih University. The staff of the department is generally relatively young; most are from Irian Jaya and share a keen interest in improving the lives of the people of the province. In addition, there is a fairly large number of very enthusiastic undergraduate anthropology students from all over the province.

Assistance in developing the department has been provided for the past few years by the Canadian-funded Eastern Indonesia Universities Development Project, for which I have served as the anthropology consultant since 1991. In addition to working on long-term training of local staff, curriculum development, and the creation of national and international linkages for the department, each year I have given a training course in field research techniques, assisted by an anthropologist from Jakarta, the capital of Indonesia. Research topics have been selected through consultation between the department and myself and have focused on applied issues deemed to be of primary importance to the people of Irian Jaya.

The first course was general in nature and included a very short period of fieldwork in the village of Doyo Lama, on the shores of nearby Lake Sentani.

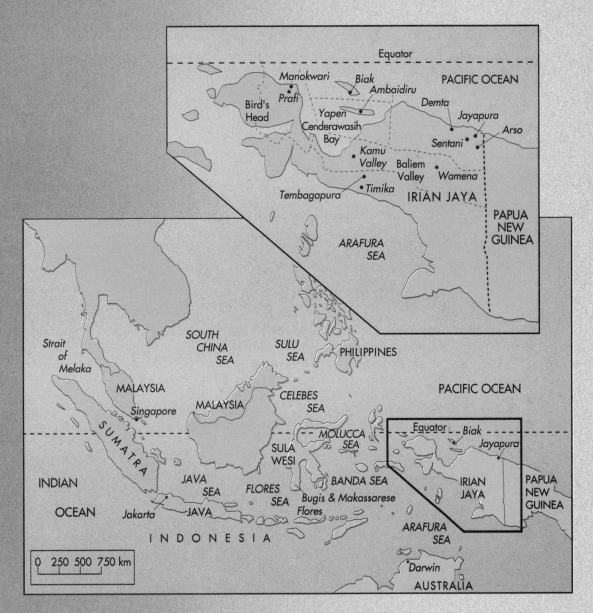

Irian Jaya is Indonesia's easternmost province, occupying the western portion of the island of New Guinea in the Southwest Pacific.

Since then courses have focused on specific topics concerned with adaptational problems and socioeconomic development.

In 1992 course participants were sent in teams to carry out research on different topics in three sites. One team focused on socioeconomic relations in the capital of Jayapura's main market at Hamadi. Of particular interest here were relations between indigenous Irianese and migrants, largely Bugis and Makassarese from the Indonesian island of Sulawesi, who dominated the sale of food and other commodities in the Hamadi market. A second team conducted research among people living around the large oil palm project at Arso, south of Jayapura. The oil extracted from these palms is used in cooking oil and as an additive in some foods. The communities around the plantation are ethnically very mixed, including migrants from different parts of Irian Jaya and from elsewhere in Indonesia as well as a small indigenous population. The researchers focused on the adaptation of the migrants and indigenous peoples to the oil palm project, including economic activities and ethnic relations. What has emerged from this research is a very complex picture of ethnic relations. There are far more interactions among members of different ethnic groups than what had been expected. The research team also gained a sense that some groups of Irianese (such as the Dani) were adapting far more successfully than others.

The third team was sent to Demta to conduct fieldwork in the neighboring fishing village of Ambora. Demta is the site of a large logging operation. The actual logging takes place some distance away and the logs are brought to Demta to be loaded on ships and sent to mills elsewhere. The research concerned relations between the villagers and the logging operation and with the impact of this enterprise on the village. In this instance, the researchers found relations to be poor. They heard many complaints from the villagers about their treatment by the loggers and went away with the feeling that, with the help of an applied anthropologist, the company could have avoided many of the problems and created a much better atmosphere for all.

The research sites for the 1992 course were relatively close to and connected by road with Jayapura, the province's largest town and its administrative and commercial center. In 1993 two research teams were sent to more remote parts of the province where important export-oriented industries have been developed in previously very isolated regions. One group went to study a migrant settlement at the province's other large oil palm project at Prafi, and the other group went to Timika, where the local economy is dominated by the Freeport copper and gold mine.

The 1993 studies, focusing on migrants' relations with indigenous people and the impact of mining, reflect major concerns in the area. As already mentioned, the Indonesian government's policy of promoting migration to Irian Jaya has been controversial and has generated many social problems. To develop expertise in this area, we selected Prafi, the site of a large migrant program. The study at Prafi took place in Wariori village, a community that was settled initially in 1986 by migrants from the islands of Java and Flores. In general the study concerned the adaptation of the migrants and their relation with local Irianese and the local environment. One particular topic of interest was the weaving of cloth by the Flores migrants for sale to the Irianese. The demand for cloth is strong among the Irianese, who do not weave. Upon marriage, they pass the cloth from the husband's group to the wife's, an exchange also known as bridewealth. Also used for other ceremonial purposes, this cloth quickly became a major source of income for the Flores migrants and thus an important aspect of relations between the migrants and indigenous peoples.

Freeport's mining operations around the remote mountainous site of Tembagapura are an extremely important part of Irian Jaya's economy. The company is one of Indonesia's largest corporate tax payers and the largest single source of tax revenue for the province. The mine employs thousands of workers from overseas, from elsewhere in Indonesia, and, increasingly, from Irian Jaya itself. The mine's infrastructure (including buildings and roads) covers an extensive area in southern Irian Jaya, and, as with most large mining operations, the Freeport operation has had a significant environmental and social impact on the region. The immediate vicinity of the mine is the traditional territory of the Amungme, many of whom have now been resettled from their original mountain habitat to the lowlands around the town of Timika (see Cook 1988). Many of the Amungme, a relatively small group, feel overwhelmed by the scale of

An anthropologist from Cenderawasih University interviews staff at the cooperative in the village of Opiaref, which supplies carvings for Biak's tourist market.

change going on around them. Relations among the Amungme and the mining company and migrants attracted by the mine have at times been difficult and communication among the different parties has frequently proven inadequate.

The Cenderawasih University anthropology department has given high priority to developing its ability to conduct impact studies relating to mining in regard to Freeport and other mines likely to be developed in the province in the future. The department's efforts in this regard have received encouragement from Freeport, which itself has initiated a number of programs in recent years to promote social and economic development among local communities. The 1993 study looked at the adaptation of the Amungme to their new setting as viewed by different segments of Amungme society, such as youths, women, and community leaders. It was a very preliminary study, intended as the first of many studies in the area.

A new area of growing importance for Irian Jaya is tourism. The number of tourists visiting Irian Jaya in recent years has been very small, fewer than 2,000 a year. Government planners and private sector investors, however, have set about to change this situation dramatically. They intend to create a major tourist industry on the island of Biak, which is connected by air to Hawaii and Los Angeles. One 400-room resort is due to open in 1995 and there are plans to construct several other hotels in the same vicinity with a total of over 2,000 rooms. The area selected in eastern Biak was occupied by the small village of Marau; a handful of other tiny villages are nearby. Our study sought to provide baseline profiles of these villages immediately before the onset of large-scale tourism. One of the villages, for example, has a number of carvers who presently supply the island's small tourist industry with Biak-style souvenirs. The carvers sell largely through a cooperative which markets primarily through an airport concession. The opening of nearby hotels will create a potential market many times larger.

For 1995 the department plans research in the village of Ambaidiru, a small mountain village at an altitude of 900 meters on the island of Yapen. The villagers are linguistically and culturally distinct from other Yapen islanders who live mainly along the coast. Ambaidiru is known primarily for its coffee production, introduced to the village by the Dutch in the 1950s. The coffee beans are carried on peoples' backs down a mountain trail to the coastal town of Serui, where the village cooperative roasts and packages them. Production has been limited and the villagers have had difficulty in finding adequate markets. This situation may be about to change, however, as the village is integrated into a regional development plan supported by the Indonesian government and the United Nations Development Programme (UNDP) aimed at promoting agricultural and marine resources in part by linking them to the market expected to come with the arrival of large-scale tourism on Biak. In addition, construction has begun on a road linking Ambaidiru with Serui. The purpose of the anthropological study of Ambaidiru is to provide a sociocultural picture of the community in relation to present economic practices, thus helping to promote the satisfactory incorporation of the village into the emerging regional economy.

In addition to the research discussed above, I have also been involved in an ongoing survey of the material culture of northern Irian Jaya with Naffi Sanggenafa, the head of the anthropology department in Jayapura, and Anto Achadiyat of the University of Indonesia in Jakarta. The research has involved interviews with a variety of craftspeople, especially carvers in an effort to understand the current sociocultural dynamics of craft production in the area. Among the aims of the research is assessing the sustainability of the production of various crafts and finding appropriate ways to promote such activities.

One of the plans for later in the project is to restudy Prafi, Biak, and Ambaidiru. By that time, Ambaidiru should have a road and large-scale tourism should have arrived on Biak. While predicting how things will be in Irian Jaya even a few years from now is difficult, given the pace at which things are changing it seems a safe to say that anthropological research has an important role to play in the changing face of Irian Jaya.

2 ETHNOGRAPHIC RESEARCH

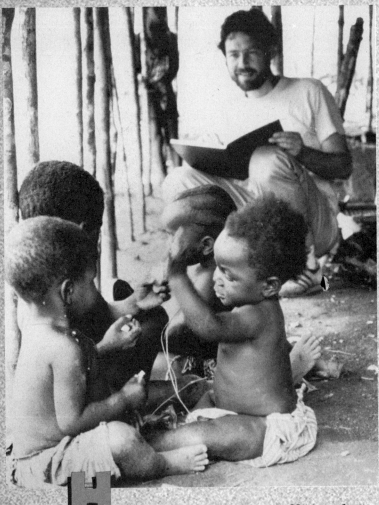

How can we obtain sufficiently good information to support or refute anthropological theories? Because of the ethnographic method of **participant observation**, refined by anthropologists over the past hundred years, we now have a much clearer picture of the lives of other peoples. Employing this method, a researcher lives with a group of people and observes their daily activities, learning how they view the world and witnessing firsthand how they behave. This form of immersion ensures that the people studied are regarded not only as abstractions for analytical purposes, but also as real people living within a complex setting.

To intimately understand a group of people, an anthropologist must spend more than a few days or weeks with them. Even after a year of systematic research, communicating with them in their own language and sharing as much as possible in their lives, an anthropologist is just beginning to appreciate and understand their way of life. But only through such experiences can we move away from static and stereotypical views of people and begin to understand what culture is all about.

◄ PREPARING FOR FIELDWORK ►

While today's anthropologists may spend years living with the people they are studying, they may spend even more time preparing for field-work. Their preparation includes the surprisingly complex matter of choosing a topic and narrowing its focus.

Choosing a Topic: Studying Small-Scale and Large-Scale Societies

Anthropologists' research interests often are inspired by their own life experiences. Anthropologist David Maybury-Lewis provided the following description of what sparked his interest in the native peoples of South America, which eventually led him to live among the Xavante of Brazil:

> As an undergraduate I once took a course in the discovery, conquest, and settlement of Spanish America. I marveled then at the skill of the early transatlantic navigators and at the audacity of the conquistadors; but what intrigued me the most were the first accounts of the American Indians. I conceived a romantic desire to know more about some of the people who had inspired such highly coloured narratives and who still, four hundred years later, seemed remote and exotic in a world jaded with travelogue. [1968: 13]

Field-worker studying children among the Efe people of the Ituri forest in northeast Zaire, Africa.
This man was actually a psychologist who was a member of a team doing anthropological field work.

Some people have been drawn to anthropology by their experiences with different cultures. Decisions about specific research projects, however, usually require more impersonal consideration. For example, projects may come about as a result of gaps in the ethnographic literature. The study of relatively isolated, nonindustrial societies historically has been a major concern of anthropology. These **small-scale societies** are characterized by an adaptive strategy that features localized social interaction and the exploitation of local resources. Studying these small-scale societies helps us to understand the human condition and improves our understanding of specific developments on the frontiers of the expanding industrial world system, developments such as those on Rabi Island in Fiji described by Hans Dagmar (see "Focus on Anthropologists"), which may be poorly comprehended otherwise. Especially where the culture of people in small-scale societies is not well known, the priority for anthropologists is to fill out the "ethnographic map" of the area by doing holistic descriptions of these peoples, gathering information on such topics as their physical environment, history, technology, productive activities, food and drink, daily routines, sexual practices, social and political organizations, medical beliefs, and religion. The goal is to understand the totality of their lives.

Once a basic familiarity with the societies of a region has been established, in-depth research can follow. At this point, instead of addressing all aspects of a culture, the field-workers will focus on a specific issue. These may include such topics as political leadership, religious beliefs, or the impact of economic development.

Anthropologists also conduct fieldwork among people who are more thoroughly integrated into the global structure constituting the world-system. In contrast to small-scale societies, such **large-scale societies** are much less localized in orientation and much more dependent on extensive and highly specialized interchanges of goods, ideas, and people. Today, most research by sociocultural anthropologists is conducted among such people—among rural farmers or peasants as well as urban dwellers.

As with students of isolated societies, anthropologists studying those more integrated into the wider world initially focused on filling in the ethnographic map of these societies before moving on to more specialized studies. Until fairly recent times, studies of peasant villages or urban neighborhoods tended to treat these communities as if they, too, existed in isolation, with little or no reference to social and economic relations beyond the local level. Such studies were influenced by the more traditional studies of more isolated peoples. Contemporary anthropological studies, however, take into account the links between the community being studied and the wider society, such as the imposition of political changes from the outside or the encroachment of the tourist industry. Anthropologists see members of these communities as actors in a local setting and as participants in a much larger social system.

Narrowing the Focus

Once a topic is selected, an anthropologist must struggle with two problems: How might the information sought be explained? From whom should it be gathered?

FORMING A HYPOTHESIS. One primary aim of anthropology is to be able to explain why people act and think as they do. In pursuit of this goal, anthropologists continually pose, test, and reformulate hypotheses.

As introduced in Chapter 1, a **hypothesis** is a tentative statement that something observed, such as a pattern of behavior, is caused by a particular set of factors. An anthropologist may observe, for example, that people are moving from rural areas to a city. A hypothetical explanation might be that two major factors are causing this shift: (1) declining employment in the countryside because of the mechanization of farming,

Anthropologist David Maybury-Lewis (second from right) among the Xavante, a small-scale society in Brazil. Dr. Maybury-Lewis is director of the Center for Cultural Survival, an organization that links research to action on behalf of indigenous peoples seeking to protect their resources and safeguard their futures.

and (2) increasing opportunities for employment in the city because of an increasing demand for industrial and service workers.

To test the hypothesis, an anthropologist collects and analyzes ethnographic data. On the basis of these data a researcher rejects or accepts the validity of the hypothesis or recognizes the need to modify it. In trying to explain rural-urban migration, an anthropologist would probably find that other factors, such as improved transportation and the desire for better education, contributed to the process.

Anthropologists often pose hypotheses to test whether findings in a specific setting have wider applicability. David Aberle (1966), who conducted research among the Navajo of the American Southwest, extended his specific research findings to a consideration of the wider consequences of people's involvement in a specific type of religious movement. In the 1930s, the Bureau of Indian Affairs discovered that many Navajo pasturelands were becoming eroded because of overgrazing. The bureau then ordered a significant reduction in livestock, the

mainstay of the Navajo economy. The measure was designed to protect the long-term interests of the Navajo, but in the short-run the policy nearly bankrupted some of the sheepherders. Aberle found that those affected by reductions in herd size tended to join the Native American Church, which stressed the use of peyote, a hallucinogenic plant, to gain access to supernatural power. Moreover, Navajo who had become more integrated into mainstream American culture were less likely to join the Native American Church than those who had more traditional outlooks.

These findings led Aberle to hypothesize that in general, the type of religious movements found among oppressed peoples was associated with how the people were incorporated into the wider social and economic system. He argued that "transformative" movements, such as the Native American Church, that preach withdrawal from the world will be found in a particular context. This is, they would occur where people's lifestyles have been severely disrupted and where the disruption of traditional life and

HANS DAGMAR

FOCUS ON ANTHROPOLOGISTS

In his work Hans Dagmar tries to combine anthropological research and practical assistance to people caught in processes of radical social and economic change. Between 1972 and 1984, he spent two separate one-year periods and several shorter ones among Aborigines in northwestern Australia. In the course of this fieldwork, he became closely involved in the Aborigines' efforts to regain control of land and to improve their living conditions. In 1985, with his wife and younger son, Dr. Dagmar lived on Rabi Island in Fiji and went back for shorter visits in 1986, 1988, and 1993. During the last two periods, he cooperated with local fishermen in setting up small-scale commercial fishing projects.

∧∧∧∧∧∧∧∧

Fieldwork on Rabi Island: An Experiment in Development

I n a bustling street of Suva, the capital of Fiji, a brass sign marks the entrance to the "Rabi Council of Leaders." Here, in 1985, I began fieldwork to address problems of the development of Rabi Island, more than 200 kilometers away, in the northeast part of the country.

The council office is located in a block of shops and offices owned by the people of Rabi. On the office's teleprinter, messages from the council's Australian-based economic adviser indicate the results of investments in overseas stocks and bonds.

The Rabi Council of Leaders are the elected representatives of the Banaban people, who now number more than 4000.

Banabans fish and plant for a living on Rabi Island, some 72 square kilometers in size. In 1945, the Banabans bought Rabi from a private company exploiting coconut plantations; at the same time, there was no longer a native Fijian population on the island. Settling on Rabi, the Banabans left behind their tiny and isolated home island, Banaba, or Ocean Island, more than 2000 kilometers away from Fiji, in what is now the Pacific nation of Kiribati. In 1900, intensive phosphate mining began on Banaba, throwing the fishing and fruit-gathering Banabans headlong into the colonial economy. The ensuing history of these people is an extraordinary tale of its leaders learning to bargain for royalty payments, culminating in the 1970s in a lawsuit against the British government aimed at seeking compensation for the destruction of their homeland. Although they lost their court

case, the Banabans were given an "ex gratia payment" by the British, a capital sum stipulated not to be touched, but to be invested and the interest used by the Rabi Council for essential services and development of Rabi Island.

Since the payment of phosphate royalties had ceased after termination of mining in 1980, the council was looking for new ways of providing for the fast-growing number of Banabans. My research was seen as a possible contribution to this effort. Although I was well aware of the burden of such expectations, I did not want to back away from the task. Thorough anthropological fact-finding is a most useful basis for development planning.

It was the council's explicit wish that I pay attention to the people's perception of the council's role in the development process. As I was soon to find out, on Rabi there was growing uneasiness among the

Banabans about their low standard of living and the council's performance in remedying the situation. As one informant explained:

> Development seems to be so late here; it should have picked up long ago. We Banabans have looked to the past so much, everything seemed to revolve around the court case. I remember the British did a study on development on Rabi, but nothing really came of it. In those days the council was concentrating on getting justice.

After arriving on Rabi, I began a survey of the economy and social organization of Banaban households with my wife and two Banaban assistants (a man and a woman). We formed two teams and visited every household on the island. Of course, we could permit ourselves this approach only because of the limited size of the Rabi population. After nearly 500 interviews, we not only had a useful body of census material, we also had been able to show our faces and explain what we were doing in all four villages and smaller settlements of the island. Apart from gathering factual data on such things as types of crops planted, methods of organizing agriculture and fishing, and patterns of income and consumption, we also had sought information on the people's attitudes and aspirations regarding future development of their community. Suppositions

Dr. Hans Dagmar (third from right) with the 1985 Rabi Council of Leaders, Rabi Island.

gained from the survey were then taken as the basis for a more informal and largely open-ended interview schedule with which we approached a sample of households and experts in various fields of Banaban life.

Between sessions of interviewing, and considerably helped by the presence of my family, I had ample opportunity to learn more about Banaban life by participating in family gatherings and other social events through a network of friends that we gradually developed. Performing various types of administrative tasks for the council and participating in many of its meetings increased my insights into council operations.

After one year of fieldwork,

and contrary to popular belief in Fiji, I had detailed evidence that well over half the Banabans were desperately poor, even according to the standards of developing countries. But, as a contribution to attempts to raise standards of living, was it enough to have charted Rabi's social and natural resources, the wider regional impediments to development, and the limitations of the people and its council in resource management?

From an anthropological point of view, it was also necessary to offer an interpretation. In fact, the chairman of the council, a man with exceptional leadership qualities, had asked for such an interpretation soon after I began my fieldwork. He put it in the following terms:

The past will be explained by us. We will tell you how our economic enterprises went down. We will tell you about all this and then you can ask us questions. You will get answers from the councillors, from the old people, and then you can use these answers for suggestions for the future.

Showing keen insight, the chairman brought up two key characteristics of the anthropological research enterprise, first, that research is all about asking questions and, second, that understanding the present necessitates inquiry into the past. As for the latter point, if anything had become clear to me during my work with the Banabans it was that the past was bearing heavily down on these people. Ever since settling on Rabi, the Banabans had also retained ownership of the island of Banaba. It was the Rabi Council who, with full support of the people, had managed to maintain a "two-island identity" for more than 40 years, thus securing a moral and actual entitlement to relatively large payments of phosphate money. But the reverse side of the council's skillfully played political role was a one-sided focus on the world outside Rabi, hence, a strong reliance on outside "experts" (including myself) and a view of development primarily in terms of finance. Increasing the cash flow to the Banabans became a measure of development. To secure this the council

invested in enterprises outside Rabi, all of which were failures. An accompanying effect of the Banabans' focus on "foreign" politics and finance was their strong dependence on their Council and the moneys the Council distributed to them (on an individual family basis).

While delving into the Banaban past was of critical importance in understanding their failure at local economic development, it was insufficient for fully coming to grips with the impediments to such development, not so much because it was difficult to ask appropriate questions about the subject, but simply because, for reasons explained above, hardly any economic development had actually taken place on a village level.

Going beyond "pure research" and urged on by many informants who felt that their situation was worsening, I worked out a modest experiment aimed at shifting the development emphasis to one of cooperation between the council and the people in small, locally controlled forms of enterprise. Supported by the Council, I found an agency that was willing to finance a commercial fishing project. In 1988 I returned to Rabi and, after months of very close consultation with the Banaban fishermen, presented a detailed working plan for the project. It was essentially based on local control with explicit strategies for continuous adaptation by the local management group as the project was unfolding and new

information and special requirements of the fishermen emerged.

But, again, history seemed to overtake the Banabans. When funds for the project arrived, the council did not use them to equip and organize local fishermen; rather, they chose to invest in a large-scale commercial fishing enterprise in the capital, Suva. The joint venture ended in financial disaster.

The new Council's neglect of the needy fishermen and their families was symptomatic of things to come. While the history of the Rabi Council of Leaders unmistakably bears signs of a growing rift between the elected leaders and the common Banabans as well as an ever-increasing and alarming mingling of money and politics, the conduct of the Council elected in 1991 turned out to be the low point in the self-administration of Banaban affairs. By the end of 1991, when essential services of Rabi were on the verge of breakdown and total economic chaos threatened their lives, the Banaban people violently rose against their Council. As a result, in 1992 the Rabi Council of Leaders was dissolved by Fijian Presidential Decree.

Thus my attempt to shift my research emphasis from pure fact-finding to research and development was left stranded by the financial and political intrigue of local leaders. Moreover, I must add sadly that a more communicative and trusting relationship between the donor agency and this anthropologist might have prevented the squandering of project money by the Rabi Council. Yet, the experiment is not over. Deeply impressed during a visit to Rabi in 1993 by the impoverishment of local communities and the unbroken desire of the people to ameliorate their situation through their traditional fishing skills, I decided to make another attempt, this time without any involvement of local administration or donor bureaucracy. Presently, through direct funding to fishermen, a first pilot project of mixed subsistence and commercial fishing is underway. The results of this will be studied and hopefully serve as an impetus to financial support for a greater number of local communities.

forced incorporation into a largely alien society had not been accompanied by an acceptable new social status for the population. Testing such a hypothesis requires research in other settings and provides stimulus and direction for further fieldwork.

DETERMINING WHOM TO QUESTION. If, like David Aberle, a researcher decides to study the Navajo, he or she must ask some fundamental questions. Who are the Navajo? Should only those living on the reservation be included, or should the study also include Navajo who live in nearby towns or more distant cities? Should all individuals who consider themselves Navajo be included, even if they are not considered Navajo by a majority of other Navajo? Should persons be studied who do not consider themselves Navajo, but who are considered Navajo by others according to some standards, such as kinship? Deciding whom to study is not as simple as it may seem.

The people a researcher decides to include in a study are called its **population.** A population may be determined by several criteria. One is the problem being addressed. If an anthropologist is interested in studying urban migration, for example, he or she would be likely to select persons who had migrated to cities. Those who had not migrated might also be examined to explore why some left while others did not. The population may be determined by one or more other criteria: location or length of residence in the city, place of origin, ethnicity, social class, reli-

gious affiliation, or occupation. Selection of a population to be studied also may be influenced by social, residential, or environmental characteristics of the area being studied. A researcher may select a village as an appropriate population, or perhaps valley dwellers, or a group of kin because these appear to be relevant units of analysis in the particular context. Another basis for selection of a population might be local ways of classifying people, such as ethnic classification.

In general, while caution must be exercised in specifying the population to be studied, it is equally important to be flexible. Part of this flexibility involves recognizing that the study of a particular group of people may require talking to others who influence or interact with them.

◄ RESEARCH TECHNIQUES ►

Precisely how anthropologists conduct their investigations depends on a variety of factors. One is the setting of the fieldwork. Urban research poses problems that are different from those encountered in a village in an isolated mountain valley. In the city the researcher is faced with problems associated with the greater number and variety of people, while in the mountain village an important concern may be finding enough to eat or avoiding diseases. A second factor is the personal inclinations and theoretical biases of the researcher. Researchers with a psychological or cognitive perspective are likely to conduct their fieldwork in a different manner from those who stress social behavior and interaction; the former would emphasize people's statements and ideas, the latter, the people's actual behavior. A third factor is the problem being studied.

There is no single formula for anthropological fieldwork; each problem and research setting is distinct. Anthropologists rely on different approaches according to their different projects. Nevertheless, some general characteristics are common to most anthropological research: observing, questioning, and probability sampling.

Participant Observation

Understanding culture requires attention to how people perceive the world as well as to how they behave in it. However, people's statements about their activities are not always accurate or sufficient explanations of their behavior. Whether consciously or subconsciously, an informant's reporting of events is likely to be selective and distorted in some way. If at all possible, the researcher should view people's behavior directly, but even direct observation does not ensure objectivity, for anthropologists, too, are subject to human biases.

The above points are highlighted by the controversy surrounding assertions by anthropologist Derek Freeman (1983) that Margaret Mead's influential work on Samoan culture is inaccurate. Freeman argues that Mead was duped regarding her depiction of sexual freedom among Samoan adolescents by Samoans who told her tall tales of casual love affairs. Moreover, Freeman feels that Mead's distortions were related to biases in her theoretical outlook and her desire to present an appealing picture of "primitive" life. Many anthropologists disagree with points raised by Freeman in regard to his criticisms of Mead, his own theoretical assertions, and his depiction of Samoan society (see Brady 1983; Shankman 1983). Such a controversy illustrates just how difficult it is to achieve

a reasonable level of objectivity in reporting and interpreting ethnographic data even among highly trained, skilled anthropologists.

To appreciate the complexity of culture, an ethnographer initially must record events, ideas, and conditions in as much detail as possible. Deciding which data are relevant and searching for patterns can come later. Recording people's behavior thoroughly and systematically requires certain skills. Learning to take notes quickly and unobtrusively under conditions that are less than ideal is useful. Anthropologists also often use cameras and tape recorders; however, trying to keep a tape recorder working in a tropical rain forest may pose problems. Social difficulties may arise as well. Some people may not want their picture taken or their statements recorded. In each setting, the anthropologist must learn the most appropriate way to obtain accurate records of people's actions and statements.

All people impose restrictions regarding who may observe certain of their actions. The fieldworker must be sensitive to the privacy and wishes of the people being studied. Overzealous attempts to view restricted behavior can ruin or terminate a research project, besides violating the rights of the individuals being studied.

What anthropologists are allowed to observe in a society may change. Many Australian Aboriginal societies, for example, have strict restrictions governing who may observe or participate in religious functions. In the past, after building up sufficient rapport with the people, anthropologists usually were allowed to attend and even photograph the most sacred of these. As long as they had little direct contact with any society besides their own, the Aborigines did not care what the anthropologist did with the material. In recent years, however, as Aborigines have become more integrated into the larger Australian society, they have been upset to see pictures of secret rituals and sacred objects in various publications. Today, many Aborigines are much more cautious about allowing anthropol-

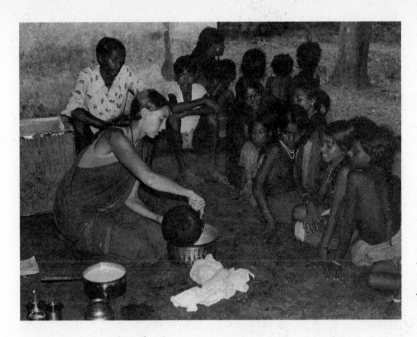

An anthropologist preparing ground-
nut milk in India observes as she
participates in the local culture. This
method of studying another culture is
known as participant observation.

ogists to view their rites. Anthropologists have
tried to limit public access to the collected material that Aborigines deem sensitive.

Questioning

Much of anthropological research consists of
asking people questions about their actions. The
level of questioning depends on the anthropologist's prior knowledge of a culture. Upon being
introduced to a new and relatively unknown
culture, the anthropologist is likely to ask basic
questions—how food is properly eaten, for example, or how kin should behave toward one
another. When he or she feels sufficiently at
home in the culture to move on to more sophisticated ideas, subtler questions may be posed,
such as how the population deals with deviations from expected behavior, why some behavior seems contradictory, and why certain people
eat as they do.

At the outset of fieldwork, the anthropologist
may not know the language or languages spoken
by the people being studied and may have to
rely on interpreters. Fortunately, anthropologists
often can begin their language training before
leaving for the field. Some universities have native speakers on their staffs who help train
prospective researchers. There are also language
tapes and written material for many of even the
rarest of languages. Learning the rudiments of a
language in advance saves time and helps to
avoid some of the initial difficulties associated
with entering a foreign culture. When advance
preparation of this kind is not possible, anthropologists spend the early period of their fieldwork striving to become fluent in a new
language.

Asking questions takes more than simply
learning basic grammar. The field-worker also
must learn *how* to ask questions in a society. Most
societies have prescribed ways of asking questions, often depending on the question and the
relative status of the person being addressed. The
social setting within which the question is being
asked also is usually important. For example, it

∧∧∧∧∧
Author Michael Howard with fellow anthropologist Boedhi Hartono in Irian Jaya, Indonesia, questioning an informant as a method of research. Knowledge of the local language and familiarity with the culture are useful in such a questioning session.

may be considered bad form to bring up a particular topic in the presence of women or children, or the question "Is sorcery practiced in your village?" may not be appropriate in a formal interview, especially if a sorcerer is among those present.

FORMAL QUESTIONING.   Although sensitive topics are usually best discussed in informal conversations, some questions can be dealt with more systematically. Anthropologists use structured questionnaires to generate survey data on such topics as residential and landholding patterns, the distribution of wealth and income within a population, and people's attitudes or beliefs on topics ranging from religion to kinship. The question asked may require a specific answer ("How old are you?"), or it may be open-ended ("How do you feel about employees with AIDS?").

Before a questionnaire can be used in a meaningful way, the anthropologist must have some experience with or knowledge of a culture. Dutch anthropologist Hans Dagmar (au-

thor of the focus section on Rabi) described the process that preceded his formal questioning of Aborigines living around the Australian community of Carnarvon as follows:

During the first two months of fieldwork I collected material solely by means of participant observation including numerous informal talks and unstructured interviews. After about two months I was able to draw up a list of almost all Aboriginal households in the area. From this list I then made a selection of households the adult members . . . of which I planned to interview with open-ended questions. In this I enquired about factual matters such as knowledge of Aboriginal culture, kinship relations, housing, education, employment, income and participation in voluntary associations and asked for opinions about Aboriginal traditional culture, internal relations within the Aboriginal community, the Aboriginal position in the institutions of the wider community and relationships with Whites including such associations of Whites as government departments.

Since it was of great importance to conduct these interviews in a genial atmosphere I took extra care to be properly introduced to my respondents. Most of them I had become acquainted with during the first months of my stay in Carnarvon and to those I did not know well enough I asked to be introduced by a close relative or good friend. [1978: 13–14]

INFORMAL QUESTIONING. Even when formal techniques are used, anthropologists usually derive a great deal of information in a less formal manner. Julia Crane and Michael Angrosino (1974) point out that anthropologists' best interviews often are the result of chance encounters. While conducting research in the Caribbean, one of them noticed an old man out in front of his house, gathering stones and arranging them in patterns. His daughter-in-law was in labor, he told the anthropologist, and newborn babies were especially susceptible to wandering demons who might have been sent by family enemies. The stones would keep any such demons from entering. Through this chance encounter, the anthropologist gained insight into the people's beliefs concerning the supernatural, social relationships within the family, and village factionalism.

Similarly, when I (Howard 1977) began work in southern Belize with Mayan Indians, little effort was made to obtain information about their prehispanic religious beliefs because the existing literature stated that these beliefs largely had disappeared. Initially, this view seemed true, since the people rarely discussed such things. One evening, however, while I was visiting one of the older members of the village, a younger person present asked for a story. The "story" turned out to be a Mayan creation myth. This and similar events alerted me to pay more attention to prehispanic religious beliefs and practices. Through informal questioning, a very different picture of

the beliefs of these people slowly emerged—one in which many prehispanic aspects of their religion continued to play an important role.

Probability Sampling

The picture painted by formal and informal questioning is most valid when the entire population is questioned, or at least, a sizable portion, but when the population is large, interviewing everyone becomes impossible. To avoid collecting data from a nonrepresentative segment of a large population, the anthropologist can use **probability sampling**—selecting a segment of the population, the responses of which are taken as a miniature, relatively unbiased replica of the larger population.

One basic sampling technique is the **random sample.** This method involves selecting for questioning a significant number of persons from the entire population. All members of the population should have an equal chance of being selected to ensure that the sample is as random and unbiased as possible. For example, all names could be placed in a bowl and the desired number to be questioned drawn out. A random sample is best used when dealing with a relatively homogeneous population, such as a group of army recruits coming from similar areas and backgrounds. Ideally, a researcher will interview a wide enough spectrum of people to gain an impression of how the population as a whole would have responded to the questions.

When a population contains a number of distinct subgroups, the researcher may wish to collect data separately from each one. This is called a **stratified sample.** In studying a small Pakastani village, John Honigmann (1970: 277) determined from an initial survey that the village was stratified into six levels: noncultivating landlords, cultivating landlords, tenant cultivators, craftspeople, tradespeople, and domestic servants; and also included Marwari, a Hindu enclave in this otherwise Muslim community, and transient Brahui speakers living on the village outskirts.

Consequently, Honigmann used a stratified sample of forty subjects from each category.

In certain projects, such as trying to reconstruct the history of a people from oral sources, anthropologists employ **judgment sampling.** Rather than talking to everyone or to some randomly selected population, they collect data from a limited number of key informants, selected on the basis of criteria deemed critical to the research; for example, age, gender, education, experience, reputation for reliability, or length of residence in a particular locale. I used judgment sampling in seeking to piece together the history of Australian Aborigines living in and around the city of Perth (Howard 1981). After reviewing the written material available (newspaper accounts, diaries, government reports), I surveyed the local Aboriginal population to discover as many likely informants as possible. Preliminary interviews with those who could be contacted and who were willing to be questioned yielded information on a range of basic topics. The sample was then narrowed to those who seemed most knowledgeable and reliable for further interviewing on specific topics.

< CONDUCTING FIELDWORK >

Anthropological fieldwork requires unusual personal adjustments. The research setting is not a library or a laboratory; the objects of study are not abstractions, but fellow human beings with whom the anthropologist must live and interact. The intensity of social relations brought about by this type of research leads to emotional commitments and to unique ethical dilemmas. In addition, the anthropologist often must learn new rules of behavior and new means of physical and psychological survival.

Gaining Entry

Rarely can anthropologists simply move into an area and start their research. To begin with, the governments' institutions, and even sometimes communities of many countries require some form of research permit. Obtaining one may be little more than a formality, or it may turn into a difficult and drawn-out procedure. On the positive side, this practice of prior clearance helps to ensure that research by outsiders reflects the perceived needs of the country or group being studied rather than just the needs of the researcher.

While research permits obviously serve useful purposes, they also can be used as a form of censorship to forestall research that could work against the interests of a segment of the society. For example, Fiji has long been dominated by a chiefly elite from the eastern part of the country (Howard 1991a). To shore up its paramountcy, this chiefly elite has attempted to ensure that writing and research on Fiji favorably reflect it and its role in Fiji's history and Fijian society. One means of doing this has been through the selective issuing of permits to foreign research workers. Permits have been granted readily to those wishing to conduct research in eastern Fiji on topics that reflect favorably on the social order dominated by the eastern chiefs. However, permission to conduct research on more sensitive topics has been more difficult, if not impossible, to obtain. For example, researchers have been actively discouraged from conducting research among indigenous Fijians in the western part of the country, who have a history of resistance to eastern chiefly rule. This control of research has resulted in an ethnography of Fiji that is biased toward the views of those most loyal to the country's ruling elite.

Even when official permission has been granted to work with a group, projects may not always be successful. Since anthropological research requires delving into the most intimate parts of a people's culture, the researcher must establish good rapport with his or her subjects. The anthropologist must be candid about the research aims, at the same time convincing the people that he or she does not represent a threat to their well-being. Given an honest opportunity to decide whether they want to be studied, people will not feel later that they have been tricked. Honesty in this matter is also important for the sake of future research in the area.

Convincing people that the researcher is not a threat can be far from easy. Gerald Berreman found that the Pahari, who live in the hills of northern India, were very suspicious of outsiders. Most outsiders who contact the Pahari are government agents, despised and feared for their extortions and interference with local affairs. "As the variety of officials has proliferated," Berreman (1972: xx) noted, "any stranger . . . may be a government agent, and as such he is potentially troublesome and even dangerous." Many people have a limited number of categories for outsiders—government official, missionary, bandit. Such categories often limit interaction to superficial interchanges. In some cases, being female may help in gaining entry.

To escape negative stereotyping, the fieldworker must get beyond the role of outsider and be brought more closely into the local society. Complete immersion is usually impossible, and from the standpoint of maintaining objectivity it is undesirable, but the anthropologist may be able to occupy a position somewhere between outsider and native. Berreman found that after he had stayed four months in the Pahari village and had made a speech about the need for Americans and Indians to know one another better, opposition to his presence began to wane. "Although I remained alien and was never made to feel that my presence in the village was actively desired by most of its members, I was thereafter tolerated with considerable indulgence" (Berreman 1972: xxvii). Many initial problems disappear as the field-worker's actions come to seem less exotic and as it becomes clear that no harm has resulted from his or her presence.

Survival

When fieldwork is carried out in poor and isolated areas, mere physical survival can be a problem. Even when conditions are not severe, decisions about what to eat and where to live may affect the research.

Isolation from markets may make procurement of food difficult. This was attested to by David Maybury-Lewis, who described dining with his wife on gathered fruit and rice provided by a Xerente villager in Brazil:

> Both of us ate ravenously, ignoring the children who gathered to watch the performance. I could feel my stomach distending as I forced more and more food into it. It was a habit we had learned since our arrival. When there was food, eat as much as you can. You never know when you will eat again. A couple of lean days had persuaded us of the truth of this unspoken aphorism. Today we had the sensation which Sherente [Xerente] cherish and which is much celebrated in their stories: the pleasure of feeling our bellies grow big with food. [1968: 52]

Large quantities of food can sometimes be brought into the field, but doing so creates other problems. It hinders rapport with people by stressing the anthropologist's relative wealth. Also, one who has such a surplus usually is expected to share these goods with others. Not to do so is considered bad manners. Stocks meant to last for months may therefore dwindle quickly. In some circumstances, the aims of a research project can interfere with food sharing. For example, when Richard Lee (1969) studied a group of San in the Kalahari Desert, his intent was to examine their patterns of foraging and food distribution, but he was forced into the role of miser, standing apart from the San's custom of sharing, since accurate data collection required denying them access to his stores. This made other aspects of his research more difficult to carry out.

An alternative is to live off the land in a way similar to that of the people being studied. One difficulty with this option is that the field-worker may strain an already overexploited environment. Problems like these usually arise only in extreme circumstances, however. Most field-workers are able to feed themselves without experiencing serious problems.

Deciding where to live and what to live in during fieldwork depends on a number of factors. First is the type of society being studied. Most desert-dwelling Australian Aborigines now live in relatively stable settlements; anthropologists who live with them frequently use trailers. With more mobile foragers, like those in the Amazonian region of South America who erect very temporary camps, anthropologists are forced to live much as the people do, keeping their possessions to a minimum.

When an anthropologist is studying villagers or town-dwellers, he or she must decide whether to live with a family or to establish a separate household. Living with a family may allow greater insight into daily activities, but the field-worker's close ties with that family may inhibit other social relations. In the case of forest-dwellers who all reside in a single longhouse or Inuit living in a communal igloo, there may be no choice. Even in a village with a large number of individual households, no one may be willing to take in an outsider. Surplus houses also may be in short supply. Berreman (1972) described the house he shared with two to four water buffalo as inferior to those of most villagers. A researcher may even have to construct a house.

Sometimes anthropologists must cope with health problems. A radical change in climate or diet frequently requires a period of adjustment, which may be accompanied by intestinal disorders. Severe diseases, such as malaria or hepatitis, abound in some research areas. While illness may be a way of gaining firsthand knowledge about a people's curing practices, or their compassion, there are rarely any other benefits. In fact, by becoming ill the anthropologist may be perceived as a threat. Charles Wagley discovered this while conducting research among the Tapirapé of Brazil: "The Tapirapé are not compassionate toward a visitor to their village when he is ill; they become nervous, fearing retaliation if he should die, and they fear that his disease will spread, as well it might" (Wagley 1977: 16). An anthropologist can minimize health problems by knowing what to expect and by carrying a supply of preventive medicines.

Field-workers often undergo mental strains. For many, the initial period of entry is a difficult and anxious time. Fear of failure and of not gaining rapport with the people are common. The researcher may not know the rules of behavior in the society and may find it difficult to know how people are interpreting his or her actions and statements. In many ways, the beginning field-worker is a clumsy and unknowledgeable child—a status hard for most university-educated adults to accept.

Fieldwork among people of any poor or isolated region, like the San of the Kalahari Desert, means doing laundry by hand, as Nancy DeVore demonstrates. The water was obtained from a source six miles away. Drinking water had to be boiled.

The psychic distress caused by the strain of adjusting to a culture so different from what one is used to is referred to as **culture shock.** It is brought on by sudden immersion in an unfamiliar culture with different rules of behavior and different interpretations of actions and statements (see Meintel 1973; Nash 1963). A person suffering from culture shock may experience anything from annoyance over such things as strange foods being served at odd times or people being late for appointments to disorientation in attempting to adjust to new lifestyles or fear of people and even trauma.

Although initial anxiety usually wears off as the field-worker's understanding of the people and their culture improves, psychological stress often persists. The intensity of social interaction required by participant observation in a small, closely knit community may be hard to handle for a person raised in a large-scale society, where more individual autonomy and privacy is allowed. To escape the strain of being continually "on stage," researchers periodically get away from the fieldwork setting.

Not all anthropologists encounter these problems. Some individuals adjust better to stressful situations than others; also, some fieldwork conditions simply are easier than others. Even the most trying research, however, is not without personal and intellectual rewards. In time, anthropologists become accepted by most of the people they study and often develop friendships that ease the stresses. Also, learning about another culture is a worthwhile endeavor that adds to our understanding of human diversity.

Acquiring a Broader Worldview

During the early part of this century, under the influence of Franz Boas and Bronislaw Malinowski, fieldwork became established as the "rite of passage" for aspiring anthropologists. It transformed the neophyte into a full-fledged practitioner. What the student of anthropology had learned from books and lectures was put to the test and given a grounding in the world beyond the university. Many of today's anthropologists feel that their work is much more than simply a job. It is, according to Claude Lévi-Strauss, "with music and mathematics, one of the few true vocations" (1961: 58). It is ethnographic fieldwork that provides entry into the vocation.

In addition to promoting professionalism and producing ethnographic data, fieldwork can also play a role in consciousness-raising. Ideally, participant observation forces the field-worker to examine his or her assumptions about the world. Participant observation extends people's view of the world, revealing the complexity of human existence and the variety of possible interpretations of situations. People who were strangers or mere abstractions become real in a way not possible through films, books, or television.

In a poor southern Tunisian village we will call Shebika, a number of young Tunisian researchers found their education and beliefs put to a rude test by the realities of the villagers' struggle for existence on the edge of the desert. Plans for development that in the capital city had seemed logical and simple to put into practice lost validity in Shebika. The group of researchers "lost the typically optimistic self-assurance which it had picked up from the ruling class in the capital city and realized what a gap there is between political programme and social reality" (Duvignaud 1970: 213). Their fieldwork taught them that plans for change had little chance for success if they were not based on a thorough understanding of people gained through participant observation.

The harsh reality of Shebika also made more tangible the concept of the unity of humankind. Shebika's inhabitants were flesh-and-blood people. Along with this recognition came one of obligation: "We can't but feel responsible for these people who are part of ourselves"

(Duvignaud 1970: 218). Fieldwork, then, may not only increase the researcher's awareness of the realities of poverty and the difficulties of bringing about change, but also can bring home more imperatively the desperate need for change. Unlike the humanism of the distant intellectual, the humanism of the anthropologist who has done fieldwork is grounded in practical experience and an awareness of concrete situations (Hans Dagmar's "Focus on Anthropologists" box earlier in the chapter also makes this point).

The anthropologist's probing and systematic questioning can also lead the subjects of their research to look at and reflect on their own culture more carefully. The process of consciousness-raising among the researched is exemplified by Colombian anthropologist Gerardo Reichel-Dolmatoff's work with Antonio Guzmán, a Desana Indian from the isolated Vaupes region of Colombia. Guzmán was educated by missionaries and attended high school. He served in the army and eventually moved to Bogotá, the capital of Colombia. Unlike many persons of Indian origin, he never sought to hide his Indianness. He has sought "to find balance, a way of life that would permit him to become a member of Colombian Creole culture without losing his identity as a native Indian" (Reichel-Dolmatoff 1971: xiv). Working with Reichel-Dolmatoff to make sense of the Desana belief system, Guzmán began to discover "for himself relationships in his own culture that he had not established before" (1971: xix):

> There can be no doubt that for the informant this work involved a profound self-analysis and a detailed reevaluation of his traditional culture and of the urban civilization to which he was becoming acculturated. Everything that was discussed during our interviews necessarily reaffirmed his traditional attitudes and put him, up to a point, in conflict with his present way of life and his ambitions for urban education. Now, while describing and discussing his own culture, he discov-

ered in it values and goals that, under the influence of his formal schooling, he had denied but whose permanent validity manifested itself with more and more insistence. [Reichel-Dolmatoff 1971: xx]

In this instance, the informant not only gained insights into his own culture, but he also gained a greater appreciation of the value of this culture in the modern world, something his Western education had sought to undermine.

< ETHICAL ISSUES IN FIELDWORK >

By and large, anthropologists hope that the data they gather will benefit humanity. Anthropologists also generally feel obligated to help the people among whom they have lived and studied—those who have befriended and assisted them in their work. It is not always easy, however, to tell whether anthropologists' actions really are helpful, and long-term consequences are difficult to predict.

Cora DuBois conducted research in the village of Atimelang on the Indonesian island of Alor in 1938. She had done no apparent harm to the people by the time she left, and she had taught them a little about the outside world and provided them with a bit of excitement. As DuBois recalled, shortly after the Japanese occupied the island of Alor in 1942,

> Word reached the Japanese command in Kalabahi that the village leaders of Atimelang were claiming that America would win the war. This could have been nothing but the most innocent fantasy to my friends in Atimelang since they had never even heard of the United States prior to my arrival. But to the Japanese, suffering from all the nervous apprehensions of any occupying power in a strange and therefore threatening environment, such talk could only mean rebellion . . . so the Japanese sent troops to arrest five of my friends in Atimelang. . . In Kalabahi

they were publicly decapitated as a warning to the populace.

There is no end to the intricate chain of responsibility and guilt that the pursuit of even the most arcane social research involves. [1960: xiv–xv]

Although such instances of anthropologists causing extreme harm are rare and more often they succeed in helping people learn skills or how to defend their rights, anthropologists must be sensitive to the potentially adverse effects of their work. By acting as informants for government administrators or corporate employees who want information about isolated regions of a country and its cultural minorities, anthropologists may benefit the people with whom they are working, by correcting misinformation or acting on their behalf. They may also unwittingly supply information that can be used against the native populations. Anthropologists sometimes are privy to such illegal activities as smuggling, tax evasion, and the brewing of illegal beer. This raises questions about maintaining confidentiality regarding the sources of such sensitive data and not publicizing information that is likely to harm people.

Discretion also is required in publishing the results of fieldwork. While the majority of anthropological publications have not had harmful effects on people, there have been exceptions. In a comprehensive published account of a society, data might be included that for the sake of the society would better have been left out. An account of an impoverished East African society displaced from its original homeland, for example, noted that a significant part of the people's economy is concerned with the smuggling of stolen cattle. The account was sufficiently detailed to allow govern-

Members of the Cenderawasih University anthropology department, Irian Jaya, Indonesia. Because many people once labeled "illiterate" can now read, and most former colonies now boast institutions of higher education, anthropologists from industrial countries should make their data available to these people. Anthropologists must also be more sensitive than ever in their manner of writing up studies.

ment agents to move against the smugglers—a situation that raises serious ethical questions.

A basic issue related to the previous example concerns the audience anthropologists address. While academics and some other citizens of industrial nations are the primary readers of anthropological writing, increasingly those studied by anthropologists and those living close to them are likely to read these accounts. Many people once labeled "illiterate primitives" now read, and most former colonies now boast institutions of higher education and even anthropology programs. Anthropologists from industrial countries should make their data available to these people. Most anthropologists today are careful to see that their work gets back to the national archives of countries where they have worked and, if possible, to the residents of the actual communities. Some have written books in the local language to be read and distributed among the people who were studied. This, of course, means that anthropologists must be more sensitive than ever in their manner of writing up studies.

In most instances anthropologists are confronted with few ethical dilemmas concerning the sources of their financial support for research. As several anthropologists who worked in Thailand during the 1960s discovered, however, there are exceptions here also. These anthropologists were funded by a United States government agency to conduct fieldwork among isolated hill-dwelling peoples. The prospect was appealing because ethnographic data on these people were sparse. Eventually the anthropologists learned that the information they were collecting was being used for military purposes. This led a number of those involved to quit the project, feeling that the application of their work was not in the best interest of anthropology or the people being studied (see Jones 1971).

One of the issues raised in the Thailand situation is the propriety of secrecy in anthropological fieldwork. Is it *ever* proper for anthropologists to hide the sources of their support from the people they are studying, or not to tell them the purpose of their research or the uses to which it might be put? Most anthropologists consider it imperative that persons who are the subjects of anthropological research be provided with a clear understanding of these matters from the outset. Secrecy about such matters is ethically questionable and harmful to the reputation of anthropology.

S U M M A R Y

Cultural anthropologists' principal method of conducting research is participant observation, which requires that a researcher live with the people he or she is studying. The anthropologist begins by selecting a general area of interest. Anthropologists gather information on relatively isolated small-scale societies as well as on subgroups of larger societies. Then they focus on specific topics and locales.

Preliminary research usually is general. Once anthropologists have a fairly good idea of the area, they begin to focus on more specific problems in their research. They formulate hypotheses to explain what they expect to find and define the population to be studied.

In actually conducting participant observation research, anthropologists often face physical difficulties in recording information and social constraints regarding what they may view or record. A good deal of fieldwork consists of asking questions, and anthropologists must learn the appropriate ways to question people in a society. Anthropologists ask questions formally through questionnaires as well as informally through conversations. Since it is not always possible or desirable to speak to everyone in a population, anthropologists frequently resort to probability sampling techniques—random sampling (which gives all members of a population an equal chance of being selected), stratified sampling (which selects subjects from particular groups), or judgment sampling (which focuses on a limited number of key informants).

Anthropologists must always get the permission of the people to be studied to conduct their fieldwork and sometimes that of government or institutional officials as well. Since the anthropologist is to live among the people being studied, he or she must build good relations with them.

A number of problems associated with living in the field relate to food, residence, health, and mental stress. However, fieldwork turns people into full-fledged anthropologists, and it can also help broaden their view of the world in a concrete way.

It is difficult to assess the consequences of an anthropologist's work. To avoid possible ill effects for the people studied, anthropologists must be very careful about the disposition of the information they gather. Their responsibility also includes ensuring that the people they study have access to the results of the research.

Population   A group of individuals from whom data are obtained as part of a research project.

Probability sampling   A research technique in which the responses of a selected segment of the population are taken as a miniature, relatively unbiased replica of the larger population.

Random sample   A significant number of people selected from a population on a random basis to serve as subjects in a research project.

Small-scale societies   Societies characterized by highly localized social interaction and the exploitation of local environmental resources.

Stratified sample   A significant number of people selected from distinct subgroups within a population to serve as subjects in a research project.

KEY TERMS

Culture shock   The psychic distress caused by the strain of adjusting to a culture very different from what one is used to.

Hypothesis   A tentative statement that something observed, such as a pattern of behavior, is caused by a particular set of factors.

Judgment sampling   Collecting data from a limited number of key informants who have been selected on the basis of criteria deemed critical to research.

Large-scale societies   Societies characterized by a high degree of social complexity and dependence on extensive and highly specialized interchanges of goods, ideas, and people.

Participant observation   A research method that entails living among a group of people, observing their daily activities, learning how they view the world, and witnessing firsthand how they behave.

SUGGESTED READINGS

General books on anthropological methods:

Bell, Diane, Pat Caplin, and Wazir Jahan Karim, eds. 1993. *Gendered Fields: Women, Men and Ethnography.* New York: Routledge.

Bernard, H. Russell. 1988. *Research Methods in Cultural Anthropology.* Newbury Park, CA: Sage.

Briggs, Charles L. 1986. *Learning How to Ask.* New York: Cambridge University Press.

Crane, Julia, and Michael Angrosino. 1974. *Field Projects in Anthropology: A Student Handbook.* Morristown, NJ: General Learning Press.

Devereux, Stephen, and John Hoddinott, eds. 1992. *Fieldwork in Developing Countries.* Boulder, CO: Lynne Rienner.

Epstein, A.L., editor. 1967. *The Craft of Social Anthropology.* London: Tavistock.

Foster, George M., et al., editors. 1979. *Long-term Field Research in Social Anthropology.* New York: Academic Press.

Pelto, Perti J., and Gretal H. Pelto. 1978. *Anthropological Research: The Structure of*

Inquiry. New York: Cambridge University Press.

Smith, Carolyn D., and William Kornblum, editors. 1989. *In the Field: Readings on the Field Experience.* New York: Praeger.

Spradley, James P. 1980. *Participant Observation.* New York: Holt, Rinehart and Winston.

Stull, Donald, and Jean Schensul, editors. 1987. *Collaborative Research and Social Change: Applied Anthropology in Action.* Boulder, CO: Westview Press.

There are a number of valuable personal accounts of fieldwork, including:

Alland, Alexander, Jr. 1976. *When the Spider Danced: Notes from an African Village.* Garden City, NY: Doubleday.

Dumont, Jean-Paul. 1978. *The Headman and I: Ambiguity and Ambivalence in the Fieldwork Experience.* Austin: University of Texas Press.

Fernea, Elizabeth W. 1976. *A Street in Marrakech.* New York: Doubleday/Anchor. (fieldwork among Moroccan women)

Malinowski, Bronislaw. 1967. *A Diary in the Strict Sense of the Term.* London: Routledge and Kegan Paul. (early fieldwork in Melanesia)

Maybury-Lewis, David. 1968. *The Savage and the Innocent.* Boston: Beacon Press. (fieldwork in central Brazil)

Read, Kenneth E. 1980. *The High Valley.* New York: Columbia University Press. (fieldwork in Papua New Guinea)

CULTURE AND COMMUNICATION

The exchange of information is one of the most universal features of life and is an essential part of the adaptation of any species to its environment. Organisms are almost

➤ How human language differs from communication among animals

➤ Whether language influences culture or culture influences language

➤ What general kinds of variation occur within a language

➤ Why a person would speak one language in one context and another language in another context

➤ What historical linguists study

➤ How the promotion of literacy can have political implications

constantly transmitting and receiving information. Without effective means of communication, an eagle cannot locate its prey, a flower cannot attract a bee, a salmon cannot find its spawning site. Getting food, avoiding danger, and finding a mate all hinge on sending out the appropriate signals at the right time and on picking up essential information from the environment. A failure in communication can result in loss of resources, injury, or even death.

Information exchange is also a feature of human adaptation. Unlike other animals, whose ability to adapt to the environment is largely fixed by genetics, humans have an extraordinary ability to learn and to modify their behavior. The human adaptive strategy—which relies on technology, social organization, and values and beliefs—is unique, depending largely on the expansion and reorganization of the human brain that occurred in the course of biological evolution. Human intelligence makes information exchange among humans a highly elabo-

rated part of their life; in particular, it makes possible language. Without language, culture as we know it—the customary, learned manner in which human groups organize their behavior and thought in relation to their environment—would not exist.

How is human communication related to culture, society, and the human adaptive strategy? This question and others are the focus of the anthropological subfield known as **linguistic anthropology.** In this chapter, we will explore aspects of communication that anthropologists study to further a holistic understanding of human life.

< THE COMMUNICATION PROCESS >

Communication occurs whenever information is exchanged between a sender and a receiver. Information is transmitted by a sender by means of signals, such as a song, a sentence, a

Mayan stela, or carved stone pillar used for commemorative purposes by the ancient Mayan people of Central America and Mexico. Arduous research deciphering the inscriptions like those shown here have helped us to understand the culture and social organization of the Mayan people, especially their warfare.

chest-thumping display, or a scent. At the other end, the information is received as a message.

Sending and Receiving Messages

As we all know from personal experience, what a signal means to the sender is not always what it means to the receiver. One person may smile at another to signal approval or friendship, for instance, but the message received may be quite different: "You are making fun of me," or "You think I am acting like a fool." The potential for misunderstanding exists in all communicative transactions.

Sending signals of one kind or another is inevitable. Simply by existing, any plant or animal betrays information as to its size, shape, and location. Even camouflaged, organisms continue to emit signals. The flatfish, or sole, can alter its skin color to match the color and texture of the ocean floor, but it cannot camouflage its odor and electrical field, signals that mean "dinner" to a shark that swims close enough to detect it.

Since it is impossible to avoid sending signals entirely, the trick is to transmit appropriate information to appropriate receivers at appropriate times. From the point of view of the sender, the key to success lies in effective *impression management:* If signals must be transmitted, let them be to the advantage of the sender. In many instances, good impression management requires that signals be true. In other cases, it may be to the advantage of the sender to transmit purposely misleading signals.

Through impression management, the sender of signals hopes to control, in some way, the response of the receiver. However, there are limits to this power. Like the sole, an organism may be unable to control all the signals it emits. Another difficulty lies in the fact that a sender cannot always determine who the receivers will be. A drug dealer needs to communicate the nature of his or her business to potential customers, but the signals used to do this also are likely to attract the police. A third problem is the one we mentioned earlier—the sender may intend one thing by a signal, but the receiver might get a message that means something else entirely.

Redundancy

For both senders and receivers, there is some uncertainty in all communication. Neither senders nor receivers have complete control over the meaning of the information they exchange. However, uncertainty can be reduced by **redundancy**—the repetition or reinforcement of a signal or message. An angry man, for example, may reinforce his verbal signal—"I'm mad as hell at you"—with other signals, such as a forceful tone of voice and aggressive gestures.

A receiver of contradictory or misleading messages also may be helped through redundancy. If we are not certain of someone's sincerity, for instance, we will watch carefully for consistency in the signals the other person emits. If what a person says is not reinforced by how he or she says it, we are likely to suspect the person of a lack of truthfulness. Even with overlapping cues, clear mutual understanding is rare.

Communication and Sociability

Effective communication is basic to the survival of all organisms, but some require more complex systems of information exchange than others. An octopus does not require a sophisticated system of communicating. Interactions with other octopuses are rare and not particularly complex. Octopuses that meet attempt to drive each other away, retreat, or mate. The signals required for these simple interactions need not be elaborate.

Communication is far more complex among social animals. Ants, bees, penguins, elephants, and primates, such as baboons, gorillas, and humans, face their environments collectively rather than as individuals. Survival depends not just on the adaptive abilities of the individual but also on the

^^^^^
Redundancy helps in basketball. Coach Pat Riley talks and gestures, reinforcing his verbal signal.

sex, parenting, grooming, defense, and food-procuring; the same two individuals also may be competitors over resources. As they work together or compete in a diversity of contexts, their behavior must vary according to the situation. This complexity in role relationships requires a corresponding sophistication in communication.

While the communication systems of any social animals are always fairly well developed, some have systems that are more highly elaborated than others. Wolves, for example, have a more complex system of information exchange than ants. Most of the ant's behavior is genetically controlled, whereas wolves are much less the prisoners of their instincts. Humans are virtually devoid of genetically determined instincts and depend instead primarily on culturally learned patterns of behavior.

^^^^^
A group of closely related female rhesus macaques sit together, grooming one another in relaxed physical contact. The role relationships of social animals such as these primates are complex and call for a corresponding sophistication in communication.

ability of the members of a group to coordinate their behavior and integrate their activities in the pursuit of common objectives. This teamwork depends on efficient communication: Members of a group have to know what each is up to in order to work together effectively.

Communication complexity increases not only with the importance of interactions, but also with the number of roles each actor plays. The repertory of roles that loners such as octopuses play in their simple, brief encounters is very limited. The role relationships of social animals are considerably more complex. In a social setting, two individuals are likely to play many roles. At various times, they may be partners in

The adaptive advantage in learned behavior is flexibility, which refers to responsiveness to change or adaptability. Because of the human capacity for learning, we can alter our activities and procedures quickly to meet diverse and unstable environmental conditions. But it is not enough for individuals to be able to change their behavior. Rather, successful adaptation requires the maintenance of maximum behavioral flexibility at the group level. To alter their activities in coordinated group fashion, social animals need to have flexible systems of communication. Among ants, much of the information exchanged takes the form of information-bearing chemicals, called *pheromones,* each of which probably has only one meaning. This one-for-one correspondence places a significant limitation on the flexibility of any communication. In contrast, humans communicate mainly through symbols. As we will see, symbols represent the ultimate in communicational flexibility, for their meaning is not fixed or automatic.

‹ COMMUNICATION › AMONG HUMANS

Humans rely more on learning, engage in a greater variety of activities, and play more diversified roles than any other animal. Of all societies, those of humans are the most complex. It is no wonder, then, that human systems of communication are so flexible and highly developed. Humans exchange information through a wide variety of channels—sight, touch, sound, and smell—but the most important mode of human communication is verbal.

If anything can be considered the most basic element of culture, it is language. Language allows us to exchange detailed information about conditions both inside and outside ourselves. Culture is transmitted from generation to generation primarily through language, and a person's language greatly influences how he or she perceives the world. It is impossible to imagine what human life would be like without it.

Signs and Symbols

All communication is based on signs. A **sign** is anything that conveys information including physical objects, colors, sounds, movements, scents, and even silence. Among many animals, the meaning of a sign is *biologically determined*. A cricket does not need to learn how to chirp, nor does it need to learn what chirping by other crickets signifies: The meaning of chirping is part of its genetic makeup. In addition, the sign systems of most animals are *closed:* Different signs cannot be combined to create new signs. Such animals cannot combine a sign that means "I want to mate" with one that means "danger," for example. For these animals, each sign functions independently. Such sign systems place considerable limitations on the flexibility and range of information exchanged.

Not all animals are limited to communicating through sign systems that are closed and determined; some primates have communications systems that are based on symbols. Human communication, for example, is based entirely on symbols. A **symbol** is a sign whose meaning is *arbitrary.* Its significance is determined not by a genetic "program" but by social convention and learning. Words, whether written or spoken, are symbols, as is a cross, a coat of arms, or a flag.

Because the meaning of a symbol is arbitrary, different symbols may be used to mean the same thing. What English speakers call *a dog* is called *ein Hund* by German speakers and *anjing* by speakers of Indonesian. Conversely, any particular symbol may have different meanings in different cultures. The swastika, for example, has highly negative connotations today in Western cultures because of its association with Nazis, but to Buddhists and Hindus it signifies peace and good fortune, and to the Navajo, it is associated with the sun. The meaning of any symbol is determined by culture, not by genes.

The flexibility of human communication is increased further by another characteristic of symbols: they may be *multivocal*—that is, often they have multiple levels of meaning. To the

In Navajo culture, the swastika, as depicted on this nineteenth-century Navajo blanket, signifies the sun. In contrast, the rise of the Nazi party in Germany and its subsequent impact on the world—including, as shown here, neo-Nazi groups in the United States—has made the Nazi swastika a symbol of evil for many.

Christian, for example, a cross is a highly multi-vocal symbol. It may signify hope in a life here-after, relief from suffering in this life, or the desirability of moral behavior. By providing a single focal point to which a diversity of experiences may be related, such a symbol may help to integrate a variety of ideas.

A symbolic system of communication is also *open*. Unlike other signs, symbols can be combined with one another to produce entirely new meanings. Rather than being restricted to a limited set of signs, humans can invent new terms and concepts freely, as when the words *smoke* and *fog* are merged to form *smog*—a new symbol with a new meaning.

Symbols also are *abstract*. The term *book* refers not only to the object you are reading but to all other like objects. This aspect of symbol use enables humans to generalize about things and events to a degree far beyond the capacity of other animals.

Because human society involves such complex relationships and because human adaptation requires responding collectively to rapidly changing conditions, it is essential that human communication systems be equally complex and flexible. Symbols are the most complex and flexible devices for communication yet formed, allowing humans to adapt them to whatever purposes necessary.

Language and Speech

The terms *language* and *speech* often are used interchangeably, but there is a distinction between them. **Speech** consists of patterned oral behavior—a concrete, observable phenomenon. **Language**—a system of communication using symbols for information exchange—however, is an abstraction. Language exists only in people's minds; therefore, it is not observable. Just as the values, beliefs, and assumptions of culture guide and condition cultural behavior, so the code of a language generates speech behavior.

The capacity for language and speech is innate in all humans. All normal human beings are, in fact, programmed for linguistic interaction. Parents do not have to force their children to learn to talk in the same way that they enforce toilet training or table manners. Linguistic skills are something human children are motivated naturally to acquire. The human brain is organized in such a way that humans are programmed for "symboling," for communicating through signs that have arbitrarily assigned meanings. In addition, all normal human beings are endowed with a special kind of vocal apparatus that allows them to make the range of sounds required for speaking any language.

The configuration of the anatomical complex on which speech depends—the lips, teeth, palate, tongue, and larynx—occurs only in humans. But apparently humans are not the only animals with the capacity for language. Some other primates, especially chimpanzees, have demonstrated mastery of rudimentary language skills (see, for example, Fouts and Budd 1979; Patterson and Linden 1981; Premack and Premack 1983).

Elements of Language

Human languages have two main levels of structure: sound and grammar. The analysis of a language's sounds is called **phonology.** Grammar has two dimensions: morphology and syntax. The **morphology** of a language determines how simple sounds are organized to form units of meaning; **syntax** determines how words are strung together to form statements.

PHONOLOGY. To describe a language, linguists must first determine what sounds it uses. Humans are capable of making a wide range of vocal sounds, but no one language makes use of them all. Some languages are based on a larger number of sounds than others. In English, for example, there are 45 distinct meaningful sounds, whereas in most Polynesian languages there are only about 15.

The smallest linguistically significant units of sound—units that alter the meanings of the words in which they occur—are called **phonemes.** In English, [p] and [b] are considered separate phonemes because one cannot be substituted for the other without changing the meaning: pat and bat have distinctly different meanings.

A phoneme may consist of a single sound or a number of closely related sounds. For example, the [pʰ] sound in pike and the [p] sound in spike are pronounced slightly differently: the [pʰ] sound in pike is aspirated (that is, it is accompanied by expelling air), while in spike the [p] sound is unaspirated.* In English, the difference is not given any meaning, so speakers are largely unaware of it. Such variations of a single phoneme that do not affect meaning in a language are called **allophones.** In contrast, in T'ai, aspiration can make a difference in meaning. Thus, T'ai recognizes the unaspirated [b] sound such as in the word bahn (house) as a separate phoneme from the aspirated [bp] sound as in the word bplah (fish).

MORPHOLOGY. Single sounds can be significant linguistically, but in most cases they do not have meaning in and of themselves. To create meaning, sounds are combined with one another to form morphemes. **Morphemes** are the smallest combinations of sound that convey meaning, such as prefixes, suffixes, and stems.

We have seen that not all sound contrasts are recognized as linguistically significant in a particular language. Some contrasts are considered separate phonemes, while others are allophones of a single phoneme. Similarly, at the level of morphology, variations that have the same meaning

---

*Brackets around letters, as in the case of [pʰ], are used to indicate minimal sound units. The small raised [ʰ] indicates an aspirated sound.

will be considered *allomorphs* of a single morpheme. For example, the prefixes *in-, un-,* and *non-* all indicate negation of what follows; therefore, they are considered allomorphs and not distinct morphemes.

Unlike English and other European languages, in many languages the pitch at which a syllable is pronounced determines meaning. These are known as tonal languages. In T'ai, for example, there are five tones: midtone, falling tone, rising tone, high tone, and low tone. Just how important the change in tone can be is exemplified by the words *glai* pronounced with a midtone and meaning "far," and *glai* pronounced with a falling intonation and meaning "near." Likewise, the word *mai* pronounced with a falling intonation means "not," while *mai* pronounced with a rising intonation means "silk."

SYNTAX. All languages have standardized conventions for combining words to form statements that make sense to other speakers of the same language. These conventions are called the *rules of syntax*. The English sentence, "If you use the light meter properly, you'll get a good picture," can be translated into German by substituting German words for English, but for a German speaker to make sense of the statement, the words would have to be rearranged as well. In German, the statement would be, "Wenn Sie den Belichtungsmesser richtig gebrauchen, dann muss es ein gutes Bild geben." Translated back into English, but keeping the German syntax, the statement reads, "If you the light meter properly use, then must it a good picture give."

The rules of syntax are not learned in a fully conscious manner. All native speakers of English "know" the rules of syntax in that language, yet few could say exactly what these rules are. But the fact that a seven-year-old child can talk and be understood by others is proof that the child has, somewhat subconsciously, acquired a basic knowledge of syntax.

Other Modes of Communication

Language is not the only means by which humans exchange information. In conversation, for example, humans communicate not only with words but also through facial expressions, voice tones, and gestures. Style of dress and grooming also may be interpreted as messages by others, and even the ways in which people organize the space around themselves can have communicative significance.

Kinesics is the study of gestural communication, or "body language" (Birdwhistell 1960). Since all humans are essentially alike physically, much of our body language has universal meaning. For example, a smile probably conveys roughly the same range of messages in any part of the world. However, kinesic communication is influenced by culture, so some gestures or poses can mean one thing in one culture and something else in another (see Morris, et al. 1979). In Western cultures, it makes no difference whether an individual uses the left hand or the right when he or she gives someone a piece of candy. In many Asian cultures, however, to offer anything with the left hand is considered an insult, or at least bad manners. Likewise, different gestures can convey the same meaning in different cultures. In northern Italy, as in the United States, a person shakes his or her head from side to side to mean "no," but in southern Italy and Greece the same meaning is communicated by an upward jerk of the chin.

While most of us are to some extent aware of how interaction is influenced by body language, we are probably less conscious of the ways in which information is exchanged through patterns of spacing. **Proxemics**, or the study of the cultural use of space, focuses on the "geometry of interaction" (Hall 1966). Spatial arrangements help to define interactions, such as the degree of formality or intimacy involved. In some interactions, such as a job interview, people are likely to maintain a considerable distance from one another. In contrast, the conversational distance

▲▲▲▲▲
The use of space is defined differently in Japanese and American cultures. In the United States, bathing traditionally is not communal. Note that in the Japanese communal bath, the bathers still find ways, however subtle, to create distance between themselves.

between two good friends discussing a personal matter is more likely to be very close.

The "appropriate" use of space and the meaning of spatial arrangements are defined differently from culture to culture. For example, in a London post office, stamp buyers are expected to stand in a queue without any physical contact with the others in line and patiently await their turn at the window. In Spain, however, queuing is virtually unknown. People crowd up to the window; there may be considerable body contact, even some elbowing.

Another dimension of nonverbal communication involves bodily adornment. Everything about a person's appearance—such as clothing, hair style, jewelry, makeup—influences interaction with others. Conventions of dress and grooming serve as ready indicators of social status; moreover, they affect behavior, especially interactions between strangers. A person wearing a police uniform will elicit behavior different from that provoked by someone in a clown's suit. Bodily adornment thus helps to define particular situations within a cultural tradition.

Differences in dress and grooming often are important for cross-cultural interaction. In highland Guatemala, for instance, each Indian village traditionally had its own special customs of bodily adornment. However, such styles of dress all fit within a general type identified cross-culturally as "Indian," thus serving to emphasize the cultural distinctiveness of all Indians in contrast to non-Indians. Scott Nind, an early European resident of southwestern Australia, found that not knowing the language of bodily adornment in another culture can confound cross-cultural understanding. In his discussion of initial contact between Europeans and Aborigines, he noted that the Europeans' preconceived notions about native adornment and social organization led them to misinterpretation:

> We endeavoured to discover whether they had any chiefs, and for a long time believed they had: indeed we had fixed upon two or three individuals to whom we supposed that rank belonged. The natives whom we selected were fine, tall active men, much painted and ornamented. . . . We subsequently discovered that they were all single men, which accounted for their constantly ornamented appearance. [Nind 1831:40–41]

< LANGUAGE AND CULTURE >

It is impossible to comprehend a culture without taking into account its language, probably its single most important element. It is also impossible completely to understand a language independent of its cultural context. As expressed by anthropologist John Beattie (1964: 31), "A people's categories of thought and the forms of their language are inextricably bound together." Despite the many ways in which culture and language influence each other, however, their integration is not absolute. Each has many unique properties that are not directly, or even indirectly, influenced by the other. People with cultures that are otherwise very similar may speak different languages, and similar languages may be spoken by people with very different cultures.

Cultural Influence on Language

There has been little research into whether culture affects the grammatical structure of a language, but it is not particularly difficult to show that social and cultural factors can influence its vocabulary. Inuit (Eskimo), Saami (Lapps), and various other native groups who live in the far north, whose livelihoods and even lives may depend on snow, have the ability to distinguish many different types of snow conditions. In contrast, native Fijians traditionally had no word for snow until one was created in the nineteenth century, following the arrival of Europeans. However, Fijians do have "distinct words for each species of coconut, and for each stage in the growth process of the coconut" (Clammer 1976: 31).

In any language, the elaboration of a category of words is related to the importance of the category to the society, to the real-world diversity of the category, and to the uses to which the category must be put. The Samal of the southern Philippines, for example, have words for more than 250 kinds of fish. This is partly because fish are a main source of food and cash for the Samal. It is also because many different types of fish are found in the waters off the coast where the Samal live.

All languages have both highly abstract and highly specific concepts. However, languages differ in this respect. Languages such as Mandarin and English, associated with societies having an extensive division of labor and spoken by large populations, tend to have elaborate general vocabularies. Such English words as *administrator, mammal, society,* and *rights* are not found in the vocabularies of many small foraging societies, but they do have their counterparts in Mandarin.

Also, research indicates that vocabulary may be influenced by cultural, environmental, *and* physiological factors. This appears to be true, for example, of color terms. While all languages have highly specific words for colors (such as *peach*), not all distinguish as many colors or have the same number of general color words. Thus, the Hmong of Southeast Asia use the same term for blue and green. Also, while some languages have as few as two general color words, *warm-light* and *cool-dark,* others, such as English and Hungarian, have as many as 11 or 12. Berlin and Kay (1991) found that the number of color terms in a language increases in association with greater economic and technological complexity. Kay and McDaniel (1978) have shown that the order in which general color terms are added as societies develop reflects the physiology and neurology of the eye. "Orange," for example, is never found in a language without both "red" and "yellow," reflecting the neurological characteristics of the human eye. The appearance of "orange" is not merely a reflection of neurology, however, for it also tends to be associated with societies with standard dyes and pigments as well as formal schooling. The color vocabulary, then, reflects not only the pan-human exposure to color in the environment and the generally pan-human perception of color, but also the differential need of societies to talk about color.

Linguistic Influence on Culture

On the other side of the language/culture coin, language may determine or influence certain aspects of culture. In at least one way, language clearly helps shape our cultural practices: Every language helps to shape our perceptions of the world. Language establishes categories by which things considered the same or similar can be distinguished from those considered different. The categories of one language will never be precisely identical to those of another. In English-American culture, a person's mother is called by one kinship term (*mother*) and the mother's sister by a different term (*aunt*). The Iroquois use the same term for both the mother and her sister. Such linguistic differences influence cultural behavior. English-Americans relate to aunts differently than to mothers, but Iroquois are expected to relate to both in much the same way.

Some anthropologists have gone further and claimed that we are virtual prisoners of language. The classic expression of this is known as the **Sapir-Whorf hypothesis,** named for the anthropological linguists Edward Sapir (1884–1939) and Benjamin Whorf (1897–1941). According to the Sapir-Whorf hypothesis, the structure of thought and that of language are closely related:

> Human beings do not live in the objective world alone, nor alone in the world of social activity as ordinarily understood, but are very much at the mercy of the particular language which has become the medium of expression for their society. . . . The fact of the matter is that the real world is to a large extent unconsciously built up on the language habits of the group. No two languages are ever sufficiently similar to be considered as representing the same social reality. The worlds in which different societies live are distinct worlds, not merely the same world with different labels attached. [Sapir 1929: 209–14]

The Sapir-Whorf hypothesis maintains that the tyranny of language goes beyond mere influence on the way people relate to their experiences; it forces them to perceive the world in terms that are built in to their language. If this view is correct, speakers of different languages will have correspondingly different conceptualizations of how reality is constructed.

Certainly language places some limitations on how a person can express his or her thoughts. For example, since verb tenses are a basic structural feature of the English language, almost any statement made by an English speaker must specify whether an event is happening now, has already happened, or will happen in the future. However, a speaker of Indonesian—which does not conjugate verbs according to number, person, or tense—is not forced to make the same kind of time specifications that are required in English. In Indonesian, one cannot say "I went to the store." Instead, one says, "I go to the store" whether that action occurs in the present or occurred in the past. According to the Sapir–Whorf hypothesis, the structural contrasts between the two languages give English speakers and Indonesian speakers different views about the nature of time. The English language stresses periodicity by dividing time into distinct categories of past, present, and future, whereas in Indonesian time is seen as flowing and continuous. However, even though statements might be easier to make in one language than in the other, there are probably no thoughts or ideas that cannot be expressed in both languages. Indonesians can add a qualifier such as "yesterday" or "this morning" to their tenseless statements.

Although language and culture influence each other in many ways, both obvious and subtle, difficulties arise whenever one tries to show that culture *determines* language, or vice versa. The Sapir-Whorf hypothesis has helped to generate interest in investigating connections between language and culture; it has also generated a great deal of controversy. As yet, the hypothesis remains unproved.

< LINGUISTIC VARIATION >

Comparisons between languages in an effort to discover cross-cultural influences are complicated by the lack of clear-cut boundaries between languages. Further, some languages are spoken in many different dialects, and some ways of speaking are combinations of other languages. Linguistic experts find it very difficult to determine how many distinct languages are now in use.

Distinct Languages

How many languages are spoken in the world today? Estimates range from 5,000 to 6,000, but no one is really certain (see Table 3.1 for a list of the number of speakers of the world's major languages). As many as 3,000 different languages used by South American Indians alone have been named in the literature, but this high number is deceptive. Problems in identifying separate languages are many. In the South American studies, a single language has been identified by more than one name. Furthermore, it is frequently difficult to tell whether the language described by one linguist is the same as that described by another. Some languages named are now extinct; other categories overlap or are inappropriate. Once such categories are eliminated, there appear to be only 300 to 400 Indian languages currently spoken in South America. Yet as Sorensen (1973: 312) has concluded, "the linguistic map of South America remains impressionistic at best." Similar problems exist elsewhere.

One primary problem confronting anyone who wishes to compile a list of world languages (for example, see Ruhlen 1987 and Voegelin and Voegelin 1977) is defining what constitutes a separate language. Generally, the primary criterion for a distinct language is *mutual intelligibility*. Within any population individual competency in a language will vary, but for the most part speakers of the same language should be able to understand one another. One common way of measuring the degree of difference or similarity between two speaking traditions is to compare their vocabularies. While vocabulary alone does not tell us all that we need to know about how languages are related, it is the major factor influencing mutual intelligibility. Vocabulary comparisons frequently are made through a carefully

TABLE 3.1
Major Languages of the World

Name	Total Speakers, Native and Nonnative (in millions)
1. Mandarin (China)	952
2. English	470
3. Hindi (India)	418
4. Spanish	381
5. Russian	288
6. Arabic	219
7. Bengali (Bangladesh; India)	196
8. Portuguese	182
9. Malay-Indonesian	155
10. Japanese	126
11. French	124
12. German	121
13. Urdu (Pakistan; India)	100
14. Punjabi (Punjab, Pakistan; India)	94
15. Korean (Korea; China; Japan)	75
16. Telegu (Andhra Pradesh, Southeast India)	73
17. Marathi (India)	70
18. Tamil (India; Sri Lanka)	69
19. Cantonese (China, Hong Kong)	66
20. Italian	63

constructed list of *core terms* found in every language: words such as *woman, head,* and *rain.* Words used for such core terms in each language tradition are then compared to find similarities, but even when such a systematic method is used, there is still the problem of determining where to draw the boundary. How similar must two language traditions be to constitute a single language? How different must they be to be considered two distinct languages? Morris Swadesh (1971) developed a scale for determining the boundaries of linguistic units based on percentages of shared words. Despite such techniques, however, disagreement continues over deciding what constitutes a separate language.

Dialects

Further complicating the problem of distinguishing distinct languages, individual languages are not spoken or used in uniform fashion. Variations occur within any language tradition. A **dialect** is a patterned language variant that is associated with a geographically or socially distinct speech community or speech context. The hundreds of thousands of Russians who came to live in the secret towns created for technicians in the former Soviet Union to work on biological and nuclear technology rarely interacted with people outside their own communities, creating a situation where, as noted by one writer, "even the language secret-city dwellers speak is different—more educated and self-consciously literary than that of the open cities" (*Economist* 1993-94: 68).

People who speak different dialects of the same language should be able to understand one another; the point beyond which they cannot communicate should mark the boundary between two separate languages. These distinctions are not always clear, however. An English-speaking person from Alabama and an English-speaking person from Boston usually can understand each other, though they may find the other's pronunciation and grammar a bit peculiar. Their variations on a single language are known as *regional dialects* and are usually easily identifiable.

As studied by **sociolinguists**—who focus on the relationship between language and social factors— distinctive conventions of language usage also may be associated with factors such as class, ethnicity, or situation. These language patterns are known as *social dialects.* The contrasting speech styles of English cockneys and members of the English upper class are social dialects. Classbound social dialects are found in most societies where class or caste distinctions occur. In fact, speech differences of this nature often are cultivated for the very purpose of helping to define or maintain a separation between classes or castes. Any person coming from a lower-class background who hopes to rise in society knows from experience that "nothing stigmatizes a class more indelibly than its language" (Bolinger 1968: 138). Being able to "talk right" is almost always a critical factor in social mobility.

Other social dialects may occur in connection with such factors as religion, occupation, or age. The speech style of a minister will differ from that of a dockworker. The unique speech conventions of American teenagers provide a familiar example of the age-related dialects found in most cultures.

Frequently, social dialects are linked with particular social situations. In many cultures, the same people use one distinct dialect on formal, public occasions, and another in private conversation. Presumably the style of speech Abraham Lincoln used when he chatted with his family was not the same as what he used in the Gettysburg Address. How a particular social situation is defined can have an important impact on patterns of speech.

Individual speakers of a language may use several dialects in different contexts. The number of dialects used by a person will to some extent reflect the number of groups he or she associates with that have or require different modes of speech. The range of variety in individual speech

A classic contrast in English social dialects occurs in My Fair Lady when cockney Eliza Doolittle is coached in speaking "proper" English by Professor Higgins. The differing speech styles of the cockneys and the upper class have always been significant in class-conscious English society.

systems tends to be greater in large-scale societies simply because there are more kinds of people—members of different ethnic groups, classes, and subcultures.

Gender and Language Variants

Men and women too can have different speech patterns. This may simply be a matter of distinctions between what is considered "polite" language appropriate for women or mixed company and "coarse" language used in all-male company. But the differences can be more involved. In Japanese society, for example, there are definite male and female variants. In American society, communication between men

and women has been described as cross-cultural. According to Tannen (1990), while women speak and hear a language of connection and intimacy, men speak and hear a language of status and independence. Speaking different "gender-lects," American men and women suffer the damaging effects of contrasting conversational styles.

The Garifuna (Black Carib) of the Caribbean coast of Central America also possess very distinct male and female dialects. The original Garifuna came about from a mingling of runaway male slaves and Carib-speaking Indian women. Their different origins continue to influence the speech patterns of men and women. The women speak the same dialect as the men, plus one that is used only among women. The difference between these two dialects has led investigators to conclude, erroneously, that they were separate languages. In fact, even in languages that have male and female variants, the differences are often superficial linguistically though they may be socially significant.

Pidgins and Creoles

In addition to dialectical variations within languages, there are variations known as *pidgins* and *creoles* that reflect contact between language traditions. Until very recently, the study of pidgins and creoles was assigned a relatively minor place in linguistic analysis. Linguists and nonlinguists alike viewed them as marginal or inferior forms of speech. Many laypeople saw them as crude attempts by mentally inferior people to mimic the speech of supposedly more advanced people. Few students of language hold such views today. Creoles are now recognized as the dominant languages of several countries, and they have been afforded official status in Haiti, Papua New Guinea, Vanuatu, and Sierra Leone. John Holm (1989) listed 94 pidgins and creoles in his survey. Because of their social and political importance in the world today and the recognition that they can tell us a good deal about the dynamics of linguistic contact and change, creoles have become the object of study of a number of language experts (see Thomason and Kaufman 1988).

A **pidgin** is a simplified hybrid language developed to fulfill the communication needs of peoples who have no common language. The use of pidgins tends to be limited to particular situations, such as intercultural commerce and migratory labor. Normally a pidgin is not the native language that any of the speakers use in a domestic setting, although sometimes it comes to serve as the native tongue of persons who are socially marginal. The term *pidgin* was first applied in the mid-nineteenth century to a speech form that had evolved in China as a result of interaction between Chinese and British and American traders in Canton. The imperial Chinese government, wary of outside influence, forbade the Chinese traders to learn the language of the foreigners or to teach their language to these foreigners. This situation forced both groups to communicate in a simplified manner as a way of getting around the ban. Pidgins are now recognized as a widespread phenomenon that may occur whenever there is sustained contact among members of societies speaking different languages.

Despite considerable variation, there are features common to most pidgins. In all pidgins the emphasis is on efficient and unambiguous communication. Pidgins usually simplify such things as gender and plurality, and they tend to reduce redundancies. For example, "the two big newspapers" becomes "tupela bikpela pepa" (two big paper) in the pidgin spoken in Papua New Guinea. Pidgins, however, also may develop distinctions not normally found in the original language. The vocabulary of most pidgins is relatively limited, reflecting the needs of the specific culture-contact situation.

When a pidgin becomes the mother tongue of a society, it is referred to as a **creole.** Pidgins become creoles for two primary reasons. In some instances, people are cut off from their mother tongue and the pidgin comes to assume linguistic

primacy. Such a process occurred with African slaves who were brought to the Caribbean, where they were cut off from other speakers of their native languages. Another possibility is that pidgin becomes identified with achievement of a higher social status, which encourages people to speak it instead of their native tongue. This is essentially what has happened in the case of pidgins spoken in parts of Melanesia, especially among those who have moved from their villages to town.

In the process of creolization, the language is changed, since it now must be "large enough to encompass all the communication needs of its speakers" (DeCamp 1971: 16). It must become sufficiently complex and sophisticated to be usefully applied in a full range of social situations. This process typically involved expanding the vocabulary and evolving more elaborate syntax. Creoles themselves have changed in recent decades as they have gained legitimacy. This is especially evident in the growth of written creole for everything from newspapers and books to advertising. It has also gained greater recognition as a form of literary expression as poets, novelists, and dramatists in developing countries have sought to express their own experiences more accurately.

◄ LINGUISTIC CONTACT ►

We have seen that linguists face many challenges in studying linguistic variation. In addition, it is difficult for them to map the regions of the world where particular languages are spoken because of overlapping. Even within very small communities, there may be speakers of more than one language or very distinct dialects living together; moreover, individuals themselves may speak more than one language.

Patterns of Contact

Patterns of social interaction result in the creation of linguistic communities. A **linguistic community** consists of any group within which communication occurs, having a recognizable communicational boundary (Gumperz 1962). In southern Belize, for example, the linguistic community consists of members of six major ethnic groups, each with its own distinct cultural traditions and languages: Spanish-speaking Hispanics from Guatemala and Honduras, Mopan-speaking Mayans, Kekchi-speaking Mayans, Creoles who speak Belizean creole, Garifuna who speak Garifuna, and a mixed group of mostly English-speaking expatriates. Because linguistic ability, inclination, or economic necessity are sometimes lacking, not all members of each ethnic group communicate with members of the other groups.(In fact, some individuals are fluent in all of the languages spoken in the region.) Yet by and large, these groups do interact and communicate regularly—a pattern that has increased as a result of greater educational opportunities, the building of roads, and increased economic integration of the region. In particular, an increasing percentage of the population speaks English in addition to one of the other languages.

Within a linguistic community, a number of subunits can be identified. In particular, there is the **speech community,** which Dell Hymes (1972: 54–55) has defined as a "community sharing rules for the conduct and interpretation of speech, and rules for the interpretation of at least one linguistic variety." Members of a single speech community share a common set of ideas about language and its use. These concern forbidden topics of conversation, procedures for making requests, means of expressing humor or irony, standards for the duration of silence and level of voice within conversations, and so forth. In southern Belize the residents of a number of small mixed Mopan- and Kekchi-speaking villages may be seen as a single speech community because of their shared perceptions of the social use of language. This was not always the case. Not many years ago the Kekchi and Mopan formed distinct speech communities, but over the years, through intermarriage and migration, they have come to form a single speech community.

Links between speech communities are formed on the basis of interaction and social ties among people across community boundaries. Such linkages, referred to as **speech networks,** often are formed because of economic factors. Bilibili Island of the Viataz Strait of Papua New Guinea, for instance, is inhabited by about 250 traders and potmakers. Individual islanders have trading partners on other islands who speak different languages but with whom they are able to communicate. While the speech network of each islander is limited to a few trading partners, the islanders as a community have ties with a wide range of different speech communities.

Colonialism has served as an important mechanism for the diffusion of languages. European colonialism during the past few centuries resulted in the establishment of English and French as global languages. These were the elite languages of administration and commerce. Among colonial subjects, economic and political success became identified with the ability to speak one of these languages. For some local elites, as in India, these languages came to supplant their native languages as the primary means of communication and thus served to distance these people further from other members of their society.

In the postcolonial world, English has emerged as the dominant world language that links people and markets with the global community. As mentioned in the section "Communication and Technology" at the end of this chapter, modern telecommunications has enhanced this process. Satellite and cable television carry American news, music, and soap operas in English around the world. As businesses are drawn into the global market, they too tend to rely on English, especially for electronic communication. Likewise, scholars and scientists the world over have come increasingly to use computer networks such as Internet to exchange and search for information, and most of the communication flowing through such networks is in English. One important aspect of this technological revolution is that extensive linguistic contact is less reliant on the actual movement of people than ever before. No longer does a person need to be in physical contact with an English speaker or even to be able to read English to be intensively exposed to the language.

Diglossia and Multilingualism

Frequent contact with people of other language traditions may lead individuals to speak more than one variant of a single language or more than one language (see "Focus on Anthropologists"). Charles Ferguson (1959) coined the term **diglossia** to describe situations where two varieties of one language ("standard" forms, dialects, pidgins, or creoles) are spoken by persons in a speech community under different conditions. Use of more than one variant may have important cultural meanings. In Haiti, for instance, the vast majority of people speak what is commonly referred to as Haitian creole (derived from French), but the middle class and elite speak both Haitian creole and standard French. Standard French clearly is assigned a higher status in Haiti than creole, and an ability to speak standard French is a requirement for upward social mobility. Even among the elite, use of the two speech forms depends on the relative social positions of those speaking and the setting of the speech situation. For diglossic Haitian elites:

> Creole is used exclusively in private informal situations such as among peer groups of children and adolescents and between parents at home; French is used exclusively in formal public situations, such as in administrative proceedings or in official speeches. Both Creole and French are used interchangeably in private formal situations (receptions, conversations with mere acquaintances) and public informal situations (in shops, in conversations with friends). [Valdman 1975: 66] .

Where both French and creole are used, patterns of use signal subtle shifts of roles and attitudes among speakers.

Individuals who speak more than one language are relatively common in most societies, a fact that English-speaking American students taking their first foreign-language class sometimes find amazing. Multilingualism develops for a variety of reasons: growing up in a home where more than one language is spoken, schooling, traveling for work or some other reason to an area where another language is used, or living in border areas or mixed ethnic communities. Although an ability to speak more than one language may be little more than a convenience for the speaker, it also may have considerable social and psychological significance. When use of one's mother tongue results in stigmatization or deprivation of economic opportunities and political rights, the ability to speak another language (that of the dominant culture) may greatly enhance a person's social status and well-being.

In many countries, an ability to speak English is viewed as an important criterion for employment. In Cambodia, for example, Khmer is the indigenous language of most people, and French was the language of colonial rule. Use of French went into decline during the unsettled period of the 1970s and early 1980s. Under the Pol Pot regime (1974-79) and subsequent Vietnamese influence until the early 1990s, Cambodia was relatively isolated from the rest of the world. During the past few years Cambodia has become increasingly integrated into the larger global community, and this has had an impact on language patterns. French foreign assistance to Cambodia has focused on support for public education, in part out of a desire to revise the French language among Cambodians, and French is now the language of instruction in virtually all public schools. It is English, however, that most Cambodians wish to learn as a second language. As a result of this desire and the dominance of French in public instruction, numerous makeshift private English schools have emerged, especially along one street in Phnom Penh, the capital, known as "English Street." Typical comments of young Cambodians are, "I learn French at school, but English is the international language" (Wilkinson 1993) and "Only English will make it easier to find a job" (Thayer 1993).

People's ability to speak languages learned after their initial language often is influenced by the first language. **Linguistic interference** occurs when familiarity with multiple languages or dialects results in a speaker's deviating from speech norms—when a person "has a funny accent" in one of the languages. Linguistic interference is often a major problem for persons learning a second language for purposes of social mobility or acceptability—for Saami (Lapp) trying to become assimilated into Norwegian society, for example. The Saami in Norway constitute a distinct ethnic group with cultural traditions and a language that are markedly different from those of Norwegians. Because of their minority status and unfavorable treatment by Norwegians, many Saami seek to conceal their ethnic identity in public by avoiding Saami dress, modes of behavior, and speech, but the Norwegian that they speak tends to be noticeably different from that spoken by native Norwegian speakers. This interference makes it impossible for them to disguise their ethnic identity entirely.

Usually social and cultural considerations determine when a multilingual speaker uses a given language. In a study of ethnicity in a mixed Saami-Norwegian township in northern Norway, Harald Eidheim (1971) found three spheres of social interaction: the public sphere, the closed Saami sphere, and the closed Norwegian sphere. Although Saami was the domestic language in 40 of the 50 households, Norwegian culture and language predominated in public. Even when all of the persons in a public place are Saami, the language used generally is Norwegian. In a Saami-owned store the owner will respond in Norwegian to anyone speaking to him in Saami. Saami is, however, spoken in the closed Saami sphere—interaction with kin and other Saami at home, in one's neighborhood, or occasionally in more public locales. When Norwegians enter a closed Saami sphere, however, people usually switch from Saami to Norwegian. Eidheim (1971: 60) explains: "The Norwegian not only regards Lapp [Saami] as an inferior language in a general sense, but also judges it highly improper and challenging if it is used in his presence." When Saami wish to speak Saami in public places, they are careful to move away from others and to speak briefly in low voices, switching immediately to Norwegian when a person of unknown or Norwegian identity approaches.

◄ HISTORICAL LINGUISTICS ►

Another way of studying languages is to look at the patterns by which they change. Like the rest of human culture, language is inherently dynamic; no language remains fixed. Just as societies and cultural traditions can merge or diverge or become distinct, so can languages. In other words, languages evolve: They undergo systematic changes partly in response to conditions in the environment (especially the social environment) and partly as a result of forces within the language themselves.

Evolution is not an inevitable process leading from simple to complex. Any culture that exists today has aspects of simplicity and complexity at the same time, and the same is true of language. For example, Indonesian has no verb tenses. Standard English contains a fairly large number of verb tenses, but American black English exhibits even greater complexity in its verb tenses than standard English.

Except for pidgins, all languages in the world today are fully developed, fully able to meet the communicative needs of their speakers. Evolutionary trends can be identified, however. Persons in small-scale societies are capable of communicating as wide a range of concepts as people in large-scale societies, but their normal communicative needs usually are met with a more restricted vocabulary. As social

JOAN GROSS

FOCUS ON ANTHROPOLOGISTS

Joan Gross is a linguistic anthropologist at Oregon State University. She has conducted ethnographic fieldwork in Belgium, Puerto Rico, and Morocco on multilingualism and the role of verbally artistic forms. She spent two years in Morocco with her husband, David McMurray, a social anthropologist, where she gave birth to a son. Her study concentrated on language use.

∧∧∧∧∧∧∧∧

Multilingualism in Morocco

For someone raised in a monolingual environment, it is difficult to imagine living in a society where one has to speak and understand many different languages depending on the situation, the person being addressed, and the topic of conversation. Most Americans associate knowledge of foreign languages with years of training in school, but throughout the world people pick up other languages without attending school because it is a social or economic necessity. Furthermore, Americans tend to associate language with a nation state, whereas in many places in the world, people in a single country do not share a language.

When my husband and I first arrived in Rabat, Morocco, in the winter of 1985, we immediately started intensive lessons in Moroccan Arabic. This is a variety of dialectal Arabic called Darija, and it is the primary language of the Arab portion of Morocco, which includes all the major cities. Darija exists in a diglossic situation with Classical Arabic, or Fusha. Fusha is used where literacy has traditionally played a role. It is considered a sacred language, since it is believed that the Prophet Mohammed received the Holy Koran from God in this language. Prayers are said in Fusha. Political speeches by the king are in Fusha. School lectures are mostly in Fusha, although they will probably be discussed in Darija. Children do not begin to learn Fusha until they attend school, whereas Darija is learned as a mother tongue. Very seldom is Darija ever written, and Fusha is never used for informal communication.

Both varieties of Arabic arrived in North Africa with the Arab invasions in the eighth century. The population living in North Africa at the time was Imazighen, or Berber. Many of these people assimilated to the language and culture of the Arab conquerors throughout the centuries. However, a large number of Imazighen still live in the rural parts of Morocco, especially in the mountain ranges. For the most part their language, Tamazight, is unwritten, although in prehistoric times a writing system was developed, and this survives in some areas for use in magic spells. On occasion, Imazighen use Arabic script to write personal letters or poems in Tamazight. No books or newspapers have been allowed to survive in this language.

After six months in Rabat, we finally received permission to proceed to our field site in northeastern Morocco. Quite proud of our ability to get by in Darija and the response it got us in the Arab parts of the country, we tried it out in Nador. People generally answered us, but saw no particular merit in our speaking Darija because for them it was just another foreign language. We quickly redirected our language lessons away from

Darija and toward the local variety of Tamazight.

The language conditions that prevailed in the populous Arab portion of Morocco to the south were definitely not the same as in the north. The role of Fusha was similar, but instead of Darija, the Tarifit variety of Berber (locally called Tamazight) is learned as a mother tongue. Since the schools are run by the Arab government, Darija, not Tamazight, is used to explain formal lectures and readings in Fusha. Tamazight speakers have to learn Darija and Fusha simultaneously upon entering school.

The other language that permeates the school system of Morocco is French. The French colonized the major part of Morocco between 1912 and 1956. After independence, Moroccan schools were based on the French model, with most subjects being taught in French. Gradually the government has been trying to change this through a process called "arabization," but French is still an important part of most people's education. The north, however, was colonized by the Spanish; in Nador, Tamazight speakers have been trading with the nearby Spanish city of Melilla for centuries. Furthermore, the northern region is one that many people leave in order to earn higher wages in Europe. Typically, they leave most of their family back home and support them with their wages

Linguistic anthropologist Joan Gross (right), who spent time in the homes of women in Morocco to learn the local languages and their social setting, here helps prepare food for her son's naming feast.

earned in Europe, returning home at a later date. Because of this, it is not unusual to run into people who speak French, German or Dutch, or even a Scandinavian language in addition to Spanish, Darija, and their native language, Tamazight. Yet, they may never have been to school and may not know how to read and write in any language.

Language is a complex issue in Morocco. Fusha is considered to be the richest and most beautiful language, but few people know it well. While there is understandable resentment toward European colonial languages, it is hard to get ahead economically without knowing at least one of them. The native language (which

varies from region to region) is considered esthetically and expressively inferior and is seldom written. Moroccans adapt to this sociolinguistic situation by learning as many languages as possible. No one is considered educated without being at least trilingual. Besides speaking their native language, university students can read and write Fusha and French and generally one other European language. English has entered the scene recently as an international language, especially of computer technology. American products and music add to its prestige.

In Nador, I spent most of my time with women in their homes. Language was often a topic of conversation, even among this segment of the population, which is considered to be the most cut off from public life, and hence the most monolingual. Frequently they mentioned that while Imazighen learned Arabic, the Arab bureaucrats sent by the government to Nador never bothered to learn Tamazight. They bragged about the various foreign languages their children were learning in school. A few of the older women had been to Spanish schools as children and therefore could speak Spanish. Younger ones in school could speak French. Others had never been to school, but even these women usually had some knowledge of Spanish, and they all said prayers in Fusha, even though some words probably were not understood.

Popular culture is sometimes more important than national borders in linguistic matters. In the afternoons, after houses had been cleaned and meals prepared, women got together with their friends to drink sweet mint tea and eat together. Sometimes they painted each others' hands and feet with henna and prepared sweets for upcoming parties. But most of the time they simply gossiped and watched television. The favorite programs were soap operas. Soap operas are about secular concerns and therefore constitute an informal situation for language use. So in the Arab world, the language is dialectal, rather than Fusha.

However, Arabic soap operas all seem to come from Egypt, which means that they are broadcast in Egyptian dialectal Arabic and not Moroccan Arabic. One day, while watching soap operas, I told the women I was sitting with that I couldn't understand anything. One old woman who had recently come from the village and who didn't have a television set voiced a similar problem, but the other women were shocked. "But you speak Darija!" they exclaimed. I qualified my linguistic abilities saying that I could get by in the Moroccan variety of Arabic, but this was Egyptian. "Oh, you know Moroccan!" they replied. "That's so difficult. We only understand Egyptian."

complexity increases and the need arises to express new ideas, existing words may take on different or additional meanings or be joined to form new words, or entirely new words may be borrowed or invented.

The study of how languages change is known as **historical linguistics.** The fate of a language and the ways in which it changes primarily reflect the history of its speakers, especially their contact with speakers of other languages.

Evolutionary Processes

One of the evolutionary processes that has been identified is **extinction.** As a result of subjugation of a people through conquest or other forms of forced change, languages may cease to be spoken. In the British Isles, for example, Pict and Cornish fell into disuse as those who spoke them either died or were absorbed into English society. Linguistic extinction does not necessarily mean that the society or persons who originally spoke the language have ceased to exist, although this may well be the case. Although still culturally distinct in many ways, only about one-fourth of Canada's Aboriginal inhabitants are able to converse in an Aboriginal language. With the introduction of writing, which allows for the preservation of languages in printed form, extinct languages can be revived if social factors favor such a development. Before a language disappears entirely there is frequently a period of bilingualism, and it may take several generations for the language to become extinct. About half of the estimated 5,000 to 6,000 languages spoken in the world today are spoken by no children, however, and therefore are probably doomed to extinction within a few years. In fact, as few as 300 languages seem to have a secure future.

An extinct language may be replaced by a newly created language (as in creolization) or an already existing one. The latter is an expression of **linguistic expansion,** the spread of a language among a new population. As languages expand, they pick up traces of neighboring languages. Borrowing of words and other aspects of speech from other languages is especially noticeable in languages that have undergone considerable expansion, such as the major European colonial languages. When the Europeans subjugated indigenous peoples in North America and South America, for example, they picked up a number of native American words and incorporated them into their language—in the case of English, producing words such as *tobacco, potato, chocolate, hammock,* and *raccoon.* The global influence of the English language has meant not only that many people learn English, but that English has influenced their own languages as well. Thus, the 1992 French dictionary produced by the Academie Française recognized thousands of English-derived words, such as *bookmaker* and *cowboy,* that had entered the French language since the last edition in 1935.

Linguistic multiplication refers to the process of differentiation within a language—the development of variant forms. Frequently it is a by-product of expansion. As the use of Latin spread with the expansion of the Roman Empire, for example, dialectical variants evolved, partly as a result of contact with other languages. Subsequent isolation of variant-speaking populations as the empire disintegrated led to a deepening of these differences until distinct languages evolved—the Romance languages.

Reconstructing Language History

Linguist Derek Bickerton (1990) argues that primitive language evolved as the minds of humans and other species sought to understand the world around them. He cites as survivals of such rudimentary communication the simple one- and two-word utterances made by small children and adults seeking to communicate with one another. The appearance of fully developed language coincided with the emergence of modern humans, who possessed the necessary anatomy, some 200,000 years ago. This original language community appears to have lived in Africa. As modern humans dispersed across the globe, starting some 50,000 years ago, new languages evolved.

Tracing the history of human languages is difficult. The first system of writing, cuneiform, was developed only about 3200 B.C., and even today there are languages that do not exist in written form. Despite the lack of firm data, however, it is still sometimes possible to reconstruct the grammars and vocabularies of the ancestral forms, or *protolanguages,* and to reconstruct the process of linguistic evolution. Hypothetical protolanguages can be reconstructed by comparing the grammars and vocabularies of the contemporary descendants of the original tongue. These reconstructions are supported by the recognition that languages are systematically structured; hence, the changes that occur must be correspondingly patterned and systematic. The *comparative method,* as this approach to linguistic reconstruction is called, makes considerable use of **cognates**— words that have evolved from a common ancestral word. The English word *hound* and the German *Hund* are cognates, as are *to* and *zu* and *mine* and *mein.* Regularities in the slight differences among cognates are analyzed carefully to deduce the major patterns of protolanguages.

Just as it may be possible to reconstruct extinct languages, it may also be possible to estimate the dates at which two languages diverged. For this purpose, Morris Swadesh (1971) developed a method known as **glottochronology,** or sound dating. This approach is based on the assumption that linguistic changes are orderly, and that the rate of linguistic change is essentially uniform. If the core vocabularies of two related languages are compared and differences between them counted, a rough estimate of when the split occurred can be determined. The ability to arrive at such dates is of particular use in trying to reconstruct the early histories of peoples, including their migratory patterns and contacts with other peoples. In this regard, glottochronology is sometimes used in conjunction with archaeological work to confirm patterns indicated by the material remains or to offer possible explanations for archaeological findings.

While not all scholars agree with Swadesh's methods and assumptions—the main critics of glottochronology challenge the idea that rates of linguistic change are as constant as Swadesh supposes—overall, considerable progress has been made in reconstructing the history of human language. For example, current evidence indicates that the protolanguage for most European languages, called proto-Indo-European, originated in a portion of Turkey known as Anatolia. As speakers of the proto-Indo-European language spread across Europe and western Asia, starting some 8,000 years ago, new linguistic forms developed. We can trace modern English and German, for instance, back to what is called Western Germanic (see Figure 3.1). This and Northern Germanic (from which the Scandinavian languages are derived) can in turn be traced back to Balto-Slavo-Germanic, which is also antecedent to the Balto-Slavic languages (Latvian, Russian, etc.). Balto-Slavo-Germanic is one of the four major branches of proto-Indo-European (along with Celto-Italo-Tocharian, Arayano-Greco-Armenic, and Anatolian).

◄ PLANNED LINGUISTIC CHANGE ►

Linguistic change often is not simply a result of indirect sociocultural pressures but is brought about through the implementation of conscious policy. Because of its role in creating or denying opportunities and forging loyalties, language is closely related to economic and political life.

Therefore, those concerned with building nations or empires, promoting economic development, or converting people to particular beliefs commonly have set about to devise linguistic policies to promote their goals. In this regard Robert Cooper argues that language planning "is typically, perhaps always, directed towards nonlinguistic ends" (1989:35).

Language planning can take a number of forms. Three of these are setting language standards, creating a national language, and conducting literacy campaigns.

Setting Language Standards

Efforts at standardization of languages are often linked to the emergence of a strong state and the creation of state institutions, such as public schools. A number of countries have officially recognized bodies such as the Academie Française, which seeks to set standards for spoken and written French. The process of standardization is usually accompanied by the compiling of dictionaries and grammars. The assertion of such standards is rarely simply a matter of trying to reflect existing patterns, but often also has important social and political implications. Thus, what is deemed correct, to some degree will also reflect status and power relations—correctness being associated with those of higher status and with more power. It is such a consideration that in recent years has led English-speaking feminists to strive to eliminate what they perceive to be the *androcentric* bias in the English language.

In addition to concern with standards for an entire language, often specific groups within a linguistic or speech community may wish to set standards for certain elements of a language that are relevant to them. This is especially true of professionals such as accountants or lawyers. Thus, in preparation for Hong Kong becoming part of China in 1997, the Hong Kong government established the Bilingual Laws Advisory Committee. Even though almost all inhabitants of Hong Kong are Cantonese-speaking and less than half are bilingual in English, for the past 150

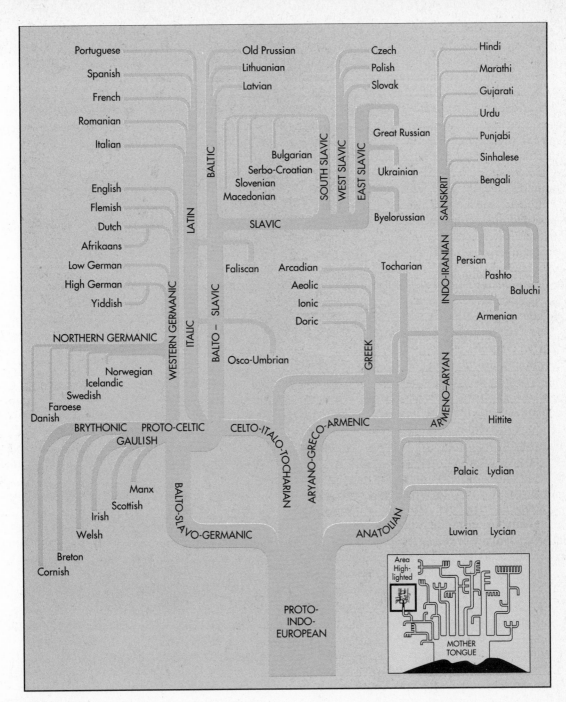

FIGURE 3.1
The origins of modern languages. The language tree best established by linguists is that of proto-Indo-European, possibly just one branch of a larger tree that arose from a few ancient "mother tongues."

David S. Merrill, U. S. News & World Report.

years the colony's common law has been conducted in English. The committee's task is to translate laws and legal terms from English into Cantonese, starting with the creation of a glossary of some 5,000 terms. This has not always been an easy task. For example, English common law recognizes two types of lawyers: solicitors and barristers. There are important status differences between the two; this is reflected in how Cantonese popularly refer to them as well: "lawyers" and "big lawyers," respectively. The committee sought to define them officially according to function, as business lawyers (solicitors) and advocate lawyers (barristers). This decision, however, was overturned by the Legislative Council, some of its members being lawyers, which preferred to keep the status distinction (Karp 1993).

Creating a National Language

The populations of most countries exhibit considerable linguistic diversity. This is especially true of developing countries, where national boundaries often are more the result of colonial conquest than cultural or linguistic affinity. Such diversity can be measured in terms of **linguistic density,** the number of languages spoken within a population. The Melanesian countries of the southwestern Pacific have the greatest linguistic density in the world. The 3.5 million inhabitants of Papua New Guinea, Solomon Islands, and Vanuatu speak more than 900 indigenous languages in addition to various local pidgins and the colonial languages French and English. Likewise, of the 660 indigenous languages spoken by Indonesia's 175 million people, 250 are spoken by the one million Melanesian inhabitants of the Indonesian portion of New Guinea. Even in much larger, more developed countries, however, linguistic diversity can be considerable. Although the United States possesses a dominant language (English) spoken by most of its inhabitants, other languages are also widely spoken.

These include languages such as Spanish, Cantonese, and Hindi spoken by migrant populations and a large number of indigenous languages such as Navajo and Hopi. Faced with such situations, national governments generally try to promote one or two languages as *national languages* to help create or strengthen a sense of nationality among the inhabitants.

Creation of a national language, however, can be extremely difficult. Moreover, it can have a profound and inequitable impact on segments of a linguistically heterogeneous country. Malaysia, for example, has three main ethnic groups, speaking distinct languages—Malays (62%), Chinese (29%), and Indians (9%). Under British rule from the latter part of the nineteenth century until 1957, English became the language of government and education. After independence the Malay majority sought to promote Malay as the national language over a ten-year period, while recognizing English as the "second most important language." The promotion of Malay reflected the nationalist sentiments of a newly independent country as well as the state of ethnic relations in Malaysia, whereby use of the language of the ethnic majority took priority over considering the use of English as a bridge between ethnic communities.

The National Language Act of 1967 required that all educational instruction be conducted in English. Secondary school instruction in English ended in 1981. Nationalist sentiments in regard to language policy, however, have come up against economic problems. Since 1981 an increasing number of graduates have found their employment prospects reduced by their poor English language skills, English fluency, being much sought after in the private sector. As one recent graduate noted: "It is impossible to secure a good job in Kuala Lumpur [the capital] without good English" (Vatikiotis 1991: 30). Those desiring to gain fluency in English turned to private schools. This pattern assumed an ethnic dimension as Malays predominated in public schools and non-Malays, especially Chinese, predominated in private schools. Instruction was also in Malay in the universities, and a growing number of students began going overseas to study in English-speaking countries. By 1991 the number of students studying at overseas universities was about 40,000 in comparison to some 60,000 studying in Malaysia. Not only did this result in graduates from Malaysian universities finding themselves at a disadvantage in seeking employment in the private sector in relation to those educated abroad, but the numbers studying overseas were creating an economic burden on the country as well (around US $1 billion a year).

By the early 1990s, economic pressures forced the Malaysian government to rethink its language policies in regard to the use of English. In particular, the government had come to see the English language as closely linked to its desire to achieve developed-country status. Neighboring Singapore had used the English proficiency of its population to strengthen its role as a regional financial center. Malaysian Prime Minister Mahathir called English "a tool to develop [the] nation" (Vatikiotis 1991:28). As the government took steps to reintroduce English-language instruction in science and economics classes, the Duputy Minister for Education justified the new policy: "We should recognize the different roles played by the languages. One is to do business, the other to establish an identity" (Vatikiotis 1993). Similar developments are taking place in many other countries around the world. Given the extent to which greater wealth tends to be associated with those linked to the largely English-speaking global economy, such dualistic linguistic policies have important implications in literacy.

Literacy

Another important aspect of language that is frequently linked to socioeconomic change and development and the subject of language planning is **literacy,** the ability to read and write in a given language. Numerous writers, planners, and politicians have argued that literacy is a crucial part of development because it allows greater participation in politics and the economy. According to Blaug (1966), on a world scale the map of illiteracy and that of poverty have striking parallels. While governments, scholars, and planners make a connection between literacy and development, many others are becoming aware of the correlation between the ability to read and getting ahead economically. Thus, writing critically of Africa's ruling elites, Amadi (1981: 178) argues: "Literacy . . . remains one of the few methods of gaining admission into the new ruling class"; it "allows individuals to acquire the much talked-about three Ms: mansion, mistress, and Mercedes." Once one is literate, these things do not come automatically, but without literacy, access to them virtually is ruled out.

While the above definition of literacy may serve in a very general way, it leaves unanswered the important question of when a person is considered literate. This issue was addressed in an expanded definition by UNESCO (1957), which argues that a person is literate when "he [or she] has acquired the essential knowledge and skills which enable him to engage in all those activities in which literacy is required for effective functioning in his group and community, and whose attainments . . . make it possible for him to continue to use these skills." In this regard, it is more common to speak of *functional literacy* than simply of *literacy*. Furthermore, the UNESCO definition emphasizes that to be considered literate a person must be able to function independently; one must be able to read and write after leaving the classroom. Needless to say, measuring levels of literacy with any degree of accuracy is extremely difficult. This difficulty is related to what Amadi (1981: 178) refers to as *cosmetic literacy*. For example, some people may

Literacy is linked to socioeconomic change and development. Here an Inuit woman reads a native language newspaper while ice fishing.

possess books, degrees, and academic titles, but show little deep-seated understanding.

As with the establishment of a national language, promotion of literacy in a particular language can have important political implications. During the nineteenth century, Christian missionaries in Fiji, who were responsible for introducing literacy to the local population, could have translated the Bible into any of 15 distinct dialects. They chose only one, however—one that was associated with the group most closely aligned with the British. This dialect subsequently became established as the written version of Fijian, to the detriment of those speaking other dialects, and helped to augment the dominant position in political and economic terms of the group whose dialect had been chosen. Moreover, promotion of literacy in their respective languages by colonial powers like France, England, or Spain has helped maintain ties between these countries and their former colonies long after independence. One response

to this in some countries has been to promote writing and literacy in a more indigenous language.

Literacy was promoted actively by Christian missionaries in many parts of the world in the eighteenth and nineteenth centuries. Reading the Bible was seen as an essential part of spreading Christianity. It also had the effect of promoting the acceptance of values associated with the dominant colonial powers; some commentators argue that it played a crucial role in the spread of colonial rule. In the twentieth century, Christian missionaries have continued such work among tribal peoples, but more often the task of promoting literacy has fallen to national governments. Thus, in 1919, the new government in the Soviet Union passed a decree making it obligatory for everyone between the ages of 8 and 50 to learn to read and write; the government subsequently set about establishing centers around the country and organizing a mass campaign to promote literacy.

Over the past few decades massive literacy campaigns have been launched in a number of developing countries such as Brazil, Cuba, Nicaragua, Tanzania, Ethiopia, Vietnam, and India (see Arnove 1981, Bhola 1981, Prieto 1981, Bannerjee 1992, Lieten 1992, Rao 1993). In these countries, such campaigns have been linked to the desire to promote rapid socioeconomic development. India's National Literacy Mission was launched in 1988, focusing on women and persons belonging to the lowest castes and tribal groups in rural areas. In addition to teaching basic literacy skills, the mission has aimed at promoting awareness of the "values of national integration, conservation of the environment, women's equality, family planning . . . and making them aware of the causes of their deprivation to enable them to move towards the amelioration of their condition through organisation and participation in the process of development" (Banerjee 1992:445).

Literacy campaigns, such as those in the countries mentioned, often have been highly successful in promoting basic literacy. In 1980, some 50,000 young people took part in Nicaragua's National Literacy Crusade. They succeeded in helping to reduce the basic rate of illiteracy from over 50 percent to around 13 percent. In many developing countries, however, very large proportions of the population remain illiterate in even a basic sense. In Africa, where the problem is the worst, 54 percent of the population is illiterate; in several African countries the illiteracy rate is between 85 and 90 percent. Unfortunately, according to recent UNESCO figures, in many countries the percentage of people who are literate in the population is declining, since literacy programs have not been able to keep pace with population growth.

< COMMUNICATION AND > TECHNOLOGY

For thousands of years human communication has involved the use of technology, first writing and other graphic forms and more recently such things as radios, televisions, and satellites. We'll look briefly at the development of these technologies, their cultural consequences, and the role they have played in the integration of human society.

Writing and Printing

Whereas speech enabled the earliest humans to externalize thought, the invention of *writing*—the process of forming visible marks, letters, or characters that represent ideas or words—allowed people to preserve that thought. Early forms of writing were executed through carving on wood or stone, painting on wood and papyrus, and incising into clay tablets. Through these simple technologies, ideas and information could more easily be communicated across space and time.

Pictorial representation, such as that carved on ivory by Inuit, served as forerunners of writing. These drawings represented objects or a series of objects, such as the canoe, human figures, and dwelling drawn by Native American hunters on a piece of wood, a work that has been interpreted as a story about the success of a hunt (Gelb 1963: 47). A true system of writing does more than represent objects, however; it represents words. According to Gelb (1963), picture writing first came to incorporate phonetic elements when cultures, such as that of the ancient Sumerians, developed a need to represent proper names using symbols for the sound of the name. In Sumer, among other ancient civilizations, a *logosyllabic* system of writing evolved, which added to symbols (logographs) for objects, numbers, and personal names the signs that expressed the sounds of words not given to pictorial representation. With the development of syllabaries, a far smaller number of characters was needed to deal with a combination of sounds in the language.

The Phoenicians and later the Greeks contributed toward the use of speech sounds as opposed to syllables as the segments for writing, bringing writing even closer to the spoken language. An alphabet involves a system of letters and other characters; when the Greeks, around the ninth century B.C., divided consonants from vowels and began writing each separately, alphabetic writing as we know it today appeared.

The Western world owes the diffusion of alphabetic writing throughout the West to the Romans, who adapted the Greek alphabet to Latin. In fact, although the Koreans may have developed an alphabetic system independently, it seems that all other alphabets derive from the Greek. In countries as widepread as Malaya, Indonesia, and Tanzania, local languages can be transcribed by using the Roman alphabet derived from the Greeks, though the Arabic alphabet is used in these countries, too. The significance of a true alphabet such as Greek is not that it links characters to any particular sounds, but that it enables the transcription of the sounds of any language (Mengham 1993).

Writing was useful to early centralized governments in recording state affairs and assets, such as food surpluses and tribute. In the Mayan culture, a system of *hieroglyphic* writing, comprising highly stylized pictures, came into use not just for keeping state records but especially for recording such things as the royal conquests, genealogies, and marriages of the Mayan elite. In short, writing came into the service of both economic and political systems.

Writing and the evolution of printing, which involves the reproduction of visible images, have been major forces in creating the modern world and have been essential in the development of the postindustrial world. Despite the rapid growth of the web of modern electronic communications in the world, books and journals remain the chief sources for the transmission of ideas. Many of the electronic media tend to simplify thought; rather than being substitutes for the printed word, "They feed on it, usually transmitting snippets of thought as an obbligato to pictures or as teasers for ads" (Barnet and Cavanagh 1994). Even if the interlinking of electronic text across global databases some day renders the printed word less important than the computer screen, words will remain the cornerstone of communications.

Evidence of the earliest printing, dating to around 1500 B.C., comes from the remains of a palace in Crete, but the Chinese used moveable type and are credited with inventing paper, and the Chinese also made ink for printing. In 1440, the German printer Johann Gutenberg developed a printing press that became one of the most significant technological develop-

ments in history. Before the press, in the West and in other areas of the world, nearly everyone except small religious and political elites were illiterate, and most people knew little of the ways of life of people even in neighboring communities. After the press, literacy became more widespread. First in the West, then elsewhere, with some exceptions, the printing press was influential in opening the way to industrialization and all the lifestyle changes that has entailed.

While literacy has become widespread in the West and elsewhere, limitations on literacy have occurred for a variety of reasons. Before the invention of the printing press, there were technical restrictions on literacy, since written materials had to be copied by hand and were, therefore, relatively scarce. In his discussion of what he calls restricted literacy, Jack Goody (1968: 11–20) points to situations in which written texts are kept secret, such as when they are associated with magic and the sacred. Saberwal (1991:733), in a survey of literacy in India, points to economic limitations, including poverty, and normative restrictions, such as the exclusion of untouchables from literacy. Thus, the pattern of literacy in a society reflects technical, economic, and cultural factors.

New Information Technology

Hall and Preston (1988: 30) identify writing and printing as the first main phase of information technology. They see the "new" forms of information technology as (1) a category that includes the telephone and the early electronic technologies of radio and TV; and (2) the microelectronic technologies (computers and such office equipment as the facsimile machine, or fax). In addition, they point out that these two new forms converge into a single system of information processing and exchange. This integration of

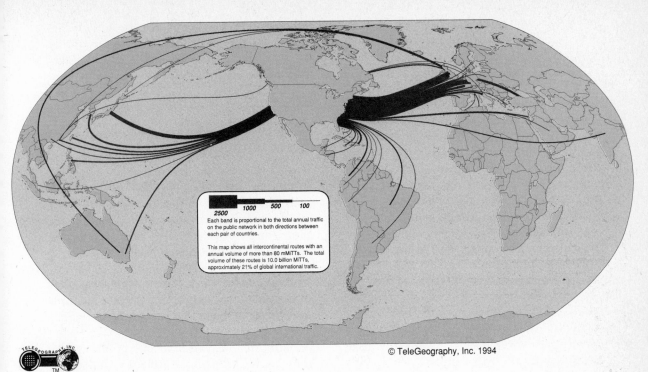

FIGURE 3.2

World Communications Flow. Societies today are an integrated part of a world system. Modern telecommunications link even formerly isolated societies.

TeleGeography, Inc., Suite 1000, 1150 Connecticut Ave., N.W. Washington, D.C. 20036

computers and telecommunications has been significant in influencing the world economically, politically, and culturally, especially in regard to globalization.

Much of the modern commercial world has become dependent on telecommunications, which allow for the transmission of messages at great speed. For example, satellite technology used for commercial telecommunications facilitates business transactions by carrying thousands (even hundreds of thousands) of telephone conversations simultaneously across continents. Transnational corporations based, for example, in the United States use this new communication technology to coordinate production, financial,

marketing, and customer service operations that may extend from Dallas to Mexico and Malaysia.

The commercial use of telecommunications has benefited some societies more than others. Although some information theorists believe that technology will ensure that economic development is spread equally throughout the world, in fact, many historical and cultural differences remain between those countries that possess advanced information technologies and those that do not (Lyon 1988:105–122). Because of their colonial past, many countries have remained economically dependent on the West. Some countries, such as India and Singapore, have been able to take advantage of their relationships with former colonial powers to begin to develop information infrastructures. Others, however, have been handicapped in certain ways.

There have been various problems in using and gaining access to telecommunications technology in some countries. For instance, the presence in a developing country of a transnational corporation may not guarantee that a developing country will have access to the technical expertise to develop its own communications industries. Also, in many countries, phone lines, if they even exist, may break down, and fax messages delivered to capitals in a developing country may depend on goat carts or rusty buses to reach the interior of the country.

Political relations are also influenced by telecommunications and have become dependent on them (Goldstein 1994:410–411). Access today, especially in developed societies, to global television, fax machines, and computer networks—all of which allow people to keep tabs on what their government is doing—may make the emergence of a repressive government less likely. In Thailand in 1992, after the government had shot at demonstrators and cut off their phones lines, continued resistance to the repressive military regime was made possible in part by the prodemocracy forces' use of cellular phones and fax machines (Goldstein 1994:415). Transmissions of many kinds—telephones that use satellites and fax or modem messages—travel across national boundaries without regard for them, contributing to the increasing reach of people and businesses beyond state authority.

However, modern communication technology can also serve national governments (Goldstein 1994: 411–413). Because of the increasing global flow of information, many governments have focused more on information as an instruments of power. Control of the dissemination of information (for example, the United States' Voice of America shortwave radio network picked up in developing areas where it informs people of the outside world), the intelligence gathering operations of gov-

ernment agencies, and the use of satellite reconnaissance to learn about foreign countries are examples of governments' interest in information control.

Mass Communications and Global Culture

The mass media have been especially influential in transmitting information and shaping opinion and culture. Radio and, increasingly, TV—both important for the vividness and sense of immediacy they provide—reach even poor rural regions of the developing world. People on a remote island in the Philippines now gather at a local hangout to watch *Rambo* on videotape, and in Colombia, travelers on long distance buses are kept awake at night watching *Robocop* (Barnet and Cavanagh 1994:27).

With the increased wiring of the world through such things as cable TV and fiber-optic technologies, we can see the rise of what has been called the **global village** (McLuhan 1989). To some extent, however, this concept of a world-wide electronic community of mind glosses over vast differences that still exist in ethnic and national consciousness. Marketing people tend to see the world not as a single global village but as many clusters of consumers sharing a common lifestyle of consumerism despite their national or ethnic differences. The global village view also tends to ignore vast differences between the rich and the poor. The majority of people on the planet still cannot afford to buy the consumer items they see glamorized on TV advertising, and more than half the people in the world still live in countries with fewer than one telephone per 100 persons (John Maxwell Hamilton, in Barnet and Cavanagh 1994:337). Yet the global village concept is a significant way of summarizing the fact that many people across the world are now wearing the same kinds of

Africans in a rural village watching television. Modern mass media play a dramatic role in integrating such small-scale societies with the modern world.

clothes, watching the same news, and tuning in to the same music.

This linking of the world through communications has brought numerous benefits not the least of which are the corporate benefits from turning the world into a kind of global shopping mall. Local peoples can also benefit; improved medical care aided by telecommunications, for example. At the same time, many non-Western countries have resisted what they see as the invasiveness of a global culture that is based so largely on white, European civilization, though the Japanese and other groups also have a hand in it. The dominance of this Western-influenced culture, and especially the United States, around the world is known as **cultural imperialism**, a term used particularly by those countries who fear this cultural influence threatens to overwhelm local cultures.

The widespread use of the English language and the overseas marketing of U.S. films and television programs are examples of global Western influence. A number of non-Western societies have become dependent on the importation of communications technology and technicians from the West. While countries such as Japan have adopted much of American culture, from rock music to baseball, with little clash with Japanese identity, countries such as Iran have tended to view telecommunications as an instrument of the spread of dangerously modern cultural values, including the independence of women, sexual promiscuity, and challenges to the authority of elders.

A very powerful force in the development of a transnational culture has been international sports. Sports champions are honored across national borders and sometimes even serve to open avenues to cooperation among different nations. Globalization as a result of sports was much in evidence when the author was watching the summer Olympics with a group of Irianese in Irian Jaya over Indonesian television. Rather than simply being an invasion of Western culture, a much more complex process was involved. The programming was handled by an Indonesian television crew covering the Olympics that focused on those items of special interest to an Indonesian audience, especially such sports as badminton and women's tennis, where Indonesia did relatively well. Women's tennis, in particular, was entangled in issues relating to women in sports in a Muslim society. In addition, the coverage in the context of Irian Jaya can be seen as having a role in Indonesian nation building.

In summary, communication, enabled by new forms of electronic technology, has become a global affair that in many ways transcends national and local cultural differences. At the same time, however, it may underscore those very differences. In any case, the day that telecommunications will create a truly global identity or a democractic explosion in the accessibility of knowledge is still far ahead of us.

SUMMARY

The increased intelligence and symbolic thought that were made possible by human biological evolution are the basis of much of human communication. Communication is a highly elaborated feature of our culture and our adaptive strategy.

Although all communication is essential to social life, inaccuracies arise between the sending and receiving of messages. An organism trying to control the impression it makes may use redundant messages to get its point across.

While communication among loners can be simple, social animals require a much more complex system of communication. Humans possess the most complex and flexible system of communication, its flexibility being based on the use of symbols. Human language and speech are unique, but other animals too may possess some capacity for language.

Our language is a complex system of patterned sound. This includes phonemes, the smallest meaningful units of sound, and morphemes, the smallest meaningful combinations of sounds. Language also includes rules, or syntax, for combining sounds to convey meaning. Humans also communicate by means of gestures (kinesics), the use of space (proxemics), and bodily adornment.

Language and culture are closely interrelated, although neither totally determines the other. Culture influences language in a number of ways; in general, those things that are of most cultural significance receive the most linguistic attention. Language, in turn, provides shape to a people's lives, although probably not to the extent argued by the Sapir–Whorf hypothesis, which says that language determines how we think about things.

There are thousands of languages in the world today, although the precise number is difficult to determine because of poor data and ambiguity about what constitutes a separate language. In addition to different languages, there are also regional and social dialects, pidgins (simplified hybrid languages developed to fulfill communication needs of those having no common language), and creoles (pidgins that become mother tongues). Another problem in determining linguistic boundaries is related to linguistic contact. Individuals often are multilingual and in different situations may be called upon to use a range of distinct speech forms, as in the case of diglossia. Such contact sometimes interferes with an individual's use of certain speech forms. It also can produce changes in the languages themselves.

Through contact and other means, languages are constantly changing. Some aspects of linguistic change are explored through the study of historical linguistics, which is concerned with the processes of linguistic extinction; expansion and borrowing; and multiplication, as well as with the reconstruction of protolanguages and patterns of linguistic change. Finally, linguistic change in the modern world often is brought about as a result of conscious planning to promote national languages and literacy.

Communication, enabled by new forms of technology, has become a global affair. In many ways telecommunications transcend national and cultural differences, although in other ways it may underscore those differences. Linking the world through communications has brought numerous advantages, but some countries see it as cultural imperialism, the imposition of a dominant European and U.S. culture.

KEY TERMS

Allophone   Variation of a single phoneme that does not affect meaning in a language.

Cognate   A word that has evolved from a common ancestral word.

Creole   A pidgin that has become the mother tongue of a people.

Cultural imperialism   The imposition of culture by more dominant societies on weaker ones.

Dialect   A patterned language variant that is associated with a geographically or socially distinct speech community of speech context.

Diglossia   A situation in which two varieties of one language ("standard" forms, dialects, pid-

gins, or creoles) are spoken by people in a speech community under different conditions.

Extinction   In a linguistic context, the evolutionary process in which a language ceases to exist.

Global village   The world as it is linked into a single community through electronic communications.

Glottochronology   The technique of estimating the date at which two languages diverged from a single language through the comparison of core vocabularies.

Historical linguistics   The study of how languages change.

Kinesics   The study of gestural communication.

Language   A highly flexible and complex system of communication that allows for the exchange of detailed information about both exterior and interior conditions. As a creative and open system, new signals may be added and new ideas transmitted.

Linguistic anthropology   The branch of anthropology that concentrates on the study of language.

Linguistic community   Any group within which communication occurs having a recognizable communicational boundary.

Linguistic density   The number of languages spoken within a population.

Linguistic expansion   The spread of a language throughout a population.

Linguistic interference   Deviation from speech norms resulting from familiarity with multiple languages or dialects.

Linguistic multiplication   The process of differentiation within a language; the development of variant forms.

Literacy   The ability to read and write in a given language.

Morpheme   The smallest combination of sound that convey meaning.

Morphology   The study of how simple sounds are organized to form units of meaning.

Phoneme   The smallest linguistically significant unit of sound. Phonemes cannot be substituted for one another without changing meaning.

Phonology   The study of a language's sounds.

Pidgin   A simplified hybrid language developed to fulfill the communication needs in the absence of a common language.

Proxemics   The study of the cultural use of space.

Redundancy   The repetition of reinforcement of a signal or message.

Sapir-Whorf hypothesis   The proposition that language influences culture by forcing people to perceive the world in terms that are built into their language.

Sign   Anything that can convey information, including physical objects, colors, sounds, movements, scents, and even silence.

Sociolinguistics   The study of the relationship between language and social factors, such as class, ethnicity, age, and gender.

Speech   Patterned verbal behavior.

Speech community   A subunit of the linguistic community, characterized by shared rules and the interpretation of at least one linguistic variety.

Speech network   Links between speech communities formed on the basis of interaction and social ties among people across community boundaries.

Symbol   A sign, the meaning of which is arbitrary, being determined by social convention and learning.

Syntax   Standard conventions for combining words to form statements that make sense to other speakers of the language.

SUGGESTED READINGS

Among the numerous general studies of languages:

Bauman, R., and J. Sherzer, editors. 1989. *Explorations in the Ethnography of Speaking.* New York: Cambridge University Press.

Eastman, Carol M. 1990. *Aspects of Language and Culture.* San Francisco: Chandler and Sharp.

Holm, John. 1988. *Pidgins and Creoles—Volume I: Theory and Structure.* New York: Cambridge University Press.

—. 1989. *Pidgins and Creoles—Volume II: Reference Survey.* New York: Cambridge University Press.

Hymes, Dell. 1974. *Foundations in Sociolinguistics: An Ethnographic Approach.* Philadelphia: University of Pennsylvania Press.

Schieffelin, Bambi, and Elinor Ochs, editors. 1987. *Language Socialization Across Cultures.* New York: Cambridge University Press.

Thomason, Sarah Grey, and Terrence Kaufman. 1988. *Language Contact, Creolization, and Genetic Linguistics.* Berkeley: University of California Press.

Trudgill, Peter. 1983. *Sociolinguistics.* New York: Viking Penguin.

More specialized studies of language include:

Brenneis, Donald, and Fred R. Myers, editors. 1984. *Dangerous Words: Language and Politics in the Pacific.* New York: New York University Press.

Cooper, Robert L. 1989. *Language Planning and Social Change.* New York: Cambridge University Press.

Goody, Jack. 1985. *The Logic of Writing and the Organization of Writing.* New York: Cambridge University Press.

Grillo, R. D. 1989. *Dominant Languages: Languages and Hierarchy in Britain and France.* New York: Cambridge University Press.

Jackson, Jean E. 1984. *The Fish People: Linguistic Exogamy and Tukanoan Identity in Northwest Amazonia.* New York: Cambridge University Press.

Merlan, Francesca, and Alan Rumsey. 1990. *Ku Waru: Language and Segmentary Politics in the Western Nebilyer Valley, Papua New Guinea.* New York: Cambridge University Press.

Philips, Susan U., Susan Steele, and Christine Tanz, eds. 1987. *Language, Gender and Sex in Comparative Perspective* . New York: Cambridge University Press.

Siegel, James T. 1987. *Solo in the New Order: Language and Hierarchy in an Indonesian City.* Princeton: Princeton University Press.

Siegel, Jeff. 1987. *Language Contact in a Plantation Environment: A Socio-linguistic History of Fiji.* New York: Cambridge University Press.

Smalley, William A., Chia Koua Vang, and Gnia Yee Yang. 1990. *Mother of Writing: The Origin and Development of a Hmong Messianic Script.* Chicago: University of Chicago Press. [Laos]

Street, Brian V., ed. 1993. *Cross-cultural Approaches to Literacy.* New York: Cambridge University Press.

PATTERNS OF SUBSISTENCE

o survive we must eat. But unlike other animals, we humans are rarely satisfied with getting food by gathering or killing whatever we come upon by chance. We desire more security, more stability, and often simply more to eat. Accordingly, we spend a good deal of time learning how to acquire food and exploring ways to increase the amount available. In some instances food procurement is done individually, but more often it involves group efforts. Closely related to the procurement process is the manufacture of implements to assist us in gathering, capturing, or producing food. While a few other animals have devised simple tools to help them in acquiring food, humans have developed tools much more intricate and sophisticated than those employed by any other species.

Human existence is more than a matter of eating, of course. We expect to obtain a much wider range of things if we are to live as "humans" and not as "animals." The so-called necessities of life are not only those things that we need to survive; often they are amenities defined by cultural prescription—companionship, clothing, shelter, means of transportation. We also produce many things that are not necessities—videos, frozen yogurt, and Nikes do not sustain us, although we may sometimes think they do. Even people with relatively simple technologies and few material possessions produce an assortment of toys, trinkets, and other nonessentials.

What ways have humans devised to procure the fundamental things they need or want? How are these subsistence activities related to the physical and social environment? In this chapter, we will look at the features of the major patterns of subsistence. We will also look at changes in these patterns, particularly those resulting from contact between people that is a result of the creation of the world system.

< SMALL-SCALE FORAGING > SOCIETIES

The economic basis of human society for most of the period since *Homo sapiens* appeared some 300,000 years ago and spread across the continents was **foraging**—collecting wild plants, hunting wild animals, and fishing for subsistence. Adaptations based on more intensive use of resources, agriculture and domesticated animals, evolved only within the past 10,000 years. Over the past 10,000 years the number of societies relying on foraging has diminished, and few foraging societies exist in the world today (see Figure 4.1).

The popular view of foragers is that of people barely surviving on the edge of extinction. The contemporary societies that have contributed to this image, however—the Inuit, San, Aborigines of central Australia, and similar societies—are far

A pig ceremony among the Dani tribe, a small-scale farming society of Irian Jaya.

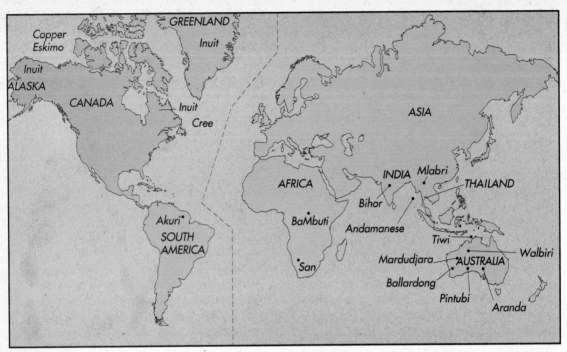

FIGURE 4.1

Locations of Some Recent and Contemporary Foraging Peoples. Those few small-scale foraging societies that for the most part survived through this century are found almost exclusively in marginal areas of the world, such as Arctic regions (Inuit) and deserts (Australian Aborigines and San). Yet these foragers are not simply relics of the Stone Age; they have been influenced by the modern world system.

from typical of foragers prior to contact with nonforaging societies. Most foragers previously lived in more hospitable environments with ready access to sufficient food sources so that it was possible to meet their subsistence needs with only a few hours of work per day; real scarcity and hardship were rare.

Archaeologists working in Europe and the Middle East in recent years point to a *preagricultural revolution,* in reference to the cultural intensification that took place among some foragers, predating the emergence of agriculture. This "revolution" included advanced food storage capabilities, long-distance trade, greater residential stability, and limited social hierarchies (Henry 1988). For example, archaeologists have uncovered beads and other indicators of social hierarchy

in Western Europe dating 32,000 years ago and evidence of permanent settlements dating 26,000 years ago. In central Russia, 20,000 years ago people lived in increasingly permanent settlements and used mammoth bones to build large structures for shelter and storage.

Over the thousands of years since the advent of agriculture, many foraging societies have modified their strategies, at least to a limited extent, to include relations with nonforaging peoples with whom they interchange goods and ideas. While these foragers might have been suspicious or even fearful of neighboring nonforagers, their relations usually were not overly hostile and, in fact, were often characterized by a degree of complementarity when, for example, forest products like wild animal skins were traded for goods such as salt or metal. In fact, some foraging adaptations are probably possible only as a result of relations with agriculturalists. Thus, no foragers appear to have been able to live in rain forests without access to large amounts of cultivated food obtained from nonforagers (Bailey, et al. 1989). Most important, such relations allowed foragers, by and large, to maintain a relatively stable adaptive strategy in which change took place gradually.

As the pace of global change has accelerated since the last century, most of the remaining foraging societies have either disappeared or been forced to radically alter their adaptive strategies. Today these groups are to be found almost exclusively in the harshest and most remote areas of the world—regions that no one else wants to occupy and where competition with nonforagers is at a minimum (for example, Arctic regions and the deserts of Australia and southern Africa; see Figure 4.1). Contemporary foraging societies differ in many ways from earlier ones because they have evolved for thousands of years, usually in contact with and under the influence of nonforagers. These modern-day foragers are not simply relics of the Stone Age; their lifestyles are influenced by the contemporary world, and they are active participants in the modern world system.

There are three basic types of foraging adaptation (Martin 1974): pedestrian hunting and gathering, equestrian hunting and gathering, and aquatic foraging. Although all are associated with relatively small-scale societies, aspects of the people's lives differ considerably.

Pedestrian Hunters and Gatherers

Most foragers are *pedestrian hunters and gatherers,* hunting wild animals and gathering wild edible plants on foot. Contemporary and recent pedestrian hunters and gatherers include most of the foragers in Australia, the BaMbuti and San of central and southern Africa, the Cree and similar groups of northern Canada, and the Punan and other isolated tribes of Southeast Asia.

In most of these societies men hunt and women gather food, and there is little else in the way of labor specialization. The relative importance of hunting and gathering for these societies varies, but gathering generally provides the bulk of what is eaten. This means that women usually contribute the largest share of the food consumed, and with this contribution goes a greater equality of gender than is found in most other societies. Women also commonly are responsible for food preparation, although men may prepare game. However, the roles of men and women in foraging societies are likely to overlap. Among the San, for example, gender roles, such as gathering food or collecting water, are for the most part exchangeable (Draper 1975). Even when hunting is the preserve of men, women can play a significant role. Thus, among the Matsigenka of southeastern Peru, women contribute a small but "crucial detail in the production of the hunting weapons," resulting in their labor becoming "a necessary prerequisite for the accomplishment of the so eminently male hunting" (Rosengren 1987: 25).

Most pedestrian hunters and gatherers are organized into small nomadic groups known as *bands,* which wander from place to place to meet subsistence needs, rather than residing in a fixed locale. The optimum size of a band for efficient use of resources is between 15 and 25 individuals, depending on the environment. Kinship plays a prominent role in recruitment to band membership. In fact, kinship often is the principal medium for expressing social and economic relations. It is likely to be through kinship that a person acquires the right to use specific territories for foraging purposes.

The members of a foraging band may range over a territory from less than one hundred up to a few thousand square miles, according to environmental conditions and population density. Not all foragers, however, have been mobile. In some environmentally favorable areas, foragers

!Kung San women and children of the Kalahari Desert return to camp after gathering food and water. Anthropologists today are more carefully studying the roles and influence of women as gatherers in foraging societies.

were able to live sedentary lives. Groups living in coastal California, for example, who subsisted primarily by collecting acorns, were able to live in settled villages, but most foragers appear to have been nomadic.

Although the band is the primary group for social interaction and economic production and exchange among foragers, larger social groupings also are important. Bands usually are allied to a number of other bands with which they share cultural features, speaking similar dialects or languages and exchanging members through marriage. The bands within this larger group may meet periodically when available resources permit. During these meetings major religious ceremonies are performed, marriages arranged, goods exchanged, and disputes settled (or initiated).

The technology of pedestrian hunters and gatherers is not complex. Because, for most, their mobility depends on their ability to carry all of their possessions themselves, they accumulate relatively few material goods. Such constraints limit differences in wealth, limiting the development of social inequality and de-emphasizing individual ownership. Foragers do recognize differences in individual skill, allowing for a limited degree of specialization in the manufacture of implements or performance of social and religious functions, but in these small-scale societies a person is rarely able to become a full-time specialist.

THE FORAGING MLABRI: "A CULTURE FOR SALE."   While some societies have, at least until recently, retained a distinct identity as pedestrian hunters and gatherers, under increasing pressure from the outside world their subsistence patterns have been significantly modified. The Mlabri, for example, who number around 150 people and now live in the forests of northern Thailand near the Laos border (see Pookajorn 1992), formerly subsisted by hunting small game and gathering eggs, honey, and edible plants. Virtually all their material requirements were provided by plants found in the forest—banana leaves, rattan, bamboo, and the like. They lived in groups of 12 to 25 people and foraged within about a 20-mile radius, moving camp every four to ten days. Such movements helped to ensure that they did not overhunt or gather too much. They also believed that it reduced the chances of children and older people being attacked by tigers.

The Mlabri have known about agriculture and for a long time had limited contact with neighboring slash-and-burn farmers who lived a more sedentary lifestyle. Traditionally they exchanged a variety of forest products (such as rhino horn, herbal plants, and wild animals) with these farming people for such items as salt, cloth, steel, and tobacco. The Mlabri were not, however, attracted to the way of life of these people, which they believed to be offensive to the spirits. If they were to settle and farm, they believed, the spirits would send a tiger to destroy them. Accordingly, they resisted initial efforts by missionaries and others to settle them.

Since the 1960s, however, external sources have made their hunting and gathering adaptation unsustainable. The primary factor has been severe deforestation, which has depleted the plant and animal resources to the point that the Mlabri can no longer feed themselves from these sources. Deforestation has also reduced the territory available to the Mlabri, and this situation has been made worse with the government's creation of forest reserves where Mlabri have been arrested as poachers. Moreover, agriculturalists, especially from the Hmong hill tribe, have moved into Mlabri territory in greater numbers.

To meet their subsistence needs, many Mlabri have been forced to work as laborers for the farmers who have moved into their forests.

The Mlabri have a very poor understanding of the value of their work and are paid relatively little by their employers. Thus, according to one report, three young Mlabri men and their mother were given only one pig and some rice for clearing over 30 acres of land for a farmer (Thaitawat 1990). Even an American missionary living there in 1990 was paying them only 80 cents a week to work on his coffee plantation.

The Mlabri have also become involved in the tourist industry. The missionaries encouraged them to sell handicrafts, but they received little for their carved bamboo and other simple jungle products. Recently, the Mlabri have received groups of trekkers and been brought down from the hills to meet tour groups. They have also been taken on tourist promotion campaigns and even put on display in Bangkok department stores. Their compensation for these activities is minimal, a pig or two or perhaps some rice, knives, and cloth. They have become what Thai critics have referred to as a "tourist attraction promoted by unscrupulous businessmen" (*Bangkok Post,* 1992) or "a culture for sale" (Panyacheewin 1990: 31).

Equestrian Hunters and Gatherers

Hunting from horseback is nearly unknown today except for purposes of sport, but this subsistence pattern was widely used by societies in the Great Plains of the United States and Canada and the pampas of South America from the seventeenth until the nineteenth centuries, after Europeans introduced the horse to the New World.

Equestrian hunters and gatherers differ from their pedestrian counterparts in size of social units, the degree of social and economic inequality, and, of course, their mobility. Equestrian groups usually have been larger, more mobile, and more likely to develop a social and political hierarchy or system of rank.

Before they adopted the horse toward the end of the eighteenth century, the Patagonians of southern Argentina had lived in small, localized groups along the coast (Williams 1979). By allowing greater mobility, adoption of the horse created a shift from reliance on coastal resources to an emphasis on hunting rhea (a type of ostrich) and guanaco (a type of llama). Adapting to the annual migratory patterns of these animals, the Patagonians moved from the coastal plain across the Patagonian plateau, and into the foothills of the Andes each year. Their society underwent a number of changes as the Patagonians formed larger, highly structured groups. The size of these groups varied during the year. While moving across the plateau, they formed bands of 10 to 15 men and their dependents, each group totaling about 70 people; the size met the labor requirements of their hunting activities on the game-sparse plateau. At either extreme of their migratory route, game was more concentrated, and a number of these bands would gather, forming a group of around 350 people possessing a common identity.

Aquatic Foragers

Aquatic foragers, who rely heavily on fishing, may form even larger, less egalitarian societies, with more elaborate material cultures. Rather than following game on foot or horseback, these foragers settle near waters rich in marine life, where they gather shellfish, net and trap fish, and in some areas, hunt sea mammals by boat. Today this strategy is still used by native peoples of the northwest coast of North America, such as the Kwakiutl and Haida, though these people now supplement their foraging activities with wage labor and commercial fishing.

Historical accounts of the Haida provide a picture of this adaptation and an extreme example of the degree of social inequality that can accompany aquatic foraging. Traditionally the Haida fished (primarily for salmon and halibut),

trapped game, and gathered berries and roots. They possessed an elaborate fishing technology, including canoes more than 50 feet long. With these boats they ranged over hundreds of miles—not always for subsistence purposes, but sometimes to raid other peoples. Their society was divided into kin-based groups. It was also highly stratified, with chiefs, servants, and even slaves. This life-style was supported by an abundance of resources and a technology that allowed a relatively large number of people to live in villages of plank houses, some of which could accommodate more than 100 people. In 1840 some 8,000 Haida lived in a handful of permanent villages.

Some aquatic foragers have been in contact with nonforagers for a very long time, and, while taking on many of the characteristics of their neighbors, have also retained distinctive characteristics. The Hezhen of northeastern China are the only tribal minority in China whose adaptive strategy is based on fishing. Their activities were recorded in Chinese histories dating back some 1,300 years ago. Today there are around 1,400 Hezhens (their population dropped to 300 in the 1940s). While they retain their own language, they have lived in mixed sedentary villages with majority Han Chinese for many years and also use the same written and spoken Chinese as the Han. As with the Haida, contemporary Hezhen subsist in part on the sale of fish, although under different marketing conditions. Some of them have also sought to live by selling folk art—in this case, their unusual fish-skin clothing and ornaments.

< SMALL-SCALE FARMING > SOCIETIES

Although rather elaborate technologies and social structures could be built on a foraging lifestyle under certain circumstances, and although, at its simplest, foraging met subsistence needs with limited effort, most of the world's people have moved away from this adaptive pattern in favor of agricultural production. The cultivation or domestication of plants for subsistence usually could support higher population densities than was possible with foraging, enabling people to lead a more sedentary life.

Food Production Practices

Subsistence farmers in small-scale societies rely on human or animal labor and employ simple tools. This type of production is sometimes referred to as **horticulture,** a term for any kind of garden cultivation. This type of agricultural adaptation evolved with the earliest period of plant domestication some 9,000 to 10,000 years ago. Over the past few thousand years more intensive forms of agriculture have evolved along with the development of market economies associated with large-scale societies, but horticultural production remains an important subsistence activity among many people on the margins of the modern world-economy today.

A common horticultural method among small-scale farmers is **slash-and-burn cultivation,** a form of *shifting cultivation*. A few thousand years ago this type of cultivation was practiced by peoples all over the world. Today other agricultural techniques predominate throughout much of the world, although slash-and-burn cultivation does continue to support millions of people, primarily in equatorial tropical regions.

The slash-and-burn technique entails cutting down the natural growth on a plot of land, burning it, and then planting crops in the burned area. Most tropical soils are very poor and rapidly lose nutrients. Burning woody growth produces a layer of ash that provides needed nutrients for crops. The soil fertility is rapidly depleted, however, and after one or two plantings the plot is left alone for a number of years until natural growth has again become lush

enough to be burned. This *fallow period* may last only a few years in some areas or several decades in others depending on environmental conditions. After burning, it is common for a number of different crops to be sown together, a pattern known as *intercropping.* Often root crops, cereals, and shrubs are sown together in a manner that simulates the original forest cover and protects the soil from erosion. Once planting is completed, little is done to the field until it is time to harvest.

The adaptational strategies of shifting cultivators vary. Two of the most common are *rotational shifting cultivation* and *pioneer shifting cultivation.* Land rotational shifting cultivation entails using roughly the same pieces of land in sequence, returning to a plot of land once the forest cover has recovered sufficiently to allow it to be farmed again. This type of cultivation is practiced by the Karen and Lawa of the Thailand-Burma border area, who complete a cultivation cycle over a period of eight to ten years. This pattern of land use allows the Karen and Lawa to live in relatively stable villages—some are 300 years old or even older—and is also characterized by careful management of agricultural and forest land, since there is an expectation that the villagers will remain in the area for a very long time. In contrast, pioneer shifting cultivation involves a constant process of opening up new land for cultivation and leaving behind land once it is no longer fertile. This pattern was commonly practiced by the Hmong as they migrated across southern China, northern Vietnam and Laos, and then into northern Thailand. Careful land management is less crucial to such a strategy, as long as new land is available.

Shifting cultivation has become increasingly difficult to maintain over the past few decades in the face of population growth, deforestation, the creation of parks, and other factors that have limited the amount of land available. Few frontiers remain for pioneer shifting cultivators, and even rotational shifting cultivators have had to reduce their cycles. One solution is to adopt

Slash-and-burn agriculturalists in the Amazon cut and burn the ground on a plot of land and then plant their crops on the burned area. Once practiced by people all over the world, shifting cultivation is now restricted largely to equatorial tropical regions.

more intensive agricultural practices. Thus, many Karen have come to rely increasingly on stationary irrigated paddy rice farming, but this requires more inputs, new skills, and secure title to the land (something denied to many shifting cultivators in modern states). Where farmers persist with shifting cultivation they usually must reduce the fallow cycle and are therefore forced to use land before it is really ready for cultivation. As the situation worsens, soil erodes and weeds take over from other plants. The result in many parts of the world is a treeless and eroded landscape in which "the cycle of regeneration to forests has thus been permanently broken" (Hands 1972:31).

Not all small-scale farmers practice these methods of shifting cultivation. In the higher altitudes of central Mexico, for example, a modi-fied system is practiced that involves tilling, weeding, and shorter fallow periods. Some small-scale farmers employ more intensive methods, especially in more fertile environments, such as the banks of rivers and lakes. They may also use animal waste for fertilizer or crop rotation to allow prolonged use of fields.

Many small-scale farmers augment their diet with wild game or fish and plants. In addition, they often possess a wide variety of domesticated animals for consumption and transportation. Domesticated animals can assume a very important place in the subsistence base and in the overall social system. Among the Tsembaga of the New Guinea highlands, pigs are eaten only on special occasions, such as major rituals and during illness (Rappaport 1967). Pigs help clean garbage around Tsembaga settlements, and their rooting activities in fallow gardens hasten the reforestation process. They are also one of the primary items of exchange: Feasts in which pig meat is distributed are of considerable importance in creating and maintaining social and political alliances.

Social Organization

People practicing shifting cultivation live in camps or villages of various sizes. Both the size and stability of such settlements are influenced by the local ecology and population pressure. People living in areas with poor potential for agriculture and relatively long fallow cycles usually live in small villages, moving every few years to remain close to their fields. Where more intensive use of the land is possible, shifting cultivators usually live in larger, more stable villages. The growth of villages may also result from external pressure. This happened in the Amazon as European expansion pushed indigenous peoples closer together.

As with foragers, the societies of most small-scale farmers are organized around kinship, which plays a vital role in ordering social and economic relations. Land usually is owned by villages or kin-groups, and a person's place of residence and access to land are determined by ties of kinship. In many ways the family is the primary unit of production and consumption in these societies, but a good deal of work is also carried out communally. Important tasks, such as clearing fields, harvesting crops, and building houses, are often done by large groups rather than by individual families.

The technologies of small-scale farmers are rarely much more complex than those of foragers. Specialization in performing tasks is rare; age and gender are the most important factors determining the kinds of activities people engage in. Among the Mundurucu, small-scale farmers of the Brazilian Amazon, women are responsible for the more tedious types of work, which also provide most of the subsistence base.

Their work includes most agricultural labor, virtually all domestic chores, and the preparation and distribution of food. Men, on the other hand, hunt and fish, take care of occasional heavy agricultural work, and conduct the village's external affairs.

Although women tend to do much of the cultivation in societies practicing horticulture, their status depends even more on their control over the products of labor (Sanday, 1974). Rules of kinship (such as whether men or women inherit land) and the extent to which men are absent from the community (for example, away waging war, leaving much of the subsistence to women) affect the relative positions of men and woman. In those societies where women are able to inherit land and engage in much of the subsistence, their social positions will be higher.

Because of their more sedentary lifestyle, small-scale farmers accumulate more things than foragers. However, the humid tropical environments in which many shifting cultivators live discourage accumulation, since many items are subject to rapid disintegration. In part because of this lack of durable goods, differences in wealth in these societies are minimal. A strong emphasis often is placed on sharing of food and possessions. Sharing ensures that every villager has enough to eat and promotes village solidarity. Despite the lack of differences in wealth, members of these societies are not always social equals, for while accumulation of durable wealth may be limited, status differences can come about through the exchange of goods and services.

◄ PASTORAL SOCIETIES ►

In areas of low and unpredictable rainfall, which are not well-suited for agricultural production, animal herding, or **pastoralism,** is a useful adaptation. Found in many parts of Asia, Africa, and Europe, animal herding was uncommon in the Americas until the arrival of Europeans. In some pastoral societies, only the herders move with the herds, while other members live in settled villages growing some crops; in other pastoral societies everyone moves with their migrating herd. We will consider these two pastoral variants separately, for they shape cultures in different ways.

Transhumance

In this form of adaptation, only the herders move with the herds. **Transhumance** consists of limited crop production near a village and migratory herding of animals. This pattern is found, for example, among certain Mediterranean societies, the Navajo of the American Southwest following European contact, and various groups in the drier

areas of southern Africa and in the foothills of the Himalayas of South Asia. The relative importance of herding and farming among transhumants varies a great deal. While some transhumants rely a great deal on their herds, others do not. Among the Nuer of southern Sudan, for example, Turton (1980: 78–79) estimates that cattle account for less than 20 percent of dietary requirements, while farming and fishing account for the remaining 80 percent. This is not to deny the importance of cattle, however, which serve as a vital emergency resource in an environment where rainfall is highly erratic and crops can fail, as well as occupying a central role in the symbolic and ritual life of these people.

Around the Mediterranean, with its pattern of long summer droughts and wet winters, a pro-

Pastoral nomads living in regions not suited to horticulture or transhumance build their subsistence around movement with grazing herds. Here pastoral nomad goatherders near Cairo, Egypt, live a mobile way of life, depending on their animals for subsistence.

duction system has evolved based on cereals such as wheat and barley, tree and vine crops such as olives and grapes, horticultural production of fruits and vegetables, and grazing sheep and goats. In the more impoverished Mediterranean environments, the grazing of sheep and goats has assumed particular importance. The sheep and goats are grazed on coastal plains during the wet winter and spring and moved to the highlands when lowland vegetation dries up during the summer. The people live in sedentary villages. For those living in the lowlands, male shepherds spend a good deal of time away from the villages grazing their animals on distant pastures. Grazing is conducted by the family, and cooperation in the community beyond the family level is rare. Moreover, conflict between families is common as families compete for scarce resources and attempt to defend family honor and well-being. In such pastoral societies, men often control work, property, and politics, animal herds are passed from fathers to sons, and the father rules the household. Women, often excluded from such patterns of control, including that over the herds, occupy a subordinate status in the society.

Pastoral Nomadism

In regions even less suited to horticulture or transhumance, peoples have built their subsistence patterns around nomadic movement with grazing herds. **Pastoral nomadism** is an economic adaptation and life-style characterized by lack of permanent habitation and primary dependence on the herding of animals for subsistence.

The development of pastoral nomadism followed the domestication of the horse in the Asian steppes and the camel in southwestern Arabia, both around 3000 B.C. Over the next 2,000 years or so, pastoral nomads spread into the drier areas of northern and eastern Asia and Africa. They occupied the high mountains, lowland deserts, and dry steppes, which were sparsely populated by more sedentary populations. The use of horses and camels for food and transportation allowed a more mobile pattern based on animal grazing than had been possible before. Pastoral nomadism developed in other parts of the world too, such as among the Saami of northern Europe, whose economy centers on reindeer herding.

SUBSISTENCE ACTIVITIES. Movement is a central feature of pastoral nomadism. Because of seasonal variation or unpredictability in the weather, pastoral nomads must move their herds to take maximal advantage of available pasturage. Many pastoral nomadic societies in the Middle East follow a traditional route, or "tribal road," over a widely diverse landscape. Typically the pattern entails gradual movement from a low-lying area, where they are close to sedentary peoples, to high and isolated mountain pastures.

Pastoralists herd many kinds of animals, and the extent to which they are involved in agricultural production varies considerably. Pastoralists also vary in self-sufficiency: those in Africa concentrate on meeting their own daily food needs, whereas in the Middle East they try to produce a marketable surplus that can be exchanged for other goods. Nevertheless, all pastoral nomads depend to some extent on nonpastoral products, such as grains and fruits.

SOCIAL ORGANIZATION. Among pastoral nomads, animals are usually owned by individuals or family heads, and the primary unit of production and consumption is the family. Families, however, must work with larger groups for efficient use of resources and often for protection. Families are part of individual herding groups, or *camps*. The size of the herding group will depend on factors influencing optimum herd size and composition and on the distribution of age and gender differences within the human group. The composition of the herding group is constantly in flux. In addition to seasonal changes associated with herding requirements, groups change as individuals mature and as herds grow.

Above the camp level of organization, pastoral nomads commonly are grouped into larger social alliances, usually on the basis of kinship. The primary form of alliance is the *tribe,* sometimes formed through presumed descent from a common founding ancestor or perhaps through an alliance of associated kin-based groups. Tribes vary in size from a few hundred to several hundred thousand individuals. In the past, primarily because of the influence of central governments and pressure to organize into larger groupings for purposes of warfare, tribes sometimes joined to form larger *confederacies.* These confederacies tended to be highly unstable.

Within pastoral nomadic societies the division of labor is based primarily on age and gender. Much of the labor associated with herding and agriculture is done by men, but women, too, often play an important role in herding. Studies of some East African pastoral societies have demonstrated that women sometimes engage in herding even large animals and have also pointed to a range of herding-related activities carried out by women, including carrying water and feed for the animals, caring for sick and young livestock, and processing or milking the animals (Wienpahl 1984, Dahl 1987). In addition to any herding activities, women are responsible for domestic tasks and for producing items associated with the home, such as handwoven rugs. Specialization within a group is rare, but group members may depend on many goods and services produced by people who are not pastoral nomads—itinerant traders and craftspeople, sedentary workers, and merchants.

Despite their mobility, pastoral nomads are able to accumulate possessions because they can carry them on large pack animals. Also, since most pastoral nomads are integrated into national economies, they are able to accumulate wealth in the mobile form of general-purpose money. The ability to accumulate wealth and the need to coordinate the movement of large numbers of people and animals and their access to scarce resources have led to greater differences in social status among pastoral nomads than among other small-scale societies. Status differences have also resulted from contact with centralized authority.

Since the nineteenth century the number of pastoral nomads has declined because of the expansion of more intensive systems of land use and pressure to settle from central governments. There are still, however, several million pastoral nomads in the less fertile parts of North Africa and the Near East. For these people, pastoral nomadism remains the optimum adaptive strategy in such difficult environments. An example of how pastoral nomads in Tibet have, through sophisticated adaptive strategies, managed to survive and even created a secure existence in a sometimes hostile environment is provided in the "Focus on Anthropologists."

< LARGE-SCALE SOCIETIES, THE > WORLD SYSTEM, AND INDUSTRIALIZATION

The subsistence patterns we have looked at so far involve relatively small-scale human groups. Large-scale societies are more often associated with intensive agriculture. The establishment of relatively dense populations arose following the founding of village farming communities between 8000 and 6000 B.C. as agricultural production was intensified in certain parts of the world. There were only a few centers where early states were formed. These included the so-called cradles of civilization in the Near East, the Far East, and the New World. In these settings, previously autonomous villages were incorporated into larger political units, cities grew, and commerce beyond the village level assumed greater importance. Between A.D. 1 and A.D. 1000, the centers expanded north in Europe beyond the Mediterranean, south of the Yangtse River in China, and into southern Africa. In the New World, the civilizations in Mexico and the Andean region of South America spread into

MELVYN C. GOLDSTEIN AND CYNTHIA M. BEALL

FOCUS ON ANTHROPOLOGISTS

Melvyn C. Goldstein is the John Reynolds Harkness Professor and Chairman of the Department of Anthropology at Case Western Reserve University. He is also the director of the university's Center for Research on Tibet. Dr. Goldstein's research has taken him to India, Nepal, and China. He is currently engaged in projects in Tibet and the Mongolian People's Republic. Cynthia M. Beall is Professor of Physical Anthropology in the Department of Anthropology at Case Western Reserve University. She has conducted extensive research on human biology and adaptation to high altitude in the Peruvian and Bolivian Andes and the Nepalese Himalayas, and is currently conducting research in this area in Tibet and the Mongolian People's Republic. Professors Beall and Goldstein are the authors of Nomads of Western Tibet: The Survival of a Way of Life *(University of California Press, 1990).*

∧∧∧∧∧∧∧∧

Nomads on the Roof of the World

T ibetan nomadic pastoralists—*drokba*—exemplify an ancient and successful lifestyle in which domesticated animals are used to convert natural vegetation into food, clothing, and shelter for their owners. The owners do no farming, nor do they feed their animals fodder; rather, they move their tents and herds several times a year to ensure that their livestock obtain adequate grass and water.

Between 1986 and 1990, we spent about 20 months in Tibet (the Tibet Autonomous Region of China), living with and studying a group of nomadic pastoralists in Phala, about 300 miles west of Lhasa, the capital of Tibet. In a world characterized by farmers and hostile

governments pushing pastoralists into increasingly marginal environments, Tibet's nomads are fortunate to still live in their traditional habitat—Tibet's *changdang*, or "northern plateau."

There they have lived with their herds of yak, sheep, and goats for untold centuries, not just eking out a meager existence, but actually producing substantial surpluses that were the backbone of Tibet's sophisticated religious civilizations. One of our research goals was to learn how they accomplished this without destroying their grassland environment.

The formidable changdang is truly the "roof of the world." Encampments range from 16,000 to 17,000 feet above sea level, and temperature lows reach well below zero—in winter, 30° to 50° F. In midsummer, temperatures still hover around

freezing. Sitting in tents in winter, we were struck by the ferocity of the climate—while a roaring fire warmed our fronts, the relentless cold tugged at our backs, reminding us that the fire was only a small point of warmth in a world of bitter cold.

These harsh conditions, however, have actually served the nomads by protecting them from the competition of agriculturalists seeking to expand production. Farming is simply not a viable alternative to herding. If there were no nomads on the changdang, the land would revert to the wildlife.

Life on the changdang is not easy. Because Tibetan livestock feed entirely on natural vegetation, the animals must be taken to graze every day, regardless of the weather. Similarly, lactating animals must be milked every day. The sight of nomad women milking their yaks as a storm deposits a layer of snow on their backs, or of a herder returning in the evening so numb with cold that even opening a tent flap is difficult, epitomizes the hardship of pastoralism on the changdang.

The nomads of Phala, however, view things differently. They laughed when we referred to the hardships and insisted that their way of life was far easier than that of farmers, who had to plow the soil and weed the fields. As one of them explained to us: "Look, it is obvious that we have a very easy life. The grass grows by itself, the animals reproduce by themselves, they give milk and meat without our doing anything. So how can you say our way of life is hard?"

The Phala nomads actually do have a great deal of leisure time, but they are not passive bystanders. Their success depends on their active adaptation to changing conditions. They cannot alter the cold or wind or snow, but they can compensate for it by adjusting how and where they herd.

Having no farms (and there being no outside migration for jobs), these people depend completely on their livestock, which they view as a perpetual source of wealth. It is a simple view—if they can provide the herd with proper water and grasses, the animals will provide the nomads the means to survive as well.

On a cold day, anthropologists Cynthia Beall and Melvyn Goldstein with Tibetan nomadic pastoralists.

The nomads' animals do this by yielding a wide variety of products.

As sources of food, the herd provides milk and meat products. Milk production, however, is highly seasonal. The sheep and goats (87 percent of the herd) give milk only from June to September, so there is an abundance in summer and an inadequate supply in winter and spring, when only yaks are lactating. To compensate, the nomads process the milk, converting the quickly perishable summer milk into storable butter and cheese.

During the peak summer milking season, women boil each day's fresh milk and set it aside overnight to become tart, smooth yogurt. The next morn-

ing, they eat some and churn the rest for about an hour to produce butter. When sewn tightly in "football-size" packets made from sheep stomachs, this butter can be stored for up to a year. The remaining milk solids are reboiled to produce a soft, tart cheese. Some of this is also eaten fresh, but most is dried in the sun. The resulting crumbly, rock-hard cheese can be stored indefinitely. The nomads, therefore, have developed an effective dairy-processing system that enables them to spread the summer abundance of milk calories throughout the year.

Meat, another important component of the nomad diet, is also harvested in a manner to maximize its caloric value. Rather than slaughter animals throughout the year, the nomads cull their herd for food at the end of fall. This is when the good grazing of summer and fall has built the largest store of fat on the animals. The nomads argue (correctly) that to slaughter livestock earlier or later would result in less meat and fat per animal. Also in late fall there is no problem storing the 20 or so animals most families slaughter, since temperatures are already well below zero.

The nomads' animals also provide the raw materials essential for clothing, shelter, and fuel. Life on the changdang requires a portable dwelling that can stand up to the terrible wind and hailstorms that are common in this area. The Phala people weave the coarse black belly-hair of yaks into material that they sew into their windproof and durable tents. As for clothing, 8 to 10 sheepskins or goatskins are used to make the nomads' heavy winter robelike dress, the fleece worn on the inside. Their pants are made from heavy woven wool or from sheepskin or goatskin, and their boots have yakskin soles and woolen leggings. Similarly, winter hats are generally made from lamb's fleece, and ropes, bags, and gear for their horses come from the wool, cashmere,

and leather they harvest from their livestock.

The herds also provide fuel, critical for cooking and heating. There are no trees (or even shrubs) on the changdang, and life would not be possible without the dung of animals. Thus, the nomads have a free and inexhaustible source of energy that requires little work to collect.

Intrinsic to nomadic pastoralism is moving camp. In Tibet, yak, sheep, and goats can be used as transport animals. Having their own source of transport also means the nomads can easily trade with other segments of the society; in fact, half of their total caloric intake comes from barley they obtain from farmers living about a month's walk to the southeast. In its traditional trade system, the nomads carry a variety of items, including wool; goat hair; skins of yak, sheep, and goats; butter; and live animals. They return laden with barley and other foods, such as tea and cooking oil. They also obtain items such as wooden utensils, metalware, swords, and jewelry.

The transport animals serve still another function. They enable the nomads to exploit the enormous salt flats on the

Tibetan plateau. From a distance these look like vast snowfields, but up close they are recognized as salt deposits about one foot deep. This salt is literally there for the taking, but the task is not easy. The Tibetan nomads traditionally obtain salt in the spring, the round trip from Phala to the northwest salt flat taking 70 days. Then, the salt is transported for another month to the south to be sold.

Wild animals also play a part in the pastoral adaptation. Phala has substantial herds of antelopes, gazelles, and blue sheep—all of which are considered edible by the nomads, but they are not usually hunted heavily. When times are good, most nomads adhere more strictly to their Buddhist values and refrain from killing. However, when times are bad, literally everyone hunts. Thus, in a sense, the wildlife acts as a stockpile, used little until conditions warrant it.

The nomadic pastoralists of Phala serve as an excellent example of the nomadic pastoral mode of production. Through a sophisticated and highly efficient system of breeding, rearing, and harvesting livestock, they secure for themselves a stable and satisfactory existence in an environment that is often hostile.

surrounding areas. Much of the growth in these centers was related to more systematic and intensive agricultural production, accompanied by population growth.

Beginning in the fifteenth century, European exploration, expansion, and colonization altered human society further by creating a more integrated world system. Peoples came into contact with one another to an unprecedented degree. Crops and farming techniques spread over wide areas, and commercial exchange and urbanization expanded greatly.

The formation of larger-scale societies was further encouraged by the development of industrial methods of production. During the second half of the eighteenth century the economy of Britain, and to a lesser extent the economies of Western Europe and New England, were transformed by a series of mechanical inventions, especially the steam engine and innovations in textile manufacturing. This **Industrial Revolution,** a shift from slow hand methods of production to mechanized factory and agricultural production, resulted in major social changes whose impact was eventually felt throughout the world.

As societies adopted machine technologies, they shifted from traditional subsistence activities to newer methods that greatly increased the quantities of food and other goods that each worker could produce. Those people not needed in food production could specialize in other activities, move from rural areas to urban areas where jobs were concentrated, and use the money they earned to trade for their subsistence needs. Contemporary large-scale societies using this general strategy differ in degree from small-scale societies in a number of ways. The large-scale societies are characterized by reliance on machines rather than human or animal labor, intense use of resources, large and more concentrated populations, specialization of work, emphasis on trade, interdependency of populations, and inequalities in wealth and social status.

Recently the world economy has entered a phase that can be referred to as the *second industrial revolution,* also known as the postindustrial revolution, a technological revolution related to developments with computers and telecommunications. This technological revolution has made global production much easier and resulted in greater global integration of production and sales and a marked expansion of world trade. It has also introduced an unprecedented pace of change in which patterns of employment and demands for skills are constantly being altered with the result that many existing jobs are being made redundant over a short period. While there is still a need for low-skilled workers, the demand for higher levels of skill, especially in service work, has gone up sharply, one result being that the wage differential between high-skilled and low-skilled workers has widened. There are other social consequences as well. In particular, the countries of East and Southeast Asia that have been able to take advantage of the new global economy have undergone a period of rapid economic growth with few historical parallels. The social impact of this process in this part of the world has been tremendous as many traditional values and practices have come under pressure to change. In Singapore, for example, economic development has coincided with a rejection by many women of their traditional roles in relation to their families and marriage—many women marry late or not at all and in general lead lives far more independent of their families than was the case in the past.

Women in industrial societies have been exploited as menial factory laborers or excluded from industrial work, often with the belief that women are biologically unfit for physical or machine labor. On the other hand, since the advent of the information and service economy in the mid-twentieth century, in which muscle, once argued to be a prerequisite of industrial work, can no longer be considered a factor, women's place in the work force has been changing. Because of their historical devaluation in the workplace, women can offer skilled work for lower wages than men.

Although a great deal of production in large-scale societies is done by machine and by highly specialized workers, this is not the only means of production. In fact, some adaptive strategies employed in many large-scale societies are modern

Fishing is a subsistence activity that continues to be important in large-scale societies. Dipping for salmon in the traditional Yakima method in Washington State is shown in contrast to industrial-scale fishing, seen here in American Samoa with a Korean fishing boat's catch to be processed at a tuna cannery.

versions of those of small-scale societies that have changed in accordance with their progressive integration into the new encompassing social and economic environment.

Foraging in Large-Scale Societies

The collection of wild foods persists in large-scale societies, although the methods of collection and distribution are often different from those used in small-scale foraging groups. Groups who retain ties with their small-scale foraging past are likely to continue their practices of collecting wild foods. For example, Cree Indians in Canada today collect wild rice and trap beavers, selling a portion of what they forage to enable them to purchase industrially produced goods such as chain saws and rifles.

One activity in particular continues to be significant in large-scale societies—fishing. While some fishing continues to be carried out through relatively simple means (such as those used by some native peoples like the Haida along the northwest coast of North America),

most modern fishing, which can be called *industrial fishing,* employs industrial technology and considerable mechanization. Tuna fishing in the Pacific is done in boats costing millions of dollars with sophisticated electronic equipment and even helicopters.

Other foraging adaptations are unique to large-scale societies—adaptive strategies by "foragers" who are excluded from the mainstream of social and economic life. These are the beggars, the so-called bag ladies, and others who live off of what others discard or give away.

Peasants and Peasant Farming

In Africa, Asia, Latin America, and even parts of Europe, hundreds of millions of farmers in large-scale societies can be classified as peasants. The family farm is the peasant's basic unit of production and social organization. Although wage laborers are sometimes employed, the individual family provides most

The Loos family planting rice, near Vientiane, Laos. In Asia, one of the early centers for the development of agriculture in the world, individual peasant families continue to farm, growing rice partly for their own consumption and partly to sell on the market.

labor, and farming is carried out with a relatively simple technology and minimal reliance on mechanization. The farm furnishes the bulk of the family's needs, as well as a surplus for redistribution to nonpeasants through sale, taxation, or some other means.

Peasants are part of an encompassing stratified society. One of the most significant features of peasants' lives is their underdog status—their domination by outsiders. They serve as primary producers for urban markets and rural elites, but they have little control over the means of distribution and little political power. The result is often poverty. But not all peasants are equally poor, and peasant societies themselves are stratified as a result of differential access to land, markets, and other sources of wealth.

Since peasants are incorporated into the wider society in such a disadvantageous manner their relations with nonpeasants are characterized by extreme defensiveness. They see themselves as continually having to defend against external forces. Sometimes this defensiveness turns inward in the form of extreme suspicion and jealousy of one another; this, in turn, may

lead to high rates of homicide and other forms of violence within peasant communities. But peasants are not always merely defensive nor are their frustrations always taken out on one another. Periodically, peasants band together in revolt against the established order, as witnessed in the course of the leading revolutions of the twentieth century (see Chapter 12).

Plantation Agriculture

In a sense, peasants are small-scale farmers who have been incorporated into large-scale societies. However, a great deal of the world's agricultural production is not the result of peasant labor but of farming enterprises on a much larger scale. One form of large-scale agricultural enterprise is what Philip Curtain (1990) refers to as the *plantation complex*—a system of large-scale commercial agricultural production created to supply a distant market in a different kind of society. Another important feature of the plantation complex is that its population is not self-sustaining, and personnel must be re-

Work on a tea plantation in India requires considerable hand labor as well as machinery.

cruited externally (through the use of force or by contract).

The origins of the plantation complex are to be found in sugar-growing enterprises in the eastern Mediterranean established in the twelfth century. The plantation complex developed further with European colonial expansion in the Americas during the sixteenth century, and later in Africa and Asia. Plantations served primarily to provide the major industrial centers in the northern latitudes with crops that could be produced solely, or more cheaply, in the tropics or subtropics—such crops as rubber, sugar cane, coconuts, sisal (a fiber used for rope and other forms of cordage), and coffee. Most of these crops require years of maturation from planting to first yield, and after several yields production may fall off and replanting may be required. All of the products of a plantation are exported, in part to pay for the importation of machinery and food required to maintain the plantation.

Plantation production is labor-intensive. Plantations require large, disciplined, but not especially skilled labor forces. In North and South America the labor was supplied initially by slaves imported from Africa. In other areas, and during the latter part of the nineteenth and twentieth centuries in the Americas, labor was either supplied by the existing local populations or imported from such countries as India and China. The workers on a plantation may reside in compounds on the premises or in neighboring villages and towns. Their living quarters tend to be kept separate from those of the managerial staff, reflecting the hierarchy of social and economic relations.

Large-Scale Mechanized Grain Farming

Large-scale agriculture does not always require a large labor force. The type of agricultural production that has come to dominate the nontropical regions of the world—and that recently has been spreading into the tropics as well—is exemplified in the large-scale, mechanized grain farm. In the manner of plantations, grain farms focus on growing only one or two crops, and the products are usually exported to distant markets.

Unlike plantations, however, these large grain farms are capital- rather than labor-intensive; that is, they depend on capital investments for inputs of fertilizer and mechanical equipment while requiring relatively small amounts of labor.

The form of ownership and social organization of these enterprises usually depends on the encompassing economic system. In many socialist countries during the twentieth century the enterprises have been collectively or state-owned. Despite recent market-oriented reforms in many of these countries, collective farms remain an important part of their economy. In Russia, for example, while there are now around 260,000 private farmers, each farming an average 38 hectares of land, there are still 25,000 state or collective farms, cultivating as much as 15,000 hectares each (*Economist* 1993b:61). In market-oriented countries, the owners are commonly corporations or private individuals, although they may also be communal groups, such as the Hutterites in North America.

Ranching

Yet another subsistence pattern of large-scale societies is *ranching,* a ranch being a large farm devoted to the raising and grazing of cattle, sheep, or horses. Ranching originated in medieval Europe, especially in the activities of Spanish sheepherders. Their work gave rise to institutions such as the rodeo and to much of the equipment, attire, and vocabulary of ranching. Today ranching is confined largely to the drier regions of the world where Europeans have migrated over the past few centuries. As in plantation agriculture, the impetus behind the spread of ranching was the demand in the northern industrialized countries for goods that could be produced more cheaply elsewhere.

Most ranches occupy land that is not suitable for agriculture and, moreover, has a low *carrying capacity,* that is, can support only a small number of animals per acre. This situation is changing, however, as innovations in agriculture increasingly have made farming in such inhospitable regions more feasible. The result in some cases is a mixture of ranching and agriculture; in others, ranching has been replaced by agriculture.

Ranching is highly specialized; most ranchers raise a single type of animal, usually cattle or sheep. Unlike the technologically unsophisticated ranches of the past, today's ranches commonly employ a wide array of industrial products. The low carrying capacity of ranch lands results in low population densities and considerable social isolation. Ranching cultures reflect this situation with an emphasis on individualism, isolationism, and hospitality. Ranches have few permanent residents, with the majority of laborers hired seasonally for roundups and shearing. Small, less affluent family-owned ranches usually have a limited division of labor and will be run on a fairly egalitarian basis. In contrast, large, corporate-owned ranching operations generally exhibit a great deal of specialization, and social relations tend to be hierarchical.

Nonfood Production Patterns

In large-scale societies, more goods are produced than in small-scale societies, and in greater variety. Also, production and distribution are more specialized. There are two principal systems of manufacturing in large-scale societies: craft production and industrial production. *Craft production* can be carried out within relatively small social units, even within a single village, with limited external trade. By contrast, *industrial production* represents a considerable leap in scale of production, degree of specialization, and reliance on extensive exchange networks.

Craft production before industrialism tends to be family based, both men and women contributing to the production of crafts for domestic use and for sale or barter. With the advent of wage labor as a result of industrialization, craft production declines as people seek employment as wage laborers. Craft-produced goods are replaced by industrial goods although craft production does not necessarily disappear, especially in poorer communities, but it does tend to become more exclusively the domain of women than of men. In a study of craft production in India, for example, Maithreyi Krishnaraj found that overall craft production has declined, but that where it continues "women are today engaged more than men" (1992:WS7). Except for the garment industry, there is a market preference for male labor, and men are more likely to "seek alternatives to craft work through wage labour either within or outside the village" (1992:WS7), while women continue in more traditional productive activities that are progressively less remunerative than men's. One result is that traditional caste and family rights and obligations continue to apply to women more than to men.

Industrial production uses energy sources other than human or animal to operate machinery for the extraction and conversion of resources. It requires a relatively large and diverse labor force and relatively large amounts of capital. Limited industrial production (such as metallurgy) has occurred in various societies for thousands of years. Only during the past 200 to 300 years, however, since the beginning of the Industrial Revolution in eighteenth-century England, has it become a dominant feature of economic production. Since that time industrialism has been one of the driving forces behind the creation and expansion of the present world system.

Industrial production can be understood only in reference to the wider world system and to the history of its expansion. Industrial production beyond Western Europe and North America is a relatively recent phenomenon and, in much of the developing world, dates only from World War II. Wherever it has developed, industrial production has contributed to the growth of cities as people migrate from the countryside in search of work. The type of industry within a single country is primarily a reflection of that country's place within the international division of labor. Access to natural resources, transportation, technology, and labor make a difference as well. In the more developed nations, industrial production tends to be more highly mechanized and more skill-intensive,

whereas in less developed countries industry continues to rely more heavily on less skilled labor.

The Mixed Blessing of Industrialization

While industrialization has increased productivity, it has been a mixed blessing, particularly for those unable to share in its products and for those employed in tedious and dangerous jobs. Many of the political and economic struggles in the world today center on problems related to industry—the distribution of the wealth created by industry, working conditions, and industrial pollution. In fact, recent increases in productive capability through the use of computers and highly sophisticated electronic technology have in many ways only made matters worse. The new technology has resulted in many benefits, but it has also allowed for greater concentration of wealth, drastically altered the structure of employment, and exacerbated environmental problems.

S U M M A R Y

Subsistence activities are the strategies human groups employ to procure and produce the fundamental things they need or want. Subsistence patterns are influenced by environmental factors, physical and social, including the scale of the society. At least in the past, small-scale societies have tended to be restricted, while large-scale societies are more extensive, ultimately forming part of the international division of labor.

There are three major small-scale subsistence patterns. The first is foraging, the hunting and collecting of wild foods. Foraging activities can be subdivided into three subtypes: pedestrian hunting and gathering, which involves hunting wild animals and gathering wild edible plants on foot; equestrian hunting and gathering, which entails the use of horses; and aquatic foraging, which focuses on fishing. The second pattern, small-scale farming, involves the use of human and animal labor and simple tools. Shifting cultivation is a common small-scale farming method, especially in the tropics. One widespread form of shifting cultivation, the slash-and-burn technique, entails cutting down the natural growth on a plot of land, burning it, and then planting crops in the burned area. Shifting cultivation has become increasingly difficult to maintain over the past few decades because of population growth, deforestation, and other factors that limit the amount of land available. Pastoralism, the third pattern, practiced by peoples who subsist primarily on herding animals, has two main forms: transhumance (limited crop production near a village and migratory herding of animals) and pastoral nomadism (characterized by lack of permanent habitation and primary dependence on the herding of animals for subsistence).

In large-scale societies, foraging, especially fishing, continues to be a significant activity for some people, though increasing pressure from the outside world had led to significant modifications in foraging patterns. Common forms of agriculture are peasant farming, plantations, large-scale grain farming, and ranching. The two principal systems of manufacturing are craft production and industrial production.

Although industrialization has increased productivity it has also become the focal point of many of the political and economic struggles in the world today.

KEY TERMS

Foraging   A subsistence pattern that involves collecting wild plants, hunting wild animals, and fishing.

Horticulture   A subsistence pattern involving the use of human or animal labor and simple tools to cultivate gardens.

Industrial Revolution   The shift from slow hand methods of production to mechanized factory and agricultural production that resulted in major social changes eventually felt throughout the world.

Pastoral nomadism   A subsistence pattern involving primary dependence on the herding of animals and lack of permanent habitat.

Pastoralism   Economic adaptation involving animal herding.

Slash-and-burn cultivation   A form of shifting cultivation in which the natural growth is cut down and set afire to prepare land for the planting of crops. As new sections of land are cleared, the old are left until they have returned to a more natural state.

Transhumance   An economic adaptation and lifestyle characterized by subsistence based on limited crop production and migratory herding of animals and by residence in a permanent village

SUGGESTED READINGS

Small-scale foraging societies:

Bailey, Robert C. 1991. *The Behavioral Ecology of Efe Pygmy Men in the Ituri Forest, Zaire.* Ann Arbor: University of Michigan.

Berndt, Ronald M., and Catherine H. Berndt. 1970. *Man, Land and Myth in Northern Australia.* East Lansing: Michigan State University Press.

Brody, Hugh. 1981. *Maps and Dreams: Indians and the British Columbia Frontier.* Toronto: Douglas and McIntyre.

Chapman, Anne. 1982. *Drama and Power in a Hunting Society: the Selk'nam of Tierra del Fuego.* New York: Cambridge University Press.

Gordon, Robert J. 1991. *The Bushman Myth: The Making of a Namibian Underclass.* Boulder, CO: Westview Press.

Hoffman, Carl. 1986. *The Punan: Hunters and Gatherers of Borneo.* Ann Arbor, MI: UMI Research Press.

Leacock, Eleanor, and Richard B. Lee, editors. 1982. *Politics and History in Band Societies.* New York: Cambridge University Press.

Lee, Richard B. 1984. *The !Kung: Foragers in a Changing World.* New York: Holt, Rinehart and Winston.

Small-scale farmers:

Dwyer, Peter D. 1990. *The Pigs that Ate the Garden: A Human Ecology from Papua New Guinea*. Ann Arbor: University of Michigan Press.

Feil, Daryl K. 1987. *The Evolution of Highland Papua New Guinea Society*. New York: Cambridge University Press.

Harner, Michael J. 1972. *The Jivaro: People of the Sacred Waterfalls*. New York: Natural History Press.

Murphy, Yolanda, and Robert Murphy. 1974. *Women of the Forest*. New York: Columbia University Press. (Amazonian Brazil)

Sutlive, Vinson H., Jr. 1978. *The Iban of Sarawak*. Arlington Heights, IL: AHM.

Wagley, Charles. 1977. *Welcome of Tears: The Tapirapé Indians of Central Brazil*. New York: Oxford University Press.

Pastoralists:

Behnke, Rah H., Jr. 1980. *The Herders of Cyrenaica*. Urbana: University of Illinois Press. (Libya)

Cole, Donald P. 1975. *Nomads of the Nomad: The Al Murrah Bedouin of the Empty Quarter*. Arlington Heights, IL: AHM.

Galaty, John G., and Douglas L. Johnson, editors. 1990. *The World of Pastoralism: Herding Systems in Comparative Perspective*. New York: Guilford Press.

Ingold, Tim. 1976. *The Skolt Lapps Today*. New York: Cambridge University Press.

Irons, W., and N. Dyson-Hudson, editors. 1972. *Perspectives on Nomadism*. Leiden: E. J. Brill.

Peasants:

Brintnall, Douglas E. 1979. *Revolt Against the Dead: The Modernization of a Mayan Community in the Highlands of Guatemala*. London: Gordon and Breach.

Deere, Carmen D. 1991. *Households and Class Relations: Peasants and Landlords in Northern Peru*. Berkeley: University of California Press.

Eklof, Ben, and Stephen Frank, editors. 1990. *The World of the Russian Peasant*. Boston: Unwin Hyman.

Evans, Grant. 1990. *Lao Peasants Under Socialism*. New Haven: Yale University Press.

Hefner, Robert W. 1990. *The Political Economy of Mountain Java*. Berkeley: University of California Press.

Pearse, Andrew. 1975. *The Latin American Peasant*. London: Frank Cass.

Potter, Sulamith Heins, and Jack M. Potter. 1989. *China's Peasants: The Anthropology of a Revolution*. New York: Cambridge University Press.

Sorensen, Clark W. 1988. *Over the Mountains Are Mountains: Korean Peasant Households and Adaptation to Rapid Industrialization*. Seattle: University of Washington Press.

Industrial society:

Applebaum, Herbert A. 1981. *Royal Blue: The Culture of Construction Workers*. New York: Holt, Rinehart and Winston.

Bourgois, Philippe I. 1989. *Ethnicity at Work: Divided Labor on a Central American Banana Plantation*. Baltimore: Johns Hopkins University Press.

Chibnik, Michael, editor. 1987. *Farmwork and Fieldwork: American Agriculture in Anthropological Perspective*. Ithaca: Cornell University Press.

Despres, Leo A. 1991. *Manaus: Social Life and Work in Brazil's Free Trade Zone*. Albany: State University of New York Press.

Nash, June C. 1989. *From Tank Town to High Tech: The Clash of Community and Industrial Cycles*. Albany: State University of New York Press.

Pappas, Gregory. 1989. *The Magic City: Unemployment in a Working Class Community*. Ithaca: Cornell University Press.

Stoller, Ann Laura. 1985. *Capitalism and Confrontation in Sumatra's Plantation Belt, 1870–1970*. New Haven: Yale University Press.

5 ECONOMIC SYSTEMS

ow do anthropologists view economic patterns? In addition to their more obvious features described in the last chapter, subsistence patterns are based on more abstract principles of production, ownership, and exchange. In this chapter we will look at the basic economic systems, the organizational and institutional structure of systems that people have developed to supply themselves with the necessities and niceties of life, but that in turn constrain people in their actions and beliefs.

◄ SYSTEMS OF PRODUCTION ►

When our early ancestors picked up a stone, chipped it, and put it on the end of a stick to turn it into an implement for hunting and fighting, they produced a weapon. **Production** involves the significant transformation of an object for cultural purposes. An act of production often entails physically changing an object, but it may simply be a matter of rearranging objects to alter their nature or function, such as piling stones to make a wall. But production is more than an act of transformation: It is a systematically ordered series of acts set in a particular social and environmental context. It takes place within an ecological framework, requires the recruitment of workers, and is affected by the organization of the society, which it in turn influences. Anthro-

pologists are not so much concerned with the productive act itself as they are with the *system of production* of which the act is but a part.

Production varies considerably from one society to another. In our own society, the production of weapons usually involves several successive transformations of a number of objects to produce an implement that is much more complicated than a chipped stone on a stick. Those people who produce a missile will be trained and organized in a different manner from those making a spear. The difference reflects a more complex technology and division of labor than that of our spear-making ancestors.

The contrast between systems of production with the capability to produce spears and those able to produce missiles reflects the process of change that systems of production undergo. There are three processes that occur in the development of a system of production: *adaptation, expansion,* and *intensification.*

Adaptation in this context refers to the initial response to the opportunities and constraints of an environment. Thus, when the ancestors of present-day Polynesians first settled islands such

Systems of production in the modern world system draw upon resources and markets over much of the world, often with the potential for environmental destruction. In the Serra Pelada gold mine, Brazil's "Klondike," men struggle up slippery ladders, carrying sacks of unwanted soil in the process of excavating the earth.

An example of a relatively simple production process: These Indian men of Ecuador, South America, spin wool.

as those of Hawaii and New Zealand, they set about to employ their existing knowledge in order to maintain themselves and survive in these new environments. Expansion refers to the spreading out within the environment largely as a result of population growth. Ancestral Polynesian migration across the Pacific itself was an expansion of a system of production that already existed in mainland and neighboring island Southeast Asia, and expansion continued as they occupied more and more islands as well as more of the land areas of the islands themselves.

Intensification involves altering a system of production so that it is capable of greater productivity. In the rice-growing areas of Asia, intensification can be associated with the change from rice production based on

slash-and-burn agriculture to that based on irrigated paddy fields. While paddy rice production requires a larger labor input than slash-and-burn production, generally the output is much higher. Slash-and-burn agriculture is therefore usually associated with, and is arguably best suited to, areas with relatively low population densities. This is not to say that population density is the only factor leading to intensification, but it is often an important consideration. Intensification involves altering social and political relations as they are related to how labor is organized and how what is produced is distributed. The change from systems of slash-and-burn agriculture to more intensive forms of agricultural production, for example, is commonly associated with the rise of more hierarchical forms of political organization, such as the Polynesian kingdoms of Hawaii and Tahiti.

< THE ENVIRONMENT AND > PRODUCTION

Systems of production are influenced by the local ecology as well as by the social, political, and economic environment. Production by small-scale producers is especially attuned to the local ecology on which they must rely for most of their raw materials. Foragers such as the Mardudjara of Australia and small-scale farmers such as the Tsembaga of New Guinea obtain most of their food and the raw materials for their hunting and farming implements as well as for their clothing and shelter from their immediate environment. Production is constrained by their knowledge of local resources and their ability to transform these resources into desired objects. Over thousands of years these societies slowly improved their productive capability, by gaining better knowledge of local resources and through technical innovations—adding such things as spear throwers to improve their hunting capability, in the case of the Aborigines, and new crops, in the case of the New Guinea farmers. Such changes represented only limited modifications of the overall system, however, and did not alter the close connection between production and the local environment.

Even systems of production associated with small-scale societies over time have important consequences for the environment—they are not environmentally neutral. Patrick Kirch notes in the islands of the South Pacific that "the island landscapes recorded by early European voyagers had been extensively modified through the introduction of exotic biota, by forest clearance and habitat modification, erosion and deposition of sediments, and faunal and floral extinctions" (1989:39). Before the arrival of Europeans, deforestation was a serious problem on many Pacific islands. The most dramatic example is Rapanui (Easter Island), where the collapse of the society responsible for producing the well-known large stone figures can be closely linked to rapid deforestation brought about by domestic consumption for firewood, canoe building, house construction, and other uses. Such deforestation took place over centuries, however, and at a much slower pace than the destruction of forests taking place today with the use of modern industrial technology.

Systems of production associated with large-scale societies are more flexible in adapting to ecological conditions because of the growth of commerce, which allows them to draw upon resources and markets over much wider areas, and their command of greater technical knowledge. Such productive systems are able to produce more from their environment. For example, employing relatively simple hand tools, the Kalinga and other peoples of the northern Philippines were able to mine limited amounts of gold from the soils and rivers of their mountainous environment prior to the arrival of Europeans. Since the early part of this century, however, modern technology has allowed mining companies to produce far greater amounts of gold, making the Philippines one of the world's leading producers of gold.

Their technological flexibility makes large-scale societies less dependent on local environments. In fact, sometimes their adaptations are highly dependent on resources drawn from outside their environment. Many communities in the Arctic depend on external sources for heating fuel, clothing, building materials, food, and mechanical devices like snowmobiles. Their technological capability, however, also increases their potential for environmental destruction. The environmental damage from centuries of gold mining by the Kalinga was minimal, while modern mines over the past few decades have caused considerable damage to the local environment as well as harming farms and fish ponds in the distant lowlands as a result of the polluting chemicals that have been carried off in rivers.

~~~~~
Human action can cause ecological problems that threaten a system of production. The Anasazi culture of New Mexico, whose prehistoric cliff dwellings are seen here, dealt unsuccessfully with erosion that destroyed the top soil and ruined the irrigation system on which Anasazi agriculture depended.

◄ MAINTAINING PRODUCTION ►

Keeping a system of production going, whether in a small-scale or a large-scale society, is not always easy. Disruptions such as wars and environmental crises must be dealt with, a steady supply of workers must be maintained, and labor and rewards must be distributed in satisfactory ways.

Dealing with Disruptions

Production systems usually have mechanisms for dealing with temporary or regular disruptions, such as droughts or other natural disasters. Foragers maintain alliances with other groups of foragers so that they can use the resources of other groups if their own are depleted. Small-scale producers also often have types of foods that they can turn to in emergencies—items that would not be consumed under normal circumstances. In our own society we adjust to disruptions by turning to alternative sources and by storing reserves. We also provide for the primary producers, especially farmers, through disaster relief supplies and funds.

Many of the forces disrupting production result from natural causes and can be dealt with in a manner that does not have long-term effects on the system of production. Human action itself, however, sometimes causes ecological problems that threaten the maintenance of the productive system. Many societies in the past contributed to their own demise by abusing the lands they lived on. The Anasazi culture of the Chaco Canyon in New Mexico (A.D. 1000 to 1200), for example, was advanced for its time, but eventually fell because of environmental degradation (see Gumerman 1988). Abrupt deforestation for fuel and building materials led to erosion that destroyed the topsoil and ruined water channels used for irrigation. Eventually, the agricultural system collapsed. Soil erosion and deforestation are severe problems in much of the world today, threatening the well-being of societies scattered far and wide, and perhaps even global society as we know it.

Replacing Workers

Another fundamental requirement of any productive system is the replacement of people. All systems of production have ways of maintaining a steady supply of productive humans. This means ensuring that people are produced in the first place and produced in the appropriate numbers. Then they must be made productive, usually through socialization whereby children of a society are tutored in the appropriate values and knowledge. Many small-scale societies have sought to limit population growth through infanticide, abortion, and various means of birth control. These practices, along with relatively high infant mortality rates, kept the world's population growth at a slow rate for tens of thousands of years, minimizing population-related stresses on economic adaptations. This situation began to change dramatically several hundred years ago; particularly since the 1940s, rapid population growth has been one of the major problems confronting many poorer countries.

While many poorer countries face severe economic problems because of the speed with which their populations are growing, many developed countries are facing problems because of their low or negative rate of population growth. For a variety of reasons, more affluent people tend to have fewer children, and today many countries in Europe and North America must meet their labor requirements by importing workers from other parts of the world. Importing workers occurs in the modern world system as a result of economic inequalities and labor requirements. In the modern world such movements began as Europeans developed plantations in the New World and set about meeting labor needs through the acquisition of millions of slaves from Africa. In the latter part of the

Mexican immigrant laborers harvest aloe plants in south Texas. Labor requirements in the United States combined with severe economic problems in Mexico lead to the import of workers to the United States.

nineteenth century, following the abolition of slavery, India and China provided millions of workers for construction, mining, and agriculture for the expanding colonial capitalist economies. The long-term effects of such migrations are seen in the large numbers of descendants of these migrants found scattered across the globe far from their ancestral homelands.

Labor migration is hardly a thing of the past. The more prosperous economies of Europe have attracted migrants from southern Europe and the Middle East. In the 1970s and early 1980s, oil-rich countries in the Middle East recruited large numbers of workers from India, the Philippines, South Korea and elsewhere. The Gulf War of 1991 drew international attention to the five million migrant workers in the Middle East (over half in Saudi Arabia). Countries such as the United States, Canada and Australia—and, to a lesser extent, even Japan—continue to receive millions of workers from poorer countries around the world. In fact, the United States accepted more immigrants in the 1980s than in any previous decade in its history (7.3 million immigrants and a few million more illegal immigrants). As in the past, not all of those who come to work remain, though many do.

While clearly contributing to the economies of the countries they migrate to, what of the countries the migrants leave behind? Such migration deprives poorer countries of skilled personnel and often adversely affects these countries' ability to recruit needed skilled workers.

Dividing Labor and Rewards: Gender and the Division of Labor

There is little that is natural about the types of work people do or the value assigned to a type of work. Both the *division of labor* and its rewards are products of their sociocultural setting. Continuity in a system of production requires

that people accept or at least acquiesce in these practices. Such acceptance is more common in small-scale societies than it is in large-scale ones. The trade union movement and women's rights movement are examples of how people have questioned existing patterns of employment and rewards in modern large-scale societies. Even in small-scale societies, however, compliance may not be automatic. Like their American counterparts, Mundurucu and Mardudjara women complain about being given the most boring and least prestigious tasks.

In most instances, in both small-scale and large-scale societies, little comes of people's complaints. Rather than seeing their problem as an aspect of the system, protesters frequently focus on individuals—the bad or unfair headman, foreman, king, or president. Changes in personnel may alleviate conditions, but such a change is unlikely to significantly alter the system of production itself. In fact, such periodic reforms often serve to strengthen a system rather than to change it.

Sometimes, however, significant changes do occur. This may be the result of changes in the environment of the system of production. Because of changes in external market conditions, for example, a task that was of little importance may assume greater importance to the extent of altering the productive system. In many of the highland communities of Guatemala, men produce the bulk of the economically significant products through agriculture; women tend to do domestic chores and market produce. Women also weave and make ceramic pottery—crafts that receive relatively poor rewards within the communities. External markets for pottery and woven goods may emerge, however, because of improved transportation, development programs, or an influx of tourists. As a result, women's activities may assume more importance. In some cases, for example, the increased importance of ceramic production has resulted in groups of mothers and daughters replacing groups of farm-working men as the primary unit of production, with men assuming the marketing role. Such changes have reduced the significance of male bonds beyond the family while strengthening bonds between women engaged in ceramic production.

Changes in systems of production may also result from interplay between problems within the system and environmental changes. During both World War I and World War II, labor shortages in countries like Britain and the United States temporarily created large numbers of employment opportunities for women in areas of traditional male employment. These changes played an important part in altering the sexual division of labor and helped to serve as a catalyst for the modern women's movement—which has brought about even greater changes in the sexual division of labor. All systems of production have internal problems that can lead to basic changes under pressure.

◄ DISTRIBUTION AND EXCHANGE ►

It is not enough simply to produce things—there must be a system for distributing them. Individuals have different needs, tastes, and desires, and often there is either not enough of something to go around or a surplus to be disposed of. How to distribute products and resources is one of the fundamental questions facing all societies, and it may be the most important source of human conflict.

Ownership

Central to an understanding of distribution and exchange is the concept of **ownership**—acknowledged supremacy, authority, or power over a physical object, process, or idea. Ownership within any society is rarely a simple concept. In our society, we say that people own their homes. Yet through various ordinances and social constraints, the state and a person's family and neighbors have a good deal to say about decisions regarding the house. Under many circumstances, police and other public employees can enter the premises regardless of the owner's wishes. The bank that holds a mortgage on a house also has rights over it; failure to pay taxes can result in a loss of ownership. Oil companies may be able to drill holes on the site, mining companies can burrow under it, and city and state governments can tear it down to build a road, park, or civic building.

Among the Pintubi, a group of foragers in the Australian desert, ownership is denoted by the term *kanyininpa,* which may be translated as "having," "holding," or "looking after" (Myers 1982: 83). The term is used to refer to possession of physical objects ("I have two spears"), to the relationship of parent to child ("my father looked after me and grew me up"), and to the rights individuals or groups may hold over sacred sites (which may be water holes, large rocks, or caves), religious ceremonies, songs, and designs. Ownership among the Pintubi entails both control and responsibility. A person controls or "owns" a child or sacred site, but that person also has responsibilities associated with these possessions. The idea of ownership is tied to an encompassing moral order, known as the "Law," which dictates what these responsibilities are.

Ownership of land for the Pintubi comes about through the inheritance of sacred sites and the territory associated with them. It entails obligations to perform rituals linked to the sites. Failure to carry out such obligations does not merely affect a person's status in relation to the land and society, it threatens the entire moral and social order of the Pintubi. It is easy to see how such concepts are at variance with those of the Europeans who came to settle in Australia, and how such differing concepts of ownership have led to conflicts and misunderstanding.

Wealth is unequally distributed among Arabs in the Middle East. Traders on the floor of the stock exchange in Kuwait City, where oil provides great wealth, contrast sharply with Palestinian men and women in a food kitchen.

The Distribution of Wealth: Inequality and Development

No matter how ownership is defined, some people seem to own more than others in all societies. Unequal distribution of **wealth** (objects or resources that are useful or that have exchange value) is a universal characteristic of human society. Minor inequalities exist within many small-scale societies, especially when comparing men and women. As the productive capability of societies increases, greater inequalities result. With the rise of greater inequality have evolved mechanisms of social control (police and military) that support unequal accumulation.

Beyond such general tendencies, there is considerable variation. For example, wealth was much more equally distributed among the Mardudjara Aborigines, a foraging group who lived in Australia's harsh Western Desert, than among the Tiwi, who lived in the more abundant environment of Australia's north. Likewise, some modern industrial societies exhibit greater degrees of inequality than others. Thus, wealth is much more equally distributed in a country like

Denmark than in, say, the United States. But overall, inequality is far greater in even the most egalitarian modern industrial society than in societies such as that of the Tiwi.

Inequality on a worldwide scale in the modern world has led to the division of countries into those perceived as "developed" (rich) and those called "underdeveloped" or "developing" (poor). Developed nations include industrial nations of Europe and North America as well as Japan. A wealthier group of developing nations includes the industrialized former socialist nations of Eastern Europe, some of the wealthier oil-producing nations (such as Saudi Arabia), and a few other better-off states like Singapore. The remainder of the underdeveloped group includes about 120 countries, encompassing the bulk of humanity, characterized by relatively low standards of living, high rates of population growth, and general economic and technological dependence on wealthier industrial nations. Wealth is divided very unequally in many of these countries—a small wealthy elite controls the bulk of the national wealth, with some individuals having at their disposal millions if not billions of dollars, while the majority of rural and urban poor may possess barely enough to stay alive.

Patterns of Exchange

The distribution of wealth within a society is the result of processes of **exchange,** the pattern of trade that exists in resources, goods, ideas, and services. Economic exchange is a universal aspect of human society. Individuals in all social settings depend on others for satisfying some of their needs or wants, and our life cycle from birth to death requires that resources and ideas continually be transferred to meet changing circumstances. The process of exchange is based on principles of **reciprocity** (the mutual exchange of goods and services) and takes on various form, such as systems of redistribution and market exchange.

RECIPROCITY. The concept of reciprocity is important in understanding exchange and social relationships in all societies, although reciprocity is especially characteristic of small-scale societies. Different forms of reciprocity reflect the degree of social closeness between the partners in exchange. Anthropologist Marshall Sahlins (1965) has delineated three forms of reciprocity: generalized, balanced, and negative reciprocity. *Generalized reciprocity* refers to gift-giving without any immediate expectation of return, such as the exchange of food within domestic groups. Among foragers, some parties may provide more food at one time, while others contribute more at another time; in the long run, the give and take, which has no deadlines, balances out. We also find this form of reciprocity in our own society, in which parents provide for their children without keeping account of what is given or without expecting an immediate or specific return. *Balanced reciprocity* involves a more explicit expectation of immediate return, as when a San trades a Tswana an animal hide for a negotiated quantity of tobacco (Marshall 1961) or Mayan farmers exchange equal amounts of work in the field with one another. We engage in a form of balanced reciprocity when we offer gifts at birthdays; we express our friendship in doing so, but there is a strong sense of social obligation on the part of the receiver to reciprocate a gift of similar value at the appropriate time. *Negative reciprocity* is an attempt to take advantage of another by forcing that person to exchange something that he or she may prefer to keep, or trying to ensure that what one receives is of greater value than what one gives in exchange. It may involve such behavior as manipulation, cheating, haggling to get the better of the bargain, or theft. Negative reciprocity is the least sociable—impersonal and sometimes even hostile—form of exchange.

REDISTRIBUTION. *Redistributive systems of exchange* entail first the accumulation of wealth and then its redistribution. Redistribution can take many forms, among which are taxation and gift-giving. All societies large enough to support a government that includes an administration to provide infrastructural services (such as roads and port facilities) have developed methods of collecting wealth from their members to support the services provided. In our society, and in many others, one of the primary means of accomplishing this is **taxation.** Individuals, according to various criteria, surrender part of their wealth to the government, which in return is expected to do such things as defend them from external threats and provide for law and order, infrastructure (roads and other permanent works), and welfare services.

The **potlatch** is a form of redistribution found among native peoples of the Northwest Coast of Canada and the United States. Banned by authorities in Canada until the 1950s, it has undergone a revival among many Northwest Coast native peoples. Through a potlatch, individuals and groups seek to enhance their status by elaborate and, at times, dramatic feasts and gift-giving ceremonies. Similar forms of competitive feasting and gift-giving are common among

A contemporary potlatch among Kwakiutl Indians of the Northwest Coast. By redistributing wealth, the sponsor of a potlatch validates his rank, enhances his social status, and reinforces political ties. The redistribution of perishable goods ensures that they do not go to waste.

small-scale agricultural and fishing societies, serving as a focal point of economic exchange among members of different social groups.

Among the Kwakiutl of British Columbia, the gifts traditionally presented in a potlatch in-cluded slaves, canoes, blankets, various manufac-tured articles, and highly valued shieldlike sheets of copper. Hudson Bay Company blankets were the most common gift in the late nineteenth and early twentieth centuries (several thousand

People buy and sell goods at a market in Kampala in Uganda, Africa. In market exchange, impersonal supply and demand take priority over kinship and social status.

blankets might be presented at a single potlatch), and they served as the basic unit of account; thus, the value of goods was expressed in blankets. The feast itself was sponsored by an individual on such occasions as a marriage, the birth of a first child, or the initiation of one's sister's son into a secret society. It earned the sponsor a high-status title.

A person would prepare for a potlatch by accumulating the needed items largely through loans (on which interest was paid) from relatives. At the potlatch, goods would be distributed to members of one's own kin-group, related kin-groups who had been invited, and often to people from other communities. This meant that goods were redistributed within one's own community and outside of it. Intercommunity distribution of food through the potlatch ensured that surplus perishables did not go to waste. Members of the elite competed keenly to outdo each other in their largesse, and through the potlatch a person could advance in social standing. Moreover, those invited were not simply the recipients of goods; they were placed in

the potlatcher's debt, thus increasing that person's influence and prestige.

MARKET EXCHANGE. Market exchange involves the buying and selling of goods. The dominant feature of these transactions is price-setting, which is based more on impersonal economic factors such as supply and demand than on personal factors such as kinship and relative social status. Market exchange comes to dominate especially where economic transactions are conducted among strangers. In the modern world, it has come to be the primary system of exchange.

Media of Exchange

Money is used as a medium of exchange where the depersonalization of market exchange occurs. The term **money** refers not so much to the physical thing itself, but more important, to the qualities associated with it—durability, transferability, and acceptability over a wide range of functions. As Belshaw (1965: 9) notes, all these functions depend on the characteristic of *liquidity,* "the relative ease with which a commodity . . . can be exchanged."

There are two basic types of money: special-purpose and general-purpose. The term **special-purpose money** refers to objects that serve as a medium of exchange in only limited contexts and that are interchangeable for only a particular range of goods and services. Cattle, pigs, jewelry, and cloth are common forms of special-purpose money. The people of the Bird's Head region of Irian Jaya, for example, use cloth for a variety of exchange purposes (Elmberg 1968). Such cloth is not worn, but is used only for exchange. Cloth is the central item in marriage exchange. Those who must give cloth in marriage transactions accumulate cloth prior to the marriage through trading partners. Cloth is also used to pay fines. Thus, the Karondori assess a fine of 150 bolts of cloth and two pigs to be presented to the offended party in the case of elopement with another's wife. Cloth is also a symbol of wealth, and some wealthy people appear to go out of their way to commit marriage offenses since payment of the fine "is actually an opportunity to exhibit their wealth" (Sanggenafa 1990: 96).

General-purpose money differs from the more limited versions of money in its comprehensiveness. In a society using general-purpose money, most material things and services can be bought or paid for with this one medium of exchange. This form of money makes it easier to conduct economic exchanges with strangers. One's wealth, work value, and even thoughts can be assessed in monetary terms that are widely shared.

Introducing general-purpose money into societies where it had not been previously used leads to considerable changes. For example, the substitution of general-purpose money for cattle in marriage transactions in East Africa allowed young men greater personal freedom. In the process, it also undermined patterns of parental authority and the political system based on clan

alliances. In addition, it contributed to the breakdown of herd management by kin groups. The introduction of market exchange by means of general-purpose money into economies throughout the globe has been part of the spread of the modern world system. General-purpose money is one of the most tangible forces integrating societies into the world economy; the flow of money produces both direct and indirect effects on almost all aspects of people's lives.

Even though general-purpose money has become the dominant medium of exchange in most economic systems, reciprocal exchange and special-purpose monies continue to be employed to a limited extent even in developed industrial societies. An example of this is the exchange of Harley-Davidson parts among groups of bikers in the United States. Although the bikers are integrated in many ways into the wider economy, within the group the exchange of Harley-Davidson parts plays a significant social and economic role. Maintenance of the bikes—which are the primary symbols of group identity—relies largely on a barter system, a system that reduces their dependence on the encompassing market economy. In one Texas group, the Bandidos, to overhaul a member's bike, friends

> visit other bikers, even several who are not Bandidos. The parts come in, almost all of them from trades with other Harley riders. A few items, like piston rings, they buy from the dealership, though neither of them enjoys giving the dealer their trade. In their eyes, Harley dealers are little more than profiteering pirates. [Reaves 1978: 214].

Regional and World Commerce

Economies are almost never completely self-sufficient. **Commerce,** or the exchange of goods, between different countries or regions is a feature of virtually all economic systems. The

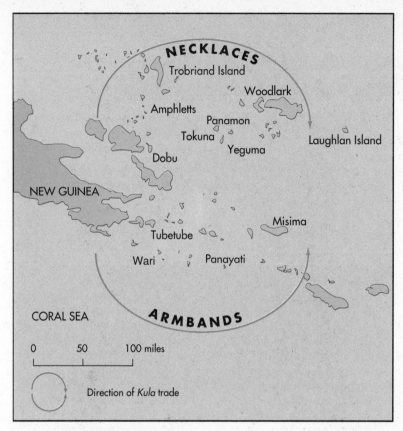

FIGURE 5.1
The *Kula* exchange system, or trade ring. In this elaborate exchange system among the Trobriand Islanders of the Southwest Pacific, necklaces are exchanged clockwise from island group to island group around the ring and armbands, exchanged for the necklaces, move counterclockwise.

quest for resources and markets beyond the confines of one's own society is certainly not new. Salt, for instance, has been an important item of trade in many parts of the world for thousands of years. For those living away from the sea, salt must be obtained either by trading with those who have access to sea salt or with those who possess inland sources such as brine springs. The area inhabited by the Kelabit of the interior of northeastern Borneo contains such springs. The salt they obtained from these springs was traded with the neighboring Kenyah for iron knife blades and carved handles, which the Kenyah obtained from the Apo Kayan in return for Kelabit salt (Schneeberger 1979:53–61). But the scope of world commerce today is unprecedented, as is the extent to which people's lives

are influenced by world commerce. Even in small, relatively isolated villages people today produce for distant markets and consume goods, including salt, from the far corners of the globe.

Despite the many changes and growing complexity of commercial relations, even in the past, members of small-scale societies commonly engaged in often quite intricate exchange with members of other societies. The inhabitants of the small islands along the north coast of New Guinea, in part because of their elatively poor resource base (Tiesler 1969–70), traditionally engaged in complex trading expeditions to different islands and to the mainland. They developed trading systems within particular regions. The best known of these is the *kula* trading system of the islands off New Guinea's east coast

SANDRA NIESSEN

FOCUS ON ANTHROPOLOGISTS

Sandra Niessen first visited the Batak region of North Sumatra during 1979–1980 to do doctoral fieldwork (State University of Leiden) and returned again in 1986 and 1990. She has been researching the social significance of the local, handwoven textiles, the technology of their production, and their design and composition. Increasingly, she is relying on a historical perspective to understand the dynamics of the persistence of this woven phenomenon. Currently she teaches in the Department of Human Ecology at the University of Alberta.

∧∧∧∧∧∧∧∧

North Sumatran Weavers in a Global Economy

N umerous weaving villages are clustered around the central market town of Tarutung in the Silindung Valley, just south of Lake Toba in North Sumatra, Indonesia. I visited each in turn to document their textile production. Each specializes in a particular type or types of cloth. It is easy to locate the weavers as they sit on the floor of their veranda, their backstrap loom tensed between the railing and their lap. If they weave inside their home, the clatter of the wood gives them away as they beat the weft between the warps. The lengthy process of yarn preparation takes place out of doors, beside or behind the house. By Friday the cloth is finished. Early on Saturday morning, either the weavers themselves or their

marketing agents head for the market where they sell their newly finished cloths to the market stall proprietors. Later in the day, the visitor to the market can parade past more than 60 of these stalls, draped in a wide variety of colorful cloths not only from the Silindung Valley but from as far as the expansive market network extends. Tourists can't resist buying one or two as souvenirs to have sewn up into jackets or whatever is fashionable, but mostly these textiles are sold to the Bataks themselves. Certain cloth types are deemed indispensable as ritual clothing and gifts to mark their life-cycle rites, and others as finery to be worn on modern-day dress-up occasions such as church-going or the visit of a political dignitary.

The Silindung Valley is overpopulated. Its fertile lands are packaged ever smaller as its population expands. The lack of rice land translates into a heavier reliance than ever before on the sale of handwoven

cloth at the market. Almost all the money earned from the sale of the textile is spent on more yarn to weave the next cloth. The little that is left over goes into groceries. The sale of this week's cloth at the market is frequently the buffer against indebtedness, even hunger. In the northern part of Samosir Island in the middle of Lake Toba, and on the northwestern shore of the lake, where the farmland has never been very fertile, an arrangement has existed for at least 100 years, perhaps much longer, whereby those with the poor farmland weave for the neighboring group with fertile lands. Weaving fills in the gaps created by infertile lands or an insufficient harvest.

It is no wonder that several weavers regarded me with suspicion when I came, notebook in hand, to observe them at work. It seemed far-fetched to an academic like myself that their suspicion rested on fears that, after learning about their arts, I would return to my country, mechanize Batak textile production, and undercut them in the market. The women (all Batak weavers are female) were in no sense naive. They were suspicious of the recapitulation of a pattern with which they were familiar—sometimes desperately so and sometimes cagily so.

At the turn of this century, at the height of the Industrial Revolution, British traders sailed to Southeast Asia in search of markets for their expanded textile production. They collected examples of indigenous textiles and noted which were the most popular and where, so that they could put their industrial machinery to work and undercut the sales of the local industry based on handweaving. European cloth rose to prominence in the Southeast Asian trade while many sectors of Indonesian cloth production collapsed. Bataks began to wear the cheaper, imported cloth, and indigenous clothing production for daily wear eventually stopped altogether. It was only for ritual and ceremonial purposes that weaving was able to maintain itself. This is the most dramatic example of how the Batak weaving craft was undermined by outsiders who documented their tastes and their technology.

In the early decades of this century, the Batak stole a little back from their market competitors using semimechanized looms that the Dutch colonial

Anthropologist Sandra Niessen with a weaver of the Silindung Valley in North Sumatra. Initially, the weavers here were suspicious of Dr. Niessen, fearing that after she learned their arts, she would return to her country to mechanize Batak textile production, and then undercut them in the market.

authorities set up in certain Batak towns. With them, they were able to produce cheap sarongs for daily wear. Recently, however, Batak owners of these factories have adapted their looms to compete with Batak handweavers. They are able to mass-produce some of the more important ritual textiles that are normally handwoven. Because of local poverty in the Batak area, significant segments of the population purchase these inferior but cheaper factory-produced items. The weavers specializing in those particular cloths have had to compete with machinery, and the difference in the quality of their work is drastic. The profits of their labors are barely worth it. In fact, several

cloth types are rarely found in their handwoven version any more.

This example of how industry has stolen the Batak means of livelihood is one that every weaver is well aware of, and that she is reminded of every time she surveys a textile stall in her local market. Early in the 1980s, an urban Batak from the Silindung Valley saw new marketing potential in her culture's handwoven cloth. Together with an expert designer, she produced fashionable clothing and even shoes and handbags made with local handwoven fabrics. She began to successfully promote them in Europe and Japan and won a provincial prize for her efforts to help women in North

Sumatra. As her orders increased, however, she could neither stockpile enough hand-woven textiles nor produce them quickly enough to meet the time demands of her buyers; she began to consider mechanically producing the very cloth that she was purchasing from the small producer. When I left in 1986, she had not yet made her decision. Since then, from North America, I have watched machine prints of Javanese batik designs hit the western ethnic market in the form of jackets, shirts, dresses, bags, and so on. When I returned to Sumatra in 1990, I noticed that ethnic Chinese manufacturers had begun to print Batak textile motifs on T-shirts for sale at the major tourist spots in the Batak area. I overheard many weavers discussing whether this would be the trend to put them out of business for good.

Batak weavers are suspicious of the interest that foreigners take in their cloth production no doubt also from personal experience of the importance of their foreign cloth to their own design successes. Batak weavers themselves are adept at the strategy that, used against them, can undermine their own production. For at least 100 years, they have been stringing their looms to make cotton variants of textiles once produced in Aceh, north of the Batak territory. The Acehnese variants were fine, silken cloths, coveted by all Bataks and within the means of only the most wealthy. Today, the Batak variants of these cloths are so common as to have become indispensable in Batak ritual. There is evidence that Batak weavers also borrowed Malay styles from the coast and rendered them locally into an array of variations now considered to be traditional Batak cloth. Most likely, regional variation in many Batak textile types attests to the success that their weavers have in borrowing designs.

Nai Ganda, a weaver I knew in the Silindung Valley, was obviously inspired by new designs that fit her aesthetic criteria, and liked to reproduce them on her own loom. Her penchant to interpret foreign designs in her own way also made good marketing sense. On Saturdays, in her own market stall, she kept a sharp eye on which cloth designs were doing well, and which were falling out of fashion. She always hoped that her latest design would be swept up in local demand so that she would make a healthy profit.

My own stock of photographs of Batak museum textiles that I brought with me for identification turned out to be a source of design inspiration for some weavers. Old, forgotten motifs, and motifs from neighboring regions were scrutinized, and sometimes jealously guarded from the eyes of neighboring weavers. There was a strong sense that she who put it on the market first would profit most.

Currently, the bestsellers in Batak hand-woven cloth include outfits comprising matching shouldercloth (*slendang*) and hipcloth (*sarong*). These outfits are executed by the best Silindung Valley weavers with the finest and highest-quality yarns, and are Batak versions of outfits typical and common among the neighboring Malays and Javanese. They are pricey and only the wealthier urban Bataks can afford to purchase them; nevertheless there is much local pride in these products. Even the wife of the Indonesian president owns such an outfit, the local weavers are proud to relate. Not only can the weavers compete within the realm of local high fashion, but they see their sales expanding beyond just the Batak population and winning a little of the Javanese market.

Batak successes in the marketplace are evident from their cloth design repertory, but are not as spectacular in trade history as the successes of their European competitors. Winning in the local fashion scene is currently one of the weaver's most important strategies since none of them has access to cheaper materials or faster technology by which to undercut her neighbor's production. She knows, however, that anyone with these capacities who decides to make and market distinctively Batak textiles can put them all out of work and reduce most of them to abject poverty.

△△△△△
Arab dhows at Goa, India, unload merchandise. Networks of seagoing trade have linked areas of the Indian Ocean, the Pacific, and the Western world for centuries.

(see Malinowski 1922, Leach and Leach 1983). Participants in the kula system undertook difficult voyages in canoes to carry out ceremonial exchanges of prized necklaces and armbands with trading partners on other islands. Armbands and necklaces circulate in opposite directions (see Figure 5.1), thereby helping to sustain an extensive trading network among numerous islands. Thus, Trobriand Islanders give armbands to people on Dobu and receive necklaces from them. Trading partnerships are inherited from kin and establish important social and economic relationships. The exchange of the necklaces and armbands is accompanied by elaborate feasts, the presentation of other gifts, and bartering over a range of goods on the side.

Between larger-scale societies, shorter on ceremony, commerce is characterized by a more constant flow of greater quantities and varieties of goods and more extensive commercial networks than exchange between small-scale societies. The growth of early empires was accompanied by such networks. After 1200 B.C. the ancient Phoenicians, for instance, became masters of trade routes throughout the Mediterranean that were linked to routes stretching as far as India. Cloves from the eastern islands of Indonesia were carried by Arab sailors and overland cara-

vans at great expense to the Roman Empire for use in cooking and to scent the air in temples. In the New World, the Aztecs of central Mexico were at the center of an extensive trade network over which goods traveled from all over Mexico and Central America and even from northern South America.

European maritime exploration was concerned primarily with securing trade routes and eventually the sources of goods around the world. Columbus sailed to the New World not simply out of curiosity but in search of trade. Europeans' search for raw materials and new markets for their products transformed the world and formed the basis for the modern world system. The colonial period was one in which European imperial powers sought to create a world suited to their economic needs, and the postcolonial societies studied by anthropologists today are both a reflection of and a reaction to this colonial transformation.

Terms such as *globalization* and *the global economy* highlight the commercial interconnectedness of the modern world economy (see "Focus on Anthropologists"). This is especially apparent in the electronics industry. It is hard to find a village anywhere in the world without several radios and cassette tape recorders and probably a television set as well. The raw materials—metals, petroleum products, and the like—used to produce a single radio or television may come from dozens of countries. The individual components may be made in Malaysia, Mexico, Taiwan, or any of a number of countries, while the entire unit may be assembled in yet another location. Once assembled, the radio or television may pass through several countries before ending up in someone's home in the highlands of Papua New Guinea or the Amazonian jungle

◀ RELATIONSHIPS BETWEEN ▶ PRODUCTION SYSTEMS

Relationships between systems of production fall into three basic types: symbiotic complementarity, hierarchical complementarity, and open competition. These categories are not mutually exclusive. All relationships between systems of production will include aspects of each. But these categories represent fundamental differences of emphasis; they also are linked with social and political relationships between groups.

Symbiotic Complementarity

Symbiotic complementarity refers to different systems of production complementing each other, each providing goods and services needed by the other, without one being dominant. The groups involved in this mutual economic interdependence are usually relative social equals and politically independent. Symbiotic complementarity is relevant primarily to small-scale systems of production. Increasing scale tends to lead to more unequal or competitive relationships.

Symbiotic complementarity can take many forms. Sometimes two groups use the same land at different seasons for different yet complementary purposes. For example, some pastoral nomads in the Middle East who summer their herds in the mountains bring their animals down to winter them on the stubble left by

sedentary farmers after the fall harvest. The animals are fed, and they fertilize the fields in the process. Additional complementarity is provided by the nomads' provision of animal-derived products such as wool and cheese to the farmers in exchange for agricultural products.

Groups occupying completely different areas may complement each other by providing items not available in their respective environments. Forest-dwelling foragers such as the Maçu of South America and the BaMbuti of Africa provide forest goods such as medicinal and edible plants and game to agriculturalists who live beyond the forest, in return for agricultural and industrial products.

In both of these instances situations may arise leading to inequality. Pastoralists sometimes dominate farmers by gaining ownership of their land. The BaMbuti and Maçu are not always treated well by their neighbors, who consider them to be inferior, but both groups are able to maintain a good deal of social and political autonomy. Such relationships are not static, however. The habitat of the BaMbuti is being destroyed by commercial loggers and land-hungry farmers, and the Maçu increasingly find their land and lives encroached on by settlers, government officials, and missionaries.

Hierarchical Complementarity

When systems complement one another but relationships are clearly unequal, often characterized by domination and exploitation, the relationship is one of *hierarchical complementarity*. This pattern is associated with increasing social scale and the formation of states and empires. A common pattern here is a powerful state with a relatively developed economy dominating the resources, products, or markets of less powerful states with less developed economies. Such domination may be direct, as in the case of colonialism, or indirect through the control of strategic resources and the manipulation of local politics.

West Africa provides an example of an evolving structure of hierarchical complementarity. Prior to European incursion, West Africa was made up of a number of small empires and city states, which engaged in long-distance trade, and numerous independent villages of subsistence farmers. Beginning in the sixteenth century, Europeans established themselves along the coast and initiated trade with the local African states, exchanging European manufactured goods (especially weapons) for slaves captured in the interior. The slaves were intended for the colonial economies of North America and South America. The African states involved in this trade became organized along military lines, several expanding their spheres of influence over other states and over the agricultural villages, which supplied most of the slaves. When the slave trade was abolished in the nineteenth century, the West African states shifted to providing agricultural products for European markets. During the latter part of the nineteenth century the European powers assumed direct control over these states and oriented the local economies even more thoroughly to suit European economic requirements.

Open Competition

Open competition emerges when groups with different systems of production come into conflict over access to the same desired resources. This pattern also is related to increasing social scale and commonly takes the form of one system of production engulfing and destroying another. Today this usually involves conflicts between large-scale industrial societies seeking access to resources and thereby threatening the economies of small-scale societies.

Brazilian Amazonian Indians like the Mundurucu and Yanomami until recently lived as relatively autonomous foragers and farmers. During the past few decades, however, their habitat has attracted outside attention as a source of timber, mineral resources, pasture, and farm-land. Many of those who have sought to resist such incursion have been killed, forced to retreat ever deeper into the jungle, or placed on reservations. On the reservations, they are able to maintain something of their traditional way of life, and in some cases are given time to better adapt to the new environment, but few of the reservations have proven to be secure sanctuaries. Off the reservation, those who have survived have been forced to find new ways to subsist—working as servants, menial laborers, beggars, and prostitutes—as their traditional economic adaptation disappears.

S U M M A R Y

Economic systems consist of patterns of production, ownership, and exchange. Production, an ordered series of acts set in a particular social and environmental context, involves the transformation of an object for cultural purposes. Anthropologists are interested in the system of production of which the act is a part. Production systems must cope with disruptions and environmental crises, arrange for regular replacement of workers, and divide labor and distribute rewards.

Ownership—acknowledged supremacy, authority, or power over a physical object, process, or idea—tends not to be absolute; ideas of ownership can be complex. Considerable differences in how much is owned exist among and within societies. Differences in the distribution of wealth within societies are greater in large-scale societies.

Wealth is distributed within and among societies in patterns of exchange. There are three basic patterns: reciprocity, redistribution, and market exchange. In reciprocal exchange, people trade one kind of good or service for another. Redistribution takes such forms as taxation, gift-giving, and potlatches. Market exchange is characterized by the buying and selling of goods through the use of special-purpose or general-purpose money.

Today few societies are isolated from the world economic system. Groups are often drawn into contact with others through commerce. Relationships between systems of production may reflect symbiotic complementarity (each system provides for the needs of the other), hierarchical complementarity (one system dominates or exploits the other), or open competition (involving conflict over access to some desired resources).

Special-purpose money A medium of exchange used in only limited contexts and only for a particular range of goods and services.

Taxation A form of redistribution of wealth in which individuals of a society surrender part of their wealth to the government in exchange for services provided them.

Wealth Objects or resources that are useful or that have exchange value.

K E Y   T E R M S

Commerce The exchange of goods among different countries or regions.

Exchange Trade in resources, goods, ideas, and services.

General-purpose money A medium of exchange that can be used to pay for a wide range of goods and services.

Market exchange The buying and selling of goods.

Money A medium of exchange characterized by durability, transferability, and acceptability over a wide range of functions.

Ownership Acknowledged supremacy, authority, or power over a physical object, process, or idea.

Potlatch An elaborate, at times dramatic, feast and gift-giving ceremony performed among native peoples of the Northwest Coast of North America; it is a form of redistribution of wealth.

Production Significant transformation of an object for cultural purposes.

Reciprocity The mutual exchange of goods and services.

S U G G E S T E D   R E A D I N G S

Among relevant general works on economic anthropology are:

Clammer, John, editor. 1978. *The New Economic Anthropology.* London: Macmillan.

Humphrey, Caroline, and Stephen Hugh-Jones (eds.). 19 92 . *Barter, Exchange and Value.* New York: Cambridge University Press.

Plattner, Stuart, editor. 1989. *Economic Anthropology.* Stanford: Stanford University Press.

Sahlins, Marshall. 1972. *Stone Age Economics.* Chicago: Aldine.

Seddon, David, editor. 1978. *Relations of Production.* London: Frank Cass.

There are a large number of studies of particular aspects of economic anthropology and case studies in economic anthropology, including:

Appadurai, Arjun, editor. 1986. *The Social Life of Things: Commodities in Cultural Perspective.* New York: Cambridge University Press.

Babb, Florence E. 1990. *Between Field and Cooking Pot: The Political Economy of Marketwomen in Peru.* Austin: University of Texas Press.

Beals, Ralph. 1975. *The Peasant Marketing System of Oaxaca, Mexico.* Berkeley: University of California Press.

Carrier, James G., and Achsah H. Carrier. 1989. *Wage, Trade, and Exchange in Melanesia: A Manus Society in the Modern State.* Berkeley: University of California Press.

Clark, Gracia, editor. 1988. *Traders Versus the State: Anthropological Approaches to Unofficial Economics.* Boulder, CO: Westview Press.

Cooper, Eugene. 1980. *The Wood-Carvers of Hong Kong: Craft Production in the World Capitalist Periphery.* New York: Cambridge University Press.

Durrenberger, E. Paul, and Nicola Tannenbaum. 1990. *Analytical Perspectives on Shan Agriculture and Village Economics.* New Haven: Yale University Southeast Asian Studies.

Halperin, Rhoda, and James Dow, editors. 1977. *Peasant Livelihood: Studies in Economic Anthropology and Cultural Ecology.* New York: St. Martin's.

Howard, Michael C. 1991. *Mining, Politics, and Development in the South Pacific.* Boulder, CO: Westview Press.

Leacock, Eleanor, and Helen I. Safa, editors. 1986. *Women's Work: Development and the Division of Labor by Gender.* South Hadley, MA: Bergin & Garvey.

Lehman, David, editor. *Ecology and Exchange in the Andes.* New York: Cambridge University Press.

Mintz, Sidney W. 1986. *Sweetness and Power: The Place of Sugar in Modern History.* New York: Viking Penguin.

Sherman, D. George. 1990. *Rice, Rupees, and Ritual: Economy and Society Among the Samosir Batak of Sumatra.* Stanford: Stanford University Press. (Indonesia)

Smith, Waldemar R. 1977. *The Fiesta System and Economic Change.* New York: Columbia University Press.(Guatemala).

6 SOCIETY

Wolf children, a few hermits, prisoners in solitary confinement, and those stranded on desert isles aside, most of us spend a great deal of time in the company of other humans. It is generally as a group that we adapt to our surroundings and seek to ensure that our subsistence requirements are met. How we perceive the world and how we behave in it are largely reflections of our interaction with others. **Society** is an abstraction of the ways in which interaction among humans is patterned.

In the last chapter we looked at how people produce, distribute, and exchange things. This chapter focuses on the social dimension of adaptation: What are the varied ways in which people order their interaction with the human environment?

◄ LOOKING AT SOCIETY ►

To figure out how society works, anthropologists study both the structure and the function of social events or processes. In their analyses, they look at varying levels of interaction—from whole societies linked by the world system down to the interaction of two individuals.

Analyzing Social Structure

The term **social structure** refers to the patterned interrelationship of the parts of society in a complex whole. When we look at the structures of whole societies, we see that groups that pursue similar subsistence strategies tend to have similar social structures. Their similarities will be modified somewhat by local conditions and historical circumstances, such as the availability of particular resources and weather patterns. For example, Kekchi Mayan communities in the highlands of Guatemala and the lowlands of southern Belize have similar kinship, economic, and religious structures, but, since land is more abundant in southern Belize, these structures are more flexible there than in Guatemala. Despite such differences, these communities share with other small-scale societies a characteristic way of organizing people into social units that is different from that found in larger-scale societies.

In a very general sense, we find that small-scale societies exhibit a high degree of internal cohesiveness. Such cohesiveness relates to the fact that people in these societies interact largely on a face-to-face basis, and it is reflected in their limited division of labor. Everyone is familiar with everyone else, does much the same thing, and undergoes similar experiences. In addition to this *homogeneity*, or similarity, among people, there is also a great deal of overlap in the units

Vietnamese workers and children near Hanoi, acting out the roles expected of them in their society.

of social structure. Among the Shoshone, the family and the foraging group are virtually one and the same. In contrast, as societies become larger they begin to lose their homogeneous nature, and the social structure comes to be made up of a greater array of more specialized parts. In a traditional Amazonian Indian village most of the process of food production and exchange is carried out within a single family. In contrast, in our own society food production involves the farms, ranches, and laboratories where food is produced, and a variety of other supportive institutions. Transportation and exchange of food are handled by yet other specialized institutions.

Analyzing Social Functions

By **function** we mean the purpose and effects, the intended and actual consequences, of particular beliefs and actions. While one function may be of primary importance, most beliefs and actions serve a variety of functions, depending on the point of reference. Marriage, for example, performs different functions for the individuals getting married, for the couple's respective families, and for society as a whole.

Social scientists distinguish two categories of social function: manifest and latent. **Manifest functions** are the purposes or results that are most obvious and that are explicitly stated. The manifest function of washing clothes is to get them clean. **Latent functions** are the less apparent purposes. Women's clothes-washing may perform a latent function as a means of assessing their social standing in relation to their peers in terms of skill and diligence; as a form of drudgery, it may also symbolize the society's belief in the inferiority of women in relation to men.

The Individual and Society

In looking at the parts of a society, we can start with the individual. The individual is the building

Tibetan girl winnowing millet. The manifest function of this activity is to separate chaff from grain; a latent function is to prepare the child to become an adult.

block of society, because in one sense society is the product of its members' actions. The members of a society do not act alone, however. Individuals are social actors whose behaviors are influenced by the social environment. It would be more accurate, then, to view society as the representation of the collective behavior of its members. Much of this collective behavior is highly patterned, conditioned by social forces that both spring from and transcend the individual.

Because society has no tangible existence, any permanence or regularity that it does exhibit will depend on the repetition of people's actions. Society has to be continually recreated by individuals. The pattern that we associate with the family in rural Japan, for example, exists only insofar as individual Japanese continue to group themselves and behave in ways associated with their particular family structure.

Society is the product of decisions people make concerning when, how, and with whom they are going to interact. Such individual decisions are influenced by a number of factors, some of which may be based on existing social patterns. One of these factors is individual perception: how individuals view their environment and the situation within which they must act, and what they perceive their options to be. Another factor is historical precedent, because what a person does is almost always influenced by what has been done in the past. The weight individuals give to this continuity depends on the extent to which they consider past actions to be relevant in their current circumstances and the degree to which they interact continually with the same people and the same physical surroundings. A third factor is a person's or group's goals. We interact with others to achieve some end. Should our goals or those of the group change, so will the pattern of our social behavior.

Social Relationships

We use the term *relationship* for any regularized pattern of action between individuals. By placing such patterns in a social context, we arrive at the concept of a **social relationship.** The interaction between a woman and her daughter may be termed a mother-daughter relationship and can be expected to have certain regularities within a particular society. However, rather than thinking about *the* mother-daughter relationship in a society in some idealized sense, we should recognize a range of mother-daughter relationships, depending on the life cycle and the varying circumstances of the two individuals involved. The relationship of an American mother and her preschool daughter will change as the child grows and becomes an adolescent. How much variation there will be in relationships is likely to depend on social scale, but even in small-scale societies there will be some variation.

Two primary questions need to be asked about social relationships: Who are they between? What are they about? (Beattie 1964: 36). Answers to these questions are often expressed in terms of status and role. **Status** is social position—what people are in relation to one another, such as the statuses of student and teacher. Social scientists make a distinction between an ascribed status and one that is achieved. An *ascribed status* is assigned, usually on the basis of birth. A girl born to Nuer parents automatically becomes a Nuer as well as a female. An *achieved status* is attained through the actions or decisions of individuals on an optional basis. One becomes a teacher in our society as a result of an individual decision, then successfully completing a course of training and managing to find employment. A status can have both an ascribed and achieved quality. To be born heir to a throne does not automatically mean a prince will become king.

The part a society expects one to play in a given relationship is a **role**—a set of activities that are thought to have some purpose and function in a particular context. A king is expected to govern; a subject is expected to submit to the king's authority. Such expectations cannot be understood in isolation, however. Precisely how a king or a subject is expected to behave will be defined by historical tradition and the contemporary situation. The status of kinship in the society will also be a factor. A king may be expected not only to govern but also to intercede with the deities on behalf of his subjects or to give his blessing to certain brands of cookie

Traditional Hawaiian chiefs in cloak and head-dress. Although Hawaiian chiefs inherited their status genealogically, it was not entirely ascribed, since their practical success in leading their people helped contribute to their chiefly status.

their subjects, and such relationships can influence the respective roles of king and subject. Furthermore, individuals usually occupy a number of different statuses and perform a range of roles, any one of which may influence the others. The king may also be a father, a member of a cricket team, a husband, and an airplane pilot.

Social scale is an important factor affecting statuses and roles. In small-scale societies with relatively little specialization, the range of distinct statuses and roles available to an individual is much more limited than in large-scale societies. Among desert-dwelling foragers such as the Shoshone, almost the only distinctions made are those of age, gender, and kinship. Furthermore, statuses and roles may overlap, forming a few clusters that are ascribed to individuals. All middle-aged Shoshone men, for example, can be expected to occupy more or less the same status and perform roughly the same roles. In sharp contrast, a middle-aged man in a large-scale industrial society can be anything from a wealthy and powerful business leader to an impoverished vagrant.

Institutions

Institutions are practices that are based on similar principles and that display some degree of regularity. While there are many principles around which institutions may be organized, anthropologists identify four of major significance (Beattie 1964). Some institutions deal with *economic and property relations*—with the ways people produce and distribute things. Among these institutions are farms, banks, and markets. There are institutions concerned with *social control*—with politics and law. Government, courts, and the police fall within this category. In the third category are those concerned with the *supernatural*—with magic and religion. These include the church, monasteries, and witches' covens. The fourth category consists of institutions, such as the family, based on principles of *kinship*—relations created by descent and mar-

or tea. Such expectations are not static. Both the status and the role of Queen Elizabeth II are a far cry from those associated with King Henry VIII; the difference reflects changes in the English economy, the emergence of new forms of social stratification, and the transformation of the English state.

Roles do not take place simply in pairs. Kings also have relationships with those who are not riage. Anthropologists have been especially interested in institutions based on kinship because of their central role in small-scale societies. We will discuss kinship in more detail in Chapter 8.

Any institution is likely to involve to some degree more than one of these organizing principles. The family, for example, is also concerned with social control, with economic and property relations, and, in many societies, with the supernatural. These are secondary concerns, however, rather than primary organizing principles for, in this case, the family.

The process by which regularized patterns are created is referred to as **institutionalization,** or the standardization of patterns of joint activity. For example, when a religious prophet or cult leader succeeds in regularizing people's beliefs and practices according to his or her teachings, this type of religious belief and the social group that forms around it can be said to have undergone institutionalization. One common way of institutionalizing social relations is through kinship.

Social Networks

Despite the social shaping of relationships, individuals do not act entirely in a patterned, stereotypical fashion. Individuals are never merely passive actors playing out social roles. People can act creatively, and part of that creativity involves the use of their social environment. To better understand how people both use and are influenced by their social environment, anthropologists turn to **social networks**—the bonds and links that form the social web within which we act (see "Focus on Anthropologists").

Whether trying to find a new job or a spouse, we continually mobilize potential links that exist within our personal social network. Analysis of this dimension of social life—the interpersonal links among people—is an important complement to the study of institutional-ized relationships. It allows us to look beyond the formal structures of bureaucracies or kin-based groups and see more clearly how such institutions actually function.

Patterns of recruitment to social networks can differ from one society to another. In the small Mayan villages of southern Belize, a person's social network is built up primarily on the basis of kinship and *compadrazgo* (social links created by sponsorship of children in rites like baptism and confirmation) and to a more limited extent on the basis of less formal friendship. Many of the links created in village settings such as these are *multiplex*—formed on the basis of more than one criterion. For example, a person may be linked to another on the basis of kinship, *compadrazgo,* and friendship. This multiplication of criteria tends to intensify links, enhancing the extent to which individuals are willing or can be expected to honor obligations or to feel free to exercise rights implied in the links (Mitchell 1969: 27). The Maya of southern Belize feel much more secure in asking individuals with whom they have multiplex ties to help with farm-related work than they do individuals with whom they have fewer ties.

People in large-scale societies also form multiplex links, but their personal networks are also more likely to contain a variety of links formed on the basis of a single criterion, such as employer and employee. We refer to such links as *simplex*. Simplex links also occur in small-scale societies, but there is a tendency to try to strengthen them through additional criteria. The Maya of southern Belize commonly seek patrons among merchants and government officials to assist them in their commercial dealings and dealings with the government (Howard 1977). They seek to strengthen their relationship through *compadrazgo*, asking their patron to sponsor their child. This *compadrazgo* link, however, does not carry with it the same expectations as do *compadrazgo* links formed with members of one's own community. One would not

DIANE Z. WILHELM

FOCUS ON ANTHROPOLOGISTS

Diane Z. Wilhelm did fieldwork among Irish street traders in 1987 and returned for a short visit in 1991. She has also studied the Araucanians in Argentina and Chile and the people of the Appalachian Mountains in North Carolina. She is currently Professor of Anthropology at Middlesex County College (MCC) in New Jersey and Director of the MCC field school in cultural anthropology in the Picuris Pueblo in New Mexico. Dr. Wilhelm is also past president of the Society for Anthropology in Community Colleges.

∧∧∧∧∧∧∧∧∧

Dublin's Illegal Street Traders: Female-Centered Support Groups and Networks

S treet traders in Dublin, Ireland, have been an integral part of the local scene for centuries. They constitute a unique occupational subculture within the working class. Dublin street trading has traditionally been an activity carried on primarily by women, and most traders were either born or have married into trading families. Traders with flat Dublin accents can be heard loudly crying their wares every day of the week except Sunday and in all kinds of weather.

At different times in history, traders have been classified as legal or illegal, depending on circumstances. Today some operate legally and some illegally. The legal traders have licenses

and fixed stalls. Many are kin to the illegal traders but are not in the social network, or web of interpersonal links, of the illegals because there is considerable friction between the two groups over the issue of licensing. Because of city council restrictions, a trader who has been arrested for not having a license cannot be granted one. Since the illegal traders are those who have been arrested on those grounds, they are not now able to obtain licensing.

My study focused on one group (a *group,* as opposed to a *network,* has a definite structure of roles and a boundary). This group comprises about 20 women who are illegal street traders. They lack fixed stalls but sell their fruits, vegetables, or flowers from prams. These women represent more than the survival of a quaint Dublin subculture. Although their trading is part of a family tradition, realistically, in a bad economy, it is also one of the few avenues open to them for making a liv-

ing. Most of these women's husbands are unemployed and on public assistance. The women are pragmatists; their street trading represents a rational response to economic conditions.

The illegal Dublin street trader is enmeshed in a tightly knit network of reciprocal relationships with other traders, many of them kin. (A *network* is ego-centered and lacks group structure and boundary.) This network provides the material and emotional support vital for the success of the trader. The network also functions to help traders cope with the problems of survival in a difficult inner-city environment. In contrast to inner-city dwellers in the United States, who are often recent migrants, Irish street-trading families, according to their own oral tradition, have lived here for perhaps as long as 500 years. This fact reflects the strength and durability of their networking.

Although there are probably several hundred street traders in

Dublin, the illegal traders are concentrated on one major street and adjacent side streets in a fashionable downtown shopping district. There are about 75 regulars, supplemented on Saturday by occasional traders. However, the effective support group for each trader numbers about 20 and each can call upon a wider network when the need arises.

Among the group that I studied, a boundary mechanism that helps define the group was being included or excluded in the daily lunch at a local cafe. Conversations in the cafe indicated that members perceive themselves as part of a group. For example, whenever an unfamiliar name entered the conversation, someone would invariably turn to me and comment, "She's one of us" or "She's not one of us."

This daily meeting provided an opportunity to reaffirm group membership by discussing traders in other groups, emphasizing through gossip that they were not part of this particular group. No traders from other groups ever entered the cafe during this time.

Group membership, mutual obligations, and cooperation were further reinforced by what went on during the meal. For example, the money taken in by each woman was counted out. This task frequently fell to one woman, my key informant, who was clearly a leader in the group. Also during the meal, the trader nearest the door

Irish street traders, who form a network of women, peddle their wares on Dublin streets.

would get up to make a sale at any pram outside which attracted people, return with the money, and hand it over to the owner of that particular pram, serving to reaffirm the cooperative relationships among the women.

Ties were further reinforced and mutual obligations incurred through children and younger siblings' visits to the cafe, often to ask for money. If the mother or sister were not there, the child was given money by another relative and frequently sent on an errand. This reemphasized the link of kinship as well as the economic relationship within the network.

The social cohesion of the group of 20 women is also a result of their social interaction in contexts other than eco-

nomic. Almost all the women live in public housing on the same street, a few blocks from where they sell. At home, they are involved in a constant round of activities, such as visiting back and forth and borrowing children for chores. Each morning, for example, many of the group would gather at one home to have a cup of tea and plan the day's selling.

In addition, on a typical Sunday night, several of the women would meet at the house of my key informant around 7 p.m. Fashionably dressed, they would then begin the ritual of putting final touches to makeup or hair. Being a woman, I was included in this ritual. The routine entailed visits to several other homes for a new brand of perfume or hair spray. This grooming ritual engenders a particularly strong feeling of intimacy among the women.

A group of about five women would then go to a small pub on the corner where they met other traders from various groups, including their own. No men were present, and the women moved constantly around the room, stopping briefly to chat at different tables. Important information about prices in the wholesale market, earnings, the police, and families was exchanged. Several collections were taken up for women in financial difficulties. It was apparent from this socializing that each of the women studied also had a network that extended into other street trader groups, and included, as well, helpful local individuals. This network was utilized for the benefit of the street trader and her group.

After about an hour, the group of five women would move on to a larger, "singing pub" several blocks away. This pub consisted of one large room in which men were also present. However, the introductions indicated that the men at the table were brothers to the women. That some were also married to some of the women was incidental.

The singing pub provides yet another opportunity to reaffirm group membership. There is friendly competition among the groups of traders as people are called upon to sing, and each

group takes great pride in the proficiency of its singers. At this pub also, several collections would be taken up for women with troubles.

Among the financial hazards of street trading is the constant risk of being arrested. The fines imposed may be heavy, but more important perhaps, the trader's pram and merchandise may be confiscated. The pram will be returned upon payment of a fine, but the merchandise is a total loss. In addition, no income is earned during the time spent at the police station; if a court appearance is required, another day is lost with no income from selling. If a heavy fine is imposed and the trader cannot pay it, she may be sentenced to a short jail term. Finally, the trader is also required to pay the equivalent of a taxi fare for the ride in the police vehicle.

The illegal street traders are also at an initial disadvantage. Since they must push their prams and cannot therefore load them too heavily, they are unable to buy goods in the wholesale market at the larger discount given to volume buyers. All this, of course, reduces their profit margin. To minimize these difficulties, the traders employ a variety of strategies.

Perhaps the most important strategy is the establishment of a partnership with another trader. The two women pool their money to purchase goods at the wholesale market, enti-

tling them to a larger discount. At the end of the day the money taken in is split between them, regardless of which one has sold the most. Although most of the traders seem to have a regular partner, some days they will partner with another woman.

Another advantage of a partnership is that each woman watches the other while they are selling. If the police head for one pram, the other will swiftly transfer most of the merchandise to her pram and leave, thus salvaging the investment. This in fact often occurs. However, it is also true that sometimes the partner will not be alert or, seeing the police, will run rather than try to transfer the goods. Although this is cause for complaint, it does not seem to be cause to end the partnership.

Another strategy to reduce the risk of confiscation is to keep a limited amount of merchandise on the pram and store the rest nearby. This enables the traders to purchase more in the wholesale market without risking their entire stock. However, to do this, the trader must leave the street and walk to the storage place, thus reducing selling time.

When a trader has sold her stock for the day, she will then sell the merchandise of a friend, not usually a partner. She will turn over all the money made from the sale of that merchandise to the other trader. This probably functions to create and cement bonds and gives the trader a wider network of support when she in turn needs it. Traders also exchange information about the location of police and try to plan their movement to minimize encounters.

Obviously, since the traders are arrested frequently, these strategies do not work perfectly. However, without the social and economic network within which the traders are enmeshed, illegal street trading would be impossible. It is only this female-centered network that enables them to function at all.

think of asking one's patron to help clear a field or put fresh thatch on a roof. We can say that the content of the *compadrazgo* link in these two situations differs.

< SOCIAL GROUPINGS >

We use the term *group* very broadly in common discourse, but anthropologists are much more careful in their use of the word. When referring to a group, anthropologists usually mean what more specifically can be labeled a corporate group. A **corporate group** is theoretically permanent; its members are recruited on the basis of recognized principles, have common interests or property, and have norms or rules fixing their rights and duties in relation to one another and to their property or interests. A patrilineage is a corporate group to which members are recruited on the basis of kinship, the principle being descent through the male line from a common ancestor (see Chapter 8). A business corporation is also a corporate group, but one that recruits people for specific purposes on the basis of their possession of desired skills and their acceptance of particular modes of behavior.

Although both the patrilineage and the business corporation are corporate groups, membership in the former is ascribed, whereas membership in the latter is nonascriptive. This important distinction bestows groups with significantly different characteristics.

Ascribed Groups

In **ascribed groups,** membership is acquired at birth and is nonvoluntary. Assembling people into multipurpose groups on the basis of ascribed categories is the chief principle of group formation in small-scale societies. With increasing social scale, groupings become more voluntary and specialized. The most common types of ascriptive multipurpose groupings are based on age, gender, and kinship.

AGE-BASED GROUPS. Age is a universally important factor determining social behavior. All societies possess a series of recognized age-based categories, or **age grades.** Most societies at least divide their members into categories associated with youth, adulthood, and old age, and in many these grades are further refined. Behavior expectations are associated with each of the age grades, and sometimes they are accorded specified rights and privileges. However, individuals within the same grade do not necessarily function as a corporate group.

In a number of small-scale societies, especially in Africa, those belonging to the same age grade are formed into corporate groups. These groups, known as **age sets,** are composed of individuals of similar age and of the same sex who possess a common identity, maintain close ties throughout their lives, and together pass through a series of age-related statuses. The structure of age sets varies from one society to the next. Some follow a linear progression, in which those born during a specified period belong to a single set that

∧∧∧∧∧
Age-based groups in U.S. society are largely voluntary and specialized. These young men in Los Angeles form an age-based group that is associated with the behavioral expectations of a gang.

1963). At age 12, boys who have grown up working closely together leave their parental homes and move to a village of their own. They continue to return to their parents' homes for meals and to their fathers' fields to work until they marry and set up their own households at about age 25. Younger brothers of the village founders join the community until it becomes large enough for the members to decide to close admittance. After a decade or so, when there are a number of new age-set villages in the area, the fathers will hold a ceremony to hand over full political authority to their sons.

GENDER-BASED GROUPS.   All societies categorize people by gender, as well as by age. In small-scale societies, people are automatically divided into gender-based groups that serve many purposes, such as carrying out subsistence activities delegated to one or the other sex. Large-scale industrial societies also commonly possess a range of gender-based groups (such as the League of Women Voters, the Boy Scouts, fraternities, and sororities), but membership in these is usually more voluntary and the groups serve a narrower range of purposes. During the past few decades, for example, concern for women's political rights and welfare has led to the formation of thousands of specialized voluntary groups focusing on such things as violence against women, harassment of women on the job, the needs of single mothers, and equal employment opportunities.

Again, within small-scale societies the structure and significance of gender-based groups can differ a great deal. In Amazonian Brazil, the Mundurucu household contains a gender-based group consisting of several closely related women of two generations. Usually the women are from the same village and have grown up together. They carry out most of their productive tasks as a group—gardening, preparing manioc, and cooking together. It is a secure group that is to a very large extent self-sufficient.

moves through a series of grades as the members grow older. Others adhere to a cyclic pattern, in which new members are periodically accepted. In some societies, age sets are fairly unimportant, performing a limited range of functions and exerting little influence on the overall functioning of society. In other societies, they are of tremendous importance.

The Nyakyusa of southeastern Africa have a well-developed system of age sets (Wilson

Gender-based groups in two cultures: An example of a gender-based group in a large-scale society is the fraternity. Here making a pledge cake deteriorates into a food fight between present members and pledges. In a small-scale society: Kuikuro Indian men paint up for a tribal dance in their men's house, a common gender-based feature of these societies. The use of a men's house, from which women are excluded, often functions to maintain men's control of special forms of ritual and knowledge.

The males in a Mundurucu village have moved there from other villages upon marriage. When not engaged in subsistence activities, they spend much of their time in a central men's house, a common feature in small-scale farming societies. Men's groups are not as well integrated as women's, since the men come from different villages and different kin groups. Also, male economic tasks are performed alone or in small groups, further diminishing their unity.

Changes brought about by integration into larger societies have served to undermine gender-based groups such as those of the Mundurucu. The Mundurucu have become increasingly dependent upon the collection of rubber to meet their economic needs, especially to earn money to purchase consumer goods from traders. Rubber trees are widely scattered, and many Mundurucu now live as isolated nuclear families to be nearer rubber-collecting areas. Some have moved to a mission settlement. Such moves have resulted in the breakdown of the prior pattern of separate gender-based groups and their replacement by new forms of association.

Voluntary Associations

Special-purpose groups, the members of which are recruited on a nonascriptive basis, are a common feature of life in large-scale industrial societies. These **voluntary associations** are found less often in small-scale societies, where most groupings tend to be ascriptive. Nevertheless, several types of voluntary association may be found in small-scale societies.

VOLUNTARY GROUPINGS IN SMALL-SCALE SOCIETIES. Specialized *military associations* are formed in some small-scale societies that engage in warfare regularly, although kinship groups and age sets are more likely to be the primary military units. The Cheyenne traditionally had five such societies: the Fox, the Dog, the Shield, the Elk (or Hoof Rattle), and the Bowstring (or Contrary), each with its own leaders, costumes, songs, and dances (Hoebel 1978).

Secret societies are another form of voluntary grouping in small-scale societies. The Poro society, found in Liberia and Sierra Leone, is an example of such a group (Little 1965/66). Members of the Poro society are said to have close contact with the supernatural and to possess magical powers. Its leaders come from among those who hold public power, and the society serves to support their public statuses. Young men who are initiated into the society attend "bush school" in an isolated part of the forest for several years, where they learn secret rituals and the society's version of the history of their people, as well as a variety of useful survival skills.

There are also *religious cults,* like those of the Tupi-Guarani of Brazil reported by early European explorers and settlers (Lanternari 1963: 171-181). Tupi-Guarani prophets would gather large numbers of followers and then set off in search of a promised land. The so-called cargo cults of the South Pacific (see Chapter 13) provide another example of this type of voluntary association.

VOLUNTARY GROUPINGS, URBANIZATION, AND INDUSTRIALIZATION. Voluntary associations have developed in large-scale societies in response to two processes: urbanization and industrialization. The dislocation, alienation, and depersonalization of modern, large-scale societies have given rise to the formation of voluntary associations directed toward the varied interests of those living in these societies. While anthropologists have studied a wide range of such associations, they have been especially interested in those formed by ethnic minorities and recent migrants to cities.

Recent urban migrants frequently form associations on the basis of region, ethnicity, religion, or line of work. These associations sometimes play an important role in securing employment and social services for their members, but their precise roles can vary a great deal. Moreover, anthropologists have questioned the actual importance of these associations to members of the community within which they exist. Abner Cohen (1969), in a study of West African ethnic associations, found that only a small percentage of the total number of migrants actually joined these associations and that for many of those who did join, the associations' activities were of little relevance to their daily lives. Cohen's study alerts us to the need for caution when placing modern voluntary associations in the context of life in large-scale societies.

Voluntary associations, of course, need not directly affect the daily lives of their members to exert a great deal of influence on them. We can see this in the case of trade unions, a form of voluntary association that arose out of the new work conditions of large-scale industrial societies. Unions have influenced the lives of workers in many countries indirectly by having had such an important effect on the evolution of acceptable conditions of work and more specifically through individual negotiations that set wages and work standards. Workers are reminded of the importance of unions when negotiations take place or disputes occur. A similar point can be made concerning political parties. Indirectly, political parties influence almost every aspect of the lives of people in modern states; yet most people in these societies do not directly participate in these associations and are directly concerned with them only when elections take place. In this way, we can see that they differ a great deal from the ascriptive groups of small-scale societies where the link between daily life and association is much more direct and constant.

S U M M A R Y

As social creatures, humans shape and are shaped by their social environment. These interactions can be analyzed by looking at their structure or functions. *Social structure* refers to the patterned

⌃⌃⌃⌃⌃

Voluntary associations: The Cheyenne Lance Society (photograph taken in the late 1880s). A social and military group, the Lance Society, also known as the Coyote, was part of a ruling group along with chiefs. The group also served a police function on buffalo hunts. U.S. veterans of the 82nd and 101st Airborne Divisions, who parachuted over France at D-Day during World War II, do not perform the same roles in society as did the Cheyenne, but they do form voluntary associations for such days of remembrance as this.

interrelationship of the parts of society in a complex whole. By *function* we mean the purpose and effects, the intended and actual consequences, of particular beliefs and actions. Within a society, beliefs and activities may serve certain obvious, or manifest, functions and less obvious, latent, functions.

The individual is the basic building block of society. Society is the result of the decisions individuals make about when, how, and with whom they are going to interact. Social relationships—regularized patterns of action between individuals—are often institutionalized according to the status and role given to those involved. *Status* refers to social position—what people are in relation to one another—while *role* refers to a set of activities that are thought to have some purpose and function in a particular context.

Individuals organize or are organized into various kinds of groups. They are born into ascribed, nonvoluntary groups on the basis of age, gender, and kinship. Such groups tend to be rather strictly adhered to and multipurpose in small-scale societies. Voluntary associations are more common in large-scale societies, where they may serve a variety of functions.

KEY TERMS

Age grade   A series of recognized age-based categories in a society.

Age set   A corporate group formed by the individuals in an age grade; members are of similar age and the same sex, possess a common identity, maintain close ties throughout their lives, and together pass through a series of age-related statuses.

Ascribed group   A group in which membership is acquired at birth and is nonvoluntary.

Corporate group   A theoretically permanent group whose members are recruited on the basis of recognized principles, have common interests or property, and have norms or rules that fix their rights and duties in relation to one another and to their property or interests.

Institution   Social practices that are based on similar principles (for example, economic relations, social control, the supernatural, and kinship) and that display some degree of regularity.

Institutionalization   The process by which regularized social patterns are created.

Latent function   A purpose or result of particular beliefs or actions that are not especially apparent nor explicitly stated. (Compare with *manifest function.*)

Manifest function   A purpose or result of particular beliefs or actions that are most obvious and that are explicitly stated. (Compare with *latent function.*)

Role   The part a society expects an individual to play in a given relationship; a set of activities that are thought to have some purpose and function in a particular context.

Social function   The purpose and effects, or intended and actual consequences, of particular beliefs and actions.

Social network   The bonds and links that form the social web within which we act.

Social relationship   A regularized pattern of action between individuals placed in a social context.

Social structure   The patterned interrelationships of the parts of society in a complex whole.

Society   An abstraction of the ways in which interaction among humans is patterned.

Status Social position; what people are in relation to one another.

Voluntary association A special-purpose group whose members are recruited on a nonascriptive basis.

SUGGESTED READINGS

Banton, Michael, editor. 1965. *The Relevance of Models for Social Anthropology*. London: Tavistock.

Beattie, John. 1964. *Other Cultures: Aims, Methods and Achievements in Social Anthropology*. New York: Free Press.

Bernardi, Berdardo. 1985. *Age Class Systems: Social Institutions and Polities Based on Age*. New York: Cambridge University Press.

Boissevain, Jeremy, and J. Clyde Mitchell, editors. 1973. *Network Analysis: Studies in Human Interaction*. The Hague: Mouton.

Burnham, P. C., and R. F. Ellen, editors. 1979. *Social and Ecological Systems*. New York: Academic Press.

Firth, Raymond. 1964. *The Theory of Social Structure*. London: Athlone Press.

7 SOCIALIZATION

To the Semai, a small group of relatively isolated forest-dwellers in Malaysia, the thought of becoming angry is absurd. "We do not get angry," they explain (Dentan 1968: 55). Of course, the Semai *do* get angry on occasion, but they deny the existence of such an emotion within their culture.

WHAT TO LOOK FOR

➤ The kinds of things learned during socialization and enculturation, and how they are important to society

➤ How worldview can differ depending on the type of society

➤ How worldviews and values are manifest in the personality of individuals

➤ How socialization varies with the different phases of life

➤ How members of a society identify deviants, and how deviants consider themselves

Indeed, their cultural values minimize the likelihood of their becoming angry. They see themselves as nonviolent people. Almost from birth they are taught to avoid aggression and to feel shame for aggressive behavior. Should an individual hurt someone physically or emotionally, the injured party has the right to ask compensation, and more than likely the aggressor will endeavor to make up for the ill-feeling he or she has caused.

The Semai attitude toward aggression seems peculiar to most people in American society, where anger and hostility are everyday aspects of life. To many brought up in a Western cultural tradition the Semai may seem weak and cowardly, or perhaps carefree and naive. Either perception reflects the Westerner's own cultural views concerning violence and anger. Both Western and Semai attitudes are part of cultural traditions that have been shaped by distinct historical and environmental conditions. How do people acquire such attitudes, and how is acquiring them related to the larger society? This chapter looks at how individuals become part of their society.

⌃⌃⌃⌃⌃

A classic American rite of passage, or ritualized transition between an old and a new status, is the graduation prom, seen here in a high school group in Texas.

‹ SOCIALIZATION AND › ENCULTURATION

The general process by which we learn social roles from others is known as **socialization.** While part of what is learned is a result of formal instruction, much socialization occurs simply through interacting with others. As we learn to behave as members of a particular society, we undergo a process of **enculturation** by which we learn the rules and values of the culture.

We acquire an image of the world that is highly conditioned by the practices and beliefs of those around us. We are taught how to categorize the physical and social world and what these categories mean. The Semai categorize animals according to their habitat; fish, whales, and turtles are all in the same category. Likewise, the categories into which they divide their social and physical world differ from our own in many ways and carry with them many attitudes that are very different from those of Westerners. They consider thunder squalls, for

Toddler carried in basket on father's back, Kunming, China. This child is beginning to acquire an image of the world by the beliefs and practices of those around him.

instance, unnatural and caused by human action (Dentan 1968: 21–22), rather than being natural phenomena over which humans have little control.

Socialization results in a degree of uniformity among the members of a society as they come to share values and attitudes. But there will always be considerable variation. Variation reflects in part the particular statuses and roles individuals occupy within a society. In addition, there is always some room for individual choice and individual peculiarities, especially in large-scale societies, where pressure to conform is less than in small-scale societies. Not all Semai are alike, but close and continuous interaction and the fear of

disapproval lead to a high degree of uniformity. More options are available to those living in large-scale societies, where there is a wider range of potential statuses and roles to occupy and greater opportunity for social mobility. The presence of options does not mean that they will be realized, however. People exhibit a great deal of uniformity within segments of large-scale societies—such as those associated with class, community, or ethnicity. This is as true of elite society in Philadelphia as it is of Mexican-Americans in East Los Angeles; in both cases, the pressures toward conformity to group expectations are considerable.

Socialization begins at birth. Although the early years of life are especially important in shaping an individual's views, the process continues until death. As people grow older, their place in society changes, and they must learn new modes of behavior. Expectations of children differ from those of adults, and as people achieve adult status they must learn how to behave in accordance with new expectations. What these differences are, and how great, will vary from one society to another; but there will always be differences.

Socialization is also influenced by changes within the environment. Societies and the settings within which they exist are changing constantly, and people must adapt to these changes. The kinds of adjustment people make will depend partly on the nature of the changes taking place and partly on prior behavioral patterns and views of the world. For example, the introduction of television in the 1940s altered socialization patterns as TV came to function as a source of information, a mediator between members of a household or between individuals and the outside world, and a baby-sitter for millions of children. But its impact on society was not uniform. Reactions to television varied according to age, gender, class, ethnicity, and a host of other factors.

In a very broad sense our biological characteristics set limitations on what we can do and see and how we can view the world. We cannot fly unaided, we can eat only certain foods, and we can see in only a specific range of the light spectrum. Within these limitations, however, a tremendous potential remains for innovation and imagination. There are also individual biological differences, for each person is born with a unique configuration of inherited tendencies and physical characteristics that will influence how he or she behaves. How important individual biological differences are will vary according to their nature and the social context. To be blind in an urbanized society is far different from being blind among a group of desert foragers.

◄ WORLDVIEW AND VALUES ►

What we learn within a particular society is part of the adaptive strategy of its members. This strategy is reflected in their way of looking at life, their ideas about how best to go about doing things, and their notions of right and wrong. These broad views and ideas are part of a society's **cultural orientation.**

Cultural Orientation and Adaptive Strategy

The basic perceptions and behavioral patterns encouraged within a cultural tradition reflect the overall adaptive strategy of a society's collective membership. In dividing game, Semai are careful to divide portions equally and to distribute them widely. The man who kills an animal gives portions to the heads of a number of households. In return, he can expect to receive game from at least some of these people on other occasions. Central to the Semai exchange system are the ideas that one should not calculate what one receives and that one should share whatever one can afford (Dentan 1968: 49).

Such values ensure that food is distributed to all members of the society and thus provides a sense of security for those unable to support themselves because of ill health or injury. This is part of the Semai's collective egalitarian adaptive strategy.

Since perceptions, values, and attitudes represent strategies for dealing with specific environmental conditions, they will be affected by changes within the environment. Many of the environmental changes faced by the members of small-scale societies today are related to the expansion of the world system. For example, the introduction of money among the less isolated eastern Semai greatly altered their exchange system and their views about the nature of exchanges. Unlike food, money does not spoil and is easy to hide, so it is easier for people to be selfish (Dentan 1968: 50). Such changes do not necessarily spell the immediate end to a culture's existing values, but increasing integration into the world system does serve to increase pressure for change. While many Semai continue to adhere to their values of sharing, greater integration into Malaysian society is likely to result in their becoming more competitive and aggressive.

Worldview

The basic cultural orientation of the members of a society—the way in which people perceive their environment—may be referred to as their **worldview.** As Robert Redfield (1952: 30) noted, a person's worldview is the organization of ideas that answer the questions, "Where am I?" "Among what do I move?" "What are my relations to things?" Worldview concerns the fundamental assumptions of a people about the nature of the world, as expressed more or less systematically in their philosophy, ethics, ritual, and scientific beliefs (Wallace 1970: 142–143). Not all members of a society adhere to the same perceptions or beliefs, but a society's worldview is thought to represent the shared understand-

Through this spirit mask of the fire dance, New Britain Islands, Papua New Guinea, these young tourists are being exposed to a worldview that differs considerably from what they know back home.

ings of that society's culture as a whole.

The Desana, a small group of foraging and farming Tukano in southern Colombia (Reichel-Dolmatoff 1971), provide an example of a worldview and how it is expressed. The central theme of the Desana worldview is the biological and cultural continuity of their society. This desire for continuity permeates all their activities and attitudes. As the Desana see it, this goal can be achieved only by minimizing competition through a system of strict reciprocity in all relationships with members of their society and with the animals. In their division of labor—men hunt and women are responsible for agricultural production—more prestige falls to the men, for the Desana view themselves as hunters, not farmers. But this contradiction with the goal of reciprocity is mediated through religion. During ceremonial gatherings, to emphasize their mutual interdependence, those of each sex place themselves "under the reflection" of the light (red or yellow) symbolic of the opposite sex. Reciprocity is emphasized in craft pro-

duction, too. Although individuals specialize in producing canoes, manioc graters, baskets, and pottery, the Desana emphasize the mutual and equal exchange of goods rather than competition, profit, or exploitation.

People living in similar types of societies share broadly similar views of the world. How foragers in the deserts of Australia view the world resembles the perceptions of foragers roaming Africa's Kalahari desert. Likewise, it is possible to speak of a worldview of those living in modern industrial societies in the West and to some extent globally. This situation is complicated, however, by differences such as those associated with social class. Oscar Lewis (1966) developed the concept of the *culture of poverty*—common cultural attitudes and life-styles that he found among poor people in industrial and industrializing nations: a feeling of helplessness, a withdrawal from political activity, and an orientation toward immediate consumption. Lewis's idea of a culture of poverty has many shortcomings, but it does point out that living in impoverished circumstances with little real chance of improvement may lead to certain shared perceptions of the world.

Some writers divide worldviews into two very different types: "primitive" and "civilized." We will refer to these as *indigenous* worldviews and *metropolitan* worldviews.

THE INDIGENOUS WORLDVIEW. The *indigenous worldview* is a personal view of the universe in which humans are seen as united with nature (Walker 1989). The physical world within which humans find themselves is seen as animate; thus, humans relate to animals, trees, bodies of water, and other nonhuman things as they do to other humans. As a part of nature, humans assume the responsibility for maintaining the natural order of things, rather than trying to dominate or change nature (Wallace 1970: 142). Their efforts find expression through ritual.

The indigenous worldview reflects the close social relationships that the members of small-scale societies maintain with each other and the close relationship with nature that their technology and adaptive strategies entail. Australian Aborigines, for example, assign religious significance to the entire physical landscape and see themselves as united with animals and with particular territories through kinship and ritual. Their religion emphasizes the unchanging aspect of the universe. Furthermore, it not only makes them a part of nature, but it also requires that they perform rituals to maintain the natural order. (See also "Religion and the Environmental Movement" in Chapter 13 for a discussion of indigenous societies' relation to nature, especially as seen from the point of view of the environmental movement.)

THE METROPOLITAN WORLDVIEW. The *metropolitan worldview,* by contrast, reflects the more impersonal nature of social relationships in large-scale societies—as exemplified in our relationships with the government—and a technology that allows people to distance themselves more from nature. In many ways, it is the opposite of the indigenous worldview, though instances of both types of worldview may be found in large-scale societies. Instead of emphasizing the unchanging nature of the universe and placing humanity within this natural order, the metropolitan worldview stresses our separation from nature and our role as its conqueror. Instead of living in harmony with the desert or the forest, we seek to dominate it, to transform it to suit our perceived needs.

Values

Bound up in the worldview of a culture are the values of its members. **Values** are emotionally charged beliefs about what is desirable or offensive, right or wrong, appropriate or inappropriate. Within any society there will be a variation in the values held by individuals. Even within our own families we are unlikely to have precisely the same values as our parents or siblings. With work associates or neighbors, value differences may be even greater.

Despite individual variation, many common values are often held by residents of a region or by members of a social class or ethnic group. In our own society we speak of national values, middle-class values, or city values, recognizing that different life-styles can be associated with different value orientations. In each of these cases, the values will be related to the particular setting, history, and adaptive strategy of the people. Peoples with long histories of warfare or military conquest will possess a range of values associated with militarism and aggression: a willingness to sacrifice and to pledge blind obedience to those in command.

In most cultures, it is possible to identify a set of central values that are systematically related. These *core values* provide the basis for social behavior and for the goals pursued by the members of a society. The Japanese emphasis on duty, respect, and filial piety provides an example of such core values.

Many core values of a culture do not apply equally to all members of the society. This is true, for example, of values associated with men and women in Hispanic society; for example, *machismo* (manliness, bravery) and *verguenza* (modesty, bashfulness, shame). Moreover, just what constitutes the core values of a society may be subject to controversy and people's definition of core values may reflect their political status in the society. Mouer and Sugimoto (1986) are critical of attempts to portray values such as those associated with consensus and acceptance of hierarchy as being universally accepted in Japanese society. To them, this portrayal reflects the view of the Japanese conservative elite and obscures the fact that Japan's history has largely been one of conflict. A similar argument can be made concerning the promotion of consensus-oriented values as core values in other parts of the world. In the South Pacific, the notion of the "Pacific Way," with its emphasis on consensus and harmony, has been closely tied to the aspirations of political elites desirous of stifling criticism and holding onto power (Howard 1991a: 54–55).

Core values may be resistant to radical change, but they are not static. Under certain circumstances they may change drastically in a short time. Changes in values are generally associated with a changing social or environmental context. Japanese values that place women in a subservient position to men have come under increasing pressure to change in recent years as a result of the country's economic prosperity, greater educational opportunities, and increasing exposure to cultures characterized by greater equality in male-female relations.

≺ PERSONALITY ≻

In the individual, worldview and values manifest themselves in the personality. The term **personality** refers to personal beliefs, expecta-tions, desires, and values derived from the inter-action of physiological and environmental influ-ences. Anthropologists approach the study of personality by looking at its various components and trying to discern their meanings and causes in their social context. Thus, most anthropolo-gists focus their studies of personality on social and environmental, rather than physiological, factors. One component that receives a good deal of attention is emotion. In her study of Inuit life in northern Canada, for example, Jean Briggs (1970) found that in trying to adapt to life in a harsh environment, the Inuit have pro-moted sociality by avoiding expression of anger.

An individual's personality has unconscious as well as conscious aspects. The unconscious as-pect involves a core of values, attitudes, and ori-entations of which we are largely unaware. This core serves as a "blueprint" for the conscious as-pect of our personality, which includes the over-all view that we have of ourself—our **self-con-cept.** Self-concept is based, among other things, on a person's perception of how others view him or her. In forming a self-concept, individu-als usually choose to emphasize certain person-ality traits over others. What the individual comes to emphasize tends to coincide with more general cultural values. Thus, most Semai would include an image of themselves as nonag-gressive as part of their self-concept, in keeping with the more general Semai values concerning the avoidance of aggression.

Personality Types

We all like to think we are unique, and to a de-gree we are distinct. Nevertheless, it is possible to generalize about personality types in a popu-lation. However, we must be careful to avoid stereotypic thinking and rely instead on careful analysis in making such generalizations. In com-piling personality types, anthropologists usually focus on what they find to be dominant themes in the personalities they study, at the same time recognizing that individual personalities will be more complex and varied.

David Riesman (1953) distinguished three personality types in the United States: tradition-oriented, inner-directed, and other-directed. The *tradition-oriented personality* is most commonly associated with small-scale societies, where the majority of activities are routine, rather than with life in large-scale societies, such as the United States. Even in large-scale societies, however, such personalities may exist—often within subcultures such as the Amish in the United States. Values and behavior in these societies are oriented toward and legitimatized on the basis of tradition. Riesman maintains that because tradition alone does not suffice to give direction to life for most people in large-scale societies, the other two personality types are more common.

The *inner-directed personality* is characterized by a strong conscience and a sense of righteousness, as exemplified by the Puritans of colonial New England. A person with such a personality is compulsively driven and is the ideal type to expand a frontier, to conquer other peoples, and to exploit resources with a fervent single-mindedness. It is a type of personality that was presumably common in the early years of American history, when the nation was expanding. Yet the Puritan strain is still strong in American society, as seen, for example, in views about abortion, state-sponsored art with sexual themes, and the advocates of "political correctness." In contrast, the *other-directed personality* is characterized by ambiguous feelings about what is right and wrong. Other-directed personality types are more adaptable, and are more responsive to the actions and expectations of others. To Riesman, this type of personality is more suited to the United States of the latter half of the twentieth century.

Riesman's personality types do not coincide with the personalities of any particular individuals; they indicate tendencies or themes associated with personalities. Also, they point to the important relationship between personality and a society's environment and adaptive strategy.

Modal Personality

There is a range of personalities and of personality types within any society. The **modal personality** of a group encompasses the central tendencies of those personality characteristics found within the population. It is, in a sense, the average personality type found within a group, an average that should be based on careful sampling of the population. The modal personality of a group will not be identical to the personality of any of its members; it represents merely a general tendency or pattern that is particularly useful for comparative purposes.

Attention to modal personality can be useful in trying to understand social relations between groups. Mayan Indians and non-Indians living in Guatemalan communities can be seen to have very different modal personalities. The Mayan orientation is often characterized as passive and fatalistic. By contrast, the non-Indians' attitude toward their surroundings, and especially toward others, is more aggressive, as they seek to overcome what they perceive to be obstacles or problems. These differences are a result of radically different historical and social circumstances. The Mayans are a powerless and impoverished people who were conquered by the ancestors of the non-Indians, while the socially dominant non-Indians are descended from those who conquered Guatemala in the sixteenth century. Their differing modal personalities not only reflect different social and historical situations, but also represent cultural factors that serve to perpetuate differences between Indian and non-Indian, especially their different political and economic statuses. Not all Mayans are passive or fatalistic, however, and at times large segments of Mayan society have been provoked to violence not only to defend themselves but to improve their status within Guatemalan society.

The fatalism of Guatemalan Indians and the nonaggressiveness of the Inuit are not determined by biology; they are attitudes learned through interaction with others. To look at how values, attitudes, and beliefs are transmitted and how personalities are formed, we will turn in the next section to the dynamic side of socialization.

< SOCIALIZATION THROUGH > THE LIFE CYCLE

Socialization is continuous. It lasts from birth to death, and according to some cultural traditions, continues even after death. Within any society, this process tends to follow a pattern associated with the **life cycle:** birth, maturation, old age, and death. Precisely how these periods are divided and interpreted, however, varies from one society to another.

Childhood in some societies is seen as a single continuous phase, lasting until the onset of puberty. In other societies it is divided into a series of clearly defined phases. The Mardudjara Aborigines, for example, divide early childhood into distinct stages, with a particular label for each: newborn, able to sit up, only just walking, walking properly, no longer breast-fed, and no longer carried. After that, a person is simply referred to as a child until the person becomes an adult. The precise age at which childhood ends also varies among societies. In different societies the beginning of adult life may be variously defined as the onset of puberty, the time of marriage, or an age determined almost at random, as in our own society.

In Europe during the Middle Ages there was only a single division between infancy and adulthood, with a person becoming an adult between the ages of seven to nine. By this age most people had attained most essential knowledge, and the Roman Catholic church argued that this was when you could know God. The idea of a transition period, adolescence, developed following the advent of the printing press and the spread of mass education. This was a period in which people gradually learned to read and write and to master various skills. When this transition period began and ended has varied and has often been somewhat hazy historically. Some analysts of popular culture have argued that the introduction of television and the mass media, in part by taking away many of the "mysteries" of growing up, has served to undermine this transition phase and that Western society is witnessing a return to a simple division between infancy and adulthood.

Even death is not treated the same way in all societies. The Judeo-Christian tradition, for example, views the period after death as linear: Death is considered to lead to a permanent existence in a noncorporeal, or spiritual, state. To Hindus, on the other hand, death is part of a cycle in which the spirit of the deceased eventually will be reborn.

However life's phases are defined, socialization will not be the same at different periods of the life cycle. Our experiences and requirements change with age. In any society the experience of a one-year-old child will be limited and his or her needs fairly basic—affection, feeding, and looking after. This situation contrasts sharply with that of middle age, when a person possesses decades of prior experience and has much greater and more complex social and psychological needs than those of a child. From the society's point of view, its members' statuses and roles vary throughout the life cycle, and each individual must become socialized to change in his or her social position. In our society, we say that adolescents need to learn to behave like adults and we refer to the adjustments people must make upon retirement.

Childrearing, Family Influence, and Gender Identity

Early childhood experiences are the most critical in forming an individual's personality and in socializing the individual to the ways of the society. These early experiences are, for the most part, unstructured and unplanned. Much of early childhood socialization is not the result of acts explicitly aimed at shaping the child's view of the world, although some acts will be. Rather, most of what goes on in the socialization process during this period is informal, as people feed, care for, and play with the child.

The range of people influencing a child can vary a great deal from one society to the next and among different groups within the same society. To free the mother and father from the "burden" of childrearing, elites in large-scale societies often leave early childrearing largely to nurses or nannies. Childhood socialization among the urbanized middle classes of these societies usually takes place within the confines of the nuclear family. In contrast, in many small-scale societies virtually everyone in the community assumes some responsibility for looking after children. Thus, unlike most Western children, Australian Aboriginal children are not separated from the rest of the community. The life of the camp goes on all around the child, and all adults take an active role in his or her rearing, whether they are the child's parents or not.

How those involved in childrearing interact with the child also varies. In contrast to societies such as our own, where children are subject to stricter discipline, the Semai community indulges its infants. Physical punishment is rare, consisting merely of a pinch on the cheek or a pat on the hands. This does not mean that Semai do not seek to control the behavior of their children. Instead of using physical means, they instill fear in their children—fear of strangers, of evil spirits, and of violence in nature.

Whatever they may be, the child's experiences are internalized and organized unconsciously, gradually shaping the personality of the emerging adult. Early childhood relationships shape our personality for the remainder of our lives, despite our growing independence from those who raised us.

The continuing influence of early childhood socialization is seen in gender identity (Chodorow 1974). Women are universally responsible for most of early childcare. Both males and females begin life by developing a close bond with the female(s) responsible for rearing them. For the female, this mother-daughter relationship becomes internalized as a core element within her personality although it may not be easily accepted. In our society, for example, in spite of many changes in attitudes toward women in recent years, women's identity is still devalued relative to men's. However, a woman is not likely to be unclear about her identity.

The male's personality, on the other hand, is shaped by a rejection of this bond, by a desire to establish a separate identity and to escape from the dependency of early childhood. He comes to define himself largely in negative terms—that which is not female; his insecurity about his identity may lead him to take steps to prove his masculinity.

In industrial societies where the father is absent a good deal of the time, the male comes to identify with a fantasized masculine role more than with his father as a person. The male therefore becomes a fairly isolated individual, interacting with others largely on the basis of role stereotypes. In contrast, the female, whose identity does not require that she reject her bonds with her mother, lives in a social world of more concrete relationships. She is less concerned with individuality and identifies readily with her mother and other females. In recent years, this pattern has been subject to change as male and female labor become less distinct. Under some circumstances, females have been drawn into the isolated male pattern. On the other hand, males often find themselves socialized to behave in a less individualistic manner by their female co-workers.

Rites of Passage

Although much of our socialization takes place gradually, during certain times of transition the social shaping of our lives is accelerated. Some of these transitions may be closely associated with biological developments, such as first menstruation; other transitions, such as school graduation

^^^^^^

Childrearing and the influence of the family on the child differ in different societies. Very young Fijian children enjoy every comfort and attention from indulgent parents, other adults, and older children, but they soon take on the responsibilities of childcare themselves. An upper-class English child may not be indulged as much by parents, but, as shown here, receives the attention of a nanny, who socializes the child in the ways of English culture.

or marriage, are influenced by sociocultural factors. For both the individuals involved and the society as a whole, these transitions are important and often rather stressful. Marriage is thus a period when individuals and groups must adjust to a new set of relationships and roles.

Transitional periods frequently are occasions for ceremonies that focus on the importance of the person's change in status and affirm his or her new place in society. The rituals associated with these transitions are called **rites of passage.** These rites are composed of three stages: separation, transition, and incorporation (Van Gennep 1960). First the individual is symbolically and often physically separated from society and his or her normal place in it. Separation is followed by a transitional stage in which the person is suspended between the old and the new. Finally, there is the ritual incorporation into the new social position as the individual reenters society.

The college graduation ceremony in our own society provides a good illustration of the

stages of a rite of passage. We begin by having the graduates wear distinctive costumes and separating them from the others present. During the transitional stage, ritualized speech-making takes place in which graduates are provided with words of wisdom intended to help them as they leave a protected environment for the wider world. The speeches are followed by the handing out of diplomas, after which the graduates and parents mingle and the graduates once again become part of the normal order. But now they occupy a new status: They hold a college degree.

In addition to affirming an individual's movement through stages in the life cycle, rites of passage may serve to reinforce, through ceremony and speech, some of the dominant values of a society. A marriage ceremony can thus be used to emphasize values associated with social, economic, or political relationships. Likewise, the graduation ceremony instills in the graduates a sense of belonging to a community—a community from which they have been estranged during their years of study—and reminds the graduates of their responsibilities toward the community.

Male and Female Rites of Passage

Many societies, especially small-scale societies, have distinct rites of passage for males and females. Mardudjara Aboriginal males must pass through a series of rites in order to achieve adult status and to become acquainted with the major teachings of the religion that permeates their lives (Tonkinson 1978). The first male initiation occurs when boys are young adolescents; it involves the piercing of the nasal septum. Several years later the most significant and elaborate rite, that of circumcision, takes place. Over a period of six to eight weeks the initiate is kept in seclusion from females and from noninitiated males, is not allowed to speak, and is considered symbolically dead. During his silent "death," the initiate is exposed to dances, myths, and sites of religious significance. After the circumcision ceremony, ideally performed by two mother's brothers, the initiate remains in seclusion until his penis has healed, at which time he is reborn and resumes his life among the living.

A year after circumcision, young men undergo another ritual: *subincision,* which entails cutting the penis lengthwise. The initiates are again secluded and taught more of the intricacies of Mardudjara religion. With completion of this rite, a youth achieves full manhood, the right to participate in sacred affairs, and the right to marry. Over the next decade young men progress through a series of additional initiation stages associated with religion. Their progress through these stages depends on their reputation

In Rio de Janeiro, teenage surfistas ride atop a train speeding through the hills. This behavior is part of a rite of passage that marks the boys' passage into manhood. The risk they take ducking electric lines at just the right moment is part of the test of their mettle.

among older men, who expect younger men to provide them with meat, to participate willingly in activities, and to avoid causing trouble.

In addition to their function as a means of religious instruction and as markers of a person's movement through the life cycle, these rites emphasize and reinforce Mardudjara views concerning the status of elders. The rites link the status of older males with religion, ensuring that disrespect shown to older males will also be interpreted as disrespect for the people's religious beliefs. Throughout the rites older men expect and are usually afforded absolute obedience, and this attitude carries over into daily life. The rites also define and enforce the distinctions that exist in male-female relationships. Since females are excluded from participation in most aspects of these rites, the rites serve to emphasize the separation of male and female roles, statuses, and labor characteristics of Mardudjara society.

Women also commonly undergo distinct rites of passage marking life transitions. Particularly important in many traditional societies are rites associated with the first menses, which is seen as the transition to womanhood. While female puberty rites may be relatively simple or not overly traumatic affairs in some societies, in other societies (such as in north and east Africa, Papua New Guinea, parts of Southeast Asia, and central Australia) women undergo puberty rites as severe as any facing males. Such severe rites carried out on women (by women) include *clitoridectomy*—the removal of all or part of the clitoris—and *infibulation*—sewing together the lips of the vagina. Between the ages of 3 and 7, for example, Bugis girls are subjected to ear-piercing and clitoridechtomy, while boys are circumcised between the ages of 10 and 15.

Various reasons have been advanced for the presence of severe male and female puberty rites. In general, scholars recognize that they are associated with the assertion of male authority. Thus, even though performed by women, severe

female puberty rites in patrilineal societies may be associated with the desire of males to control female sexuality in order to preserve the lineage and male status. Likewise, severe male rites may ensure that young males are removed from the world of women in which they were raised and are brought firmly into the world of men. Beyond this, such rites are usually associated with societies facing the constant threat of warfare or pursuing an expansive military strategy and/or extreme resource constraints.

The persistence of these rites in the modern world has been the subject of considerable comment and debate. This is particularly true of severe female puberty rites, which continue to be practiced on millions of girls and women annually in some 20 countries in Africa and the Middle East (see McLean and Graham 1985). Since the early 1980s the Foundation for Women's Health and Development has campaigned against these practices both as a threat to female health (such as excessive bleeding and tearing during childbirth, sometimes leading to death) and as an expression of the oppression of women within the overall context of the underdevelopment of their societies. More recently, the World Health Organization has also launched a campaign against female "genital mutilation." Other women defend these practices, stating that they ensure fertility, guard virginity, and fulfill religious obligations (this based largely on the false notion that female circumcision is prescribed by the Koran). Male practices, like subincision, have come under attack from Christian missionaries and health officials (who point to the risk of infection) and have been defended largely on the basis of preserving cultural identity and traditions.

Education

Another important mode of socialization is **education,** systematic instruction or training. Through education individuals are given instruction in beliefs, ways of behaving, and the means of producing things according to the cultural traditions of their society. People are not simply taught history, reading, or weaving; rather, they are given a distinct view about these things or a specific way to perform tasks. As Jules Henry (1963: 32) noted: "The function of education has never been to free the mind and the spirit of man, but to bind them." The history taught in American schools represents a distinctly American view; it does not provide a student with a completely unbiased account of past events. This holds true not only for how material is presented, but also for what is left out. Students learn about the westward expansion of the United States more from the perspective of the pioneers than from the native Americans at whose expense the expansion took place.

INFORMAL AND FORMAL EDUCATION. In nonindustrial societies, most educational instruction is given by example; learning results from observation and imitation of relatives, peers, and neighbors. Children see how adults perform tasks and how they behave. At first, children's imitation is in the form of play—making toy bows and arrows, shooting at insects, or making mudpies. Play slowly disappears as children begin to take a more substantial role in community work. From an early age, children accompany their parents on their daily round of activities, watching and then assisting until eventually they are able to perform required adult tasks on their own. Some education in small-scale societies is more formalized. This is especially true of more esoteric subjects such as magic, curing, and playing a musical instrument. Sometimes formal education is also more universal, as when all Mardudjara Aboriginal male children are isolated for weeks and given instruction about religious and legal traditions in preparation for initiation into adulthood.

In large-scale societies, formal education is more pervasive. Individuals are instructed formally in a wider range of topics, and they spend more time in schools. This is not necessarily because there is more to learn; rather, it reflects a shift of emphasis in the way people are taught and who is responsible for their instruction, in keeping with a greater division of labor. In most large-scale societies some governmental authority or nonfamilial institution, such as the church, assumes a primary role in education, resulting in a loss of instructional autonomy at the family or community level. Under state control, education functions not simply to provide instruction, but also to promote homogeneity and a sense of identification with the state that supersedes more local and personal loyalties.

The governments of many newly independent states that have emerged since the 1940s have emphasized formal education. Such education is used to provide technical skills to lessen dependence on foreigners and to promote a basis for economic development. Since many of these states include peoples from very different backgrounds, schools also are used to promote a sense of nationalism and to reduce cultural differences.

EDUCATION AND ECONOMIC ADVANCEMENT. For individuals in most societies, education is often an avenue to desired economic rewards and social status. In many very poor countries, the potential social and economic rewards available to the educated can be substantial; the alternative is extreme poverty.

In many underdeveloped countries, the "white collar" jobs available to the educated allow them to live a lifestyle of relative affluence, similar to that of their counterparts in developed industrial nations, in contrast to the impoverished majority. Such desirable positions, however, are scarce, and the cost of the education required to attain them is considerable. Tuition and board for a year at a grammar school can easily amount to more than the yearly earnings of most parents—and the cost of attending university is even greater. Nevertheless, the potential rewards of education prompt many parents to devote all their available resources and even to go into debt to provide for their children's education. In some instances, entire communities will pool their incomes to support a student, hoping that they will be rewarded when their native son (or occasionally daughter) lands an influential position. As the character in Nigerian Chinua Achebe's novel *No Longer at Ease* notes:

> A university degree is the philosopher's stone. It transformed a third-class clerk on one hundred and fifty a year into a senior civil servant on five hundred and seventy, with car and luxuriously furnished quarters at nominal rent. . . . It raised a man from the masses to the elite whose small talk at cocktail parties was: "How's the car behaving?" [Achebe 1960: 91]

As the number of highly educated people in a country increases, it becomes more difficult for those with higher education to find suitable employment, especially when universities produce more graduates than can readily be absorbed in the work force. This is in part a result of people's aspirations for individual socioeconomic advancement outpacing the productive capability of their society to support white-collar workers. Competition for scholastic achievement to gain economic advancement can become intense, creating considerable stress for children and their parents. In Japan, for example, as noted by one researcher, "Most mothers today want to become mothers of Tokyo University students" (Watanabe 1992). Admission to a good university in Japan is viewed as a way for one's child to obtain a secure and prestigious job in the government or a large corporation. But the competition, which begins at the kindergarten level, allows children little or no leisure time and is turning many of them into physical and emotional wrecks who develop diseases associated with adults: by the fifth and sixth grades a growing number of children are losing their hair and

developing bald patches, and a large percentage are in danger of developing ulcers or high blood pressure. In today's global economy in which desirable employment is linked to ever higher educational levels, such competition and accompanying side effects are likely to become more widespread. For many poorer countries, however, this has yet to become a problem; rather they continue to suffer from a shortage of trained personnel at the higher levels.

EDUCATION'S EFFECT ON TRADITIONAL VALUES. Western-style education frequently conflicts with the traditional values of non-Western peoples, which may cause serious social problems. At the university level, education patterned on Western models often creates an educated elite whose values are more Western than the values shared by the majority of their fellow citizens. Such education can serve a positive role in the process of development, but it can also encourage the elite to view indigenous segments of their society as uncivilized barbarians rather than as people with whom they share a common bond.

Western education in societies with non-Western cultural traditions may also promote sociocultural marginality. That is, it may lead students to become disenchanted with their traditional culture but not fully integrate them into the new, leaving them marginal to both the old and the new ways of life. Until recently, it was common practice in rural Australia for missionaries or government authorities to take Aboriginal children away from their parents and place them in schools, usually run by Christian missionaries. At the schools, the children were encouraged to reject their cultural heritage and to adopt the views of the missionaries. Almost no attempt was made to adapt the curriculum to the cultural needs of the Aboriginal children. As a result, the children performed poorly and learned little that was of use to them in either the white or the Aboriginal world. As a result of their formal education, many of these children lost their attachment to traditional Aboriginal culture. Since they did not fit into white culture either, they became people "in between" (Sackett 1978: 39–40).

As the shortcomings of traditional Western education in non-Western settings have become apparent to educators in recent years, reformers have sought to develop alternative approaches that better fulfill the needs of particular populations. Such reform requires an understanding of traditional local educational practices, as well as a thorough knowledge of the people being educated and their needs. Anthropologists, with their understanding of culture and their focus on the integration of sociocultural factors, are seeking to assist by providing analyses to help foster reform.

Socialization in Adulthood

The period up to adulthood is the most important time for the incorporation of values and the formation of an individual's personality. But socialization does not stop at this point. Three patterns of socialization are of particular significance in adulthood: the reinforcement of values associated with one's society, learning how to adjust to new phases in the life cycle, and learning how to adapt to changes in one's environment.

REINFORCEMENT OF VALUES. During our early formative years we are socialized to accept the core values and views of our society. As we grow older our experiences widen, we are faced with more choices, and life becomes more uncertain. We may then be inclined toward different values and attitudes. Such tendencies to change are countered by the lasting effects of our early socialization, general social pressures to conform, and other forms of continuing socialization.

One means of reinforcing core values and views is through public gatherings in which members of a society are subjected to desired messages as a group. Group sharing of the experience makes the individual concretely aware of being part of society. Among Australian Aborigines, periodic gatherings for religious ceremonies are the most important means of reminding individuals of the dominant values of their society. In these dramatic representations of mythical events, the members of the society as a group are made to feel as if they are a part of the mythical events through which the world was created. Public gatherings in our own society serve similar purposes. In Fourth of July parades, for example, millions of people join in a celebration of American patriotism.

Western-style education of Aboriginal children in Australia is imparted here by an Aboriginal teacher. In the past, formal schooling among Aborigines trained them in little they could use in either their world or that of white people.

People's adherence to prescribed values and views is also reinforced in other ways. In our daily interaction with those around us, public values and attitudes are a constant topic of conversation. In most societies today, continual reinforcement comes from newspapers, magazines, radio, and television as well. The news reports that we receive, the fashion articles that we read, and the music that we listen to all channel our perceptions and, frequently, reinforce the prevailing values of our society. Through the media in our society we are pressured to consume, compete, and get ahead—and encouraged to view such behavior as the most rational possible.

ADJUSTING TO LIFE-CYCLE CHANGES.   As we mature, we must adjust to new phases in the life cycle, coming to terms with new roles and physical changes. Sometimes these changes are small, as when a person receives a minor promotion at work. In other instances the changes may be considerable, as when a person retires from a job that has been the focal point of his or her

life for 40 years. The greater the change, the greater the need to adjust and the greater the need to learn.

Adjusting to new statuses and learning new roles are characteristically different in small- and large-scale societies. In most small-scale societies the range of roles and statuses available is relatively limited and fairly well known. There is room for individual choice, but the basic guidelines are quite well established. Among the Mardudjara Aborigines, for example, everyone is expected to marry and have children. Fairly rigid rules determine potential spouses. The prospective bride and groom probably have known each other for years by the time they actually marry. Learning how to behave in their new role is relatively simple for the bride and groom, for they were able to observe in detail the interaction of married couples in the camp as they grew up. Family and other kin also are likely to give them a great deal of advice about how to behave. Also, because life in the camp is so public, their behavior will be subject to continual scrutiny and comment by other members of the community.

An American couple continues their education at an elder hostel. Socialization does not end in later life, nor does formal education necessarily.

In large-scale societies, the range of statuses and roles is much greater. True, there are limitations, and chances are that the life of a Bolivian tin miner's son will be very much like his father's, but for most people there is much more potential for variation than in small-scale societies. In our own society, a substantial minority do not get married, and many of those who do marry do not have children. The life-style of parents is a poor indicator of what their children's lives will be like, except in very general terms. That a person is an accountant who married his childhood sweetheart and lives in a well-appointed suburb where he plays golf or tennis on the weekend tells us little about the lives of his children once they leave home. Chances are that they will lead lives roughly similar to those of their parents, but they are also likely to pursue other occupations and some may lead very different lives.

Although some of the socialization for new statuses and roles in large-scale societies is carried out by parents or kin, much is not. Where labor is highly specialized and generational differences exist, teachers and professional counselors assume an active role in socialization. There is a limited amount of advice that a mother who is a secretary or cook can give her son or daughter about adjusting to life as a lawyer. Literacy and the mass media also change things, because written sources or the radio or television offer guidance. Furthermore, role models include not only acquaintances, but also a much wider assortment of celebrities and public figures—to say nothing of fictional characters—than is available to those in small-scale societies. For these reasons, socialization to changing roles in large-scale societies is far less personal than in small-scale societies.

ADJUSTING TO ENVIRONMENTAL CHANGES. In addition to trying to adjust to the more predictable changes that accompany growing older, we must also come to terms with changes in our world (see "Focus on Anthropologists"). For those born in relatively isolated, small-scale societies, integration into the wider world can be traumatic. Sometimes the trauma is so great that people cannot adjust. Many of those who have perished as a result of contact with Western civilization did not die from disease or murder, but from loss of the will to live in a world that is too different from the one they know. Age is often an important consideration in adjusting to environmental changes; the younger members of a society are usually better able to cope with drastic changes.

Adapting to changes in the world around us can be hard even for those brought up in a Western cultural tradition, especially for older people who have formed fairly rigid ideas about how the world should be. Most people in a society like ours do adjust, however grudgingly, partly because we are socialized to expect and, to some extent, even to desire change. Our flexibility is also made possible by our reliance on a relatively wide range of impersonal socializing devices. Socialization based on the personal experiences of parents and others of older generations with whom we are acquainted has its limitations in dealing with completely new circumstances. Adjustments to such changes are made easier by being able to draw on the experiences of a much greater range of people through books and the media and through the use of professional counselors.

◄ DEVIANTS ►

In all societies there are standards for judging behavior as appropriate. Views about what constitutes an ideal person and a normal person are fairly well established. The normal person usually is not expected to live up to the ideal. In fact, to do so can lead to criticism: "Who does she think she is, acting so prim and proper?" Those who are judged to be normal simply are

JAMES LOUCKY

FOCUS ON ANTHROPOLOGISTS

First working in highland Guatemala in 1973, before the onslaught of tourists or of massive political repression, James Loucky has continued to work with the Mayan people both in their homeland and in exile. Using a mix of observation and time-recall methods, he has documented the significance of children in their rural household economy. Since the mid–1980s, Dr. Loucky's research has focused on Mayan families now living in the United States and Canada. Currently he teaches at Western Washington University.

∧∧∧∧∧∧∧∧∧∧

Central American Refugees: Learning New Skills in the U.S.A.

E nrique's public schooling in Los Angeles ended the day he was jumped on the way home. Demanding that the 15-year-old join their gang, several youths forcibly tattooed a mark on his arm before letting him go. Filled with a fear that he had not experienced since fleeing Guatemala with his family several years earlier, he never returned to school. At the urging of his parents, he attended night school for several months until the family left for the perceived safety of a farm community, where Enrique now labors in the fields alongside his father.

The contrast between the remote mountain villages of highland Guatemala and inner-city neighborhoods in the United States could hardly be more

striking. In addition to being uprooted from traditional means of adaptation and learning, Mayan refugees living in cities such as Los Angeles confront challenges in the areas of social and economic roles, language, and values. As with the immigrants and refugees preceding them, how well they adjust to the new conditions and the stresses of a major metropolitan area depends largely on the children and their achievement in school.

When I first went to Guatemala, I became fascinated with how fully the Maya utilize natural resources available to them, and I quickly realized how important children are in this way of life. From an early age, Mayan children begin running errands and caretaking, gradually assuming responsibility for an increasing variety of food-gathering, cultivation, and food-processing tasks. By adolescence, they are working nearly as intensely as do adults. Parents and older

siblings offer encouragement, and the children soon come to realize that their help is essential to an interdependent family effort.

The skill acquisition and value formation inherent in this informal education provides a built-in cultural intervention for a population at risk. However, the pressure that comes from having insufficient land also prevents many Mayan children from attending or staying in school. In contrast to their socialization in the work setting, the possibility and efficacy of socialization by formal means is far less apparent.

During the 1980s, Guatemala's glaring social inequalities escalated into popular unrest, which the military countered with brutal and massive repression. Tens of thousands of Maya fled scorched-earth campaigns, kidnappings, and forced recruitment into the fighting. Many joined other Central Americans in the movement north, eventually settling in communities throughout Mexico, the United States, and Canada. Several thousand now live in urban barrios west and south of downtown Los Angeles.

Ironically for Guatemalans, the insecurity and fears related to poverty and violence in Central America have been replaced by new uncertainty and danger in the inner city of Los Angeles. People crowd into one- or two-room apartments in aging brick tenements, doubling up with extended kin or even unrelated people to pay the high rents. Most Maya over the age of 15 toil for 50 to 60 hours a week doing menial sewing work in the sweatshops of the garment district. They are underpaid and have little job security. When not in school, Mayan children stay in or near the apartment, since street crime and drug dealing can make even the front steps or hallways dangerous places to play.

Completely removed from their natal circumstances, these children quickly find out that they need to learn new skills and ways of thinking. Their economic value is clearly not as evident as in the normally occurring family structure of highland Guatemala. However, as I developed close relationships with the Mayan refugee community through my work with a cultural organization they formed in 1986, I saw how the children continue to play an essential role in contributing to the family's well-being. They fa-

Mayan refugees enjoying the marimba during a community fiesta. Community activities such as this, less structured than schooling, serve as a form of education that helps to empower and transform immigrants in the United States.

cilitate household management by helping to clean and by taking care of younger brothers and sisters. As they get older, they take on part-time jobs and do mending at home.

The competence of children in Los Angeles, compared with that of children in Central America, increasingly revolves around schoolwork rather than physical labor, yet it is of no less benefit to the family, both immediately and in the long term. The children's school attendance is often the main sustained contact recently arrived families have with the institutions of their new society. Children daily cross the threshold between home and host society and play a valuable culture-broker role by translating and channeling English and

other information from classroom to home. In this way, they help to expand their family's skills and resources and provide an anchor in the midst of change.

So, while their activity lacks the survival significance it has in rural Guatemala, and while they tend to be ignored by researchers and politicians alike, immigrant children are still best viewed as integral parts of an interdependent family. They both influence and are influenced by their family's adaptation to Los Angeles, helping to enhance mutually effective social interaction. Education is thus part of a strategy for holding together and furthering the family and an actualization of the age-old immigrant dream of "something better" for their children.

Guatemalan parents laud the benefits of school, particularly as it promotes proficiency in English. However, there is considerable variation in the degree of success Central American children achieve in Los Angeles schools. For some children, the student role is new, home-study space is limited, and parental role models are few. Intergenerational conflicts emerge as the children acquire new roles and power that may be disturbing to their non-English-speaking parents. The classroom itself can create cultural conflict. Quick second-language acquisition is required. Teachers often lack knowledge of the students' cultural background or misperceive their insecurity or cultural differences as lack of intelligence or motivation. For some children, academic underachievement may snowball into low self-esteem as they blame themselves for falling further and further behind.

By contrast, other immigrant children are incredibly creative and resilient, in some cases progressing toward higher education despite (and perhaps in reaction to) traumatic uprooting, family separation, or privation. These successes can usually be traced to families that offer a supportive environment for schooling. This may include effective management of joint space and activities, frequent encouragement, and early inculcation of faith to maintain a positive view of the future. However, individual children differ; for example, one indigenous Guatemalan girl won a scholarship to college, while her sister dropped out of school in the seventh grade.

Their minority status and their concern about the disruptions they frequently experience have led Guatemalan refugees in Los Angeles and in other communities across North America to try to maintain their cultural identity. Social ties and cultural competency have been reaffirmed through nonformal educational means, such as music, dance, language, lore for children, and fiestas. Though less structured than schooling, community activities to restate and re-create culture are examples of the diverse ways in which education both empowers and transforms immigrants in the United States today.

expected to behave in ways generally deemed acceptable and to hold views that are not considered too strange or threatening. Normal people are allowed a few peculiarities and occasional slips, but there are limits. Behavior that goes beyond these limits is considered deviant, and those who think or act in ways radically different from the norm, especially if they do so with some consistency, are considered **deviants.**

Identifying Deviants

Anthropologists are concerned primarily with how members of a society as a group reach a consensus about deviance. Definitions of deviance vary a great deal from one society to the next. A person labeled crazy in one society might be considered gifted or normal in another. In our society if you catch someone trying to cheat you and become angry, you are considered to be behaving normally, as long as anger does not lead you to act too violently. Semai or Inuit would view such anger as deviant.

All cultural traditions allow leeway for rationalizing occasional improprieties. For example, although the Semai consider violence abnormal, many took an active part in the British campaign against communist insurgents in the 1950s. Some Semai justified their action by attributing it to temporary insanity, to "blood drunkenness." In this way they avoided labeling themselves as deviants and upheld the Semai view that violence is wrong.

How members of a society define deviance usually reflects their collective experience over generations and their adaptive strategy. Semai or

Inuit consider violent individuals to be deviant because they are seen as threats to an adaptive strategy that stresses harmonious social relations. Early childhood socialization fosters the transmission of such perceptions over generations. These learned attitudes toward deviance are reinforced in later life by the actions and statements of others with similar views. Experiences that result in frustration and insecurity may also shape attitudes toward deviance because the deviant acts of others often are seen as related to one's own problems. To a Mayan Indian, frustration in hunting or in courting is likely to be related to the work of a sorcerer. In our own society we are likely to blame bums, hoodlums, and drug pushers for our problems; but the list of "troublemakers" is long—for some people it extends to rock musicians and homosexuals.

Members of small-scale societies, because of their relative homogeneity, tend to exhibit a high degree of consensus regarding deviance. Most Mardudjara Aborigines would agree about which acts and individuals were deviant. There is usually a good deal less consensus in large-scale societies because of the greater diversity of socialization patterns, individual experiences, and goals. For instance, while some members of American society consider it deviant to drink anything alcoholic, most Americans do not.

Groups also can be singled out as deviant. Members of small-scale societies usually reserved this designation for communities or groups outside their own. Thus, the members of a particular kin group or community may be seen as "a gang of cutthroats and cheats" or "a den of thieves." More heterogeneous large-scale societies commonly contain groups that are designated deviant. Throughout Europe, the Romani Gypsies are seen as such a group, as are motorcycle gangs like the Hell's Angels in North America.

Definitions of deviance and attitudes toward deviants are not static. They can vary according to one's place in the life cycle. While it may be acceptable for an American male to be something of a "hell raiser" in his teens, to continue such behavior into middle age is viewed with disfavor. Moreover, attitudes can change significantly over time in the face of social change. For example, during the Cold War hysteria of the 1950s many people in the West considered anyone with communist leanings a deviant who threatened the social order. As the Cold War waned in the 1960s, communists seemed less of a menace, and Americans turned their attention to other deviants, more relevant to current problems—rapists, welfare cheats, robbers. Such changes in defining deviance are often related to attempts by particular members of a society to promote their views about deviance and, as in the case of the so-called "witch hunts" against suspected Communists in the 1950s, definitions of deviance can assume a political dimension.

The Deviant's View

To this point, we have been discussing how people identify others as deviant. But what about the deviants themselves? Do they see themselves as deviants, as normal people, or as unjustly censured members of society? While there are people who consider themselves to be witches, often those accused of witchcraft do not agree with their accusers. Likewise, while some members of a society might consider prostitutes to be deviants, the prostitutes themselves (for example, those involved in organizations like Coyote in the United States, POWER (Prostitutes and Other Women for Equal Rights) in Canada, and the All India Prostitute Welfare Organization in India) may not share such a view. Citing the fact that prostitution was legal by licensing in 56 countries, in the late 1980s the Indian association called on the government to legalize prostitution and to set up a body to protect prostitutes' rights. The president of the Delhi chapter ran independently in the 1991 national election in one of the city's wealthiest and most conservative constituencies in an effort to draw attention to the problems faced by India's estimated two million prostitutes.

While people may agree with a society's general view of deviants, they may be unwilling to identify themselves as deviant. Middle-class persons in our own society who engage in acts that are generally held to be deviant, such as stealing or smuggling, may not consider themselves deviant. This is in part because they have a stereotyped vision of what a deviant is like ("the criminal type"), and this differs considerably from their own self-image. A similar situation can exist with groups considered to be deviant by most members of a society. Those who belong to the Ku Klux Klan certainly do not consider the group to be deviant. In fact, they feel that it functions to uphold the fundamental values of American society.

Many deviants accept the general consensus regarding their status. This is not surprising, since deviants take their cues about how to identify deviants from the same cultural tradition as do those around them; should their acts lead others to see them as deviant, they are likely to agree with the label. Billy the Kid was quite aware of his deviant status, just as the Hell's Angels are of theirs. In fact, some people may gain satisfaction from being labeled deviant.

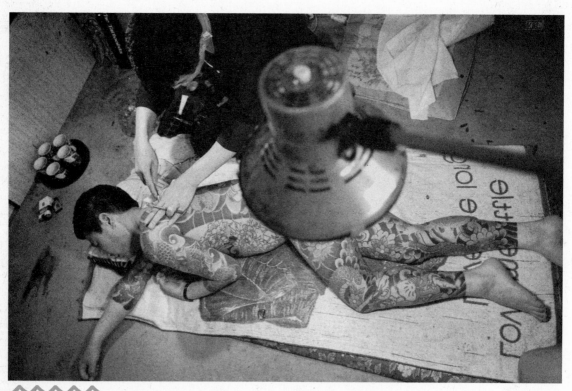

Members of the Yakuza, a Japanese organization resembling the Mafia, are socialized into their criminal group and even develop trademarks of their position. They practice "ybitsume," an enforced discipline whereby the member chops off the top joint of his little finger as a sign of obedience. Another trademark is body tattooing, shown here, performed during elaborate ceremonies. The Yakuza's impact is felt from small sidestreet businesses to the largest corporations and to the highest levels of Japanese government.

By and large, deviants are still members of the wider society and are influenced by its cultural traditions. Indian or French prostitutes still share much of their respective cultures, just as Maori biker gangs in New Zealand have many distinctively Maori characteristics. In fact, deviants may be so labeled not because of their rejection or transgressing of cultural values, but because they exaggerate certain values, as in the case of the "patriotism" of the Ku Klux Klan.

Within the wider society, deviants often form distinct groups or subcommunities with their own adaptational strategies, values, and methods of organization. The *hijras* of India and Pakistan (eunuchs, transsexuals, hermaphrodites, and transvestites), for example, function as a caste, form household units, and employ fictive kinship ties creating extensive networks (Nanda 1990). These *hijras* have rituals associated with joining the group (a castration ritual modeled on female rites surrounding birth) and later life crises. They are organized hierarchically under the leadership of a single guru, with transvestites occupying the lowest status. They support themselves by singing and dancing (women are not allowed to dance in public in Muslim Pakistan) at celebrations for newborns and newlyweds. People believe that by virtue of their sexual impotence they will bring good fortune by blessing a marriage with a son, and a son with prosperity. Many *hijras* also work as prostitutes. Often viewed as a social evil, they may serve positive functions for individuals: "The hijras may provide a social outlet for transsexuals and sexually confused men in a society where psychotherapy and sex-change operations are out of the reach of all but the ultra-rich" (Kroeber 1989). Since the early 1980s, when the All-India Hijra Welfare Society was formed, *hijras* have actively sought to improve their place in Indian society.

As individuals become members of deviant groups or subcommunities, they become socialized to a new set of values and expectations. Those sent to prison for the first time undergo a process of socialization as they adjust to prison life. The adjustment can be considerable, especially if the prisoner comes from a segment of society in which imprisonment is uncommon. Such an adjustment may be only temporary, as with "white collar" criminals who are likely to assimilate into law-abiding, middle-class society upon their release. On the other hand, it may result in a more fundamental transition. Some inmates of prisons and psychiatric hospitals become so thoroughly socialized to the ways of the institution (becoming, in a sense, normal in the institutional context) that they later cannot adapt to life on the outside. Those who undergo such thorough transformations are likely to remain deviants from the perspective of the encompassing society, unless some other drastic change of circumstance forces or encourages them to move in another direction.

SUMMARY

The general process by which we learn social roles from others is known as *socialization*. As we learn to behave as members of a particular society, we undergo a process of enculturation by which we learn the rules and values of the culture. Members of different societies learn to view themselves and their world in different ways. The basic cultural orientation of the members of a society is called their worldview. A society's worldview is linked with its adaptive strategy and its environment. Similar economic circumstances produce roughly similar worldviews, as exemplified in Lewis's culture of poverty. Very generally, worldviews may be divided into the indigenous and the metropolitan: the former views things in largely personal terms, the latter more impersonally. Within any cultural tradition, it is possible to isolate core values, which are fundamental in providing shape and meaning to people's lives.

On the individual level, culturally learned attitudes are expressed in the personality. Personality is based on a set of core values of which we are largely unaware, with a conscious aspect that includes our self-concept. Although each personality is unique, it is possible to generalize about personalities in particular societies. Thus, some anthropologists have described personality types, such as tradition-oriented, inner-directed, or other-directed. In seeking to describe the average personality of the members of a society, anthropologists use the concept of modal personality—the central tendencies of the personality characteristics of members of a given society.

Worldviews, values, and personality develop throughout the life cycle by way of socialization. The life cycle is divided and defined differently in different societies. However childhood is defined, socialization during this early period is critical in forming an individual's personality. Transitional periods in the life cycle are often marked by rites of passage, which may ease a person's move into the next stage of life and may be used to reinforce cultural values.

In most societies, education plays a significant role in socialization. In small-scale, nonindustrial societies, education is largely a matter of observation and imitation, with little specialized instruction. In large-scale societies, education is conducted more formally in specialized institutional settings. Since World War II in particular, Western-style education has spread throughout the world, with important consequences—some good and some not so good—for the nations concerned.

Even after formal education ends, socialization continues in adulthood. The culture's values are reinforced, and the person continually learns how to adjust to life cycle and environmental changes.

Although these processes tend to shape people who conform to the group worldview, values, and personality, there is always some deviance from these patterns. How members of a society define deviance is largely a product of their collective experience over generations and of their adaptive strategy. Those identified as deviants may or may not define themselves as deviant, but they are clearly still members and products of their society.

KEY TERMS

Cultural orientation A society's broad views about life, how to do things, and right and wrong.

Deviants Those who think or act in ways radically different from the norm, especially if they do so with some consistency.

Education A mode of socialization including systematic instruction or training.

Enculturation The process by which we learn the rules and values of the culture.

Life cycle The cycle of life that begins with birth and continues through maturation, old age, and death, periods that are divided and interpreted differently depending on the society.

Modal personality The central tendencies of those personality characteristics found within the population.

Personality The personal beliefs, expectations, desires, and values of an individual derived from the interaction of physiological and environmental influences.

Rites of passage Rituals associated with transitions from one phase or social position in life to another.

Self-concept The overall view that an individual has of her- or himself.

Socialization The process by which we learn social roles from others.

Values Emotionally charged beliefs about what is desirable or not, right or wrong, appropriate or inappropriate.

Worldview The basic cultural orientation of the members of a society.

Suggested Readings

Among the general works on socialization and psychological anthropology are:

Barnouw, Victor. 1973. *Culture and Personality.* Homewood, IL: Dorsey Press.

Berry, John W. 1976. *Human Ecology and Cognitive Style.* New York: John Wiley.

Bock, Philip K. 1989. *Rethinking Psychological Anthropology.* San Francisco: W. H. Freeman.

Rosenberger, Nancy R. (Ed.) 1992. *Japanese Sense of Self.* New York: Cambridge University Press.

Schwartz, Theodore, Geoffrey M. White, and Catherine A. Lutz (eds.) 1992. *New Directions in Psychological Anthropology.* New York: Cambridge University Press.

Stigler, James W., Richard Shweder, and Gilbert Herdt, editors. 1989. *Cultural Psychology: Essays on Comparative Human Development.* New York: Cambridge University Press.

Wallace, Anthony F. C. 1970. *Culture and Personality.* New York: Random House.

Whiting, Beatrice B., and Carolyn P. Edwards. 1988. *Children of Different Worlds: The Formation of Social Behavior.* Cambridge: Harvard University Press.

Case studies include:

Briggs, Jean L. 1970. *Never in Anger: Portrait of an Eskimo Family.* Cambridge: Harvard University Press.

Burbank, Victoria K. 1988. *Aboriginal Adolescence: Maidenhood in an Australian Community.* New Brunswick: Rutgers University Press.

Dentan, Robert N. 1968. *The Semai: A Nonviolent People of Malaya.* New York: Holt, Rinehart and Winston.

Herdt, Gilbert H., editor. 1982. *Rituals of Manhood.* Berkeley: University of California Press. [Papua New Guinea]

Hsu, Francis L. K. 1984. *Rugged Individualism Reconsidered.* Knoxville: University of Tennessee Press. [United States]

Kolig, Erich. 1989. *Dreamtime Politics: Religion, World View and Utopian Thought in Australian Aboriginal Society.* Berlin: Dietrich Reimer Verlag.

Nanda, Serena. 1990. *Neither Man nor Woman: The Hijras of India.* Belmont, CA: Wadsworth.

Ottenberg, Simon. 1989. *Boyhood Rituals in an African Society: An Interpretation.* Seattle: University of Washington Press. [Afikpo of Nigeria]

KINSHIP AND DESCENT

When anthropologist Laura Bohannon (1966) lived with the Tiv in West Africa, she tried over three pots of beer one rainy day to tell the story of *Hamlet* to the local chief and the men of his homestead. One of her biggest

> How anthropologists graphically represent kinship to show relationships between members of a kin group

> The fundamental types of relationships in kinship

> How and why societies limit the range of persons through whom descent can be traced

> The significance of descent and kin-based groups in traditional, small-scale societies and how that significance changes in the face of greater social scale and integration into the world system

problems lay in trying to explain Shakespeare's story in ways that made sense within the Tiv's concept of kinship and the behaviors expected of kin. She tried to explain why Hamlet was unhappy because his mother remarried soon after his father's death: "It is our custom for a widow not to go to her next husband until she has mourned for two years." Her listeners objected, "Two years is too long.....Who will hoe your farms for you while you have no husband?" And when Bohannon explained that Hamlet stabbed his would-be father-in-law Polonius through a curtain on the mistaken assumption that it was his mother's new husband, his father's younger brother, her listeners were outraged:

> For a man to raise his hand against his father's brother and the one who has become his father—that is a terrible thing. . . . If your father's brother has killed your father, you must appeal to your father's age mates: they may avenge him. No man may use violence against his senior relatives. [1966: 207, 212–213]

Despite their inability to interpret Hamlet in identical ways, Bohannon and the Tiv both recognized the importance of kin relationships in the story, for **kinship**—social relations based on culturally recognized ties by descent and marriage—is a feature of all human societies.

The reasons for this universality are biological. Human infants are helpless and depend on the care of others for a prolonged period, and bonds arise among people in relation to these conditions. But while biology provides the basis for kinship, the ways in which people define and use kinship are determined by sociocultural considerations, not biological ones. When anthropologists study kinship, they look at social relations and cultural definitions. Rather than being universal, these vary widely. We now turn to answering the questions of how, in different societies, people with the same biological or marital relationship may be defined differently,

Bafu African chiefs dressed for a council meeting. The design and colors used in their clothing are symbols of the social status and rank of the wearers.

labeled differently, and classified variously as kin or nonkin.

◄ KINSHIP DIAGRAMS AND ► ABBREVIATIONS

Before we start to unravel the complexities of differing interpretations of kinship, we need to cover a few preliminaries: the fundamental elements of kinship diagrams and the abbreviations anthropologists use when writing about kinship. They do not use drawings of family trees. These often artistic reconstructions show graphically how family members are related over generations, but they are not particularly useful for showing all of the intricacies of a kinship sys-

tem. The branches can become quite muddled after a few divorces and remarriages. Moreover, many family trees are hard to understand until we can figure out the creator's particular logic for diagramming Faced with the need to understand and compare a wide variety of kinship systems, anthropologists have developed a standardized notational system (see Figure 8.1). At the heart of this system are six basic symbols:

1. A triangle to indicate a male;

2. A circle to indicate a female;

3. A square to indicate unspecified gender;

4. A vertical line to indicate descent, as from parent to child;

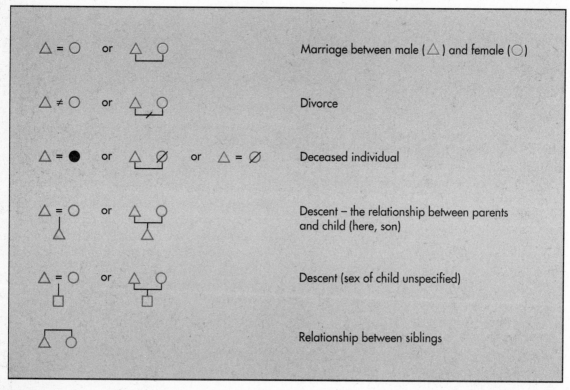

FIGURE 8.1
Standardized notations for diagramming kinship relations.

5. A horizontal line with descending vertical lines to indicate codescent, as in the case of siblings;

6. An equals sign or a horizontal line with ascending vertical lines to indicate marriage.

It is often necessary to use other symbols as well. For deceased persons, the symbol may be darkened or a line drawn through it. Divorce is represented by drawing a slash (/) across the horizontal bar of the diagram. Kinship diagrams may be centered on a particular person. This person is referred to as *ego,* the individual from whose point of view relationships are being traced.

Anthropologists also have devised shorthand notations to indicate the relational statuses of persons:

F for father   M for mother   S for son
D for daughter B for brother   Z for sister
H for husband   W for wife   C for child

Other relationships can be indicated by combining these abbreviations. This is especially important because of the ambiguity in kinship terminology. Thus, what we call uncles would include mother's brothers (MB), father's brothers (FB), mother's sister's husbands (MZH), and father's sister's husbands (FZH). In many other kinship systems, these distinctions are important; therefore, a shortened version of what are sometimes cumbersome combinations is very useful. A hypothetical family is diagrammed in Figure 8.2 with the relevant notation.

◄ KINSHIP CATEGORIES ►

In their study of kinship, anthropologists are concerned with two separate, but interrelated, types of relationship: consanguinity and affinity. **Consanguinity** refers to biological relationship, that of "blood"; those so linked we call *consanguines.* **Affinity** concerns relationships formed through marriage; people linked in this fashion are *affines.* Not all societies view blood relatedness in the same way. In some societies a child is considered to be related by blood to its mother only; in others, a child is related by blood to the father.

While there are different views about who should be categorized as blood relations, even more disagreement exists when we turn to more distant relatives. Take our father's brother, our uncle, for example. Some societies make no categorical distinction between him and our father; others use the same term for both of them and one of our cousins (FZS). How people categorize kin varies greatly. The variations are far

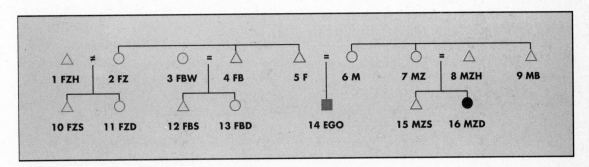

FIGURE 8.2
A hypothetical family diagram. Ego (14, the center point of the diagram) has no brothers or sisters. Ego's father (5) has a sister (2) and a brother (4). Ego's father's sister (2) and father's sister's husband (1) are divorced. Ego's mother has a sister (7) and a brother (9), but only the sister has married. Ego's mother's sister's daughter (16) is deceased.

from unlimited, however. There are a few general principles around which most categorical systems are built.

Defining Parents, Siblings, and Cousins

Two fundamental relationships in any system of kinship are those between parents and children and those between siblings. After all, these are the most immediate biological links that we possess. However, biology only provides the basis for these relationships. Definitions of these relationships are culturally constructed.

In our society, a distinction is made between the actual biological father, the socially and legally recognized father, and the mother's husband. The same person may occupy all three statuses, but not necessarily. When we talk about someone's father we usually mean his or her social father, who may or may not be the biological father. When divorced couples remarry, for the sake of clarity we sometimes use such terms as *stepfather* and *real father*. In other societies, things can be even more complex. The Nuer allow women and even ghosts to assume the status of social father, and in some South Asian societies a group of brothers may be viewed collectively as social fathers of a single individual.

Definitions of siblings may be equally complicated. In our society siblings are often related by blood, but this is not always the case. We often make no distinction between siblings who are a couple's natural offspring and those who are adopted, or between children of a couple from previous marriages and those of the present one, although such distinctions are possible. The situation becomes much more complex in societies that allow individuals to have more than one spouse at the same time. Some societies also distinguish siblings according to relative age. In Thailand, for instance, different terms are used for younger and older brothers or sisters. In yet other societies siblings and cousins

are categorized together. In this case, the same terms will be used for sisters and all female cousins and for brothers and all male cousins. The Cheyenne, for example, draw no distinction between siblings and cousins, but within the family they differentiate between older and younger siblings (Hoebel 1978: 29–30).

Cousins, the children of a parent's sibling and his or her spouse, are also basic to any kinship system. In our society virtually the only distinction made is between those cousins considered too close for sex or marriage and those who are felt to be sufficiently distant. Although the reasons for making such a distinction are often couched in biological terms, the distinction in fact represents a strictly cultural pattern. In other societies, paternal cousins may be considered different from maternal cousins. Also **cross-cousins,** children of a parent's sibling of the opposite sex (e.g., children of the father's sister), may be considered different from **parallel-cousins,** children of a parent's sibling of the same sex (e.g., children of the father's brother) (see Figure 8.3). These distinctions are not random. They are deeply rooted in people's cultural traditions and social structures. The distinction that many societies make between kinds of cousins may be related to inheritance patterns and strategies. Many of the distinctions are also products of particular kinship systems and the manner in which descent is traced.

Principles of Descent

The organization of kinship systems involves **descent,** socially recognized links between a person and his or her ancestors. It is largely through descent that our range of kin expands beyond the narrow limits of our siblings and parents and their siblings.

Many societies limit the range of persons through whom descent can be traced. One of the most important reasons for doing this is to control access to resources. In this way, descent becomes a part of a society's adaptive strategy. The most restrictive way of tracing descent is

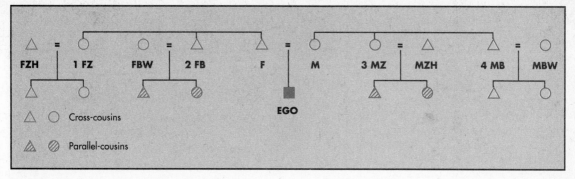

FIGURE 8.3
Cross-cousins and parallel-cousins. Ego's cross-cousins are the offspring of ego's father's sister (1) and ego's mother's brother (4). Ego's parallel-cousins are the children of ego's father's brother (2) and ego's mother's sister (3).

unilineal descent—through a single line, male or female. Unilineal rules of descent affiliate a person with a line of kin extending back in time and also into the future but select only those kin who are related through male or female lines. We refer to the tracing of descent through female lines as **matrilineal descent.** According to this principle, children of each generation trace descent from their social mother, and only those who are related through female lines are considered part of the same kin group (see Figure 8.4). Descent traced in a similar manner through male lines is referred to as **patrilineal descent** (see Figure 8.5).

Unilineal descent patterns tend to be found among more affluent or stable foragers, certain small-scale farmers, and pastoral nomads. Which form of descent is adopted depends in part on environmental factors. For example, farming societies adhering to the principle of matrilineal descent generally are located bordering on' or outside of forested areas (Aberle 1961) and in areas where large domestic animals are absent. Population pressure and competition for scarce resources usually is absent or minimal among these peoples. As a result, warfare is infrequent or totally absent, as are the psychological and social results—aggression, competition, strong differentiation between public and private spheres, devaluation of women, and female infanticide. The environmental conditions that allow for matrilineal systems globally have decreased over the past few centuries. In a survey of slash-and-burn farmers, Martin and Voorhies (1975) found that only 24 percent were matrilineal. They suggest that the frequency was much higher in the past under more stable conditions, arguing that matrilineal descent tends to disappear when people are confronted with problems of expansion, competition, or intensification of production.

A few small-scale societies define kinship in less restrictive terms, yet continue to adhere to notions of lineality. Some trace descent separately through both male and female lines. According to this principle of **bilineal descent** (sometimes known as double descent), an individual may trace descent patrilineally for some purposes and matrilineally for others. Other societies recognize both matrilineal and patrilineal descent, but it is up to the individual to choose between them. This principle is referred to as **ambilineal descent.** Finally, in some societies women trace descent through female lines and men trace descent through male lines, a principle referred to as **parallel descent.**

Another form of descent predominates in large-scale societies, foraging societies occupying harsh environments or experiencing pressure from nonforaging peoples, and family-oriented transhumants and farmers living in fairly poor

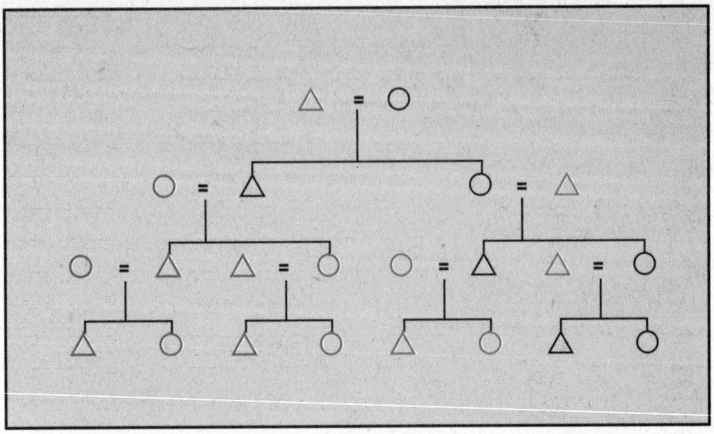

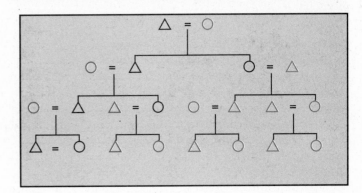

FIGURE 8.4
Matrilineal descent. The symbols outlined in black in this diagram are all related through the female line to a common ancestor.

FIGURE 8.5
Patrilineal descent. The symbols outlined in black in this diagram are all related through the male line to a common ancestor.

environments. This pattern, often called **cognatic descent,** allows a person to trace descent through all ancestors, male and female. All relatives on both sides are considered kin.

No matter what principle of tracing descent is employed, people in all societies promote or play down relationships according to circumstances. If the chance of an inheritance exists through a particular line of descent, the relevant links become important. If potential embarrassment lies in ties to a certain line, those links will more than likely be ignored. In his discussion of Tunisian villagers and nomads, Jean Duvignaud notes that people use and manipulate genealogies "like a game of chess" (1970: 72). The Tunisians seek association with an unproven ancestor because of the prestige it brings by link-

ing them with sacred genealogies and the pillaging tribes that came out of Egypt in the twelfth century. The people recite genealogies at great length, seeking to create a reality "by dint of rationalization, by the apparent coherence of a chain of marriages and connections and inheritances" (1970: 145), and yet these claims often have no basis in fact and they change with some frequency. In some instances family trees are bought or negotiated for. Young men sometimes wander from family to family, laying claim to a series of genealogies in the process.

The situation is not as fluid in all societies as it is in Tunisia. Some societies are very careful to maintain genealogical integrity. In most instances, however, it is best to see the way people trace descent as a reflection of current circumstances rather than as historically accurate accounts of the past.

Systems of Labeling Kin

Not only do societies figure descent differently, they also apply different labels to their relatives. Although a vast array of kinship terminologies are to be found around the world, anthropologists have been able to isolate a limited number of patterns in the ways people label kin. We will now review some of the more common of these patterns.

The system employed in our own culture and commonly associated with cognatic descent systems is known as the *Eskimo system* (see Figure 8.6). In this system cousins are distinguished from brothers and sisters, but all cousins are placed in the same category. Aunts and uncles are distinguished from parents and are labeled separately according to sex. Unlike most other systems, in the Eskimo system no other relatives are referred to by the same terms used for members of the nuclear family—mother, father, brother, sister. This restrictiveness may be related to the fact that societies using it usually lack large kin-based groups and thus emphasize small family groups instead.

The *Hawaiian system* (see Figure 8.7) is the least complex system, using the smallest number of terms. All relatives of the same gender in the same generation are referred to by the same term. Thus, all female cousins are referred to by the same term as ego's sisters and all male cousins

by the same term as ego's brothers. Likewise, all known male relatives of ego's parent's generation are called by the same term, as are all female relatives of this generation. This system is often associated with ambilineal descent, which allows for a person to be affiliated with the kin group of either father or mother, or with nonunilineal systems. At the other extreme is the *Sudanese system* (see Figure 8.8), which makes the most distinctions possible. It uses distinct terms for all cousins on the basis of their relationship with ego, for example. The Sudanese system is associated with societies possessing a complex division of labor, marked social stratification, and patrilineal descent groups.

The *Omaha system* (see Figure 8.9) is the one usually associated with patrilineal descent. It uses the same term for a number of kin of the same generation within the patrilineal group. For instance, ego's father and father's brothers are all given the same label. Distinctions are not made in regard to most maternal relations, however. Ego's mother, mother's sister, and mother's brother's daughter are all assigned the same title, as are the mother's brother and mother's brother's son. Within ego's generation, different labels are applied on the basis of gender. Male siblings and male parallel cousins are all given the same title, and ego's female siblings and female parallel cousins are lumped together under another label.

The *Crow system* (see Figure 8.10) is to a degree the matrilineal equivalent of the Omaha system. The primary difference between the two

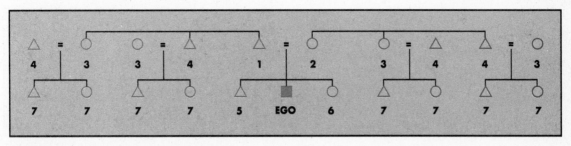

FIGURE 8.6
Eskimo kinship system. Symbols with the same number are referred to in the same way by ego.

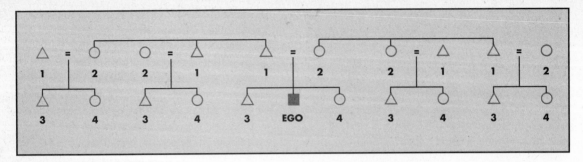

FIGURE 8.7
Hawaiian kinship system.

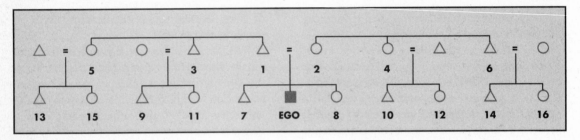

FIGURE 8.8
Sudanese kinship system.

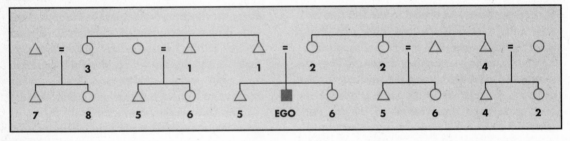

FIGURE 8.9
Omaha kinship system.

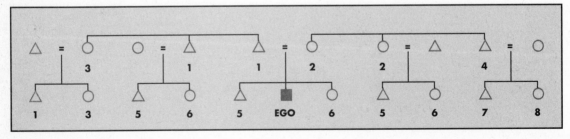

FIGURE 8.10
Crow kinship system.

is that in the Crow system relatives in the father's matrilineage are labeled together (F, FB, and FZS under one label and FZ and FZD under another), while generational distinctions are made on the mother's side. Accordingly, ego's mother and mother's sister are given the same name, ego's female siblings and female parallel cousins are given one name, and ego's male siblings and male parallel cousins are called by one name.

Finally, the *Iroquois system* (see Figure 8.11) is similar to the Crow and Omaha systems in the way persons of ego's parents' generation are treated: Ego's father and father's brother are assigned the same name, and ego's mother and mother's sister are likewise merged. The primary difference between the Crow and Omaha systems and the Iroquois system is in the way cross-cousins are treated. In the former systems they are given separate terms or merged with the previous generation. In the Iroquois system male cross-cousins are categorized together (FZS, MBS), as are female cross-cousins (FZD, MBD). This pattern may be linked with societal preferences for cross-cousin marriage, since cross-cousin marriage and Iroquois terminology are often found together (Goody 1970).

◄ DESCENT AND KIN-BASED ► GROUPS

People use kinship for two primary social functions. First, kinship serves as a medium for transmitting status and property from one generation to the next. We refer to this process as **inheritance.** In virtually all societies people leave something that is coveted and needs to be distributed upon their death. To avoid chaos, the members of a society almost invariably devise rules for the inheritance of social and material property; quite often these rules are stated in terms of kinship. Second, kinship serves as a principle by which to establish and maintain social groups. In small-scale societies kinship is frequently the primary or sole means through which groups can be formed. In large-scale societies, kinship tends to be only one of many means of forming groups.

Kin-based groups themselves can be formed for a variety of purposes. They are often property-owning bodies, with the ownership of land, animals, ceremonial objects, and other forms of property vested in the collective membership. They may also provide a basis for mutual aid, with their members helping one another in anything from agricultural labor to burying the dead. They may also serve military purposes, or ceremonial ones, or even political and administrative functions. The most basic kin-based group is the family, which will be discussed in the next chapter. For now, we will look at kin-based groups beyond the family level.

Unilineal Descent Groups

Unilineal descent is one of the most common principles used in the formation of such kin-based social groups. Membership in unilineal kinship groups generally is ascriptive: A person becomes a member at birth. Its ascriptive nature allows for the formation of discrete social groups, dividing everyone in a society into members and nonmembers. The four basic types of groups that are based on unilineal principles are indicated in Figure 8.12.

These groups are lineages, clans, phratries, and moieties.

LINEAGES. A **lineage** is a group of kin who trace descent from a common ancestor or ancestress through known links. When descent is traced through the male line the group is known as a **patrilineage;** when descent is traced through the female line the term **matrilineage** is used.

Lineages often form a corporate group. In many small-scale societies, lineages serve a primary role in the distribution of wealth and political power. Among the Nuer, inheritance of cattle—their most important form of wealth—

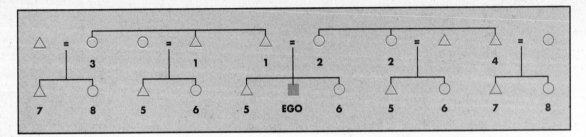

FIGURE 8.11
Iroquois kinship system.

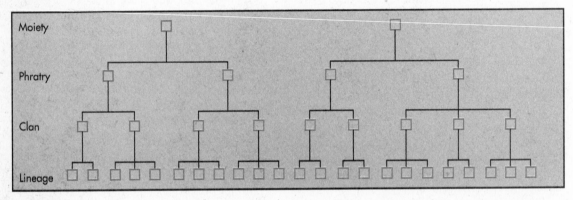

FIGURE 8.12
Unilineal descent groups. Lineages, clans, phratries, and moieties are groups that can form an organizational hierarchy. A lineage is a subdivision of a clan, a clan is a subdivision of a phratry, and a phratry is a subdivision of a moiety. Societies are not always subdivided into four groups, however; some societies may have only one or two of these groups

takes place exclusively within the lineage, from father to son or brother to brother. In many societies, land is held jointly by lineage members. Lineage members frequently cooperate economically. It is often the responsibility of lineage members who are better off to ensure that others in their lineage who are poor, infirm, or elderly are cared for. Religious life in lineage-based societies commonly emphasizes the worship of lineage ancestors.

Lineages can also exist in large-scale societies. Historically, lineages have been a common feature of Chinese society. The Tang lineage of Hong Kong was formed in the mid-eighteenth century as a result of economic competition

with neighboring groups (Watson 1985). Those who came together to form the lineage had already lived in the same area and been closely related to one another for at least three centuries. It required particular circumstances, largely economic, to lead these people to form a lineage. The Tang lineage has been dominated by a small landlord-merchant elite. Despite such marked inequality among lineage members, the lineage has been held together by the perceived advantages of membership in a large group as well as by egalitarian rituals that serve to reinforce membership bonds.

Lineages can be divided and subdivided into smaller segments. This process of division,

Headquarters for the Tang Clansman Association are located in this office building in Hong Kong. The office serves as a business, social, and cultural center for the members of the Tang lineage, which is dominated by a small landlord-merchant elite of Hong Kong but held together partly by rituals that stress the values of membership.

known as *segmentation,* takes place as the generational distance from the founding ancestor increases. Segmentation commonly occurs as a result of stresses produced by the growth of lineages and is a normal feature of many lineage-based societies. The nearly one million Tiv of northern Nigeria believe that they are descended from a single male ancestor who lived some 14 to 17 generations ago (Bohannon and Bohannon 1953). The sons of this ancestor and male descendants in succeeding generations are viewed as the founding members of a series of sublineages. The process of lineage segmentation continues up to about three or four generations from the present living elders, at which point segmentation is supposed to cease. This final subdivision forms *minimal lineage segments,* which serve as the primary political and residential units among the Tiv.

Alliance and competitiveness among sublineages in societies such as the Tiv is based on degrees of relatedness. Using Figure 8.13 as an example, each minimal lineage (*H-O*) is an autonomous unit. Members of *H* and *I* will normally have little to do with one another. Should a member of either minimal lineage

come under attack from, say, a member of *J,* however, members of both *H* and *I* would be expected to act in concert against a common enemy because of their common ancestor *D.* Likewise, all of those who are descended from *B* would be expected to be allied against those who are members of groups tracing descent from *C.*

When members of a lineage split into distinct segments, they do not always continue to view themselves as being part of an encompassing lineage They may form separate lineages. In some societies this process of *lineage fission* takes place with regularity, as siblings in each generation split off and found new lineages. In societies where lineage fission is common, descent often is not traced more than a few generations—perhaps only as far as the living representatives of a generation.

Whether segmentation or fission is the predominant pattern is in part due to environmental considerations (Onwuejeugwu 1975). In West Africa, for example, both patterns are found, but usually in very different settings. Where population growth and expansion occur but resistance is met from outsiders, segmentation is likely to

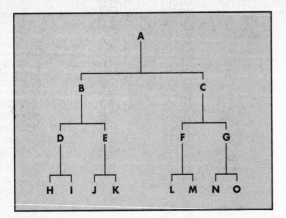

FIGURE 8.13
A model of segmentation. *A* represents the founding member of a series of sublineages (*B-O*). *H-O* are minimal segments—the products of the final subdivision of the lineage. Among the Tiv, a minimal lineage segment serves as the primary political and residential unit. In segmentation, all sublineages consider themselves part of a single lineage.

develop. The threat of external opposition makes it disadvantageous for groups to become too autonomous. With the segmentary model each sublineage can pursue its own interests during peaceful periods, while being able to form readily into larger units when threatened by or preparing to threaten others. Where expansion and external threats are minimal, lineage fission is more likely to predominate.

Lineages may also be ranked. Such ranking reflects status differences within a society. The Lawa of northern Thailand, for example, possess ranked lineages. Before their subjugation by the Thais several centuries ago, the Lawa possessed small kingdoms and controlled trade in such important goods as iron and salt. While they no longer have any royalty and only a few culturally distinct Lawa communities remain, most remaining communities have lineages, known as *samang,* that are said to be descended from their last king or one of the princes and that are ranked above other lineages (Kauffmann 1972). The eldest member of the samang, called the

"great samang," oversees matters of traditional law, directs agricultural rituals, and is afforded numerous privileges, such as the right to receive a piece of all big game killed by hunters or the leg of any pig sacrificed. The great samang is also considered to be the guardian of Lawa culture: "without *samang,* the Lawa say, they would be forced to live in the jungle like monkeys" (Kunstadter 1966:69).

CLANS. In contrast to a lineage, a **clan** is a group of kin who believe themselves to be descended from a common ancestor but who cannot specify the actual links back to that ancestor. In some societies, clan members form close-knit groups not unlike lineages. Often, however, as in most Scottish clans today, clan members are widely dispersed, rarely interacting on a clan-wide basis. A point of unity for clan members commonly is a shared **totemic emblem**—an animal or plant (see also Chapter 13, under "Totems").

Those recognizing membership in a clan can be expected to acknowledge certain mutual obligations, but these may be very limited, such as providing mutual aid should the need arise. The Western Apache, for example, trace descent matrilineally and live in small farming settlements. In the past, those who worked in the early settlements took the name of the particular site. As the population grew, people moved away from these farms but continued to be known by the name of the original home. Clans formed among people who identified their common ancestry through the settlement names. The clan members sometimes have rights to clan lands, but the primary function of the clan is to serve as a basis for mutual aid (Kaut 1957).

Clans often encompass a number of localized lineages. The Yakö of eastern Nigeria, for example, have small landowning patrilineages (they also have matrilineages, which serve other functions). Patrilineages occupying a section of a village are usually united by common clan membership. Each clan has a ritual leader who is in charge of the clan shrine and presides over informal meetings of lineage elders and notables. Under normal circumstances members of Yakö clans recognize their common descent. When disputes arise over household sites or agricultural land, however, lineage members tend to emphasize their distinctiveness (Forde 1964).

PHRATRIES. **Phratry** organization divides a society into three or more groups normally composed of several clans. These groups may or may not be exogamous. In many instances phratries do not serve important social functions. Historically, however, they have been important among a number of native societies in North America. In prehistoric times, for example, Aztec phatries not only served as a basis for common ceremonial activities, but also performed significant political functions. They are also found among a number of native societies in the United States and Canada, and in some instances they continue to have important roles.

The Hopi of Arizona have clans composed of matrilineal lineages. These clans are totemically named after some object in nature; they are land-owning groups, and they are the basic ritual units controlling ceremonies and owning ritual paraphernalia. Each clan has a clan house where the female head of the clan normally resides and where ritual objects are kept. A clan is also part of a group of linked clans, or phratry. Eggan (1950: 64–89) lists 12 phratry groups among the Hopi, each with from three to seven clans.

Hopi phratries are not linked as descendants of a common ancestor, but as a result of common experiences during wanderings in the mythical past are seen as partners. Despite the lack of a common ancestor, members of a Hopi phratry are viewed as kin, and marriage is not

Tsimshian chiefs of the wolf crest (clan emblem), Giltadamaxs 1903: Andrew Nass, shirt with coppers; John Nass in white; James Skean, chilkat blanket; Philip Nass, chilkat blanket with neck ring; Charlie Brown in shirt with inverted face and holding drum.

allowed within phratries. The phratries have no economic, political, or ritual functions. As Eggan (1950:62) notes, however, phratry organization "does serve to tie clan units together into larger structures and furnishes a mechanism for dealing with clan extinction, since 'partner' clans normally take over the ceremonial obligations" of linked clans that cease to exist. On the negative side, Eggan (1950:62–63) points out that rivalries also develop "between clans within the phratry which may cause serious trouble and even disorganization."

MOIETIES. Many small-scale societies are divided into two **moieties,** distinct unilineal descent groups that perform reciprocal functions for each other. Where moieties exist, members usually must marry members of the opposite moiety, and moiety affiliation is often an important consideration in religious or ceremonial activities. The Mardudjara Aborigines have moieties based on patrilineal descent, and at large ceremonial gatherings they group themselves into two "sides," each performing distinct roles in the ceremonies. Among the Seneca Iroquois of North America, each moiety performs mourning rituals on behalf of the other. In some North American native societies, moieties competed against one another in games of lacrosse. Moieties are frequently associated with dualities in the universe: land and water, night and day, sky and earth, war and peace. Accordingly, moieties may be assigned names that identify them with these dualities.

Bilineal Descent Groups

In societies with bilineal systems, which trace descent both matrilineally and patrilineally, an individual is a member of both his or her mother's and father's lineage. This could conceivably cause confusion, but these lineages in most instances perform separate functions. Among the Lodagaba of West Africa, for example, a person inherits immovable property, such

as land, from his father's side and portable property such as money or grain from his mother's side (Goody 1959). Despite this separation of functions, it is often difficult for these societies to form descent groups of much depth.

Cognatic Descent Groups

Whereas lineal descent provides a ready basis for groups with nonoverlapping memberships, cognatic descent is much more messy. With cognatic descent individuals can be members of more than one group at the same time, and any person can serve as the founder of a group. Thus, all of ego's grandparents might be the founders of separate groups, and ego could be a member of all of them. From the perspective of the individual, such a system offers adaptive advantages because of its flexibility, which offers ego a range of choices, but the system makes it difficult to form unified groups, and property and loyalties can be widely and almost randomly dispersed.

There are two ways to approach the formation of groups on the basis of cognatic descent. In the *ancestor-focused* approach, groups are formed by tracing descent from ancestors. In the *ego-focused* approach, groups are formed around a shared relative who is not an ancestor. The network of persons linked to ego through ego-focused cognatic principles is called a **kindred** (see Figure 8.14). One of the distinguishing features of a kindred is that no two individuals except siblings (and double first cousins) will have the same potential kindred. Furthermore, a kindred cannot persist beyond the life of the person upon whom it is centered.

Kindreds are rarely able to function as a group. The members of a kindred will have divided loyalties, and their allegiance to ego's kindred will depend largely on the strength of ego's personality and what ego is asking them to do. Kindreds tend to be loose collections of people who come together at ego's urging on occasion for some particular purpose. The kindred is not a landholding group, and it has little to do with inheritance or the ownership or distribution of most forms of property.

Kindreds are common among the tribal peoples of island Southeast Asia who traditionally lacked states. Emphasis in these societies was placed on ideas of family gift-giving and obligation. Male prestige was associated with war and especially head-hunting, and kindreds often served as the basis for recruiting head-hunting parties. One of the main activities of kindreds among the Iban of Borneo in the past were head-hunting raids. When an individual decided to stage a raid he would go around recruiting the members of his kindred. Each time the composition of the raiding party might be dif-

ferent. Among the Kalinga of the northern Philippines, kindreds served to form vengeance parties when someone was killed, as a means of sharing meat, and as occasion for other forms of assistance.

The ancestor-focused approach allows for the formation of groups that are more like groups formed on the basis of lineal descent, but it requires the imposition of some kind of restriction. The most common type of restriction has to do with residence. A person may have the right to membership in a number of groups but is able to exercise that right only by living in a group's territory. Individual New Zealand Maori, for example, may have a great number of cognatically rec-

Funeral of a noble, Sulawesi, Indonesia. These people, the Torajans, practice cognatic descent, allowing individuals to build extensive kinship networks by linking themselves with ancestral homes known as tongkonan. *These kinship ties are seen in the funeral feast shown here, in which large numbers of kin involve themselves in elaborate preparations and the days of activities that surround the funeral.*

ognized ancestors and may belong to a number of different descent groups, but in practice a person can reside only with one of these groups, and for males this is usually the father's group.

◄ THE SIGNIFICANCE OF KINSHIP ►

The importance attached to kinship varies from one society to the next, although in very general terms it may be said to decrease in the face of greater social scale and integration into the world system (see "Focus on Anthropologists"). Within a single society it can vary in significance among individuals and segments, and this can change with time.

In Western societies, the importance of kinship varies a great deal from one family or individual to the next, depending on circumstances and outlooks. For many of us in these societies, kin are an assortment of grandparents, aunts, uncles, and cousins, some of whom we have never

met and some of whom we encounter only on rare occasions. A few of our relatives may be important to us, or they may have been at some time in the past—our grandparents whom we visited on holidays, a cousin who was a childhood friend, an uncle who gave us a summer job—but for the most part they are fairly marginal to our lives. This is, of course, not true for everyone. Those of us who reside in the same town or neighborhood as did our great-grandparents or even great-great-grandparents are likely to have a large number of relatives whom we encounter frequently and who assume a large role in our lives. If our family is wealthy, or if a distant cousin dies leaving us a fortune, kinship can become quite significant. Among white families, kinship networks are very important channels influencing the flow of wealth and power.

The importance of kinship in Western societies is not to be understood simply by reference to wealth or power, or even friendship, although these certainly are considerations. For a great

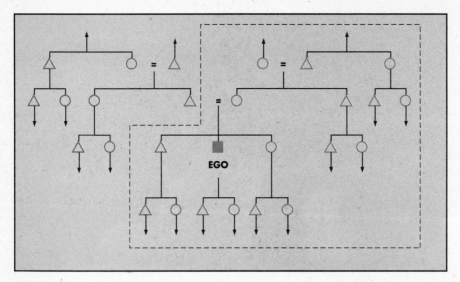

FIGURE 8.14

A kindred. A kindred is a group that is formed using ego-focused cognatic descent principles: People are related to a living person (ego) through both male and female lines. This diagram shows ego's kindred; ego's mother's kindred, however, is composed only of those within the dashed line. (Arrows indicate continuation of the lines.)

many people what makes kinship important is its durability. Like other social institutions, kinship has a permanent quality that allows it to transcend individuals and their actions. It helps to provide us with a sense of security, with roots, in a world that is otherwise always changing and in which we may feel alienated. We may enjoy the feeling that we are related to hundreds, even thousands, of people in other parts of the country, even if we know nothing about them as individuals. Some of us delight in going through telephone books when stranded in strange towns or airports, looking for persons with whom we share surnames—and perhaps calling them to see if we are related. All these potential relatives can have practical value. If our car breaks down outside Gila Bend, we might try to find a cousin to ask for assistance. Chances are that he or she would help us, provided the demands were not too great.

Kinship can provide us with a sense of security by establishing links with the past, through a variety of ancestors. Almost every family claims to be related to at least one national hero, although it is rarely clear exactly what the connection is. Many families have purchased from mail order firms coats of arms with an accompanying booklet telling of a few famous ancestors. Such coats of arms and claims of relationship to the once rich and famous have little practical importance, but they may make people feel a little more significant. A person's ancestors can be of practical importance, however. Being a descendant of an early settler in the United States or Canada, even if the ancestor in question might have been a rather unsavory sort, often can be used to social advantage. The Daughters of the American Revolution and members of many similar organizations consider their ancestry of considerable significance. Ancestry is also of relevance, for example, in land claims associated with early Spanish land grants throughout the southwestern United States.

Important as kinship can be in Western societies, it pales in comparison with the signifi-

A refugee Cambodian family living in the Tenderloin district of San Francisco. Although integration into the modern world system can be said to reduce the significance of kinship, for some communities in America, such as many Asian immigrant groups, kinship continues to offer a strong source of security and sense of roots and can even determine one's role and status in society.

cance it is afforded in other societies. In many African, Asian, and New World indigenous societies kinship is a fundamental factor in a great deal of social interaction. For millions of people around the world, kinship remains perhaps the most important social factor influencing their lives, for in many ways it determines their role and status in society. In many societies to be without kin reduces a person to the status of outcast, with no hope of having a normal life,

DAVID S. TRIGGER

FOCUS ON ANTHROPOLOGISTS

David S. Trigger has carried out research with Aboriginal communities in the Gulf of Carpentaria region of northern Australia since 1978. His doctorate and subsequent publications have focused on the politics of Aboriginal/non-Aboriginal relations, and he has completed many research consultancies concerned with land claims, mining developments, and community relations. Since 1986 he has taught in the Department of Anthropology at The University of Western Australia and broadened his research to include media studies and the politics of competing ideologies about land use.

∿∿∿∿∿∿∿

Kinship, Land Rights and Aboriginal Culture in Australia

In 1980 I was told by an elderly Aboriginal man from a coastal part of northern Australia about the very earliest phase of his ancestors' interactions with white people. His father had explained to him how whites, remembered as having come from the sea in a ship, were perceived as deceased relatives. They were thought to be returning from the domain of human spirits, located somewhere in "the middle of the sea." The Aboriginal people are said to have cried with sorrow for the white men, calling out kin terms for father and father's brother. They fed the whites with high-status marine meat foods (including dugong and sea turtle) and ensured their safe transition into the territory of neighboring groups.

This initial response to the newcomers has been reported for many parts of the Australian frontier. However, conflicts of interest and violence often followed, the indigenous people catching on to the purpose and methods of the Europeans as colonization proceeded. The imperative within Aboriginal society to incorporate all meaningful social relationships within an idiom of kinship could be said to have continued since first contact times. Yet it has rarely been reciprocated by the colonizers and their descendants. As in North America and other similar settings where European settlement has occurred, white Australian culture neither recognizes nor values the idea that kinship relations can be extended outward from the immediate family to encompass other social relationships and aspects of life.

This difference in emphasis upon the idea of kin relatedness is evident in the history of conflict over Aboriginal land rights.

Through large-scale agriculture, pastoralism, and mining, white Australians have treated land largely as an impersonal commodity of crucial importance in economic terms. Yet, for Aboriginal peoples, the economic importance of land is typically regarded as complementary to its intrinsic spiritual significance. And there is a sense in which land itself is incorporated within the intimate world of kinship, for important totemic entities (often known in English as "dreamings") within the landscape are commonly conceived as sharing the same spiritual essences as the family members to whom one traces genealogical connections. The spirituality of deceased ancestors can be aligned particularly closely with the perceived spirituality of key dreamings inhering within the land.

Thus, Aboriginal people with whom I have conducted research may use kin terms when calling out to powerful dreamings believed to be located within the topography and general environment. These can be occasions when considerable emotion is expressed in relation to the dreaming entity; I have witnessed some individuals cry openly when visiting an important site for the first time after a long absence. Senior men and women have introduced younger visitors by referring to how they stand to the dreaming in kinship terms. "Your two grandsons are here," announced a man during a site visit in 1985, when addressing an important totemic force believed to inhabit the local landscape.

On this occasion, I was also introduced in terms of my "kin" relationship to key people present and the dreaming itself. Like many anthropologists (and others) who have established meaningful social ties with Aboriginal communities, I had long been incorporated within a broad social network articulated through the idiom of kinship. For me, this began in 1978, when an influential elderly man announced he would call me "younger brother," thereby immediately providing a way for all members of the community to determine a kin-like relationship with me by reference to their relationships with the old man. While, over the years, those people with whom I have worked and lived most closely have chosen to do this with more conviction and enthusiasm than others, the principle that social interaction

Anthropologist David S. Trigger (second from left in foreground) doing field work with Aboriginal communities in the Gulf of Carpentaria region of northern Australia, found that Aboriginal people believe their relationshi with land is of the same philosophical order as the relationship with kin.

should proceed through the template of kinship has been quite clear.

Among Aboriginal people of the Gulf Country, certain land can be referred to as "my father country," "my mother country," "my granny country" and so on. In one sense, this reflects that speakers trace personal connections to such areas through their father, mother, grandmother, or other senior relatives. Apart from inheriting rights to lands through their four grandparents, people express intensely felt sentiments and memories about the places of birth, death, burial and life activities of a wide range of relatives when articulating their historical connections with the land and its features.

Furthermore, the actual character of a person's relationship with a tract of land (and the spiritual forces embedded within it) is understood through the idiom of kinship. This is illustrated particularly well when people describe their "mother country" as their "milk," thereby fusing the notion of nurturance provided by one's mother with the nature of the relationship to her country. Conceiving relations with land through a discourse of kinship thus encompasses sentiments very different from those forming the basis for a predominantly economic perspective on land and its resources.

During the past two decades, there have been increasing attempts at recognition of

Aboriginal land rights by some Australian governments and courts. Different Aboriginal groups have presented claims in a range of ways, some explaining their kin-based relations with land in greater detail than others. In 1982 I prepared land claim documents for the Nicholson River area, in the Northern Territory adjacent to the border with the State of Queensland. While an earlier case not far to the west had involved people claiming only their fathers' estates, the Nicholson River people successfully sought legal recognition for individuals' affiliations to their mother's country, as well as to the estate of their patriline. By 1989, when the Robinson River case was heard (this land being located between the two earlier claims) there was lengthy consideration given to including further ties to land as well. Would it be plausible to have people seek legal confirmation of their rights to their mother's mother's or father's mother's estates? What about the highly significant association some individuals felt for the place regarded as where their spiritual "conception" had occurred?

As the anthropologist engaged to do the research for this case, I discussed with the Aboriginal claimants how the Northern Territory legislation requires that a *collective* and *primary* spiritual responsibility for the land be demonstrated. However, such legally defined concepts do not necessarily equate well with the complex set of relations to land within Aboriginal society. The burden of achieving translation between the two very different bodies of cultural knowledge often falls particularly upon the anthropologist. In the Robinson River case, the claimants did not, in the end, seek to have a diverse set of genealogically defined rights to land recognized. They were able to prove that there were "traditional owners" for all the land claimed by relying solely upon patrilineal connections between different clans and estates.

In 1992, further impetus was given to the process of Aboriginal claims to land.

The High court of Australia ruled that, according to common law, native title to a small island off the northeast coast of Queensland had not been extinguished through the process of European colonization. Where else on the continent a similar native title continues to exist has now become a matter of national importance. Not surprisingly, some sectors of the wider Australian society have reacted negatively to the prospect of increasing numbers of such claims, allegedly because of fears about economic consequences of Aboriginal aspirations for land rights. Thus, different cultural perspectives on how land is valued continue to divide Aboriginal sentiment from those held by most other Australians. While the general view regards land predominately as a secular "resource" with economic potential, Aboriginal people remain firm in their conviction that people's relationship with land is of the same philosophical order as the relationship with kin.

marrying, adequately meeting subsistence needs, or being taken care of in old age. For all of these things one must depend on kin. In small-scale societies it is common for everyone to be categorized as either kin or stranger. Kinship in such a society forms the basis of political, economic, and even religious organization. Often in these as well as in many large-scale societies, especially Africa and east Asia, ancestors are a fundamental part of the social order. Ancestors are seen as taking an active part in the lives of their descendants, bringing them good luck if respected and ill fortune if mistreated or ignored.

The differences between the role of kinship in Western societies, where kinship is a sometimes useful but rarely crucial part of social life, and in societies where it is a fundamental feature of social life reflect basic differences in adaptive strategies of these societies. In what are sometimes referred to as kin-based societies, for example, kinship serves as a primary organizing feature for the production of goods and services. People work together and exchange what they produce on the basis of kinship, and largely in accordance with behavioral expectations linked to kinship. There is, thus, little segregation of kinship and economic roles.

In the essentially urban-industrial societies of the West, kinship plays a relatively small part in production and exchange beyond the level of the nuclear family. Productive activities and exchange are organized and governed according to principles that are not closely tied to kinship. People are recruited to work largely on the basis of the skills or knowledge they possess, although kinship too may play a part. There is a feeling, however, that family and economic roles *should* be kept separate—people are expected to avoid bringing personal problems into their place of work or showing favoritism to a relative. Roles often overlap, of course, and kinship commonly affects how we behave at work in practice.

As those societies where kinship serves as a key element in their adaptive strategy have been incorporated into the modern world system, the role of kinship generally has been reduced. Before the advent of European colonial rule, for example, much of rural Africa was composed of small agricultural and pastoral societies, each made up of a collection of kin-based groups. Members of these groups worked largely on a collective basis. Land and other forms of property were owned by the groups and administered by senior members of the groups. Under European colonial rule, this system was replaced in many parts of Africa with one dominated by wage labor and production for market instead of group consumption. Where the solidarity of the kin-based groups broke down as people sought to own property

and accumulate wealth on an individual basis, the significance of kinship in their lives was generally reduced.

Incorporation into the world system does not demolish kinship's significance, but kinship begins to assume more of an optional nature. Nevertheless, for many of those who have been impoverished by incorporation into the world system, kinship continues to be of considerable significance by providing one of the few sources of security available through the promotion of mutual assistance. In addition, elites too often find kinship useful as a means of securing and enhancing wealth.

S U M M A R Y

While biology provides the basis for kinship, the ways kinship is used and defined are determined by sociocultural considerations. Even consanguineal, or blood, relationships with parents, siblings, and cousins are defined differently in different societies.

One way to understand varying kinship patterns is to study how descent is perceived. Some societies figure descent unilineally—through either male (patrilineal) or female (matrilineal) ancestors and descendants. Other societies use bilineal descent (patrilineal and matrilineal descent for different purposes), ambilineal descent (allowing a choice between patrilineal and matrilineal descent), or parallel descent (males follow patrilineal and females matrilineal descent). A form of descent found in many large-scale societies, as well as certain small-scale societies, is cognatic descent, which allows a person to trace descent through all ancestors, male and female.

The "same" relatives are also given different labels in different societies. The many relatives we call cousins, for example, are given more explicit labels in some other naming systems. The major kin-naming systems are Eskimo, Hawaiian, Sudanese, Omaha, Crow, and Iroquois.

Kinship has two main social functions: inheritance and group formation. In order of increasing inclusiveness, kin-based groups formed on principles of unilineal descent are lineages, clans, phratries, and moieties. A lineage is a group of kin who trace descent from a common ancestor or ancestress through known links. A clan is a group of kin who believe themselves to be descended from a common ancestor but who cannot specify the actual links back to that ancestor. A phratry is one of three or more groups of a society comprising several or more supposedly related clans, often serving no important social functions, while the term *moiety* refers to distinct unilineal descent groups that perform reciprocal functions for each other. Societies using cognatic descent principles may form ancestor-focused cognatic descent groups or ego-focused kindreds.

Differences in the significance of kinship reflect societies' differing adaptive strategies. In kin-based societies, kinship serves as a primary organizing feature for the production of goods and services. Increased integration into the world system tends to lessen the importance of kinship.

K E Y   T E R M S

Affinity   Relationships formed through marriage. (Compare with *consanguinity*.)

Ambilineal descent   Tracing descent in which both male and female lines are recognized; it is up to the individual to choose between them.

Bilineal descent   Tracing descent through male lines for some purposes and female lines for other purposes.

Clan   A group of kin who believe themselves to be descended from a common ancestor but

who cannot specify the actual links back to that ancestor.

Cognatic descent   Descent traced through all ancestors, male and female.

Consanguinity   Relationships that are the result of biology (those of "blood"). (Compare with *affinity*.)

Cross-cousins   Children of a parents' sibling of the opposite sex. (Compare with *parallel-cousins*.)

Descent   Socially recognized links between a person and his or her ancestors.

Inheritance   The process by which status and property are transmitted from one generation to the next.

Kindred   A network of individuals linked to ego through ego-focused cognatic principles.

Kinship   Social relations based on culturally recognized ties by descent and marriage.

Lineage   A group of kin who can trace descent from a common ancestor or ancestors through known links.

Matrilineal descent   The tracing of descent through the female line.

Moieties   Two distinct unilineal descent groups dividing a society that perform reciprocal functions for each other.

Parallel-cousins   Children of a parent's sibling of the same sex. (Compare with *cross-cousins*.)

Parallel descent   A means of tracing descent through female lines only, in the case of women, and through male lines only, in the case of men.

Patrilineal descent   The tracing of descent through the male line.

Phratry   One of usually three or more social units within a society normally composed of several clans.

Totemic emblem   A symbolic representation linking individuals or groups with human ancestors, plants, animals, or other natural phenomena.

Unilineal descent   Tracing descent through a single line, male or female.

SUGGESTED READINGS

General works:

Fox, Robin. 1984. *Kinship and Marriage: An Anthropological Perspective.* New York: Cambridge University Press.

Goody, Jack. 1989. *The Oriental, the Ancient and the Primitive.* New York: Cambridge University Press.

Harris, Christopher. 1990. *Kinship.* Minneapolis: University of Minnesota Press.

Tcherkézoff, Serge. 1987. *Dual Classification Reconsidered: Nyamwezi Sacred Kinship and Other Examples.* New York: Cambridge University Press.

Case studies:

Aschenbrenner, J. 1975. *Lifelines: Black Families in Chicago.* New York: Holt, Rinehart and Winston.

Epstein, A. L. 1981. *Urbanization and Kinship.* New York: Academic Press. [Zambia]

Hiatt, L. R. 1965. *Kinship and Conflict: A Study of an Aboriginal Community in Northern Arnhem Land.* Canberra: Australian National University Press.

Singarimbun, Masri. 1975. *Kinship, Descent and Alliance Among the Karo Batak.* Berkeley: University of California Press. [Indonesia]

Stack, Carol B. 1975. *All Our Kin: Strategies for Survival in a Black Community.* New York: Harper & Row.

Strathern, Andrew. 1972. *One Father, One Blood: Descent and Group Structure Among the Melpa People.* London: Tavistock. [Papua New Guinea]

Watson, Rubie S. 1985. *Inequality Among Brothers: Class and Kinship in South China.* New York: Cambridge University Press.

SEX, MARRIAGE, AND THE FAMILY

Among humans, the interaction between men and women involves more than occasional sexual encounters and sharing of food. Male–female relations are, in fact, an integral part of most aspects of social life. Every human society

> The kinds of restrictions societies place on sexual activities, and the institutionalized ways of getting around the restrictions

> The relationship between sexual behavior and sacred or secular power

> Homosexuality as a *social construction*

> How anthropologists view marriage and the marriage process

> The types of family groups in different societies

has developed institutions to regulate these relations, two of the most universal being marriage and the family. These institutions may be found in all societies; however, as with so many human institutions, the form they take can vary a great deal, as can the functions they serve. How are sexual relations conditioned by society? What are the varied forms and functions of marriage and the family? This chapter focuses on answering these fundamental anthropological questions.

‹ CULTURAL ATTITUDES › ABOUT SEX

The Bounty's welcome off Point Venus was characteristically Polynesian. The Tahitian men and girls swarmed by the hundred from their canoes up the sides of the Bounty, cluttering the upper deck, climbing the rigging, scuttling down the ladders, chattering, laughing, shrieking. . . . Soon they were busily trading, and the minor chieftains exchanged gifts of live hogs and fruit for hatchets and mirrors. The coconut

harvest was at its peak and the crew all drank deeply of the restorative milk as they bartered and made their choice of the girls who showed off their bodies with uninhibited enthusiasm. . . . As the sun went down over Point Venus the native men were ordered ashore. Only the lucky chosen girls, sometimes two to a man, were allowed to remain, sharing hammocks or lying linked with their lovers on deck through the hot night. [Hough 1972: 106–107]

Much to the delight of the sailors who accompanied Captain Bligh to Tahiti in 1788, Tahitian attitudes about sex were different from those in Europe. The way the sexual favors of local women were bestowed on these sailors would have been unthinkable in Europe. No wonder many of the men on the *Bounty,* especially after ten months at sea, felt that they had arrived in paradise. For their part, the Tahitians found the arrival of the *Bounty* exciting, but their behavior toward the Europeans was not particularly extraordinary. In fact, it was quite in keeping with their traditional views of hospitality.

The royal wedding of Japanese Crown Prince Naruhito to commoner Masako Owada on June 9, 1993, received much attention in the world press. It symbolized many important values in Japanese culture.

The views and actions of Europeans and Tahitians alike in this situation illustrate the social and cultural nature of sexual relations. Sex may be a basic biological drive, but it is also one that humans have manipulated and conditioned. Sexual relations are influenced by personal preferences, but these preferences are rarely a matter of personal taste alone. Whom we have sex with, whether we have sex with the opposite or the same sex, what the act means, and even how it is performed will be influenced by social and cultural considerations. Anthropological cross-cultural research on sexuality has helped to expose many of the ethnocentric biases of Western society and demonstrated the extent to which seemingly deviant non-Western sexual practices exist within a rational moral framework (Davis and Whitten 1987).

The sexual drive and the attachments formed as a result of this drive are fundamental to human society: They are the basis of biological reproduction and part of the glue that holds society together. Our sexual drives function in a contradictory fashion, though, for while they promote bonds between persons, they can also result in competition, frustration, and ill feeling. Fearing chaos, we have managed to create from these tensions and contradictions a degree of order. We seem to rebel at the thought of sexual anarchy—even our orgies tend to be structured. Although some nineteenth-century writers searching for the origins of human behavior postulated a state of nature in which there was random mating, no evidence supports the presence of this "primitive promiscuity" in any society. In all societies that we know of, humans have sought to control this biological drive and to create a sexual order that is socially and not biologically determined.

In the process, sex has come to be treated as a scarce resource that is employed in a strategic manner in accordance with the goals and conditions created by the social environment. For Inuit males, traditionally the sexuality of their wives could be used to strengthen important social ties with other males. For Mundurucu fe-

males sexuality is a means of acquiring and holding a husband; in extramarital relations their sexuality can be used to seek revenge with the hope of improving existing relations or of destroying them and creating new ones. The relations and strategies of individuals engaged in sexual intercourse cannot be viewed in isolation from the society within which they live, for the patterns and norms governing sexual exchanges vary in each social setting.

Sexual Restrictions

Societies differ in the degree to which they *restrict* sexual activities, which activities are restricted, and which people are defined as acceptable partners. Most groups, however, have institutionalized ways of getting around these restrictions.

DEGREES OF RESTRICTIVENESS. At one extreme of the restrictions placed on sex, we find groups such as monastic orders in which sexual relations are prohibited entirely. One of the fundamental characteristics of such a "sexless" society is that its members must be recruited from without. Therefore it depends on societies that do not prohibit sexual intercourse. Slightly less extreme are those societies that restrict relations between males and females to the minimum necessary for survival. A number of societies in highland New Guinea, such as the Maring, are noted for marked hostility between the sexes. Their religious beliefs, economic activities, and even living arrangements emphasize this antagonism, as do their attitudes toward sex. Maring men feel that sex leads to physical dissolution and that sexual intercourse, except on rare occasions:

> will cause a man's skin to become loose, wrinkled, and ulcerated, his flesh to waste away, his thoughts to become fuzzy, and his belly bloated. Some men say that it also causes coughing and the spitting up of phlegm. Youths worry that it will stunt their growth or even cause them to shrivel,

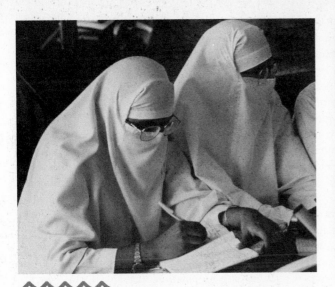 

(left) In Islamic societies, values concerning female sexuality have generally been more restrictive than those in other societies. These women of Pakistan are shown in full chadar, the whole body covered except for the eyes. (right) Off the coast of Papua New Guinea, on the island of Losuia, teenagers dance at a yam-harvest festival. Although some societies allow more freedom for sexual behavior and expression, all societies impose some kinds of restrictions.

loosen their hair, blemish their skin, and leave them generally weak and unattractive. [Buchbinder and Rappaport 1976: 21]

More common are societies that attempt to limit sexual intercourse to married couples and to limit the number of potential spouses available to a person during the course of his or her life. Such restrictiveness can be associated with the maintenance of group boundaries and may be linked with a high value placed on female virginity (Schneider 1971). Where female virginity is so highly prized, tests are often devised as proof of a woman's premarital chastity. In many Muslim countries and in parts of the European Mediterranean the blood-stained sheets of the nuptial bed are displayed the day after the wedding as "proof" of the bride's virginity.

Among Greek pastoralists such as the Sarakatsani, women are expected to remain virgins until marriage, "and even married women must remain virginal in thought and expression" (Campbell 1974: 270). A Sarakatsani girl who has a premarital love affair is supposed to be killed by her father or brother, although in practice she is usually spared. Divorce is virtually unheard of, and can occur only if the marriage has not been consummated. The Sarakatsani place considerable emphasis on family solidarity, and "the sexual, reproductive, and working capacities of women belong exclusively to their families." To the Sarakatsani, female sexuality represents a threat to family honor; there are few better ways to shame a family than to seduce one of its women.

Not all societies are so restrictive about sexual relations. In fact, there appears to be some correlation between social scale and restrictiveness. In small-scale foraging and farming societies sexual relations are often much more open, especially prior to marriage, than in large-scale societies.

Among the Melanesian Trobriand Islanders sexual relations are relatively free and easy within certain bounds. Trobriand sexual behavior follows a general pattern according to age. Parents take no special precautions to prevent their children from witnessing their sexual activities, and from a very early age children engage in genital manipulation and oral stimulation of the sex organs. Once they are old enough, boys and girls begin to have intercourse: "It is their play to *kayta* [to have intercourse]. They give each other a coconut, a small piece of betelnut, a few beads or some fruit from the bush, and then they go and hide and *kayta*" (Malinowski 1929: 48).

Upon reaching adolescence, Trobriand boys and girls assume a more serious part in village life and are treated more like adults. In recognition of their emerging sexuality, brothers and sisters are separated from each other and from their parents. The boys move into a house with bachelors or widowed male relatives or friends, and the girls go to live with other female relatives. Adolescence marks a transition from the playful sexuality of childhood to the more serious relations that will precede marriage. The setting of lovemaking also changes, from the bush to some prepared "cozy corner" in a bachelor's or yam storage house. These liaisons eventually become more permanent, and marriage is usually preceded by a period in which a couple becomes publicly recognized as lovers. Even at this stage, however, sexual relations are not exclusive, and either partner will in all likelihood have occasional relations with others. But at this point a certain degree of decorum must be observed. The couple will share a bed on a regular basis, but they will not have their meals together, nor are there any services to be mutually rendered. This relationship is seen as a nonbinding preliminary test of compatibility before a decision is made concerning marriage.

Even people as relaxed in their sexual practices as the Trobriand Islanders usually take a very unfavorable view of extramarital relations. Adultery is a serious matter, and killings and suicides commonly result from marital infidelity. To them the bond of marriage implies a more exclusive relationship than "sweetheart" relationships; it is also seen to involve the couple's kin, who may take a hand in disputes arising over cases of adultery. Among the Trobriand Islanders as well as the Sarakatsani, adultery is seen as an affront to individual and family reputation. To the less restrictive Trobriand Islanders, marriage changes things; however, marriage changes very little for the uniformly restrictive Sarakatsani view of sexuality.

Not all societies take such a dim view of adultery, however. Among the Mundurucu of Amazonian Brazil, a woman is expected to acquiesce to her husband's advances, but a Mundurucu husband's control of his wife's sexuality is limited. Divorce among the Mundurucu is relatively common and marital fidelity is seen as an exception rather than the norm (Murphy and Murphy 1974: 153). This situation partly reflects the considerable personal autonomy of women, although males in Mundurucu society are dominant in certain spheres. Other societies take an even more liberal view of extramarital sex, often emphasizing its role in expanding or strengthening social relations. The Toda of southern India consider a husband who would restrict his wife's sexual relations as immoral. Somewhat more restrictive than the Toda is the practice among many Arctic-dwelling peoples, such as the Chuckchee of Siberia. Chuckchee husbands offer their wives as sexual partners to friends on a reciprocal basis.

People's public as well as private attitudes concerning acceptable sexual behavior can vary a great deal within a single society. This is especially true of large-scale societies. Such variation is found both among individuals and from one segment of a society to another. Differences based on gender and age are common. So too are differences according to religion, ethnicity, and social class.

Values concerning sexual restrictiveness within societies also change over time. The spread of Islam in South and Southeast Asia from the twelfth century brought with it much more restrictive values concerning female sexuality than had existed previously in these regions. In the West such changes can be seen in the so-called sexual revolution of the 1960s and 1970s. The modernizing middle classes of developing countries like Mexico and India now also seem to be undergoing a similar, although far less extreme, "revolution."

Sexual attitudes in India have undergone significant changes over the years. The Indian elite of a thousand years ago were fairly liberal in their attitudes, as exemplified in the *Kama Sutra* and the temples of Khajuraho (mostly built by a Rajput warrior clan, the Chandallas, between A.D. 950 and 1050). Growing Islamic influence after A.D. 1100 led to the introduction of much more restrictive values, such as the notion of *purdah* (seclusion of women). Within the last few decades India has witnessed the rise of a new middle class. This class initially had relatively conservative sexual values, comparable to those of middle-class Victorian England. These attitudes currently are undergoing considerable change. In particular, attitudes of young, educated, middle-class women toward sex have altered.

DEFINING ACCEPTABLE PARTNERS.   Even with societies that do not restrict sex to marriage, certain considerations pattern relations by placing restrictions on sexual exchanges or channeling the personnel involved. Concepts of physical beauty can be quite influential. There are a few negative concepts that are almost universal. Trobriand Islanders are not unique in their notion that "no one would sleep with" anyone who is diseased or deformed. In highly stratified societies, however, considerations such as wealth or social status can modify even these views, and in almost any society there will be those who do not share such views.

Most ideals of attractiveness are not universal. The Trobriand Islanders classify obesity as a disease, placing those who are obese in the category of someone with whom no one would sleep. But Rumanika, the nineteenth-century

Ideas of physical attractiveness differ from culture to culture and even between groups within the same society. These bikers, here to celebrate the 90th anniversary of Harley Davidson, display the tattoos and other signs of their status as a group.

king of Karagwe (near Lake Victoria in central Africa), "kept an extraordinary harem of wives who were so fat they could not stand upright and instead grovelled like seals about the floors of their huts" (Moorehead 1960: 47). In this brief account, the chronicler clearly shows his own bias about the attractiveness of obese women. Ideals of attractiveness also change within cultures over time. Among the Apo Kayan of Sarawak, women traditionally were tattooed as a mark of rank and a sign of beauty.

Following World War II, as a result of Christianization and greater contact with the outside world, tattooing declined and eventually was no longer practiced. As noted by one heavily tattooed 80-year-old Apo Kayan woman: "In the past, this was a sign of beauty. But today, tattooing is against our religion (Christianity). Anyway, the younger ones feel it is not only painful but also a waste of time" (Ritchie 1989).

There are often more precise social constraints placed on choice of sexual partners as well. Included here are **incest taboos,** or rules prohibiting sexual intercourse between specific categories of kin. Sanctions such as the threat of social ostracism, castration, imprisonment, or death, are usually involved. Such prohibitions are usually bolstered by myths or beliefs, like the idea commonly held in our society that the offspring of incestuous matings will be mentally retarded or physically deformed.

There are no universally tabooed categories of sexual partner. The choice is made in most instances on the basis of social and cultural rather than biological reasons. Even prohibitions against mating within the nuclear family (father-daughter, brother-sister) have not been adhered to in some societies under certain circumstances. Various forms of intrafamilial sexual relations occurred and were seen as legitimate at least for the aristocracy in ancient Persia (Iran), Egypt, Hawaii, and Peru; in Athens before the time of Solon; and among pre-Mosaic Hebrews (Vivelo 1978: 217–218).

While prohibiting sexual relationships between certain kin, some societies also encourage sex between specific kin. This is particularly true of small-scale societies. Ronald Berndt (1978: 14) notes that among the Aborigines of Arnhem Land in northern Australia, "Pre- and extra-marital liaisons . . . usually brought together persons who were formally related to each other in acceptable ways—so that their union would not normally contravene the preferred patterns of betrothal and marriage." This was as true of brief encounters as it was of more durable "sweetheart" relationships. In large-scale societies the role of kinship in choice of sexual partners may be slight, but other factors such as ethnicity, religious affiliation, or social class commonly affect individual choices of partners.

SIDESTEPPING THE RESTRICTIONS. An interesting feature of all these restrictions is that the members of many societies have devised legitimate means of getting around them. This can be seen as an attempt to acknowledge and order the effects of human frailty and the desire to taste forbidden fruit, although more prosaic functional explanations usually apply as well.

Many societies have highly structured ways of sidestepping their own sexual restrictions. An example of this is ritual sexual license, known as *gurangara,* which was an integral part of one of the major Aboriginal rituals in northern Australia, the Kunapipi or Gunabibi (Berndt 1951). Sexual partners in the *gurangara* included persons who are normally taboo to one another, such as those who called each other mother-in-law and son-in-law. According to the participants in the *gurangara,* its functions were to cement bonds of friendship, especially between members of different groups, and to draw women further into the sacred scheme of the ritual.

In some societies, gang rape is seen as a legitimate punishment for female transgressions, creating a situation in which normal sexual prohibitions are suspended. Such a punishment functions to symbolize male dominance; it also legitimizes a number of normally deviant activities. This form of punishment is meted out by Mundurucu men, for example, to women who have seen the men's sacred flutes (which are kept hidden from public view in the men's house) and to women who are openly aggressive sexually (since these women are perceived as a threat to male dominance). The rape may involve 20 or more men, including those who normally would be prohibited from having sexual intercourse with the woman, such as her parallel cousins.

Sex as Power

An important aspect of sexual behavior and ideology is their relationship to sacred and secular power.

SEX AND SACRED POWER. The link between sex and religious belief and ritual is manifest in many societies. The precise nature of the relationship can vary between viewing sex as a negative, threatening force and seeing it as a positive force promoting well-being and fertility. Australian Aborigines fall into the second camp—as exemplified in Kunapipi fertility rituals. By contrast, some peoples view sex as pollution. Sarakatsani shepherds are careful to wash their hands after sexual intercourse to avoid contaminating the milk of the sheep (Campbell 1974: 26). The Wogeo of New Guinea feel that they must be periodically disinfected of the negative effects of sexual intercourse. Menstruation is thought to purify women; the men "menstruate" by slitting their penises until they bleed (Hogbin 1970: 88–89).

Attitudes regarding the religious nature of sex are not always consistent within a culture. Many of the Kekchi and Mopan of southern Belize avoid sexual intercourse before and for some time after clearing their fields and planting crops to avoid contamination and to ensure the well-being of the young plants. Some individuals among the Kekchi and Mopan, however, take a different approach: A husband and wife may simulate or actually have intercourse at each corner of their house the night before planting to promote fertility. Such mixtures of attitudes may be a result of historical mixing of peoples. Thompson (1930: 50) argues that the use of intercourse by some Kekchi and Mopan as a fertility rite may be a surviving practice of the Chol, a group assimilated several centuries earlier.

Attitudes within a single belief system may also vary according to the context: Roman Catholics stress chastity for priests and nuns, for example, but promote fertility among the lay population. Similarly, while sex between males and females may have negative connotations in many Melanesian societies, such societies sometimes have a more positive view of male homosexual relations. This is seen in the widespread custom of male mentorship, which focuses on the perceived power of male bodily fluids (Herdt 1984).

SEX AND SECULAR POWER. In the secular realm, sexual relations often reflect the distribution and nature of power in a society. Sex provides a stage for those wishing to demonstrate or compete for power. Thus, the relative status of males and females is commonly expressed through the sex act itself. For example, Mundurucu male ideology and public behavior express the belief in male superiority, and this theme carries over into sexual intercourse:

> Orgasm is sometimes reached by women, but it is our impression that in most cases climax is experienced only by the male. . . . Women are subservient to men in sex, the wife has no choice but to accept the husband's advances, and male satisfaction is the goal. There is little foreplay, and sexual encounters are brief in consummation. . . . The woman, then, usually derives far less satisfaction from the sex act than does the man, but she also understands that sex is the means by which one gets a husband and then holds him. [Murphy and Murphy 1974: 153]

Sex among the Mundurucu can be seen as a rather unequal exchange by which women gain or hold onto husbands or lovers in return for their acceptance of male superiority. Similar patterns of sexual behavior can be found in other societies where women occupy a subordinate status, and to some extent in our own.

In contrast to the Mundurucu situation is that found in traditional Southeast Asian societies in which women were afforded considerable power in sexual matters. This is most dramatically seen in the painful surgery undergone by males in parts of Borneo and the Philippines to allow them to insert metal pins to increase the woman's sexual pleasure. When the astonished sixteenth-century European explorer Antonio Pigafetta (1524/1969: 43) asked men why they did it, the response was because women wished them to and would not have sex with them otherwise. Anthony Reid (1988: 146) argues that the power of Southeast Asian women in sexual matters was a reflection of the relatively high degree of female autonomy and their economic importance.

Males occupy a superior status in Trukese society in Micronesia, but Trukese women are far from subservient. Trukese males strive to attain a macho image through a reputation for sexual prowess. Prowess, however, is not measured simply by the number of conquests or children that a man can boast. A Trukese male is expected to bring his lover to orgasm, often under very difficult conditions. Failure to satisfy one's lover can lead to ridicule and loss of reputation. Ward Goodenough has characterized sexual intercourse among Trukese lovers as "a contest in which the partner who first achieves orgasm is said to lose to the other" (1949: 619).

Power is also a factor in determining with whom people have sex, especially in societies with marked differences in status and wealth. The chances that a poor black male in Nova Scotia or Alabama will have sexual relations with an upper-class white woman are fairly remote because they move in different circles and because their society's values discourage such relations. However, sexual relations between social classes can be used strategically to exploit or overcome inequality. Exploiting inequality, males of more powerful segments of society are often

able to use their status to sexual advantage. Medieval European lords, for example, sought to exploit their position through the custom of *droit de seigneur,* by which they asserted the right to have sex with newly married women of lower status before the women had sex with their husbands.

From the perspective of those on the bottom, sex may provide a means of gaining status or wealth. Until slavery was abolished in the nineteenth century, for slave women in Brazil and elsewhere in the Americas, one of the few ways to escape from the rigors of life as a field slave was by becoming the mistress of a slaveowner. In less extreme circumstances, members of many low-status minority groups in Western industrialized nations like our own seek out sexual partners and mates from higher-status groups to escape the hardships associated with their status.

Sexual relations with those who are wealthier and more powerful can have mixed effects on the adaptive prospects of less powerful groups. While sexual relations with those of higher status may improve things for the individuals directly involved, they may have only a slight or even an adverse effect on the lower-status group as a whole. It can be argued that those who seek wealth or an improvement of social status by sexual means actually undermine the status of the group they are identified with by further exposing it to humiliation at the hands of those who are more powerful. Situations are rarely clear-cut, however. Faced with a dramatic loss of population and of the traditional basis of their livelihood, many groups of indigenous peoples in the Amazonian Basin have had to decide whether to retain their standards and probably doom their societies to eventual extinction, or to make an effort to survive by prostituting themselves to those who have taken their lands and brought disease.

Economic modernization in poor countries affects sexual relations, particularly the position of women and attitudes toward them (Alam 1985; Mink 1989). Although modernization often offers women greater freedom from traditional patterns of male domination and opportunities outside the home, economic development can also lead to the weakening of traditional means of support for women, such as family and neighborhood. It might also undermine traditional roles such as wife, sister, and mother and emphasize women as objects of sexual attention. The "sexualization of women" can lead to further drawbacks for women; for example, encouraging men to leave older spouses for younger, more physically appealing women.

PROSTITUTION. The hiring of a person for sexual intercourse, or *prostitution*, is not found solely in modern large-scale societies. Because it is linked with the emergence of inequality, it dates from a relatively early period of social evolution. In many early hierarchical societies it was associated with religion: In India, groups of young women, usually from poorer families, became servants of the Hindu goddess of fire, Yellama. These women, known as *devadasis,* were offered by their parents as a result of dreams or in hope of being rewarded by wealth or male children. Bhattacharji (1991: 510) comments that the number of *devadasis* "swelled from the pious wish of rich patrons who desired to earn merit for the next world by buying girls for the temples." The *devadasis* were barred from

Women in a house of prostitution in the Amazonian rain forest, where economic development is taking place. Prostitution here offers at best a reprieve from the extreme poverty and other conditions associated with economic restraint on women.

marriage and had few legal rights, but could gain wealth and position by serving as mistresses of the nobility (the offspring of such unions, however, were not entitled to inherit property from their father).

With the rise of more secular forms of hierarchy, urbanization, wage employment, and related developments came the advent of more secular forms of prostitution (such as houses of prostitution in ancient ports and trading cities). The social upheaval that was associated with the Industrial Revolution in Europe led to a veritable boom in prostitution as young women moved to cities in search of scarce employment opportunities. Today prostitution is widespread throughout the industrialized and industrializing world.

In Thailand, for example, as a result of the AIDS epidemic and its close association with prostitution, the government of Thailand and international aid agencies have supported a large number of research projects employing anthropologists and other social and medical scientists to study sexual relations, especially in regard to prostitution, in the hope of discovering ways of coping with the AIDS crisis. Among these studies are those by Pongpaichit (1982), Kanato (1990), Santasombat 1992), and Van Landingham, et al. (1993).

The use of prostitutes among Thai males is widespread and has become a major source of the spread of AIDS. In a survey of technical school students in the town of Khon Kaen in northeastern Thailand, Kanato (1990) found that 82 percent of the male students had sexual experience, while for females the figure was 30 percent. This reflects a double standard by which males can be sexually promiscuous without stigma, but for females this is not the case. For most Thai males their first sexual experience is at a brothel. They are introduced to prostitution by their peers or elders. After marriage it is generally accepted, though perhaps begrudgingly by their wives, that men will engage in extramarital relations, and most of these are with

commercial sex workers or minor wives (*mianoi*). Male sexual activity with commercial sex workers is viewed as a leisure activity, a means of having fun, usually with a group of friends. In response to questions by anthropologists, men have also stated that it is a way to release tension and express power, since they are able to do things to prostitutes that they would not do to their wives.

Estimates of the number of prostitutes in Thailand vary widely from an exaggerated two million often cited in the foreign media to an official welfare department figure of 60,000. In between are figures by researchers in the field, ranging from a conservative 100,000 to a probably inflated 500,000 to one million. This is out of a total female population in Thailand of around 28 million. While these figures represent a sharp increase in the number and percentage of prostitutes that existed in Thailand before the rapid industrialization of the 1960s, they are not especially high for industrializing or industrialized societies. In Canada, for example, estimates of commercial sex workers run as high as 13 percent of around 14 million females.

Researchers in Thailand have not only looked at factors relating to the use of prostitutes, but also at the prostitutes themselves, where they work, and what leads to their recruitment. Prostitutes in Thailand work in a variety of settings, including brothels, membership clubs, tea houses, cocktail lounges, karaoke bars, and massage parlors, as well hotels, pubs, restaurants, and barbershops. Moreover, they are found not only in cities and larger towns but also in many rural settings such as cattle markets, farmers' markets, and military bases. There are three categories of prostitutes: (1) professional commercial sex workers, or those who sell sex for money as a form of employment, live in a brothel, and are under the control of a pimp; (2) optional commercial sex workers, who have a legal profession (such as bar hostesses, nude show dancers, escorts, masseuses, waitresses, or hair dressers), where sex for the client and worker is an option; and (3) opportunistic commercial sex workers (such as students or models) who involve themselves from time to time.

Prostitutes in Thailand are recruited in a number of ways. Some become prostitutes voluntarily, approaching employers such as brothel owners on their own. Others are bonded through payments to their parents or guardians. These payments may amount to anywhere from $120 to $800. The girl is expected to work off the bond while also being paid a wage on a per customer basis. Females are also recruited through deception by being forced into prostitution after being lured away from home with the promise of some type of high-paying job. Finally, especially in the case of children, they may be kidnapped, although this practice is not as prevalent as it was in the past.

The income of prostitutes varies from $4 to $10 per customer in a teahouse or brothel (the number of customers varying on average from six to 15 per day) to as much as $80 or more for a single customer for the evening in a cocktail lounge. With rural wages being around $2 a day and urban wages from $4 to $8 per day, it is not difficult to see the economic attraction of prostitution. Moreover, families and entire villages may perceive economic benefits from prostitution. In many northern Thai villages the children who leave to work as prostitutes are referred to as "grateful children" or "dutiful daughters," since they bring back lots of money for their families and even for upkeep for the community temple. Culturally they adapt to this situation by developing a double standard for behavior of their children outside and inside the community.

The financial incentives that draw people into prostitution reflect important changes in Thai society brought about by rapid industrialization. Industrialization has resulted in greater economic inequality, including a sharp disparity between poorer rural areas and wealthier urban areas. Thus, the majority of prostitutes are recruited from relatively poor rural areas. In addition, both traditional and newer cultural values contribute to the acceptance and growth of prostitution.

Among the traditional values still adhered to are those that place women in a subordinate position and that relate to a double sexual standard for men and women. This situation is perpetuated through media images of women as sex objects and in subservient roles. Newer values include those associated with consumerism and the increasing demand for goods that cannot be acquired through traditional means of earning a living. Also relevant are changes in social structure, such as the rise of two-income families, in which supervision of children is reduced, and increased temporary and permanent migration, which loosens traditional constraints. Kanato's (1989) study of the northeast found that increased migration has meant that more women are away from close observation and control, and in towns in particular they are able to hide the fact that they are prostitutes from their neighbors.

Within rural areas, anthropologists have sought to discover reasons for different patterns of recruitment to refine the general picture of prostitutes coming mainly from those areas. In a comparative study of two northern Thai villages, Santasombat (1992) found that, in the case of the one that had many of its young women working as prostitutes, the reason was linked both to deforestation as a result of logging concessions that hurt agricultural production and to outside values promoting a level of consumerism that cannot be supported by agriculture. In this community, procurement of daughters is seen as a profitable supplement to agriculture, and has become part of their adaptive strategy. In another village, where procurement has been resisted and few young women leave, the study found stronger village leadership and a good source of water for agriculture throughout the year.

One particular concern to anthropologists is the growing number of prostitutes among the hilltribes of northern Thailand. A government survey of brothels in the northern Thai city of Chiang Mai showed that 36 percent of the prostitutes were ethnic Thai, 29 percent were from hilltribes, and 33 percent were Shan (an ethnic group from Burma). Increasing prostitution among hilltribes is related to many problems, such as a lack of legal rights to land, lack of citizenship, poverty, and inequality. However, the pattern is not uniform among the different hilltribes, but is found mainly among the smaller hilltribe groups rather than the larger groups. These small tribes also seem to suffer from greater rates of drug addiction and in general seem the most vulnerable to changes in Thai society. Although the larger hilltribe groups have many differences among their cultures, including attitudes toward sex and levels of wealth, they have been able to retain a stronger degree of social cohesion than the smaller ones.

Prostitution in Thailand also has international dimensions. The most publicized of these is sex tourism. Although the vast majority of prostitutes in Thailand work exclusively with Thai clients, over the past few decades foreign clients have increased. The impact of foreigners is most noticeable in the case of child prostitutes (aged 9 to 15), who comprise around 20 percent of the total. Researchers estimate that 60 percent of those patronizing child prostitutes are Westerners, mostly from Western Europe. Thus, the reasons for this form of prostitution are to be found in part by looking at other cultures.

Another international dimension stems from the fact that Thailand is much wealthier than its neighbors. As a result, many prostitutes are now recruited from poorer neighboring countries, especially Burma (as many as 30,000), and also from southern China (Yunnan) and Laos. More recently, thousands of young Russian women, mostly aged 16 to 18, have come to Thailand on tourist visas to work as prostitutes and earn extra money during their school holidays. Most of their clients are Thais who are "crazy about things from overseas."

Finally, many Thai women are recruited to work in wealthier countries, the largest number (around 5,000) in Japan. Other countries include Hong Kong, Macao, Singapore, Brunei, Taiwan, Saudi Arabia, Syria, Iraq, Turkey, Kuwait, Germany, Greece, the Netherlands, Switzerland, and Austria.

Today, as in the past, prostitution in most parts of the world is linked with poverty and limited employment prospects for women. The vast majority of India's two million prostitutes, as in other poor countries, are recruited from impoverished families in poor rural areas to serve wealthier urban-dwellers. For such women, the only other employment available is in households as domestic servants or in industrial sweatshops, where wages are generally much less than what they can earn as a prostitute. Of course, not only poor women become prostitutes. Again, however, the motivating factors are related to their constrained social roles (especially in terms of employment). Although some women may become relatively wealthy as prostitutes, most do not. In most cases prostitution offers at best a partial reprieve from extreme poverty.

Sex is not simply a matter of recreation or producing offspring or heterosexual love. It is an inextricable part of the totality of human society; above everything else, it is a social and cultural phenomenon. A similar point will be made in the next section, about homosexuality, the practice and social acceptance of which are shaped by sociocultural conditions, and again in the following section on marriage, also very much a part and a product of human society and culture.

Homosexual Behavior

Anthropology has not always been open to researching homosexuality. In fact, until recently, anthropologists have been somewhat reluctant to pursue an area of study that, laden with the prejudices of American and European society, lacked complete legitimacy and might even result in the censure of one's colleagues. Not until the 1960s, with the emergence of the gay movement in the United States, did homosexuality begin to gain serious attention as a field of study in cultural anthropology. Now an increasing interest is reflected in the mushrooming analyses and published works and in ethnographic studies of homosexual behavior, identity, and related subjects (Weston 1993).

Despite the late development of this area of study, anthropology has proved capable of providing significant insight. In particular, anthropology has much to offer in the way of revealing and exploring the wide variation in sexual behavior across cultures, applying sociocultural explanations to that behavior, and recognizing Western assumptions and prejudices that get in the way of understanding what gender, male and female sexuality, and same-sex behavior mean in other cultures.

Although there is some biomedical evidence that genetics, hormonal influences, and even brain function and anatomy are related to the development of an individual's sexual orientation, anthropologists tend to see homosexuality, like other sexual practices, as occurring within and shaped by its sociocultural context. Culture is seen as working on biology to shape the sexual behavior and attitudes of individuals. Expressions of female homosexuality, for example, may be encouraged in one culture but punished in another. As a result of work done from this point of view, a tremendous variation in sexual behavior and attitudes has been documented across cultures, calling into question notions about what is "normal" in sexual development. Related to this perspective is the viewpoint that homosexuality, like all forms of sexuality, is socially or culturally constructed. According to this point of view, the body and its

functions and sensations are potentials or limits that are culturally mediated (Vance 1991: 879).

In the social sciences, **social construction** refers to the way individuals shape, or construct, reality through social interaction.

Each culture, according to its own concepts and categories, constructs an understanding of the world, so that what is taken for granted in one culture may not be real in another. If people believe, as many do in our society, that homosexuality is a sin, a disease, a crime, and, for males, a sign of effeminacy, then sin, disease, crime, and effeminacy become a part of reality to those people, even though other cultures regard homosexual behavior in the appropriate context as a source of social approval and even manhood for a young man. Similarly, many Native American societies constructed a gender role other than male and female. It was manifested in the androgynous "two-spirit" (the older, now largely discredited term was *berdache),* a morphological male who mixed the behavior, dress, and social roles of women and men and might become a wife to a man (there are also reports of women marrying women). For these people, this alternative gender became a reality.

The social constructionist approach leads us to question our own categories. Clearly, in other cultures, homosexual behavior is not a matter of individual pathology, as it has been considered in the Western medical model. Similarly, Jeffrey Weeks (1977) has argued that whereas homosexual behavior is universal, homosexual identity is restricted to certain historical periods and cultures. In addition, in the example of the "two-spirit," which represents a separate gender to many Native Americans, our notion of "the opposite sex," based on anatomical differences, is seen as the social construction that it is (Williams 1986).

Just as other attitudes toward sexuality vary with the society that constructs them, so does the degree of acceptance of homosexual behavior. There is in fact a broad range of permissiveness or restrictiveness across cultures. For example, among the Azande of East Africa, as discussed in greater detail below, young male warriors were expected to have homosexual relations with boys, whose families approved of the relationship. In spite of numerous changes in contemporary U.S. society in recent years, many Americans still disapprove of homosexual behavior, and within an occupational group such as the armed forces, such behavior has been punishable by severe peer pressure, including violence, and by discharge.

Some anthropologists believe that a society's acceptance of homosexuality is related to the extent to which a society values population growth. A society that seeks a larger population and sees homosexuality as limiting population may be more likely to disapprove of same-sex behavior. According to Herdt (1984: 169), for example, societies in New Guinea that strongly encourage ritualized homosexuality among men seem to be refugees from more heavily populated areas. Dennis Werner (1979) has shown that a society that opposes having large numbers of children is more likely to tolerate forms of sexuality, such as homosexuality, that are not reproductive.

Azande society before European colonization provides an example of how social arrangements allow and even encourage forms of homosexual behavior. British social anthropologist E. E. Evans-Pritchard explained both male and female homosexual relations among the Azande of the Sudan in pre-European days in terms of certain social conditions found at that time.

Male homosexual relations among the Azande occurred between young unmarried warriors living in military barracks at the royal court and boys aged 12 to 20, warrior apprentices who would someday soon join the military companies to which their one-time husbands belonged as warriors and husbands themselves. The young warriors lived apart from women. Their sexual relations with boys

took place within a prescribed institutional context. "Boy marriage," in which the bachelor warrior would refer to his young male companion as "my wife," formed a legal union between the warrior and the boy. A warrior would turn over some form of wealth (a *bridewealth*; see "Marital Wealth Transfers" on page 213), passed from his group to the male companions' parents, and perform services for them just as he would had he married their daughter. What's more, a good son-in-law might expect to be rewarded with a daughter later. For the Azande, there was no distinct division between heterosexuality and homosexuality as there is in North American society.

The boy wife not only served his husband sexually (the Azande, scornful of anal penetration, told Evans-Pritchard that intercourse was accomplished between the boy's thighs) but also as a female wife would by, for example, drawing water for him and bringing him cooked food from home. At court the bachelor warrior had no mother or sisters to look after him.

This boy marriage practice, according to Evans-Pritchard, was a consequence of the scarcity of marriageable women in Azande society. In those days, the nobility and richer commoners were able to keep large harems because they had readier access to the necessary bridewealth than did the poorer men. For many younger men, forced by limited resources to marry late, and without recourse to younger women, who were married at a very young age, sexual satisfaction with a woman meant resorting to adultery. This, however, carried the severe risks of a stiff fine for the offender's father or, worse yet, bodily mutilation for the offender. Given these conditions, it became customary for young men to take a boy wife.

A homosexual practice for women was also a result of Azande polygyny. In this society, a woman was part of a large household with other women, and some received little sexual attention from the common husband.

Adulterous intercourse, however, was even riskier for a young woman in pre-European Azande society than for a man. A man's wives were secluded and watched over, and the penalty for adultery—or even its suspicion—was death. The lesbian relationship, as told to Evans-Pritchard by males only, consisted of two wives shutting themselves off from the others, one playing the female role and the other, with an artificial male organ made of a cut sweet potato or manioc root tied around her stomach, playing the male role. As Evans-Pritchard pointed out, what the male-dominated Azande society encouraged among their young men, they condemned among women.

Anthropologists have not limited their studies of homosexuality to past or small-scale societies. They have also conducted studies of homosexuality in large-scale contemporary societies such as the United States, Japan, Thailand, Mexico, and Brazil. Many of these studies have sought to provide a more accurate picture of the complexities of homosexual communities and social relations among homosexuals. Thus, a study of the resort of Cherry Grove, a long-standing homosexual community in the eastern United States, challenges common perception of a homogeneous homosexual community by pointing to class and racial divisions (Newton 1993). Among the important differences in this community are those between property owners and renters. Other anthropologists have studied working class female homosexuals in Buffalo, New York (Kennedy and Davis 1993), kinship ideologies among homosexuals (Weston 1991), and Mexican-American homosexual culture (Carrier 1992).

< MARRIAGE >

Marriage can be defined as a socially sanctioned sexual and economic union between men and women. In some societies, this definition can be expanded to include unions between members of the same sex.

Marriage as an Adaptive Measure

The near universality of marriage in human society appears to be the result of an adaptive response to several problems common to the human species. One of these is the human infant's prolonged period of dependency. Especially in labor-intensive foraging and agricultural societies with a minimal division of labor, this dependency places a severe burden on the person (usually a woman) responsible for childcare, since it interferes significantly with subsistence activities. During this period, the person tending the child becomes, in turn, dependent on others. Marriage is the most common way of ensuring that the child and its caretaker are supported.

The second problem marriage seeks to solve is sexual competition. Unlike females of other species, mature human females are more or less continuously biologically receptive to sexual activity, which leads to a greater likelihood of disruptive rivalry among men and among women. Some scholars (mostly male) have argued that sexual competition is a reproductive and economic threat to the survival of society and that the relative stability provided by marriage is the best way of coming to terms with this threat.

A third adaptational factor encouraging marriage is the division of labor based on gender. Among foragers—the primary human economic adaptation for millions of years—men usually hunted large game and women gathered edible plants and killed smaller animals. Numerous authors argue that such a pattern best meets the needs of a foraging society. Among the Mardudjara Aborigines, women gather food in groups if possible, which allows them to share childcare responsibilities. Mardudjara men, on the other hand, usually hunt alone or in pairs without children to care for because hunting requires far greater mobility than the slow-paced foraging activities of women. Marriage ensures that men and women gain access to the fruits of the other's labor. Marital partners share with each other the food that they find.

Some scholars also suggest that marriage was traditionally, and in some instances still is, a means to gain dominance over women. Thus, although female foragers could meet most of their own subsistence needs, marriage ensured that males gained access to the substantial products of female labor and thereby reduced their own workload. In our own society, there is considerable debate over the labor performed by housewives and their dependency on male wage-earners. Many feminists argue that the housewife is an exploited laborer who performs necessary and often very tedious services for which she is compensated only to the extent to which her husband sees fit.

The adaptive advantages of marriage may diminish as social scale increases, so that marriage becomes increasingly optional. Members of many small-scale societies assume that all adults will marry and that the only unmarried adults are either looking for a spouse or have lost their spouse and are too old to remarry. The Mundurucu, for example, have no social roles for bachelors or spinsters, and those who are unmarried are viewed with distrust as potential spouse-stealers or adulterers (Murphy and Murphy 1974: 145). In large-scale societies such as our own, parents, relatives, and peers usually place pressure on individuals to marry. But it is also possible to be accepted in our society without ever having been married. This liberalization reflects the increasing degree of specialization in these societies and the diminishing importance of kinship and might lead one to speculate that marriage will eventually disappear. Such a development is not likely to occur in the near future, however, for sufficient pressures and adaptive advantages remain to ensure that most people will choose to marry.

Anna Gould, the youngest daughter of American financier Jay Gould, became a countess when she married Count Marie Ernest Paul Boniface de Castellane in 1895. Upon marrying, the count acquired access to Anna's yearly income of about $650,000 from her trust fund. In spite of this income, by the time this picture was taken in 1900, the couple had run up debts totaling $4.5 million. Anna left the count shortly after this, went to France, and married the count's cousin, the Duc de Talleyrand-Perigord.

Marriage as Formation of Alliances

Marriage is rarely just a matter of uniting two individuals. Those joined in wedlock have kin and friends who are affected by the creation of the relationship, and the act has other broad implications as well. More often than not, marriage unites a wide network of people, providing a relatively durable bond or series of bonds of widespread social importance.

In rural Newfoundland, for example, the network of people united by marriage may include most of the community's inhabitants as well as those of surrounding communities. Furthermore, these people may make up the most important element of the newlyweds' social environment. In large-scale, urbanized settings such as Toronto or New York, such networks tend to be much more dispersed and can be quite small; interaction may consist of no more than an exchange of cards at birthdays and Christmas. But in all societies, the social links created by marriage may potentially serve a variety of purposes: to form economic units (such as fishing crews in Newfoundland), to establish political alliances (as in the Kennedy clan), and to expand the number of persons to go to for money, a job, or a place to stay while traveling.

MARRIAGE AS EXCHANGE.   Viewed from a group perspective, marriage becomes an *exchange* of personnel and resources that creates alliances based on reciprocal rights and privileges. Not only is there an initial exchange of people and wedding gifts, but there are usually expectations of future transactions among those associated with the married couple. These expectations may be little more than the promise of help should the need arise, or they may entail a firm commitment to assist in warfare or political struggles. They may also involve a pledge to reciprocate at some future date with the exchange of yet another male or female in marriage.

Anthropologist Claude Lévi-Strauss (1969) has argued that marriage in small-scale societies serves as a generalized exchange system centering on the exchange of women between groups. Lévi-Strauss makes a distinction between what he calls elementary and complex systems. *Elementary systems* are those in which the rules specify into which category or group of persons one should or should not marry. For example, the prescribed form of marriage among the Mardudjara is between cross-cousins. For a man, these include mother's brother's daughters and father's sister's daughters; for a woman they include mother's brother's sons and father's sister's sons. Marriage to any other category of person is considered wrong and possibly incestuous (Tonkinson 1978: 48–49). In *complex systems* the rules state whom one cannot marry, but they do not specify whom one should or must marry. A complex system might prohibit one from marrying certain categories of kin or social strata, but otherwise the possibilities are left open.

Lévi-Strauss makes a further distinction between systems in which the exchange is direct and those in which the exchange is more indirect. The simplest system is that of *direct exchange,* whereby group A gives its women to group B, and group B provides wives for group A. Such exchanges can take place immediately within the same generation or be delayed over generations: Group A gives group B wives in one generation and group B reciprocates in the next. *Indirect exchange* occurs when women move in one direction only. Group A gives wives to group B, group B provides wives for group C, and group C provides wives to group A, forming a circle of marriage exchanges. The so-called marriage alliance cultures of Southeast Asia, such as the Batak of Sumatra, are an example of societies in which indirect exchange plays an important social role. Such societies emphasize giving and receiving gifts within and between social groups. Spiritually and ritually, wife-giving lineages are viewed as superior to wife-receiving lineages. Givers and takers are bound to each other through a series of gifts and counter-gifts of women, food, textiles, jewelry, and livestock. These alliances form the focus of village social life.

ENDOGAMY AND EXOGAMY. **Endogamy** refers to a rule that one must or should marry within one's own group or category. **Exogamy** refers to rules or preferences for marrying outside of a social group or category. Basically, exogamy links groups together, while endogamy isolates groups and maintains them as distinct units.

The distinction between endogamy and exogamy depends on how one's own group is defined. In our society, we tend to marry people outside our own kin group but within our own socioeconomic stratum. A wealthy industrialist would not be imprisoned for marrying someone of blue-collar background, but social pressures and practices help to maintain strata endogamy. The family (nuclear or extended) is the primary exogamous unit in our society, and it is primarily between families, usually of the same social stratum, that marital exchanges take place.

Social strata in our society are not, of course, homogeneous. There are different kinds of groups within a social stratum, and marriage can serve in forming alliances between these segments. This can be illustrated by marriage patterns among the wealthy elite of the United States and European nobility during the latter part of the nineteenth century and early twentieth century which were endogamous in terms of social strata but exogamous in terms of nationality. The newly affluent Americans of this period were seen as rather crude by the more established elites of their own country. In Europe, the newly rich found poorer aristocrats who were all too willing to trade their family name for a share of American wealth (Fowler 1993). The principal marketplace was the Riviera:

> Daughters of the American rich could
> here be traded for the esteem that went

with older landed wealth and title, or sometimes merely the title. By this single simple step the new wealth achieved the respectability of age. And the anciently respectable got money, something they could always use. So inevitable was this bargain that they were negotiated by the scores, and brokers—often impoverished women of imagined social rank— appeared to make the deals. . . . By 1909, by one estimate, 500 American heiresses had been exported for the improvement of the family name, along with $220 million. [Galbraith 1977: 68]

Perhaps the most notable of these exchanges was between the Vanderbilts and the Churchills. Cornelius Vanderbilt was able to arrange to have his daughter marry into the Churchill family, one of the most honored in British history, for an initial payment of $2.5 million. With this (and eventually another $7.5 million), he was able to help rid his family of its robber-baron stigma and transform it into one of high repute.

Australian Aborigines also seek marriage partners outside of their immediate group for strategic reasons. The alliances created through such marriages serve to give them access to a wider hunting and gathering range. For desert-dwelling Aborigines, faced with the ever-present threat of scarcity and draught, such a strategy especially makes sense.

Families or social groups do not always favor a strategy of seeking alliances through marriage with others. They may instead follow a narrowly defensive endogamous strategy, usually in an effort to maintain a group's identity and wealth. One way of achieving this is to prescribe marriage to certain categories of cousin. Among patrilineal Muslim peoples in the Near East and North Africa, for example, the preferential marriage for a male is to his patrilateral parallel cousin (his father's brother's daughter). This marriage practice ensures that property is kept within relatively narrow bounds, overcoming the threat to maintenance of family wealth posed by Islamic law, which calls for inheritance by sons and daughters. It also creates a strong social group of allied brothers and their children, particularly useful in the hostile and faction-ridden social environment in this area. Such a social environment, however, is to some extent a product of the isolationist principles by which these groups are formed and separated from others in the first place. The result is a cycle in which the practice of patrilateral parallel cousin marriage encourages factionalism, which in turn promotes this form of marriage.

Number of Spouses

Societies typically prescribe not only whom one should marry, but also how many people one may marry. In our own society, a person who is married to more than one spouse at the same time is known as a bigamist; if caught, he or she can be imprisoned. Many societies, however, allow men to have more than one wife, and some allow women to have more than one husband. In fact, historically the practice of allowing a person to have more than one spouse has been accepted in the vast majority of societies. There are no natural reasons for either practice. Whether a society tries to restrict marriage to a single spouse or encourages persons to have more than one spouse reflects the particular way that society has evolved. Such practices also change over time as conditions change. Some societies that formerly allowed plural marriages no longer do so, one reason being the spread of European colonialism and the Christian morality that accompanied it.

MONOGAMY.   The form of marriage in the United States and other Western industrial nations is **monogamy,** the state or custom of being married to one person at a time. Monogamy is not simply a norm in these societies; it is prescribed. Plural marriages are illegal. In societies where divorce is fairly common, individuals may enter into a series of marriages—marrying, divorcing, and marrying again—but still they may have only one spouse at a time. We refer to this pattern as **serial monogamy.**

POLYGYNY AND POLYANDRY.   Many other societies prefer not to limit the number of spouses available to a person to one at a time. The practice of having more than one spouse at the same time we call **polygamy.** There are two principal types of polygamy: polygyny and polyandry.

The term **polygyny** refers to marriage between one man and two or more women simultaneously. Historically, polygyny has been common to many societies around the world. The possibility of polygynous marriage in a society, however, does not mean that all adult males in that society will have more than one wife. For them to do so in most cases would be a demographic impossibility. In a survey of the Mardudjara Aborigines, inhabitants of Jigalong in Western Australia, Tonkinson (1974: 46–47) found that despite the preference of married men for two wives, only 11 of the 40 married men in the sample had polygynous marriages. Among the Tiwi of northern Australia (Goodale 1971; Hart and Pilling 1979), some older males may marry up to one or two dozen women, while others will have only one wife and younger men may have to wait until their late thirties to marry. Tiwi males do not necessarily remain celibate before marriage, but their sexual relations with women are considered illegitimate.

Jealousy and interpersonal rivalry among co-wives is recognized as a potential problem in most societies with polygynous marriage. Maintaining separate households for each wife is one way of trying to avoid conflict. Among the Plateau Tonga of Zambia, husbands with more than one wife not only place their wives in separate dwellings, but also divide their property among them. A husband's demonstration of a noticeable preference can cause conflict in any polygynous situation. The Tanala of Madagascar have dealt with this by ruling that a husband must spend a day with each of his wives in succession or be accused of adultery; a slighted wife is entitled to sue for divorce and receive considerable alimony.

Another common means of reducing jealousy among co-wives is to assign the wives hierarchical statuses. The senior wife among the Lacandon of southern Mexico is the only female allowed to enter the family shrine when specially prepared ritual offerings are to be presented (Tozzer 1907). In other societies, the older wife can dictate to the younger.

The potential for tension is especially acute when the co-wives share no other social bonds except the one with their husband. One strategy for getting around this problem is for a man to marry sisters, in the belief that they will get along well since they are accustomed to cooperating and living together in the same household—a belief that sometimes proves to be false. In the practice of **sororal polygyny,** marriage to one woman gives a man the right to claim her younger sister in marriage, sometimes without additional ceremony or payment. Sororal polygyny is found most often in societies with patrilineal descent groups, where co-wives are bound not only as siblings but also by the duties imposed on them by lineage affiliation.

While the practice of polygyny is not as widespread today as it once was, it persists nevertheless, especially in countries with substantial non-Christian populations. Islam, for example, does not advocate polygyny, but the Koran does make provision for a man to take up to four wives under certain circumstances. These circumstances include war, which may result in a population with more women than men; insanity; physical debility or serious illness; and inability of a wife to bear children. In the case of wealthy and powerful individuals, however, the provisions under which polygyny is allowed may be overlooked or loosely interpreted.

It is estimated that as many as 25 percent of the men in Africa have more than one wife, despite attempts by Christian churches to end the practice and its stigmatization among many urban-dwelling, educated Africans. According to Hazel Ayanga (1986), men report looking for second wives because the first wife is too busy with an outside job to run the household. They want a less educated, more manageable second wife. Others simply state that they have a second wife because they "think it's fun." Also, since divorce is frowned upon in Africa, it is easier to take a second wife than to divorce the first. Looking at it from a woman's perspective, Ayanga noted: "When a young woman becomes a second wife, it's usually on the understanding that the first wife is going to be sent away. . . . But most of the time this doesn't happen and you end up being a second wife" (1986: 10). Some of the potential complications are avoided when the two wives are physically separated, as when one is in town and the other is in the village. In fact, the two may not even know one another.

Antipolygamy laws were enacted under Christian influence in the United States and Canada, supported by passages in the book of Genesis and by New Testament passages in which Jesus and Paul affirm the "implicit" message of monogamy. Yet polygamy continues to be practiced by a handful of small religious groups including fundamentalist Mormons, a voodoo group called Yoruba, a Jewish organization called Black Israel, and some Muslims.

Early Mormons considered many wives a sign of God's goodness and favor, and supported polygamy on practical grounds as increasing their number. Mormon church leaders, however, abandoned polygamy during the latter part of the nineteenth century in the face of legal problems with U.S. authorities as Utah moved toward statehood, since federal law prohibited the practice. But not all Mormons were willing to abandon polygamy. Citing historical precedent among Mormons and Old Testament passages such as those referring to King Solomon and his hundreds of concubines, one Mormon sect known as the United Order Effort refused to

Polyandry is a rare form of marriage, found mostly in South Asia. Shown here is a polyandrous family in Nepal: two grooms at left, bride swathed in veiling, during ceremonial tea-drinking at wedding.

give up the practice. After being excommunicated by church authorities, in 1947 sect members established a community in an isolated part of British Columbia where they continue to practice polygamy despite its illegality. One of these families, for example, consists of a man, his five wives, and 45 children. They live in a single house in which each wife has her own bedroom, but the husband does not have a bedroom of his own.

Polyandry, marriage of one woman to two or more men at the same time, is a rare form of marriage. The majority of societies where polyandry has been found are in South Asia: Tibet, India, Nepal, and Sri Lanka. The most common form of this type of marriage is **fraternal polyandry,** in which a group of brothers share a wife. Nancy Levine (1988) describes one such polyandrous household among a group of ethnic Tibetans in Nepal. The household was composed of three generations, including three brothers and their wife and their five sons and their wife. In most such households, the eldest brother, as the first-married, is accorded a higher status and exerts some authority in household affairs. In the case of the group

studied by Levine, the brothers sought to determine paternity of children, placing a great value on male offspring. This is not always the case. Thus, among the Pahari of northern India, studied by Gerald Berreman (1962), biological paternity was disregarded.

There are various practical reasons for the custom of fraternal polyandry beyond the simple weight of tradition. Among the Pahari, for example, there may have been a shortage of women. In other cases, the custom seems related to situations where men are away to make war or to trade much of the time. Polyandry ensures that at least one man will always be at home. The women Levine (1988) studied commented that polyandry provided them with the security of knowing that should one husband die, there would always be another. She also pointed to several other important implications of fraternal polyandry: It serves to maintain a low rate of population growth; it prevents the dispersal of property, especially land; and it serves to maintain a united group of brothers, and often their male offspring, as the core of a highly self-sufficient household unit. Anthony Walker (1986) relates the practice of polyandry among the Toda of southern India, among whom polyandry disappeared almost a century ago, to an imbalance in the sex ratio brought on in part by the practice of female infanticide.

Not everyone in societies that allow polyandry practices it, and, especially today, not everyone looks upon it favorably. Although polyandry remains the ideal form of marriage among the Nyinba of northwestern Nepal, herders and traders who number around 1,300, only about half of the marriages at present are polyandrous. The rest are monogamous. Positive comments about polyandry point to it being "just like insurance for the wife" and how it contributes to the accumulation of wealth by limiting the partition of land and creating a strong work unit among brothers. Others view it differently, however: "I want one rich, active husband who is a good trader" or "Polyandry is no good. There's too much work for one woman. It's too hard trying to take care of many husbands equally" (Dunham 1993: 82). As for the future, notes one older woman, after commenting on the declining practice of arranged marriage: "Polyandry is our custom and we will continue it as long as possible . . . for as long as it works" (Dunham 1993: 86).

The Marriage Process

Marriage cannot be treated as a single event; it is a process that occurs over time. The process essentially has three parts: finding a potential spouse (or spouses), securing the marriage, and maintaining it. All societies have norms about what course this process is supposed to take and sanctions against extreme deviations. Practices vary, however, and the norms themselves undoubtedly change over time.

CHOOSING A SPOUSE. In many societies personal choice in selecting a spouse is limited. In small-scale or village-level societies, for simple demographic reasons there are unlikely to be many potential spouses. In a village of 200 people, no more than one or two dozen choices are likely at best. If the village population is relatively stable and families have been intermarrying for generations, the number of possible marriage partners will be reduced even further by rules of exogamy. Those unable to find a spouse locally will be forced to look elsewhere. Young Kekchi men from the highlands of Guatemala sometimes spend a couple of years traveling about northern Guatemala and southern Belize as itinerant merchants; they look not only for a little adventure and a way to earn money but also for a mate.

Systems of marriage exchange, such as those discussed earlier in the chapter, are one way of overcoming local shortages of potential spouses. Another way is to seize mates from elsewhere. *Marriage by capture* typically involves the capture of women from groups perceived to be hostile. Capturing wives was once fairly common among small-scale farmers in Melanesia and Amazonian South America, where the practice was closely related to warfare, and it is still practiced by some peoples in these areas. Capturing a woman does not always automatically make her a man's wife, however. Among the South Fore of New Guinea, for example, for the marriage to be recognized, the man still has to provide appropriate payment to the woman's kin (Glasse 1969: 22).

Whether spouses are drawn from the local population or from elsewhere, it is common practice in many societies for marriage to be arranged by one's family or kin. Among the Bena Bena of highland New Guinea, for example, marriage is seen as the responsibility of the division of a clan to which a man belongs. A man decides after consulting with other members of his kin group that it is time for his son to be married, and a search for a bride is begun. The marriage arrangements may be made by the father, but they are just as likely to be made by his brother or some other member of the kin group, or in some instances even by more distant relatives (Langness 1969).

Australian Aborigines essentially have two means of arranging marriages: wife bestowal and mother-in-law bestowal (Maddock 1972: 46–54). In *wife bestowal,* a man is given a wife (often a widow). In *mother-in-law bestowal,* a woman becomes a man's potential mother-in-law with the promise that he will be able to marry a future or existing daughter when she is old enough. Meanwhile, the man waits, often for years, currying favor with his "in-laws" until the time for marriage arrives. During this long wait things can go amiss. The "mother-in-law" may die before having a daughter, the daughter may die, or one of the parties may try to back out. In general, the bestower gains a great deal from the arrangement because of the dependent relationship it establishes; the young man must endure it because of the relative shortage of potential spouses in these small societies. The right to bestow a daughter or mother-in-law may be assigned to the father or brother of the girl or the girl's mother's brother. Bestowal, however, is never decided on by a single individual, although there may be one person who has the final say. Also, the girl herself is unlikely to remain entirely silent in the matter.

Arranged marriage is still widely practiced around the world. In Japan, an estimated one-quarter of marriages today involve parental mediation, where great care is taken to examine the social, educational, and financial backgrounds of the prospective partners. In Indian society, the majority of marriages are arranged. Marriage arrangements traditionally have been the responsibility of one's parents, although today a young man may take an active part—calling the parents of a girl whose picture he has seen or placing an advertisement in the newspaper: "Handsome Delhite, British degree, suitable government position for sophisticated virgin 22 years old. . . . " Families and unmarried individuals also sometimes resort to professional matchmakers and even matchmaking services in the search for a spouse. In any arrangements, such factors as caste, relative wealth of the family, educational background, citizenship, and employment prospects or position held of those being matched will be important considerations (see "Focus on Anthropologists").

As Indian communities have grown around the world (in North America, England, Australia, New Zealand, Fiji, the Caribbean, and South and East Africa), the marriage market has taken on international proportions. Thus, overseas Indian parents of Gujarat origin (a state in India) will sometimes send a daughter on a chaperoned world tour to explore marriage possibilities—the preference being a spouse whose family came from the same caste. Or an Indian male or his family living in Australia, for example, may hear of a family in Fiji with a marriageable daughter. They will contact her parents who, if interested, will supply her photo. If things go well, the girl's father may then travel to Australia to arrange the marriage.

MARITAL WEALTH TRANSFERS. Once a man has obtained the right to marry a woman, he may be expected to perform tasks, called **bride service,** for his bride-to-be's parents. This service may be little more than bringing his future wife and her parents corn and firewood for a few months, as is expected among the Kekchi of southern Belize. By contrast, the man may be expected to live with his future in-laws and work for them for several years, the traditional practice among Kekchi in highland Guatemala. Bride service may continue for some time after the couple is married, or in some instances it may begin only after the marriage takes place. The most common reason given for the practice of bride service is that it compensates the family of the bride for losing one of its members.

In most societies, it is customary to exchange more than just people through marriage. Money, labor, animals, and land may be

MIRIAM SHARMA

FOCUS ON ANTHROPOLOGISTS

Miriam Sharma combines a personal interest in rural India with academic study of the area. In the summer of 1965, she made her first visit to her in-laws' village as a recent bride. It took an entire day to travel the 50 miles from Delhi by bus and horse tonga, finally culminating in a bullock cart ride across the fields. She returned to live there as a bahu (daughter-in-law) with her husband's extended family from January to August in 1976. Fieldwork in North India brought her to Arunpur village (near Banaras) for a year, during 1968 to 1969, to study village politics. From October 1986 to April 1987 she lived in a Rajasthan village researching the connections between class and gender relations. She is a professor of Asian studies at the University of Hawaii and is currently restudying changes in Arunpur over the past two-and-a-half decades.

^^^^^^^^^

Arranged Marriage, Family, and Gender in a North Indian Village

When I arrived in Kota village in June 1965, preparations were well under way for the impending marriage of my husband's sister, Dropa. She was 19 years old and had studied up to the fifth grade; her marriage had been arranged to a young man of 24 years. He had a job on the Indian Railways and came from a village some 15 miles away. She and the groom-to-be had never met or even seen each other from a distance.

Following several days of the bride's family's purchasing necessary items for the marriage, contracting cooks in charge of feeding all the guests attending the marriage, making arrangements to accommodate visitors coming from outside the village, and undertaking the prescribed prenuptial rituals for the bride, the groom and his party of male relatives finally arrived. After their welcome, they retired to rest and were served refreshments, followed by an elaborate feast. The actual marriage ceremony took place in the middle of the night. The next morning saw a lengthy farewell and presentation of many gifts by the women of the house to the groom. My sister-in-law departed after an emotional scene; there was much weeping by all in the family. Then, Dropa, with her head and face covered, got into a taxi alone with a group of strangers to whom she was now forever bound. She was going to an unknown village and new home.

Three days later, I went with my husband and his younger brother to bring Dropa back to Kota from her *sasural* (in-laws' place). There, to my amazement, I found her laughing and talking with her husband and some of his younger relatives, while keeping silent and covering her face with her *sari* before all others. This spirited young woman was suddenly practicing *pardah* (veiling). How, I wondered, could she have acquired such a quiet demeanor so quickly? How could friendship have transpired so quickly with a man she had just met and "did not even love!"

Such was my initiation into the system of arranged marriages that occurs almost universally in India—whether in the villages or the cities; whether among Hindus, Muslims, or other religious groups; whether among the very poor or the westernized elite. Of course, I later came to learn that there are many variations. Urban middle-class families may arrange for the boy and girl to meet beforehand at a restaurant, highly educated professionals may have matrimonial ads placed in a newspaper, and recently, even some villagers are beginning to request photographs of prospective brides and grooms, which are passed eagerly from one kin and friend to another. There are also important differences between the north and the south relating to marriage between relatives and within the same village. But the basic pattern and logic of the arranged marriage system was everywhere the same.

Marriage is the most important event in the life of Indians and is closely linked with ideas of honor, caste purity, patriarchy, and the status of women. The honor of men rests in their women and may be violated by the women's conduct. This has meant that men have a direct interest in controlling a women's sexuality and marital norms. Men marry to carry on their name, while women are transferred from one family to another. The rite of *kanya dan* (literally "gift of a virgin") during the marriage ceremony symbolizes this and the devotion of the wife toward her husband, as a "god." At that time the bride and her dowry are given away by the father (or uncle) to the groom.

Sad faces are seen after the marriage ceremony in Kota village when the young wife leaves her village to go to live in the unknown village of her in-laws.

Women's purity and the legitimacy of children are critical. These conditions ensure that the reproduction and socialization of the young take place only in the patriarchal family. Paternity is important because it is the male heir who carries the family name, honor, and property. Marriage also regulates social relations among castes, because these are endogamous (in-marrying) groups with prescribed norms relating to purity. In India, as in other traditional patriarchal societies, the status of both the child and the woman depend on the man.

My fieldwork experiences and life as a village *bahu* (bride) showed me the importance of these many ideas and beliefs that are invested in the institution of marriage. I began to understand why it is not primarily an affair between a boy and a girl. As a matter of fact, as in Dropa's case, they have little, if any, say in the matter. It would have been considered shameless for them to ever speak of wanting to be married or to directly ask questions once the arrangements were being discussed. All the arrangements and selection of a partner lie with the family members, although they may inform or consult with the person involved. Marriages are often used as a way to strengthen already existing relationships or to create new alliances between different families. They are often arranged with a view to enhancing status and prestige.

Dropa's life and status were suddenly and traumatically changed by her marriage. She had been socialized to accept her role as "some man's" wife and to cater to the needs of males—her father, brothers, future husband, and even adult sons. Modesty of dress and demeanor became second nature as she learned reticence before males and avoidance of public notice. She was protected by and dependent upon the men in her conjugal home, but still enjoyed a certain freedom in her parent's home, where there was no question of veiling before anyone.

The only males she came to develop fond and affectionate relations with were her brothers, male cousins, and those relations formed through marriage of her brothers and cousins. Knowing their daughter would one day marry and leave for her husband's home, her parents regarded Dropa as a cherished guest in the family. She was clothed and trained by her parents for the benefit of her future husband's family. While she may depend upon her father and brothers to make gifts to her from time to time, she has no share in their land.

Dropa's marriage had taken place when she was 19, but the talk about her marriage began when she reached puberty. It was just such talk and the frequent references in jokes and songs that helped prepare Dropa for that day. A number of joking relationships in her husband's home (especially with his younger brother) helped her to adjust and feel less lonely.

Despite the legal age for marriage being set at 18 for females and 21 for males, early marriage often takes place to ensure protection and purity of the bride. This is more common among lower castes where poverty forces young girls to work outside the home and the parents fear for their safety. A second marriage ceremony (the *gauna*) takes place several years after the formal betrothal, when the girl reaches puberty and she is sent to her husband's home. While chastity for unmarried girls and fidelity for a wife are the ideal, quietly committed sins are not uncommon in village India. Elopement, love marriages, and premarital sexual activity are also strongly disapproved, but not unknown.

But how are marriage partners selected in rural north India? What do parents look for in a bride and groom? The rules and regulations of the Hindu caste structure sanctify arranged marriages and provide strict rules to promote and preserve endogamous marriage within the caste. The rules also prohibit marriage between those claiming a common descendant. In north India they also require that the marriage partner come from outside the village (exogamy). Muslims have fewer rules, restricting marriage only beyond the nuclear family; marriages between cousins are even encouraged.

Hypergamy, or marriage with a man whose family is of a superior status, is a common practice among the Hindu upper castes. This has the unfortunate effect, however, of putting a new bride (*bahu*) in double jeopardy in her husband's home. Not only does she have the lowest status and responsibility for most menial and time-consuming tasks, but the lower status of her natal family also reinforces her subordinate position.

A family looks for a bride with the qualities of docility, obedience, modesty, hard work, and homemaking skills, as well as the potential to be a good wife, mother, and daughter-in-law. She should not have any physical handicap and should be of pleasing appearance. A boy is expected to have some education, a good job, or income from family land, and not to have any bad habits (drinking, carousing, or gambling).

Parents of all castes, classes, and religions in village India aspire to arrange the marriage of their adolescent child in a similar way. Family members, other kin, or close relations serve as intermediaries and as matchmakers in helping to find an appropriate partner. Older, married women and their connections in other villages are often important. Men start asking about available mates for their children among in-laws and other relatives and discuss the virtues of each candidate with their womenfolk.

A relative—traditionally, the barber—will be sent to the village to see a prospective bride and learn about her and her family. If she is acceptable, then the father, other family members, or go-betweens will meet and agree upon the marriage. A major part of the discussion—especially among upper and more well-to-do castes—will focus on the exchange of gifts, marriage expenses (including the feast and number of people to come in the groom's party), and the dowry to be provided with the bride. A Brahman priest is consulted to examine the horoscopes for any possible obstacle to the match. Small, monetary gifts are exchanged, with larger gifts forthcoming during the *sagai* (engagement ceremony).

The person who acts as the matchmaker has primary responsibility for the marriage and may suggest to various kin where a good match may be made. This person (most often a male) plays an important role in smoothing over any last-minute difficulties that may arise, especially relating to the timing of the marriage and the dowry. There is much bargaining and giving and taking during marriage negotiations as material wealth is transferred to accompany the daughter into her new home. This may include cash, clothing, jewelry, household items, and, for the affluent, appliances (refrigerators, television), and motor scooters or motorcycles. Boys may be persuaded to marry into a lower-status family by the inducement of a large dowry. Unfortunately, with this runaway dowry system (illegal by law), women often become virtual pawns to be played carefully in the whole game of status-building among upper castes. While villagers have not taken to the horrible practice of actually murdering those brides who are thought to bring too little dowry—there are increasing incidents of "bride-burnings" or "dowry deaths" in urban areas—harassment of brides is not unknown.

Marriage in India differs significantly from the institution as it is commonly known in most Western cultures, although even in India this form dates mostly from the end of the nineteenth century. Of particular note is the lack of choice and romantic love as elements in marriage for the boy and girl, the de-emphasis on the union of the couple, and the emphasis on the wider network of familial relations that marriage entails.

It is not clear that our model of free choice based on the possibility of an enduring romantic love is a better model for India. People in India are struggling for more opportunities, choices, and ways to empower women to exercise more control of their lives, but this may lead in different directions as far as marriage is concerned.

The Nuer of East Africa use cattle as bridewealth. Cattle are passed from the husband's group to the wife's, promoting the alliance between clans and redistributing cows throughout the society.

exchanged by individuals or groups. This exchange may take the form of **bridewealth,** or **brideprice,** in which wealth of some sort is passed from the husband's group to the wife's. Like bride service, it is sometimes considered payment for the loss of the bride's companionship, labor, and fertility. In recognition of the loss of fertility, for example, in some societies in Irian Jaya the relatives of a married woman continue to receive gifts from their in-laws after marriage for every child she has (Baal 1975). The practice

of bridewealth or brideprice is especially common in societies with patrilineal descent groups, where it can be viewed as compensation for transferring the woman's labor and potential offspring to her husband's group. Bridewealth is rarely paid in societies with matrilineal descent groups, where the children automatically become members of their mother's group.

Among the Nuer, as many other pastoral societies, young men use their family's cattle for bridewealth. The family itself may not have enough cows and may have to borrow cows from other relatives, widening the network of those involved in the exchange. The cows are then distributed to relatives of the bride's father and mother. The exchange of cows reinforces the alliance between patrilineal clans formed as a result of the marriage and also promotes redistribution of cows throughout Nuer society.

Many Asian and southern European societies have a different exchange custom, called **dowry.** The dowry is usually seen as the woman's share of her inheritance from the group of her birth which is taken with her upon marriage. For example, among the Sarakatsani of Greece, parents are expected to contribute to the establishment of their children's new households (Campbell 1974: 44–45). Family wealth—animals, money, and goods—is held in common, with the idea that eventually it will be distributed among the family members as inheritance. Upon marriage, a son usually continues to reside near his parents in an extended family group, and wealth is still held in common. A daughter, however, leaves to live with her husband and his family. The dowry that she takes with her upon marriage is her portion of the family estate. As a result, both the husband's and the wife's family provide roughly equal amounts toward establishing the new household.

Dowry has been an important part of marriage in Indian society and remains so today despite having been outlawed in 1961 and despite protest from many women's rights groups. Such opposition is based on social problems associated with the practice. For example, there are reports of young women killing themselves because of fear that their parents will be unable to provide them with dowries. Another problem is the practice of parents demanding increased dowries of their daughter-in-law's family after marriage. Such demands are sometimes accompanied with threats to kill the bride, or they may lead her to commit suicide. Linked to this are thousands of cases each year in India of brides being burned to death, beaten, tortured, or starved because

their families failed to supply the level of dowry promised at the time of marriage or subsequently demanded. In a case in a rural Indian community, a woman's mother-in-law and brother-in-law were sentenced to hang for burning her to death because her family had failed to provide a radio and bicycle promised as dowry. The husband was jailed for life. Such practices are often associated with growing consumerism. Notes one commentator, "Many prospective grooms' families, unable to afford what they want, wait for the time when they can zero in on their would-be in-laws to fulfill their desires" (Sarkar 1993:40).

BRIDEPRICE CUSTOMS IN THE MODERN WORLD. The monetization of economies has affected brideprice customs in many parts of the world. The introduction of general-purpose money often breaks the hold that parents and other kin have over the exchange since money, unlike traditional forms of wealth, is more likely to be individually owned rather than owned by the family or group. Also, the introduction of money often creates inflationary cycles, whereby ever-greater amounts are paid, usually as a result of competition for prestige. Such inflation is possible where the supply is not subject to the same constraints as more traditional forms of wealth. It is commonly associated with migratory labor.

Throughout much of Papua New Guinea, payment of bridewealth in cash has supplemented and often replaced exchanges involving more traditional forms of wealth, such as shell-money. But there have been reactions against this trend. The Tolai of New Britain (east of New Guinea), for example, "look on such practices with contempt, and see in them the reduction of marriage to a purely commercial transaction" (Epstein 1969: 216). The only time that they will use cash instead of shell-money is when outsiders marry Tolai women. The Tolai are very much a part of the

∿∿∿∿
As part of the Bugis wedding ceremony, the groom (left), dressed in "adat" costume, recites his vows as administered by an imam.

modern world system, but they have not allowed market pressures to destroy an important part of their culture.

THE MARRIAGE CEREMONY. Marriage is formalized by different means in different societies, but in all cases there is some publicly recognized act or rite. The act may be a very simple one. After coming to an understanding with a woman, a young Brazilian Tarirapé male will deposit a load of firewood at the woman's family dwelling as a way to publicly announce their intention to be married (Wagley 1977: 157). He then moves his hammock next to her hammock and becomes part of the household.

Agricultural societies with more elaborate patterns of social differentiation often have more elaborate ceremonies. The Bugis are an Islamic farming people of southwestern Sulawesi who have also migrated extensively to other parts of the Indonesian archipelago. Their society is characterized by strongly hierarchical social relations with status based on birth as well as individual achievement. They form bilateral kin groups based on birth and marriage, and on leader-follower alliances. Competition for higher status is strong among the Bugis, and they jealously guard whatever position they have achieved. Weddings serve as a setting for competition and the manifestation of hierarchy as statuses are displayed in public.

A Bugis marriage is surrounded by a number of events and requires the participation of a large group of people (Millar 1989). The formal process begins with an engagement meeting at which the marriage proposal is accepted by the bride's family and the bridewealth is decided. Preparation for the wedding ceremony usually begins a few weeks beforehand. For important weddings, family and friends are formed into task committees that take responsibility for jobs, including construction of the reception area, sending invitations, preparation of decorations, arranging housing for out-of-town guests, collection of utensils and chairs for the event, arranging entertainment for the reception, and allocation of seating.

On the day of the marriage ceremony, the bride is dressed and seated in a secluded spot, while preparations go on around her and the formal guests and the *imam* (a Muslim religious leader) arrive and are fed. At the same time, at the groom's house, the groom's party is fed (but not the groom) and special foods are prepared to take to the bride's home. The groom and his party then leave for the bride's home, the groom led by an elder who serves as the wedding father. As the groom's party is seated, the groom is led off to be married. After the groom repeats the Islamic marriage vows and signs the marriage contract, the brideprice is announced. Consisting of "rankprice," this comprises units of outdated currency of little value that serve to mark a woman's rank by descent and "spending money," which includes money and often jewelry in an amount commensurate with the wealth and prestige of the bride's parents (a percentage of this is given to the bride's father). The groom is then led to his bride amid a large number of onlookers. Where the groom first touches his bride is viewed as an indication of the kind of relationship the couple will have. He then places a ring on her finger before being led away to shake hands with her parents. After a wedding meal, the groom is taken back to the bride for a playful ritual of sarong exchange. The groom then departs, and the couple is not allowed to begin living together until the balance of the spending money is received and public sittings are held.

For several days prior to the public sittings, the bride and groom separately receive guests who are fed and leave gifts. The day before the public sittings, 50 to 200 women gather to cut up the cow (or cows) that has been slaughtered for the event and to help prepare dishes for the reception. After the workers are given an evening meal, the reception eve begins. This includes a reading from the *Life of the Prophet Muhammad,* a cleansing ceremony, and a vigil. The bride and groom are each formally dressed for the cleansing ceremony, and are seated before bowls of water and henna leaves. The bride and groom place their hands palm upward on a pillow as individuals approach them and place henna leaves dipped in water in their hands. After the ritual, the men present begin the evening vigil, talking and playing games through the night.

The next day there are two public sittings. At the first sitting the groom is escorted by his party to the bride's home in the late morning, where he and his bride sit on a decorated seat and receive guests. After this the groom is escorted by the bride's party to her home for the second sitting. The sittings include meals, speeches, and entertainment, and guests are seated according to their respective statuses. The elaborateness of the sittings depends of the social status of those involved, and the number of guests at each may be anywhere from 50 to over 1,000. After the sittings, the couple stays at the bride's place for the first night but do not sleep together. The next day the couple is supposed to pay a visit to the graves of the bride's ancestors. Later in the day a group of the groom's relatives (other than his parents) take the couple back to the groom's place for the "three nights' stay" (which now may last only one night), which consists of further gatherings and meals. Next the couple is taken by the groom's parents back to the bride's place for the final ritual, the formal meeting of the in-laws. This concluded, and after a few courtesy calls on relatives who assisted in the wedding, the couple may relax.

ESTABLISHING A RESIDENCE. Once a couple is married, where will they reside? In our own society, the ideal residence is their own dwelling, which may or may not be near either set of parents. We refer to such a practice as **neolocal residence.** The pattern fits with our overall economic system—we sell our

⋀⋀⋀⋀⋀
Iban longhouse, Borneo. Among the Iban, after marriage a couple may choose to live with either the husband's or the wife's family group.

labor and move where jobs are available—and with our lack of extended corporate kin groups. Neolocal residence is associated not only with geographical mobility but also with financial independence. A newly married couple who are poor or unemployed or who otherwise lack the capital to support themselves often reside with one set of parents until their financial situation improves, but in general the goal of a married couple remains living on their own.

Neolocality is not a universal residential preference. In many societies newly married couples do not aspire to owning their own homes and living independently. In societies where social bonds among closely related males are important, the couple usually resides with the husband's group and even in the same household as other male relatives of the husband. Wives in such situations may find themselves cut off from their natal group (group of birth) and may become permanent members of their husband's group instead. We refer to such a pattern as **patrilocal residence.** This is the predominant pattern in virtually all patrilineal

societies, as well as a small number of matrilineal societies.

Among peoples with matrilineal kin groups, it is common for a woman to live with her own group after marriage and for her husband to come to live with her. This is a **matrilocal residence** pattern. This form of residence may be particularly beneficial for women, allowing them to form strong social units for work and mutual support. The man in this case, however, does not give up membership in his natal group, as does the woman in patrilocal residence. A man in this type of society exercises authority in the group of his birth over his sisters and their children because he occupies the important status of mother's brother. Because of this status, a particularly powerful mother's brother sometimes can establish residence with his natal group, taking his wife with him.

The T'ai, the predominant population of Thailand, favor matrilocal residence upon marriage (Skinner 1975; Potter 1980). This is especially true in regard to the youngest daughter, who is expected to stay with her parents and care for them. In return, she inherits the parent's home. A man's association with his wife's family is strengthened by his reliance on their family spirits for protection rather than on those of his parents. Even though a man may live with his wife's family, he retains the rights to inherit land from his own family, but to do so he must move back to his parent's household. Also, if space is inadequate, the couple may move out of the home of the bride's parents after a token period.

Another form of residence found among matrilineal societies is **avunculocal residence.** In this case, the couple live near the husband's mother's brother. In such societies, the residential unit includes a group of brothers and their sisters' sons. Divale and Harris (1976) argue that this pattern is associated with warfare and male dominance; it is a practice that can shift to patrilocality should the brothers begin to allow some of their sons to remain with them after marriage.

There are other types of residence too. In **ambilocal residence,** the couple has a choice of living with or near the parents or kin of either bride or groom. **Bilocal residence** (also known as dual residence) is somewhat different: The couple is expected to live for a period with or near the bride's parents and for another period with or near the groom's. The T'ai Lü of northern Burma, Laos, and northern Thailand (known as the Dai in southern China) traditionally practiced bilocal residence, which they refer to as "three years ago and three years come." Accordingly, the newly wed couple lives for three years with each set of parents. This helps to maintain the production level of each family, aids in caring for the elders, and allows the couple to gain land and accumulate money for their future separate household. The practice has been breaking down over the past few decades, however, as couples have tended to prolong residence with one or the other set of parents.

Residential patterns are not always rigidly prescribed or uniform. Among the Kekchi of southern Belize, there is a patrilocal bias in residency, but the situation is very mixed and fluid (Howard 1977). During the first few years of marriage, a couple may shift between patrilocal and matrilocal residence a few times before settling down more permanently. Where the couple settles can be determined by personal factors, such as inability to get along with in-laws. Villages are often divided into factional groupings, and choice of residence can also be related to the formation of factional alliances. In such cases, not only may the sons of a factional leader live near him, but also the leader may convince his daughters' husbands to live nearby. There are physical considerations, too. Because of heavy rainfall during the rainy season, houses must be built on high ground, and the hilly terrain places a premium on suitable residential sites and sometimes limits the number of residences that can fit on a site.

REMARRYING. After the marriage is legitimatized, much of married life centers on the family, which we take up in the next section. The final part of the marriage process concerns events after a person's first marriage ends, either through divorce or death. While in a large-scale society such as our own there is considerable variation in what people do once they are no longer married—from starting new careers to enjoying the single's life to getting remarried, in many societies patterns are more institutionalized, especially for widows and widowers.

In the remarriage custom called **wife inheritance,** when a man dies, his heir (usually his next of kin) is expected to marry the widow. Wife inheritance is found in conjunction with patrilineal and matrilineal descent, where it is customary for a man's brother or some other member of his lineage to marry his widow after he dies. In a matrilineal system a man inherits from his mother's brother, and one of the things that he may inherit is the obligation to care for the deceased's wife or wives. The rationale for this custom is that since the marriage involved the dead man's group, a member of that group should replace him. When found in conjunction with polygyny, with

patrilineal descent groups, and usually with patrilocal residence as well, the custom is commonly referred to as the **levirate.** This practice
ensures that the widow's children continue to belong to the patrilineage. A complementary practice is the **sororate,** in which a man marries the
sister of his deceased wife. It, too, is associated
with polygyny, patrilineal descent groups, and patrilocal residence, and is sometimes a natural extension of sororal polygyny.

Ghost marriage is a related practice found
in some African societies. Among the Nuer, the
brother of a deceased man may marry an unmarried woman "to the name of" the deceased.
The children of this marriage are considered
children of the dead man, and thus his heirs
(Evans-Pritchard 1940). The Zulu of South
Africa have two forms of ghost marriage
(Gluckman 1950: 184). In one, when a man
who is betrothed dies, his fiancée is married to
one of his kinsmen and she then bears children
for the dead man. In the second form, a man
"wakens" a dead kinsman who has not been betrothed by marrying a wife to his name.

All of these practices reflect a belief that
people should remain married until they
clearly are too old to function properly in society. While they serve to limit personal freedom and can be seen to emphasize the low
status of women in these societies, they also
function to provide security for those who are
widowed. In some situations today, however,
the tradition of wife inheritance is subject to
abuses that relate to changing values. In
Zimbabwe, for instance, wife inheritance may
be used by relatives to seize the mobile property of a couple (televisions, furniture, etc.)
when the husband dies, leaving the widow
destitute (Chandler 1986).

Many societies stop short of dictating who is
to marry a widow, while formulating rules to ensure that someone is responsible for taking care
of her. A Kekchi widow may be taken care of by
her own kin, by her husband's, or by her own
children, depending on circumstances, but it is
expected that someone among her relatives will
care for her. If she is not too old, she is expected
to remarry, but there are no more restraints on
her selection of a new spouse than if she were
marrying for the first time.

There are, however, societies that discourage
widow remarriage. The Roman Catholic
Church discourages remarriage of widows and
widowers, and in former times priests were
empowered to refuse to sanctify unions in
which one or both partners had been married
previously. Among the Sarakatsani, because the
family into which a woman has married does
not want to lose her labor, her children, or
their honor (since she would be having sexual relations with someone from another
family), it is extremely difficult for a widow
to remarry.

Even more extreme are instances where
spouses are killed or kill themselves upon the
death of their husband or wife. A well-known
example of this was the Indian practice of *sati*
(or suttee): self-immolation of a widow in the
belief that a faithful wife who follows her husband into death becomes a demi-goddess (see
Datta 1988). Based on a religious cult, the
practice gained increasing support among
the Indian priesthood and aristocracy from the
fourth century B.C. It was not universally supported, however, and the British set about to
ban it in the nineteenth century. It spread
among the common people in later years, and
is still practiced on rare occasions in rural villages, despite being illegal. In recent years, sati
temples have been established in parts of India
and support for sati has been found within
conservative political movements (see Joseph
1991). Thousands of people turned out to
honor an 18-year-old widow as she was forced
to commit *sati* by her relatives in a village in
Rajastan in 1987. Such developments can be
seen as a reaction to the pressures of modernization. The spread of sati temples, for example,
coincided with steps taken by the national

government to reserve a percentage of local government seats for women.

Similar to *sati* was the Fijian practice of *loloku,* whereby the wife or wives of chiefs were strangled beside their deceased husband (Williams 1858: 189–190; see Mariner 1827: 273). There are also a few societies in which husbands were killed upon the death of a wife, such as the Natchez of the Mississippi region. This custom was associated with matrilineal societies, in which female aristocrats married commoners.

The practices we have discussed are for the most part tied to kin groups with vested interests in what happens to widows of their members. These practices can be expected to be maintained only as long as the social conditions that generated them remain. In many parts of Africa, for example, the erosion of corporate kin groups has led to the end of related forms of remarrying widows.

Divorce, too, is a reflection of social and economic processes in a society. The near impossibility of divorce among the Sarakatsani, for example, fits their overall pattern of social organization and their attitudes toward the family and toward women in general. By contrast, the ease with which Mundurucu women can divorce their husbands is related to the social and economic autonomy of Mundurucu women and to their matrilineality and matrilocal residence pattern. In our own society, a higher divorce rate can be linked to ideological and economic changes concerning the role of women and the nature of the family in recent decades.

⊰ FAMILY GROUPS ⊱

One of the functions of marriage is the creation of the family. Families may exist independently of marriage, but it is through marriage that families usually come into being as socially recognized, le-gitimate entities. An intimate kin-based group that consists of at least a parent-child nucleus, the **family** is the minimal social unit that cooperates economically and is responsible for the rearing of children. Various people may be added to the parent-child nucleus, forming an economically cooperating, child-rearing family group that may or may not share the same dwelling.

Types of Family Groups

The "typical American family" so thoroughly incorporated into our ideology consists of a husband, a wife, and two or more children, all of whom live in a single detached household. However, this image does not typify families in American society today. There are single parents with children, and there may be other relatives living with the family. If we look at families in other societies, we find that the American ideal is, in fact, rather rare worldwide.

The **nuclear family** is composed of a man, a woman, and their children. This group is not the ideal in societies that practice polygyny or polyandry, nor is it considered normal in most societies with unilineal kin groups. The nuclear family group is fairly rare among small-scale agriculturalists and, in fact, occurs infrequently among any rural peoples. The nuclear family group is most often found in segments of societies like the United States where housing is not in short supply and where social mobility, the hunt for jobs and improved social status, and the existence of specialized support systems (such as schools and nursing homes) reduce the central caring role of the family. It is also associated with more marginal foragers, whose precarious economic adaptation favors organizing into small, very mobile units for most of the year.

Since few environments encourage the existence of small independent social groups, more common types of family organization are those referred to as complex or compound. Polygynous marriage leads to the creation of **polygynous family groups,** consisting of a man, his wives, and their children. The members of this family group sometimes live in the same household, each wife perhaps having her own territory centering on her fire hearth. Since this living arrangement often exacerbates tensions, however, co-wives more often have separate dwellings. This results in matricentric households, in which each wife lives in her own dwelling with her own children.

Polyandry leads to the creation of **polyandrous family groups.** All the members of a polyandrous family group—a woman, her husbands, and children—may live under a single roof, or the husbands may jointly occupy a separate men's hut.

There are also various forms of **extended family groups,** in which two or more families of at least two generations live together. Extended family groups are common to pastoral and agricultural societies where household labor demands require more than one adult man and woman. A *patrilocal extended family group* consists of a man and

Although a traditional ideal in our society has been a family of two parents and two or three children, an ideal represented in television's "Leave It to Beaver" family, there is great variation in this family pattern in our society.

his sons and their wives and children. A *matrilocal extended family group* consists of a woman and her daughters and their husbands and children. An *avunculocal extended family group* consists of a man, his sister's sons, and their wives and children.

Extended family groups play a significant economic role in the adaptive strategies of many societies today. In Africa, for example, extended families provide important support services in the face of economic hardship and political upheaval. The growing number of individuals who depend on the few members able to earn a living, however, places considerable strain on the structure. Commenting on this stress in the face of Africa's almost overwhelming problems, Blaine Harden (1991) says of the extended family: "Like a bridge that has borne too much high-speed traffic for too many years, its foundations are cracking."

Finally, there are **joint family groups** in which two or more relatives of the same generation and their spouses and children live together. The *fraternal joint family group* is a common example of this type; it consists of at least two brothers and their wives and children.

While one or two of these family groups may represent the normative ideal of a society, in practice many of these forms may coexist in the same social setting. In Kekchi villages in southern Belize, it is common to find nuclear families, various extended and joint family groups, and even an occasional polygynous family group (usually curers who have inherited wives from deceased patients). In each case, the pattern reflects the strategies of people in relation to their broader social environment—the size of the village, factionalism, the social network of the married couple, and how long they have lived in a village.

The Development Cycle

Family groups are formed and evolve in accordance with the ongoing cycle of birth, maturation, and death. There are three main phases, or stages, in this development cycle (Fortes 1958). First is **expansion.** It begins with marriage and lasts until all children of the family are born and raised to reproductive age. The duration of this phase is limited primarily by the length of time a woman is fertile. During this period the offspring are highly dependent on their parents.

The second phase is **dispersion and fission.** This may overlap with the first phase, for it begins with the first marriage of one of the children and continues until all the children are married. Where it is customary for the youngest child to remain to take over what remains of the family estate, this commonly marks the beginning of the final phase. The third, or final, phase, **replacement,** includes the death of the parents and their replacement in the social structure by families of their children.

At any given time, the phase a family group is going through may influence its residential patterns. Among the Iban of northern Borneo, a couple may choose to live with the wife's or husband's family group, depending on where they are in the cycle. If one of the spouses is the last child remaining in the family after the others have married and left, for instance, he or she stays on as prospective heir.

Precisely what happens in the final stage, as well as residential decisions throughout the cycle, often depends on inheritance customs. In some societies, the oldest child inherits most or all the property. This is referred to as **primogeniture.** Younger siblings are either dependent on the oldest or are left to seek their fortunes on their own. In other societies, the youngest (usually male) child remains in the natal household and inherits the property of the parents. This is referred to as **ultimogeniture** and usually leads to that child's taking over directly from the parents when the cycle begins anew. Such a child is also usually expected to care for the aged parents.

As with other aspects of the institution of the family, the form that family groups take and the cycle of their development vary from society to society. This variation reflects the larger environment of which the family is a part.

Acquiring Children

Children are an important element determining the form and evolution of family groups. How many children there are in a family depends partly on environmental factors. In earlier times in the United States and Canada, when old age was even more precarious than it is now, when the cost of having a child was insignificant, and when more people lived in the country, families tended to be larger than they are today. As more people moved to the city, as young children became more a financial burden than an asset and as pension and welfare systems took the place of family support for the elderly (to name a few contributing factors), families began to get smaller. In general, urbanization and industrialization create conditions favoring smaller families.

The way people acquire children may be a matter of chance, but often it is not. Family planning is a widespread practice. The Tapirapé traditionally limited the number to three living children, and even stipulated that no more than two could be of the same sex. This policy was maintained by a prohibition on sexual relations between a couple during the first year after they had a child, and by the practice of infanticide. It was not that the Tapirapé disliked children; rather they did not "want to see hunger in their eyes" (Wagley 1977). They recognized that feeding more than three children is difficult, and sought to ensure that those children they had were well provided for. Postpartum sex taboos (prescribed restraint from sexual intercourse after the birth of a child), infanticide, and abor-

tion are relatively common means of limiting the number of children people have, or at least spacing them.

Family groups do not always obtain children naturally. Adoption is another way of obtaining children through socially prescribed methods. In Western societies adoption is handled either through relatives or by an adoption agency. Children are brought to the agency for various reasons by their parents or agents of the state. Although the practice is changing, great efforts are still made to keep the natural parents and the adoptive parents from knowing each other. Adoption does not always take place through an agency, however, and the adoptive parents are not always strangers to the adoptee. Over half of the adoptions in the United States, for example, are by relatives— the adoption of illegitimate children by their grandparents, the adoption of stepchildren, and the adoption of children of divorced or deceased relatives.

In many Pacific island societies adoption is a transaction between close relatives. Traditionally there are no formal legal procedures. Furthermore, the natural parents are not stigmatized; on the contrary, they are usually considered generous. Whereas the natural parents in Western societies are usually unwilling or unable to assume parental responsibility, in these Pacific societies the natural parents of adopted children are generally quite capable of caring for their children. They give up their children to be adopted either out of obligation or out of a desire to help someone. In Nukuoro, an island in the Federated States of Micronesia, the act of adoption reflects the interdependency of relatives (Carroll 1970). Relatives are expected to be willing to share all of their resources, including children, especially when one of the relatives is in need.

There is another way of obtaining children: stealing or capturing them. This practice is found primarily among small-scale agriculturalists, such as those in Amazonian South America and New Guinea, where relations between groups are tense and warfare is endemic. Sometimes the need to steal children is related closely to practices that limit population growth. Relations between the sexes among peoples of the Trans-Fly region of New Guinea, for example, are so limited and hostile that in some of these societies homosexuality is the norm instead of heterosexuality. The birth rate among these people is so low that they are forced to raid their neighbors in order to perpetuate their population. In Western societies there is also the usually illegal practice of child purchase.

For the world's poor, the most important factor influencing the number of children a family has is not the number of children produced, adopted, or stolen, but the number who live through early childhood. For many small-scale indigenous societies, newly introduced diseases have had devastating effects, killing large numbers of children as well as their parents. Where there is high infant mortality, parents may seek to have a large number of children so that at least some will survive. While disease and malnutrition still lead to the deaths of millions of children every year, improved health conditions overall have resulted in dramatic increases in population in many developing countries. Combined with the breakdown of traditional family planning strategies and the inaccessibility of new birth control techniques—often too costly or difficult to obtain, the result is often relatively large families.

SUMMARY

Male-female relations are conditioned by their social and cultural environment. The most basic element of male-female relations is sex. Our culture has a profound influence on how we perceive sex and with whom we have it. Societies vary in the degree to which they restrict sex and how they define acceptable partners. In most societies, there are some socially acceptable means of getting around the usual restrictions. An important aspect of sexual behavior and ideology is their relationship to sacred and secular power.

Just as other attitudes toward sexuality vary with the society that constructs them, so does the degree of acceptance of homosexual behavior. There is in fact a broad range of permissiveness or restrictiveness across cultures. Population and social arrangements can affect a society's tolerance or encouragement of homosexual behavior.

Marriage is a socially sanctioned sexual and economic union between men and women. It is an adaptive measure, related to such factors as the prolonged period of dependency of human infants, sexual competition, the sexual division of labor, and, perhaps, male domination. It is also a means to the formation of alliances. Systems of marital exchange between groups may be elementary or complex, direct or indirect, endogamous (marriage within one's social group or category) or exogamous (marriage outside of a social group or category).

Although one spouse at a time is the only form of marriage allowed in our own society, monogamy is not universal. Two forms of plural marriage, or polygamy, are found in many societies: polygyny (marriage between one man and two or more women simultaneously) and polyandry (marriage of one woman to two or more men at the same time). Our version of the marriage process is not universal either. Societies place varying restrictions on the choice of a spouse. The terms of the marriage may involve bride service or brideprice. The actual ceremony can vary a great deal in elaborateness. After the ceremony, residential possibilities include neolocal, patrilocal, matrilocal, ambilocal, bilocal, and avunculocal residence. Last, there is the question of what happens when a spouse dies or a divorce takes place. Many societies have institutionalized remarriage through practices such as levirate, sororate, and ghost marriage.

In our society, the traditional family includes husband, wife, and children. This nuclear family does not provide the only way of grouping close kin, however. In addition to the nuclear family group, there are four principal types of complex or compound family groups: polygynous, polyandrous, extended, and joint. The family group is not static; it follows a rhythmic cycle of expansion, dispersion, and replacement. Expressions of this pattern are influenced by a number of things, including inheritance customs such as primogeniture and ultimogeniture. Expansion involves the acquisition of children, either through natural procreation, adoption, or capture. How many children a family has and how they are obtained are influenced, like all of culture, by environmental factors.

In Chapters 6 through 9 we looked at the primary components of society and have examined how individuals become a part of society. These chapters were essentially concerned with showing how a society is put together. In the following three chapters we will shift our attention toward the forces that threaten to pull society apart and look at how these threats are dealt with: We begin in Chapter 10 with ethnicity and social stratification.

KEY TERMS

Ambilocal residence Residing after marriage with or near the parents or kin of either bride or groom.

Avunculocal residence Residing after marriage near the husband's mother's brother or father's brother.

Bilocal residence Residing after marriage with or near the bride's parents for a period and,

for another period, with or near the groom's parents.

Bride service Service performed by a future husband for his bride-to-be's parents.

Bridewealth (brideprice) The passage of wealth of some sort from the husband's group to the wife's as a result of marriage.

Dispersion and fission The second phase in the development cycle of a family that begins with the first marriage of one of the children and continues until all the children are married.

Dowry The woman's share of her inheritance from the group of her birth, which is taken with her upon marriage.

Endogamy A pattern, preference, or requirement that marriage be within a social group, class, or category.

Exogamy A pattern, preference, or requirement that marriage be outside a social group, class, or category.

Expansion The first phase in the development cycle of a family that begins with marriage and lasts until all children of the family are born and raised to reproductive age.

Extended family group A residential group consisting of two or more families of at least two generations.

Family The minimal social unit that cooperates economically and is responsible for the rearing of children.

Fraternal polyandry A marriage pattern in which a woman is married to a group of brothers.

Ghost marriage The custom in which a woman is considered married to, or may simply bear children in the name of, a man who is deceased.

Incest taboo A rule prohibiting sexual intercourse between specific categories of kin.

Joint family group A residential group consisting of two or more relatives of the same generation and their spouses and children.

Levirate The custom of a brother of a man who has died, or some other member of his kin group, marrying his widow.

Marriage A socially sanctioned sexual and economic union between members of the opposite sex (occasionally between members of the same sex).

Matrilocal residence Residing after marriage with the wife's kin.

Monogamy Marriage of one person to one other person at a time.

Neolocal residence Residence of a couple after marriage in a new household, not linked to the households of either of their families.

Nuclear family A group composed of a man, a woman, and their children.

Patrilocal residence Residing after marriage with the husband's kin.

Polyandrous family group A group resulting from a polyandrous marriage, consisting of a wife and her husbands and children. The men live under a single roof with their wife or jointly occupy a separate men's hut.

Polyandry Marriage of a woman to two or more men at the same time.

Polygamy Marriage to more than one spouse at the same time.

Polygynous family group A group resulting from a polygynous marriage, consisting of a husband, his wives, and his or their children, all living in a single household or, occasionally, the wives living in separate dwellings.

Polygyny Marriage between one man and two or more women at the same time.

Primogeniture The practice whereby the oldest child inherits most or all the parents' property.

Replacement The third, or final, phase in the development cycle of a family that includes the death of the parents and their replacement in the social structure by families of their children.

Serial monogamy The marriage pattern in which an individual enters into a series of marriages, but still has only one spouse at a time.

Social construction The process by which individuals shape reality through social interaction.

Sororal polygyny The custom that, upon marriage to a woman, a man acquires the right to claim her younger sister in marriage.

Sororate The custom of a man marrying the sister of his deceased wife.

Ultimogeniture The practice whereby the youngest child remains in the parents' household and eventually inherits their property.

Wife inheritance The custom of an heir of a deceased man marrying his widow.

SUGGESTED READINGS

Bledsoe, Caroline H. 1980. *Women and Marriage in Kpelle Society.* Stanford: Stanford University Press. [Africa]

Collier, Jane F. 1988. *Marriage and Inequality in Classless Society.* Stanford: Stanford University Press. [Plains Indians]

Croll, Elisabeth. 1981. *The Politics of Marriage in Contemporary China.* New York: Cambridge University Press.

Edwards, Walter. 1989. *Modern Japan Through Its Weddings: Gender, Person, and Society in Ritual Portrayal.* Stanford: Stanford University Press.

Goody, Jack R., and S. J. Tambiah, editors. 1973. *Bridewealth and Dowry.* New York: Cambridge University Press.

Kilbride, Philip L., and Janet C. 1990. *Changing Family Life in East Africa: Women and Children at Risk.* University Park: Pennsylvania State University Press.

Levine, Nancy E. 1988. *The Dynamics of Polyandry: Kinship, Domesticity, and Population on the Tibetan Border.* Chicago: University of Chicago Press.

Millar, Susan B. 1989. *Bugis Weddings: Rituals of Social Location in Modern Indonesia.* Berkeley: University of California, Center for South and Southeast Asian Studies.

Parkin, David, and David Nyamwaya, eds. 1988. *Transformation of African Marriage.* Manchester: Manchester University Press.

Potash, Betty, editor. 1986. *Widows in African Societies: Choices and Constraints.* Stanford: Stanford University Press.

Potter, Sulamith H. 1980. *Family Life in a Northern Thai Village: A Study of the Structural Significance of Women.* Berkeley: University of California Press.

Schuler, Sidney R. 1987. *The Other Side of Polyandry: Property, Stratification, and Nonmarriage in the Nepal Himalayas.* Boulder, CO: Westview Press.

Slater, Miriam K. 1977. *The Caribbean Family: Legitimacy in Martinique.* New York: St. Martin's.

Tapper, Nancy. 1991. *Bartered Brides: Politics, Gender and Marriage in an Afghan Tribal Society.* New York: Cambridge University Press.

Watson, Rubie S., and Patricia Buckley Ebrey. 1991. *Marriage and Inequality in Chinese Society.* Berkeley: University of California Press.

Baal, J. van. 1975. *Reciprocity and the Position of Women.* Assen, the Netherlands: Van Gorcum.

Carrier, M. 1992. "Miguel: Sexual Life History of a Gay Mexican-American." In G. Herdt (ed.) *Gay Culture in America*: 202–224. Boston: Beacon.

Dunham, Carroll. 1993. "The Many Husbands of Tsering Zangmo." *Discovery*, January:80–86.

Evans-Pritchard E.E. 1970. "Sexual inversion among the Azande." *Am. Anthropol.* 72(6):1428–34.

Fowler, Marian. 1993. *In a Gilded Cage: From Heiress to Duchess.* New York: Random House.

Herdt, Gilbert H., ed. 1984. *Ritualized Homosexuality in Melanesia.* Berkeley: University of California Press.

Kanato, Manop. 1990. *Becoming "Opportunistic" Commercial Sex Workers: An Anthropological-Epidemiological Study.* M.Sc. thesis, McMaster University.

Kelly, R.C. 1976. "Witchcraft and Sexual Relations: An Exploration in the Social and Semantic Implications of the Structure of Belief." In *Man and Woman in the New Guinea Highlands,* eds. P. Brown and G. Buchbinder, 36–53. Special Publication, no. 8. Washington, DC: American Anthropological Association.

Kennedy, E.L., and M.D. Davis. 1993. *Boots of Leather, Slippers of Gold: The History of a Lesbian Community.* New York: Routledge.

Lindenbaum. S. 1972. "Sorcerers, Ghosts, and Polluting Women: An Analysis of Religious Belief and Population Control." *Ethnology* 11:241–253.

Newton, E. 1993. *Cherry Grove, Fire Island: Sixty Years in America's First Gay and Lesbian Town.* Boston: Beacon.

Phongpaichit, P. 1982. *From Peasant Girls to Bangkok Masseuses.* Geneva: International Labour Office.

Potter, Sulamith H. 1980. *Family Life in a Northern Thai Village: A Study of the Structural Significance of Women.* Berkeley: University of California Press.

Santasombat, Yos. 1992. *Mae Ying Si Khaai Tue (Woman Sell Yourself): The Community and*

Commercial Sex in Thai Society. Bangkok: Institute of Local Community Development.

Sarkar, Jayanta. 1993. "Indian Crusader Seeks to Halt Child Slavery." *Far Eastern Economic Review*, 8 July: 62.

Skinner, William G. 1975. *Change and Persistence in Thai Society*. Ithaca, NY: Cornell University Press.

Vance, C.S. 1991. "Anthropology rediscovers sexuality: A theoretical comment." *Soc. Sci. Med.* 33:8, 875–84.

Van Landingham, Mark J., Somboon Suprasert, Werasit Sittitrai, Chayan Vaddhanaphuti, Nancy Grandjean. 1993. "Sexual Activity among Never-married Men in Northern Thailand." *Demography* 30 (3):297–313.

Weeks, Jeffrey. 1977. *Coming Out: Homosexual Politics in Britain from the 19th Century to the Present*. London: Quartet Books.

Werner, Dennis. 1979. "A Cross-Cultural Perspective on Theory and Research on Male Homosexuality." *J. of Homosexuality* 4:345–62.

Weston, Kath. 1991. *Families We Choose: Lesbians, Gays, Kinship*. New York: Columbia University Press.

Weston, Kath. 1993. "Lesbian/Gay Studies in the House of Anthropology." *Annu. Rev. Anthropol.* 22:339–67.

Williams. Walter L. 1986. *The Spirit and the Flesh: Sexual Diversity in American Indian Culture*. Boston: Beacon Press.

ETHNICITY AND SOCIAL STRATIFICATION

About the Aborigines of York, Western Australia in the late nineteenth century, police constable David E. Hackett reported (in Curr 1886–1887, 1:342–343),

The Ballardong say that some remote tribes to the eastwards are cannibals, and that they mark children at their birth who are eventually to be eaten. . . . I am convinced, however, that little dependence can be placed on stories of this sort respecting cannibalism; what we positively know being that most tribes practiced it more or less, and that nearly all stoutly deny the fact, and accuse their neighbors of it.

None of the Ballardong had ever actually eaten anyone, but they were prepared to believe anything that cast their eastward neighbors in a bad light. The Ballardong had no clear evidence that their neighbors were cannibals, basing their beliefs instead on misinterpretation of the purpose of circumcision (for the Ballardong did not circumcise, a practice which, of course, had nothing to do with cannibalism). But the Ballardong's unfounded beliefs reinforced their perception of cultural differences between themselves and Aborigines living to the east and supported a feeling of group identity among the Ballardong by helping them to define themselves as distinct. Such beliefs in a we-they dis-

tinction are central to **ethnicity**—selected perceived cultural or physical differences used to class people into groups or categories considered to be significantly distinct.

Hackett's statement reveals not only the Ballardong's prejudices, but also the prejudices of white Australians toward Aborigines. His remark about Aboriginal cannibalism is based no more on observation than was that of the Ballardong, but most white Australians during the nineteenth century were certain that Aborigines did eat each other. European settlers simply assumed that the practice of cannibalism was a feature of most "savage" societies; the claims fit with their commonly held stereotypes, and proof was by and large not thought necessary. Such beliefs helped white settlers to justify their maltreatment and displacement of Aborigines.

How are people and groups differentiated from one another? In this chapter, we will look at two closely related dimensions of sociocultural differentiation: ethnicity and social stratification. In doing so, we will turn our attention to forces that threaten to pull society apart. A wide range of factors is involved in these ways of differentiating people, for ethnicity and social stratification influence and are influenced by almost

Living by scavenging in a dump in metropolitan Manila, the Philippines. Despite reforms in recent years, inequality has remained a marked feature of Philippine society.

235

all aspects of our lives. Both are dynamic processes that continually adapt to the ever-changing conditions in the world around us.

◄ ETHNICITY ►

Ethnicity, or ethnic group affiliation, is one major basis on which to draw we-they distinctions. Ideas about ethnic groupings involve concepts of race, people's perceived ethnic identity, ethnic symbols, and relations among ethnic groups.

Race: Symbol of Nonbiological Differences

Categorization of humans according to physical or racial characteristics took place among very early human societies. Prehistoric cave paintings in various parts of the world and decorations on ancient Egyptian tombs refer to people with different physical characteristics. Anthropologists find that people often make distinctions between groups according to observed or presumed biological differences. Usually one's own type is considered normal—the Yanomami call themselves "true men," the Aboriginal inhabitants of southwestern Australia refer to themselves as "the people"—as compared with all others. The concept of **race,** or categorization according to physical traits, is virtually universal. But so also is the mistaken belief that the physical features chosen for purposes of categorization reflect differences in behavior or intelligence.

As European civilization spread across the globe, race became the subject of systematic scientific enquiry. It became an important issue as Europeans encountered people who differed so much from themselves as to raise doubts about their humanness. From the great variety of observable physical differences, Europeans developed universal classifications. Carolus Linnaeus (1758–1759) divided all humanity into four races: White, Yellow, Negro, and Indian. In colonized areas where there was concern over the products of *miscegenation,* or sexual mixing of

these presumed races, racial categorization became even more complex. The Spanish carried such racial classification to an extreme in their American colonies. In eighteenth-century Mexico, for instance, the Spanish created 16 racial categories based on degrees of mixture among European, Negro, and Indian (Mörner 1967: 58).

As in the case of colonial Mexico, such classifications often were used to determine the political and legal rights and economic statuses of people. More generally, it was common to rank races. The noted philosopher David Hume (1748) stated that since Negroes were the only race not to have developed a major civilization, they were "naturally inferior" to whites. Since Hume's time, of course, Europeans discovered that the people of Africa had developed important civilizations. Even today, many people think that humanity is divided into a small number of distinct races and that their differences reflect social and intellectual as well as physiological differences. Using such perceived differences to determine people's position in relation to one another is known as **racism.**

Racism in small-scale and large-scale societies is significantly different. In small-scale societies, it entails hatred or violence of strangers—those outside of one's own society. This is true of large-scale societies as well, but in these societies racism commonly involves oppression of groups within one's own society. This is to be expected, since larger societies may incorporate a greater heterogeneous mixture of people than do smaller ones.

Race as a biological concept has come under considerable attack in recent years. No fundamental biological differences have been found among contemporary races, and race appears to be equally insignificant as a determinant of social or cultural differences. No longer important scientifically, race continues to be of relevance as a sociocultural phenomenon. Race stands as a symbol of nonbiological differences—a reflection of cultural differences, different religious beliefs, and economic inequality and exploita-

Much of a "racial" minority's identity arises from their experience with economic inequality and perceived injustice. Here protestors demonstrate against the mayor of New York City. They want the mayor to stop racist attacks on squeegees, many of whom are young African Americans, who race out into stopped traffic to wash a car windshield and then demand to be paid for the service.

tion. As Brazilian anthropologist Verena Martinez-Alier (1974: 6) has noted: "Strains and tensions in society that may be the result of a variety of factors are often justified and rationalized in terms of racial distinctions."

Ethnic Identity

Buoyed by optimism concerning the prospects for rapid global change during the decades immediately following World War II, some social scientists believed that racism and ethnicity were rapidly disappearing throughout the world. They felt that race and ethnicity were ceasing to be significant issues in Western industrial nations and that they would soon be irrelevant elsewhere, as countries became more urbanized and industrialized.

However, in both industrial and industrializing countries, predictions of the demise of racism and ethnicity have been incorrect. If anything, ethnicity has undergone a period of revitalization. Many people thought to have lost their sense of **ethnic identity**—awareness of themselves as a group and of how they differ culturally from others—once again are pro-

claiming their pride in being members of distinct ethnic groups with their own cultural traditions. As conflicts in Sri Lanka and Eastern Europe have demonstrated, ethnicity remains a central fact of political life.

The persistence of ethnicity is tied to identity formation in early socialization. As young children, we learn to value certain aspects of the cultural traditions of our society. We acquire what may be called primordial, or original, attachments to a particular way of life, and in the process learn to value that way of life more than other ways. In other words, we become *ethnocentric.*

While our ethnic identity may be rooted in early childhood socialization and in the perceived cultural traditions of our society, the significance of this identity at any given time will, for the most part, reflect current situations. For example, the resurgence of ethnicity in eastern Europe, as exemplified in struggles for political separation from existing states, is not simply a reflection of primordial attachments to cultural traditions. Such attachments are important, but recent ethnic militancy in these countries is primarily a reaction to current political and economic conditions, such as

The persistence of ethnic conflict in certain areas of the world, including Bosnia in the former Yugoslavia, demonstrates the continued political importance of ethnicity and ethnic identity. In this picture, a United Nations peacekeepers' tank follows a group of Bosnian refugees.

the collapse of communist regimes and major economic disruptions.

Western countries, too, have witnessed increased ethnic awareness. This is seen, for example, in the case of indigenous peoples in countries such as the United States, Canada, and Australia. Census figures in Australia in 1987 showed 225,000 people identifying themselves as Aborigines. In 1981, the figure was only 160,000. Since the population growth rate for Aborigines is three percent per year, how can such a rise be accounted for? Part of the answer is fairly simple. In 1987 Aboriginal census workers were hired to help count fellow Aborigines for the first time. State institutions often play a role in ethnic identification in this way, some-

times creating or encouraging such identification where previously it was weak or nonexistent. But the increased self-identification among Aborigines also was brought about by the work of Aboriginal political activists. The clearest example of this was in Tasmania, where most Australians believed the last of its Aboriginal inhabitants had died in the nineteenth century. In recent years, however, Aboriginal political activists in Tasmania have struggled for recognition of local Aborigines, and people of Aboriginal ancestry in Tasmania increasingly have come forward and identified themselves as Aborigines.

Ethnic identification may result from the imposition of ethnic categories by others rather than simply from a process of self-identification.

The creation of such categories is a common feature of state formation, especially where linked to colonial expansion. For example, Australian Aborigines did not see themselves as Aborigines until they were treated as a single ethnic group by their European conquerors. Similarly, the Makah are a native American tribe that was created around 1870 by the United States government from an aggregation of formerly autonomous villages. In such situations, it may take time before the people categorized began to assume their new identities. If there is no pressure to do so, they may never adopt them.

Ethnic Symbols

To lump others into ethnic groups—or to see oneself as part of an ethnic group—usually involves the selection of particular aspects of a culture as characteristics defining ethnic identity. For example, how people speak, what they eat, how they build their houses, and what they wear all serve as markers identifying members of a distinct ethnic group. Often there will be clusters of symbols, only some of which will be seen as essential for defining identity. This is especially true when physical differences exist between populations. In the southern United States, for example, it is possible to list numerous traits associated with the black population, although few of these are universal. The essential characteristic is that of skin color.

The significance of ethnic symbols may vary a great deal from one group to another and even among members of a single ethnic group. Not all whites in the southern United States have the same views about black ethnic identity, and their ideas will not correspond entirely with the blacks' own views. Also, while poorer blacks may view certain foods and patterns of behavior toward kin as part of being black, upwardly mobile blacks may not. Indeed, the latter may wish to identify more with the dominant white culture and thus may assume characteristics identified with that culture. To some extent, use of ethnic symbols will depend on a person's strategy in a particular situation. Identification with the characteristics of the dominant culture is part of the process of **acculturation,** whereby members of one culture adapt aspects of another culture as a result of culture contact and incorporation into a larger system.

The evolution of ethnic symbolism is related to efforts to define ethnic groups in relation to one another. Defining groups becomes especially important under conditions of national integration— the incorporation of groups of people at one time relatively autonomous and distinct into an encompassing state structure. For example, when the Kekchi- and Mopan-speaking Maya, who today occupy the southern part of Belize, moved into the area from Guatemala during the latter part of the nineteenth and early twentieth centuries, they had little contact with members of other ethnic groups in Belize—Garifuna, Creoles, whites, Chinese, and others. Since World War II this situation has changed markedly, as the Kekchi and Mopan progressively have been integrated into the multiethnic Belizean society (Howard 1980). As a result, they have had to consciously define their ethnic identity—to develop an idealized picture of what it means to be a Mopan or Kekchi Maya. They have also developed conscious ideas about what it means to be a member of one of the other ethnic groups. These images, known as "basic value orientations" (Barth 1969:14), include the Maya's view of themselves as hard-working and honest in contrast with "lazy" Creoles and Garifuna and "crafty and dishonest" East Indians and Chinese. Among the values of the Maya were those emphasizing sociocultural homogeneity, playing down differences among themselves.

Out of this general picture of what it is to be a Maya, the Mopan and Kekchi selected specific symbols to characterize their identity. The symbols chosen were items, institutions, or practices that they perceived as central to their life-style and to the social fabric of their communities. These included growing maize and black beans, practicing reciprocal labor exchange, wearing certain kinds of clothes, and eating certain foods. The thatched hut emerged as a particularly important symbol of Maya identity, in contrast with the corrugated-metal-roofed houses of board or brick common among non-Maya. Construction of a thatched house traditionally has involved reciprocal labor exchange and the use of local forest products, whereas corrugated-metal-roofed houses are built by paid laborers and require the purchase of externally produced building materials. When constructed by individual Maya for their own use, the latter type of house came to be seen by other members of the community as a means of flaunting one's wealth and social superiority. As a result, those who built such houses were stigmatized by other Maya.

In the face of the rapid change in southern Belize in recent years, the use of ethnic symbols by the Maya has changed. Dress, for example, now almost never serves as an ethnic marker, for the men no longer wear distinctive clothing, and fewer and fewer women have the inclination or can afford to wear the traditional clothes.

A limited range of ethnic symbols is often important to members of ethnic groups living away from their homeland. This can be seen in the case of overseas Scots and their wearing of kilts and playing of bagpipes. The Scottish kilt, which was banned after the Battle of Culloden in 1746 as part of the repression of local Gaelic culture, was revived in the nineteenth century by Walter Scott and other romantics who promoted it as a symbol of Scottish patriotism. In the process it was changed from a single piece of cloth worn around the waist and over the shoulder to the skirt form in which it is worn today. The nineteenth century style kilt went out of fashion in Scotland when it was mocked by other nationalists as a substitute for a true struggle for power, but continued to be popular among overseas Scots wishing to retain some symbol of their ethnic identity. Until recently, kilt makers sold more kilts to overseas customers than to local ones—a situation that has begun to change as the domestic market has grown with the revival of Scottish nationalism in recent years.

Ethnicity and Religion

Religious differences are often an important part of contrasting ethnic identities. Lowland peoples of South and Southeast Asia, for instance, over the centuries were converted from more localized animistic religions to major religions such as Hinduism, Buddhism, and Islam as a result of conquest, trade, and their appeal to local elites. The more isolated highland peoples, however, tended to retain their animistic beliefs, that is, beliefs in the existence of spirits that dwell in nature. Religious differences between highland and lowland peoples were among the things commonly viewed as setting these peoples apart. Later, during the nineteenth and early twentieth centuries, under the influence of European colonial policy that gave Christian missionaries a role in extending colonial authority to these upland peoples, members of these tribes, such as the Nagas of eastern India, the Karen of Burma, and the Toraja of Indonesia, converted to Christianity. The Christianity of these tribal peoples was often modified by local beliefs and made an integral part of these people's lives and of their ethnic identity. After independence, such religious differences continued to set these people apart from the national non-Christian majorities.

Religion, ethnicity, and politics can become a very potent mix. The spread of Islam across southern Asia, northern Africa, and into the corners of Europe resulted not only in countries where today the majority of the people are Muslim, but also in instances where Muslims constitute significant ethnic minorities. This is seen dramatically in the case of the former Yugoslavia, where the spread and later collapse of the Ottoman empire left in its wake a Muslim minority amid a largely Christian population that has found itself at odds with various Christian groups anxious to create ethnically based states. Islam spread through island Southeast Asia as well, and at present the majority of people in Malaysia and Indonesia are Muslim. In addition, the neighboring states of Thailand and the Philippines have Muslim minorities on their southern borders who are viewed as distinct ethnic groups and who have had a history of difficult relations with the respective Buddhist and Christian majorities. Both countries have witnessed armed rebellions among their Muslim minorities that advocated separation from the encompassing states. In the case of the Philippines, after decades of violent confrontations a political compromise was reached in the 1980s allowing for the creation of an autonomous region in areas with a Muslim majority.

Ethnic Relations

Ethnic identity is primarily a product of interaction among members of social groups who perceive themselves to be different. While it may be of little importance to members of small-scale societies who rarely interact with members of other societies, for those living in large-scale societies it is often very significant. Especially in urban areas, a person is likely to encounter people of different ethnic identities at work, while shopping, or in the course of other daily activities. Whether we-they distinctions arise depends on factors that promote either **boundary maintenance**—the process by which ethnic distinctiveness is maintained—or **assimilation**—the process by which cultural distinctions between ethnic groups are minimized or eliminated. These factors include marriage patterns, patterns of occupational specialization, demographic characteristics, and politics.

MARRIAGE PATTERNS. Marriage within an ethnic group maintains ethnic boundaries because it enhances group homogeneity (and

Marriage across ethnic boundaries may promote assimiliation or create new ethnic groups. Shown here after their marriage, Michael Jackson and Lisa Maria Presley exit a children's hospital in Budapest, where they distributed toys and other goods.

hence, indirectly, group distinctiveness). By contrast, marriage across ethnic boundaries *may* promote assimilation. For example, faced with a shortage of women in the 1960s, the Tapirapé of central Brazil began to intermarry with the neighboring Carajá speeding up the loss of a distinctive culture by the Tapirapé (Shapiro 1968). Young Tapirapé males who marry Carajá women form important social bonds with their Carajá in-laws by joining them as commercial fishers and ceasing to live as Tapirapé agriculturalists. Both Tapirapé and Carajá nevertheless remain part of an encompassing ethnic category—Indian—that distinguishes them from non-Indian Brazilians.

Rather than assimilating one group into another, marriage between members of different ethnic groups may lead to the creation of new ethnic groups. In colonial Mexico, for example, there were 16 ethnic categories that were generated from only a few initial groups—Spanish, Indian, and African (categories themselves representing a synthesis of an earlier plethora of ethnic divisions)—as a result of *miscegenation*.

OCCUPATIONAL SPECIALIZATION OR COMPETITION.   Within multiethnic settings occupational specialization often is a feature of ethnic groups, playing a significant role in the maintenance of ethnic distinctiveness. Although this specialization may promote interdependency between ethnic groups, relations between the groups are not necessarily harmonious or egalitarian. For example, the nomadic Baluchi pastoralists of southern Iran and Pakistan historically have dominated other non-nomadic ethnic groups who share the same territory. Many non-Baluchi agriculturists farm as sharecroppers on land owned by the Baluchi.

Members of different ethnic groups may compete for jobs. When people from rural areas move to the city, they often seek assistance from members of their ethnic group who live in the city. The central figure in Nigerian novelist Chinua Achebe's *No Longer at Ease* is supported while at school in England and assisted in getting a job upon his return home by members of a voluntary association of his tribespeople. In his study of the Liberian city of Monrovia, Fraenkel (1964) described how tribal-based voluntary associations function to exploit and maintain a monopoly over particular occupations.

DEMOGRAPHY.   **Demography,** or population characteristics such as birth rate and geographical distribution, also influences ethnic relations. For example, rapid population growth among members of a particular group may put

pressure on them to expand their place in a society at the expense of another group. Conversely, a group's rapid loss of population may invite others to exploit a perceived advantage. Greater numbers do not always mean greater power, however. Tension may be created when relatively small ethnic minorities are able to dominate the politics and economy of an area at the expense of much larger groups. South Africa serves as a prime example, where some four million whites dominate around 20 million blacks and two million people categorized as "colored" (mixed). On the other hand, when larger groups do gain economic and political ascendancy, and when their interests and those of the smaller groups conflict, they may feel little compunction about oppressing ethnic minorities.

POLITICS.   Ethnic relations influence political activities and are also affected by them. To the extent that people's use of ethnicity is related to their desire to enhance their position, ethnicity may be seen as inherently political. The Saami of Norway, by choosing which language to employ in multiethnic settings (see Chapter 3), and ethnic associations in Monrovia which seek to monopolize occupations, are at least indirectly acting politically. The political role of ethnicity often is even more direct; in many settings, ethnicity is central to political dialogue. This is especially true in postcolonial societies where diverse peoples were brought together under colonial rule. In Fiji, for example, ethnic differences between the descendants of Indian immigrants and the indigenous population, each making up roughly half of the population, have provided a focal point for political competition for many years (see Howard 1991a). In settings such as this, ethnicity overrides or obscures other differences, such as those associated with social class.

In South Africa, during the early part of this century the Afrikaaner minority (descendants of early Dutch settlers) found themselves progressively losing out to the English community. To reverse this trend, the Afrikaaners sought to build an alliance among white South Africans based on race and promoted policies aimed at curtailing the rights of nonwhites. In particular, they sought to restrict land ownership and to relegate nonwhites to the role of servile laborers. By 1948, through an alliance with some whites of English origin, the Afrikaaners assumed control of the government. Through the 1950 Suppression of Communism Act, supported by a wide spectrum of the white population during a wave of anticommunist hysteria, they suppressed any organization or individual opposed to them or their policies. At this time, the Afrikaaners also began to enforce the apartheid policies of ethnic separation and domination (brought to an end in 1993), and their political success was translated into greater economic prosperity for the white community as a whole.

International Tribes: Ethnicity and World Commerce

Not only has ethnicity not disappeared around the world as countries become more industrialized, but ethnicity has played a critical role in the rise of some ethnic groups to prominence in today's international commerce. Ethnic identity and the revitalization of old ethnic ties resulting from the end of the Cold War have been powerful forces in contemporary global business. Joel Kotkin (1993) has shown how, just as in the past certain ethnic groups have dominated commerce, today certain groups have achieved unusual success in the world economy. He argues that five geographically dispersed groups are notable for displaying certain characteristics that have made them what he calls "global tribes." These five groups, while not the only groups today who have crossed national borders with both economic and cultural effect, are the Jews, the British (and their progeny in North America), the Japanese, the Chinese, and the Asian Indians.

Even with their different histories and cultures, these groups share the following principal characteristics, as defined by Kotkin:

1. A strong sense of ethnic identity and interdependence.

2. The creation of a global network based on mutual trust and other cultural values that serve as adaptive strategies in the world economy.

3. An emphasis on technical and scientific knowledge combined with an open-mindedness that promotes scientific and cultural development necessary for succeeding in the late twentieth century global economy.

Keep in mind that each of these groups possesses all of these characteristics. For our purposes, however, in the following discussion based largely on Kotkin, we can look briefly at three of the groups to illustrate one of the above three characteristics.

The Jews are the oldest of global tribes. Long possessing a historical sense of uniqueness, they provide a good example of the first characteristic. Their biblical legacy, including a descent myth that begins with the story of Abraham, combined with a millennium of experience with hostile neighbors in many different countries, has sustained among them a strong sense of ethnic identity. Having been itinerant traders for generations, without a land to return to, Jews developed a strong sense of dependence among themselves and a willingness to learn from others and adapt. A tradition of self-help—seen, for example, in the United States in the early part of this century when they created more than 500 benevolent societies to provide Jewish immigrants with such assistance as insurance, burial plots, and summer camps for children—has been a significant adaptation in their group survival.

The adaptations of Jews as an ethnic group also allowed them to emerge as skilled entrepreneurs and innovators. Today still, their ethnic awareness serves them in a highly competitive world economy where a sense of belonging remains a social and economic asset.

The Japanese, too, have a strong sense of ethnic identity, but they also illustrate the related creation of a global network of trust. Kotkin describes the Japanese diaspora as one by design: commercial and demographic necessities have led them to disperse. Since the late nineteenth century, when Japan first rose as a modern nation, the Japanese have become like a single world city stretching from Bangladesh to London where they have developed practical skills of overseas survival.

This Japanese global dispersion is now linked by banks, trading companies, media, and special schools that teach their young people the Japanese spirit. Like other Asians overseas, the Japanese are not culturally isolated, but in most major world cities have access to Asian-language broadcasts, newspapers, and shops that sell, for example, videotapes in Japanese. Among the other institutions the Japanese have created abroad that allow them to work together outside their national borders are hotels or spas where they stay, golf courses owned by their countrymen, and a widespread network of Buddhist temples.

For all their cosmopolitanism, the Japanese, however, also illustrate the provincialism that characterizes all the global tribes. In some ways, in fact, they are one of the most insular of the global tribes. Having been very successful at developing a network of mutual trust among themselves, they also stand out for their failure to accommodate non-Japanese within their cultural network and economic development strategies. Racism, of course, exists among the other groups, too, but other countries have not had the centuries of isolationist history that promoted an especially strong sense of ethnic superiority among the Japanese. Related to this, as Fernandez (1993) has pointed out, Japan has resisted becoming proactive in minority and immigrant rights as, in comparison, the United States has. Although there have been many problems with diversity in American society and business, the United States, because of its extensive experience with immigrants and minorities, may be better positioned to embrace diversity in competing as a global economic power (Fernandez 1993).

Finally, the British and the British empire, as Kotkin makes clear, have been a particularly powerful force in shaping the modern world. Like the Jews, the British have been adaptable and open to learning from other cultures. From the eighteenth through the middle of the twentieth century, the United Kingdom and the United States have been foremost in giving the world the primary inventions associated with industrialization. The British diaspora, especially in the United States, has been behind not only the essential scientific and technological standards of the contemporary world economy, but also those of language, political economy, and business practice. The ascendant Asian groups—notably the Japanese, Chinese, and Asian Indians—have been served by the technological and commercial paths laid down by the Anglo-Americans.

The more successful of the global tribes have shunned politics out of choice or because it was prohibited. Not the nation state, but increasingly the more cosmopolitan mechanism of the transnational corporation or financial conglomerate, for example, has become their medium of expression. In fact, these groups flourish in an increasingly denationalized and demilitarized world economy. Kotkin quotes one Tokyo executive who, in reference to this evolution of the global economy, said that with such changes someday "there will be no Japan, only Japanese" (1993: 12). The same might be said for the other international tribes.

< SOCIAL STRATIFICATION >

As the South African example illustrates, ethnicity can be closely linked to economic and political inequality. The Afrikaaners used ethnicity as a means of attaining power and of defining the relative socioeconomic statuses of groups of people, assigning nonwhites lower statuses than whites. Ethnicity is not the only basis for inequality in South Africa, however, and even among whites there is a great deal of inequality in terms of wealth and power. Virtually all societies have developed some degree of inequality through the process of **social stratification**–the division of members of a society into *strata* (or levels) with unequal wealth, prestige, and power.

Increasing social scale, productive capacity, and specialization of labor all increase the potential for stratification. In small-scale foraging and farming societies there is little specialization and a relatively small food surplus to appropriate. Accordingly, differences in wealth and power in these societies are limited. In contrast, more intensive forms of agricultural and industrial production, and attendant increases in social scale and division of labor, result in far more potential for inequality.

Beliefs Supporting Stratification

Systems of social stratification are accompanied by beliefs that obscure or legitimate inequality. These beliefs maintain the existing system of stratification by drawing attention away from threatening areas and emphasizing common bonds or interests. Widespread adherence to egalitarian ideals in the United States, for example, has obscured perceptions of inequality and the existence of a ruling class wielding a great deal of power. Such a ruling class comprises a small group that dominates the wealth of a country and holds considerable political power. In addition to sharing economic and political interests, the group has a high degree of social and cultural unity. Writing of the wealthy amilies that he argues make up the core of the ruling class in the United States, for example, G. William Domhoff (1974: 86) notes that they "are part of interlocking social circles which perceive each other as equals, belong to the same clubs, interact frequently, and freely intermarry." In some societies differences between

social strata are promoted as part of the natural order of things: Louis XIV of France said he ruled by the will of God, and the Nazis in Germany sought to rule as representatives of a supposedly superior race. In feudal societies, those on top view the world as hierarchically ordered and consider themselves part of a "natural" aristocracy; the peasants are encouraged to accept their position likewise as part of a natural order.

Ideologies supporting systems of stratification also are linked to notions of exchange. In all societies, those who have less wealth and power are taught to think that they are getting something in return that justifies existing differences. Aboriginal women give up a portion of the food they gather to men, who in turn perform rituals to ensure the survival of the world. The serf in medieval Europe gave a large part of his crop to his lord for protection.

Conflict Versus Stability

The potential for conflict exists in all stratified systems. As long as members of a society feel that the exchange is fair and as long as belief in the supportive ideology is maintained, a degree of stability is possible. If a particular segment of society becomes dissatisfied with the arrangement, however, it may seek to change things. The likelihood of this happening in small-scale societies is minimal. Inequalities are not as glaring as in large-scale societies, pressure to conform is strong, and few alternative views are available. The differences between strata in large-scale societies are much greater and tensions are more pronounced. Also, the increased heterogeneity in experience, socialization patterns, and views of those in large-scale societies increases the likelihood of conflict. While fundamental changes in systems of stratification in large-scale societies are rare, tensions as expressed in riots, protests, and rebellions can lead to reforms and gradual changes.

Adherence to an existing system of stratification is associated with the stability of a people's overall adaptation. Should the essential features of their adaptation begin to change, the traditional system of stratification will be threatened. The rise of the modern world system, the Industrial Revolution, increased population, and a number of other factors combined in the late eighteenth and early nineteenth centuries to undermine the aristocratic hierarchy that prevailed in Europe, replacing it with a system of stratification linked to capitalist production. Thus, as adaptive and economic patterns evolve, so do the ways in which the members of a society are stratified. (See "Focus on Anthropologists.")

◄ SYSTEMS OF STRATIFICATION ►

While stratification is found in all societies, the forms it takes differ both in degree and in kind. In egalitarian societies, stratification is minimal. In nonegalitarian societies, people differ with respect to *wealth, prestige,* and *power* (components of stratification that are not necessarily correlated) according to systems of hierarchical ranking, caste, feudalism, or class.

Egalitarian Societies

The least stratified of societies are known as egalitarian because people tend to treat each other as equals. **Egalitarian societies** are characterized by few individual or group differences with respect to wealth and power. Many foraging and small-scale agricultural societies are relatively egalitarian. Norms in these societies emphasize sharing and ideals of interpersonal equality. This is not to say that social stratification is nonexistent in these societies. Although the Copper Eskimo of northwestern Canada traditionally emphasized equality, for example, they were not blind to the existence of differences. Some individuals were held in high esteem for personal qualities such as hunt-

ing or spiritual abilities; the *ataniq* organized hunts; and shamans (those in direct contact with the spirit world) were sometimes feared because of their ties to the gods (Damas 1972). Similarly, the Mardudjara-speaking Aborigines of Australia are stratified according to gender and age, and individuals can attain high status as curers or "law-men" (those responsible for maintenance of traditional rules and rituals). In comparison with nonegalitarian societies, however, such differences are insignificant.

The egalitarianism of small-scale societies frequently is undermined by contact with more hierarchically inclined societies. As a result of contact with Indian Hindu society, the Bihors (foragers of the Chota Nagpur plateau of central India) have come to possess an array of officials—headmen, priests, curers, conveners of meetings, and so forth—all of whom occupy higher positions than other members of Bihor society (Sinha 1972). Often this transformation from egalitarian to nonegalitarian society is part of colonial expansion. White settlers in southwestern Australia made changes among the Aborigines to ease administration of these conquered people: they created "kings" and gave them brass plaques to wear around their necks to signify their status (Howard 1981).

The egalitarian ideal does not necessarily disappear in large-scale societies. A degree of economic and social equality may be maintained within segments of the larger society. The egalitarian norm tends to be most pronounced among those occupying the lower socioeconomic strata of large-scale societies—peasants, industrial workers, and pastoral laborers. Among peasants, egalitarian beliefs find expression in a worldview termed the "image of the limited good" (Foster 1965). Those who hold this view believe that a limited amount of wealth is available; by gaining more than one's share of this wealth one deprives someone else. This is not to say that all peasants within a village will, in fact, have equal resources or the same social status. Those who do have more, however, are careful

^^^^^

An Inuit shaman in Point Hope, Alaska, chants a song for good luck in hunting whales. The bones in the background are whale ribs; the drum is made from sealskin. Although part of an egalitarian society, shamans are accorded more respect than others because they are believed to be connected with the gods.

not to flaunt what they have; moreover, they are expected to share some of their surplus with others.

Since the eighteenth century, individuals and groups in a number of industrial societies have adopted ideologies proclaiming social equality as their goal. These ideologies include various forms of communist, socialist, anarchist, and utopian thought. Their theories have been put into practice in communes, cities, and nations with varying degrees of success.

Rank Societies

In contrast to egalitarian societies, many societies divide people into hierarchically ordered groups that differ in status and perhaps in occupation and wealth. Often this hierarchy is ac-

cepted fatalistically by those in the lower as well as in the upper strata as being part of the natural order.

Members of **rank societies** differ in prestige according to a series of graded ranks. In ancient Panama, for instance, high chiefs ruled a number of villages. The high chiefs were respected, traveled by litter, had the sole right to wear many fine ornaments, possessed large and well-provisioned households, and were given elaborate funerals that included the sacrifice of servants. Below the high chiefs were others of high rank: aristocrats who served as administrators; warriors who served under the aristocrats, controlling villages; and a lesser group of commoners who had achieved social advancement for their own lifetime for prowess in battle. Under the elite were the rest of the commoners, primarily farmers who provided

MARK MOBERG

FOCUS ON ANTHROPOLOGISTS

Mark Moberg holds a Ph.D. in cultural anthropology from the University of California, Los Angeles, and is an assistant professor of anthropology at the University of South Alabama in Mobile. Since 1985 he has also conducted research on development and local-level politics in southern Belize, Central America. His current research examines immigration and ethnic conflict in that country's commercial banana industry.

∧∧∧∧∧∧∧∧

Development and Stratification in a Garifuna Village in Belize

In late 1985, I arrived in Hopkins, Belize, to begin research on the role of agricultural cooperatives in rural development. Hopkins is an idyllic Garifuna village of some 1,000 residents on the Caribbean coast of southern Belize. The surrounding hinterland of Stann Creek district is a sparsely populated region where rural residents formerly made their living from subsistence agriculture and wage labor. Although some citrus fruit was grown for export as early as the 1920s, not until nearly a half-century later did the region become heavily involved in world markets for the crop. By the late 1960s two local factories began producing orange and grapefruit juice concentrate for export.

Attracted by new cash-earning opportunities, many Stann Creek farmers were soon planting citrus trees to fulfill the factories' demand for produce.

In the 1970s and 1980s what had once been a moderately profitable strategy for small farmers underwent dramatic growth. As consumption patterns in the developed countries shifted toward "healthier" eating habits, orange and grapefruit juice consumption soared in the United States and elsewhere. In Belize, these world market trends resulted in rising producer prices for citrus, which soon became far more profitable than traditional crops such as rice and corn.

For all the enticements of citrus production, small farmers in Hopkins were frustrated by its high costs. Because of their heavy reliance on fertilizers, agrochemicals, and machinery, citrus farmers face major expenses in establishing their groves (known locally as citrus "walks") and keeping the trees

free of pests and undergrowth. More than five years elapse between the time trees are planted and the time of their first commercial crop. During this period a farmer could expect to spend about $750 per acre in establishing a citrus walk. Thereafter, annual maintenance costs range between $200 and $250 per acre. In Hopkins, where the average household income above subsistence needs was only about $500 in 1985, few farmers could afford to establish citrus walks. As a result most were confined to traditional crops that cost little to produce but yielded poor returns when sold.

Enter the Hopkins cooperative, part of the focus of my study. In the 1970s agencies from the United States, Canada, and Great Britain began providing direct development aid to "grassroots" organizations of the rural poor in many parts of Central America, including Belize. Development policymakers viewed cooperatives, credit unions, and cottage industries as sources of livelihood and economic growth that would benefit the poorest citizens of developing countries. For their part, many Belizeans reacted to the availability of such funds by flocking to established cooperatives and forming new ones of their own. While many of these ventures have been unsuccessful, in part because development grants were spent on personal consumption, others have created dramatic new income opportunities for their members.

Viewing development aid as a way to overcome their limited resources, 21 villagers chartered the Hopkins Farmers' Cooperative Society Ltd. in 1983. Shortly thereafter they submitted grant proposals to several "grassroots" development agencies in the United States and Canada. One such proposal was funded, establishing a rotating credit fund that would enable co-op members to plant citrus trees on their farms. Farmers purchased seedlings, fertilizer, herbicides, and other inputs from the cooperative on credit, and were not required to begin repaying their loans until their first citrus crops were sold to the processing factories. By 1986, each member had about five acres of citrus trees, and by 1988, the first oranges were being sold to the processing plants.

Anthropologists have studied the effects of agricultural development on the rural poor in

Members of the Hopkins Farmers' Cooperative work together in clearing new farms. The residents of Hopkins continue to describe the divisions among them in terms of political affiliation rather than class, though lasting economic disparities have replaced what were once merely political labels.

many parts of the world. While policymakers herald the "modernization" of agriculture as a means of promoting development, anthropological studies demonstrate that novel crops and agricultural technologies often have unexpected adverse effects for the rural poor, including increasing disparities of wealth and further impoverishment for the poorest farmers.

I was attracted to Hopkins in part because of the prominent role that a cooperative made up of small farmers had taken in the process of agricultural change. Initially, I hypothesized that by channeling development aid directly to the poor, the cooperative would allow Hopkins residents, regardless of income, the opportunity to invest in commercial agriculture. As a result,

I anticipated that Hopkins would avert some of the social stratification associated with citrus production in other areas of Stann Creek district. What I failed to anticipate was the social and political context in which the cooperative operated, which, in fact, prevented the benefits of the grant from being evenly distributed throughout the community.

While Hopkins was a relatively egalitarian village until the advent of citrus farming, it was by no means free of divisions among its residents. In recent years, Hopkins has been heavily targeted by outside politicians seeking support from the rural electorate. As the largest village in rural Stann Creek district and the largest Garifuna settlement in the country, Hopkins has become critical to the careers of aspiring national office holders. Politicians have sought such support by awarding local voters with patronage, such as jobs on work projects, land titles, and other official favor. As a consequence of such intense political campaigning, residents of Hopkins have been polarized into two feuding factions affiliated with national political parties—the People's United Party (P.U.P.) and the United Democratic Party (U.D.P.). Each faction operates as a cohesive bloc, seeking benefits for its members and control of the village council, the local governing body that channels resources from the national government to the community.

Although violence rarely occurs between members of the two groups, strong political sentiments make for often argumentative relations across factional lines. One resident described the effects of such factionalism on community social relations: "Some years aback we was all brothers and sisters here. Now you want to kill your best bally [friend] for what the politicians them promise you. They break they promise, but we have to live with the poison they spread."

I became aware of these factions in the course of studying the cooperative. Several weeks after arriving in the village, a prominent local foe of the cooperative had reported me to the district police as a "communist

alien," apparently because of my visible association with cooperative members. Later, one of the farmers confided that he had initially feared I was a CIA agent sent by the national government (then under U.D.P. control) to break up the cooperative. Months passed before I was able to dispel such rumors about my activities, and I was forced to distance myself somewhat from the cooperative in order to build rapport with nonmembers. From the rumors that circulated concerning my affiliation and objectives in the village, it had become clear that the cooperative was a primary arena for local factional infighting.

When the Hopkins cooperative was formed in 1983, it was open to all members of the village, but many viewed it from the first as a P.U.P. organization since this was the affiliation of the organizer and most of its members. The few U.D.P. members who initially joined later dropped out, citing hostility from other members and an inability to work with them. Others who applied for membership out of interest in adopting citrus had their requests denied. In the factionalized community setting, U.D.P. residents claim that they have been refused membership because of their party affiliation.

Meanwhile, major economic benefits have steadily accrued to cooperative members as their citrus trees matured. Because of citrus sales, cooperative mem-

bers by 1989 were earning approximately twice the average farm income of nonmembers. More recent world market trends indicate that Hopkins' path to development through export production may be less promising in the long term. Much as Hopkins farmers reacted to high producer prices by planting citrus trees, so did their counterparts throughout Latin America. In 1992 a glut of citrus products on the world market forced producer prices in Belize to their lowest point in 15 years. These trends may limit the extent of stratification between citrus growers and traditional farmers in Hopkins, but they also point to the perils of basing development on the needs of an often volatile world market.

Policymakers continue to see cooperatives as a way of bringing development aid to the rural poor. The case of Hopkins illustrates, however, that development always takes place within the context of village politics, as well as markets over which the rural poor have little control. Even an economically egalitarian community has subtle divisions that may become the basis of stratification. The residents of Hopkins continue to describe the divisions in their midst in terms of political affiliation rather than class. Residents on both sides of Hopkins' political boundaries recognize, however, that lasting economic disparities have replaced what were once merely political labels.

services for those above them—fishing for the elite, planting their crops, fighting for them, and building their houses. The lowest stratum consisted of slaves, who were captives of war (Helms 1976).

In a rank society, those of higher rank tend to be wealthier, to live in better houses, and generally to live a more comfortable life than those of lower rank, who provide them with goods and services. In exchange for this support, the higher-ranking members undertake public services and sometimes are expected to redistribute some of their wealth through feasts and religious ceremonies.

Kinship is an important criterion in determining status in rank societies. Individuals generally are born into a particular stratum, and often there are ranked kin groups. Upward mobility is sometimes possible for individuals who show exceptional aptitude in warfare or religion. Religion plays an important role in many rank societies. Priests are afforded high status, and the elite justify their special position on the basis of religion.

Historically, the formation of rank societies was associated with intensification of production by farming communities and, in some instances, by foraging societies (such as the Kwakiutl of western Canada). This increased productive capability allowed for greater specialization, increased organizational complexity, and greater population density.

Rank societies consisted of confederations or a number of centrally administered villages; thus, they can be associated with the transition from small-scale societies to large-scale societies. Warfare and competition among rival elites often played an important role in the expansion and development of rank societies (and in their subsequent transition into larger sociopolitical units, such as empires or states). Sometimes, the development of rank societies was stimulated by contact and trade with larger societies.

European colonial expansion destroyed or enveloped many rank societies. In western Panama, members of rank societies who were not slaugh-

Before the arrival of Europeans, Fijians had a ranking system consisting of commoners and chiefly families. Although the introduction of a European colonial administration in the nineteenth century changed Fijian society, today the traditional system of stratification is still seen in the continued influence of chiefly families. Here Ratu Mara, of an old chiefly family, and at the time of this photo prime minister of Fiji, plays golf.

tered by the Spanish in the sixteenth century, or killed by diseases introduced by them, fled into the mountains or were incorporated into the Spanish colonial state. Eastern Panama was out of the main thrust of Spanish conquest and colonization. The indigenous people, the San Blas Cuna, though they suffered some disruption, were able to adjust more gradually.

The creation of the modern world–system has not put an end to all systems of stratification based on rank. In some parts of the world, traditional systems of rank remain a significant part of contemporary patterns of stratification. Indigenous ranking systems were often employed by European colonial powers to establish control over populations through a pattern known as **indirect rule,** whereby ranking individuals in the native population assisted foreign colonial authorities administer those under their charge. This was the case in Fiji (see Howard 1991a), where the chiefs held a variety of posts under the British from the 1870s until independence in 1970. After independence, the highest-ranking chiefs were able to assume dominance in the new government, holding such posts as prime minister and governor general and forming a body known as the Great Council of Chiefs, which was granted important powers under the constitution. The Fijian state today is very different from the warring chiefdoms of the early nineteenth century, but the traditional system of ranking does continue to exert an influence on contemporary Fijian politics.

Caste Societies

Rank societies are divided primarily horizontally, with only limited differentiation found within strata, especially at the lower levels. In some parts of the world, however, as social stratification (and along with it, the division of labor) became more complex, societies developed the practice of dividing individuals at birth into one of a number of occupationally specific, largely endogamous (individuals marry within the group), and hierarchically ordered groups known as **castes.** Caste systems are elaborations of rank systems. Perhaps the most comprehensive and striking example of a caste system is found in India. Other examples are provided by preindustrial Japan and by several precolonial societies in northern Africa.

The Indian caste system probably evolved in northern India more than 2,000 years ago out of

In a caste system, individuals are divided at birth into closed, occupationally specific groups. These groups are stratified. Members of the lowest group, the untouchable caste, are considered to be unclean and perform work regarded as polluting.

a blending of the indigenous Harappan civilization of chiefdoms unified by a priesthood and the nomadic Aryan tribes that invaded northwestern India around 1500 B.C. Hindu religion and culture and the related caste system developed out of the mixing of these two peoples and the emergence of larger, more hierarchical, and urbanized societies.

Hindu religious beliefs rationalize and stabilize the caste system. It divides society into four categories of caste, called *varna,* on the basis of occupation. The varna are ranked according to their relative purity—the extent to which their members are considered in a sacred sense to be clean or unclean. The highest varna is occupied by Brahmins—priests and scholars, who are held to be the purest. Below the Brahmins in descending order of status and purity are the Kshatriyas, or warrior castes; the Vaisha, or merchant castes; and the Shudras, or castes of artisans and menial workers. A fifth group, occupying a position below the four varna, consist of Harijans (or untouchables), who perform work held to be too polluting for others. According to Hindu belief, the varna into which a person is born reflects the quality of his or her actions in a previous life.

Hindu beliefs also provide guidelines for the behavior of caste members. Higher-caste persons will not accept food or drink from the polluted hands of those belonging to a lower caste. Likewise, in the past there were proscriptions against having sexual relations with or marrying members of lower castes. Also, higher-caste members are expected to avoid consuming polluting substances, such as meat or alcohol. While members of all castes are supposed to try to live up to many of the Hindu ideals of behavior, those of the higher castes are expected to come closest to ideal behavior.

Previously, Indian castes functioned within rather narrow localities—a village, or at most, a few linked villages. Within this setting, the population would be divided into a series of exclusive castes numbering from a few to 20 or more, called *jati,* ranked according to their place within the varna hierarchy (the relative ranking often being subject to dispute among the jati). These were the most important focal points of caste identity. Each local caste or jati formed a closed, endogamous descent group with an occupational specialization that it offered in exchange for the products and services of other castes. Each caste group usually lived within its own quarter; untouchables lived either on the fringes of villages or in a separate hamlet altogether. Often a dominant family or caste controlled the arable land and monopolized the use of physical force.

In northern India, relations between higher and lower castes often took the form of *jajmani* relationships—patron-client relationships between families of different castes. The jajmani system served as a means of economic exchange within village settings, both reflecting and helping to maintain the relative inequality of castes. Especially important was the giving of grain by members of the dominant castes to families in exchange for services.

The Indian caste system often is presented as highly static—as an unchanging social structure in which a person's status and occupation are determined at birth. This is certainly not true in independent India, nor was it entirely true prior to or during British colonial rule. The British, for example, brought about significant changes in the caste system to better suit their own administrative and economic needs. They promoted classes of people who owned land privately to higher-caste statuses, in part as a means of increasing revenues from taxes. The advancement of this group of people led to widespread debt peonage and encouraged migration to towns and plantations (and later overseas) in search of wage employment, causing further disruptions to the caste system. There are also many instances of castes seeking to enhance their status within the caste system, especially among elites within a particular caste. This was the case with the rajabanshi caste movement in north Bengal (1910–1947), in which elite members of this caste sought to attain kshatriya status by gaining greater representation in public offices. Significantly, while elites of this caste were striving for upward mobility, communists in 1946 sought support from poorer members of the same caste, who were mainly sharecroppers, in their efforts to challenge the caste structure (Swaraj Basu, cited in Bhowmik 1992: 1247).

India became independent in 1948, and the decades that followed have seen further changes in the caste system as a result of urbanization, industrialization, political reforms, and other factors. New employment opportunities in the industrial and service sectors and increased education also have undermined caste-imposed limits on economic advancement.

Nevertheless, caste remains important in India. Most Indians marry within their own jati, which serves to reinforce many other caste practices and values. Caste also plays a role in competition with relation to land, wealth, business, education, and politics. Social change and reforms in Indian society in recent years have sometimes exacerbated tensions between castes—at times spilling over into violence. In 1991, for example, upper-caste Indians in one community went on a rampage, torturing and killing dozens of Harijans, after a Harijan let his foot touch a Brahman—viewed as an insulting act of defilement. Since many of the police themselves were also from higher castes, no arrests were made. As members of localized castes have come into contact with those from similar castes in cities and towns and in new occupations, new castes have evolved—super-castes that fuse or incorporate the more specialized local castes. Nevertheless, caste now takes its place among many other factors, such as those associated with a modern class society, in shaping the pattern of social stratification in contemporary Indian society.

Slavery

Slavery refers to a form of labor that entails holding a person in servitude as property. While some nineteenth-century evolutionists associated slavery with a particular stage of evolution, in particular the emergence of the state, slavery has in fact existed in many different types of society and assumed many different characteristics. The slave status often is reserved for members of other societies or ethnic groups considered inferior to one's own, but, especially in large-scale societies, poorer members of one's own society may also become slaves. Despite differences in its importance, slavery is a dominant feature of stratification in certain societies.

Slavery was found in many rank societies, although it was rarely the dominant form of labor.

Slaves in such societies were usually employed to perform domestic chores and were recruited by raiding neighboring peoples. Slavery assumed far more importance in certain early states of the Mediterranean and Middle East, such as ancient Egypt and Athens. It was the dominant form of labor in these states and was closely associated with the rise of commodity production and of a merchant class. Writing on the early Mediterranean, Will Durant comments that "it is as difficult to begin a civilization without robbery as it is to maintain it without slaves" (1939: 10). In ancient Athens, while free citizens did some manual work, much of it was carried out by slaves whose ranks included unransomed prisoners of war, victims of slave raids, criminals, and infants rescued from exposure. The Athenians saw foreigners as natural slaves and even the poorest free citizen had a slave or two. In early states elsewhere, however, such as in China and Middle America, while forms of slavery existed, it was not of such great importance.

Slavery was also important to the economy of ancient Rome, whose armies brought home large numbers of slaves. During the latter years of the Roman Empire, however, the importance of slavery declined. The importance of slavery in Europe diminished even more under feudalism as serfdom increased (see the next section). But it did not completely disappear—there were still household slaves in England in the twelfth century; the Germans employed captured pagan Slavs as household slaves and sold them to the Muslims and Byzantium; and even the Popes of Rome used slaves on their estates, and generally approved of making slaves from those who were not Christians. While slavery was not the dominant form of labor in the Muslim states and empires of Asia and North Africa—in fact, Islamic law forbade the sale or enslavement of Muslims—slaves (many of them from Africa) were commonly used in domestic service and for other purposes.

Starting in 1593, European colonies in the New World began to rely heavily on slave labor shipped from Africa. Over a little more than two centuries around 11 million African slaves were brought to the New World (at least that many again did not survive the trip from Africa). Plantation economies such as those of Brazil, Cuba, Puerto Rico, and the American South can be characterized as slave-based, and their system of stratification centered on the master-slave relationship. The slave trade was outlawed by most European countries in the early nineteenth century, but some of the plantation economies of the New World continued to employ slave labor into the second half of the century.

Although outlawed universally today, slavery persists in many parts of the world in illegal factories, mining operations, plantations, and the like— the bulk of those employed in slave labor being children. The carpet industry of India and Pakistan has received considerable attention for employing children (between 75,000 and 300,000 in India) under harsh conditions described by critics as "semi-slavery" (Wagstyl 1992) or "the modern form of slavery that is bonded labour" (Satyarthi 1993).

Feudal Societies

Various agrarian societies, as they have increased in scale have evolved systems of social stratification that can be termed **feudal.** Within feudal societies, those who work the land differ from those who support themselves by appropriating some of the produce and labor of the agriculturalists. This division is reflected in the pattern of social stratification. In medieval Europe those who worked the land are often referred to as serfs or vassals, while the primary group appropriating their surplus are referred to as lords. The lord provided military protection and served as a patron for the serf. In return, the serf was expected to provide the lord with a substantial amount of his agricultural produce and to render numerous services. There is some degree of reciprocity in the lord-serf relationship and each had specified rights and duties regarding the other. But the relationship was not a balanced one—the lord clearly got the better end

Feudal society in Europe. Serfs, who tilled the fields, provided a large portion of their agricultural produce to the knights and ladies.

of the deal. In addition, there were individuals who provided services for the lord (such as court jesters, armorers, and domestic servants) who were supported out of the surplus appropriated by the lord. Another group that appropriated agricultural surplus was the clergy.

Feudalism is associated with the rise of chiefdoms or the breakdown of larger centralized political authority. In western Europe, feudalism emerged out of the chaos that ensued after the death of the emperor Charlemagne (A.D. 768 to A.D. 814). In India, China, and Japan, feudalism was linked to the rise and decline of various empires and the struggles for power among warlords. Feudal societies are prone to warfare and instability. It was partly out of a desire to secure protection and a degree of stability that relations between lord and vassal arose, because lords provided military protection to the farming population and assumed the rights of government.

With the rise of modern capitalist societies and the nation-state, feudalism has disappeared in many settings. Where it has survived, it has done so within the context of the modern world, and is therefore different in many ways from earlier forms. The modern feudal societies provide a large part of their product to external markets rather than being largely self-contained, as in the past. Thus, what is produced by these societies and the value that is placed on products depend more on external market conditions than on local needs.

In Latin America, feudal relations took hold where the authority of Spanish colonial or postindependence governments has been weak. The **hacienda** exemplifies feudalism in Latin America. In highland Peru, where this feudal system continues, there are three classes of persons: the landlord, or *hacendado*; the tenant-workers, called *colonos;* and the administrators or foremen hired by the hacendado (Long 1975: 268). While the hacendado has legal control of the land, it is the colono who works most of it. The colono pays for the use of the land in labor—working on the hacendado's land, working as a servant in his house, and periodically clearing roads and water channels and carrying out repairs around the hacienda. Performance of these services usually leaves the colono only enough time to satisfy basic subsistence requirements. Besides providing the colono with a small plot of land, the hacendado is expected to give small amounts of money for the work done on the hacienda, provide alcohol and cigarettes for those involved in collective work parties, provide pasturage for the workers' animals and access to firewood for cooking, and feed people working for the hacienda.

Modern feudal systems are unstable in the face of an expanding modern world system. For the elite owners of land, for example, there is the option of replacing feudal labor-intensive methods with more mechanized production, or replacing such a paternalistic system of labor with a more flexible system of wage employment. For the serf, there are also options. There is the possibility of moving to town or finding employment elsewhere. Also, most governments in recent years have sought to take a more active role in the affairs of those regions characterized by feudalism. The Peruvian government, for example, has sought to implement land reform and to exert greater control over agricultural production through administrators.

Modern Class Societies: Production, Wealth, and Class Consciousness

The development and spread of Western industrial capitalism has given rise to a fourth system of social stratification based on free labor and individual ownership of property. Strata in such societies are composed of **classes,** which are defined primarily in relation to the means of production. In this case, classes are defined in relation to the process of production within an industrial capitalist system.

Classes arose with the Neolithic revolution, associated with the development of farming and stock raising, and the rise of civilizations. The creation of agricultural surpluses supported nonagricultural classes, and leadership resided in a class of persons who could manage surpluses and coordinate activities within and between communities. Modern classes developed first in response to the growth of extensive trade within and beyond Europe largely between the fifteenth and seventeenth centuries, and then assumed greater importance with the rise of industrial production beginning in the early eighteenth century. The first period can be referred to as the era of mercantile capitalism and the second as industrial capitalism. During this time the system of stratification based on capitalist relations became established and then consolidated.

Class distinctions arose in particular between those who controlled commerce and owned factories on the one hand and those who provided productive labor in return for wages on the other. Modern classes have accompanied the diffusion of industrial production from Western Europe and North America to the rest of the world over the past two centuries.

Membership in a class is determined by the means by which people acquire wealth rather than by wealth per se. In a capitalist industrial society, there are two primary classes: one composed of those who sell their productive labor in return for a wage, and the other of those who own the means of production. Included in the first class are workers engaged in the production of agricultural and industrial goods, the **proletariat**—factory workers, farm laborers, and the like. Also included are those whose labor is concerned with the movement or distribution of what is produced. This group includes such occupations as clerical worker, truck driver, and dock worker. The second primary class, the **capitalist,** is made up of those who own the means of production; they appropriate value or wealth from what is produced (i.e., profits) and control of the circulation the wealth that is appropriated.

Often closely related to the capitalist class are wage earners in supervisory or management roles. There are also those employed in various technical positions (such as engineers) and others whose class position is more ambiguous—a reflection of the complex division of labor found in modern industrial societies. All these people are sometimes labeled *middle class.*

Another important segment of modern class-based societies consists of those at the margins or beneath the other classes. These people serve as a reserve army of surplus workers who can be employed when the need arises. Braverman described the reserve army as follows:

[It] takes a variety of forms in modern society, including the unemployed; the spo-

radically employed; the part-time employed; the mass of women who, as house-workers, form a reserve for the "female occupation"; the armies of migrant labor, both agricultural and industrial; the black population with its extraordinary high rates of unemployment; and the foreign reserves of labor. [1974: 386]

In many societies, the role of domestic (largely female) unpaid labor within this reserve army is especially important in that it supports relatively low wages paid to members of a household employed in wage labor. Another form of such support exists where laborers receive goods and services from relatives who are active in semi-subsistence agriculture. The laborers themselves may resort to subsistence agriculture when wage labor is not available.

Members of the capitalist class are generally wealthier than those of the wage-earning class, but this is not always the case. Moreover, there are wealth differences within classes. The wealth of wage earners is determined largely by how much they are paid for their labor. Their pay is influenced by a number of factors: how much their work is considered to be worth by members of the capitalist class, the relative demand for their particular skills, and the political power they exert as a result of unionization or lobbying. Highly skilled laborers usually are paid more than semiskilled and unskilled laborers. Workers in countries where labor is abundant and political rights of workers are few may be paid much less than workers in comparable jobs in countries where labor is more scarce and where workers have more political power. Textile workers in many Asian and Latin American countries, for example, are paid less than $1 an hour, while in the United States they may be paid $10 or more an hour.

Wages of even the best paid of such laborers, however, are considerably less than those earned, for example, by managers of large corporations. Thus, the top 30 executives in the United States earn 178 times the average pay of the lowest paid workers in their corporation—the ratio in Japan and continental Europe, in contrast, is only 21 to 1 (Nankivell 1992). Also, laborers' wages tend to be much lower than those in some technical fields such as medicine. Relative wage differences between the working class and middle class vary considerably from one country to another. Thus, in many developing countries, members of the middle class earn a great deal more than factory workers. In developed countries, the gap between the wages of the middle class and those of factory workers is much smaller, largely because of the better bargaining position of factory workers in these societies.

The wealth of capitalists comes principally from their *profits*—the difference between what goods cost to produce and what they can be sold for. The actual wealth of individual capitalists depends on the success they have in finding and controlling sources of profit. Some capitalists may be completely unsuccessful in their search for profits, and others may be able to find only small sources. In contrast, the wealthiest capitalists control enormous sources of profit. There are more than 200 individuals and families with fortunes worth more than US$1 billion—mostly in the United States, Japan, Canada, and Western Europe. When he died in early 1993 at the age of 88, Japanese businessman Taikichiro Mori was considered the world's wealthiest capitalist. His wealth, based largely on real estate holdings in Tokyo, was estimated to be around US$13 billion. His son, Minoru Mori, has since been named president of Mori Building Co. Ltd. At the time of his death in 1992, American Sam Walton, founder of the Wal-Mart discount stores, left behind an equally impressive fortune. The five members of the Walton family possess a fortune estimated to be in excess of US$23 billion.

Whereas in rank, caste, and feudal societies people are aware of their precise position in the social hierarchy, in modern class-based societies consciousness of class position often is ambiguous. **Class consciousness** evolves through the

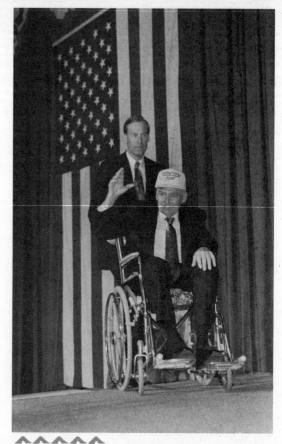

Wal-Mart founder Sam Walton in a wheelchair pushed by his son. When Walton died, he left the five members of his family a fortune estimated in excess of US$23 billion. The actual wealth of such capitalists depends on their success in finding and controlling sources of profit.

perception of common interests. For example, for those engaged in industrial production and, later, service work, class consciousness came about largely through the organizing and actions of labor unions. Class consciousness among capitalists is promoted by bodies such as chambers of commerce. For the middle class, things are more ambiguous, but they, too, sometimes form associations to promote their specific interests—for example, as consumers or home-owners.

People do not always see themselves as members of a distinct class. They may view themselves instead as individual actors, or they may see themselves as belonging to a specialized segment of society with its own distinct interests—bankers, lawyers, or electricians. Such views reflect important ideological values in capitalist societies that stress individual achievement. Alliances across class boundaries based upon perceived common interest also serve to undermine class consciousness. In many countries the most significant alliance is between the capitalist class and the military. In return for creating optimal conditions for corporate profit (for instance, by stifling labor unrest), the military may be rewarded with higher wages, better living conditions, and greater amounts of military equipment.

Relations between the two primary classes have an underlying competitiveness regarding the distribution of wealth. In capitalist industrial societies, this tension underlies any surface stability and occasionally breaks out into open conflict. For example, in the Russian Revolution of 1917, industrial laborers, peasants, members of the middle class, and others revolted against the Russian aristocracy and those members of the capitalist class allied with it.

Communist Societies

The Russian Revolution of 1917 led to the founding of the first modern **communist society,** a society based on the public ownership of the means of production and distribution. In this century communist governments were established in about 30 countries. These countries varied considerably in terms of population, level of economic development, and political institutions. They varied from giants such as China and the Soviet Union to small states such as the Congo and Mongolia (with fewer than two million people each), from the relatively developed countries of Eastern Europe to some of the poorest countries in the world, such as Ethiopia, Laos, and Cambodia. Their political

structures have included the relatively liberal governments of the former Yugoslavia and Hungary on the one hand and the highly authoritarian regimes of North Korea and Romania on the other. During the 1980s and early 1990s, most communist countries underwent dramatic changes, putting an end to communist rule.

But even if they varied in terms of the kind of communist society they created or aimed to create, they shared certain characteristics—at least in theory. They shared a stated goal of creating a society in which inequality of wealth and hierarchies of status and power are minimized. They also relied more heavily than most capitalist societies on state planning and other forms of state intervention in the economy. And private ownership of the means of production was replaced to a greater degree by state or collective ownership than in capitalist societies.

In practice, communist societies were not egalitarian. Yet the transition to communism did bring about important changes in social stratification, making it different from that in capitalist societies. The former ruling classes were eliminated, whether they were landed aristocrats or wealthy capitalists. Most communist societies inherited extensive peasantries. Collectivization of farms and industrialization led many peasants in these countries to move to towns to become urban workers. For those remaining in the countryside, life changed in many ways as they were incorporated into a more centralized state structure. Among the middle sectors, communism created a need for expertise in planning and management as the government administration assumed a central place in the daily lives of people. Greater educational opportunities also served to produce a larger middle class of technical and professional people.

Taking Hungary as an example, during the immediate postwar era efforts were made to change the country using the former Soviet Union as a model. This had a major impact on social classes as the old capitalist-feudal class structure was transformed into one more in

Russian middle class family jogs past the Kremlin. The rise of a middle class in the former Soviet Union was a significant influence in the political change that led to the breakup of that country.

keeping with communist ideals and the Soviet model. The subsequent period of extensive industrialization and collectivization of agriculture in the 1950s created a much larger group of industrial workers. As peasants came to work in cooperatives, they resembled industrial workers. A new stratum of professionals and white-collar workers also arose, initially coming mostly from the working class.

Social stratification in communist Hungary was shaped largely by how occupations were positioned in the structure of redistribution (of goods, services, and income). Kolosi and Wnuk-Lipinski (1983) identified four main socio-occupational categories in Hungary: unskilled and semiskilled workers, skilled workers, white-collar workers, and professional workers (including managers). The socio-occupational status of the parents did not necessarily influence the status of their children. In fact, social mobility was high. As in other communist countries, education served as the main channel of social mobility. Moreover, Kolosi and Wnuk-Lipinski found that membership in socio-occupational categories did not correlate neatly with socioeconomic strata, as indicated by material living conditions and other criteria. The position of many skilled workers was identical to that of many professionals.

Whereas social stratification may have been blurred in communist countries such as Hungary (in part because of the absence of both an impoverished underclass and a super-rich ruling class), differences did exist. Of considerable importance in the 1970s and 1980s was the rise of a large middle class in communist countries such as the former Soviet Union and those of Eastern Europe. Real incomes rose significantly in the 1960s and 1970s (2.2 times in the case of Hungary between 1960 and 1978), resulting in a more prosperous stratum of intellectuals, managers, scientists, doctors, lawyers, technicians, and other professionals. With increased prosperity came greater consumer and political demands that proved difficult to meet in the face of conditions of economic decline or slow growth in the 1980s. Such pressure was a crucial factor contributing to the fall of communism and to the emergence of new patterns of social stratification in these societies.

SUMMARY

Ethnicity and social stratification are two major ways in which humans divide themselves into we-they groupings. Ethnicity is a complex of ideas about race, perceptions of ethnic identity, ethnic symbols, and relations between ethnic groups. The notion that observed physical differences such as skin color are biologically related to different ways of behaving is now discounted by scientists, yet it is still an important influence on people's perceptions of racial "groups."

Consciousness of ethnic identity—of belonging to some group that is physically and/or culturally distinct—has not disappeared either; in fact, it is resurfacing in some areas. Often this sense of ethnic identity is expressed through selected symbols. Religious differences are often an important part of contrasting ethnic identities. Consciousness of ethnic identity is a factor in commerce, having contributed to the success of what Kotkin calls the "global tribes" in global commerce.

Ethnic awareness arises through the interaction of groups that perceive themselves to be different. Factors that determine whether boundaries will be maintained or distinctions eliminated (assimilation) include marriage patterns, occupational competition or ethnic-group specialization, demographic features, and politics.

Social stratification, though sometimes linked to ethnic distinctions, is a different way of classifying people. In stratified societies, people are divided into broad categories, or social strata, with unequal wealth, prestige, and power. Such divisions are legitimatized by a society's beliefs, but may change if the society's fundamental adaptation changes.

Stratification differs in degree and kind from one society to another. The least stratified of societies are called *egalitarian*. In ranked societies, people are divided into strata that differ in prestige. In societies with caste systems, people are born into occupationally specific, hierarchically ordered groups. Slavery is found in many stratified societies, and was especially important to many early states. Feudal societies divide people into two primary strata: those who work the land and those who appropriate the products of their labor in return for certain services. Industrial class-based societies have evolved distinctions between wage-earners and those who own the means of production. Such distinctions were modified in the case of communist societies, in which inequality was based largely on occupation and level of skill.

KEY TERMS

Acculturation The process by which members of one culture adopt aspects of another culture as a result of cultural contact and incorporation into a larger system.

Assimilation The process by which cultural distinctions between ethnic groups are minimized or eliminated.

Boundary maintenance The process by which ethnic distinctiveness is maintained.

Capitalist One of two primary classes in a capitalist industrial society that includes those who own the means of production.

Caste One of a number of groups in societies that are hierarchically ordered (some regarded as "higher" than others), largely endogomous, and occupationally specific. A society assigns individuals to castes at birth.

Class A social stratum, or level, defined primarily in relation to the means of production in a capitalist industrial society.

Class consciousness Awareness of class position based on perceptions of common interest.

Communist society A society based on the public ownership of the means of production and distribution.

Demography Population characteristics such as birth rate and geographic distribution; a factor influencing ethnic relations.

Egalitarian societies Societies characterized by few individual or group differences with respect to wealth and power.

Ethnic identity A group's awareness and definition of its cultural differences.

Ethnicity Selected perceived cultural or physical differences used to class people into groups or categories considered to be significantly different.

Feudal societies A system of stratification found in some agrarian societies in which those who work the land differ from those who support themselves by taking some of the produce and labor of the agriculturalists.

Hacienda A large estate, especially in a Spanish-speaking country, characterized by a feudal system of social stratification.

Indirect rule A system of colonial rule by which ranking individuals in the native population assisted foreign colonial authorities in administering those under their charge.

Proletariat Those who sell their productive labor in return for a wage, one of two primary classes in a capitalist industrial society.

Race Categorization of people according to physical traits. Race in fact represents not biological but cultural differences.

Racism Using perceived biological differences or those believed to be the result of biology to determine people's position in relation to one another.

Rank societies Societies in which members differ in prestige according to a series of graded ranks.

Slavery A form of labor that involves holding a person in servitude as property.

Social stratification The division of members of a society into social strata, or levels, with unequal wealth, prestige, and power.

SUGGESTED READINGS

Among the works on ethnicity are:

Banton, Michael. 1967. *Race Relations.* London: Tavistock Publications.

Barth, Frederick. 1969. *Ethnic Groups and Boundaries.* Bergen/Oslo: Universtetsforlaget.

Beckett, Jeremy, editor. 1988. *Past and Present: The Construction of Aboriginality.* Canberra: Aboriginal Studies Press.

Cultural Survival. 1987. *Southeast Asian Tribal Groups and Ethnic Minorities.* Cambridge, MA: Cultural Survival.

Fried, Morton H. 1975. *The Notion of Tribe.* Menlo Park, CA: Cummings.

Howard, Michael C., editor. 1989. *Ethnicity and Nation-building in the South Pacific.* Tokyo: United Nations University.

Schryer, Frans J. 1990. *Ethnicity and Class Conflict in Rural Mexico.* Princeton: Princeton University Press.

Warren, Kay B. 1978. *The Symbolism of Subordination: Indian Identity in a Guatemalan Town.* Austin: University of Texas Press.

Works on social stratification include:

Berreman, Gerald D., and Kathleen M. Zaretsky, editors. 1981. *Social Inequality: Comparative Developmental Approaches.* New York: Academic Press.

Earle, Timothy, editor. 1991. *Chiefdoms: Power, Economy and Ideology.* New York: Cambridge University Press.

Finney, Ben R. 1973. *Polynesian Peasants and Proletarians.* Cambridge, MA: Schenkman.

Godelier, Maurice, and Marilyn Strathern, editors. 1991. *Big Men and Great Men: Personification of Power in Melanesia.* New York: Cambridge University Press.

Helms, Mary. 1979. *Ancient Panama: Chiefs in Search of Power.* Austin: University of Texas Press.

Meillassoux, Claude. 1991. *The Anthropology of Slavery: The Womb of Iron and Gold.* Chicago: University of Chicago Press.

Rousseau, Jérôme. 1990. *Central Borneo: Ethnic Identity and Social Life in a Stratified Society.* Oxford: Clarendon Press.

Sanday, Peggy R. 1981. *Female Power and Male Dominance: On the Origins of Sexual Inequality.* New York: Cambridge University Press.

Stavenhagen, Rodolfo. 1975. *Social Class in Agrarian Societies.* New York: Doubleday/Anchor.

Strathern, Marilyn, editor. 1987. *Dealing with Inequality: Analysing Gender Relations in Melanesia and Beyond.* New York: Cambridge University Press.

Wasserstrom, Robert F. 1983. *Class and Society in Central Chiapas.* Berkeley: University of California Press.

POLITICS AND POLITICAL ORGANIZATION

11

In all societies there will be competition for resources—land, money, labor, and so forth—and disputes over how they are to be acquired and used. In adapting to harsh environments, foragers such as the Inuit and the Mardudjara Aborigines emphasize cooperation in the acquisition and distribution of goods. Despite their emphasis on noncompetitiveness, there are rivalries among these peoples and competition for prestige, spouses, and the like. At the other extreme, in large-scale societies like the United States, competition and aggressive social relations are a fundamental part of the adaptive strategy.

Competition goes beyond gaining actual possession of resources. It also involves attempts to control others' ideas concerning how goods are distributed and the ways in which competition takes place. While there is relatively little disagreement over such matters among the members of small-scale societies, often in large-scale societies many competing ideas and many groups or individuals seek to assert their particular view. The ability to influence or control how people perceive things, how they behave, and how things are distributed involves **power,** or the ability to act effectively on people or things. The competition for power is called **politics.**

Almost any action or statement may be political or have political implications. Shaking hands or kissing a baby may signify nothing more than a wish to demonstrate friendship or affection, but when these actions are intended to influence power relations, they become political acts. Viewed from such a perspective, politics is a universal of social existence. But politics is not the same in all settings. Despite some underlying similarities, politics among Amazonian Indians, urban-dwelling Canadians, and Javanese rice-farmers is very different. How do different environmental conditions, forms of social organization, and cultural traditions produce particular political goals and means of achieving these goals? In this chapter, we examine beliefs about and patterns of competition for power. We also look at who takes part in politics and at the relationship of political organization to the adaptive strategies of societies.

◄ THE BASES OF POLITICAL POWER ►

The struggle for power and the ability to wield it are central to politics. We say that parents have power over their children, that people have power over their pets, or that a government has

Societies have to deal with questions about how political power is transferred. Here Jean-Bertrand Aristide (left) is shown returning to Haiti to become the country's president after three years of military imposed exile. Major General Jean-Claude Duperval (right) took over as head of Haiti's armed forces after military ruler Raoul Cedras resigned and left the nation.

power over people. What we mean is that they can influence what others do, that they can cause others to behave according to their own designs. When the designs and interests of those in power coincide with those over whom they have power, an air of benevolence or irrelevancy is created. If a boy acts in accordance with the will of his parents, for example, it is largely irrelevant to him that they have the power to punish him. Similarly, when a government places persons we consider threatening to our well-being in prison, we are likely to view the use of power in a good light. The ultimate coercive nature of power is thus often masked. The ability of those in power to coerce is not always hidden, however. When those in power find their wishes are contravened, they may resort to force. The use of force will be considered in the next chapter. First we examine more subtle expressions of the struggle for power: political ideas or norms (authority, ideology, symbols) and political contests.

Political Ideas

Politics is based not simply on brute force but also on **political norms**—ideas about appropriate political goals and behavior. Through a process of political socialization, people develop goals within a specific environment and learn preferred means of achieving them. Although these norms may not be strictly adhered to in practice, they influence political behavior.

Authority

Among the most fundamental political norms are those concerned with **authority**, the right (versus simply the ability) to make a particular decision and to command obedience (Smith 1960: 18). Authority reflects the acceptable or tolerable bounds and contents of power—a government's right to tax certain activities and, *up to a certain level,* to police the activities of citizens in certain spheres and *according to accepted procedures,* and the like. What is acceptable or tolerable, though, is not simply a matter of voluntary

Among the Kababish Arabs of the Sudan, the sheikh, or headman, here seated in his tent, holds power within the tribe. The sheikh and his lineage gain authority through favorable ties with the national authorities of the Sudan.

consent on the part of the governed. Any government controls sufficient resources (personnel and wealth) to allow it to influence what people perceive to be the scope of its authority. Any powerful group or institution is able to manipulate notions of authority.

Within any society there are likely to be distinct realms of authority. Talal Asad (1970) distinguishes two major realms of authority among the Kababish Arabs, pastoral nomads of Sudan: the household and the tribal. Power within the household sphere is held largely by the male household head on the basis of his role as husband, father, and manager of the family enterprise and its animal property in particular. Power within the wider, tribal sphere is held by a *sheikh* (chief or headman) and the lineage of which he is a member. The sheikh and his lineage gained authority by cultivating ties with the colonial and later national authorities, who rewarded them with administrative posts. These posts allowed them to control access to and allocation of significant resources, such as water. The majority of Kababish feel that members of the sheikh's elite lineage are entitled to their authority to speak for the Kababish, to collect taxes, and to make other political decisions. The elite themselves base their authority on historical precedent (in the past, members of other kin groups pledged their allegiance to the sheikh in return for his protection) and on the legal rights associated with the offices they hold. It is clear, however, that such authority is also based in part on the power of the elite to enforce their will.

Ideology

When ideas consciously and systematically are organized into some form of program or plan, they can be said to constitute an **ideology.** Political ideologies are concerned with the distribution of power: the maintenance, reform, or overthrow of the existing structure. Australian Aboriginal law, for example, serves as political ideology by justifying existing power relations between the sexes, between the generations, and between different social groups. In recent history, various capitalist and socialist ideologies have been concerned with maintaining or changing power relations—for example, between feudal holders of power and capitalist owners of wealth and, in turn, between the owners of the means of production and those who sell their labor.

There are two forms of ideology: organic and rationalistic (see Rudé 1980). An *organic ideology* consists of ideas held by members of a society (or segment of a society) about how the world is or should be ordered based on their historical experience. This includes commonly held ideas about what constitutes a just government in terms of taxation, law enforcement, and the like. A *rationalistic ideology* consists of a program of ac-

tion based on observation or introspection, or both, by those seeking ordered sets of laws of social behavior. Examples of the latter can be seen in the eighteenth-century revolutionary ideologies found in France and the United States, inspired by the Enlightenment philosophers and the interests of the emerging capitalist class pertaining to the nature of government, ideologies such as those enshrined in the U.S. Bill of Rights. Each form of ideology may contain elements of the other. Ideas from rationalistic ideologies creep into popular beliefs through sermons, political speeches, the printed word, radio, and television. Rationalistic ideologies in turn contain distilled elements of organic ideologies: folk wisdom based on people's experiences, ideals, and dreams.

As small-scale societies have been incorporated into the modern world system, their members have been subjected to the rationalistic ideologies of large-scale industrial societies. The indigenous peoples of the United States and the former Soviet Union, for example, have been subjected to the respective ideologies of these states through coercion, education, and the offering of political and economic incentives. Receptivity to these ideologies has varied. Members of societies with traditions of cooperation and an emphasis on homogeneity have been unreceptive to the individualism and competitiveness of capitalist ideologies. However, others with traditions of entrepreneurship and trade have had little trouble accepting such ideas.

Political Symbols

Political ideologies and politics in general rely heavily on symbolic imagery. Most Americans, for example, are familiar with the time-honored symbols of their country: Uncle Sam, the flag, the national anthem, and catch-phrases dealing with patriotism and equality. Similarly, the communist government of the former Soviet Union relied on statues and portraits of Lenin, the hammer and sickle, use of the color red and other images and words associated with revolution, and

Political campaigners strive to stir strong emotions by deliberately surrounding themselves with the symbols of patriotism. The national flag is used in the competition for power.

fell out of favor new images came into use. Likewise, recent political changes in the former Soviet Union have brought the removal of the symbols associated with the communist regime. The same symbol can also mean different things under different circumstances or to different people. In the United States, touting "family values" in a political campaign may appeal to people's feeling about what keeps the country strong. For some, however, it is a message to white male voters to guard against blacks or empowered women.

Political Contests

Political power is not permanent. Those in power must not only contend with those who compete for their power, but also with the fact of human mortality. The members of a society, therefore, are faced with crucial questions about how power is to be transferred. Just how orderly this transfer of power may be varies from one political setting to another. **Political contests** are the processes through which power is sought and challenged and through which ideologies can be tested. While political contests can become chaotic and even violent, all societies attempt to provide some order to the processes of challenging and transferring power.

Since power is never secure from challenge, those who wish to remain in power must constantly maneuver to ward off threats to their position. Melanesian political leaders known as Big-men, for instance, build their reputation and amass wealth in pigs and other valuables by strategic manipulation of gift-giving ceremonies. The Big-man continually maneuvers to maintain or enhance his position and never really reaches a plateau on which he can rest. If a Big-man stops playing the game, stops holding pig-feasts, soon he is no longer a Big-man. Likewise, politicians in our own society never seem to stop running for office, and even absolute monarchs must always be alert to palace intrigues and signs of trouble beyond the palace gates.

reference to Mother Russia. Symbols are useful politically because they appeal to strong basic emotions—feelings of hatred, of well-being, of happiness or despair. To be able to manipulate such powerful imagery benefits those with political ambition. This is why politicians like to be surrounded with patriotic paraphernalia and why competition among politicians over identification with such symbols can be so intense.

Political symbols are based on cultural experiences and traditions, but their use reflects current political realities. Chinese politicians relied heavily on Maoist imagery as long as the revolutionary tradition associated with Mao was in favor. After the Cultural Revolution, as Maoism

▲▲▲▲▲

The Big-man, a type of leader in parts of Melanesia, achieves his power by amassing wealth in pigs and other valuables and by holding gift-giving ceremonies that enhance his reputation and influence. This Big-man of Papua New Guinea appears with one of his valuable pigs, which he will use in a continual contest for power.

Political competition is especially keen when an individual in power dies. Communities in which politics is structured through kinship usually designate a suitable heir or heirs to bring some order to this potentially disruptive situation. An eldest son or senior brother may be the preferred successor, for instance. Whatever the preference, almost always allowance is made for an alternative to avoid the risk that others will judge the normally preferred heir to be unsuitable. Despite these provisions, disputes often

erupt when the order of succession is challenged by rival heirs within the kin group, by rival kin groups, or by opportunists. Sometimes there are recognized means for handling such disputes, such as avenues of appeal to a higher authority. If things get too bad, rival groups may separate. But even once the succession is settled, underlying tensions often remain, waiting to resurface when the new incumbent dies or when some other opportunity presents itself.

Today, heredity is less relevant in most political contexts than it was in the past, at least it is not as automatic a determinant of political succession, although it can still be an important factor. Political leaders such as Lee Kuan Yew of Singapore and Kim Il Sung of North Korea, for example, sought to position their sons to enable them to assume power. In both instances, the legacy of their fathers gave the sons political advantages, but both sons have not been able to capitalize on these advantages and have yet to achieve political positions comparable to those of their fathers. On the other hand, towns, provinces, and even nations may still be ruled by oligarchies or elite families, such as the landed oligarchs of the Philippines. And it helps to be a Kennedy or a Rockefeller in American society. In large-scale societies, however, unlike kin-based societies, heredity rarely is viewed as the primary or only legitimate means for assuming power. More often it is used in combination with resources such as wealth or military power.

During the past few centuries, elections emerged in many nations as a means for transferring power. Since World War II, electoral systems have been exported to countries throughout the world under the aegis of geopolitical powers such as Britain and the United States. Despite their superficial similarities, elections have played many different roles in these often very different political environments, in many instances assuming characteristics unlike those of their countries of origin. For instance, democratic assumptions about elections—such as the belief that they allow for a greater dispersal of power—have proven rather naive. This is most obvious in countries where elected bodies are given virtually no power, such as legislatures in Latin American and in dictatorships in Africa.

◄ THE PEOPLE IN POLITICS ►

Whether electoral, hereditary, or seized by force, political power ultimately resides in people. Within most societies there are three categories of people involved in politics: the political community, the political elite, and political teams (Bailey 1969: 23).

The Political Community

The **political community** consists of those people who adhere to roughly similar political norms and goals and for the most part follow the same political procedures. Political communities may be as small as a nuclear family or as large as the British Commonwealth. Each political community is unique in some way, for it has evolved particular modes of behavior and specific potential avenues for the acquisition of power. Some degree of generalization is possible, however. Thus, we find similar patterns of political behavior among people with similar socioeconomic adaptations, and political communities in modern states can be placed within a few categories.

Individuals often belong to several political communities at the same time. These may be interrelated, as with family, town, and national community. Membership in a community is not always rigidly defined, nor do people always consider themselves members of the communities with which others choose to associate them. For example, during World War II, many people in the United States and Canada believed that the loyalties of citizens of Japanese origin were mixed because of their ancestry and that this group sought to identify with the Japanese forces with whom the United States and Canada were at war. On the other hand, Japanese living in Canada and the United States considered themselves loyal citizens of their adopted countries.

The Political Elite

The **political elite** are those within a community who wield power and leadership. Such elites exist at different levels within a political community, ranging from presidents and dictators ruling nations down to town mayors or village headmen. Sometimes the political elite consists of a homogeneous and rigidly bound group, but often its membership is more diverse and flexible. Among those included in the political elite are leaders. A **political leader** is an individual who has the power to make decisions within and for a group. Although the scope of this power and how it is maintained varies, the political power of all leaders is personal, within the broad sweep of the socioeconomic setting within which the individual leader lives. Such things as administrative office or the status of one's parents may work to the leader's advantage (or disadvantage), but the actual power a leader possesses is largely a matter of the leader's personal manipulation of available resources—connections, wealth, charisma, speaking ability, or physical strength—within this larger context (see "Focus on Anthropologists").

The leader's status is insecure in most societies. The person who has attained it is rarely able to sit back and take leadership for granted. Threats come from those who covet the leader's position and from those who are jealous or resentful of anyone exercising power over them. To achieve some security, leaders develop a network of supports. The wider and more overlapping the network, the more secure the status. One source of support for a leader is to secure a role as an **intermediary**—one who seeks to benefit from the political, economic, and sociocultural gaps between groups or significant individuals. Not all intermediaries are political leaders; but even when they are not, they often assume political

▲▲▲▲▲
Political elites range in level from presidents and their spouses to town mayors and village headmen. (top) In Australian Aboriginal society, leadership was commonly exercised by older men, such as this one, who uses a short-wave radio to call kin to a ceremony. (bottom) Hillary Rodham Clinton gives a talk at the American Medical Association.

significance. Such is the case with *ladino* (Hispanic non-Indians) intermediaries in the Tzeltal (Mayan) village of Oxchuc in southern Mexico. These individuals are able to exploit the office of village secretary for political ends: "The secretary is the strategic link between two cultures as well as between two different kinds of governments. . . . His *de facto* power derives from the potential backing he can call upon in case of need" (Siverts 1971: 390–393).

One aspect of the intermediary's power is the use of the unknown. As Siverts notes of the ladino secretary (1971: 393), the fear of the Indians "is not so much the fright of his pistol as for the possible terrors that might be called upon from the outside world. Indian informants can tell you all kinds of dramatic stories about soldiers razing hamlets and neighborhoods." In this way, while intermediaries may serve integrative functions by providing links between different groups or cultures, in the intermediary's search for power they may serve just the opposite purpose. The ladino secretary in Oxcuc helps to maintain distance between ethnic groups by promoting fear and hostility.

One form of political elite that has an ambiguous role in many modern political systems is the monarch, or sovereign ruler. The political power of monarchs varies a great deal. In the case of the constitutional monarchs of some Western democracies, the role has been reduced largely to a ceremonial one, whereas the monarchs in Asia are more powerful, such as the Sultan of Brunei, who rules as one of the last remaining absolute monarchs.

Among those monarchs who exert political influence, questions arise concerning the extent to which their position reflects the authority of the institution itself or the personality of the individual holding the office. The emperorship of Japan is an example of a monarchy "where the institution of monarchy clearly overshadows the personality of the incumbent ruler" (Tasker, Vatikiotis, and Delfs 1993:17). While the institution plays some role in other situations, the political role of most other monarchs is more a reflection of the person-

ality of the monarch. Thus, while the current king of Thailand, King Bhumibol, has been promoted as the embodiment of the Thai nation, most observers agree that his influence and popularity—exhibited when he intervened to resolve bloody conflicts between prodemocracy and military forces in May 1992 that led to the restoration of democratic government—owes a great deal to his personality. The extent to which the position of the monarchy depends on personalities is related to the importance of the succession to the throne. In the case of Japan, the political savvy of the person most likely to become the next emperor is not viewed as nearly as important a question as it is in a country like Thailand, where the succession question is of considerable political importance.

Political Teams

Political teams are the organized groups of people actively involved in politics. Within all societies there are loosely structured political groups that can be designated *coalitions,* temporary alliances for a limited political purpose (Boissevain 1974: 171). The least institutionalized of these, an *action set,* comes into being when individuals call on other people within their own personal networks to act for some specific purpose (such as to win an election). A more institutionalized form of coalition is a *faction*—a group within a larger unit that acts in opposition to some other element of the unit. Any analysis of factions must be dynamic, viewing their evolution over time. In the case of the Kekchi-speaking village of Pueblo Viejo in southern Belize, factions evolved as the village population grew, as land pressure increased, and as social and economic differences among villagers became greater (Howard 1977: 133). Initially, the factions were recruited by individuals primarily on the basis of kinship and *compadrazgo* (ritual godparenthood). Eventually they became relatively permanent features of the village, and as they did, the role of leaders who were responsible for their formation in the first place tended to wane.

The most institutionalized form of political grouping is a *political party*. Political parties are a product of modern large-scale societies and reflect the high degree of specialization in such societies. The closest thing to a party in smaller, nonindustrial societies is a multipurpose group such as a lineage or clan, which functions as a political organization in some contexts. Political parties, however, are formed with one purpose in mind: to direct the policies of a government. In addition, their greater degree of internal organization differs from that of other political groups. Parties usually are organized around particular political beliefs and interests and are more impersonal than other forms of political groups.

After World War II, political parties became more important to small-scale societies as they were integrated into the new states. For example, previously, the people of Pueblo Viejo had been little affected by party politics in Belize (then known as British Honduras) of relevance largely in the capital city. From the 1960s onward, as roads and schools were built and as political reforms reached into even the most isolated villages, agents of political parties visited the village in search of votes, and villagers in turn sought to secure the spoils of political patronage. The villagers became increasingly aware that roads, schools, and the like were political commodities, and that their own political behavior influenced the flow of these resources. Political parties have come to affect indigenous and ethnic minorities in other ways as well, playing a role in the development of communalism in many ethnically plural societies, influencing land rights struggles, and in general serving to articulate the place of these groups within the nation.

Finally, mention should also be made of the political role in modern states of multipurpose organizations that exist alongside, within, and even in opposition to political parties. Religious organizations and trade unions play an active role in politics, as do a variety of clandestine organizations and secret societies such as Masonic lodges. In Sierra Leone, for example, the small Creole elite sought to retain its political influence through Masonic lodges after the country became independent in 1961.

Women in Politics

Gender is often a consideration in political authority, legitimacy, and various forms of political participation. The role of women in politics generally reflects broader patterns of equality and inequality between the sexes in a society. Thus, in societies where women have a low status in relation to men, their political role will also be limited. However, anthropologists have long known that, while their formal role in politics in many societies may be restricted, women often exert considerable informal influence, especially as wives, mothers, and sisters of politically prominent males.

In fairly egalitarian foraging societies, such as the San, women participate more in public discussions and decision-making than is the case in more hierarchical societies, but they are not equal in the political sphere. In particular, men function as spokespersons for the group and are more likely to use violence to enforce their wishes. Moreover, contact with nonforaging peoples has undermined the political status of women in many foraging societies. For example, the male-centered view of politics held by the Europeans who colonized Australia influenced their perception of Aboriginal politics; in their recognition of Aboriginal political leaders and forms of political organization, Europeans virtually ignored the role of women.

Politics in chiefdoms and early states, for the most part, relegated women to a lowly status. In empires, such as those in India and China, women exerted political influence largely as members of the royal household. Sometimes, however, women became powerful. Among the Maratha rulers of western India during the sixteenth to eighteenth centuries women's political influence was largely "as wives or mothers within their husband's families. . . .many women schemed to have their son chosen as ruler" (Burling 1974: 60). Despite such limitations,

JACK McIVER WEATHERFORD

FOCUS ON ANTHROPOLOGISTS

J. M. Weatherford worked in the Senate as legislative assistant to Senator John Glenn (D., Ohio) in 1978–1980, after which he wrote Tribes on the Hill, *comparing the congressional organization with various tribes around the world. In addition to conducting research on politics and crime in Washington, he has worked in South America, Africa, and Europe. Two of his books,* Indian Givers *and* Native Roots, *deal with the contributions of American Indians to the world. Dr. Weatherford teaches anthropology at Macalester College in Saint Paul, Minnesota.*

∧∧∧∧∧∧∧

The Clans on Capitol Hill

My first surprise on starting work in the U.S. Senate was how small and intimate a community Congress is. As I wandered through the underground maze of tunnels, cafeterias, barbershops, and small candy stores stuck in little corners, I felt very much at home, in the same way I had on the small back streets of the Bavarian village of Kahl, where I did my doctoral research. Sitting upstairs in the formal meeting rooms or dining rooms, I sensed the same kind of political maneuvering I had seen in the bazaars and religious court sessions of the Swahili community in Mombasa, Kenya. What surprised me most, however, was how important marriage and kinship are in Washington politics, just as in nearly every community or tribe I had seen anywhere in the world.

The importance of kinship and marriage first caught my attention in the case of Senator Howard Baker of Tennessee, who held the position of Senate majority leader from 1980 to 1984. He first arrived in the Senate as a political professional following in the steps of his father and his stepmother, both of whom served in Congress before him. In his early years in the Senate, Baker served with his brother-in-law, Representative William Wampler of Virginia, and with his father-in-law, Senator Everett Dirkson of Illinois, who was then Senate minority leader. After his father-in-law's death, Baker eventually succeeded him as Republican leader. In 1982, Baker's daughter, Cissy, won the Republican nomination for the House of Representatives, but she lost in the general election to the grandson of the man her grandfather had defeated two generations earlier.

In the struggle to replace Howard Baker as Republican leader in 1985, Senator Robert Dole of Kansas clobbered his opponents. It may have been mere coincidence, but at the time of his election he was married to Secretary of Transportation Elizabeth Dole, whereas none of the opponents had such kinship ties.

The importance of kinship was not confined to the Republican party; I soon found that a high proportion of the top-ranking Democrats were also connected by blood or marriage. Russell Long of Louisiana was one of the most important senators in his position as top Democrat on the Finance Committee. He first came to the Senate fresh out of law school and took the seat made vacant by the assassination of his father, Huey Long. For a while his mother, Rose Long, had also held the same seat. Other cousins and uncles of his served in virtually every elected office in Louisiana and in the U.S. Congress. A northern parallel to the Long family is the family of Rhode Island's Claiborne Pell, who was the ranking Democrat on the Foreign Affairs Committee. His father served in the House, representing New York. Other political members of Claiborne Pell's family included former Senators William Claiborne and George Dallas, and even John Pell, who served as a minister in the British court of Oliver Cromwell in the seventeenth century. More recently, Claiborne Pell served in Congress with his cousin, Congresswoman Lindy Boggs, who replaced her husband, House Majority Leader Hale Boggs, after he was killed in an Alaskan plane crash. One of her sons worked as a major Washington lobbyist after losing his own congressional race; a daughter ran for the Senate in New Jersey; and a third child, Cokie Roberts, became congressional correspondent for the government-financed public radio and public television networks.

Not only do such clans control the two parties in Congress, some of them cross party lines. Senator Jay Rockefeller (also known as John D. Rockefeller IV) arrived in the Senate in 1985 to represent West Virginia as a Democrat, the same year that his Republican father-in-law, Senator Charles Percy of Illinois, gave up his seat. Jay's uncles, Winthrop Rockefeller (former governor of Arkansas) and Nelson Rockefeller (former governor of

Anthropologist Jack Weatherford (right) with Senator John Glenn in Glenn's office on Capitol Hill. While working in Washington, D.C., Dr. Weatherford found that just as in New Guinea and Amazonia, political alliances in the United States are only as durable as the marriages that bind them.

New York and vice president of the United States under Gerald Ford), had also won office as Republicans. Jay's wife, Sharon Percy Rockefeller, also served as chair of the board of the Corporation for Public Broadcasting as a Democrat.

In recent years, women have emerged as more important players in these political dynasties. In 1986, Elizabeth J. Patterson, daughter of the late Senator Olin D. Johnston, won election to the House of Representatives from South Carolina. Another daughter followed her father into office in 1990, when Republican Susan Molinari ran for the seat of her father, Representative Guy V.

Molinari, who left Congress to become borough president of Staten Island.

Political family ties transcend state and regional boundaries. John and Edward Kennedy represented Massachusetts in the Senate and their brother, Robert, represented New York. In 1986, a new generation of the family came to office in Massachusetts when Joseph P. Kennedy II won election to the seat of retiring House Speaker Tip O'Neill, Jr. Barry Goldwater, Jr., won election in a California district while his father served as senator from Arizona. Before becoming vice president and president of the United States, George Bush served in the

House of Representatives from Houston, Texas, even though his father had served in the Senate representing Connecticut. Ideology, party affiliation, and geography all are subject to manipulation for the individual with the right kinship and marriage connections.

I soon found, however, that just as in New Guinea and Amazonia, political alliances are only as durable as the marriages that bind them. Divorce in twentieth-century American politics looms as threateningly as it did in the court of Henry VIII of England or as it does today in the social order of a Big-man in Melanesia. This appeared rather clearly in the case of Senator Gary Hart of Colorado. After he and his sister-in-law, Martha Keys, worked together on the George McGovern presidential campaign of 1972, they won election to Congress from Colorado and Kansas, respectively. Once in Congress, Martha Keys fell in love with Andrew Jacobs, Jr., the congressman from Indiana and son of former Indiana Congressman Andrew Jacobs, Sr. Martha Keys then divorced her political scientist husband in Kansas to marry Congressman Jacobs. This started a great political clan stretching across the American heartland of Kansas, Colorado, and Indiana, a good all-American base for a presidential candidate. Representative Keys, however, failed to win reelection, and soon afterward she and second husband Jacobs divorced. The collapse of this congressional clan because of marital problems presaged the collapse of Gary Hart's presidential campaign in 1988 because of a disagreeable mixture of national and sexual politics.

Divorce might be less of a problem today if American politicians, in the manner of some tribal chiefs, were allowed to have more than one spouse at a time. As if to compensate for this lack, Congress provides itself with supernumerary aides who can inherit a position when one of the bosses dies or moves on to a higher office and does not have the right relative to take over the job. Thus, Jesse Helms of North Carolina became such a successful congressional guerilla after learning the inside workings of the system while serving on the staffs of two former senators.

Of course, the best route into office is to be related to other politicians and to be a congressional aide. Senator Nancy Kassebaum was the daughter of the 1936 presidential candidate Alf Landon, and she worked in the Senate for several years before gaining a seat. Similarly, Senator Sam Nunn worked for his great-uncle Carl Vinson, who for many years chaired the House Armed Services Committee. When Nunn was elected to the Senate, he immediately built himself a power base on the Senate Armed Services Committee, where he became a major force. After serving 10 years as administrative assistant to Senator Nunn, Ray B. Richard won election to Congress in 1982, whereupon he immediately got a seat on the House Armed Services Committee.

The relatives and former aides of congressional members together control approximately 20 percent of the seats in the House of Representatives and the Senate, holding most of the important leadership positions. And the power of these clans is increasing in the last decades of the twentieth century as the importance of the political parties declines. For most tribes, kinship is only one resource used by rising leaders; in Washington, however, kinship and marriage are fast becoming the defining criteria that determine who gets and who holds power. Once families and clans become as established and enduring as they now seem to be in American politics, they deviate from tribal politics and take a major step toward the familial politics of reigning aristocracies and royal dynasties.

Tara Bai, the widow of the ruler Rajaram (who died in 1700), assumed considerable power and gained a reputation as a skillful military leader by ruling in the name of her infant son.

In Western countries the political role of women has been an important political issue since the last century. Initially debate focused on the right of women to vote and hold office. Today attention is on the relative scale of active participation and office-holding. Changing patterns of participation by women are most noticeable in Canada and northern European countries (to a lesser extent, the United States), where women hold an increasing number of political offices.

Political participation by women is also an issue in many developing countries. While women have held important political offices, often they have done so as a result of their being the daughters or wives of prominent political figures. This is the case, for example, with all the women who have been heads of state in South and Southeast Asia. These include Sirimavo Bandaranaike of Sri Lanka, who became prime minister in 1960 after her husband, the serving prime minister, was assassinated; former prime minister Indira Gandhi of India, daughter of Jawaharlal Nehru, the country's first prime minister; former president Corazon Aquino of the Philippines, whose husband, Benigno Aquino, was assassinated by the dictator Fredinand Marcos; Prime Minister Begum Khaleda Zia of Bangladesh, whose husband was president until killed by the army in 1981; and Prime Minister Benazir Bhutto of Pakistan, whose father was executed by military dictator Zia ul-Haq in 1970.

An increasing number of women, however, hold a variety of political offices without the necessity of such connections. In Thailand, for example, politics remains almost completely dominated by men. Although eligible to vote since the end of the absolute monarchy in 1932, Thai women have rarely sought political office. This reflects male dominance in Thai society as well as the common view among women that, as one female Thai politician put it, politics "is not a very decent thing." However, many Thai women, educated and professionals in particular, are actively trying to change this situation. As a result of this growing activism, 16 women were elected to the current House of Representatives. While there are 360 seats all together, this is the highest number elected to date.

< THE POLITICAL ORGANIZATION > OF SOCIETIES

The distribution of power in a society is related to the society's adaptive strategy. In small-scale societies, power is dissipated by features such as a lack of durable goods and manufactured possessions, low population densities, and frequent moves. Only when societies become more stable and able to produce more durable forms and greater quantities of wealth does the concentration of power become possible.

Anthropologists commonly divide systems of political organization into two broad categories: those associated with *states* and those associated with *stateless societies*. The first category includes structures with centralized authority and distinct administrative machinery and judicial institutions. Within this category are entities as diverse as the United States and the Kingdom of Tonga. The second category includes systems of organization commonly associated with small-scale societies, which lack the degree of specialization of state governments.

Stateless Societies

There are two types of stateless societies: *acephalous* (or headless) *societies* and *chiefdoms*. Among those societies designated acephalous are a range of small-scale polities associated with foraging, small-scale farming, and pastoral adaptations such as the Mardudjara Aborigines, the Cree of northern Canada, and the Nuer of northeastern Africa. Chiefdoms, such as those found in precolonial Polynesia, generally are associated with relatively intensive, small-scale agriculture. Today, both acephalous societies and chiefdoms are under the jurisdiction of encompassing state organizations, although in some instances they are able to retain a fair degree of autonomy.

Acephalous Societies

The primary unit of political organization among acephalous societies consists of the people who live and work together in bands, camps, or villages. The members of these primary units commonly are organized into loose alliances, known as tribes. A **tribe** consists of a group of people who share patterns of speech and some other cultural characteristics, have a common territory, and in general feel that they have more in common with one another than with their neighbors. A tribe is usually an alliance without much centralized authority. Where tribes have become more integrated and centralized, as with many North American Indian tribes and Middle Eastern pastoral nomads, this concentration is usually a result of warfare or the design of external authorities. For instance, European colonial authorities in Africa combined many loosely organized groups and established centralized administrative structures for them, primarily to make them easier to administer.

Kinship often is so much a part of the political organization of acephalous societies that sometimes they are referred to as kin-based societies. Thus, political decision-making in such acephalous societies as the Nuer or Tallensi is structured around clans and lineages. In these societies, political status commonly is based on a person's status within the web of kinship. Lineage and clan elders may have authority to try to settle disputes and to punish wrongdoers. Kin groups such as lineages form the primary administrative units. Most affairs are handled within the lineage or clan, although it may be loosely allied with other kin groups. Alliances among kin groups are of primary political importance when intergroup disputes arise.

Relatively little power is available to individuals in these societies, reflecting their relative lack of surplus wealth and manifesting the overall egalitarian social organization and belief systems. While there may be marked differences in status and authority between males and females or between adults and youths, differences among either adult males or among adult females tend to be slight. Administration often is conducted by some form of council. These councils may be fairly specialized, but usually handle a range of legal, religious, and other administrative matters. Who may participate in a council's affairs varies. In some societies participation is open (although certain segments of the population will probably dominate the proceedings), while in others participation is more restricted. For example, among the Mardudjara Aborigines only initiated males may participate in gatherings concerned with important political, economic, and religious issues.

Chiefdoms

The **chiefdom,** the second type of stateless society, differs from acephalous societies in that its administrative structure formally integrates a number of communities. Chiefdoms may be composed of several subunits (villages, clans, and the like), each headed by a chief, subchief, or council. The office of chief generally affords the incumbent a status noticeably above other members of the society. Kinship is also important, and the position of chief may be hereditary, with the chief and his kin forming an elite stratum. Chiefs accumulate goods, usually in the form of tribute, some of which is redistributed through public feasts and doles to those in need. While usually chiefdoms are more specialized than acephalous societies, they are still a good deal less specialized than societies organized into states.

Chiefdoms were common in the South Pacific prior to European colonial rule. In precolonial eastern Fiji, tribes (known as *yavusa*) were divided into various clans (or *mataqali*). These clans were given distinctive names and over time became the custodians of particular functions. The ideal tribe would contain clans carrying out five distinct functions: a chiefly clan, a second-ranking clan that served an executive function, a diplomatic clan whose members served as official heralds and masters of ceremonies, a priestly clan, and a warrior clan. The clans in turn were subdivided into smaller units that comprised closely related families living in a defined area who acknowledged a single relative as their head. Warfare between various groups, spurred in part by chiefly rivalries, led to the formation of confederations known as *vanua*. If the vanua held together, the position of its chief gradually became hereditary. Such vanua, however, developed only after a couple of thousand years of occupation of the Fijian archipelago and, by the late eighteenth century, even the largest vanua occupied only a short stretch of coast and a couple of small neighboring islands, with its hold over subject peoples being fairly unstable (Howard 1991a: 17–18).

Population size and growth are key factors in the transition from acephalous societies to chiefdoms—and from chiefdoms to states. Higher population densities promote a greater degree of specialization and intensification of production, which in turn creates a greater potential for the accumulation of wealth and power. Acephalous organization in Africa, for example, generally is associated with low population densities, whereas chiefdoms and other more stratified systems are associated with progressively higher densities.

The status, and in fact the very existence, of chiefs is often influenced by colonial expansion. As European colonial powers conquered large portions of the world during the eighteenth and nineteenth centuries, they commonly created chiefs where there were none and altered the status of existing chiefs to aid the task of administration or to help expand their empires. When the British conquered Australia, they appointed chiefs among the Aboriginal people, who until that time had an acephalous form of political organization. While those appointed to be chiefs (sometimes referred to as "kings") were some-

King Taufa'ahau Tupou and the Tongan Queen tour the palace grounds in Nuku'alofa, Kingdom of Tonga (South Pacific), with Queen Elizabeth II of Britain. The modern kingdom was established in the second half of the nineteenth century; declared a neutral region in 1886, it became a British protectorate in 1900 and achieved independence in 1970.

times individuals of high standing in their own society, the primary criterion was their friendliness and utility to the British. In fact, appointment as a chief or king sometimes resulted in a person's ostracism from his own society.

States: Their Origin and Fall

A **state** is an autonomous integrated political unit that encompasses many communities within its territory and has a highly specialized central governing authority. This central authority claims a monopoly over those powers concerned with maintaining internal order and ordering external relations. States vary in degree of centralization, the extent and nature of the powers claimed by the state, the precise form of administration, methods of legitimating power, and levels and manner of popular participation in the running of the state.

States are perpetually changing, and anthropologists are interested in addressing questions concerning the origin, stability, and disappearance of states as well as examining the distinct types of state. Over the past few thousand years numerous types of state have evolved, including the city-states of ancient Greece, empire states such as the Mongol and Roman empires, theocratic states such as the Vatican or ancient Egypt, and more recently, nation-states such as France and Canada.

How states in general came into being has been the subject of research and debate for years. Careful analysis of the process of state formation in a range of settings indicates that the process is never reducible to a single cause. What seems to be the best approach is to isolate a range of variables that interact in the process of state formation. Claessen and van de Velde (1987) refer to this as the "Complex Interaction Model," and delineate four main factors contributing to the emergence of states: (1) dominance and control of the economy; (2) ideology; (3) societal format, which includes the number of people, population pressure, and spatial distribution; and (4) the momentum of political organization once relevant political institutions are established. Another factor would be the influence of already existing states. Related to the economic factor are the volume of available resources, the production of a surplus, and the role of trade and infrastructure (such as irrigation and roads). War and conquest may be viewed as corollaries of economic or ideological competition rather than as primary factors themselves. Population growth is relevant in terms of the number of people in relation to the means of production and the spatial distribution of the population. In this regard, the environment is important in how it influences human behavior in association with technological development and in the ways in which spatial distribution of resources affects the distribution of people.

Judith Toland (1987) discusses the role of ideology in state formation in relation to the Inca state in South America. Toland believes that pre-existing ideas about reciprocity that developed among groups occupying different ecological regions formed the foundation of legitimacy for the Inca state and its system of tribute and reward. She also notes how the Inca prepared the way for acceptance of a sacred kingship among the different populations under Inca rule through ideological innovations and the imposition of a single language (Quechua). These innovations included the inculcation of Inca values and norms and the reinterpretation of religious beliefs. The spread of Inca ideology is in turn also linked to road construction and the establishment of population centers over a wide area.

Early states are often very unstable and may rely heavily on the use of force. This was certainly true of the chiefdoms, or *matanitu*, that emerged in early nineteenth-century Fiji, comprising a number of vanua, joined together on the basis of military alliance or conquest. Mature states are able to maintain order more through a **bureaucracy,** the specialized administrative organization concerned with the day-to-day running of the state. The degree of legitimacy of the norms and values imposed by the state is also closely related to its stability.

Most modern states did not evolve on their own. They were the creations of various colonial powers, and their subsequent evolution often has involved the progressive realization of a nationality that initially was little more than an ideal. "Nation building" refers primarily to attempts to forge nations out of disparate peoples placed together in an artificial political creation. The modern Melanesian states of Papua New Guinea, Solomon Islands, and Vanuatu were created in the nineteenth century by European powers seeking to demarcate spheres of influence and control over peoples who recognized no common political bond beyond a few allied villages and who spoke hundreds of distinct languages. Today, the governments of these newly independent states are seeking to create a sense of nationhood through language and educational policies and through a bureaucratic machinery that remains sensitive to the diversity of the people within their national borders.

Destabilizing factors (such as economic inequality) are present in all states, but the more successful ones are able to overcome them, at least for a time, At some point, however, states collapse or disappear, to be replaced by similar states or occasionally by new types of states. The fall of Rome resulted not simply in its replacement but in the emergence of new types of states in Europe. Likewise, the fall of the Inca and Aztec states to the Spanish resulted in the rise of new colonial states that were very different in character. The collapse or disappearance of a state is a complex and usually prolonged process, usually influenced by a variety of internal and external factors. The Inca state did not simply fall to the Spanish. Efforts by the Inca state to impose its values and norms on those under its control met with stiff resistance. Rather than be-

coming an increasingly stable state, in its efforts to control dissent by introducing more laws and regulations at the time of the arrival of the Spanish in the sixteenth century the Inca state was "so rigid as to be hardly viable any longer" (Claessen and van de Velde 1987: 11).

Discussing the Angkor state of Southeast Asia (ninth to fifteenth century A.D.), which encompassed modern Cambodia and parts of Vietnam, Laos, and Thailand, Hagesteijn (1987) argues that a crucial factor in the collapse of Angkor was the outflow of wealth because of the inability of the state to replace patron-client and kin-based relations with more bureaucratic relations. This points to a more general problem for states concerning center-periphery relations (Yoffee and Cowgill 1988)—that is, relations between the ruler and subjects or citizens or the capital and outlying regions of a state. Stability depends on an efficient and flexible system of ensuring an adequate flow of goods to the center. The process of collapse begins when the center is no longer able to secure sufficient resources from the periphery. Reciprocity is an important consideration in that those at the periphery must believe that they are receiving the benefits they deserve. The ruler of Angkor was unable to hold the state together in

The Aztec state had its capitol city at Tenochtitlan, today's site of Mexico City. The Aztec capitol is shown here with sacred payramids and vast marketplace. The development of such a state may be explained in terms of the interplay between such factors as population, ecology, and political dynamics.

the face of feudal tendencies and growing demands on the people and environment.

The fall of states is not a problem of the past. Recent events in the former Soviet Union and Yugoslavia point to the fragility of some modern states. In addition, pressures that contributed to the fall of states in the past, such as environmental degradation (as in the case of the Anasazi civilization of New Mexico discussed in Chapter 5), continue to be relevant today in the face of concerns about overpopulation, the diminishing resource base, and atmospheric changes.

S U M M A R Y

In all societies there is competition for power—the ability to act effectively on people or things. Political power is based on authority, ideas, symbols, and contests. Authority is the right of an individual or group in power to make certain decisions and command obedience. When ideas about appropriate political goals and behavior are organized into a systematic program, they constitute an ideology. Organic ideologies stem from the direct experiences of members of the society; rationalistic ideologies are based on observation and introspection. Symbols support political ideas by associating them with strong emotions.

Competition for power takes place all the time but is keenest during political contests. Societies with hereditary access to power usually have provisions to minimize rivalries for power vacuums created by the death of a leader. Elections have been used in other societies to make moves into power more orderly, though they may not necessarily spread power democratically across the population.

The people behind political systems can be categorized as political communities, the political elite, and political teams. Political communities are people with similar political norms, goals, and procedures. The political elite are those entitled or able to compete for available power and leadership opportunities. The monarch is an example of a political elite. Teams

actively involved in politics include coalitions, political parties, and multipurpose organizations. Gender is often a consideration in political participation, the role of women in politics reflecting broader patterns of equality and inequality between the sexes in a society.

Small-scale societies tend to be stateless, with authority limited to local realms of power, whereas in many large-scale societies power is highly centralized, with specialized administrative and judicial machinery. Stateless societies may be the acephalous (headless) form or the chiefdom (hierarchically ordered communities integrated into a formal structure). There have been numerous types of states and many still face problems associated with relations among formerly distinct groups. States come into being for a variety of reasons, including factors associated with the economy, ideology, and population. Stability can be achieved by gaining ideological legitimacy and through the use of bureaucracies, but states also face destabilizing pressures. The collapse of states is a complex and usually prolonged process and can be linked to problems between the center and periphery as well as to environmental factors.

K E Y T E R M S

Authority The right—vs. simply the ability—to make a particular decision and to command obedience.

Bureaucracy The specialized administrative organization concerned with the day-to-day running of the state.

Chiefdom A stateless political structure that integrates a number of communities; it is composed of several parallel units with recognized hierarchical political roles that generally afford the incumbents a higher status than other members of the society.

Ideology Ideas consciously and systematically organized into some form of program or plan.

Intermediary One who seeks to benefit from the political, economic, and sociocultural gaps between groups or significant individuals.

Political community Those people who adhere to roughly similar political norms and goals and for the most part follow the same political procedures.

Political contests The processes through which power is sought and challenged and through which ideologies can be tested.

Political elite Those within a community who wield power and leadership.

Political leader An individual who has power to make decisions within and for a group.

Political norms Ideas about appropriate political goals and behavior.

Political teams Organized groups of people actively involved in politics.

Politics Competition for power.

Power The ability to act effectively on people or things.

State An autonomous integrated political unit that encompasses many communities within its territory and has a highly specialized central governing authority.

Tribe A group of people who share patterns of speech and some other cultural characteristics, have a common territory, and in general feel that they have more in common with one another than with their neighbors.

SUGGESTED READINGS

Boissevain, Jeremy. 1974. *Friends of Friends: Networks, Manipulators and Coalitions.* Oxford: Blackwell.

Burling, Robbins. 1974. *The Passage of Power: Studies in Political Succession.* New York: Academic Press.

Cohen, Ronald, and Elman R. Service, editors. 1978. *Origins of the State: The Anthropology of Political Evolution.* Philadelphia: Institute for the Study of Human Issues.

Earle, Timothy, editor. 1991. *Chiefdoms: Power, Economy and Ideology.* New York: Cambridge University Press.

Howard, Michael C. 1981. *Aboriginal Politics in Southwestern Australia.* Nedlands: University of Western Australia Press.

_____. 1991. *Fiji: Race and Politics in an Island State.* Vancouver: University of British Columbia Press.

Kerkvliet, Benedict J. Tria. 1990. *Everyday Politics in the Philippines: Class and Status Relations in a Central Luzon Village.* Berkeley: University of California Press.

Kertzer, David I. 1980. *Comrades and Christians: Religion and Political Struggle in Communist Italy.* New York: Cambridge University Press.

_____. 1988. *Ritual, Politics, and Power.* New Haven: Yale University Press.

Khoury, Philip S., and Joseph Kostiner, editors. 1990. *Tribes and State Formation in the Middle East.* Berkeley: University of California Press.

Lewellen, Ted C. 1983. *Political Anthropology: An Introduction.* South Hadley, MA: Bergin and Garvey.

Rodman, William, and Dorothy Counts, editors. 1982. *Middlemen and Brokers in Oceania.* Ann Arbor: University of Michigan Press.

Seaton, S. Lee, and Henri M. Claessen, editors. 1979. *Political Anthropology.* The Hague: Mouton.

Smith, Gavin. 1990. *Livelihood and Resistance: Peasants and the Politics of Land in Peru.* Berkeley: University of California Press.

Tapper, Richard. 1979. *Pasture and Politics: Economics, Conflict and Ritual Among Shahsevan Nomads of Northwest Iran.* New York: Academic Press.

Upham, Steadman, editor. 1990. *The Evolution of Political Systems: Sociopolitics in Small-Scale Sedentary Societies.* New York: Cambridge University Press

12 LAW AND CONFLICT

S o-called race riots have been a part
of American society for over a century.
One was the "Zoot Suit Riot," named for
the flashy tight-cuffed, wide-lapelled,
padded-shouldered suits popular among
Mexican-American youths during the

1940s. The riot took place in Los Angeles in early June 1943:

> Marching through the streets of downtown Los Angeles, a mob of several thousand soldiers, sailors, and civilians proceeded to beat up every zoot-suiter they could find. . . . Street cars were halted while Mexicans, and some Filipinos and Negroes, were jerked out of their seats, pushed into the streets, and beaten with sadistic frenzy. If the victims wore zoot-suits, they were stripped of their clothing and left naked or half-naked on the streets, bleeding and bruised. . . . From the affidavits which I helped prepare at the time, I should say that not more than half of the victims were actually wearing zoot-suits. A Negro defense worker, wearing a defense-plant identification badge on his workclothes, was taken from a street car and one of his eyes was gouged out with a knife. Huge half-page photographs showing Mexican boys stripped of their clothes, cowering on the pavements, often bleeding profusely, surrounded by jeering mobs of men and women, appeared in all the Los Angeles newspapers. [McWilliams 1961: 249–250]

Such a breakdown of social order is not a common occurrence, and when it does take place people feel the need to explain it. Numerous explanations have been offered for the Zoot Suit Riot. The Los Angeles police, for example, believed that the riots stemmed from sailors making advances to Mexican-American girlfriends of the zoot-suiters. California state senator Jack Tenney and the members of his Committee on Un-American Activities in California blamed the communists, relating the riot to "the current Communist Party line to stir up matters among minority groups in order to make the Communist Party appear a champion of the group" (Tenney 1943: 215).

Anthropologists and other social scientists find such simplistic answers unsatisfactory. Recognizing the complexity of human actions, they search for a range of contributing factors. The zoot-suiters themselves were to a large degree a product of World War II: As the war disrupted strong family ties, pre-draft-age youths formed into gangs. The war also heightened racial tensions: Asian-Americans were suspected

ᐱᐱᐱᐱᐱ

In Sri Lanka, civil strife breaks out between Muslims and Tamil militants, who have demanded a separate Tamil state. Here a Muslim demonstrator picks up a tear gas canister fired by police during a demonstration in Colombo. At least 15 people were injured in the demonstration to protest a Tamil rebel massacre of Muslims.

June 7, 1943: After a series of pitched battles with soldiers, sailors, and marines, these alleged zoot-suiters are lined up in chains outside the Los Angeles jail en route to court hearings. The zoot-suiters were a focal point of competition and conflict in a city where tensions had mounted as a result of World War II.

of allegiances to Japan, and blacks and Mexican-Americans moved into cities to occupy jobs previously reserved for whites. The flashy dress and undisciplined behavior of the zoot-suiters stood out in the face of such prejudice. These characteristics also seemed to be contrary to the values of patriotism and hard work being promoted to sustain the war effort. The zoot-suiters served as

a focal point of competition and conflict in a city where tensions had mounted as a result of the war. Once the riot began, it soon turned into a general racial free-for-all.

Although such a breakdown of social order can be explained, it is often viewed as disturbing and unexpected, because all societies have mechanisms designed to prevent such disturbances of orderly living. In this chapter, we look at how people view social order, how it is maintained, and how it breaks down.

< NORMS >

Most of us have fixed notions about how people should behave. Children should obey their parents, parents should support their children, drivers should stop for red lights, doctors should care about their patients, and public officials should not take bribes. Such conceptions of appropriate or expected behavior are called **norms**. Obviously, a mixed lot of conceptions fall into this grouping. While we may think of norms as part of a system, to do so presumes an order that exists only in part. Although many of our ideas about what people ought to do are consistent, not all are; people often adhere to beliefs that actually are contradictory. Norms vary from ambiguous guides such as "Be good to your parents," to very specific directives, such as "Do not covet your neighbor's wife."

People use norms in social situations in accordance with particular goals. This usage is closely related to our perceptions of social identities—what a bank teller is and does, and what it means to be a good one. People's support of norms commonly is related to what they think others perceive to be normative behavior, rather than simply their own values. Good bank tellers wear a smile and tell customers to have a nice day. Such behavior does not necessarily mean that they care about their customers or that they are happy; it shows that they are trying to live up to their image of what others expect.

Norms change continually to keep pace with new social or environmental realities. The obsequious behavior of such cinematic characters as Step-n-Fetchit in movies of the 1920s and 1930s typifies the normative expectations of many white Americans during this period regarding relations between blacks and whites. In American films today, there is a noticeable difference in how black-white relations are portrayed, a reflection of changing attitudes about how members of the respective ethnic groups should behave. The normative beliefs of many small-scale societies underwent profound changes as a result of colonialism and integration into modern nation-states. In many parts of Africa, for example, belief in allegiance to the extended kin group came

Groups, such as neo-Nazis, usually possess a set of norms that determines their behavior. This neo-Nazi, who calls himself Satan, is seen at his home in a Paris suburb, his dog "Adolf" at his side.

into conflict with new ideas favoring nuclear families and the social and economic independence of individuals. This conflict often led to the breakdown of extended kin groups and of the normative order surrounding them.

‹ LAWS ›

Members of a society frequently systematize norms and elevate them to the status of laws. A **law** is a binding rule, created through enactment or custom, that defines right and reasonable behavior. It is common for the enforcement of laws to be placed in the hands of courts or a comparable legitimate group such as certain elders in Aboriginal society. Legal systems are constantly changing as societies themselves change, and they are part of a society's overall adaptive strategy. An important aspect of any legal system is the overt or underlying threat by those in authority to use force to ensure obedience or to punish wrongdoing.

Systems of law are not exclusive to modern large-scale societies, although such societies do exhibit unique procedures for administering and codifying laws. Traditional Australian Aborigines possessed a system of laws that dictated personal relationships with the supernatural, with physical surroundings, and with other humans. Aboriginal law included the responsibility to perform rituals associated with mythical events and established conventions of behavior toward kin. These laws were not written down, but they were binding and as systematic as our written laws. Failure to adhere to these laws was believed to result in some form of punishment from spiritual beings.

Legitimacy

A law is a norm that states with relative precision what form of behavior is expected or appropriate in a specific situation. All legal systems ultimately are based on more general normative concepts, such as the god-given right of a king to rule or the right of the state to maintain

The concept of the divine right of kings once provided British royalty with legitimacy, which refers to the traditional moral system of a society.

order, and it is from these more general norms that laws derive their legitimacy. Ultimately, **legitimacy** refers to the traditional moral system of a society. Australian Aboriginal law, for example, derives its legitimacy from mythology: The laws are said to have been laid down by creative mythical beings of the Dreamtime. Reference to the supernatural for support of a legal system is fairly common; it is a feature of many aspects of the legal systems of modern Western nations ("one nation under God").

Support for a legal system also may be based on reference to a more secular idea of morality or well-being. For example, many legal systems embrace the concept of the "reasonable man":

culturally acceptable ideas about what constitutes reasonable behavior in a given situation (Saltman 1991). As Max Gluckman (1973: 83) notes: "The reasonable man is recognized as the central figure in all developed systems of law," and argues that it is equally important in non-Western systems such as that of the Barotse of Zambia, on whom his own study focused. Gluckman also notes, however, the absence of a concept of the "reasonable woman" in many legal systems, reflecting the lower legal status of women in such societies. The question of such gender bias in a legal system has received considerable attention in many Western countries in recent years (see Kennedy 1992), as highlighted during the 1991 confirmation hearings of U.S. Supreme Court Justice Clarence Thomas.

The Evolution of Laws

Laws and legal systems change in small ways in response to social or environmental conditions. For example, environmental quality and protection laws have been enacted during the past decade in response to a growing public awareness of environmental problems and a greater desire to prevent further environmental destruction. In the United States, for instance, 30 years ago, the use of unleaded gasoline and emission controls such as catalytic converters in automobiles were seen as little more than nice ideas. Today, because of increasing concern about health effects, such as respiratory problems caused by automobile exhausts, it has evolved into laws. But such changes take place on the basis of recognized principles within an overall legal structure that remains much the same. Thus, the United States now has many more laws relating to environmental protection than in the past, but its basic legal structure has not been changed in any significant way as a result. Change in a legal structure requires much more fundamental alterations in the adaptive strategy of a society, such as those associated with increasing social scale or a change in state structure, say from a monarchy to a republic. Even in

these instances, legal systems do not always change completely, and often there is some continuity from the old system to the new.

Overlapping of Legal Systems

The existence of two or more legal traditions within a single state is relatively common. In many of its colonies Britain adopted a policy of "indirect rule" that allowed subject peoples to retain many features of their own legal systems. Most British colonies had a system of native courts that reflected the legal traditions of the various ethnic groups within a colony as well as a system of British courts that dealt with Europeans and served an appellate role for the native courts. These native courts varied greatly in terms of what they recognized as crimes, how guilt was established, and what was considered just punishment for crimes or how disputes were settled. For the most part, they were not expected to follow British legal traditions. Such courts dealt with matters relating to marriage and divorce, domestic disputes, inheritance, and destruction of property among members of a particular ethnic community. British justice intervened when disputes or crimes also involved Europeans or, sometimes, when the crime was murder or involved some activity that the colonial authorities were particularly concerned about, such as cannibalism or headhunting.

Many states today recognize some forms of legal dualism, especially where indigenous minorities are concerned. For example, the Navajo living on their reservation in the American Southwest are allowed to have their own police and court system that enforces a blend of Navajo and U.S. law. In fact, the former English settler colonies (the United States, Canada, Australia, and New Zealand) increasingly recognize indigenous legal systems in matters involving native peoples. This approach can be viewed as positive, providing people with a legal system that better reflects their own cultural values and from which they are less alienated than the Western legal system. However, critics of this tendency worry that it will only further alienate native peoples from the surrounding society. In addition, some native women have expressed concerns that how these traditional systems of law are being interpreted is discriminatory against women and sets back efforts to gain greater recognition for the rights of women within native societies, including recognition of membership within tribal groups, rights to royalties and property, and political status.

Many states today are subject to conflicting views about the basic legal structures they should employ. In modern times Shariah, or Islamic law, has been enforced only in Saudi Arabia, the Gulf sheikdoms, and revolutionary Iran. But other states with large Muslim populations have faced controversy over the extent to which their laws should conform to Islamic injunctions, as well as how such injunctions should be interpreted. While Pakistan's constitution bars legislation contrary to the spirit of Islam, the practice has been for the judiciary to use common English-drived law rather than Shariah. Pressure from Islamic fundamentalists, however, led the Pakistani government to introduce a Shariah bill in 1991, under which the Islamic religious code would be given legal status. The provisions of the bill are general, calling for promotion of Islamic values and Islamization of education; but secularists are worried that it lays the groundwork for the state's abdication of constitutional authority to the fundamentalists. Opposition to Islamization of the country's laws has come from those who are Western-educated, from women's rights advocates, and even from some Islamic groups wary of how Shariah will be interpreted (see Weiss 1988).

< LAW ENFORCEMENT AND >
DISPUTE MEDIATION

It is never enough simply to establish laws. In every society, there are always individuals whose actions fall beyond established legal limits.

Furthermore, laws may be interpreted differently or not accepted by certain individuals. Therefore, societies have developed formal or informal mechanisms for enforcing their laws and handling disputes.

Attitudes Toward Laws

While all societies have ideas about proper and improper behavior and means to ensure a degree of conformity with those ideas, precisely how order and the maintenance of order are viewed can vary. To begin with, there are considerable differences in the degree to which societies have transformed their ideas about correct behavior into a set of laws. The Comanches, for example, traditionally did not possess abstract rules about appropriate behavior (Hoebel 1940). The society did not lack norms, but they had not formulated them into a roster of general laws. Societies also vary in the extent to which compliance with laws or norms is expected. At one extreme are those societies placing strong emphasis on compliance, where absolute compliance is seen as necessary for survival or to achieve goals (e.g., to withstand external threats or to create an empire). At the other extreme are societies that are more tolerant, emphasizing manipulation and bargaining. There are also differences in the kind of behavior that is tolerated. Some societies, such as the Inuit, take the theme of peace and harmony to an extreme, seeking to avoid controversy and aggressive behavior. At the other extreme, disputative and aggressive behavior may be seen as desirable, with a high value placed on individual achievement. These differences represent different adaptive strategies.

Adherence to laws is greater when laws are based on widely accepted norms. Most people in Western societies accept and comply with laws against murder of an adult or child, while laws relating to abortion are debatable. This is because there is no prevailing view concerning the rights of a fetus. Likewise, Prohibition did not succeed in the United States because norms regarding drinking alcoholic beverages were not well established in the society as a whole. As in both of these example, laws will affect some segments of a society differently from others. This is particularly an issue in states where cultural diversity is great. Laws about abortion are more relevant to women, and attitudes on the issue are related to one's religion. Drinking laws are more important to those for whom the consumption of alcohol is an option than to those who, say on religious grounds, would never consider drinking under any circumstances.

Handling Disputes in Foraging Societies

Because laws will not automatically be adhered to by all members of a society, every society has mechanisms for dealing with those who break or disagree with the laws. The need for such mechanisms is particularly pressing in large-scale societies because of their greater heterogeneity, but even small, relatively homogeneous societies require means for handling antisocial behavior and disputes.

The two major points of tension in foraging societies are sexual relations and the distribution of food. All foraging societies have rules for sharing food, but the actual division often is marked by suspicion and stress as people worry about getting their just share. Disputes over infidelity and sexual jealousy are minimized in some societies by liberalizing sexual access, but in many others they are a major source of tension and conflict. In most foraging societies the emphasis is on reestablishing social equilibrium. Because these societies are small and close-knit, many disputes are handled at an interpersonal level through discussions or fights. Other members of the society become involved informally through shaming, gossip, and ridicule.

Disputes are not always settled easily, however, and sometimes it is necessary to try to end tensions by more drastic means. A common way of easing tensions among foragers is dispersal: Bands split up to avoid further quarrels. The ease with which this occurs depends in part on environmental conditions. Where scarce resources or hostile neighbors make dispersal difficult, the prime protagonist(s) may be ostracized. Some foraging societies use more elaborate

In foraging societies, shame, gossip, and ridicule serve as ways to handle disputes and tensions. The emphasis among Inuit is on reestablishing social equilibrium through informal means.

methods of settling disputes. In many Australian Aboriginal societies, individuals accused of wrong-doing are able to get a public hearing at certain ceremonial gatherings and, in the past, could be forgiven through a ritual involving penis holding, in the case of a man, or, in the case of a woman, giving herself to the men involved in the hearing (Berndt 1965: 187–190). Reciprocity and keeping disputes from escalating are the focal points of such actions. These themes permeate much of the legal thought in foraging societies. Compensation tends to be negotiable. Groups may negotiate over the precise goods and services they are to receive. Where death is demanded, they may negotiate over who, how many, or what type of people are to be killed.

Easing Tensions Among Small-Scale Farmers

The change from foraging to farming leads to new stresses and new legal requirements. There are more people packed into a smaller space, they are residentially more stable, and they have more material possessions. In short, there is more to fight over and a greater likelihood that people will fight. The primary legal problems for small-scale farmers have to do with distribution of the surplus they produce, property inheritance, land rights, and sexual relations. Disputes usually increase as critical resources such as land become exceptionally scarce.

Small-scale farmers handle many of their legal problems in ways similar to foragers, with some important differences. Many problems are handled by kin; for example, older brothers or fellow lineage members are held responsible for a person's behavior. Shaming and ridicule also play a role. The Melanesians of Goodenough Island practice a form of shaming with food (Young 1971). A man who feels that he has been wronged will give the wrongdoer the finest and largest yam or other food item that he has with the intent of shaming the person by giving him something far better than he can reciprocate.

Even in dealing with mundane tensions and disputes, in many small-scale farming societies people also practice sorcery and witchcraft and accuse one another of practicing them.

Dispersal and ostracism also are practiced by small-scale farmers. Farmers, however, find dispersal much more difficult because of their commitment to their crops and greater population densities. In southern Belize, which until recently had a low population density, Mayan villages commonly would fragment every few years because of factional disputes. Members of factions would move to other villages or establish a new village in an unoccupied region. Ostracism is a common strategy among small-scale farmers. In southern Belize, the leading adult men of the village may decide to ostracize an individual when they believe that other means of dealing with the person have failed. The banished person must then either seek permission to reside in another village or leave the area altogether.

Formal Law Enforcement in States

Large-scale societies organized into states have different legal requirements and legal systems than small-scale societies. The diversity of wealth and status and often greater cultural diversity in states produce a greater array of tensions that must be dealt with if social order is to be maintained. The increased scale and complexity of states make reliance on informal and interpersonal means of settling disputes more difficult. While gossip, shaming, and respect for role obligations remain important means of ensuring order, the state apparatus also relies on specialized institutions, such as a judiciary and police, for defining and upholding laws. While small-scale societies can sometimes employ individuals in special judicial or policing roles, such specialization is much more pervasive in states. Another difference is that ostracism in the form of imprisonment, as practiced in states to encourage social order, is rarely encountered in small-scale societies.

How laws are enforced in a state depends largely on the distribution of power and wealth and the competition for them. Where one segment of society is able to control the state apparatus, that segment will usually use the laws and legal institutions for its own ends. For example, Guatemala today is controlled by a small elite of wealthy landowners and capitalists. This elite has passed laws concerned with property ownership and the maintenance of civil order that favor them over the majority of people and also dominate the institutions that interpret and carry out the laws—the military, police, and courts. In instances where political power is more diverse, as in Canada and the United States, there is greater competition over the passage of laws and often greater judicial recognition of the rights of a larger section of the population.

Maintaining World Order

The modern nation-state is not an autonomous entity. Most states share boundaries with other states, and all find their affairs enmeshed with those of other states through trade, cultural affinity, and the desire for power. In this world-system, it is essential to think in terms of global politics and global economics. Tremendous tensions exist between those institutions, groups, or states interacting at the international level where wealth and cultural differences are far greater than anything imaginable within most individual states. This is apparent, for example, in the case of the international oil industry and conflicts in the Middle East.

Especially during the present century, the response to the potential for chaos within the international arena has been to try to establish some ground rules that are recognized by at least a majority of the nations of the world. These include the web of treaties dealing with such things as copyright and mail. There have also been more general attempts to create order through the establishment of international forums for disputes that transcend national boundaries, such as the United Nations and the World Court. The effectiveness of such institutions is limited, however, since they possess little coercive power. In a few instances the United Nations has succeeded in resolving disputes through a military presence or economic sanctions, but for the most part it serves as little more than an arena for airing disputes and perhaps coming to some understandings through

The soldier or policeman in the state of Guatemala today helps to enforce laws; but the laws may be passed to favor the small elite of this country who use the militia or police to prop up their rule.

mutual consent. Thus, while political and economic activities have moved to a world scale, law still lags behind.

Nongovernmental agencies, too, have norms and laws involved in maintaining world order. For example, Amnesty International has achieved some success in combating the use of torture in many cultures and in promoting due process of law. Some claim that Amnesty, through its letter-writing campaigns and consciousness-raising, has secured better treatment and freedom for more prisoners than has international diplomacy. In another example, the demonstrations of the international environmental organization Greenpeace have stopped the dumping of toxic wastes in some developing countries. Finally, the Catholic and Protestant women who led the Peace Marches in Northern Ireland caused many to question whether the feud in Ireland should have gone on so long.

◄ THE BREAKDOWN OF ORDER ►

Interpersonal and social tensions are always present in any society. As we have seen, societies develop mechanisms for trying to deal with these tensions and the threat to order that they pose. When minor problems occur, usually they can be taken care of with minimal disturbance to the social order. However, sometimes things get out of hand, and social pressures or the police are not enough to prevent a major disruption. Such major breakdowns of order within a society tend to result from increasing pressures arising from underlying conflicts in the social structure, especially conflicts concerned with the distribution of wealth and power.

Political Violence Within a Society

Orderly, nonviolent transferrals of power are not common occurrences, especially when a transferral is between different groups. Those with

power want more; they are also usually unwilling to give up what they have. Likewise, those out of power often see violence as the only means of increasing their position in society.

REBELLIONS.   Eric Wolf and Edward Hansen (1972: 235) wrote that "the history of Latin America from independence to the present time is a history of violent struggles of 'ins' and 'outs'." William Stokes (1952) outlined the basic forms of rebellion common to Latin America: *machetismo, cuartelazo, golpe de estado,* and revolution. *Machetismo* (named after the long knife, the machete, carried by many Latin American peasants) is a violent seizure of power in which a leader employs a mass of armed followers. This method of obtaining power disrupts the administration and economy and may lead to substantial loss of life. In Colombia, where machetismo was common throughout much of the nineteenth and early twentieth centuries, conflicts often took a heavy toll and affected almost every aspect of people's lives. Between 1899 and 1903 alone, more than 100,000 people were killed.

The *cuartelazo* involves careful planning on the part of a small group of soldiers to seize power quickly by taking over strategic locales. This transfer can be almost bloodless, and the bulk of the population may not even know about it until everything is over. The most difficult part of the *cuartelazo* is making it stick. Staying in power requires gaining recognition from other powerful elements in the society, especially other military units.

The *golpe de estado* (or coup d'etat) is a more widespread violent overthrow of a government than the *cuartelazo*. Although the military is always involved, the *golpe* includes important civilian participation as well. The *golpe* itself is a quick attack on those in power, generally involving the assassination or immobilization of the chief executive and the mobilization of a large number of political allies.

Forceful seizures of power are found in many parts of the world besides Latin America. The South Pacific, for example, experienced its first military seizure of power when, after 17 years of parliamentary government, the elected government of Fiji was overthrown in May 1987 (Howard 1991a). This *cuartelazo* was organized by members of the former ruling oligarchy (headed by Fijian chiefs) who had lost power in a recent election, and their civilian and military allies. The actual seizure was carried out by a small group of soldiers who occupied parliament and took the prime minister and members of his party captive for two weeks, by which time the new military-civilian regime felt itself to be securely enough in power to allow their release.

These forms of political violence do not necessarily result in any structural changes in the society, or at least may not intend to bring such changes about. The Fiji *cuartelazo* for example, was intended to restore political power to the chiefs and their associates after their political party lost an election. After reviewing numerous rebellions in Africa, Max Gluckman found that most involved a process of "repetitive change," since they did not result in an "alteration in the structure of authoritative offices or the character of the personnel who hold them" (1965: 165). Rather than promoting change, such rebellions often served as a safety valve for pressures that had built up in the society. However, many rebellions do foster at least some important changes. Looking at the Fiji *cuartelazo* again, although the original intent was to restore the traditional oligarchy to power, what actually resulted was that the chiefs were forced to share power with the military, thereby significantly altering power relations within Fijian society.

REVOLUTIONS. Although political violence is fairly common within societies, actual revolutions are not. According to Wolf and Hansen (1972: 235), a **revolution** involves "fundamental change in the nature of the state, the functions of government, the principles of economic production and distribution, the relationship of social classes, particularly in regards the control of government—in a word, a significant break with

the past." The term *revolution* has been used inappropriately for a wide range of political violence resulting in relatively minor changes for the majority of people. Fundamental breaks with the past that warrant the designation *revolution* actually are very rare.

Revolutions occur infrequently for a variety of reasons. The majority's lack of power, inability to organize, or insufficient desire to mobilize are relatively simple reasons. Gluckman, in his study of African rebellions (1965), discusses another important factor: multiple and divided loyalties that make a drastic change difficult. People are caught up in a web of social relationships—kinship, patron-client, and so forth—that bind their actions and thoughts and reduce their revolutionary potential. A desire for security and a fear of the unknown are common to most members of a society. People rarely risk what little they do have in the way of family, food, and shelter in the hope of obtaining something better by breaking entirely with the existing order. Also important in constraining revolutionary tendencies are decisions by those in power to implement reforms sufficient to relieve immediate pressures and their ability to co-opt the leadership of the opposition. Even when people do rebel because of poverty or injustice, their goal often is not the revolutionary transformation of society, but merely the adjustment of the existing social order.

Revolutions are the result of very exceptional circumstances. To have a revolution, it is not enough for people to rebel; they must also create a new social order that is drastically different from what came before. It is this creative process that most distinguishes revolution from other forms of political violence.

Anthropologists have focused on revolutions since World War II, such as those in Vietnam, Nicaragua, and Ethiopia. During the 1960s and 1970s, in part in response to the war in Vietnam, American social scientists, such as anthropologist Eric Wolf, sought to explain revolutions through a *moral economy* approach (see Wolf 1968, Migdal 1968, Paige 1975, and Scott 1976). The moral economists highlighted the role of peasants in modern revolutions. Peasants were seen from this perspective as being driven to revolt in reaction to the devastating impact of incorporating agrarian societies (of which they were a part) into the modern world economy. These peasants viewed the new commercial relations within the community and with the world beyond created by their integration into the modern world economy as illegitimate in contrast to the types of social relations, especially those concerned with reciprocity (see Chapter 5, "Economic Systems") that characterized the traditional peasant economy.

Eric Wolf (1968: 290–94) argued, in particular, that what he called the "middle peasantry" was most likely to rebel, not those who were very poor or relatively well off. Middle peasants were those who owned their own land and cultivated it with family labor. They were also the primary bearers of peasant traditions. While such peasants were the most vulnerable to agricultural commercialization because of such factors as their traditionalism, lack of access to credit, and the absence of effective state mechanisms to protect their land, they also had certain advantages once they decided to resist because of their relative isolation, subsistence base, and communal structures. Other moral economy theorists have not agreed with Wolf regarding the precise role of this group of peasants in revolutions, but all point to the importance of peasants in revolutionary movements.

Peasants do not act alone when they revolt, however, and understanding revolutions requires attention to other sectors of a society as well. Walton (1984), for example, agrees that peasant involvement in revolutions is linked to the negative impact of their integration into the modern world economy, but argues that this negative impact must be viewed less from a peasant-centered perspective that encompasses the entire society, especially taking into account the problems faced by those in the middle strata in the towns and cities as well as in the countryside. In this regard, Wolf (1984: 288) notes that revolutionary leadership among peasants often comes from what he refers to as "marginal men" from among the ranks of low-level bureaucrats, professionals, teachers, and religious organizations. In a recent study of the Ethiopian revolution focusing on the province of Tigray, John Young argues that the success of this revolution (and perhaps all revolutions) required a linkage between the peasantry and revolutionaries from the urban working class and intelligentsia who had also felt the negative impact of modernization: "Without this linkage the peasant rebellion will not rise above local concerns and will be defeated" (1994: 62).

A holistic study of revolutions, as Young (1994: 63) points out, also entails a look at the role of the regime in power and how its actions create the conditions for revolt and shape the course of the revolution. Often these regimes are characterized by excessive brutality, corruption, and a lack of legitimacy among the population. This was true, for example of the Samoza regime in Nicaragua that was defeated by the Sandanista revolutionaries. As in the case of Ethiopia where the revolution was carried out largely by ethnic minorities such as the Eritreans and Tigrayans against the dominant Amhara, ethnic differences can also be important.

To broaden our understanding of revolutions, in recent years academics have also paid more attention to the role of women in revolutionary movements and to the impact of revolutions on women and gender relations. Women have fought alongside men in significant numbers in several modern revolutions such as those in Nicaragua and Ethiopia. In Eritrea's 30-year revolt against the Amhara-dominated regimes of Ethiopia, women comprised an estimated one-third of the fighting force. Life in the revolutionary army was very different for them than life as a civilian. In particular, female fighters gained considerable prestige, and they and their male comrades sought to change many practices considered discriminatory to women. Efforts were made to increase women's rights to land ownership and access to education. Female circumcision and infibulation (an operation that sews together the lips of the vagina) were discouraged, and numerous reforms were made in marriage practices, such as the banning of brideprice. Once the war ended in the early 1990s, however, traditional practices began to be reasserted, and, for many of the women who fought in the war, this aspect of the revolutionary struggle continues as they seek to retain and advance the gains that were made.

Not all revolutionary movements succeed. In fact, most fail, and social scientists also seek to understand such failures. For instance, although modern Peru faces a host of social, economic, and political problems, the revolutionaries of the *Sendero Luminoso*, or "Shining Path," have been unable to capitalize on these and overthrow the existing governments. This failure is linked to the movement's failure to retain sufficient peasant support. In a study of the leadership, ideology, and social organization of the Sendero Luminoso, Carlos Ívan Degregori (1992) notes how the movement began among a small cohesive and isolated group rather than as a broad-based mass organization or peasant rebellion. After some initial success in gaining peasant support in the early 1980s, the movement then lost much of this support. The founder of Sendero Lumineso was a university lecturer from the city of Ayachucho, and the leadership continued to be dominated by intellectuals from urban areas whose ideas failed to generate more than superficial appeal among the peasants. Ethnicity also contributed to the movement's problems. The majority of peasants in Peru are indigenous, while the movement is highly stratified with the darker complexioned indigenes at the bottom and the lighter skinned nonindigenes at the top. Such a situation sharply contrasts with Ethiopia, for example, where revolutionaries from urban areas were able to gain widespread acceptance among rural peoples and to use ethnic differences to build a forceful revolutionary movement.

Warfare Between Societies

People within a society generally try to settle their differences in a peaceful and orderly manner, although they do not always succeed. While there are numerous constraints on aggression within most societies, beyond the bounds of the society there are far fewer restraints or incentives for a peaceful resolution of differences. This is particularly relevant when the outsiders are barely considered to be members of the same species. However, those perceived to be so different may be of little social or economic relevance; hence, there is little reason to fight.

Warfare, or aggression between politically autonomous communities, most often occurs when relations break down between communities that usually interact peacefully, or when societies that have little to do with one another find themselves in contact and competition. It is wrong to say that warfare is a natural consequence of human aggressiveness: Warfare results from specific social and environmental circumstances.

Anthropologists recognize three primary categories of intergroup aggression: feuding, raiding, and warfare. The causes and patterns of each will vary from one setting to another. They will also take on very different characteristics in large-scale and small-scale societies, reflecting demographic, economic, and technological differences. In all cases, the parties involved will pursue goals in a relatively ordered fashion, seeking continuously to rationalize their actions through ideology.

FEUDING. A prolonged state of hostility between different families or groups of kin is known as a **feud**. It may take place within a society or between members of different societies.

⌃⌃⌃⌃⌃
*Schooled in rebellion, the forceful
seizure of power, members of the
Shining Path guerrilla group of Peru
lecture new recruits on the organization's ideology and code of conduct.
The lecture takes place at a training
camp in Peru's coca-growing highland
rain forest.*

The feud is the most universal form of intergroup aggression, in part because of its limited
requirements: All that is needed is enough people to find something to fight over.

Spencer and Gillen (1899: 489–496) describe a
common pattern of feud among Australian
Aborigines—the avenging party. Quarrels usually
begin when a man steals a wife from some other
group or when someone's death is blamed on
sorcery by a member of a distant group. The ag-
grieved party will then form a group to attack
those believed to be responsible. Although the
members of the avenging party enter the enemy's
camp fully armed with spears and spear throwers,
boomerangs and shields, the quarrel is usually
confined to a verbal battle, which lasts about an
hour or two. Physical violence is not always
avoided, however. Occasionally, the avenging
party will ambush one or two of the enemy and
spear them without any risk to himself. A common feature of such feuds is that acts of violence
are not necessarily carried out against specific individuals but are aimed at any individual who is a
member of the kin group, reflecting a sense of
shared responsibility. Feuds do not always end
with the first act of revenge; there may be coun-
terattacks, and the feud may evolve into a more
general confrontation between larger groups.

Feuds also take place in large-scale societies,
such as with gang rivalries in American cities.
Feuds assume particular significance where kinship and politics are closely aligned, especially
when political authority is based on heredity, as
with monarchies. The rivalry between York and
Lancaster leading to the Wars of the Roses in
England provides an example.

RAIDING.   **Raids**, surprise predatory attacks
generally by a small group on a neighboring
group, occur both among societies with similar
adaptive strategies and between societies with
different adaptive strategies. Among foragers and
small-scale farmers, surprise predatory attacks by
groups are often associated with population
pressure and competition for scarce resources.
Raids are common among small-scale agriculturalists in the more populous parts of New
Guinea and in the Amazonian basin. Raiding
also is encouraged when neighboring peoples
possess different levels of power. This may entail
those with less power and wealth seeking to
grab something from the more powerful as
well as the more powerful taking things from
those who are less powerful. An example of the
first is provided by the various nomadic groups
of central Asia, such as the Huns and Mongol-

Tartars (see Basilov 1989), who persistently raided their more sedentary neigbors like the Chinese from the third century B.C. to the fourteenth century A.D. An example of the latter is provided by the widespread practice in Southeast Asia until recent centuries of members of low land states raiding highland tribal peoples to capture slaves.

Some societies can be said to have developed specializations in raiding as a core part of their adaptive strategy. The Amazonian Mura evolved from aquatic agriculturalists to almost full-time raiders during the nineteenth century in response to new opportunities created by the Portuguese invasion and occupation of the Amazon. The Mura raided both Europeans and other Indian groups all along the Amazon River, living in canoes for long periods in isolated regions. They raised few crops of their own, subsisting primarily on fish caught in the rivers or what they could seize from others. Groups of Plains Indians in North America developed a similar adaptation on the land, utilizing the horse and developing a social organization suited to their need for mobility and frequent fighting. The horse among these Plains Indians was not only the vehicle for raiding, but also one of its objects, and it became a centerpiece of their society. Daring deeds of bravery done on horseback during raids earned prestige. A man achieved rank by the number of horses he owned and earned a bride by the number of horses he could deliver to her family.

WARFARE. Australian Aboriginal feuds or Mura raids involved relatively small numbers of people, as does most intergroup aggression among small-scale societies. Occasionally, fighting in these societies does escalate, but because of the small population and the inability of foragers and subsistence agriculturalists to afford the luxury of a prolonged period of warfare, fighting of this magnitude tends to be short-lived.

Larger, agriculturally based populations are able to carry out more protracted forms of warfare. As population pressures become noticeable, people begin to find more to fight about. For foragers and farmers living in sparsely populated areas, warfare rarely is initiated for the purpose of seizing territory (although territory may be occupied as an indirect result of fighting). Rather, wars among these peoples usually begin because of interpersonal quarrels, such as fighting over women. As population pressure increases, so does the likelihood of fights for territory.

Warfare is an important feature of life in the densely populated valleys of New Guinea. Thus, for the Dani of Irian Jaya, warfare, until recently, was a constant threat. As noted by Shankman, "most Dani activities are in some way connected with pigs, gardens, and war, and daily life revolves around these central themes" (1991: 611). Mervyn Meggitt (1977: 182), in his study of Mae Enga warfare in the eastern highlands of New Guinea, comments that "in the present and in the past, the desire of local descent groups to gain and hold arable land has been the most powerful motive impelling them to make war on each other." Mae Enga warfare usually lasts only a few days, because more prolonged periods of warfare are a severe strain on resources. The average number of participants in wars among the central Enga is about 360. Between 1961 and 1973, out of 46 incidents, the mean number of deaths was 1.6 per incident. This number may seem small, but in relation to the size of Enga society, it is far from insignificant.

Mortality and casualty rates from warfare in such small-scale societies can, in fact, involve a larger percentage of the total population than in the case of warfare between large-scale societies. The male mortality rates from warfare among groups like the Mae Enga and Dani, for example, appear to be significantly higher than those of the major countries participating in World War II (including Germany and the Soviet Union). Moreover, mobilization rates of adult males for warfare in such small-scale societies are much higher than in large-scale societies. Among peoples like the Mae Enga, virtually the entire adult male population may go to war for at least a brief period. By contrast, mobilization during World War II did not exceed 15 percent in the countries involved in the fighting.

Warfare and the evolution of the state are closely interrelated. Larger political units were created through conquest, and large states were supported through the collection of tribute from conquered peoples. Such warfare was never rationalized solely in terms of power or wealth; it always required some other form of justification. As Frederick Hicks (1979: 90) noted: "Every empire has developed some high moral principle to justify its actions and for which its people would be more than willing to risk their lives than they would be just to make their rulers rich and powerful." Thus, for the Aztecs, support for their aggression came from their religion, which "needed" sacrificial victims.

The Aztecs of central Mexico placed great emphasis on military training, as did many early empires. Both commoners and nobles were given formal military training as youths, and those who were most successful in battle were recruited to posts such as judge, constable, or steward. To remain in a state of readiness, the Aztecs engaged neighboring peoples in *xochiyaoyotl*, flowery wars, in which fighting was restrained and nobles refrained from killing one another (the only casualties were commoners).

Within societies like the Aztec, we see the emergence of the military specialist, a role generally absent in small-scale societies. Such specialization meant that a larger proportion of the male population could become divorced from direct participation in combat. Warfare was carried out by armies consisting of specialists and less-trained soldiers recruited largely to provide bulk.

Along with specialization in personnel, another important feature of the evolution of warfare in relation to increasing social scale is technological change. The most important innovation was the development of firearms. Pettengill (1981: 4–5) pointed this out in regard to the ability of professional soldiers (knights) to con-

This member of Papenal (the National Liberation Army in West Papua) fights with only a bow and arrow against Indonesian troops armed with sophisticated modern weapons. Such resistance movements of indigenous peoples against integration into modern states are fairly widespread today, as they have been in the past.

trol the peasantry in feudal Europe: "Prior to the development of the firearm, the professional soldier did not have a preponderant advantage in weaponry over the peasant when it came to small-scale combat. . . . The professional's advantage lay more in his organization and discipline in the battlefield. . . . This relative symmetry was destroyed once firearms were developed. Whoever possesses them has an enormous advantage over those who don't." Firearms were invented in Europe in the 1300s, but it was not until the mid–1500s to the mid–1600s that significant technological improvements allowed them to assume a major role in warfare and social control. They came to play a vital part not only in warfare within Europe, but also in colonial expansion into those areas of the world that did not possess firearms.

The expansion of European empires and the spread of firearms had an important consequence for patterns of warfare among small-scale societies. In the Amazon basin, societies that had in many instances not been particularly warlike were pushed together and forced to contend with the Portuguese invaders, as well as to compete with each other for dwindling resources. For example, the warfare that became endemic to the Yanomami of southern Venezuela (Chagnon 1983) is largely a consequence of their being pushed into a refuge area with relatively scarce resources. Yanomami adaptation was then influenced by the acquisition of guns by their neighbors, the Makiritare, who were thus able to dominate them. In many parts of the world, differential access to European military technology allowed some groups to control their neighbors. In Africa, those states that supplied the slave trade were able to create far-flung empires with the support of such technology. In Polynesia, petty chiefs were able to defeat their neighbors and establish island-wide kingdoms. In most of these instances, the success of the conquerors was short-lived as the Europeans who made their success possible assumed control.

Creation of the modern world system has been accompanied by warfare that is increas-ingly wide in scope. From the sixteenth century to the early twentieth century, various colonial wars around the world were part of a global competition among European states for colonies. This interstate rivalry culminated in the twentieth century in the so-called world wars. Such warfare brought the development of increasingly complex military technology, to the point that humans possess the ability to initiate wars in any point of the globe within a matter of seconds, to carry out warfare in space, and to exterminate all of humanity.

Rather than ending this chapter on such a pessimistic note, we can remember that, despite frequent eruptions of warfare, people generally have sought to live in peace. Perhaps one of the most important ideas to come out of anthropological studies of warfare is that wars are "cultural artifacts" (Mead 1967: 219); they are created by specific, nonbiological conditions. By altering these conditions, it should be possible to eliminate warfare. To do so requires that we gain a thorough understanding of the conditions that generate warfare, and it is here that social science disciplines like anthropology can play a vital role.

SUMMARY

Although political violence has always been with us, it is limited by norms, laws, and provisions for law enforcement and dispute mediation. Norms are conceptions of how people should behave. Often norms are elevated to the systematized status of laws—binding rules about behavior. Laws are legitimatized by reference to some general normative idea and perhaps by concepts of how a "reasonable man" would behave in a given situation. Both norms and laws change with the social environment.

Attitudes toward laws vary from society to society. Laws based on widely accepted norms usually meet with the most compliance. In every society, however, some people will break laws, become engaged in disputes that require legal mediation, or disagree with others over some laws.

The face of modern warfare: U.S. soldiers practice protection against chemical warfare. Creation of the modern world system has been accompanied by warfare that is increasingly wide in scope.

Ways of handling such situations are related to the society's adaptive strategy. Foraging societies handle disputes either by informal, interpersonal means or by somewhat more formal methods. Common means of dealing with disputes are dispersal or group negotiation. In small-scale farming societies, where the potential for quarrels over distribution of surplus food, property inheritance, and land rights may be greater than in foraging societies, people may use informal interpersonal methods or more formal dispersal or decision-making methods to deal with disputes. In large-scale societies people have so much to fight over that law enforcement and dispute mediation are highly institutionalized.

Despite attempts to deal with threats to social order, tensions sometimes lead to violent struggles for power. Within a society there may be repeated rebellions that change personnel in power but leave the social structure intact. There may also be revolutions, in which the social order is radically changed, often through the involvement of peasants linked with certain urban classes, but these are rare. Warfare between politically autonomous communities may be on as small a scale as an interfamily feud or as large a scale as a world war. Each kind of

warfare is linked to specific adaptations and environments. The expansion of the modern world-system and the formation of European empires have promoted patterns of warfare among some small-scale indigenous populations. An anthropological understanding can help us better understand the causes of warfare and perhaps assist in reducing the incidence of such violence.

KEY TERMS

Feud A prolonged state of hostility between different families or groups of kin.

Law A binding rule created through enactment or custom that defines right and reasonable behavior.

Legitimacy General normative concepts based ultimately on the traditional moral system of a society.

Norm A conception of appropriate or expected behavior.

Raid A surprise predatory attack generally by a small group on a neighboring group.

Revolution A break with the existing order resulting in fundamental political or economic change, especially in regard to the relationship of social classes.

Warfare Formalized aggression between politically autonomous communities.

SUGGESTED READINGS

Studies on law include:

Collier, Jane F. 1973. *Law and Social Change in Zinacantan*. Stanford: Stanford University Press. (Mexico)

Fitzpatrick, P. 1980. *Law and State in Papua New Guinea*. New York: Academic Press.

Hamnett, Ian, editor. 1977. *Social Anthropology and Law*. New York: Academic Press.

Moore, Sally Falk. 1978. *Law as Process: An Anthropological Approach*. London: Routledge and Kegan Paul.

Nader, Laura. 1990. *Harmony Ideology: Justice and Control in a Zapotec Mountain Village*. Stanford: Stanford University Press.

Newman, K. S. 1984. *Law and Economic Organization: A Comparative Study of Preindustrial Societies*. New York: Cambridge University Press.

Renteln, Alison Dundes. 1990. *International Human Rights: Universalism Versus Relativism*. Newbury Park: Sage Publications.

Roberts, Simon. 1979. *Order and Dispute: An Introduction to Legal Anthropology*. New York: Penguin.

Rose, Laurel L. 1991. *The Politics of Harmony: Land Dispute Strategies in Swaziland*. New York: Cambridge University Press.

Rosen, Lawrence. 1989. *The Anthropology of Justice: Law as Culture in Islamic Society*. New York: Cambridge University Press.

Starr, June, and Jane F. Collier, editors. 1989. *History and Power in the Study of Law: New Directions in Legal Anthropology*. Ithaca: Cornell University Press.

Studies on rebellion, revolution, and warfare include:

Boehm, C. 1984. *Blood Revenge: The Anthropology of Feuding in Montenegro and Other Tribal Societies*. Lawrence: University Press of Kansas.

Friedrich, Paul. 1970. *Agrarian Revolt in a Mexican Village*. Englewood Cliffs, NJ: Prentice-Hall.

Haas, Jonathan, editor. 1990. *The Anthropology of War*. New York: Cambridge University Press.

Huizer, Gerritt. 1973. *Peasant Rebellion in Latin America*. New York: Penguin.

Meggitt, Mervyn. 1977. *Blood Is Their Argument: Warfare Among the Mae Enga Tribesmen of the New Guinea Highlands*. Palo Alto, CA: Mayfield.

Turner, Paul R., David Pitt, et al. 1989. *The Anthropology of War and Peace: Perspectives on the Nuclear Age*. Granby, MA: Bergin and Garvey.

Turney-High, Harry H. 1991. *Primitive War: Its Practices and Concepts*. Columbia: University of South Carolina Press.

Vayda, A. P. 1976. *War in Ecological Perspective: Persistence, Change and Adaptive Processes in Three Oceanian Societies*. New York: Plenum Press.

Warman, Arturo. 1980. *We Come to Object*. Baltimore: Johns Hopkins University Press. (Mexico)

Wolf, Eric. 1968. *Peasant Wars of the Twentieth Century*. New York: Harper and Row.

Wolf, Eric. 1971. *Peasant Wars of the Twentieth Century*. London: Faber and Faber.

Young, John. 1994. "*Peasants and Revolution in Ethiopia: Tigray 1975–1989*". Ph.D. dissertation, Simon Fraser University.

13 RELIGIOUS BELIEF, BEHAVIOR, AND SYMBOLISM

One theme that has turned up repeatedly in the preceding chapters is our search for order in ideology and behavior. The social and mental order that we find among humans is not so much an innate quality of our species as a reflection of our dread of anarchy, of a universe

➤ How context—e.g., society, history, and ecology—is important in understanding religious belief

➤ How the Rastafarians' long hair exemplifies the power of culture-specific symbolism

➤ How some religious practices can have an emotional impact and ensure that the religious message becomes a part of the believers' personalities

➤ Why a full-time religious specialist would not be found in a small-scale society

➤ Whether religion can play a role in revolutionary movements

without order and meaning. Our social institutions, norms, and experiences are not always sufficient to maintain the delicate balance between order and anarchy, however. Despite all the precautions we have taken, our ability to interpret life as orderly and meaningful faces its greatest challenge when we seek answers to the ultimate questions of our existence: Where did we come from? Why are we as we are? Why must we die? In response to such questions, humans often turn to **religion,** a system of beliefs involving supernatural forces or beings that provide shape and meaning to the universe.

The term *supernatural,* as employed in our definition of religion, refers to a shift away from the secular order of reality into the *sacred,* the realm of symbolic meanings and actions through which people interpret the forces that ultimately control and give shape to the universe. Religion, then, involves the use of sacred symbols through belief and action. In studying religious beliefs, anthropologists are concerned with how people construct a religious view of the world—a religious **cosmology,** or philosophy concerned with the fundamental causes and processes of things in the universe.

How are religious beliefs related to a society's adaptive strategies? As with beliefs in general, they tend to reflect a society's view of the world from the perspective of its adaptive strategy and to pose questions in a way that has meaning within the context of this strategy. Thus, the Aboriginal Dreamtime mythology relates the ultimate questions of our existence to the actions of mythical creative beings, but the shape of the questions and the answers to them reflect a foraging adaptation in their focus on plants, animals, and landscape in relation to hunting and gathering activities. In examining the major religions found in the world today, we see products of earlier adaptive strategies. Yet, they have evolved over time so as to be meaningful in the context of modern conditions.

Buddhist temple in Saigon, Vietnam, Chinatown. One of the major religions of the world, Buddhism arose in India during a time of great social change and eventually spread throughout most of Asia and even to parts of the West.

< UNDERSTANDING RELIGIOUS > BELIEF

What concerns anthropologists is not the ultimate truth of a religious assertion, but the question of why people hold a given belief. Why, for instance, have some people selected the idea of reincarnation out of a range of possible means of dealing with death? To the extent that they can be found, answers to such questions are both complex and difficult to arrive at. In searching for answers, we must look at the particular religious beliefs and their relationship to social processes and to historical and ecological factors.

Belief Systems in Context

Religious beliefs generally are systematically centered on a core of precepts presented in symbolic form about the nature of things. It is this core that gives direction and shape to the belief system. We can see how a belief system is shaped by looking at the Rastafarians, members of a religious cult founded in Jamaica.

The Rastafarians believe that they are eternal and shall never die. They declare, "We who are Rastafarians are the disciples who have walked with God from the time when the foundation of creation was laid, through 71 bodies, to behold the 72nd house of power which shall reign forever" (Barrett 1977: 112). They also believe that the late Ethiopian emperor Haile Selassie was the prophesied Messiah; that Africans are descendants of the lost tribe of Israel; that their diaspora is analogous to the Babylonian captivity, in which they are living in exile in Jamaica, the modern-day Babylon, because of the "Whiteman," in contrast with Ethiopia, which is heaven; and that whites are inferior to blacks.

We can trace the historic origins of Rastafarian beliefs to such sources as Christianity and the early twentieth-century teachings of Marcus Garvey, an American black activist who promoted ties between New World and African blacks. The Rastafarians see the Bible as a source for many of their beliefs. They

Members of the Rastafarian cult of Jamaica attempt to adapt to their poverty and powerlessness through the belief that they are immortal and that the world order that discriminates against them will be reversed by supernatural forces. Marijuana (Ganja) is smoked as a symbol of freedom from the laws of "Babylon."

argue, however, that the Bible has been distorted by the Whiteman and that they alone are able to interpret the meaning of its contents correctly.

The Rastafarians' interpretation of the Bible is linked to their own circumstances. For instance, they base their belief in their own immortality and reincarnation on a passage from the Bible in the Book of Romans: "The wages of sin is death, but the gift of God is eternal life." This passage guaranteeing eternal life has been interpreted in many ways by different Christian sects; the Rastafarians' version is derived from the peculiarities of their life in Jamaica—their poverty, the discrimination that they have faced, and the near-hopelessness with respect to changing their social circumstances by rational means.

The Rastafarian variant of Christianity is an example of what is termed a "religion of the oppressed" (Lanternari 1963). It is an attempt by oppressed peoples to deal with their situation through the medium of religion. Such religions represent a form of rebellion, and it is from the impoverished population of Jamaica (and elsewhere in the Caribbean) that followers of the Rastafarian movement are recruited. They can be viewed as seeking to escape from their plight through faith and the promise of a reversal of the world order by supernatural forces.

Choices Available

A person's decision to become a Rastafarian often is a matter of conscious choice, but given the life of most poor Jamaicans, it represents one of only a few choices they perceive to be available. In seeking the answer to why a person chooses to become a Rastafarian, or to adhere to any other religious belief, we can look at psychological and social pressures and constraints. The Rastafarian faith offers security and hope in an otherwise insecure and often rather miserable world. The potential Rastafarian is raised in an environment of poverty and illiteracy in which individual attempts at upward mobility rarely succeed and rebellions consistently fail. That those living under such conditions will turn to such religions as the Rastafarian can be expected. To determine why a particular choice is made, we can look at what one religion offers that others do not and how each religion recruits its members.

The options available in choosing a religion vary from one situation to the next. In small-scale societies, individuals rarely have much choice in their beliefs. For example, Australian Aborigines traditionally were provided with only one basic view of the world. There was little possibility of questioning any of the fundamental tenets of this belief system. Those who lived around the various Aboriginal societies had similar beliefs, the social order and adaptive strategy were relatively stable, and their very personalities were sufficiently intertwined with these beliefs to allow little room for fundamental change. The coming of Europeans to Australia altered this situation; but even today, as with many small communities in our own society, the choices of religious belief realistically available to Aborigines living in more isolated communities remains extremely limited.

Increasing social scale presents a potential challenge to the monopolization of religious belief found in traditional small-scale societies. However, when state religions are promoted, choices may still be severely limited, as they were in Spain during the Inquisition. Even in the absence of such formal constraints, there are other limiting factors. Early socialization is one such factor, when young people are conditioned to view the world from a particular perspective and to feel that their religious affiliation is a vital part of their social identity. This religious socialization may influence one's choice of friends and potential spouses, interaction with whom further encourages retention of the initial allegiance. But, as we shall see in the final section of this chapter, there are many other forces at work to encourage change. These include culture contact, drastic changes of social status, and proselytization.

Religious Beliefs and Adaptive Strategy

As a final consideration in understanding religious beliefs, certain forms tend to be associated with particular adaptive strategies. For example, among foragers, such as traditional Australian Aborigines, religious beliefs are closely related to those things that are of most importance in their lives: the land over which they range and the plants and animals they pro-

Galileo before the Court of the Holy Office, 1633: The Inquisition, part of the institutionalized religion of the day, worked to restrict choice of belief.

cure. Aboriginal religion therefore places a heavy emphasis on the procreation of important animal species.

The Gunabibi fertility ritual practiced in northern Australia contains a great deal of procreative imagery. The sacred ground on which the rite is performed includes a large crescent-shaped pit representing the uterus of the mythical rock python, which is the central image on which this ritual is based. As part of the ritual, young boys are led into the pit and symbolically swallowed by the rock python; they later emerge reborn. Many of the objects used in the ritual are phallic. In one of the final acts of the Gunabibi, the men place two large *jelmalandji* (12- to 20-foot-long poles with pads of grass and paper bark tied to them) across the pit. The

rite represents a way to ensure the growth and perpetuation of the animals most important to the Aboriginal diet.

The adoption of agriculture results in a shift of emphasis in a people's religion. The gods, prayers, rites, and so forth now are concerned primarily with the things that influence agricultural productivity: pestilence, natural disaster, rain, time. Among the most important deities worshipped by the Maya are those associated with the weather, especially with rain. Mayan religious specialists traditionally devoted much of their effort to divining knowledge useful in planting and harvesting.

Although they are somewhat of a simplification, Anthony Wallace (1966) has proposed four basic categories of religion that he associates with particular modes of adaptation and social formation:

1. *Shamanistic,* characterized by individualistic and shamanic cult institutions and part-time practitioners, and usually found in conjunction with relatively independent foraging bands such as those of the Inuit and native Siberians. (Shamans are discussed at greater length later in this chapter in the section on religious specialists.)

2. *Communal,* in which communal religious institutions are added to individualistic and shamanic practices. Communal cults are characterized by periodic gatherings of members of a society for ceremonial purposes, often in association with the seasons, harvests, or rites of passage. This type of religion is associated with relatively well-integrated foraging societies such as the Australian Aborigines and with small-scale agricultural societies.

3. *Olympian,* which add to the communal system a hierarchically and bureaucratically organized professional priesthood that manages rituals and beliefs. This type of religion is characterized by a hierarchy of deities that usually includes a number of powerful high gods. It is associated with chiefdoms and nonindustrial states, such as those of the Aztecs and the Inca.

4. *Monotheistic,* which includes all the various cult forms but is unique in that it has only a single supreme being or concentration of supernatural beings or forces under the control of a single supreme being. This type of religion is closely associated with the growth and expansion of state organization and the centralization of power in the hands of the state.

◄ SYMBOLIC EXPRESSION ►

The Huichol of northwestern Mexico were foragers until a few centuries ago, when they adopted agriculture as a result of Spanish influence. The Huichol have retained many social and cultural elements from their foraging past, and these continue to be reflected in their religion, which centers on what Barbara Myerhoff (1970) refers to as the Deer-Maize-Peyote complex. The influence of their foraging past is represented in deer symbolism, while agriculture is associated with maize symbolism. Through such religious practices as the ceremonial anointing of maize with deer blood, these two elements of their life are united.

Symbols like the deer and maize of the Huichol draw together or focus significant elements of a people's existence, unifying the everyday with the supernatural. Such symbols objectify experience and belief; thus, they evoke our most fundamental feelings. Because symbols have the ability to unify and express the core elements of our lives, they play an important role in religion. In the following sections we look at areas of symbolic expression that include beliefs about food, totems, and myth. In Chapter 14 the related subject of art will be discussed.

Culture-Specific Symbols

Certain religious symbols may be universal, but most are culture-specific, and individuals must be conditioned to understand and appreciate them. Conditioning occurs through both informal and formal instruction, as when Aboriginal youths are taught the meanings of the marks on the sacred boards that serve as physical representations of the actions of the Dreamtime beings. This learning is enhanced by creating an environment designed to stir people's emotions when they are confronted with the symbols. Such an environment may include use of impressive architecture or other evocative settings, a stirring ritual or ceremonial gathering, or a combination of the two. For example, through physical separation, ritual, and other means, Pintubi (an Aboriginal society from central Australia) youths are already in an otherworldly state when the elders bring forth the sacred paraphernalia and tell them: "Dead men held this" (Myers 1982).

The power of culture-specific religious symbolism is exemplified in the best-known Rastafarian symbol: their long and unkempt hair, their "dreadlocks." Wearing their hair in this fashion is justified by reference to the Bible: "They shall not make baldness upon their head, neither shall they shave off the corner of their beard, nor make any cuttings in the flesh" (Leviticus 21:5). The dreadlock serves as a powerful public symbol of what the Rastafarian religion is about. It sets the Rastafarian apart as "the natural man, who typifies in his appearance the unencumbered life" (Barrett 1977: 137). But beyond this there is the association with rebellion, with a refusal to accept the world as defined by the Whiteman. As Barrett has noted, hair is used by many Jamaicans as an index of social differences. By wearing long, unkempt hair the Rastafarian is considered wild, dangerous, effeminate, and dreadful. The Rastafarian underscores contradictions within Jamaican society and represents a threat to the social order: "The hair symbol of the Rastas announces that they are outside Jamaican society and do not care to enter under any circumstances other than one of radical change in the society's attitude to the poor" (Barrett 1977: 138). The response of authorities and others wishing to maintain the status quo has been to cut off the Rastafarians' hair.

While hairstyle is assigned some symbolic significance in virtually all societies, its specific symbolic significance can vary. While many Westerners would be disturbed to see the Pope or their local minister or priest with long, unkempt hair, in many other societies a man's long hair is associated with holiness; in some societies, it is a status marker. Before the arrival of the Spanish, lowland Maya, especially those of high status, commonly wore their hair long. Under Spanish influence and pressure, the Maya cut their hair, and today most Maya view long hair unfavorably. It is only among the non-Christian Lacandon that long hair continues to be worn, and this has served to enforce other Maya's aversion to long hair because of its association with paganism.

Food Symbolism

People's dietary habits are often closely associated with religious beliefs. In many religious traditions, particular animals or plants are assigned symbolic status; in religions with food taboos, people are forbidden to eat certain foods, except perhaps in specific sacred contexts. Rastafarians have relatively strict ideas about their diet, and these ideas are tied to their religion. They are for the most part vegetarians, although they may eat small fish. Pork and beef are considered pollutants. Basically, Rastafarians favor a diet that is natural and derived directly from the earth.

The cow has symbolic properties in many societies. To many North Americans it is a symbol of wealth and well-being, but has no direct religious significance. Pastoralists in the southern Sudan and western Ethiopia, such as the Nuer and Dinka, traditionally saw their lives and those of their cattle as inextricably intertwined. Dinka perceptions of color, light, and shape are connected with the color configurations of their cattle. The centrality of the cow to Dinka culture is reflected in their religion; the cow serves as the most important element in their religious beliefs and practices. Animal sacrifice is their central religious act, and the sacrificial animal symbolizes Dinka society as the meat is divided to represent social relations on the basis of gender, age, and clanship (Lienhardt 1961). While most Hindus in South Asia do not depend as heavily on cattle for their survival as the Dinka, the cow has assumed an important place in their religion as well. To Hindus the cow is "worshipped as a symbol of warmth and moisture, as earth mother, and as a producer of milk and indirectly ghi [clarified butter], so essential in sacrifices" (Heston 1971: 192). In India, this belief

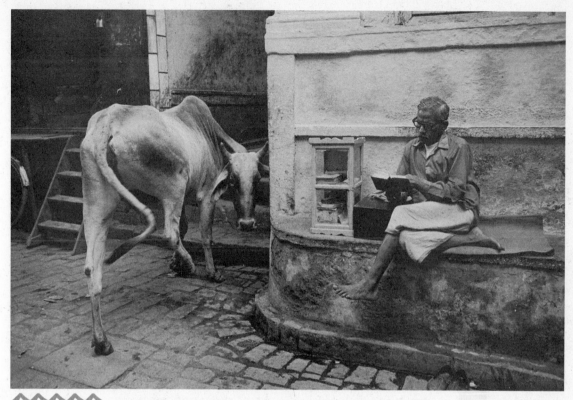

In India, Hindus have traditionally worshipped cows, which are allowed to wander freely through villages and cities. This belief and the Hindu tradition of nonviolence led to a constitutional ban on the slaughter of cattle. Today, the killing of cattle and eating of beef remain emotive issues in India.

and the Hindu tradition of nonviolence led to a constitutional ban on the slaughter of cattle, and today, killing cattle and eating beef remain very emotive issues in India, contributing to communal tensions and sometimes riots.

Totems

Australian Aborigines, like many other peoples, "conceptualize a single, unified cosmic order in which man and the natural species, ancestral beings, spirits, and other conceived entities are on equal terms. All are interrelated in a genealogical and pseudogenealogical manner" (Tonkinson 1974: 74). This view of the cosmos is referred to as *totemic.* The links between individuals and groups and particular plants, animals, and other natural phenomena are represented symbolically in the form of **totemic emblems,** and their relationship forms the basis for ceremonial and ritual activities.

Australian Aborigines recognize several varieties of totemism. Two primary types are conception totemism and ancestral totemism.

Conception totems are associated with aspects of a person's birth; for example, plants, animals, insects, secretions, or minerals of the locale where a person is believed to have been conceived may serve as conception totems. In many Aboriginal societies, there is a strong emotional bond with such totems. Since the totem and the individual are said to be of the same flesh, individuals may refrain from eating or otherwise harming those things identified as their totems. This caring bond is not universal, however. The Mardudjara of Jigalong in Western Australia feel no special attachment to their conception totem, and there are no dietary restrictions. Even within a similar environment, practices can vary. While the Aranda of central Australia place restrictions on eating their conception totems, the nearby Warramunga will eat their conception totems if they are killed by someone else, and the neighboring Walbiri assert that "men would be stupid not to eat such foods when available" (Meggitt 1962: 208).

Ancestral totems link individuals with the historical or mythical past. For the Australian Aborigines, ancestral totems are associated with activities of the Dreamtime beings. During their travels, as recorded in myth, the Dreamtime beings left objects behind; these became animated with a life force from which came spirit children waiting in plant or animal form to be born as humans. These totems place individuals within their physical environment and create a spiritual map of the terrain. It is often through these totemic beings that individuals gain access to land, in return for which they perform ceremonies at sites associated with their ancestral totems. Known as *increase rites*, the ceremonies usually involve activities aimed at procreating species of animals. Attitudes toward the treatment of plants and animals acknowledged as ancestral totems tend to be similar to those regarding conception totems. The Walbiri have no rules against eating their ancestral totems, although Meggitt (1962: 209) comments that "occasionally a man would express sorrow, in a half-joking fashion, when he ate a bird or animal he called 'father.'. . . The usual comment, accompanied by winks and smiles, was: 'What a pity—I am eating my poor father! I am so sorry for him!'" Some anthropologists claim that restrictions on the eating of totemic animals play

an important role in preserving species in a given area, but the evidence is far from conclusive.

Myth

Since at least the nineteenth century, it has been common to use the term *myth* to refer to something that is untrue: the myth of equality, the myth of democracy, and so forth. This usage reflects the secularization of our beliefs, for in its original sense, a sacred tale, a myth did not connote falsehood. For those adhering to a particular religious tradition, their myths represent received truth. Other peoples' myths may be false, but not their own. As used by anthropologists to describe a type of sacred narrative, a myth is more than just a tale. **Myths** express the unobservable realities of religious belief in terms of observable phenomena. Like other forms of symbolic expression, myths link the supernatural and sacred with the concrete and mundane.

Myths, in fact, serve a variety of functions. They may serve as cultural histories, alluding to actual events and practices in the past, such as migrations, earlier forms of social organization, and natural occurrences like meteor showers, eclipses, or floods. The events described in myths, however, may be apocryphal. Even when the myths do have historical validity, they do not simply represent records of the past, since myths use history for social and religious purposes.

Sacred history myths may serve as charters for interest groups and as justifications for particular institutions in a society. They link the present social order with a sacred past and condition behavior toward desired ends. Aboriginal youths are not instructed in their mythic traditions simply to be entertained. The myths they are told are intended to assist in producing a prescribed view of the world and an attitude toward social institutions and those responsible for maintaining the status quo that will ensure continuity of the existing social order. In this respect, myths often "constitute a conservative, socializing force

Myths link the supernatural and sacred with the concrete and mundane. In this Pueblo Indian dance, New Mexico, performed on feast day in winter, the spirits of animals and those of people are believed to be connected as one. The enactment of this belief in ritual gives assurance that the animals depended on for hunting will be plentiful.

whose function is to sanctify existing institutions and foster the values of sociality" (Hiatt 1975: 5).

The events depicted in myths deal with fundamental questions concerning the human condition from the point of view of a particular social order. Myths represent attempts to analyze the world around us and to resolve its contradictions or paradoxes. The themes that occur over and over again in myths are those associated with basic philosophical questions: the relationship between life and death, the origins of life and human society, and the strains with which people in all societies must come to terms, such as tensions between parents and children or siblings.

⟨ SUPERNATURAL FORCES ⟩ AND BEINGS

All religious beliefs recognize some named force or entity. The variety of forms these entities take is extensive, and even within a single tradition there can be many different forces or supernatural beings populating the cosmos. Following Annemarie de Waal Malefijt (1968: 146–162), we will review briefly the major varieties.

Unseen Power

Many people believe in the existence of some *impersonal supernatural force*, a power that although unseen is believed to be present everywhere. R. R. Marett (1909) referred to the belief in such a force as **animatism.** This force is conceived of as a massive reservoir of power that may infuse or possess, and perhaps be used by, individuals, gods, the forces of nature, and even natural objects. Animatism is associated with societies characterized by very different adaptive strategies. Thus, it is exemplified in the concept of *mana,* common to many religious traditions throughout the Pacific Islands; in the Hindu concept of *brahma*; in the ancient Greek notion of *dynamis*; and, more recently in Western culture, as in Henri Bergson's *élan vital*. People are rarely satisfied with leaving things up to such an ambiguous entity, however. The concept of an impersonal supernatural force is almost universally accompanied by beliefs in more precisely conceived supernatural beings.

Spirits

People in many societies believe in the existence of an almost endless number of *spirits* that dwell in animals and places or simply wander about the earth. We refer to this belief as **animism.** Because of their great number, spirits usually are viewed collectively and not given individual identities.

The number and categories of spirits recognized in a society can vary a good deal. The Gururumba of Papua New Guinea recognize only two types of spirit: those that live in the highland forest area and those that inhabit the lowlands among the riverbanks (Newman 1965: 62–63). In contrast, the Javanese have a large number of categories, including frightening spirits, possessing spirits, familiar spirits, place spirits, and guardian spirits. A culture may assign individual names to certain spirits, but even these spirits are recognized as members of a broader category of similar beings, failing to achieve the degree of individualization reserved for gods.

Spirits sometimes are of human origin. The spirit children that form the pool from which new Aborigines are born are closely tied to the human population. And many peoples recognize a category sometimes referred to as *souls of the dead*. These are supernatural beings of human origin that may for a time after death be remembered individually as *ghosts*; later they merge into an unnamed collectivity. The Walbiri Aborigines of central Australia believe that, upon death, a person's spirit becomes a *manbaraba*, "an ethereal, pale ghost, whose features resemble those of its previous owner" (Meggitt 1962: 192). The ghost remains near the tree platform where the corpse has been placed until the death is avenged (death is never considered to have occurred naturally). The ghost then dissipates, with its spirit joining the collective pool of matrispirits and patrispirits associated with particular kin groups.

The dead may retain their individual identity and continue to play an active role in society. These entities are called *ancestor souls* or *ancestor spirits*. In many societies ancestor worship is important to religious beliefs and practices. Even

today, for many Chinese and Japanese the ancestral shrine has a prominent place in the home, where the ancestors receive daily offerings and prayers. Swazi families of South Africa carry out rites to pacify ancestors on the occasion of births, marriages, deaths, the building of new homes, and family calamities.

Gods

Ancestors sometimes make it further up the religious hierarchy, being elevated to the status of a god. The term **god** or **goddess** (or *deity*) refers to a supernatural being with an individual identity and recognizable attributes who is worshipped as having power over nature and human fortunes. Most gods are of nonhuman origin. However, many human beings have either proclaimed themselves to be gods or have been considered gods by a large number of worshippers. The Rastafarians believed that the late Ethiopian emperor Haile Selassie was a living deity, for example. Such concepts are often related to systems of social stratification, as when rulers claim divinity on the basis of their descent from gods. Until 1947, the Japanese emperor was considered divine, his divinity based on a claim of descent from the sun goddess, Amaterasu Omikami. Japan's defeat in World War II and subsequent changes in the country's system of stratification ultimately ended the emperor's official divine status.

Religious systems vary widely with respect to the number of gods worshipped. As in the Christian tradition, some religions have only one god. We refer to this as **monotheism.** In **polytheism,** as in the Hindu religion, there can be an almost limitless number of gods, or perhaps a finite number arranged in a hierarchy. Monotheism is related to the development of social stratification and the rise of large-scale societies—India providing an important exception. Thompson (1970), for example, discusses

The variety of forms that supernatural forces or beings can take is extensive. Here, at a Ganpati Festival, India, appears the elephant-headed Hindu god, Ganesaha, remover of obstacles. This god is invoked in parts of India at the beginnings of new enterprises.

how the lowland Mayan god Itzam Na assumed an ever greater role during the classic period; other gods were placed under or incorporated into Itzam Na as one of its many manifestations. This process was related closely to the rise of the Mayan aristocracy. When the aristocrats' power apparently collapsed, so too did Itzam Na, and a more diverse and egalitarian polytheism reasserted itself.

An important role of the god or gods in most religious traditions is creation—the creation of the universe, of life, and of the prevailing order within the universe. For the Australian Aborigines, the creative acts of the mythical Dreamtime beings remain at the forefront of

their religious practices and beliefs. Other traditions, however, take creation more for granted, emphasizing the postcreative activities of gods. Some religions also believe in an omnipotent and omniscient god. Supposedly, this god created the universe and then more or less withdrew, leaving subsequent direction of the world in the hands of lesser deities. Such a god is called *otiose*, meaning "idle," serving no practical purpose. Otiose deities seldom have an important place in worship or ritual. The Igbo of Nigeria believe in such a god, Chuku, but there are neither priests nor shrines dedicated to its service (unlike other Igbo gods that are believed to be regular and important participants in human affairs). Chuku is called on only in cases of great distress, but even then the Igbo feel that this will do little good.

Religions that allow for a number of gods have frequently included relatively specialized gods, sometimes called *attribute gods*. Pre-Columbian lowland Maya, for example, recognized merchant gods, gods of hunting and fishing, gods of cacao growers, gods of beekeepers, a god of *balche* (a fermented ritual drink), gods of medicine and curers, gods of war, gods of poetry and music, a god of tattooing, a god of ballgame players, a god of fire, and a god of birth, just to name a few. Such supernatural departmentalization is largely a function of secular specialization in a society. Particularly important activities may have several highly specialized gods: The ancient Romans had three separate gods of the plow, since the fields were plowed three times. Activities of less importance might share a god, be lumped with some generalized deity, or do without one altogether.

Minor Beings

Finally, many religions also possess a range of divine or semidivine beings of minor theological significance. In Western Europe, these include dwarfs, elves, pixies, and the like. The traditions of the Kekchi of southern Belize populate the forests with a number of semidivine denizens. These include the *chiel*, who live in caves and in pre-Columbian ruins. They are said to live much like people, and on occasion they visit human settlements. There is also Xtabai, who shakes her breasts at young men to lure them into the forest, only to cause them to go insane. She has a male counterpart. A common character in many religions is the *trickster*. This is a semidivine being who may establish cultural practices for a group accidentally, but who basically is not concerned with human welfare. Among native North Americans, one of the best-known tricksters is Coyote: "He stole the sun, the moon, and the stars from the spirits who had them before, but he did not know

what to do with them, so he placed them in the sky" (Malefijt 1968: 161).

< RELIGIOUS BEHAVIOR > AND CONSCIOUSNESS

Religious beliefs are not simply stated: They are presented in such a way as to have a strong emotional impact. Religious specialists (about whom more will be said in the next section) attempt to ensure that a complex, multidimensional message concerning the cosmos and one's place in it becomes a fundamental part of an individual's personality. While the precise aims and methods of religious practices may vary from one setting to the next, there are features that are common to most religious traditions.

Separation

One important aspect of religious behavior is separation. It involves the recognition of two relatively distinct realms, the secular and the sacred, each of which is associated with particular actions and objects. Western Desert Aborigines in Australia categorize as "secret–sacred" certain acts, beliefs, and related objects, which are reserved exclusively for fully initiated men or women because of the danger resulting from their close association with the Dreamtime. Punishment for transgressions traditionally was severe—sometimes even death. The ideological and emotional boundary between the sacred and the secular is far less extreme in most present-day Christian religions, but there is a boundary nevertheless.

Separation of the sacred often is related to an idea of exclusiveness: Entry into this realm is special and not for everyone. To be able to enter, one has to meet special preconditions. Birth may be a factor, in which case only the chosen few are allowed entrance, or some sort of initiation may be required, as in the Christian practice of baptism. Special knowledge of esoteric language, rites, or symbols may also be important, and can be learned only from those already initiated.

The specialness of the sacred is emphasized further by how the transition from the realm of the secular to that of the sacred is marked. Frequently some form of purification is involved, ranging from abstaining from sexual relations to becoming thoroughly drunk to bathing and putting on one's Sunday best. There may be other transitional rites actually marking entry into the realm of the sacred as well, such as kneeling, praying, and crossing oneself.

Ritual

Another common feature of religious behavior is routinization and repetitiveness. Religious performances in any tradition tend to be highly routinized. While there may be variations in a Catholic mass or an Aboriginal Gunabibi ceremony, the basic format remains much the same from one celebration to the next. Within this framework we find even more precise routinization in the acting out of **rituals,** highly stereotyped, stylized, and repetitive behaviors that take place at a set time and place. This orderliness

serves to create a sense of security and stability; participants know what is happening, and they know what to expect. Members of a church know the basic order of the services and most of the parts of the services. Such routinization is evident in baptisms, communions, and marriages. Religious rituals support the basic tenets of the ordered universe as perceived within a religious tradition. Repetitive chants and the use of repetitive themes in music and discourse also reinforce the primary messages of a religion.

Altered Consciousness

Practices associated with some religions attempt to place people in an extreme emotional state, sometimes taking the form of a trance. The idea is to provide experiences or visions so overwhelming as to reinforce the individual's belief in the reality of the supernatural. There are numerous means of achieving such states of consciousness, including fasting, flagellation, sensory deprivation, breathing exercises, meditation, and ritual dancing and drumming. Certain yogic practices originating in Tibet, for example, include the recitation of *mantras*, words or sounds

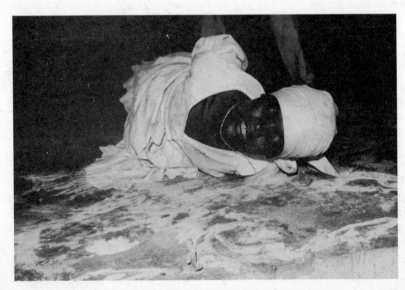

Practices in some religions attempt to place people in an extreme emotional state, even a form of trance. The idea is to provide experiences or visions so overwhelming as to reinforce the individual's belief in the reality of the supernatural. Among vodun (voodoo) practitioners in Haiti, for example, religious gatherings lead to trance states induced by drumming and dancing.

of power, in almost hypnotic fashion. By uttering the sound of a mantra associated with a deity, the person tries to transcend human thought and make contact with the deity. A trance-like state is achieved by voodoo practitioners in Haiti through drumming and dancing during special gatherings. Trances such as these are not random affairs: They tend to be culture-specific, following the rules or guidelines of the particular tradition and reflecting the behavioral norms of the culture.

A very ancient and widespread means of achieving trance-like states is the use of narcotics (see Furst 1972; Harner 1973; Schultes and Hoffman 1979). Relatively mild narcotics such as alcohol, tobacco, and marijuana are employed by many religions to assist in achieving the desired effect. Rastafarians use marijuana both for symbolic purposes and because of its mind-altering properties. They make reference to the Bible to support its use; such as, "Thou shalt eat the herb of the field" (Genesis 3:18). Other religions employ much more powerful hallucinogens to bring the individual face to face with the supernatural. The hallucinogenic mushroom *Amanita mascaria* is used by Siberian shamans to communicate with the supernatural by allowing them to go into a trance in which they believe that the soul leaves the body. Some scholars maintain that narcotic-induced soul flights may have led to the initial beliefs in souls and ghosts. According to Gordon Wasson (1972), the religious complexes in Eurasia and the New World have many roots in the Amanita-using shamanistic traditions of Siberia. Another hallucinogen, peyote, has become important in the religions of many indigenous peoples in northern Mexico and the southwestern United States (see Myerhoff 1974).

The use of narcotics in religion is related to a number of environmental and social factors. An obvious one is the availability of the plants. The widespread use of hallucinogenic plants in the New World is facilitated by the unusual number available (Schultes 1963: 147). Where plants are not available locally, trade lines can be developed. The use of narcotic plants in religion can also be linked to social structure. Narcotic plants are widely used in egalitarian societies with shamanistic traditions. With increasing social stratification, their use tends to become much more restricted. In contrast to less stratified Mexican Indian societies, where the use of hallucinogens is widespread, narcotic use among the highly stratified Aztec in pre-Columbian times was restricted to a small elite.

Historically, the popular use of narcotics for religious purposes survived only where there was little or no competition from state religions. The unrestricted use of narcotics for religious purposes threatened the monopolization of sacred truth that served as a fundamental support for state institutions. Today, the use of narcotics for religious purposes is widely opposed by secular state authorities. In the United States and Canada, for example, conflict arose between native followers of the so-called peyote cult and the government authorities who declared peyote use illegal. The 1978 American Indian Freedom of Religion Act made it legal for members of the Native American Church to use peyote in their ceremonies, but the U.S. government continues to contest the legality of growing, selling, or buying peyote.

◄ RELIGIOUS SPECIALISTS ►

In most societies, there are some people who are more skilled in the performance of certain religious tasks and who have a greater knowledge of religious traditions than others. In small-scale societies, where there is minimal division of labor, these individuals are seldom full-time specialists. They are people who must perform many of the same tasks as other members of their society, but who also do a little extra. For this, they may be afforded a status somewhat above the others. As social scale increases and the division of labor becomes more complex, full-time specialists emerge—individuals who support themselves exclusively by carrying out religious tasks.

Shamans

A type of specialist particularly common in foraging societies is the **shaman.** Michael Harner (1973: xi) has defined a shaman "as a man or woman who is in direct contact with the spirit world through a trance state and has one or more spirits at his command to carry out his bidding for good or evil." The shaman's status is highly personalistic, for it depends on perceived ability to contact and influence the spirit world rather than on knowledge of sacred lore or ritual. Furthermore, while the shaman's ritual activities adhere to a generally prescribed cultural pattern, there is a great deal of leeway within most cultures in how the shaman may carry out the task of communicating with the supernatural.

The Inuit provide a good example of shamanistic practices and beliefs (see Holtved 1967). The primary role of the Inuit shaman is to take charge of relations with supernatural beings who interfere with human life. This includes intervening to ensure a supply of game, driving away evil spirits, procuring good weather, divining the future, and curing the sick. For instance, if game were scarce, the Inuit would assume that either Moon-man or Sea-woman, who control the animals, was angry because someone had committed an offense, such as eating a prohibited part of an animal. To the Inuit of Greenland and Labrador, these offenses become dirt in the hair of Sea-woman, and the shaman must struggle to be allowed to cleanse and comb her hair before she will promise to free the animals so that they may be hunted again. The shaman communicates with such deities by entering a trance with the assistance of a drum. The shaman is assisted by helping spirits, who take a variety of forms and who are communicated with in a special language.

An Inuit usually decides to become a shaman after a dream or some extraordinary experience. The individual may try to resist the call, giving in to his or her destiny only after great mental anguish. The next step is to consult with older shamans, providing them with a gift, and then to undergo a period of instruction that lasts anywhere from a couple of days to a few years.

The initiation of a 16-year-old Mapuche woman as a shaman in Chile after an apprenticeship lasting several months. A shaman's status depends on her or his ability to contact and influence the spirit world.

During the apprenticeship, the novice meets the various supernatural beings who later will serve as helpers. Another element of the shaman's preparation is experiencing the mystery of life and death through hanging, drowning, or shooting. In Greenland, while under hypnosis the novice believes that he or she is attacked and eaten by a bear spirit, and later awakens naked on the shore of a lake.

Keepers of the Law

Very different from the shamans are religious specialists who can be designated as *keepers of the law*—individuals whose primary roles are the performance of ritual and the interpretation and maintenance of religious tradition. In small-scale societies, keepers of the law are not usually full-time specialists. The Tzotzil-speaking Maya of southern Mexico have a large number of hierarchically ranked shamans among whose primary responsibilities is curing through communication with the ancestors (see Vogt 1970). In addition, there are religious officeholders responsible for the performance of ceremonies associated with particular Catholic saints. These offices form part of the civil-religious hierarchy or cargo system. To assume his burden (*cargo*), the cargo-holder moves from his residential hamlet to the ceremonial center of the community for one year. There, those holding religious offices engage in a series of costly ceremonies for the community, spending money on food, liquor, and ritual paraphernalia such as candles, incense, and fireworks. Since the role entails withdrawal from farming and other economically rewarding pursuits, the cargo-holder is forced to live off savings and loans for the year. Such specialists, then, are able to function only on a full-time basis periodically, at the expense of their normal economic activities. Their reward is the prestige that comes with community service.

A full-time, permanent religious functionary is a luxury that small, relatively poor communities or societies rarely can support. Occasionally, older members of a small-scale society are able to devote themselves to religious activities full-time because their age precludes normal economic pursuits as farmers or foragers and the rest of the community is willing to support them. For the most part, however, full-time religious specialists, or **priests,** are found only in large-scale societies. Only societies that can support an extensive division of labor and a large nonproductive class can accommodate religious specialists on such a permanent basis. Thus, while in the United States there is an estimated one full-time religious specialist for about every 700 persons, in the poorer countries of Latin America the figure is around one per 15,000 persons. In southern Mexico and Guatemala, full-time Catholic priests visit most Mayan communities only on occasion, and one of the responsibilities of some of the cargo-holders is to collect money to pay the priest for saying mass.

Most priests can be characterized as keepers of the law because they are concerned primarily with maintaining a particular social and religious order. In fact, they can be viewed as an integral part of social order. Through their public statements, counsel, and public (as well as behind-the-scenes) maneuverings, they represent the interests of the establishment in a society. On occasion, the order they represent may come into conflict with other orders, or even with elements of their own social order, especially when secular political leaders act in ways not perceived by the priesthood to be in the interest of the church (as in the case of England's Henry VIII). In such struggles the priesthood usually acts as a conservative force. However, as we shall see shortly, not all priests play such a conservative role, and they may in fact serve as catalysts for fundamental changes.

Prophets

Perhaps the most noteworthy exceptions to the conservative role of religious specialists are prophets. **Prophets** are individuals who receive divine revelation, usually by visions or dreams, concerning a restructuring or a redirecting of some aspect of society or a people's beliefs. On the basis largely of revealed truth, prophets seek to alter the existing social order through teaching or example. They do not, however, represent a complete break with the sociocultural order around them; to some extent, they are a product of their society and its religious traditions. They do, however, represent a threat to those holding religious power (and sometimes to those holding secular power as well). The core teachings of the Christian prophet Jesus, for instance, focusing on the coming Judgment and Kingdom of Heaven, certainly represented a threat to the religious and political establishment of the time. Such ideas, however, did not break with existing Jewish beliefs so much as they sought to reform them and resembled the teachings of other reformists such as John the Baptist and cults like those of the Essenes and Nazarenes, who advocated a more ascetic approach to worship.

Because they rely on their ability to arouse loyalty and enthusiasm and their claim of direct communication with the supernatural, prophets have much in common with shamans, although the two specialists have different aims. The goal of the prophet is the creation of a new order, whereas the shaman basically seeks to ward off disruptions to human life. Success as a prophet usually leads to the foundation of a new religious institution, transforming the seer from a renegade to a person who is at least somewhat respectable, and may even become a deity and leader of millions.

◄ RELIGION AND SOCIAL CHANGE ►

Australian Aboriginal religious dogma proclaims a perfectly ordered world in which change is unnecessary. Such a claim of permanency is common to many religious traditions, as a fundamental source of their strength. Despite this emphasis on what is unchanging in the world, however, religions and the world of which they are a part are in a constant state of flux—reli-

gions both react to the changing world and often play a role in the process of change itself.

Change Through Contact or Conquest

Changes in religious belief and practices are associated with the gradual evolution of a society from one adaptive strategy or social form to another. Over the past few centuries the process has been speeded up as a result of increasing contact between societies—in particular, contact between expansive states and small-scale societies. European expansion throughout the world was not merely political and economic; it included attempts to conquer people's minds as well, largely through religion.

In establishing colonial rule around the world, the European powers profoundly influenced the religious beliefs of many peoples. Through force, or simply as a result of associating the conquerors' might with the strength of their religion, to varying degrees these peoples adopted many aspects of European religion. The result was an amalgamation of traditional and introduced elements, through a process of blending known as **syncretism,** or the conscious adoption of an alien idea or practice in terms of some indigenous counterpart (Barnett 1953: 49). (See also "Focus on Anthropologists.") In central Mexico, for example, following the Spanish conquest in the sixteenth century, Catholic and pagan beliefs were mingled to create a distinct version of Catholicism. Patron saints took on the characteristics of old pagan gods, Catholic rites were interpreted in ways different from those of the Spanish, and Catholic ceremony and ritual were incorporated into the political and economic fabric of the village (see Madsen 1967).

Today, many of these societies are again undergoing religious transformation through conversion to evangelical Protestant sects. These sects originate mainly in the United States. However, although they are in many ways vehicles for the promotion of American values, they are also adaptive responses of people to local

JOHN BARKER

FOCUS ON ANTHROPOLOGISTS

John Barker is an anthropologist at the University of British Columbia, Vancouver. He lived in Papua New Guinea from late 1981 until 1983, and again in 1986, studying religious, aesthetic, and economic change among the Maisin people. Dr. Barker is the editor of Christianity in Oceania, *a collection of ethnographic studies of Christianity in the Pacific Islands.*

∧∧∧∧∧∧∧∧

Religious Syncretism in a Papua New Guinea Village

J ourneying up the northeast coast of New Guinea in July 1907, the Anglican missionary Arthur Kent Chignell was delighted by the village of Uiaku. Distressed by the "semi-civilized" shabbiness of colonial towns and surrounding villages, he saw in Uiaku, by his account, "what I had hoped and expected to see—large villages and crowds of natives, dressed beautifully in native fashion." He went on to describe the setting of splendid tropical flora and towering golden mountains as one the likes of which he had never seen before "except in picturebooks or dreams" (Chignell 1911: 17).

When Anne Tietjen and I stepped from a small boat to the beach at Uiaku in November 1981, we felt some of the same thrill that Chignell had

experienced, despite the long passage of time. True, the Maisin people now wore European-style clothing and many were fluent in English, but Uiaku's isolation from the towns and roads of Papua New Guinea, and its clean thatched houses and clear earth plazas gave the place a pristine, "traditional" appearance. The Maisin graciously incorporated us into a daily rhythm of subsistence garden activities, punctuated by public ceremonies in which villagers exchanged bark-cloth and adolescent girls had their faces tattooed. As our new friends told us of their encounters with ancestral spirits and of the need for constant vigilance against sorcerers, I was again reminded of Chignell's early impressions. Was this the same "pagan" religion he had hoped to replace with Christianity?

Even in Chignell's time, however, Uiaku had been intimately involved with a larger world. Situated at the center of Collingwood Bay, the four Maisin communities of around

1,500 people formed a hub in an extensive coastal and interior trading network in the precolonial days. Maisin initially welcomed European government officers, missionaries, and traders to the villages after 1890, but began to resist their presence as their numbers grew. In late 1900, a government patrol routed an ambush and shot dead six Maisin men. The following year, under conditions of enforced peace, the Anglican mission built a church and school in Uiaku.

Since this early defeat, the Maisin have consistently sought opportunities within the networks established by the colonial government and mission and their successors. By the 1920s, most villagers had accepted baptism and young men were routinely leaving their villages to work for 18-month stints at distant plantations and mines. Following the Japanese invasion of 1942, most Maisin men served as laborers for the Allied forces. When the men returned, they formed councils to run the local church and to undertake economic development projects. They sent their children to new Anglican and government high schools and colleges to take advantage of the national employment opportunities opening up as the church and the government prepared for independence of Papua New Guinea from Australia. At the time of independence in 1975, the Maisin formed part of a small national elite, working as doctors, civil servants, priests, and business people in the urban centers around the country.

The "traditional" appearance of Uiaku in 1981 was thus deceptive. While around 500 Maisin lived in the village, as many as 250 more lived and worked in distant urban centers. Family members who worked in the cities regularly sent money and desired commodities, such as clothing, fishing nets, and tinned food, back to the village. This steady flow of remittances may have actually subsidized customary activities. The steady outflow of educated Maisin from the village substantially reduced the work force available to grow food and perform other necessary tasks. Money and commodities helped to make up for shortfalls in food from the gardens and wealth objects for exchanges.

By the same token, an exclusive focus on "traditional" religious ideas and such activities as mortuary ceremonies and shamanism would have resulted in a misleading impression of Maisin religion in the

A church procession in celebration of Uiaku's patron saint, St. Thomas, in December 1981. Church festivals are today the main occasions for feasting, exchanges, and customary dancing in Maisin villages.

1980s. When we lived with them, virtually all Maisin regarded themselves as Christians, and all villagers supported their church by donating money to pay the priest (a Papua New Guinean), by building and maintaining church buildings, by attending services, and by participating in church festivals—the major celebrations of the year. While the church services, which were performed largely in English, owed much more to the Church of England than to indigenous traditions, the Maisin did not regard them as foreign; they had all grown up in the church and most were second- and third-generation Christians. This was their church, a church they happened to share (as villagers told us) with millions of

other members of the worldwide Anglican Communion. It was also a church they had successfully integrated with many of their own unique traditions.

For the Maisin, as for most of us, religion is a natural outgrowth of socialization. They also turn to religion in search of answers for what Max Weber called problems of meaning: Why do we die? Why does evil happen to good people? Also, just as with the rest of us, the Maisin live in an increasingly pluralistic world; they are simultaneously members of clans, villages, Papua New Guinea, and world Christendom. People experience conundrums and crises at different levels of their social experience, and they typically respond to these problems of meaning with corresponding types of religious action. Thus, when a young person suddenly died in the village, the Maisin understood the death and sought redress in terms of local beliefs concerning sorcery and spirit attacks. When a person became seriously ill, villagers approached both indigenous healers and Western specialists for help. They understood illness not only in terms of local beliefs, but in terms of Western beliefs as well.

In attempting to make sense of their community's situation in the wider world of nation-states, capitalism, and diverse ethnic groups, the villagers referred to the church and the Christian God. "Now that Europeans and Maisin are Christians," said one woman, the wife of a church teacher and herself a traditional healer, "we are brothers and sisters and our children can now marry one another."

Christianity for Maisin in-

volves the recognition that they are members of a wider world community—a community in which the differences and inequalities that separate cultures and races can be transcended through the sharing of a common morality and faith in a single deity. At the same time, the Maisin are aware and proud of their cultural distinctiveness, which they have successfully maintained since missionaries first landed on their shores a century ago.

circumstances—offering a promise of alleviating poverty and hunger, and of personal advancement. Anthropologist David Stoll (1990) contends that, in the case of Latin America, conversion to these sects is a response to the failure of political and economic reforms and to the breakup of traditional forms of social organization. He states that "evangelical churches constitute new, more flexible groups in which participation is voluntary, where leadership is charismatic, and which are therefore more adaptable to rapidly changing conditions" (1990: 331).

Traditional indigenous religions do not always collapse as a result of conquest; people often retain much of their traditional religion. In fact, clinging to their religious heritage can serve as a source of strength for members of societies. While, in many parts of the continent, Aboriginal religion was destroyed or seriously undermined by the European conquest and subsequent Aboriginal integration into Australian society, in more isolated areas, especially in the desert interior, Aboriginal religious beliefs and practices were better able to survive. Despite decades of effort by Christian missionaries, Aborigines in many settlements, such as Jigalong in Western Australia (Tonkinson 1974), have had consider-

able success in retaining key elements of their religion. In fact, by congregating Aborigines in more permanent settlements where there is often considerable leisure time, the whites indirectly promoted indigenous religious activities.

The activities of Christian missionaries among native peoples has been the subject of considerable controversy among anthropologists. While many missionaries actively engage in defending the rights of native peoples and promote socioeconomic ventures that clearly are beneficial, at times the work of missionaries is of more questionable value to those they work among. One of the most controversial groups is the American-based Summer Institute of Linguistics/Wycliffe Bible Translators. The group's supporters point to the linguistic work that it has sponsored, including the translation of hundreds of languages into written format. The group has been attacked, by Latin American anthropologists in particular, for undermining the cultures of native peoples and promoting conservative American cultural values in a biased manner (Hvalkof and Aaby 1981; Stoll 1982). It has also come under attack for alleged links with the Central Intelligence Agency and American-sponsored counterinsurgency campaigns in the Philippines, Vietnam, and elsewhere. Critical attention has also focused on the activities of conservative evangelical missionaries in Central America and the political implications of their work in close association with governments engaged in civil wars. This is a difficult area with complicated issues. A number of anthropologists have been forced to deal with such issues because of their direct bearing on the lives of native peoples being studied.

Millenarian Movements

A weakening or disruption of the old social order, periods of social unrest, or subjugation and a loss of power frequently result in religious movements categorized as **millenarian.** Millenarian movements (sometimes referred to as *nativistic* or *revitalization movements*) espouse a belief in the coming of a new world, in part through supernatural action. These are religions born of frustration, despair, or bewilderment, which seek to cut through a seemingly hopeless situation with a promise of the millennium—a period of good government, great happiness, and prosperity. Millenarianists call for a complete change, although their actual visions are, of course, limited by their own sociocultural milieu. As Kenelm Burridge (1969: 141) has pointed out, their main theme is moral regeneration and the creation of a new kind of person. Such themes are often expressed or symbolized by a hero or prophet. Figures such as Haile Selassie, Jesus, or Buddha serve as focal points for the call for a new life.

Millenarian movements vary somewhat according to circumstance and cultural traditions. The Rastafarian movement, with its promise of return to Africa and black rule with the coming of the millennium and the Blackman's escape from Babylon, exemplifies such movements in an Afro-American context. Among Native Americans, the best-known millenarian movements are those associated with the Ghost Dance (see Mooney 1965). These are movements that emerged among the Great Plains Indians following the failure of their armed attempts to stop American expansion; the movements then spread to groups in Nevada, California, and elsewhere in the American West. The central theme is a belief that the dead will return to announce the dawn of a new day. According to some versions, the earth was to open up and swallow all the whites, while leaving all their material possessions to the followers of the cult who would be spared to live in the heavenly era brought about by the Great Spirit.

In Melanesia, millenarianism took the form of **cargo cults.** In colonizing the Pacific, Europeans deprived Melanesians of power and autonomy. In addition, they failed to meet their obligations, as perceived by the native population, to share their enormous wealth and power. The resultant cults blended Christian missionary teachings concerning the eventual millenarian resurrection of Christ with the Melanesians' own myths in which ancestors would become transformed into powerful beings and the dead would return to life. The millennium would occur when the ancestors would return in steamships or airplanes bringing European goods (the cargo) and initiating a reversal of the social order. Those on top would be relegated to the bottom, and those on the bottom would gain preeminence.

Millenarian movements commonly are associated with secular political activities. Although heavily influenced by Christian teachings, the Maasina Rule movement that began in the Solomon Islands in the 1940s was a protest over wages, racism, and British colonial rule. "Cargo" expectations existed from the beginning of the movement, but "such ideas only became pronounced during the later years of Maasina Rule, when frustration was deepening" (Laracy 1983: 33). In fact, while earlier analyses of Maasina Rule emphasized its millenarian and religious aspects, recent scholarship has focused on its role in the movement toward Solomon Islands' independence, which was achieved in 1978.

Millenarian movements are not a thing of the past. Cargo cults are still important in many parts of Melanesia, as on the island of Bougainville in eastern Papua New Guinea. Bougainville has been the scene of considerable political agitation since the late 1960s, when negotiations began with local landowners to open the large Panguna copper and gold mine, which since then has been a major source of revenue to the central and provincial governments. Disputes have continued to simmer over issues relating to division of the mine's revenues, the influx of outsiders to work on the mine, and environmental problems. The tensions created by these disputes led to the founding of a cargo cult—the "50 toea people"—opposed to foreign business interests, to town life, to intermarriage with outsiders, to the established church, and to the central government. In mid–1989 cult members joined with political militant Francis Ona to launch attacks on the mine and mineworkers. The ensuing violence led the government to declare a state of emergency and send in the army. Members of the cult were convinced that they could win the struggle, even against the army, because the ancestors with their "black

power" would intervene on their behalf (see Howard 1991b).

Religion and Revolution

The major religious traditions of large-scale societies—Christianity, Islam, and Buddhism, for example—encompass a wide range of beliefs that often are ambiguous, contradictory, and subject to differing interpretation. Such diversity allows the same religious traditions to serve the interests of those concerned with preserving the status quo and the interests of those who desire reform or change. This situation is most apparent in the case of revolutionary movements.

Within any revolutionary setting, many religious leaders will be opposed to the threat of change. Such conservative tendencies commonly are singled out by revolutionaries and attacked, as, for example, they were by Marxists who proclaimed that religion is "the opiate of the masses." During the French Revolution in the late eighteenth century the church establishment that was associated with the aristocracy was strongly criti-

▲▲▲▲▲

Millenarianism in Melanesia: Christian cross in the background, cargo cult members march with bamboo stick rifles in the belief that their "cargo" will arrive. In colonizing the Pacific, Europeans deprived Melanesians of power and autonomy and failed to meet their obligations, as perceived by Melanesians, to share their wealth and power. The resultant cult blended Christian missionary teachings about the eventual resurrection of Christ with Melanesian myth in which ancestors would be transformed into powerful beings and the dead would return to life.

In Iran, Shiite Islam is the official state religion. Since the 1979 revolution, when the exiled Islamic fundamentalist Ayatollah Khomeini returned to the country, even the Iranians who do not practice the state religion have been compelled to follow strict Islamic codes of behavior.

cized by many revolutionaries, and church property was seized. Similar developments took place during the revolutions in Mexico and Russia in the early twentieth century.

Religious leaders and religious ideologies may, however, play an active and supportive role in the revolutionary process. This was true in Europe among radical clergy involved in the sixteenth-century Peasant Revolt in Germany and the English Civil War of the seventeenth century. Radical clergy also were of significance in the North American and South American wars against European colonial domination in the late eighteenth and early nineteenth centuries. As the social forces with which many of these religious ideas and movements were asso-

ciated became dominant in their societies, these religions assumed a more conservative role in support of the new order.

Although revolutionary movements during this century were at first hostile to religion, over the past few decades religion has assumed an important place in revolutionary movements around the world. Two of the most important examples of this are liberation theology among Catholics and Islamic socialism in the Muslim world. Proponents of *Islamic socialism* claim they are seeking to bring about social justice based on the teachings of Islam. It has taken on various forms in particular national settings, including variants associated with the revolutionary Shiites in Iran (see Munson 1989) and Colonel

Mu'ammar El Qaddafi in Libya (see First 1975). According to *liberation theology*, under conditions of widespread social and economic injustice one must become committed to the political, even revolutionary, liberation of the oppressed (Ogden 1981:131). Liberation theology emerged in the 1960s under the influence of the reforms of Pope John XXIII and has become an important and controversial force throughout the developing world—as exemplified by Central American liberation theologians like Archbishop Oscar Romero (assassinated in 1980), Ernesto Cardenal (Nicaragua's Minister of Culture in the Sandinista government), and Bishop Samuel Ruiz (a key figure in events following the New Year's 1994 uprising in the southern Mexican state of Chiapas).

In both Islamic socialism and liberation theology, religions that are major parts of the cultural heritage of a people have come to serve as radicalizing forces during periods of revolutionary upheaval. Neither Islam nor Catholicism can be seen as having caused revolutions, but they have influenced the direction revolutionary movements have taken.

Religion and the Environmental Movement

Religion often plays a role in the way people relate to the environment or at least how they explain or justify that relationship. Environmentalists around the world and their critics have turned to religious beliefs for legitimation and sought the support of religious institutions and religious figures. Often, however, this support is sought without a close understanding of the religions referred to or of the societies in which they are practiced.

Depending on one's perspective, the "dominion" over nature granted to humans in Genesis 1:28 ("God created man . . . and God said unto them . . . have dominion over every living thing that moveth upon the earth") can be read as a justification of human exploitation of nature or as a message that humans are to be its caring stewards. In the environmental movement, the message of stewardship is clear, taking on strong moral and religious tones. In 1989, for example, at the St. Paul's United Church of Christ in the East Bronx, members of the congregation brought apples, barley, and flowers to celebrate Earth Day. Having praised the offerings, the pastor opened a bag of garbage and strewed it around the altar. "We trash the earth," she said, explaining her action, "yet it is every bit as sacred as any place within this church" (Carpenter 1989:66).

Although the ideals of environmentalism exist today in such churches as St. Paul's and other religious institutions, many participants in the environmental movement have rejected at least some of the tenets of the Judeo-Christian tradition that seem to deny sacredness to nature and encourage its plunder. Historian Lynn White Jr. argued in a 1967 *Science* magazine article that the Bible posits a dichotomy between people and nature, placing humans outside of nature and above it, making them its masters. Though not all Biblical scholars would agree with this position, the failings in Christianity as perceived by some scholars and environmentalists has led them to turn to or draw from other religious traditions as part of what is known as the "greening of religion" (Nash 1989).

Since at least the 1960s there has been considerable interest in Asian religions, partly for their perceived ethical implications to environmentalism. Environmentalists find a parallel between some Asian religious ideas and their own belief that there is no biological or ethical gulf between humans and nature. In Taoism, for instance, everything in nature is seen as having a purpose or potential. Mahayana Buddhists speak of the *dharma*, or "Buddha-nature," of all animate and inanimate things. Similarly, religious support for the tenets of environmentalism would seem to come from Jainism, which seeks to avoid the destruction of any life-forms, and from Hinduism, whose polytheism and beliefs in reincarnation serve as a basis for the reverence of nature.

While environmentalists find justification for their beliefs in some Asian religions, the societies in which these religions are practiced, especially as they become increasingly part of a world system that promotes economic development, do not as a whole necessarily practice ecological conservation. They may not even be environmentally aware, at least not in the same way as many of those involved in the environmental movement. In Thailand, for example, nearly 95 percent of the people are Bhuddists who hold a world view that teaches living in harmonious balance with nature and opposes killing any living things. In addition, many Thai believe in spirits associated with nature. Still, as Komin notes, Thai religious beliefs "have not stopped Thais (farmers and logging businessmen alike) from destroying seventy percent of their forest in the last twenty-five years" (Komin 1993: 268). Komin also points out that the Thais' view of the environment does not preclude dumping piles of all kinds of trash and wastes outside houses or in nearby open spaces.

In Thailand, Bhuddism is only one of a number of variables affecting peoples' relationship to their environment. The Thai view of forests provides an illustration of what is involved. Because of such factors as traditional Thai cultural categories and practices, together with the impact of a wider economic and political world, the Thais' view of forests is not the same as that of the Western environmentalist. As Taylor (1993) has shown, for example, Thai language categorizes the world in such a way that, while the domestic or familiar communal world (*baan*) is seen as a positive category, the forest and things wild or untamed (*paa*) are seen as hostile and inimical to the well-being of people. There is no sense of natural beauty in forests ("to go to the forest" in Thai means, besides its literal sense, "to defecate" or "to enter a cemetery"); all beauty is seen as residing in human settlements.

In addition, because of some tenets of Bhuddism itself, some religious leaders may be limited in what they can or will do to develop conservationist practices. Although forest-dwelling Bhuddist monks in Thailand have been able to play some role in curtailing illegal commercial logging, at least in the areas of their monasteries, they lack the ability to change villagers' ways of life, and they face the dilemma of engaging in community and environmental issues when their religious calling is one of meditative retreat from the world. Most forest monks see the wider social, political, and economic changes encroaching on the natural environment of Thailand and their forest monasteries as inevitable, and, rather than becoming involved in the worldly matters of environmentalism, they withdraw into introspection, as their Bhuddist belief in world transcendence encourages.

Another source of ideas from which environmentalists draw are the beliefs of Native American cultures. As with Asian religions, Native American religions are seen as establishing an intimate connection with—rather than division between—humans and nature. For example, according to a leader of the nature worship movement of the 1960s, Gary Snyder, Native Americans promised a sort of "ultimate democracy," with nonhuman life revered alongside humans in traditional ritual, dance, and religion. The idealized closeness of Native Americans to the natural world as perceived by environmentalists was reflected in a 1960s poster showing a Native American reflecting on the degradation of the North American continent as a result of exploitation by those who took over their lands. A tear ran down his face.

In some significant ways, the adaptive strategies of Native Americans, along with their limited populations and low-powered technologies, did make them better custodians of the environment than the whites who followed. Indian respect for an environment on which they directly depended for their survival was reflected in religious beliefs and practices which they integrated with subsistence activities. Many Native Americans saw humans and animals as social kin: bears were bear "people," for instance, and salmon were regarded as "nations."

When life was taken so that Indians could survive, it was done ritually, with gratitude, since other members of the animal species that gave Indians their sustenance would be called on in the future to give their lives. Many Native Americans also found incomprehensible white Americans' idea of "ownership" of the land or domestication of animals, herding being regarded by Indians as a form of enslavement (Nash 1989: 115–118).

Nevertheless, people living in small-scale societies like those of Native America do kill animals and in other ways exploit the environment, changing it in the process. Rambo (1985), for example, found that the Semang, a foraging people of Malaysia, although too small in scale to produce pollution at a regional or global level, do pollute the air with their domestic fires, burning of fields, and heavy cigarette smoking; pollute water with fish poison; and pollute the soil by indiscriminate dumping of rubbish. As with other belief systems, the so-called ecological wisdom of traditional cultures needs to be seen on its own terms, not on the terms of the environmental movement, with its modern Western concepts and tendency to romanticize the "noble savage."

While many Native Americans did have a closer religious relationship with their environment than many people today, that relationship stemmed in large measure from their subsistence patterns, which made them highly dependent on caring for the plants and animals upon which they depended. This dependence on and fear of a nature that could withhold, however, also let them experience their separateness from nature. Some Native American myths, for example, portrayed a division between humans and nonhumans, as seen in the failures of "marriages" between nature spirits and humans (Vecsey and Venables 1980: 18–19).

In addition, though Native Americans destroyed some aspects of their environment as do all people in the normal process of working on

the environment, in the changing circumstances associated with early contact with Europeans and the fur trade, Native Americans overhunted game animals such as beaver to near extinction (Calvin Martin 1978). In the case of such overhunting, a number of reasons have been offered for what seems to have been the Indians' loss of sense of responsibility and religious commitment to the environment, among them the social costs of new diseases introduced by whites, growing dependence on white trade items, and the emergence of a capitalistic system among Indians that led them to see animals as commodities in trade rather than "people" of nature (Vecsey and Venables 1980: 28–29). Even the Native American view of animals in pre-European contact cultures, however, did not reflect respect for all life. Native Americans respected the wildlife upon which they depended for food and which was sometimes an uncertain source. Dogs, on the other hand, were not wild, but domesticated creatures regarded as property, and though Native Americans might have had affection for them, dogs were sometimes objects of sacrifice and often treated cruelly (Vecsey and Venables 1980:29).

Whatever the exact nature of their relationship with the natural world in the past, many Native Americans today are actively involved with preserving the environment. Their reverence, however, may be a result of their present-day identification with that role as much as of their traditional beliefs (Vecsey and Venables 1980:6).

S U M M A R Y

Although religions, which assume the existence of supernatural forces or beings, are based on mystical understandings of the cosmos, their features can be analyzed on a down-to-earth anthropological level. Adherence to particular belief systems can be partially explained by local social processes, history, and environment. At the individual level, personal circumstances circumscribe the choice of a religion. For the society as a whole, the form of religion is often related to the adaptive strategy; religious behaviors and beliefs are subject to change as the adaptive strategy shifts.

Symbols are often used as concrete expressions of the core elements of a religion. How people wear their hair, for instance, is often given symbolic religious significance. In a totemic view of the cosmos, natural phenomena are seen as closely linked to humans. Myths, or sacred tales, are another way of linking the supernatural with the mundane. They may function as culture histories, as justification for the existing social order, or as attempts to deal with basic questions of the human condition from the society's point of view. In analyzing myths, we gain insight into how a social order works and how its contradictions are handled.

Religious traditions also include belief in supernatural beings. All religious beliefs recognize some named force or entity. Such beliefs include animatism—belief in some impersonal supernatural force; animism—belief in the existence of an almost endless number of spirits that dwell in animals and places or simply wander about the earth; or beliefs in one or more gods—supernatural beings with individual identities and recognizable attributes who are worshipped as having power over nature and human fortunes. We refer to the belief that there is only one god as monotheism. Belief in the existence of a number of gods is called polytheism.

Religious beliefs are presented in ways that have great emotional impact: Practices enhance a feeling of separation of the sacred from the secular; rituals repeat the basic messages of a belief system. Sometimes people seek experience of the supernatural by altering their state of consciousness. Hallucinogens are often employed in egalitarian societies that do not restrict access to sacred truths to a small elite.

Men and women who specialize in communications with the spirit world through trance are called shamans. In small-scale societies, those who specialize in keeping religious laws and performing rituals usually do so on a part-time basis. Only large-scale societies with an extensive division of labor can afford full-time priests. Keepers of the law tend to be conservative upholders of a religious tradition, whereas prophets with visions of a new way are likely to encourage radical change. Even radical change, however, is shaped by the existing social order.

A religion may change as the culture itself does. Sometimes cultures slowly evolve from within; sometimes contact with or conquest by another culture brings change in religious beliefs. A conquered people may accept the conqueror's religion, assert their own, or join the two in a process known as syncretism. When things seem particularly bleak for an oppressed people, a millenarian movement may bring hopes of a complete change. Religion may even play an important role in revolutionary movements.

Religion also often plays a role in the way people relate to the environment or how they explain or justify that relationship. Environmentalists around the world and their critics have turned to religious beliefs for legitimation, but often without a close understanding of the religions referred to or of the societies in which they are practiced.

KEY TERMS

Animatism Belief in an impersonal supernatural force, a power unseen but believed to exist everywhere.

Animism Belief in spirits that dwell in animals and places or simply wander about the earth.

Cargo cult A millenarian movement found in the southwest Pacific. Members believe that

Western material goods will be received through supernatural means.

Cosmology Philosophy concerned with the fundamental causes and processes of things in the universe.

God or goddess A supernatural spirit with an individual identity and recognizable attributes who is worshipped as having power over nature and human fortunes.

Millenarian movement A social movement espousing a belief in the coming of a new world (a millennium), in part through supernatural action.

Monotheism Belief in the existence of one god. (Contrast with *polytheism*.)

Myth A sacred narrative that expresses the unobservable realities of religious belief in terms of observable phenomena.

Polytheism Belief in the existence of more than one god. (Contrast with *monotheism*.)

Priest A person authorized, usually after a period of training, to perform religious functions. The priest is a full-time religious specialist.

Prophet A person who receives divine revelation, usually by visions or dreams, concerning a restructuring or redirecting of some aspect of society or a people's beliefs.

Religion A system of beliefs involving supernatural forces or beings that provide shape and meaning to the universe.

Ritual Highly stereotyped, stylized, and repetitive behaviors that take place at a set time and place.

Shaman A person believed to be in direct contact with the spirit world through trance and who may command spirits to do his or her bidding.

Syncretism A blending of indigenous and foreign beliefs and practices in a religion.

Totemic emblem Symbolic representation that links individuals and groups with particular plants, animals, and other natural phenomena.

SUGGESTED READINGS

Baer, Hans A. 1988. *Recreating Utopia in the Desert: A Sectarian Challenge to Modern Mormonism.* Albany: State University of New York Press.

Berndt, Ronald M. 1974. *Australian Aboriginal Religion.* Leiden: E. J. Brill.

Endicott. Kirk M. 1979. *Batek Negrito Religion: The World View and Rituals of a Hunting and Gathering People of Peninsular Malaysia.* New York: Oxford University Press.

Fuller, C. J. 1984. *Servants of the Goddess: The Priests of a South Indian Temple.* New York: Cambridge University Press.

Gellner, E. 1981. *Muslim Society.* New York: Cambridge University Press.

Greenberg, James B. 1981. *Santiago's Sword: Chatino Peasant Religion and Economics.* Berkeley: University of California Press. (Mexico)

Keesing, Roger M. 1982. *Kwaio Religion: The Living and the Dead in a Solomon Island Society.* New York: Columbia University Press.

Kipp, Rita Smith, and Susan Rodgers, editors. 1987. *Indonesian Religion in Transition.* Tucson: University of Arizona Press.

Lancaster, Roger N. 1988. *Thanks to God and the Revolution: Popular Religion and Class Consciousness in the New Nicaragua.* New York: Columbia University Press.

Lessa, Wiliam A., and Z. Evon Vogt, editors. 1979. *Reader in Comparative Religion.* 2nd edition. New York: Harper & Row.

McGee, R. Jon. 1990. *Life, Ritual, and Religion Among the Lacandon Maya*. Belmont, CA: Wadsworth Publishing. (Mexico)

Morris, Brian. 1987. *Anthropological Studies of Religion*. New York: Cambridge University Press.

Tambiah, Stanley J. 1984. *The Buddhist Saints of the Forest and the Cult of Amulets*. New York: Cambridge University Press. (Thailand)

14. ARTISTIC EXPRESSION

In recent years the definition of art, especially in the Western world, has been highly contentious. While recognizing this debate, for our purposes we can adhere to a relatively traditional definition of **art** as referring to the use of skill and imagination to produce images recognized as having an aesthetic quality. In essence, this means producing things that are considered beautiful. Of course, what is beautiful to a desert-dwelling Australian Aborigine may not be beautiful to a British accountant in London.

All art is deeply embedded in a cultural context which determines the format of expression, the nature and interpretation of reality, and the recognition of aesthetic quality. Thus, in those societies where the interpretation of the world is largely religious, artistic expression is predominantly religious. In more secular societies, such as ours, the influence of religion on art is less comprehensive. Moreover, while in small-scale societies views of beauty may be fairly uniform, in large-scale societies, with their more heterogeneous populations, such perceptions can differ a great deal. These differences can be influenced by age, class, gender, education, subculture, or a host of other factors.

The existence of so much variation, however, should not blind us to the important underlying fact that virtually all human societies engage in artistic expression. This has led Ellen Dissanayake (1992) of New York's New School for Social Research to refer to humans as *homo aestheticus,* in order to highlight how fundamental aesthetic creativity is to humans. Dissanayake argues that in much the same way as humans have a biological predisposition toward language learning, we also have a biological proclivity for aesthetic expression: "Art can be regarded as a natural, general proclivity that manifests itself in culturally learned specifics such as dances, songs, performances, visual display, and poetic speech" (1992: xii). Thus, it is not enough for humans to speak and walk upright, we also have a tendency to sing and dance.

Artistic expression can assume a variety of forms. These may include material objects such as paintings, carvings, weavings, and so forth. Such artistic expression may be set apart as in the case of framed paintings or statues placed on pedestals. It may also be integrated into the more everyday objects, like a chair or a teapot. Among Australian Aborigines, sacred objects certainly are expected to have aesthetic qualities, but it is also common to find artistry expressed

⌃⌃⌃⌃⌃

Aboriginal artist, Arnhem Land, Austrailia. Traditional Aboriginal art was bound up in the Aborigines' religious beliefs and practices. Today Aboriginal art forms have disappeared or changed and the new ones have appeared.

on secular items like baskets or spear-throwers. Art may also be expressed through drama, dance, music, poetry, or literature. Anthropological research has pointed to the near universality of dance and music among human societies, adding support to the notion that art is not merely a cultural afterthought, but a fundamental part of human existence.

◄ ARTISTIC EXPRESSION IN ► SMALL-SCALE SOCIETIES

In most small-scale societies, artists and their work are closely associated with religion (see Layton 1991: 35–40). The artist often functions as an adjunct shaman or priest who expresses myths, sacred beings, and religious principles through art. Such art may occur solely in a religious context (for example, in the performance of rituals), or it may occur in a more mundane setting (such as in the carving of religious symbols on domestic utensils), perhaps providing a reminder of or a link with the sacred. Religious art in small-scale societies can serve a variety of functions and hence can assume a range of meanings, including political. Phillip Lewis (1969: 23) notes, for example, that religious art among the Melanesian people of New Ireland is connected with wealth and power in the context of displays and exchanges of wealth at ceremonies and feasts, where such art adds to the prestige of the patron (the Big-man) whose wealth has supported the occasion.

Artistic expression in small-scale societies is influenced by a people's environment and adaptative strategy. With foraging societies, for example, there is generally less material elaboration of religious artistic expression among those living in harsher environments than among those in richer settings. Thus, there is less elaboration of artistic expression among Australian Aborigines living in the arid regions of central Australia than those in Australia's tropical north. A similar contrast is evident between the art of the for-

agers of the Great Basin of the United States, which was relatively arid, and the Northwest Coast of North America, a richer environment.

There is little scope for individuals to become full-time artists in small-scale societies. These societies are characterized by a limited division of labor and recognized artists still must engage in the more general foraging, farming or herding activities common to their society. Artists are, however, generally rewarded in some way for their creativity, often in the form of food.

Small-scale societies are not isolated and their forms of artistic expression indicate not only adaptive responses to a local environment but also their links with the world beyond. Such external links lead to the diffusion, or spread, of techniques for producing works of art and to artistic styles and motifs.

Taking weaving as an example of a technique, archaeological and historical evidence suggests that the knowledge of weaving spread very slowly around the globe. Clothing can be made from beating bark to produce a kind of cloth or by treating animal skins. These are relatively simple techniques. Somewhat more complicated is the process of weaving. The earliest evidence of weaving consists of impressions of textiles from Jarmo in northeastern Iraq dating from around 7000 B.C. (Barber 1991: 127). Gradually the knowledge of weaving developed across Europe, Africa, and Asia, often through the process of diffusion. In the far eastern parts of Indonesia (the provinces of Maluku and Irian Jaya), where people had worn little by way of clothing, cloth began to be procured through trade by prominent members of local coastal and island societies five or six centuries ago. Knowledge of weaving appears to have spread into the region only a few hundred years ago. In the eastern Indonesian province of Maluku, for example, weaving today is still carried out by the descendants of weavers whom the sultan of the island of Ternate brought to his kingdom from Buton (to the west in Sulawesi) in the

Though artistic expression can assume a variety of forms, it seems to be a fundamental part of human existence. As early as the Old Stone Age, humans were using their skills and imaginations to produce images with aesthetic qualities. Shown here are engraved and sculpted examples of European Old Stone Age (specifically, Upper Paleolithic) technologies. The objects are carved primarily from mammoth ivory or reindeer antler, except for the stone female figurine (bottom right).

seventeenth century. They produce cloth not only for Ternate, but also for people on neighboring islands such as Halmahera.

Patterns or motifs of a particular small-scale society often reflect purely local expressions as well as imported or modified versions of imported ones. Throughout Southeast Asia traditional motifs illustrate the history of migration, trade, and cultural exchange. Many of the earliest motifs are linked to the ancient Dongson culture, which flourished in northern Vietnam, a culture closely associated with the diffusion of metal and woven objects and related technologies throughout the region. Along with such objects and technology came ideas about artistic expression and, specifically, a number of motifs, for example, a boat associated with passing from one stage of life to another, especially from this life to the next, or, in some places, representing the social order (tribes, lineages, and the like). Later, artistic expression in Southeast Asia was influenced by the spread of Buddhist, Hindu, and Islamic religious beliefs and by trade with India and China. In the case of textiles, the pat-

In most small-scale societies, artists and their work are closely associated with religion. This carved figure from Nepal represents Hanuman, a Hindu monkey god of pre-Vedic origins who appears widely in the myths and art of South and Southeast Asia.

terns on cloth obtained through trade with India influenced those found on locally produced materials as far away as eastern Indonesia.

Carving and weaving are two prominent material forms of artistic expression in small-scale societies. Items can be carved and cloth woven for nonartistic purposes, but it is common in small-scale societies for even very mundane

items to be an aesthetic expression. A few years ago, for example, when I was assembling a collection of Bhutanese (Indonesian) items with David Barker, who was studying textile motifs (see Barker 1985), Barker's attention was drawn to a filthy piece of cloth in a monastery that was being used to carry firewood. Upon closer examination, the cloth turned out to be beautifully woven, with a wide range of patterns that would have taken months to produce.

Carving

Before the discovery that apes made simple tools, tool-making was thought to be one of the defining characteristics of human beings. Despite modified notions of the distinguishing characteristics of humanity, tool-making remains a very fundamental aspect of human existence. Associated with tool-making is carving, and carving is associated with a variety of forms of artistic expression. The earliest clear examples of artistically carved items found have come from the Upper Paleolithic period, beginning some 35,000 years ago. These items include bone flutes and whistles that are about 30,000 years old and a variety of carved figures from bone and antler that are around 15,000 years old and associated with the Magdalenian culture of Europe. The latter carvings decorate hunting and other implements and depict large animals as well as humans. While the precise purpose of this artwork is debated by scholars, it clearly reflects a well-developed capacity for symbolization.

Among the most widely recognized carved artistic items are masks. While masks in Western societies today are primarily associated with secular occasions, especially Halloween, historically in many non-Western societies they have served very important religious roles. In writing about Mexican masks, Donald Cordry states that "Mexican masks must obviously be recognized as art, for the primary reasons for making masks

Wooden mask from western Nepal. Masks served a variety of purposes in the societies of this area. Some represented souls of ancestors and could be used to protect a locality from danger. Others were used by shamans to assist in provoking a trance state for purposes of divination (inspired guesswork) often related to healing.

were spiritual . . . These masks were also accorded great importance within their community . . . and some masks were thought to be spiritual entities" (1980:17). Masks in west and central Africa and Papua New Guinea and neighboring islands, for example, were associated with ancestor worship, often in conjunction with male secret societies. Among the Kenyah, Apo Kayan, and Iban of Borneo masks were used for rituals with a variety of purposes, in-

cluding promoting crop fertility, healing, and catching the souls of the dead to protect the living.

In many parts of the world masks were used in healing rites. The Iroquois, for example, had masks used by curing brotherhoods known as False-Face Societies. These masks portrayed mythical beings who cause sickness. Curing rituals in which members of the brotherhood wear the masks oblige the beings to remove the illness they have caused. Similar beliefs and practices were found among other societies in North America and in Asia (especially in Sri Lanka, Tibet, and Siberia).

Mask-making was probably preceded by face painting. Cordry (1980: 78) argues that "face painting in ritual and ceremonial aspects has the same goal and so should be classified as a type of mask." He continues, that "in all likelihood, the first mask was a painted face, as natural dyes were readily available . . . and people did not require great technical skills to use them." As a result of such painting the personality of the person painted is transformed. Indian groups in northwestern Mexico continue to paint their faces for ritual purposes. The Huichol, for instance, paint their faces during peyote-gathering pilgrimages.

Perhaps because it preserves better than wood, one of the earliest carved masks is made of bone. A fossilized vertebra of a llama made to look like the head of a coyote, it was found in central Mexico and dates from around 12,000 to 10,000 B.C. (see Bernal 1968: 32). Masks made from the pelvis of cows or other large animals continued to be used into the present century in the Mexican state of Guerrero for the Mojiganga Procession announcing the start of a fiesta. Covarrubias (1954: 40) illustrates a similar mask made from a pelvic bone by the Tlingit of the northwest coast of North America.

In the past the wood used to carve masks was selected not only for its utilitarian qualities but often because of perceived special spiritual attributes. People with animistic religious beliefs

Dorte of Santiagueros, Mexico(left). Mask is worn by the main figure Santiago. Devil mask from Guerrero state in Mexico(right). The mask combines European and pre-Hispanic religious traditions, featuring a European devil with animals on his face that have pre-Hispanic meanings. The lizard symbolizes lust and wantonness. Cordry (1980:185) refers to the bat as "a powerful image within the Indian psyche" linked to the underworld and night, "when supernatural beings emerge onto the earth, a time of danger." The mask also highlights the shamanistic belief regarding a close relationship between humans and animals.

often give trees spiritual attributes. Many peoples with mask-carving traditions selected specific types of tree believed to possess spiritual power. Some North American and African peoples carved masks directly from such living trees in order to absorb the tree's spiritual power. Often the tree used for the wood is the object of ceremonial invocations and offerings. On the east coast of pre-Columbian Mexico those who cut trees for the Dance of the Voladores would first offer the tree an alcoholic drink and then ask its pardon for removing part of it (Cordry 1980: 110).

Carving masks in bone or wood is commonly done by men and often by specialists, although not always full-time specialists. Cordry refers to three categories of mask-makers in

Mexico (1980: 103–107). The first is the *santero*, who makes masks and a variety of church figures. The santero is a well-trained carver whose work is expected to have a high degree of realism. The second is the professional mask-maker who lacks the santero's training and attention to realism, but who exhibits considerable talent as a carver and at least some artistic talent. These carvers employ various motifs from Christian and pre-Christian traditions. Among both of these categories are carvers who gain individual recognition for their work regionally, nationally, and sometimes internationally. The third category is the amateur, a poor man who has made a pledge to his village's patron saint to dance on the saint's day but cannot afford to purchase or rent a mask. As Cordry (1980: 107) notes, "his mask may be an artful, naïve creation . . . , or it may be entirely without esthetic merit."

In addition to being recognized for their artistic ability, these carvers are commonly linked to the realm of the sacred. Among North American native peoples, the creation of a mask is viewed as a spiritual experience. "The artist who creates the mask is already brought into contact with the 'spirit power' that is to be represented—or the creation of the mask 'engenders' that power" (Lommel 1981: 142). In the past, Mexican mask carvers carried out their work under the influence of hallucinogenic drugs to provide them with direct contact with the spirit world.

Textiles as Art

Until recently art historians relegated the art of most small-scale societies to the category of crafts. They viewed art as the sole preserve of the "higher" civilizations and alone possessing "high" spiritual values, and crafts as a "lower" order, the result of slow, repetitive production and lacking in any lofty spiritual values (see Fraser 1966). Interesting, too, is the fact that, for the most part, art was considered to be the work of men, while what women produced were treated as crafts, including the textiles created by women in small-scale societies (with some notable exceptions, especially in Africa).

Few today would agree with this distinction between art and craft. Nowhere is the change in attitude more apparent than in the case of weaving in small-scale societies. Weaving in small-scale societies has long been the object of scholarly attention, but largely in its technical aspects and the light it shed on questions about diffusion (Howard 1994: 2). The recognition of the artistic quality of textiles in small-scale societies reflects a move away from Eurocentric, hierarchical views of art and toward greater recognition of the role of women in art.

Textiles produced by the different peoples of Indonesia have been especially important in changing Western views about the artistic value of textiles. This trend is illustrated by the 1989 exhibition of Indonesian textiles at the Metropolitan Museum of Art in New York. In his foreword to the exhibit catalog, Philippe de Montebello, the director of the museum, commented: "Like paintings in other cultures, textiles assumed an esteemed place as the greatest two-dimensional art form in Indonesia" (Holmgren and Spertus 1989:7). In a catalog accompanying another exhibit of Indonesian and other Southeast Asian textiles in 1992, Michael Brand wrote that "few other artistic traditions can better challenge some of the inadequacies inherent in the construction of art history in the West" (Brand 1992: 4). The work of anthropologists has been prominent among the numerous recent scholarly studies of Indonesian textiles that have highlighted the cultural and artistic importance of textiles in these societies (see Adams 1969, Barnes 1989, Geirnaert-Martin 1992, Gittinger 1972, Ng 1987, Niessen 1993).

In small-scale societies textiles perform a variety of functions beyond serving as clothing. In fact, some textiles are not intended to be worn at all but rather to be displayed for ceremonial purposes or used as items of exchange in bride-price transactions. Gittinger (1972) reviews the ceremonial uses of the so-called ship cloths of southern Sumatra (see photo, next page) which were used in rites of passage such as marriage, the presentation of a child to its maternal grandparents, circumcision, and funerals. They were also used as special gifts in the cycle of major ceremonies and in relation to house-building. Much like art in Western society, special textiles in Indonesian societies were also viewed as treasure. Ruth Barnes (1989: 77–81) describes being taken to view one such treasure, an antique cloth originally imported from India, on the Indonesian island of Lembata. These valued cloths were the property of clans and were brought out of storage only during special feasts held when the moon was full. When Barnes was initially taken to see the cloth, the woman who brought it down from the rafters of the clan

A ship cloth or tampan of the Kaur people of Lampung in the south of the Indonesian island of Sumatra. The cloths were used in different ceremonial contexts. The ship motif in the center is a variant of the ship symbol also found on textiles in northern Laos.

house where it was kept in a basket, decided not to open the basket since the moon was not full, referring to "something in the parcel which she called a snake, which would come out and destroy the house" (p. 78). The following day an older woman summoned Barnes back to the clan house and, assuring the anthropologist that it would be alright now, took the cloth out of the basket to be photographed in the presence of a group of excited onlookers.

Textile production has a number of technical aspects, including spinning, dyeing, and weaving. Spinning is the easiest part of the process. In recent years dyeing has often involved the use of commercially-produced dyes, but in the past (and to some extent the present) weavers in small-scale societies had to rely on natural dyes from such sources as the barks, roots, and leaves of plants and various clays and metals. Many of these dyes also required what are called mordants to chemically bond the dye to the fabrics so that it will not wash out. Knowledge of dyes and their application required a fair degree of training and offered a broad scope for different levels of skill. Weaving can be either a relatively simple task or extremely complicated and time-consuming. Small-scale societies often valued textiles that exhibited a high level of weaving skills, and only these were deemed appropriate for many important occasions.

In a community that weaves, most women will have weaving experience; in fact, that is usually the expectation. As Barnes (1989: 48) notes in the case of Lembata, however, "not all women get equal pleasure out of cloth production, or are equally good at it." Women on Lembata are taught to weave by their mothers or other female relatives. Most girls will learn to spin cotton at the age of four or five and can start weaving by the time they are 16 or 17. It usually takes a couple of years to learn the basics of the more complicated aspects of weaving. By the time they are married, most women will be able to weave simple cloths, but it is only when they are older and their children are grown that they can devote the time to producing the most valued types of cloth. The valued cloths are the ones the people themselves view as having noteworthy aesthetic qualities; the reputations earned by the women who produce them set them apart from other weavers.

In contrast to the relatively egalitarian weaving tradition on Lembata, in the past weaving on Sumba, also in Indonesia, reflected the island's hierarchical society. Textile production was usually supervised by women of the aristocracy who were responsible for designing the patterns and preparing the cloth to be dyed, but the weaving itself was carried out by slaves.

In general, textile patterns are often associated with particular communities or cultural groups, although trade and cultural interchange can dilute the distinctions. In addition, within a group certain patterns may be reserved for specific kin groups or for those of high rank. On Sumba, for example, the use of the more sophisticated patterned textiles was reserved for high-ranking families or their employees. While some textile traditions may employ only a limited range of patterns with little room for variation, others have a great range of patterns and may offer considerable room for individual innovation. Thus, the textiles of the Toraja of Sulawesi shown in the Metropolitan Museum of Art exhibition are very individualistic in character and the textiles of the Iban of Borneo are known

Front-end panel of an Iban Dayak (Borneo) man's loin cloth, or tandu sirat, dating from the late nineteenth or early twentieth century. Such textiles were important indicators of social status.

both for the individuality and for the large number of patterns (see Haddon and Start 1982).

< ARTISTIC EXPRESSION > IN LARGE-SCALE SOCIETIES

Artistic expression undergoes important changes with increasing social scale. Ancient empires and city-states were able to subsidize artistic activities to an extent that allowed for greater specialization.

Full-time specialization as an artist became possible. For example, as Thailand became established as the Kingdom of Siam several centuries ago, paintings and sculptures were produced by artists living in *sakun chang* (schools of artisans). Individuals would apprentice themselves to these schools, where they would be trained in the various techniques. Support for the better known schools came from the king and other prominent members of Thai society.

The patronage of the powerful and wealthy in large-scale societies influenced artistic creation. Under such patronage, more secular forms of art reflecting the particular interests of rulers and the state sometimes emerged alongside religious art. This was especially true in Western societies. However, until fairly recently in most societies, even in the West, religion and art remained closely intertwined. In Europe this is most clearly seen during the Middle Ages, when religious themes dominated artistic works in keeping with the central role of Christianity in the contemporary society. Historically, religion has played an even more dominant role in art throughout Asia, where art was closely associated with particular religious traditions. Thus, the traditional art of Thailand was linked to the Buddhist religion and the schools of artisans to the monasteries.

Where religion has put constraints on art, art has managed to emerge with intensity once given freedom. For example, Islam, with its law against graven images, forbade the depiction of living things among the faithful. Hence the lack of sculptures and paintings in the Muslim religious context. But no one said anything against writing, so Muslim calligraphy became a classic aesthetic endeavor. In some forms of Christianity where the Protestant reformation rejected paintings and sculptures in places of worship, the result was an absence of these things. In other more traditional modes, Roman Catholics and Episcopalians have persisted with stained glass windows, statues, and relief work. Calvinistic Protestants, who were lim-

ited in the visual sphere, sometimes compensated in the audio realm with a fairly rich blend of songs and hymns. In Africa, where dance is accepted as part of life, Christianity has had to adapt itself to this mode of expression in worship, for example, making the Roman Catholic Mass part of the ritual.

With the rise of capitalism and emergence of the modern world system, art has become increasingly secular. Beginning during the Renaissance and increasingly with the advent of the seventeenth- and eighteenth-century political and economic revolutions in Europe, artists allied themselves with those seeking to put an end to the old feudal order and the religious establishment associated with it: "By means of a change of artistic themes and the introduction of new ones, art helped to debunk a decrepid world and exalt a new one" (Sanchez Vazquez 1973: 164). As modern large-scale society became more individualistic, and as artists became more independent of religious establishments and wealthy aristocratic patrons, art itself became more individualistic. This tendency is marked by the emergence of what is generally referred to as modern art in the nineteenth century. While often associated with art in a few European and North American centers, in fact modern art was a global phenomenon with many local variants.

The emergence of modern art around the world during the last century reflects the increasing integration of the world at this time. For example, during the nineteenth century Thai monarchs sought to modernize their kingdom, introducing political reforms, new technologies, and cultural perception. In the process, Thai art changed dramatically, with Western artistic influences serving as a catalyst for the creation of a distinctly Thai style of modern art (Poshyananda 1992). Western influence included oil painting, which was a new medium for Thai artists, and greater attention to anatomical accuracy.

The Influence of the Art of Small-Scale Societies

While modern art may be different from the art of small-scale societies in regard to such features as themes, medium of expression, and degree of specialization, there are areas of overlap. This overlap is most noticeable when modern artists have been consciously influenced by the art and culture of small-scale societies. This art is identified with **primitivism,** defined by William Rubin of New York's Museum of Modern Art as "the interest of modern artists in tribal art and culture, as revealed in their thought and work" (Rubin 1984a: 1).

Primitivism in modern art developed during the late nineteenth and early twentieth centuries at a time when the art of small-scale societies was receiving considerable attention in museums and among scholars in Western Europe and North America. The most influential forms of this art were carved items such as masks and statues from sub-Saharan Africa, Polynesian and Melanesia in the Pacific, and the northwest coast of North America. Among the other relevant items was patterned barkcloth from Polynesia and Irian Jaya. Artists turning to these creations were challenging the classic formalism of Western art by exploring means of expression they perceived to be more closely linked to the unconscious and the fundamental nature of human existence.

Paul Gauguin was the first modern artist identified with modern primitivism. He idealized small-scale societies as superior to what he saw as decadent modern society. Seeking to escape the clutches of civilization, Gauguin left France for the Society Islands in the South Pacific, where he remained for all but a few years until his death in 1903. Despite Gauguin's attempt to escape the infuence of decadent civilization, as Kirk Varnedoe (1984: 179) notes, his "innovations in form and color . . . remain firmly linked to Western sensibilities of a distinctly unbarbaric kind."

A more fundamental break was to come a few years later with artists such as Henri Matisse, Maurice de Vlaminck, and Pablo Picasso. These artists saw the art of small-scale societies as an inspiration for freeing themselves from the artistic style of the day (in this case, Neo-Impressionism) and for finding ways to express fundamental aspects of the human psyche. In the case of Picasso, these aspects included "primordial terrors" such as the fear of death and disease (Rubin 1984b: 254). Picasso and other artists believed that they had found the solution to expressing such fundamental characteristics in African and Pacific art like that displayed in the Trocadéro museum, an ethnological museum in Paris. Picasso became an avid collector of such art and drew inspiration in terms of form and color especially from African and Melanesian masks. Matisse was initially influenced primarily by African carvings and later, in the 1940s, drew design and spatial inspiration from painted shields and barkcloth from Melanesia.

The art of indigenous peoples has also influenced modern artists in countries which have incorporated these peoples. There art has often served as a means of nationalist expression as exemplified in the work of Mexican artists like Diego Rivera who were part of an important artistic trend after the Mexican revolution. Rivera and Frida Kahlo had an avid interest in the art and culture of the pre-Hispanic indigenous peoples of Mexico and sought to incorporate this into their work. Much of Rivera's work portrayed images of a Mexican nation with important indigenous roots, most graphically illustrated in his murals which provide detailed accurate portrayals of pre-Hispanic Mexican society. Rivera, Kahlo, and like-minded artists of their day also promoted an appreciation of the crafts of contemporary indigenous peoples, but essentially they viewed such work as separate from art—a category reserved for work like their own. Moreover, as with Gauguin, the artistic style of Rivera, Kahlo, and similar artists remained firmly embedded in Western artistic tra-

European artists such as Pablo Picasso saw the art of small-scale societies as an inspiration for freeing themselves from the artistic style of the day and for finding a means of expressing fundamental aspects of the human psyche. Picasso, shown here, believed that in African and Pacific art he had found the solution to expressing those fundamental characteristics.

ditions. The recognition of the artistic value of the art of indigenous peoples not simply as inspiration for art but as art in its own right is a recent development still not accepted by many in the so-called art world.

Tribal Art in the Modern World

The incorporation of small-scale into large-scale societies has profoundly influenced the art pro-

duced by small-scale societies (commonly referred to as tribal art). In relation to the art of these enclave societies, Nelson Graburn (1976: 4–5) distinguishes art which is **inwardly directed,** or "made for, appreciated, and used by peoples within their own part-society," and art which is made for the outside world. Art that is inwardly directed has undergone changes that reflect transformations within these societies. Thus, although the religious aspect of this art may remain important, it is likely to have been influenced highly by the traditions and symbols of the encompassing societies. Thus, when tribal groups convert to Christianity, Christian themes commonly assume an important place in their art.

Outwardly directed art serves both as a means of generating income and as a medium for "presenting to the outside world an ethnic image" (Graburn 1976: 5). When this art is judged to be of poor quality and made for a relatively undiscerning market, it is often referred to as "tourist art." Many would argue that such works, in fact, are not art at all, but handicrafts. This art may use traditional religious symbolism, but its intended purpose is not religious. There is also outwardly directed art that is more clearly recognized as art by the larger art world using criteria such as the skill of the artist and the beauty of the work. The recognition that all contemporary tribal art is not tourist art or handicraft, which has come about only recently, has been an integral part of the greater appreciation for the value of tribal cultures in the modern world in general. Today many tribal artists have gained national and international recognition, especially native artists in North America and Aboriginal artists in Australia.

Tribal artists who produce primarily for an external market can have important inward effects on a society. The work of the famous Haida artist Bill Reid, for example, has played an important role in the cultural renaissance of the Haida people and in their claims of sovereignty for their homeland on the Queen Charlotte Islands, Canada, which they call Haida-Gwaii. Like the cedar canoe that he carved and painted for display in Paris in 1989 (see Jennings 1989), much of Reid's work utilizes religious symbolism that remains central to Haida culture.

Contemporary Australian Aboriginal Art

Traditionally, Aboriginal art was intimately bound up in religious beliefs and practices.

Most of the images created were associated with their myths and many of the art forms themselves were used in religious contexts. Although the artists were not full-time producers of art, they were compensated with food or sometimes with new knowledge about motifs. Although Aboriginal art evolved in greater isolation than many other artistic traditions, it was not completely cut off from the outside world. Thus, Aborigines in northern Australia were in contact with seafaring Makassarese from the Indonesian island of Sulawesi for centuries and the bark paintings of northeastern Arnhem Land were influenced by the patterns on batik cloth brought by the Makassarese (Berndt and Berndt 1982: 62). However, such influence was negligible in comparison with the impact of Aboriginal incorporation into the European-created state of Australia.

As the extent of Aboriginal integration into the wider Australian society has increased in recent years, traditional Aboriginal art forms have changed or disappeared and new forms have appeared. Contemporary Aboriginal art includes oil paintings, forms of modern dance and theatre, as well as written literature (see Berndt and Phillips 1973, Berndt and Berndt 1982, and Caruna 1993).

Painting illustrates well how Australian Aboriginal artistic practices have evolved. The only form of painting for which archaeological evidence exists among Australian Aborigines is found on the walls and ceilings of caves and rock shelters (see Brandl 1973, Crawford 1968, Edwards 1979, Trezise 1971, Ucko 1977, and Wright 1968). This does not rule out the possibility that painting was done at earlier dates on more perishable substances such as bark, but the oldest known examples of bark painting date only from the nineteenth century. In addition, while Aborigines in other parts of Australia painted on bark in the past, for the most part the tradition of bark painting is located in northern Australia, primarily in the region known as

Haida artist Bill Reid and assistant in their workshop. Reid's work, which can be categorized as outwardly directed art, has played an important role in the cultural renaissance of the Haida people and in their claims of sovereignty over their homeland.

Arnhem Land (see Groger-Wurm 1973a, Groger-Wurm 1973b).

Like other forms of traditional Aboriginal artistic expression, bark painting was closely linked to religious beliefs and practices. Many of the paintings illustrate mythical beings and geographical features associated with myths, used for the most part in religious contexts. In western Arnhem Land the paintings were placed in rows to be viewed by youths being instructed as to their meaning as part of their initiation. Motifs sometimes were linked to social organization, for instance, mythical motifs, sometimes associated with particular kin groups. Some bark paintings also served another purpose, such as sorcery paintings with an image of the intended victim painted with protruding stingray spines.

The bark paintings discussed so far fit within Graburn's category of inwardly directed tribal art. A relatively small number of such paintings was produced and they were not intended to last much beyond the rituals for which they were made. During the 1950s, however, the nature of bark painting began to change in response to growing outside demand for such paintings. By the 1970s bark painting had essentially been transformed into an outwardly directed art form. This change was part of the greater degree of integration of northern Aboriginal societies into the wider Australian society. Although the bark paintings themselves continued to use many mythically–related motifs, they were no longer done for use in rituals. Designs often became more stereotyped and even the bark commonly was made flatter and trimmed more neatly than was traditional. There were changes for the artists also as bark painting became a profession. The work of these artists ranged from rather poorly made pieces viewed purely as tourist art to better pieces to be sold as works of art by recognized individuals.

Another nontraditional element in Aboriginal painting is the use of commercial paints instead of the traditional natural pigments and the use of ready-made boards and canvas. Some of these

Aboriginal bark painting from central Arnhem Land by Aboriginal artist Magani of the Miljingi tribal group. The story depicted on this painting relates to humans and salt water animals and fish that are Dreamtime (mythical time of creation of the world) spirits of totemic importance to Aboriginal kin groups. The areas of cross-hatching represent the artist's country. The images in the painting are associated with the artist's birthplace or lineage and play important roles during ceremonies when the Dreamtime stories and the habits and life-cycles of the animals portrayed are retold in song and dance.

paintings have adopted traditional motifs. For example, the desert-dwelling artists of the Papunya-Yuendumu area of Western Australia began painting on canvas and board in the 1970s using motifs originally employed in ground paintings for rituals. Other Aboriginal artists have developed painting styles more akin to Western traditions. Their work is distinctive, but does not rely on traditional Aboriginal motifs for inspiration. The first and best known of these painters was Aranda artist Albert Namatjira, who was introduced to European techniques by non-Aboriginal artist Rex Batterbee and began painting watercolor landscapes in the 1930s. Namatjira's work was associated with what is named the Hermannsberg School of Aboriginal painting after the important Lutheran Mission west of Alice Springs. As noted by Wally Caruna, the curator of Aboriginal art at the National Gallery of Australia, Namatjira's work "made a major contribution towards changing negative public perceptions of Aboriginal people and laid the groundwork for the acceptance of more recent development in Aboriginal art" (1993: 106).

◄ GLOBALIZATION OF ARTISTIC ► EXPRESSION

The globalization of art that began with the emergence of modern art in the last century has become even more evident in recent years with the ever increasing integration of the modern world system (see "Focus on Anthropologists"). Artistic traditions have never been closed to outside influences, but today these external influences are greater and more immediate than ever before. Since the societies within which artists live are subject to the influence of globalization, it is not surprising that their art should reflect this process.

The globalization of art is especially noticeable in the Asia-Pacific region. Asian and Western art have a long history of influencing one another, providing inspiration in terms of

subject matter and style. Under European colonial rule, artists in some Asian countries were influenced by the artistic traditions of their particular colonial rulers. Thus, paintings in the Philippines had a Spanish flavor and in Vietnam it was French. Nevertheless, most artistic expression in the region retained a decidedly regional or national character. Today, such local identification is being diluted much more significantly and a transcultural form of art is emerging across the Asia-Pacific region alongside more culture-specific forms of artistic expression. This art has its roots in particular national artistic traditions, but increasingly both the art and the artists have become transcultural in character.

The work of Thai artist Wattana Wattanapun illustrates this transcultural tendency. Wattana began his career as an artist studying classical Thai art in Bangkok in the 1960s: "We sat in the dark temples for days and days and copied the master's works" (Howard 1994b: 64). At the same time, he also studied contemporary world art and, then, in the 1970s went to the United States to study. Since then he has moved back and forth between the two countries.

Anthropologist Herbert Phillips has commented that "Wattana's art has. . . been divided between his abstract expressionist work that met the decorative needs of American clients and his powerful social commentaries that addressed the cultural needs of those who know and love Thailand" (Phillips 1992: 135). Wattana sees himself as an artist in two worlds, but in many ways an outsider in both. He notes, however, that "being an outsider gives me more ability to view from both sides, both realms," and that "the contradictions and complications of being from one society and drawn into another makes my art perhaps a function of two worlds" (Howard 1994b: 66).

Globalization also brings a challenge to the Eurocentrism that has dominated perceptions of art. Some scholars and art critics still categorize art within a hierarchically ordered pyramid with the upper reaches reserved for the art of the majority cultures of Western Europe and the former European settler colonies of North America

MICHAEL C. HOWARD

FOCUS ON ANTHROPOLOGISTS

The Art of Carving in Northern Irian Jaya

When I first visited Irian Jaya in 1991 I already knew something of the very distinctive decorative carving traditions of the people of its northern coastal areas and offshore islands from books and museum collections (see Baaren 1968, Haddon 1937, Hoogerbrugge 1977, and Kooijman 1959; also see Greub 1992). These collections and books included a variety of older ancestor figures associated with the people's pre-Christian past, especially the so-called *korwars* (foot high figures with large, dramatic heads, actually known locally as *amfjanir*), and the fanciful carved decorations attached to the fronts of their canoes. However, these sources generally told me little about the carvers themselves or their role today. Even information on the traditional cultural context of the carvings was relatively limited. I was particularly interested in a number of questions about the current status of carvers and carving, such as did their work differ significantly from that of their predecessors?

Especially limited in the litera-ture was information on the various items, such as fish and birds, carved on or attached to the canoes that were so important in the traditional material culture of these people. There was even some confusion in the literature about what the carvings on the canoes represented, and virtually nothing was said about further cultural meanings. What I hoped was that such decorative carving was still sufficiently alive in these communities that it would be possible to study this artistic tradition as a living aspect of community life rather than solely by reconstructing past practices and beliefs.

In particular I was interested in three geographical areas with somewhat different artistic traditions (see map in the Applied Anthropology portfolio). The first included the coastal area and a few adjacent islands from the border with Papua New Guinea in the east, past the capital of Jayapura, and then roughly to the town of Sarmi in the west. The second included the communities around Lake Sentani, to the west of Jayapura and just inland from the first area. The third included the coast and islands of Cenderawasih Bay such as Biak and Yapen. One of the most notable differences in the material cultures of these areas is the motifs used for their canoes: small fish and human figures on the canoes themselves and attachments in the first area, curving designs on platforms on the ends of the canoes, and an assemblage of thin carved pieces on the fronts of the canoes in the third.

As discussed in the Applied Anthropology Portfolio, the primary purpose of my work in Iran Jaya has been training local anthropologists in social impact and other applied fields. My study of carvers had to be conducted largely on the side. The applied orientation of my general work there, however, carried over to my study of carvers. In addition to simply trying to understand the work of these carvers and its role in their cultures, I was also concerned with the carvers' economic role and their potential contribution to community development efforts in relation to both local and the emerging tourist industry. Another concern was whether carving could be sustained in the face of the rapid change in the region.

Because this interest was shared by the director of the aid project office in Irian Jaya and some of my Indonesian colleagues, the research could be conducted in a team fashion. Those who were living in Irian Jaya were able to maintain relations with some of the carvers when I was not there. More-over, while we were not able to spend a prolonged period in a single community as participant observers, since the aid project is being funded over a 10-year period, we have been able to gradually build both depth and breadth to our understanding through repeated visits to cer-tain communities and by contin-ually expanding the number of communities surveyed. Additional contextual under-standing has also been facili-tated by research done by oth-ers in a few of the communities.

Some sense of how the re-search has been conducted can be seen in the village of Tarfia on the coast west of the town of Demta. A team of undergradu-ate anthropology students from Cenderawasih University con-ducted a general social study of the village in early 1993. The head of the department and I then visited the village and talked with a few carvers as well as to others. The information that we gathered during this visit was limited. The following year we returned and were able to talk with most of the carvers; our intent was to return the following and subsequent years.

As in neighboring communi-ties, only a few families of carvers in Tarfia carved for themselves and other members of the community and occasion-ally for people from nearby vil-lages. Carving skills were taught by fathers to their sons and only those sons with demonstrated talent would continue to carve.

Carvers of northern Irian Jaya.

While the items carved were roughly similar, some of the work had distinguishing features and the carvers and community members held definite ideas about the different carvers' rela-tive talents. Within the village was evidence of a relative de-cline in demand for decorative carvings, especially true for tra-ditional decorative panels on the fronts of houses, particularly houses of important community members, which were now rarely used. Most of the carving related to canoes, but while every adult male in the commu-nity had a canoe which had to be replaced after only a few years of exposure to the sea and weather, less than half of the canoes in the village were still decorated in the traditional manner—the majority had no decoration at all. Nevertheless,

there was still significant de-mand for decorative carvings on canoes. The decorations them-selves were generally very simi-lar to pieces in museum collec-tions from the nineteenth and early twentieth centuries and employed the same motifs (vari-ous fish, birds, human heads, and clouds and stars). The carvers identified the few stylistic differences essentially as changes in fashion. The tradi-tional red, black, and white colors were still used, often as natural pigments but also some-times as commercial paints.

Some of the investigation of the carvers has fit directly into the research carried out under the auspices of the Canadian aid project with which I work. In 1994 the work I did with the anthropology department in Irian Jaya, as mentioned in the portfolio, focused on the impact of tourism on the island of Biak in relation to plans for a relatively large hotel complex on the island. Many of the remaining carvers on Biak live in one of the villages in the vicinity of the complex. In fact, they already sell carvings through the village cooperative to the limited number of tourists who visit the island or stop at its airport in transit. One member of our team of anthropologists was assigned to survey carvers in this community, including their sales and marketing techniques.

In Biak, more exposed to outside influences than many other areas where carving persists in northern Irian Jaya, very little carving is still done for local use. This decline is reflected in the virtual disappearance of active carvers from most communities. At present active carvers are found in only two communities—the one studied and another near the international airport. Canoes are still widely used, although no longer decorated as in the past, and, since canoe-related carving is not seen as appealing to tourists, almost none is done anymore. What is carved are a few items loosely based on traditional objects that are deemed suitable for the tourist market—especially small versions of the old korwar ancestor figures. Although the context of carving has changed markedly on Biak, the tourist market does seem to have kept decorative carving itself alive. A number of younger men in both villages

carve and others are learning. The growth of tourism may well encourage even more young people to carve, although their products may be the rather poor quality so-called "tourist art."

Carving has nearly disappeared from the villages close to Jayapura, other than the manufacturing of undecorated canoes and a few other utilitarian objects. In one of the villages near the Papua New Guinea border I asked a former village headman why the people no longer decorated their canoes. He said that in the past decorations were important in identifying where a canoe came from and that this was no longer necessary, especially since most people from farther away now came to the village by road and not by boat. This explanation leaves a question about why canoes are still decorated in traditional fashion in communities to the west of Jayapura that are also connected to the city by road. The disappearance or survival of decorative canoe carving may have more to do with the extent to which village populations have been changed by integration into Jayapura. In communities where canoes are no longer decorated, the young people in particular are more influenced by city ways and less interested in more traditional practices. In the village near the Papua New Guinea border, this lack of interest has prompted some older villagers to try to revive some traditional practices in the face of growing social problems among youths.

In the village of Depapre, to the west of Jayapura and connected to the city by a good road, many canoes are still decorated in the traditional manner and several families of carvers are kept busy carving and decorating canoes for their fellow villagers. When I last visited Depapre in 1994, the first large tourist group was about to arrive. In preparation, several carvers had assembled a number of canoe decorations to sell. While most followed the more traditional fashion, some were altered in a manner thought to be more attractive to tourists. As we talked with one of the carvers about his work, the local sponsor of the tourist visit came over to recommend that the carver change what he was telling the tourists. Since canoes and the decorative appendages only last a few years when subjected to the elements, after a relatively short time they can look quite old. In this case, since the tourists liked old things, the carver was encouraged to tell them that the weathered pieces (actually two or three years old) had been his father's and were 30 to 50 years old.

With the exception of Biak, the island and coastal communities of the rest of Cenderawasih Bay see very few tourists. Although carving associated with the people's pagan past is long gone, canoe decorating is widespread. Besides the lack of negative influences such as tourism and urbanization, the persistence of decorating canoes in this area may be encouraged by a government-sponsored canoe race among many of the communities as part of the independence day celebrations in August. More than just a race, the event is an opportunity for communities to show off their canoes and the people take considerable pride in how they are decorated.

I visited the island of Yapen in 1994 with two Indonesian colleagues, including the head of the Cenderawasih University anthropology department, who was raised on the island, and interviewed carvers in two communities, Menawei and Ambai. While the two are relatively close and the carvings fit within the same general pattern for the area, there are surprisingly important social and cultural differences. In Menawei carving is organized within kin groups. Only a few carving families were in each kin group and only a few motifs were associated with each carver (some passed on from father to son). In Ambai, there were dozens of carvers and no organization according to kin group. Moreover, patterns were highly individualistic, based in part on inspiration. While Menawei carvers were concerned about the lack of interest in carving on the part of younger people, in Ambai there was no shortage of young people interested in carving. Significantly, Ambai is also known for the production of basketry, beadwork, and other traditional arts and crafts, while Menawei's

repertoire is more limited.

When people converted to Christianity in the nineteenth and twentieth centuries, many carving traditions in northern Irian Jaya were eliminated; more recent cultural changes associated with greater integration into the world beyond have further reduced this art form in the region. What remains, by and large, is a tradition associated with the decoration of canoes and the newer phenomenon of essentially tourist art. While the first remains an art form primarily inner directed toward a carver's community, the second, although based on traditional patterns, is externally oriented.

There are important questions about the future of both types of carving. First, what is the likelihood of decorative carvers continuing at all? Evidence from the villages near Jayapura shows that younger members of a community may have no interest in carving, but examples from Biak, Depapre, and elsewhere lead to a more optimistic forecast. But what will they carve and what role will carving play within communities? Will decorative carving be reduced to rather pathetic, tacky tourist art? Beyond that, what are the prospects for more traditional forms persisting or for decorative carving becoming part of a vibrant tradition-based modern art?

The experience of Irian Jaya to date and of many locations around the world suggests that a growing tourist industry in northern Irian Jaya will proba-

bly generate greater production of low quality tourist art with little meaning to those producing it except as an export commodity. Nevertheless, in many cases localized indigenous art has withstood the pressures of internationalization to emerge in new forms both relevant to the indigenous communities themselves and valuable contributions to the larger art world.

In addition to carving, other traditional art forms that persist in northern Irian Jaya have shown signs of becoming more popular. During the 1920s, the work of barkcloth painters from Lake Sentani and nearby communities, known as *maro* paintings, attracted considerable attention within the art community of Western Europe (Hoogerbrugge 1992). These paintings continue to be produced today and, in fact, there is a recent resurgence of maro painting by young artists. Government-sponsored traditional dances have also helped revitalize the production of traditional bark and fiber costumes, many of which have not been produced in decades. Also numerous individuals within communities are taking an active part in promoting the traditional arts and crafts; local anthropologists, too, are hoping to play such a role. Within this context, it is likely that decorative carving will be produced not just for the tourist market, but will continue to be an important element of the cultures of northern Irian Jaya as well.

Thai artist Wattana Wattanapun. Playing a role in the globalization of art, Wattana began his career studying classical Thai art in Bangkok; at the same time, he studied contemporary world art and then moved to the United States in the 1970s to study art there.

and the Southwest Pacific. Such a view is being widely disputed today, however, as the art of Asia, Latin America, and Africa as well as of minorities within Western Europe and the former settler colonies is given greater recognition. This recognition is manifest economically in an increasingly global art market marked by a growing demand for Asian, Latin American, and tribal art that fetches prices more and more comparable to European art.

S U M M A R Y

Traditionally defined, art is the use of skill and imagination to produce images recognized as having aesthetic quality. Art is part of a cultural context that determines the form of expression, the nature and interpretation of reality, and the recognition of aesthetic quality. There is a variety of views of what beauty is, but artistic expression itself is universal.

In most small-scale societies, art has traditionally been associated with religion. In these societies, art is influenced by a people's environment and adaptive strategy, full-time artists are rare, and art forms are often linked to the outside world.

Two forms of artistic expression in small-scale societies are carving and weaving. Carving masks in bone or wood is commonly done by men and often by specialists, though not always full-time specialists. Carvers are recognized not only for their artistic ability but also for their relation to the sacred. Weaving in small-scale societies is now being recognized as an art form, reflecting a move away from Eurocentric views of art and a new recognition of the role of women. Textiles are intended not only for wear but also for display for ceremonial purposes and items of exchange in brideprice transactions and may be viewed as a treasure. Textile patterns may be associated with particular groups or classes of people, though trade and cultural interchange may blur these distinctions.

Art has also been intertwined with religion in many Western societies, but as social scale increases, artistic expression changes. Full-time specialization of artists and patronage of the wealthy and powerful are found in large-scale societies, and the rise of capitalism and the modern world system have made art increasingly secular and individualistic.

Primitivism is an art form that reflects the interests of modern artists in tribal art and culture. The art of indigenous societies has influenced a number of Western artists since the late nineteenth century. Modern artists in countries in which indigenous people have been incorporated have also been interested in tribal art.

The art produced by small-scale societies now reflects the influence of large-scale societies and the modern world. As Graburn has shown, whereas inwardly directed art is made for and used by people within their ethnic enclaves, outward directed art, made for the outside world, is sold to an external market for generating income or presenting an ethnic image. The traditional bark painting of Australian Aborigines, originally linked to religious beliefs and practices, began to change into an outwardly directed form in the 1950s in response to a growing demand for the art from outside the Aborigine communities. Globalization also influences the artists of different societies and has challenged the belief that European art is superior to art in other cultures. As the global demand for art from outside the Western world increases, so does the recognition of the artists in these societies.

K e y   T e r m s

Art   The use of skill and imagination to produce images recognized as having an aesthetic quality.

Inwardly directed art   Art which has been made for and used by people within their enclave within the larger society.

Outwardly directed art   Art that has been made largely for the outside world.

Primitivism   The work of modern artists that has been consciously influenced by the art and culture of small-scale societies.

S u g g e s t e d   R e a d i n g s

Alland, Alexander, Jr. 1977. *The Artistic Animal: An Inquiry into the Biological Roots of Art.* Garden City, NY: Anchor.

Anderson, Richard L., and Karen L. Field (eds.). 1993. *Art in Small-Scale Societies: Contemporary Readings.* Englewood Cliffs, NJ: Prentice Hall.

Barnes, Ruth. 1989. *The Ikat Textiles of Lamalera: A Study of an Eastern Indonesian Weaving Tradition.* Leiden: E.J. Brill.

Basso, Ellen B. 1985. *A Musical View of the Universe: Kalapalo Myth and Ritual Performances.* Philadelphia: University of Pennsylvania Press. [Brazil]

Berndt, Ronald M., and E.S. Phillips (eds.). 1973. *The Australian Aboriginal Heritage: An Introduction Through the Arts.* Sydney: Ure Smith.

_____, Cathrine H. Berndt, and John E. Stanton. 1982. *Aboriginal Australian Art: A Visual Perspective.* Sydney: Methuen Australia.

Brain, Robert. 1979. *The Decorated Body.* New York: Harper & Row.

Coote, J., and A. Shelton (eds.). 1992. *Anthropology, Art and Aesthetics.* Oxford: Clarendon Press.

Dissanayake, Ellen. 1992. *Homo Aestheticus: Where Art Comes From and Why.* New York: The Free Press.

Drewal, Henry John, and Margaret Thompson Drewal. 1983. *Gèlèdé: Art and Female Power Among the Yoruba.* Bloomington: University of Indiana Press. [West Africa]

Faris, James. 1972. *Nuba Personal Art.* Toronto: University of Toronto Press. [East Africa]

Forge, Anthony (editor). 1973. *Primitive Art and Society.* London: Oxford University Press.

Gittinger, Mattiebelle (ed.). 1989. *To Speak with Cloth: Studies in Indonesian Textiles.* Los Angeles: Museum of Cultural History, University of California, Los Angeles.

Glaze, Anita J. 1981. *Art and Death in a Senufo Village.* Bloomington: Indiana University Press. [Ivory Coast]

Hannah, Judith Lynne. 1988. *Dance, Sex and Gender.* Chicago: University of Chicago Press.

Hatcher, Evelyn Payne. 1985. *Art as Culture: An Introduction to the Anthropology of Art.* New York: University Press of America.

Lewis, Phillip H. 1969. *The Social Context of Art in Northern New Ireland.* Chicago: Field Museum of Natural History.

Maquet, Jacques. 1986. *The Aesthetic Experience: An Anthropologist Looks at the Visual Arts*. New Haven, CT: Yale University Press.

Mead, Sidney M. (ed.) 1979. *Exploring the Visual Art of Oceania: Australia, Melanesia, Micronesia, and Polynesia*. Honolulu: University Press of Hawaii.

Merriam, Alan P. 1964. *The Anthropology of Music*. Chicago: Northwestern University Press.

O'Hanlon, Michael. 1989. *Reading the Skin: Adornment, Display, and Society Among the Wahgi*. London: British Museum Publications. [Papua New Guinea]

Otten, Charlotte, M. (ed.) 1971. *Anthropology and Art: Readings in Cross-cultural Aesthetics*. Garden City, NY: Natural History Press.

Price, Sally. 1989. *Primitive Art in Civilized Places*. Chicago: University of Chicago Press.

Ramseyer, Urs. 1977. *The Art and Culture of Bali*. New York: Oxford University Press.

Reina, Ruben E., and Robert M. Hill, II. 1978. *The Traditional Pottery of Guatemala*. Austin: University of Texas Press.

Schevill, Margot Blum. 1993. *Maya Textiles of Guatemala*. Austin: University of Texas Press.

15 ILLNESS AND CURING

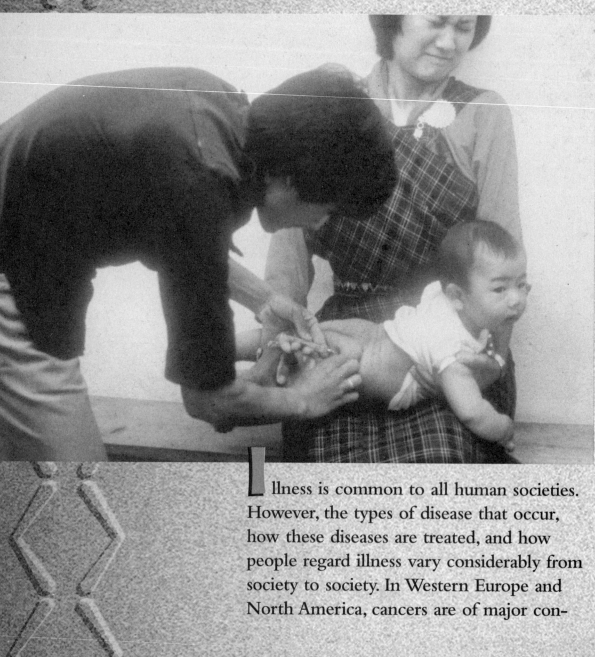

Illness is common to all human societies. However, the types of disease that occur, how these diseases are treated, and how people regard illness vary considerably from society to society. In Western Europe and North America, cancers are of major concern. In many tropical and subtropical regions, people worry more about such diseases as malaria, cholera, and dysentery. Treatment of illness in Western societies focuses on healing specific diseased organs or controlling a specific virus. In many non-Western societies, greater emphasis is placed on the social and psychological dimensions of illness.

Anthropologists emphasize that patterns of disease and methods of curing exist within particular physical and sociocultural settings. The medical systems of the United States and Nicaragua are as much a product of their respective environments as the systems of Australian Aborigines and Amazonian Indians. By **medical system** we mean "the culturally based behavior and belief forms that arise in response to the threats posed by disease" (Foster and Anderson 1978: 33). Anthropologists study the medical systems of small- and large-scale societies.

In studying medical systems, it is important to recognize a distinction between disease and illness. **Disease** refers to a pathological condition of some part of the body in which functioning is disturbed or deranged. **Illness** is a cultural concept: a society's idea of pronounced deviation from what is considered a normal healthy state. Even though beliefs about disease and patterns of incidence may be viewed as sociocultural phenomena, diseases themselves are physiological processes. Illness, on the other hand, is a broad concept referring to how people conceive of deviant mental and physical states.

◄ EPIDEMIOLOGY ►

Epidemiology is a branch of medical science concerned with the factors that determine the frequency, distribution, and control of diseases in societies. Worldwide, the leading categories of disease that people die from are cardiovascular, respiratory, infectious and parasitic, and cancerous types. However, if we compare more developed countries with poorer developing countries, we find significant differences in the relative frequencies of these types of disease. In developed countries cardiovascular diseases remain the number one killers; but the number two spot is held by cancers, with communicable diseases being relatively insignificant By contrast, communicable diseases predominate in

∧∧∧∧∧

Vaccination in Bhutan, South Asia. Although health-care settings such as this provide a specialized locale for treatment and trained practitioners, they are usually less elaborate by Western standards.

developing countries. But even in developed countries there are marked differences. While Scotland and Finland have the highest mortality rates from heart disease—over 700 and 600 deaths respectively, per 100,000 population a year—the figure for France is just over 150 and for Japan only around 50.

Epidemiological patterns are also related to gender and age. Looking again at mortality from heart disease, in Canada and the United States, while the rate for males is in excess of 300, for women it is only around 100 (a ratio that is relatively constant in other countries). In terms of age, heart disease is primarily a killer of adults. The epidemiological picture for children is different. Diarrhea is the leading cause of death among children worldwide (some five million a year), while it is responsible for relatively few adult deaths.

Whereas many of the disease-related deaths in poorer countries can be linked to poverty and poor sanitary conditions, understanding patterns in developed countries is more complex. Why do more Scots die from heart disease than the French? Smoking, high blood pressure, and high cholesterol levels are often cited as major causes of heart disease. Epidemiologists thus compare smoking and dietary habits of populations and see the extent to which they are related to the differing levels of heart disease. Recent studies, however, have pointed to personality type as an extremely important factor (Eysenck and Grossarth-Maticek 1989). In short, the epidemiologist must study a far more complex set of cultural, social, and psychological variables to interpret the different rates of death from heart disease.

One of the best-known examples of the contribution of anthropology to epidemiological research is the case of *kuru*, a disease of the central nervous system that was discovered in the 1950s among the South Fore of the Eastern Highlands of Papua New Guinea. No known treatment will cure or arrest kuru, which usually leads to death within six to 12

months. The disease was found to be unique to the South Fore, and among them it was limited to women, children, and occasionally young men.

Initial investigation revealed that the disease tended to follow family lines. Numerous hypotheses were offered to explain the disease—genetic, infectious, sociological, and nutritional—but all proved unsatisfactory (Hunt 1978). The first break came when "slow virus infections" were identified as the result of studies with sheep and chimpanzees. Such diseases appear only after a long period of incubation. Kuru proved to be the first-known human disease caused by a slow-acting virus.

The discovery of the slow-acting virus failed to explain the epidemiological characteristics of kuru, however. Why was the disease limited to the South Fore, and why to only a limited segment of the population? Also, why had its incidence changed over time? The disease first had appeared during the early part of the twentieth century, becoming more frequent up to the late 1950s and declining thereafter. Anthropologists Robert and Shirley Glasse provided a clue to the mystery (see Lindenbaum 1979). They noted that cannibalism among South Fore women was introduced around 1910, roughly the same time that the disease first appeared. In particular, eating the brains of deceased kinswomen became part of the South Fore mourning ceremonies. The brains were prepared and eaten primarily by women, with small portions occasionally being given to children of both sexes. Researchers found that the virus was transmitted in the preparation; the women who touched the mucous membrane of the brains contracted the disease either through ingestion (see Gajdusek 1977) or through handling the corpses and then "rubbing the eyes and the eyes of children with contaminated hands" (Steadman and Merbs 1982: 619). The decline of kuru was linked to the cessation in the 1960s of

The virus that causes kuru, *a disease of the central nervous system among the South Fore of Papua New Guinea, was found to be transmitted in the preparation of human brains of deceased kinswomen. Here a kuru victim is treated by "bleeding" by a medicine man.*

this ritual cannibalism. In 1986 there were only six reported cases.

Endemic Diseases

A society's characteristic diseases are closely related to its physical environment as well as to its cultural practices. Part of a population's adaptation to a particular environment entails biocultural adjustment to the local disease-causing features. Especially when the population and its adaptation are rather stable, relatively constant epidemiological patterns will emerge. One result is the development of **endemic diseases**. These diseases have a relatively low incidence but are constantly present in a given community. In our own society such diseases include the common cold, flu, and chickenpox.

Evidence indicates that during the thousands of years of our existence as foragers, disease patterns were fairly constant (Dunn 1968). The original immigrants to the New World who crossed the Bering land bridge carried few diseases with them, and in their isolation they developed tolerances for the limited selection of disease-causing agents in the New World. One of the endemic diseases to develop in the New

World was syphilis. A syndrome of the world-wide disease treponematosis, syphilis evolved as a disease that was unique to the New World, but it appears not to have been a particularly serious problem. Only after the arrival of Columbus in 1492 and the subsequent spread of the disease to Europe and Asia (the first epidemic in Europe occurred in Italy in 1494 or 1495), did syphilis take on the more severe characteristics for which it has been known since then (Crosby 1972: 122–164).

Epidemic Diseases

Migration and contact between previously isolated human populations are the prime causes of epidemics. An **epidemic disease** is one that is not commonly found in a community; it is characterized by high incidence and rapid and extensive diffusion. Perhaps the most devastating series of epidemics in world history were those brought about by the opening of regular contact between the New World and Europe after 1492. The long isolation of the New World population made it especially vulnerable to diseases brought from outside. Smallpox was one of the leading killers. Endemic to the Old World, it was a steady, predictable killer, responsible for less than 10 percent of the yearly deaths in Europe. But among people with no previous contact, smallpox will infect nearly every individual. Within 10 years of contact with Europeans, the population of central Mexico declined from 25 million to 16.8 million, primarily because of the direct and indirect effects of epidemic diseases like smallpox. The Spaniard Toribio Motolinía, writing in the sixteenth century, noted that the indigenous inhabitants of Mexico "died like bedbugs" from such epidemics (Motolinía 1950).

For centuries Mecca has been the destination for large numbers of *hajis* (pilgrims) from around the Islamic world. Such a mingling of people has provided ideal conditions for the spread of epidemic diseases on a number of occasions. Thus, the plague was carried by *hajis* to Mecca in 1865, running through the caravans and then

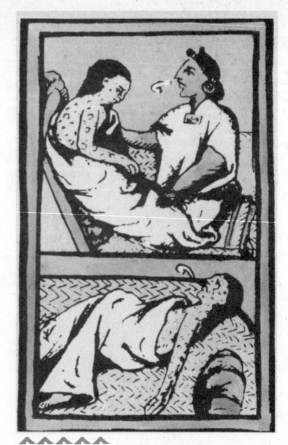

Native Americans suffering from smallpox as a result of the Spanish invasion. Smallpox epidemics took a large toll on Native American populations, which had been isolated from the outside world.

being carried back to the *hajis'* homes. In Egypt, for example, the epidemic resulted in 60,000 deaths. Spreading around the world, with cases reported as far as New York, the epidemic did not run its course until 1874. The plague subsequently recurred in Mecca in 1893 and 1902.

Epidemics are not merely something of the past, nor are they something to which those in developed countries are immune. One disease that has been spreading at an epidemic rate in recent years, especially in developed countries, is skin cancer (malignant melanoma and squamous cell skin cancer). In the United States over

500,000 new cases of skin cancer occur a year, and the number could soon be in the millions (the figure for Canada is around 50,000, an equally serious number in per capita terms). In Australia, where the state of Queensland has the highest rate of melanoma in the world, around 1,000 people die of it each year, and the number of sufferers is increasing dramatically. The epidemic has been linked to both environmental and cultural factors. In 1922, fashion figure Coco Chanel returned to Paris from a holiday "beautifully tanned." Before long the lily-white look was out, and tanned skin, which until then had been frowned upon and linked with manual outdoor labor, was in. Since then the popularity of tanning in the West has increased dramatically and has even come to be associated with good health, although it is now known to be a cause of skin cancer. Even in Japan, where skin cancer was previously very rare, the growing popularity of tanning and beach holidays has resulted in a growing incidence of skin cancer comparable to that of other developed countries (Elwood 1989). In addition to fashion trends, environmental changes also have contributed to the rise of skin cancer—primarily a thinning of the ozone layer, due mainly to chemical pollution.

The most highly publicized modern epidemic is associated with AIDS (acquired immune deficiency syndrome), which is associated with a virus known as HIV (human immunodeficiency virus). The disease is transmitted largely through sexual contact, but also as a result of intravenous drug use (as a consequence of using contaminated syringes) and the use of dirty syringes and contaminated blood in hospitals; and it is fatal. Spreading for years (after apparently originating in Africa) as a "silent epidemic," the disease was not identified until 1981. The epidemic is most advanced in Africa, followed by North America and Western Europe, and is still in its early stages in Asia, Eastern Europe, and Latin America. Of the approximately 350,000 reported cases of AIDS in some 120 countries in 1991, about 170,000 were in the United States; Uganda reported the largest number in sub-Saharan Africa (around 18,000). Since 1981, roughly half those with the disease have died. The World Health Organization estimates that there are, in fact, 12 million people who have been infected by the HIV virus, and forecasts that 20 million people will have AIDS by the year 2000—other estimates are as high as 40 million.

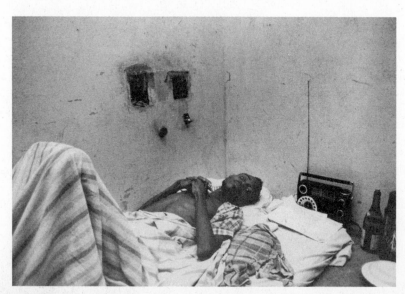

AIDS patient in Zaire. The worldwide epidemic associated with AIDS has hit the people of sub-Saharan Africa particularly hard, placing a strain on already inadequate healthcare facilities and threatening to cause economic havoc.

So far the majority of AIDS cases have been reported in the developed countries, but it is the developing world where most new cases are being reported. The problem is especially acute in sub-Saharan Africa, where the number of reported cases rose from 383 in 1985 to 91,114 in 1990. In fact, the situation in sub-Saharan Africa is far worse than these figures indicate. Health authorities now estimate that some five million adults in Africa are probably infected with HIV; in parts of East and Central Africa between 20 and 30 percent of all adults may be infected. The AIDS epidemic in sub-Saharan Africa, however, appears to have peaked in the early 1990s at around one million new HIV infections per year. In the meantime, the number of HIV infections has begun to climb dramatically in South and Southeast Asia (see "Focus on Anthropologists"). HIV infection began to appear as a serious problem in this area around 1986–87, and by 1992 there were around two million people infected by HIV, with an estimated 600,000 new infections occurring each year. By the year 2000 predictions are that half of the new infections will occur in Asia.

Because of the stigma attached to the disease and technical problems in detecting AIDS, accurate worldwide figures about its incidence are difficult to establish. Taking Zambia as an example, the government, sensitive to the country's international image, refused to recognize the disease until 1986. A major change in government policy occurred the following year, when one of President Kenneth Kuanda's sons died of AIDS. But official figures for Zambia still do not reflect the true picture. Thus, by 1989 there were still only 1,300 reported AIDS cases, while semiofficial estimates ran as high as 70,000. Moreover, as many as 350,000 are believed to be carriers of the HIV virus—out of a total national population of seven million.

Anthropologists and other social scientists are not interested solely in the relationship of sociocultural factors and disease; they are also concerned with the social consequences of diseases. Severe epidemics affect societies profoundly. For example, a popular theory argues that the sixteenth-century collapse of the various indigenous empires in the New World, such as those of the Aztec and Inca, was caused primarily by the ravages of newly introduced epidemic diseases. Equally catastrophic scenarios have been put forward for some sub-Saharan and Asian countries as a result of the AIDS epidemic. Surveys of the impact of AIDS on developing countries warn of growing economic costs not just in terms of treatment, but also because of labor shortages and declining production (Panos Institute 1992, United Nations Development Programme 1992, Gooding 1992). The more subtle effects of diseases are also significant. Endemic malaria—about 300 million people are infected worldwide—in a region may kill only a small percentage of the population, but it debilitates a much larger proportion, contributing to a general malaise that adversely affects all aspects of life.

Diseases of Development

Charles Hughes and John Hunter (1972: 93) coined the term *diseases of development* to refer to "those pathological conditions which are based on the usually unanticipated consequences of the implementation of development schemes." Such diseases can be divided into three general categories. First, there are those diseases that result from integration into large-scale industrial societies: diabetes, obesity, hypertension, and so on. For example, the people of Nauru found themselves with a dramatic increase in disposable wealth in the 1960s and even more so in the 1970s as a result of increased earnings from phosphate mining on their isolated South Pacific island (Howard 1991b). With this newfound wealth came a rise in food consumption (virtually all of it being imported and much of it high in sugar and salt content and low in nutritional value), reaching an estimated daily average of around 6,000 calories per person. By 1983, out of a total population of some 5,000 Nauruans, about 400 were known to be suffering from diabetes. Fewer than ten years later two out of every three adults had diabetes, and diabetes was the leading cause of nonaccidental death. Moreover, despite a per capita income of around US$20,000, as a result of diabetes Nauru has one of the shortest human life expectancies. Obesity is a precipitating factor in adults with a tendency toward diabetes (and certain populations do appear to have higher genetic risks of developing the disease; see Carter et al. 1989 and Heath et al. 1991). If neglected, diabetes can lead to complications like respiratory diseases, heart ailments, kidney diseases, blindness, gangrene, stillbirths, and congenital abnormalities. When the government of Nauru launched a program of medical checkups for those suffering from diabetes in 1983, some individuals had already become too ill to travel to the hospital on their own.

In the second category are bacterial and parasitic diseases, introduced or augmented by changes in the physical environment. For example, onchocerciasis (African river blindness) is a disease that traditionally has affected the population living in the Volta River basin in West Africa. Carried by a tiny blackfly, it results in reduced or total loss of vision. The disease spread to the New World, appearing in Mexico in the 1940s. In 1974 and 1975 it was reported to be spreading throughout the northwestern part of the Amazonian Basin in South America in conjunction with development projects. The indigenous population of the region proved particularly susceptible. Among some groups of Yanomami, up to 100 percent of the population became infected. Two American scientists, Robert Goodland and Howard Irwin (1975), found that the blackfly population was thriving in the cleared areas along the newly constructed Northern Perimeter Highway, which penetrated the territories of these indigenous groups.

The third category includes diseases that result from poverty, undernourishment, and unsanitary living conditions, reflecting the failure of development programs to integrate people into large-scale societies in a satisfactory manner. Diseases of development present difficult problems. Understanding the causes of the diseases helps to solve some of these problems, and anthropology plays an important role in analyz-ing the complex social, cultural, and natural factors that influence diseases. However, diseases like diabetes or onchocerciasis will not be eliminated simply through the development of wonder drugs or spraying with pesticides. Finding cures can result only from a willingness to see the disease in its total context.

◄ MALNUTRITION ►

As many as 800 million people are seriously undernourished—about one in every six humans. Understanding the causes of malnutrition and finding solutions to this problem are among the most important challenges facing scientists today. Minor cases of malnutrition can impair people's ability to perform normal daily tasks. Malnutrition also reduces resistance to disease. More severe cases of malnutrition can lead to permanent brain damage or to death. The causes of malnutrition are both cultural and social (see Foster 1992). They are related to social factors (such as economic impoverishment) that influence what people can eat and how much, and to people's ideas about what they eat (what they consider desirable food).

There are global implications of food preferences in terms of a correlation between diet and malnutrition. If all humans were to rely solely on a vegetarian diet, we produce enough food to feed 120 percent of the human population. However, if the global diet were to consist of a small amount of meat, similar to amounts commonly consumed in Latin America, we produce only enough food—if snakes, lizards, and insects are excluded—to adequately feed 80 percent of the human population. Furthermore, if we were to provide humans with the diet recommended by world health authorities, then we produce only enough food to feed 50 percent of humanity.

Malnutrition and Subsistence Patterns

In his research on foragers, Frederick Dunn (1968: 233) cites numerous studies indicating the relatively good nutritional status of more

OTOME KLEIN HUTHEESING

FOCUS ON ANTHROPOLOGISTS

Otome Hutheesing received her academic training at Leiden University, the Netherlands, where she developed a keen interest in the problems of comparative inequality, the subject of her Ph.D. thesis. After research assignments in India, Malaysia, and Thailand she became more engrossed with anthropological fieldwork among minority peoples. She taught for many years at the Universiti Sains Malaysia, while doing research on changing gender relations in various communities in Southeast Asia. In recent years she has been involved with an AIDS project among the Lisu of northern Thailand, a group of hill farmers she has known for over a decade.

∧∧∧∧∧∧∧∧

A Mountain Culture Faces Aids: The Lisu of Northern Thailand

In 1982 I became a temporary dropout from teaching in order to research changing gender relations among the Lisu minority of northern Thailand (a hill farming tribe which numbered about 18,000 people). At that time the Lisu were involved in the planting of poppies (opium), which they sold for cash. I did intensive fieldwork for three years, during which time I participated in various activities with an eye to any gender discrimination.

The fact that I was a middle-aged woman with graying hair made them bestow the rank of honorary female elder on me. Moreover, since I also distributed pills and plasters, I was perceived to be a medicine woman, a role which made me fit with ease into the Lisu way of life. At the same time I tended to resort to their traditional forest medicine and healing ceremonies whenever I had "lost one of my souls."

The egalitarian structure of female and male relations among the Lisu had deteriorated on account of opium eradication policies, and the sale of their substitute crops to the lowland markets had a devastating effect on their livelihood. In my book (Hutheesing 1990) I analyzed how their linkage with the modern commercial networks had led to a weakening of women's economic power and to the impoverishment of a majority of Lisu households. These incidents illustrated dramatically the encompassing power of the world system which had penetrated the hilly hinterlands.

Then AIDS came to be known to the mountain folk. This event brought to the fore an even sharper impact of a globalization process in which this minority people were trapped.

The routes by which the HIV virus could travel to the Lisu were opened in different ways. The low prices for the substitute crops had resulted in a flight of youngsters from the highland villages to urban areas in order to find jobs as construction workers, hotel personnel, and prostitutes. Male laborers were exposed to AIDS by visiting prostitutes in the towns and females by their work as prostitutes. In addition, the unavailability of opium, in an ironic twist of fate, brought about the introduction of heroin from Burma on which young people became hooked. As poverty and drug addiction spread, brokers emerged overnight in the mountain environment, serving to commercialize either female flesh or land—the sale of land leading to further impoverishment and greater pressure to migrate to the lowlands in search of work.

Since 1992 two men have died of AIDS in the village where I lived, while four had succumbed to the disease in a nearby settlement. In addition, one young mother had committed suicide upon learning that she and her child were seropositive. At that time I became connected with an AIDS education project for tribal people, and I sought a new way of looking at the Lisu. Anthropology came to mean acquiring a deeper understanding of people's conceptions of disease and death, sexuality and risk, contamination and communication. My work also made me ask how educating people about a new disease can be conducted in a foreign world.

Lisu beliefs regarding illness were eclectic, and their various healing practices derived from Western sources, Chinese folk practices, and some curing skills handed down from the Lisu ancestors. The Lisu sought several remedies at the same time, such as swallowing pills, getting an injection from the local teacher, and having a ceremony done as well. They were in general more interested in the symptoms than the causes of a particular ailment, and their first question upon hearing of a new disease called AIDS was "What does it look like?"

A large number of illnesses were seen by the Lisu as "arising by themselves," as "being

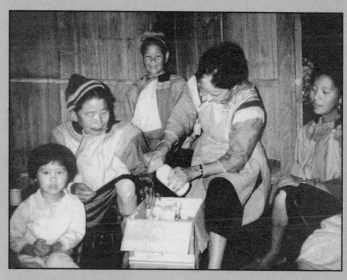

AIDS has come to the Lisu, a mountain folk of northern Thailand. The Lisu are generally more interested in the symptoms of a disease than its causes. Their first question upon hearing of AIDS was "What does it look like?"

out there." The only way to articulate these evil influences was via cosmological or environmental references. Certain diseases were categorized as "bad vapor" of the soil, others as "bad wind," and others were explained by the fact that one was born in a bad animal year. Then there were the inflictions brought about by dissatisfied ancestors or by a vampire spirit. Some of these spiritual attacks were believed to cause specific symptoms.

Within this ramshackle pattern of disease causation, AIDS was ultimately viewed as "bad fate," inflicted by their sky god who wrote the lines of destiny in one's palm. For this celestial deity no ceremonies could be carried out, as he was too pow-

erful and "too far." The mountain community members were therefore culturally ill-prepared to face the advent of AIDS, nor were they receptive to any education, since they did not grasp the idea of changing behavior for protection against the virus. The role of sexual intercourse and blood contamination was not clear to them.

The topic of sex was taboo, and in the earlier days of my fieldwork, the topic was brought up in jest and through vulgar jokes with the villagers. Sex was mainly done within the frame of procreation, and frequent intercourse was advised because the babies would grow up to be strong. Women in the early days of marriage enjoyed sex for that reason: they wanted to be instrumental in the production of healthy offspring. With more young Lisu men visiting Thai prostitutes in the lowlands, a change occurred in the idea of sex for procreation. Men perceived it to be enjoyable in itself, especially with lowland non-Lisu women.

The Lisu do not see traditional means of treatment as being effective in curing diseases related to sex with non-Lisu. In the old days adultery was considered to be contrary to custom and could invite the wrath of the senior grandfather spirit, resulting in a number of ailments. Offerings were then made to the offended spirit to remedy the ailment. However, the spirits were deemed to be incapable of dealing with the strong polluting substances associated with AIDS, which was the result of "outside" sex.

The Lisu attitude toward AIDS was also influenced by a belief that constant quarrels in the village about land, heroin addiction, and thievery had produced AIDS. I heard repeatedly that "the spirits do not like it when we quarrel, they will send us disease." In a curious way the Lisu had become aware of the ills of a world system that had plunged them into poverty and inflicted upon them contradictions and conflicts that ultimately had filtered down a disease of development into their midst.

---

traditional foraging societies. Hunger was rare and infant mortality low among these peoples, and their diets usually were sufficient to meet their nutritional needs. Hunger was also largely absent from small-scale farming societies where adequate land was available. Nathan Cohen (1989) makes the point, however, that the decrease in consumption of animal sources of protein and increased reliance on cereal grains as a result of the transition from foraging to farming reduced the nutritional quality of people's diets, exposing them to greater health problems and physiological stress. Thus, in the New World, the shift from animal proteins to maize resulted in such problems as reduced growth and anemia. Despite these problems, populations grew primarily because of increased fertility.

The extent to which malnutrition exists today among contemporary foraging societies is mainly a result of their competition for resources with nonforagers and their disadvantageous integration into modern states. In a study of nutrition among Australian Aborigines living at the Edward River settlement of the Cape York Peninsula, John Taylor (1977) noted that since the Aborigines gave up their traditional nomadic existence (which included consumption of a wide variety of natural foods) in the 1950s, their diet has been characterized by shortcomings in most important nutrients. The postsettlement diet of most rural-dwelling Aborigines consists of damper (flour and water), sweet black tea, and occasionally meat. Such a diet is lacking particularly in protein, calcium, vitamin A, and vitamin C. It provides poor nourishment, especially during pregnancy, resulting in the birth of babies of less than optimal weight and impaired resistance to disease. Health problems continue through the life cycle, and Aborigines today have far higher disease and death rates than other Australians.

Perhaps the most significant finding of Taylor's study, however, is that improvement in economic conditions for the Edward River Aborigines has not resulted in dietary improvements. In fact, just the opposite has been true. Increased earnings have been diverted toward satisfaction of demands for nonfood consumer items rather than being used for food. One problem is that Aborigines think that their diet is adequate: the flour and tea are, after all, filling. As a result of their dietary outlook and these economic changes, the nutrition of the people has deteriorated to the point where some people are unwittingly starving themselves, even though their material well-being seems to have improved.

Malnourished child being measured at an intensive feeding center, Bardera, Somalia. Civil war in this African country has left the crops and livestock devastated, resulting in famine.

For many small-scale farming societies, nutritional problems became even more serious as they were integrated into large-scale market economies. Peasant agriculturalists find a large percentage of what they produce usurped by nonagriculturalists, and what they retain plus the payment they receive for their product is rarely sufficient to meet their nutritional requirements. Their diet begins to suffer in both quantity and variety. Protein intake, in particular, tends to be greatly reduced. The protein intake of most rural peasants in Ecuador, for example, is less than half that of the Achuara Jivaro, who maintain something of their traditional subsistence adaptation in the eastern jungles of the country.

Modern agricultural techniques of large-scale societies are able to produce a tremendous amount of food, but there are also a lot of people to feed. In many developing countries, it is difficult simply to keep up with population growth, despite innovations to increase productivity. Often, however, the problem is not just a matter of producing enough food. Developing countries also face infrastructural problems in storing, preserving, and distributing food. In addition problems are exacerbated by relative socioeconomic inequality. This is not a problem faced by poorer countries alone, however. In the United States, for example, a nation with an abundant supply of food and an overfed and overweight middle and upper class, there are also millions of undernourished people occupying the lower economic rungs of society. Among the upper social classes, diets high in fat and sugar correspond to high rates of cardiovascular disease and of some forms of cancer, such as cancer of the colon, associated with lack of fiber in the diet. Among the poor, protein deficiencies mean low-birth-weight babies and, as a result, higher rates of mental retardation.

Cultural Perceptions of Food

Malnutrition also can develop in the midst of plenty because what people are willing to eat is largely a matter of cultural definition. Not only do relatively poor and uneducated people, such as the Aboriginal inhabitants of Edward River, remain unaware that their diet is lacking in vital nutrients, the same can be said of many educated and affluent North Americans.

In every society, people designate certain items from a range of edible plant and animal matter as "food." People of other cultures include in their diet things that most Westerners would never consider eating—for example, dogs, commonly eaten in parts of East Asia and the Pacific. (Ishige [1977] provides a Ponapean recipe for roasting dogs in an earth oven.) Less obvious are the numerous nutritious insects and "weeds." These are plentiful enough; but because they are not considered food, people in many societies will go hungry or even starve while living in what others would consider a veritable supermarket. The people of Bama (Ignatius 1990), for example, in China's southern Guangxi province, which claims to boast the highest concentration of 100-plus-year-olds of any place on earth, maintain that their long life is linked to a diet rich in wild grass, snakes, and lizards.

Trying to change people's perceptions of food is a difficult task; improving their dietary habits is rarely as simple as providing alternative types of food. We all know how little good it does to tell a child (or adult, for that matter), "Here, eat this, it's good for you." Cross-cultural innovations may be even more difficult, especially when there are existing prejudices against foods ("We feed that to pigs!"). Furthermore, schemes to boost nutrition through food innovations may in fact result in a deterioration of nutritional standards because of the context within which the innovation is attempted. For example, programs in poorer nations that promote the use of dietary formulas for infants distributed by transnational corporations such as Nestlé often have resulted in health problems. Mothers in these poorer countries may lack the sanitary conditions for preparing infant formula; the water, for example, is often contaminated. Moreover, the women often cannot follow the written instructions, and the price of the formula strains family budgets where breastfeeding

would be less expensive and more healthy. But the women have been told by the companies marketing the formula that the formula is the smart thing to use because it is what many women in the United States and Europe use.

⊰ MENTAL ILLNESS ⊱

All peoples recognize illnesses that take the form of mental states perceived as abnormal. **Mental illness** includes disorders caused by physiological conditions as well as those caused by unsatisfactory adaptations to sociocultural conditions at the individual level. In the latter case, mental illness is associated with stress in coping with the environment.

Stress is a feature of life in all societies. It may result from such natural causes as earthquakes or volcanic eruptions, or it may be induced intentionally, as in torture. It may also be a "normal" part of the life-cycle, such as the stresses caused by births, deaths, marriages, and the like. Beyond this are the stresses that arise from our lifestyle— those caused by commuting, unemployment, and overwork.

Patterns of Stress Disorders

After decades of careful research on mental illness in different cultures, it now appears that the major patterns of mental illness known to Western psychiatrists are universal (Kennedy 1973). However, since patterns of stress-producing situations will vary from one setting to another and because cultural methods of dealing with stress differ, the distribution of forms of mental illness varies among societies. Physical surroundings, economic conditions, child-rearing practices, religious traditions, and so forth all combine to produce particular patterns of stress. It is therefore possible (although difficult) to study mental illness from an epidemiological perspective, that is, to note distributional pat-

Life in slums such as this one in Port-au-Prince, Haiti, is difficult. The stress in coping with the environment can lead to both physical and mental health problems.

terns and search for variables in the environment that appear to influence such patterns.

In addition to universal forms of mental illness, there are unique configurations that result from particular environments and cultural traditions. These are commonly referred to as **culture-bound syndromes.** Among these disorders are "Arctic hysteria," found among a number of circumpolar peoples; "running amok," a frenzied violent behavior of males in certain Asian societies (see Spores 1988); and "koro," a fear among Chinese that the penis or the breasts and vulva will withdraw into the body. While most of these disorders are based on universal forms of mental illness, they have taken on certain unique characteristics as well.

Arctic hysteria is marked by periods of silence followed by seizures, in which the individual typically tears off his or her clothing, takes

flight, and runs about in the snow. Arctic hysteria is a variant of the universal condition known as agoraphobia (a morbid fear of being in an open space), but with certain characteristics unique to the Arctic environment and Inuit culture. Edward Foulks (1985: 307) thus writes: "While Arctic hysteria can be partially understood in universal psychological terms, a more complete understanding is offered by consideration of the unique framework of Eskimo culture." Anthony Wallace (1972) noted the important role of calcium deficiency in bringing on Arctic hysteria. Climatic factors also are important since winter conditions serve to intensify insecurity.

Studies of Arctic hysteria conducted by Foulks (1985) have provided insights into how such syndromes are influenced by culture change. Behavioral stress among Inuit today is associated with the consumption of alcohol. Foulks identified a traditional segment of Inuit society that exhibited a transformed version of Arctic hysteria involving the use of alcohol; others, however, exhibited behavior patterns that were similar to those found in the urban United States.

Social Change and Stress

Rapid social change is a primary source of stress for many people. Often the strains are temporary, but the stress may be sufficient to cause severe mental disorders. Migration commonly results in considerable stress. In an early study, Margaret Mead (1947) pointed out that migrants are frequently culturally disoriented and subject to special strains; at the same time, they lack the accustomed means of reducing tensions. The problem may be even worse if the migrant must make difficult physiological adjustments. Peruvian Indians moving to the coastal city of Lima from the Andes not only are faced with social and cultural problems of adjustment, but also have difficulty adjusting to the higher oxygen content at the lower elevation. During the initial period of their stay in Lima, the combination of factors results in a syndrome characterized by anxiety and depression, as well as by a number of circulatory, respiratory, neurological, and gastrointestinal symptoms (Fried 1959).

Migration and other forms of rapid social change can result in a state of **anomie**—disorganization of personality and a feeling of alienation. In his famous study of suicide, Emile Durkheim (1951) described anomie as a result of the abandonment of community goals and of the social rules for reaching them. In small, closely knit rural communities, people's lives tend to be highly organized and closely regulated. There are constraints, but there is also a sense of security. Movement to the city may liberate one from many of the constraints of rural life, but suddenly the individual has to live in a very unfamiliar environment, with no sure way of finding happiness in this new setting.

The changing lifestyles of the urban middle class in India, for example, have resulted in a widespread syndrome labeled "urban neurosis" among married women living on the upper floors of highrise apartment buildings. This disorder manifests itself primarily as an acute concern about security. The syndrome is linked to the feeling of isolation that such women feel as they break away from joint families to live in nuclear families with more restricted social contacts.

For many indigenous peoples around the world, rapid social change has meant the destruction of the existing social order, and, all too often, its replacement with a social order based on impoverishment and exploitation. The psychological consequences often are great, sometimes resulting in suicide or loss of a will to live. For those who persist, the stress of life under new conditions still may lead to mental illnesses that blend characteristics of disorders associated with the old and the new cultural patterns.

◄ CONCEPTS OF ILLNESS CAUSALITY ►

The ways in which people attempt to cure a perceived illness are based on their notions of what caused it. Such ideas vary widely. Within large-scale societies there are many beliefs, reflecting the complexity of the societies themselves. Such diversity is referred to as **medical pluralism**—an array of options in which a number of medical systems compete with and complement one another.

Mind-Body Dualism

Western medical traditions make a distinction between illnesses originating in the mind and those originating in the body—that is, between psychological and physiological illnesses. Other traditions have taken a more holistic approach, viewing health and illness as manifestations of the totality of a person's life. For instance, most non-Western medical systems do not have a separate category for "mental illness." Mental illness and physiological illness in such systems are placed in the same general category. To the Azande of the southern Sudan, mental illnesses are viewed in much the same way as malaria and smallpox, and all are seen as ultimately caused by sorcery. Categorical distinctions between mental and physiological illness by Western medical traditions in part reflect greater specialization (occupational and otherwise).

The traditional mind-body division of Western medicine increasingly has been called into question by Western medical practitioners themselves, who now recognize the close relationship between psychological and physiological disorders. Thus, on the one hand, it is now apparent that many physiological illnesses (such as cancer) are related to psychological problems influenced by the environment. On the other hand, research has shown that many psychological patterns are influenced by biochemical factors. Examples of the latter include some forms of depression, "possession," and perhaps schizophrenia.

Personalistic Versus Naturalistic Explanations

Not until after the sixteenth century did modern scientific concepts of disease causality begin to develop. In many parts of the world people continue to adhere to alternative beliefs. Although these alternative beliefs differ from one another, basic principles appear to be common to many of them. In broad terms, Foster and Anderson (1978: 53) have identified two major nonscientific belief systems of disease causality: personalistic and naturalistic.

In a **personalistic system,** illness is thought to be purposely caused by a supernatural being (such as a ghost or evil spirit) or a human being (such as a witch or sorcerer). Personalistic belief systems are found in small-scale societies throughout much of sub-Saharan Africa, throughout the Pacific islands, and among tribal peoples in eastern Asia. According to this system, the sick person is a victim—the object of personally directed aggression or punishment. Such a belief system

lacks a concept of accident. If a person falls from a tree and dies, it is assumed that some person or some being caused the death. This is not to say that people subscribing to such beliefs do not recognize more immediate causes of illness or injury, but they believe that other forces are at work beyond the more apparent ones. The Azande exemplify this type of thinking:

> Azande attribute sickness, whatever its nature, to witchcraft or sorcery. This does not mean that they entirely disregard secondary causes but, in so far as they recognize these, they generally think of them as associated with witchcraft and magic. Nor does their reference of sickness to supernatural causes lead them to neglect treatment of symptoms any more than their reference to death on the horns of a buffalo to witchcraft causes them to await its onslaught. On the contrary, they possess an enormous pharacopoeia . . . and in ordinary circumstances they trust drugs to cure their ailments and only take steps to remove the primary and supernatural causes when the disease is of a serious nature or takes an alarming turn. Nevertheless, we must remember in describing the Azande classification of diseases and their treatment that the notion of witchcraft as a participant in their origin may always be expressed, and that if Azande do not always and immediately consult their oracles to find out the witch that is responsible it is because they consider the sickness to be of a minor character and not worth the trouble and expense of oracle consultation. [Evans-Pritchard 1937: 479]

By contrast, **naturalistic systems** explain illness in impersonal terms, attributing good health to the maintenance of an equilibrium within the body. Illness results when the balance is upset by such natural external forces as heat or cold or internal forces such as strong emotions. Most contemporary naturalistic systems are derived largely from the medical traditions of ancient classical civilizations, particularly those of Greece, India, and China. For example, some systems are based on the concept of *bodily humors,* a belief that originated in ancient Greece. The Greeks believed that there were four humors, or fluids, in the body: blood, phlegm, black bile (or melancholy), and yellow bile (or choler). Each humor was associated with certain qualities: blood with heat and moisture, phlegm with cold and moisture, black bile with cold and dryness, and yellow bile with heat and dryness. Illness or suffering resulted when one of these humors was either deficient or excessive, or if the humors should fail to mix properly. Curing was largely a matter of restoring the balance.

In a contemporary Latin American variant of humoral pathology, illness is ascribed to an imbalance of heat and cold. This may be related to the actual temperatures of substances with which one comes into contact (such as water, air, and food), but more often actual temperature is not important, "hot" and "cold" being cultural categories. Foods are especially important in maintaining a balance between hot and cold, and the system classifies foods according to their "temperature." In a Mexican-American community studied by Margaret Clark (1970: 166), white beans, garlic, and chile peppers are considered to be "very hot"; salt, pork, and onions to be "hot"; corn tortillas, lamb, and radishes to be "cold"; and cucumbers and tomatoes to be "very cold". Illness is often attributed to eating an excess of hot or cold foods, and curing commonly entails eating things that will restore the balance.

Beliefs in disease causality rarely are so rigid as to ascribe all illness or misfortune to a single cause. Even the Azande do not ascribe certain diseases that afflict infants exclusively to witchcraft or sorcery. In fact, their ideas about the causes of these diseases are fairly vague. In part, this reflects the status of infants in Azande society. There is a high infant mortality rate, and small children are barely considered social beings, their life at this time being very tenuous.

‹ CURING ›

How people attempt to cure illness is primarily a product of social and cultural factors rather than any inherent properties of the illness itself. It is not surprising to find that cultural beliefs about causality influence how people set about to treat illnesses. If an imbalance of humors is seen as the cause, then the cure will rest in effecting a balance. The Aztec believed that headaches were caused by excessive blood in the head. Healing therefore involved the use of medicines that produced violent sneezing and nosebleeds to remove the excess blood. If this approach failed, more blood would be removed by making an incision with an obsidian point (Ortiz de Montellano 1990). If one views the cause of an illness to be bacteria or other microorganisms, the cure will probably include use of antibiotics. If sorcery is to blame, something may have to be done about the sorcerer.

The Effectiveness of Cures

Assessing the effectiveness of different healing systems is not as simple as it might seem. All healing systems seem to work at least part of the time, and all have rationales to explain their failures. Moreover, because of the psychological and cultural dimension of illness and curing, just because a cure does not work in one culture does not mean that it might not be effective in another. When an Aboriginal inhabitant of Wellesley Island in northern Australia comes down with *malgri,* an illness characterized by drowsiness and abdominal pain, said to be brought on by concern over violation of food taboos, the Aboriginal healer kneels and begins massaging sweat from his armpit into the victim's body. A belt of grass or hair then is unraveled and tied to the person's foot. The chord is run down to the water to point the way home for the intruding spirit. The curer begins to sing, continuing into the night until a shooting star (the incarnation of the malgri's eye) is seen, indicating the disposition and banishment of the spirit. The string is then snapped and the victim recovers (Cawte 1974: 110). It is doubtful that this cure would work on someone in our own culture suffering from similar symptoms, nor would it be effective necessarily if the patient was suffering from some disease with similar symptoms, but it does work for this specific illness.

All healing systems can treat at least some illnesses, but this does not imply that all systems are equally effective. Clearly, some cures work better than others, and some in fact do not work. But assessing treatments from one system to another is not an easy matter, and experience has taught many Western medical practitioners not to dismiss out of hand the curative capabilities of other systems. It was not so long ago that Western doctors scoffed at the claims of acupuncture, which is now widely judged in the West to be an effective treatment for many dis-

eases. Likewise, Western scientists are giving more attention to the medicines employed by many so-called primitive medical systems. Many of the plants and potions used in these systems may be of little value, but some are, and in fact many have provided Western researchers with valuable information in developing modern drugs. Botanist Michael Balick notes that only some 1,100 of the 265,000 known species of plants have been thoroughly studied by scientists, and he estimates that as many as 40,000 of these plants may have medicinal or nutritional value (Linden 1991: 52). Balick and others have collected thousands of plant samples from Latin American shamans in their search for drugs that can be used in treating cancer, AIDS, and other diseases.

The ambiguity that exists in all curing systems and the number of systems available create both difficulties and opportunities for healer and patient. For someone honestly trying to treat a patient, diagnosis and an appropriate cure are rarely automatic, and error is always possible. Failure to arrive at a successful cure may be attributed to the nature of the affliction or to a

Two healers in Western Australia attend an old man who is complaining of a headache. All healing systems seem to work at least part of the time, and all have rationales to explain their failures. Many Western medical practitioners have learned not to dismiss out of hand the curative capabilities of other systems.

lack of skill on the part of the practitioner. More rarely, the effectiveness of the treatment system may be questioned. If more than one system is available, the patient can resort to an alternative if the first fails. In fact, there are many instances of individuals who have been cured only after turning to another system. However, searching for cures across systems also leaves the sufferer vulnerable to "quacks." Most medical systems recognize the possibility of charlatanism, although it is more commonly acknowledged in large-scale societies. These societies have means to set standards, but such standards do not necessarily apply across systems.

Health-Care Delivery Systems

The social components of curing include aspects of the overall social structure that influence the curing process and, more specifically, what may be referred to as the **health-care delivery system** (Colson and Selby 1974: 254–257). A health-care delivery system mobilizes resources to care for those who are ill. Patient, curer, and auxiliary personnel all have role expectations. The system also includes available or appropriate technology and the physical setting within which the curing process takes place.

Health-care systems may prescribe different kinds of settings for the treatment of the ill, and within the same system settings may vary. There are two dimensions to the question of setting: privacy and specialization. Among the Azande, diagnosis takes place in public. Heralded and accompanied by drums, diagnoses of patients are considered "local events of some importance," drawing spectators from throughout the neighborhood (Evans-Pritchard 1937: 154). Hausa barber-surgeons in Ibadan, Nigeria, place their operating tables under a tree in public view (Maclean 1971: 65). By contrast, in Western medical systems a premium is placed on privacy for both diagnosis and treatment.

In many non-Western settings, healing takes place in a nonspecialized locale, such as the village center or the patient's or curer's own home.

Among the Maya of southern Belize, patients with serious illnesses traditionally are often moved into the home of the curer for the duration of their treatment, sometimes bringing their entire family with them. Treatment in a Western medical system often takes place in a specialized setting such as a hospital. Hospitals have evolved into very complex institutions, functioning as small societies with many of their own cultural attributes. Hospitals can thus be studied in much the same way as we would study a Mayan village or a South Sea island, with attention to the interplay between the external environment and the local hospital community.

In addition to prescribing the appropriate setting for treatment, every society recognizes only a limited number of people who are able to treat illnesses. Contrary to popular belief, the practice of medicine is probably the oldest profession, as well as the most universal. The role of the curer, however, varies from one society to the next. In societies with personalistic views of disease causality, there is a need for someone who is able to determine who caused an affliction and why—usually someone with ties to the supernatural. In such societies the curer usually is a shaman, sorcerer, or "witch doctor." On the other hand, societies with naturalistic beliefs require "doctors" who have learned curing skills through practice and observation of illnesses and the properties of medicines.

In most small-scale societies, curing is not a full-time vocation. There is simply not enough work, and the healer generally will engage in the same primary economic activities as other members of the society—hunting or farming— much of the time. In large-scale societies, curing is more often a full-time occupation.

Most societies also recognize specialization within the medical profession. Although by far the greatest degree of specialization occurs in Western medical systems, even very small non-Western societies commonly have different types of practitioners (see Worsley 1982: 330–331). Peasants in the Philippines recognize midwives, bonesetters, and general practitioners (Lieban

1962: 512). The Maya of southern Belize divide medical roles according to level of skill and specialty. At the lower level of skill are midwives and snakebite doctors. At higher levels are several grades of general practitioner.

Analysis of healers requires attention not only to their roles, but also to other career-related factors, such as recruitment, training, and reputation. In personalistic systems, recruitment may be by personal dream or physical affliction, such as epilepsy. Recruitment in other instances may be linked to the would-be curer's personal inclination, ability, or social status. In some cases, only the children of healers can become healers, or recruitment may be limited to members of certain socioeconomic classes. A person's gender also can be an important consideration influencing the status of a curer or the particular curing roles available. Often a combination of these factors is necessary.

For shamans or sorcerers who engage in healing, training may be transmitted by means of dreams induced by supernatural beings. In many systems, a period of apprenticeship is involved, sometimes lasting for a number of years. At the end of the training period there is commonly a rite of passage. Eric Thompson describes the training and initiation of a Mayan curer in southern Belize:

> The instructor and the initiate retire to a hut in the bush for a month so that there may be no eavesdropping. During this period the initiate is taught by his master all the different prayers and practices used in causing and curing sickness. At the end of that period the initiate is sent to meet Kisin [a deity]. Kisin takes the form of a large snake called Ochcan (otskan), which is described as being very big, not poisonous and having a large shiny eye. When the initiate and the Ochcan meet face to face, the latter rears up on his tail, and approaching the initiate till their faces are almost touching, puts his tongue in the initiate's mouth. In this manner he

communicates the final mysteries of sorcery. [1930: 68–69]

Although this sequence may be somewhat more dramatic than graduation from a Western medical school, the result is much the same: The legitimacy of the curer is sanctioned by those who set professional standards.

The ability of a curer to continue working is largely a matter of reputation. Healers generally must have a good record, although within any system a good public relations effort can compensate for a lack of success in curing patients. All systems have norms regarding appropriate "bedside manners," which play an important part in assessment of the healer. Success as a physician can have its pitfalls, however. Inuit shamans and Western surgeons alike run the risk of negative sanctions resulting from the envy of others or feelings that they have too much wealth or power.

In addition to the chief healers, health-care systems often include a number of auxiliary persons who assist in the treatment process. In Western systems these include nurses, orderlies, and assorted administrators. In non-Western systems assistance may be left to an apprentice or to readily available nonspecialists. Assistants among the Azande include musicians or chanters who provide an accompaniment to the curer's activities.

The other essential participant in any health-care system is the patient; patients, too, are expected to conform to behavioral norms. One of the most important parts of any health-care system is the interaction between the patient and those responsible for his or her treatment—an interaction based on the patient's belief in the healers' power to diagnose and cure and on the mutual understanding of what should take place. The significance of such interaction becomes especially clear when patient and curer come from different sociocultural backgrounds and communication is impaired. Among the Bomvana Xhosa of southern Africa, the diviner starts the consultation by intuitively guessing what the illness is:

He is not supposed to take "the medical history" by interviewing the patient and/or his relatives. On the contrary, he is the one who has to give answers to all the questions about the patient and the causes of his disease. [Jansen 1973: 43]

As a result of this practice, when a Xhosa patient is confronted with a Western-trained doctor's "What seems to be the matter?" the patient usually is puzzled. It is the doctor, not the patient, who is supposed to answer that question.

An important part of disease treatment in contemporary societies involves promotion of public awareness of the nature of diseases and their cures. Screening clinics, educational programs, and advertising campaigns are used in this regard. To be effective, such programs need to be sensitive to the cultures of those to whom they are addressed. Thus, in campaigning against the spread of AIDS, public health workers have had to take into account how people view sex and what they consider appropriate means of discussing sexual matters. One Swedish campaign against AIDS involves a bikini-clad woman in a "love bus" going about dispensing brochures, T-shirts with slogans, and condoms. Such an approach clearly would not be appropriate in many cultures. In the case of Uganda, priests and even the president have sought to fight the epidemic by exhorting people to limit their sexual partners. An anti-AIDS advertisement in Australia aimed at Aborigines contained the following dialogue: "What's this AIDS? This a white man's disease?" Response: "Hah! AIDS is a killer, like the pox, VD. Once yah got it, you're dead."

The Costs of Health Care

Whereas the discovery of miraculous cures used to be the primary focus of attention in Western medicine, in the past 20 or 30 years the cost of medical care increasingly has been in the limelight. Medical care costs something in all societies; what it costs, how costs are determined, who pays, and how the payment is distributed vary. Whether Western-trained physicians or African witch-doctors, healers expect some compensation for their services. Even in societies that are relatively poor in material goods, treatments can be expensive. Among the Inuit, payment traditionally ranged from the offering of a wife or daughter as a sexual partner, when the shaman was a man, to the gift of an *umiak* (a boat), a substantial fee (Spencer 1959: 308).

Curers are not always wealthy, however. Part-time healers in the Mayan community of Zinacantan in southern Mexico receive only a bottle or two of rum, a few tortillas or a loaf of bread, and a chicken or two for their work. Fabrega and Silver (1973: 54) found that the incomes of Zinacantan practitioners were roughly the same as those of other villagers, the primary difference being that the payments the curers received were not in a form that could be used readily for commercial purposes. As a result, many of the curers are among the poorest people in the village; generally, only poor people become full-time healers because of the lack of economic rewards.

In small-scale societies and many non-Western health-care systems most of the cost of being cured involves the practitioner's fee; with Western health-care systems, though, the curer's fee may, in fact, be only a small part of the overall cost. Greater specialization has meant that a wider range of auxiliary personnel must be paid for. There is also the cost of maintaining the more elaborate treatment settings—hospitals, doctors' offices, clinics, and so on. Then there is the costly research and technology that is the cornerstone of modern Western medicine. Finally there is the cost of the medicine itself. Unlike the healer who uses locally available herbs and other medicines on the basis of knowledge and traditions built up over generations at minimal cost to society or the patient, Western medical practitioners rely on medicines produced by other specialists. Western medicine devotes great effort and expense to research in developing new medicines (sometimes derived from traditional non-Western medicines) and to marketing these medicines. All these factors have combined to make Western medicine an extremely costly undertaking. The ability and willingness to devote so many resources to treating illness are a part of the adaptive strategy of a modern society.

The costliness of Western medicine is of great concern to poorer, underdeveloped countries. Spending an average of US$41 a person on health care (compared with US$1,900 in developed countries), developing countries are already having difficulty meeting the health care needs of their people. The high cost of training medical personnel is a particularly thorny issue because such expensively trained people often seek employment in developed countries, where they hope to earn more money. There is also the cost of building and maintaining hospitals and clinics. While it may be possible to find aid donors willing to finance the construction of such buildings, the cost of maintaining them usually falls on the recipient country, which may have great difficulty obtaining the necessary capital. A recent World Bank report has pointed out how high-tech medicine absorbs much of the money spent on medical care in developing countries and the extent to which such care serves primarily the wealthiest members of these societies. The report recommends reallocating funds away from high-tech medicine to basic public health and clinical services for the rural poor (World Bank 1993).

The price of medicine, most of which is produced and sold by a few large multinational firms, is another issue (see Chetley 1989; Melrose 1982). A number of developing countries and researchers have accused pharmaceutical firms of pushing drugs that are overly expensive, useless, and in some cases known to be harmful. There are numerous instances where, in order to boost sales, even potentially beneficial drugs are wrongly promoted by those companies in developing countries, with serious consequences. Silverman, Lee, and Lydecker (1982: xi) refer to "the bribery, the mislabeling, and the medically unjustified overpromotion" of drugs by such companies in poor countries. They cite, for example, the antibiotic chloramphenicol. Chloramphenicol has proven to be very successful in treating many serious diseases that plague poorer countries (such as typhoid fever). In the United States, Canada, and other developed countries, physicians are warned not to use the drug in the treatment of trivial infections because of its potentially harmful side effects. By contrast, in many developing countries, recommendations for its use are extremely broad, and few or no warnings are provided concerning its potential dangers. This has served to boost sales of the drug but has also led to its overuse, if not abuse, in treating many minor diseases.

Muller (1982) has pointed to the need for developing countries to use drugs that are both more effective and "efficient"—that is, drugs that people can afford. Wishwas Rane notes, for example:

> Nearly five million children die from diarrhoea every year. At least half of these deaths could be prevented by a simple highly effective therapy—oral rehydration (ORT). Instead millions . . . are spent on ineffective and often dangerous antidiarrhoeal drugs. [1990: 2649]

Governments and organizations in countries like India, Mexico, and the Philippines (Tasker 1988) have dealt with this situation by attempting to reduce dependency on drugs produced by foreign firms by developing their own pharmaceutical industries, tightening controls on the marketing of drugs, and exploring uses of existing traditional medicines. Success in these efforts remains limited, however.

Western medical technology poses a problem in terms of cost, appropriateness, and dependency. Poorer tropical countries often have difficulty in maintaining expensive equipment that has little tolerance for the added strains of heat,

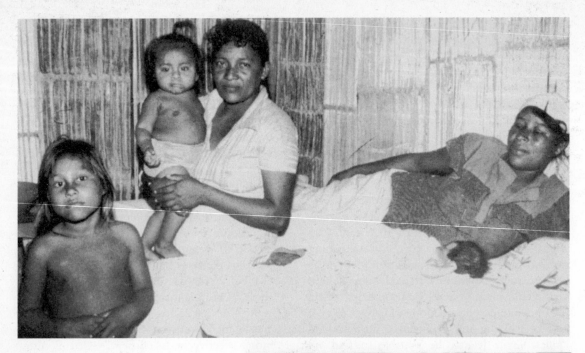

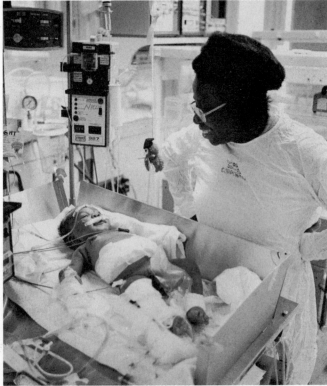

⌃⌃⌃⌃⌃

The quality of a country's medical facilities depends in large part on its wealth, just as the quality of personal health care often increases with one's ability to pay. These two childbirth sites—a health-care center in Nicaragua (top) and a high-tech center in Brooklyn, New York (bottom)—contrast dramatically in the quality of service they are able to provide.

humidity, and an undependable supply of electricity. These things can be dealt with, but often only at a great deal of added expense. The question of dependency has both an economic and a political dimension. For example, Nicaragua found itself in a desperate situation when the Reagan Administration imposed an economic embargo in the early 1980s because virtually all Nicaragua's medical technology came from the United States (Williams 1984: 72–73). While elites in developing countries can go to developed countries for treatment requiring expensive technology, this is not an option for the majority of people. Developing countries, such as India, and international agencies are seeking ways of overcoming this problem by creating their own technologies and exploring alternatives. For example, recognizing that a simple solution of salt, sugar, and water can prevent dehydration and diarrhea has saved hundreds of thousands of children in developing countries. Such agencies as UNICEF (United Nations Children's Fund) have administered this as a simple, effective treatment.

SUMMARY

Illness refers to a society's idea of pronounced deviation from what is considered a normal healthy state. Disease is a pathological condition of some part of the body in which functioning is disturbed or deranged. Both must be understood within their cultural context. Epidemiology concerns the factors that determine the frequency, distribution, and control of diseases. Epidemiologists working from an anthropological perspective have helped to uncover reasons for the occurrence of mysterious diseases, such as kuru. They have shown how environmental factors explain the incidence of both endemic diseases (diseases that have a relatively low incidence but are constantly present in a community) and epidemic diseases (diseases characterized by high incidence and rapid and extensive diffusion). The environmental context is also critical to an understanding of "diseases of development."

Malnutrition, though not a disease itself, may have debilitating or fatal effects. Its occurrence is linked to subsistence patterns: It is more common in large-scale agricultural and industrial societies than in small-scale societies. Foragers and small-scale farmers are usually malnourished only when their traditional subsistence pattern has been severely disrupted. Even in societies like our own that produce plenty of food, inequalities in food distribution reflect socioeconomic inequalities and leave many people hungry. Hunger is also linked to people's perceptions of food: potentially nutritious resources may be defined as "nonfood," and nutrition is not clearly understood, even by so-called experts.

In addition to physiological diseases and malnutrition, mental illness is recognized in all cultures. Often it is caused by the stress of trying to deal with a particular environment. Certain patterns of mental illness are universal; others are culture-specific, linked to particular physical environments and cultural traditions. Sometimes rapid social change can be so stressful that individuals become seriously disoriented or lose the will to live.

Notions of the origins of illness vary considerably. Western medical specialists have traditionally viewed mind and body as two separate systems, each accounting for its own type of illness. Other traditions have taken a more holistic approach, and Western medicine is beginning to view the two systems from a more unified perspective. Among nonscientific medical systems a distinction can be made between personalistic systems, in which illness is thought to be intentionally caused by some malicious being, and naturalistic systems, in which impersonal factors are recognized as the cause of illness.

Attempts to cure illness vary greatly, but all traditions can claim some degree of success. Precisely how and why they work is hard to prove, however. In social terms, the health-care delivery system consists of a culturally defined setting for treatment, healing specialists and their helpers, and the patient. Treatment always costs something, and in Western medical systems, in particular, a wide range of factors contribute to such costs.

KEY TERMS

Anomie   A state of disorganization of personality and a feeling of alienation.

Culture-bound syndrome   A unique configuration of mental illness that results from particular environments and cultural traditions.

Disease   A pathological condition of the body, or some part of it, in which functioning is impaired or deranged.

Endemic disease   A disease that is constantly present in a given community, but with a relatively low incidence.

Epidemic disease   A disease not typically present in a community, characterized by high incidence and rapid and extensive spread.

Epidemiology   The study of the interrelated factors that determine the frequency, distribution, and control of diseases in societies.

Health-care delivery system   A system by which resources are mobilized to care for those who are ill.

Illness   Pronounced deviation from what is considered a normal healthy state.

Medical pluralism   A situation in which members of a society are presented with an array of options in which a number of medical systems compete with and complement one another.

Medical system   A system of behavior and belief that has arisen in response to the threats posed to human health.

Mental illness   An illness associated with a mental state perceived as abnormal.

Naturalistic system   A nonscientific belief system of disease causality in which illness is explained in impersonal terms, attributing good health to the maintenance of an equilibrium within the body. (Compare with *personalistic system*.)

Personalistic system   A nonscientific belief system of disease causality in which illness is thought to be purposely caused by a supernatural being or a human being. (Compare with *naturalistic system*.)

SUGGESTED READINGS

Coreil, Jeannine, and J. Dennis Mull, editors. 1990. *Anthropology and Primary Health Care.* Boulder, CO: Westview Press.

Crandon-Malamud, Libbet. 1991. *From the Fat of Our Souls: Social Change, Political Process, and Medical Pluralism in Bolivia.* Berkeley: University of California Press.

Finkler, Kaja. 1991. *Physicians at Work, Patients in Pain: Biomedical Practice and Patient Response in Mexico.* Boulder, CO: Westview Press.

Foster, George M., and Barbara G. Anderson. 1978. *Medical Anthropology.* New York: Wiley.

Frankel, Stephen. 1986. *The Huli Response to Illness.* New York: Cambridge University Press. [Papua New Guinea]

____, and Gilbert Lewis, editors. 1989. *A Continuing Trial of Treatment: Medical Pluralism in Papua New Guinea.* Boston: Kluwer.

Golomb, L. 1985. *An Anthropology of Curing in Multiethnic Thailand.* Chicago: University of Illinois Press.

Grollig, Francis X., and Harold B. Haley, editors. 1976. *Medical Anthropology.* The Hague: Mouton.

Gussow, Zachary. 1989. *Leprosy, Racism, and Public Health: Social Policy in Chronic Disease Control.* Boulder, CO: Westview Press.

Henderson, George E., and M. S. Cohen. 1984. *The Chinese Hospital.* New Haven: Yale University Press.

___, and M. Primeaux. 1981. *Transcultural Health Care.* Reading. MA: Addison-Wesley.

Hill, Carole. 1985. *Training Manual in Medical Anthropology.* Washington, DC: American Anthropological Association.

Holden, Pat, and Jenny Littlewood, editors. 1991. *Anthropology and Nursing.* New York: Routledge.

Janes, Craig R., Ron Stall, and Sandra M. Gifford, editors. 1986. *Anthropology and Epidemiology.* Boston: D. Reidel.

Johnson, Thomas F., and Carolyn F. Sargent, editors. 1990. *Medical Anthropology: A Handbook of Theory and Method.* New York: Greenwood Press.

Johnston, Francis E., editor. 1987. *Nutritional Anthropology.* New York: Alan R. Liss.

Kunitz, Stephen J. 1983. *Disease, Change, and the Role of Medicine: The Navajo Experience.* Berkeley: University of California Press.

Landy, David, editor. 1977. *Culture, Disease, and Healing: Studies in Medical Anthropology.* New York: Macmillan.

Leslie, Charles, editor. 1976. *Asian Medical Systems.* Berkeley: University of California Press.

Logan, Michael H., and Edward E. Hunt, Jr. 1978. *Health and the Human Condition: Perspectives on Medical Anthropology.* North Scituate, MA: Duxbury Press.

Loudon, J. B., editor. 1976. *Social Anthropology and Medicine.* New York: Academic Press.

McElroy, Ann, and Patricia K. Townsend. 1989. *Medical Anthropology in Ecological Perspective.* Boulder, CO: Westview Press.

Marshall, Patricia A., and Linda A. Bennett, editors. 1990. *Culture and Behavior in the AIDS Epidemic.* Special issue, *Medical Anthropology Quarterly,* March.

Newman, Lucile F., editor. 1985. *Women's Medicine.* New Brunswick: Rutgers University Press. [examples from West Africa, Latin America, and Britain]

Norbeck, Edward, and Margaret Lock, editors. 1987. *Health, Illness, and Medical Care in Japan.* Honolulu: University of Hawaii Press.

Ohhuki-Tierney, Emiko. 1981. *Illness and Healing Among the Sakhalin Ainu.* New York: Cambridge University Press.

Reid, Janice. 1983. *Sorcerers and Healing Spirits: Continuity and Change in an Aboriginal Medical System.* Canberra: Australian National University Press.

Robson, John R.K. (ed.). 1980. *Food, Ecology and Culture: Readings in the Anthropology of Dietary Practices.* New York: Gordon and Breach.

Romanucci-Ross, Lola, Daniel Moerman, and Laurence R. Tancredi, editors. 1991. *The Anthropology of Medicine: From Culture to Medicine.* New York: Bergin and Garvey.

Simons, Ronald C., and C. C. Hughes, editors. 1985. *The Culture-bound Syndromes.* Boston: D. Reidel.

Young, James C. 1980. *Medical Choice in a Mexican Village.* New Brunswick: Rutgers University Press.

Anthropology and Modern World Development

ver the past century we have created
an ever more integrated world system with
the help of technological innovations that
have given us a productive capacity far in
excess of anything previously imagined.
The benefits we have derived from this

> How underdevelopment differs from the lack of material wealth of many traditional small-scale societies

> The kinds of problems that often result as indigenous peoples become incorporated into the world system

> The kind of roles anthropologists can play in formulating and implementing development plans

> How anthropologists work as advocates

system are considerable. We know much more about the universe, and we are better able to solve many of the problems that confront us.

Such advances have not been without their price, however. The creation of the modern world system has left great destruction in its wake and has given us the potential to do even more damage. Millions of people have been killed and millions more left impoverished and on the verge of starvation. The environment has suffered destruction on an unprecedented scale. Furthermore, despite the advances that we have made over the past century, the majority of people today have benefited little or not at all from them. Most of the products of our modern technology are available to a minority of the world's population. The modern world system has, in fact, seen a deterioration of the quality of life for hundreds of millions of people. Their previous ways of life have been destroyed, to be replaced by a life that is qualitatively and quantitatively worse.

Anthropologists have responded to these problems on a number of levels. They try to

make people more aware of the social and environmental forces surrounding them. Frequently, however, anthropologists are not content to merely describe problems and point to their causes; they often take a more active role in finding and implementing solutions. Their work as applied anthropologists may be within their own society or in other societies with which they are familiar.

◄ CONTEMPORARY ADAPTIVE ► PROBLEMS

Many of the problems in the modern world system center on adaptation. As we continue to evolve as a human society, our adaptation changes, and so, too, the adaptive problems we face. Among the most crucial problems of our age are those associated with economic inequality and poverty, ethnic and national conflict and the often accompanying violence, the denial of fundamental human rights, and the threats posed by environmental pollution. These problems are

Deforestation occurs where roads are constructed to open up a region for development in Madagascar. The natural and cultural diversity of the forests of the world are vanishing at an alarming rate.

massive and highly complex; however, past experience has shown how resourceful and adaptable human beings can be in meeting the challenges before them. With its holistic perspective and its understanding of adaptation and the world system, anthropology offers a unique vantage point for confronting the crucial problems of our day.

Development and Underdevelopment

In its most general sense, **development** means improvement in the quality of human lives. In material terms, this entails ensuring an adequate level of nutrition and suitable physical surroundings. Development means more than just meeting material goals, however. It is also important that social, political, and economic systems help realize the human potential more broadly. All societies in the world today fall short of achieving such goals. Those countries that come closest to achieving them (such as Canada, Sweden, Japan, and the United States) are referred to as developed countries. Those countries that are further from achieving these goals, especially the material ones, are called **underdeveloped**.

As noted in Chapter 5, there are major differences between the more developed and the most underdeveloped countries. While the vast majority of people in countries like the United States and Canada live relatively comfortable, if not affluent lives, in the most underdeveloped countries even the barest necessities are out of the reach of many people. This is true both in the case of the so-called LDCs (Least Developed Countries), such as Laos or Bhutan, with per capita annual Gross Domestic Products (GDP) of under $200, as it is of wealthier underdeveloped countries, such as the Philippines, with per capita annual GDPs of under $1,000. The United Nations categorizes 41 countries as LDCs. These countries have a total population of 402.4 million people, with an average per capita GDP of just over $200, compared with an average of around $900 for all developing countries. Average adult literacy in these countries is around 30 percent, which compares with about 60 percent for all developing countries. The average life expectancy is 49 years, compared with 59 years for all developing countries.

The United Nations Human Development Index (HDI), which includes a variety of factors such as those which relate to health, nutrition, and education (see Westlake 1990), is a much broader index than GDP. Ranking countries from 130 to 1, the top-ranked country on the HDI is Japan (Canada is given 126 and the United States 112). By contrast, some two dozen countries are ranked below 30 (Niger is assigned a rank of 1), while the Philippines is near the middle with 65.

Averages such as per capita GDP and the HDI highlight the disparities that exist between poorer and richer countries in general terms. What they fail to illustrate is the extent of poverty existing within both poorer and richer countries. While Canada ranks high in terms of both per capital GDP and the HDL, inequality is considerable. The richest 20 percent of Canadians controls around 70 percent of the country's wealth, while the poorest 20 percent owes more than they own (having –0.3 percent of the wealth). In percentage terms this situation is not much different from many poorer countries, such as the Philippines. Yet there are important differences. One study (see Cohen 1990) of the "intensity of poverty" in the Philippines indicated that 30 percent of the population was surviving on an average of $50 a month for a family of six (the "poverty level" in Manila for such a family being $175).

Moreover, in many developing countries, while much of the population may find itself growing richer, a sizeable percentage often falls even further behind. Thus, despite the ending of the Marcos dictatorship in 1986 and subsequent growth in the GDP, poverty in the Philippines has not been reduced. In most parts of the country, poor families receive an even smaller

Many poor countries find themselves weighed down with debt and have little to invest in alleviating poverty. One such country is Brazil, which, though its economy is developing in many ways, still suffers severe economic problems. Children like these can be seen living in the streets in the densely populated areas of eastern Brazil.

share of the income in the early 1990s than they did in the mid–1980s; this is reflected, for example, in a growth in the proportion of preschool children who are severely malnourished. The country has long suffered from widespread underemployment (the underemployed work less than 40 hours a week but desire to work more). In the early 1990s, just over 20 percent of the work force is underemployed. This is the same percentage as in the mid–1980s, which is bad enough, but to make matters worse, it represents an additional 700,000 people in real numbers because of rapid population growth. In the rural areas of the Philippines, where land-ownership is highly concentrated in the hands of a few, the vast majority have access to little or no land and

minimal employment. Almost 70 percent of families in rural areas is estimated to live in poverty.

While living standards generally have risen for many developing countries over the past decade, poverty remains widespread. Real growth in GDP for the developing world for the 1980s was 4.3 percent. However, at the end of the 1980s over one billion people still were surviving on incomes of less than $370 per year. Moreover, such growth has done little to alleviate the poverty of the poorest of the poor, many of whom, especially in sub-Saharan Africa, are worse off than they were a decade ago. Many poor countries find themselves weighed down with debt and have little to invest in alleviating poverty. Also, by the end of the 1980s, developing countries were transferring record amounts of their financial resources to the developed world. That is, the amount they were paying to service their debts to the developed world exceeded the inflow of funds from the developed world in record amounts—a deficit of $42.9 billion for 1989, up $5 billion from the year before.

THE EVOLUTION OF UNDERDEVELOPMENT. Underdevelopment is a relatively new phenomenon that differs considerably from the lack of material wealth of many traditional small-scale societies. People living in traditional Aboriginal societies had far less than many people living in modern societies, and many of their descendants living in modern Australia are also poor. But the nature and causes of the poverty of the traditional and contemporary groups are different. Small-scale foraging societies were materially poor because they had not developed technological complexity. They were **undeveloped.** By contrast, most of the poor people in the world today are poor largely because they have been unable to benefit from the wealth available in the modern world, largely by being denied access. They are poor as a result of the progressive *underdevelopment* that has accompanied the spread of the present world system.

Underdevelopment is a reflection of how people are integrated into the modern world system. The underdeveloped parts of the world are those that occupy disadvantageous positions within the international division of labor. Their resources are drained to support the wealthier portions of the world, and their people are the most poorly rewarded for their labor in extracting the resources and producing the goods consumed by the world economic order.

The historical aspect of underdevelopment is clearly illustrated by the example of Guatemala. When the Spanish conquered Guatemala in the sixteenth century, they transformed it from a relatively self-sufficient region into one that produced primarily in the interests of the Spanish conquerors. To support Spanish demands, the indigenous population was deprived of its land and forced to work on farms and in mines under adverse conditions. By providing the Indians with few rewards for their work, the Spaniards were able to export goods at a favorable rate and at the same time extract a large profit. After the demands of the export market and the local Spanish elite were met, little was left for the Indian population, which was barely able to meet subsistence needs.

Little changed for the majority of Guatemalans with independence in the early nineteenth century. By midcentury, however, the condition of most Guatemalans took a definite turn for the worse as the Guatemalan elite, with foreign interests, sought to increase the production of export crops, particularly coffee. Coffee provided wealth for a few but pushed most people even further into poverty. More land was seized from the Indians and given to wealthy coffee-growers, and laws were passed to force Indians to work on the coffee plantations for what was very little pay, even by the standards of the day. Not only did the local elite become still wealthier, but foreigners benefited as well. United Fruit, W. R. Grace, and other companies purchased large pieces of land on which to grow export crops such as bananas. These companies extracted large profits from Guatemala, while spending relatively little within the country.

Guatemala today remains a source of inexpensive labor and goods. Output is now diversified to include textiles, beef, cotton, and other agricultural products. The country is also a source of nonrenewable natural resources such as oil and nickel, the profits from which are divided between foreign corporations and the local elite. This situation has evolved at the expense of the majority of the people, as food crops have been taken out of production to make way for export crops and cow pastures, and as people are pressured to work on plantations and in factories at low wages and under unsafe conditions. Guatemala also serves as a

When Spaniards conquered the indigenous peoples of Latin America in the sixteenth century, they transformed native societies from relatively self-sufficient ones to ones that produced primarily for an international market. Production was also geared to support the Spanish conquerors, leaving the Indians in extreme poverty.

market, though small, for foreign companies. Luxury goods produced in the United States and elsewhere are sold to the Guatemalan elite. Pharmaceutical, chemical, and other companies are able to sell a range of goods, often under more favorable conditions than at home. In addition, countries such as Guatemala serve as dumping grounds for drugs, pesticides, and other items that are banned or restricted in more developed countries.

Attempts to overcome Guatemala's underdevelopment have met with little success in the face of opposition from vested interests (such as foreign corporations and the national elite) who have benefited from Guatemala's inequality and its disadvantageous place in the international division of labor. This has manifested itself in decades of social upheaval and widespread violence and denial of human rights.

DEPENDENCY. Underdevelopment is commonly linked with dependency on outside interests or powers. For instance, the majority of people in Guatemala have little control over the direction the economy takes. This lack of control commonly is related to the concentration of power in the hands of a small elite. Even in more egalitarian countries, however, people have little control over their economy. They find themselves dependent on external markets to sell what they produce and to buy what they need to survive. This dependency contributes to their underdeveloped status, since they generally receive much less for what they sell than they pay for what they buy.

Historically, when countries or communities have tried to overcome their dependent status, those who were profiting from that status often resorted to force to stop them. Sometimes, rather than using military force, less direct economic measures are taken, such as denial of access to foreign loans or the imposition of trade restrictions. Despite such hazards, countries have adopted various strategies to overcome dependency. Some countries (such as China in the 1960s and Cambodia in the 1970s) have sought to reduce dependency by isolating themselves from the rest of the world. But such adaptive strategies have been relatively short-lived and have not proven effective. Another approach has been for countries producing a commodity such as tin or oil to band together and seek ways of acquiring a greater share of the profits from the sale of the product on the world market (see Rees 1990: 181–186). While this strategy has worked relatively well for the oil-producing nations that formed OPEC (Organization of Petroleum Exporting Countries), most other attempts have not been so successful. There are few resources that lend themselves as easily as oil to control by producer cartels. Most resources are either available in too large a quantity, are not sufficiently strategic, or are produced by too diverse a group of states. A very different strategy is to seek to reduce dependency through even closer integration with developed economies, as in the case of Mexico's pursuit of trade liberalization with the United States and Canada.

In the case of NAFTA, the trade agreement among these three countries, the hope of those who support the agreement is that their people will become more equal in standards of living. As Mexico approaches the United States in standard of living, the tide of Mexican migration to the United States may decrease, benefiting both countries.

TRANSNATIONAL CORPORATIONS. The relative development or underdevelopment of countries is closely related to the activities of **transnational corporations**—corporations that may be headquartered in one country but that have divisions in a number of companies. They are a prime ingredient of the world economy in the late twentieth century and reflect the growing globalization of economic relations. The role of transnational corporations in the world economy has grown significantly since the early 1980s. Today, international trade within 350 largest transnational corporations accounts for around 40 percent of world merchandise trade, and such corporations control an estimated one-third of the world's private sector productive assets. The United Nations estimates that there are 37,000 transnational corporations, with more than 170,000 affiliates (United Nations Department of Economic and Social Development 1993). The wealth and ownership, however, is highly concentrated. One percent of the corporations accounts for almost

half of the total foreign assets of all transnational corporations, and more than ninety percent of these corporations has their headquarters in a handful of developed countries.

The adaptive advantage of the transnational corporation lies in the efficient manner in which it can reallocate resources to maximize profit on a global scale. When taxes and the cost of labor increased for companies engaged in bauxite mining in Jamaica, capital was simply shifted elsewhere. For the major industrial societies, transnational corporations help to provide a degree of stability by giving them flexible access to a wide range of markets. On the other hand, transnational corporations may have a weakly developed sense of national loyalty, and their investment and marketing strategies tend to reflect the interests of the corporation more than those of any particular country. A decision to close down a plant in a developed country and to relocate in a country where wages are lower may be of some benefit to the economy of the developed country (especially if it receives some of the corporate profits), but the benefit to those who have lost their jobs is harder to see.

Transnational corporations have succeeded in providing a great deal of wealth for many people, but this success has not been without a price. At the same time that they introduce new technology and provide some jobs in developing countries, their production methods may, in fact, put far more people out of work and increase disparities in wealth. Transnational corporations may also exert considerable political power in developing countries, not surprisingly since many of the largest corporations have annual gross sales greater than the gross national products of most developing countries. While many corporations do behave responsibly, this is not always the case. There is particular concern today about the activities of transnational corporations in regard to the environment. Some corporations exert undue pressure on governments to allow them to ignore environmental regula-

Among the global forces influencing the lives of these villagers of southeastern Pakistan is the oil drilling operation by a subsidiary of an American transnational corporation.

tions or target their investment at countries where environmental protection is weakest.

In a world where transnational corporations have enormous power that may be abused, it is important to recognize the existence of human rights groups. These groups can sometimes effect accountability on abuses. In the case of Bhopal, India, where negligence at a chemical plant resulted in hundreds dying, protests of corporate irresponsibility resulted in settlements for victims' families. More recently, a coalition of advocacy groups has been challenging the working conditions at assembly plants on the Mexican side of the U.S.-Mexican border. They

claim that birth defects among babies are a result of environmental effects on working pregnant mothers.

The Plight of Indigenous Peoples

Those who probably suffered the most from the spread of Western industrial society and the resultant underdevelopment were the indigenous peoples of newly colonized or incorporated lands: native peoples of the United States and Canada, Australian Aborigines, Amazonian Indians, and the like. As these peoples were conquered and incorporated into the world system, they lost their land, their autonomy, and often their lives. Many fought back and sometimes were successful briefly in postponing their fate. Ultimately, however, those who survived were rounded up on reservations to become wards of the state, or left to roam, broken and impoverished, on the margins of society in a land that had once been theirs.

The progressive destruction of such peoples is exemplified by the history of the Kaingang, an indigenous group in Brazil. At the turn of the century, the Kaingang lived a seminomadic existence inland from the growing city of São Paulo. As railroad construction began through Kaingang territory and as settlers started moving onto their land, clearing the forests and planting coffee trees, the Kaingang found themselves forced into a war for survival. They had tried to make peace with the settlers, but to no avail. Their subsequent attacks on railway workers and settlers led to preparations in São Paulo to launch a campaign to destroy the Kaingang, who were seen as impeding the march of civilization. Although the Indian Protection Service saved them from destruction, the Kaingang population declined from 700 to 200 between 1912 and 1916, primarily because of deaths from newly introduced diseases, such as influenza and measles (Ribeiro 1970).

The remaining pacified Kaingang were placed on a small reserve, while the man who

Banana workers hired by an American transnational corporation. Relatively low pay for workers in underdeveloped countries helps to create wealth for corporations based in the developed world.

gained control of the lands they had occupied previously became wealthy. In 1949, the state governor took away half their reserve, handing over the land to three business enterprises, he himself profiting greatly in the process. Over the next couple of decades, much of the remaining reserve land was logged by private companies and even by the government Indian agency. Most of the profits from logging went to the companies and to employees of the Indian agency, with only a small amount being turned over to the Kaingang.

The Kaingang and other local Indians began to organize a resistance movement in the 1970s, managing to expel 2,200 non-Indian families from their lands in 1977. The government response was to establish schools, with the assistance of foreign missionaries, to train Indian leaders who would be more receptive to government control. One of the Kaingang leaders of the resistance movement was killed in 1980, and other leaders were also subjected to attacks. Having weakened Indian resistance, the government initiated the construction of hydroelectric dams that would flood a large portion of the

Kaingang reserve. Squatters encroached further on the remaining territory.

By late 1984, the Kaingang once again were on the offensive, as were other native groups around Brazil (Howard 1987: 61–63). Members of the Kaingang community took part in a hunger strike that led authorities to agree to recognize their rights to a portion of the land threatened by squatters. Delays in implementation of the agreement resulted in a group of Kaingang marching on the national capital, Brasilia, in October 1984, and to their staging a nationwide march on the capital in March 1985. Finally, in January 1986 the government announced creation of the Kaingang Indian Reserve.

The problems faced by the Kaingang are common to many indigenous peoples around the world. Decimated by outright attacks and introduced diseases, they have seen what little they have left gradually taken away by those who profit at their expense. Their attempts at resistance are met with subtle maneuvers to overpower them, and if these are not successful, with a return to violence.

GENOCIDE. Many indigenous peoples have been the object of campaigns of **genocide**, the deliberate and systematic destruction of a political or cultural group. From the seventeenth to the early nineteenth centuries, for example, the settlers of Newfoundland hunted and killed the local indigenous people, the Beothucks, at "first because they were considered a nuisance, and later for the sport of pursuing such elusive game" (Horwood 1969: 72). The Beothucks' peaceful overtures were constantly met with violence, and settlers frequently would organize parties to hunt them, much as they hunted game. Genocide did not end with the early colonial era. Australian Aborigines continued to be the object of attacks into the 1920s, with organized gangs of whites attacking the Aborigines' camps and ranchers going so far as to leave out poisoned flour for them to eat.

Genocidal acts against indigenous peoples are not a thing of the past. Iraq's Marsh Arabs, who number around 70,000, face extinction as the Iraqi government drains the marshlands within which they live and subjects them to military attacks in an effort to crush all opposition to its rule. In Brazil, even though its 1988 constitution guarantees the protection of its 250,100 indigenous peoples, violence against native peoples continues. Constitutional reform called for the creation of 510 reserves for the country's 180 tribes by October 1993. Accordingly, in 1991 a 9.4 million hectare reserve was created to protect the remaining 9,000 Yanomami; and as many as 25,000 goldminers, who had brought violence, disease, and pollution into the area, were expelled. Although the reserve was created, the government allocated very little money for its administration, and several hundred miners remained. In July 1993 miners killed five or six Yanomami, and the following month 15 men, 20 women, and 38 children were found murdered. The reserve occupies an area rich in mineral deposits and political, business, and military interests are lobbying to repeal the decree creating the reserve.

When, out of desperation, indigenous minorities try to fight back because peaceful means have been denied them, their "belligerence" is used as an excuse to slaughter them. As an example, when the Embera Indians of Colombia sought to retain control of a gold mine that one of their people had discovered in the late 1970s, they were subjected to constant attacks by local landowners and prospectors. As a result of pressures from the landowners, fueled by rumors that the Embera were subversives, in early 1981 the government sent in the police. In the ensuing battle, several Embera were killed and others captured. Similarly, dozens of Indian leaders have been killed in other parts of Colombia by gunmen hired by wealthy landowners, without a single case of murder ever being brought to trial.

ETHNOCIDE. Even when ethnic minorities are not themselves wiped out, their cultural traditions may be. Maintenance of a distinct cultural identity by indigenous peoples is difficult in the face of expanding industrial society. As their resources are seized and as they are overwhelmed by the new technology, such peoples find the very bases of their societies undermined. The destruction of a people's culture carried out on a systematic basis is referred to as **ethnocide**.

Ethnocide is the result of extreme policies aimed at incorporating minorities into the dominant culture through coercion or incentive. It is based on a belief that the indigenous culture is inferior and that it should be superseded by the dominant culture, believed to be superior. Ethnocide is ethnocentrism acted on in extreme. A common means of promoting ethnocide is to force parents to send their children to distant schools, where they will learn to accept the values of the new culture. This was the case of many Native American tribes, especially in the late nineteenth and early twentieth centuries. Another tactic is to provide the first converts to the new ways with material rewards in

the hope that others will be encouraged to follow. Traditional customs also may be banned.
Such actions almost always are defended on the
grounds that they benefit the indigenous peoples—"bringing them from the stone age into
the space age." More significant, however, are the
benefits accruing to the "civilized" in terms of
access to land and other resources. The gains of
the dominant culture usually far outweigh those
of the native peoples.

Some indigenous peoples readily accept their
cultural loss, hoping for greater rewards in the
new order; others accept the change fatalistically.
However, some choose to resist. To the chagrin
of people convinced of the superiority of
Western industrial culture, not everyone em-
braces it with open arms. Many have given their
lives rather than accept the "blessings" of
Western civilization. One of the major struggles
confronting the world today concerns the right
of indigenous peoples to retain their own identities and to utilize resources that they feel belong to them in ways they consider most appropriate. In Canada, the United States, Brazil, and
Australia, the struggle focuses on *land rights*—the
right of native peoples to control what happens
on the lands they occupy and to be compensated for the lands that they have lost.

Legal and political struggles, in which anthropologists have played an important role as advocates and researchers, have led in recent years to
a number of important decisions relating to land
rights. Brazil's 1988 constitutional provision to
create native reserves was mentioned above. In
Australia, in response to a court action undertaken by Eddie Mabo, leader of the Meriam
people of Torres Strait, in 1992 the High Court
made a decision that overturned the prevailing
notion that Australia belonged to no one at the
time of British settlement in 1788 ("terra
nullis"). Following the high court decision, in
late 1993 the Australian Parliament passed a land
rights package that strengthens the ability of
Aborigines to pursue land rights claims through
the courts and provides for governments to pay

compensation and validate claims where appropriate. In Canada, a significant step toward
granting native self-rule was taken in 1992
when the foundation was laid for the creation of
the northern territory of Nunavut, some two
million square kilometers occupied by about
18,000 Inuit. As noted by one of the Inuit nego-
tiators: "The whole point is to become self-
sufficient; to determine our future rather than
always relying on others to make decisions for
us" (Kinross 1992:23).

While today the struggle for land rights in
Australia, Canada, and the United States takes
place mainly in the courts, frustration over a
sense of a lack of justice sometimes leads to violent confrontations. In 1973 protests by Sioux at
Wounded Knee, South Dakota, over the loss of
treaty rights erupted into a violent confrontation with federal authorities involving gunfire
and the taking of hostages. More recently, a July
1990 protest by Mohawks from Oka, Quebec,
escalated into a prolonged armed confrontation
in which a police officer was killed during an
assault on Mohawk barricades. Such violence is
much more common in countries where native
peoples have little recourse to the courts. For instance, the Karens, Kachin, and other indigenous
peoples have been fighting the Burmese government since that country became independent in
1948. While recently most of these tribal groups
have made fragile peace agreements with the
government, they have few legal means for seeking justice. Resistance is based on cultural as
well as economic grounds. For many of these
people, giving in is not just a matter of being
unable to dance in a certain way or dress after a
certain fashion; it means being pushed to the
bottom of the heap in the world system, following the path of the Kaingang into ever deeper
poverty.

Even in developed Western countries, granting
land rights or self-rule is not by itself sufficient to
overcome many of the problems indigenous peoples face. A survey of the attitudes of native peoples conducted by Statistics Canada after the 1991

In 1990, the Mohawk Indians of Quebec protested injustices concerning land rights. Though confrontations such as these still occur, the struggle for land rights in Canada and the United States takes place mainly in the courts.

census revealed that only a very small number of the people appeared to believe that self-government, as advocated by native leaders, would do much to overcome community problems. There was far more support for such things as "more policing" and family counseling (Johnson 1993). Moreover, some native women fear that steps such as self-rule may worsen their position. Members of the Native Women's Association of Canada, for example, have expressed concern that self-government will mean they will lose the support given them by Canada's Charter of Rights and Freedoms which forbids discrimination based on sex.

The Impact of Tourism

Often another adaptive problem for indigenous peoples is tourism. The number of international tourist arrivals in 1993 was about 500 million, and international tourism receipts reached $324 billion. In fact, tourism is now regarded as the world's largest industry. This growing industry, which involves so many economic, political, environmental, and cultural factors, can either contribute to the sustainable development of coun-

tries, by redistributing income from rich to poor areas, or exacerbate the overall problems brought upon by development (Dearden 1992: 215–16).

Tribal people hold a compelling lure for tourists from industrial countries; in fact, the few million tribal people remaining on earth are becoming major tourist attractions. Many tourists do not realize, however, that most of these peoples do not live as portrayed in the travel brochures. What often happens may well be like this description of a visit to the Yagua of Peru by one travel writer: "As a raftload of tourists nears a jungle village, the guide blasts on a conch shell, signaling the Yagua that the visitors come in peace, he says. Otherwise, he adds, they'd be speared." In fact, "The Yagua recognize the conch shell blast as the signal for something else: time to doff their rubber boots, T-shirts, and gym shorts and wriggle into loincloths and grass skirts. The tourists, after all, are expecting 'real' Indians" (Silk 1993).

Anthropologists are primarily interested in two types of tourism: *resort tourism* and what is variously called *adventure, nature, or ecotourism*. Anthropologists are most interested in these types when they have an impact on relatively

Tourism has become an adaptive problem for indigenous peoples. Here anthropologist Todd Ames works with the Moken, so-called sea nomads who live primarily on boats, near a tourist resort in southwestern Thailand.

isolated communities. Each has a different impact because of its particular characteristics.

Resorts usually entail considerable investment in infrastructure (buildings, roads, golf courses, and the like), whereas adventure/ecotourism requires relatively little new infrastructure. Resorts also seek to provide an escape from the normal life of the tourist by providing a stress-free fantasy, and therefore purposely transform their setting. In contrast, adventure/ecotourism strives to give the tourist an authentic experience in a world very different from his or her own; this type of tourism thus tries to minimize its impact on an existing setting.

When resorts are built in relatively isolated areas, they change local communities not only by transforming the landscape, but also by altering employment patterns, social and economic relations, and even world views. For example, when work on a pineapple plantation was replaced with employment at a luxury resort for the people of Lanai, a small Hawaiian island, the pattern of work changed. It became common for both parents in a family to hold jobs in the tourist industry with different shifts, since, unlike the plantation, which had operated on an eight-hour-a-day schedule, the tourist industry operates twenty-four hours a day. This in turn altered family life, affecting interaction between couples, time spent with their children, and possibly contributing to social problems, such as attempted suicide among young people (Kubota 1994).

The impact of resorts on communities can be positive. They can provide employment to areas where few opportunities previously existed. They can also create access to new services, including educational facilities. There can also be negative consequences, however. New work patterns can lead to social disintegration, and the wealth difference between tourists and locals can promote robbery, prostitution, and other social or health problems, such as those associated with AIDS, which tends to increase where tourism encourages prostitution. Pollution from poor waste treatment and excessive demand for water by resorts can also adversely affect health and other economic activities.

In promoting authentic exotic experiences, adventure/ecotourism often takes tourists into remote areas and into contact with isolated communities. Frontier areas are sought where the impact of the modern world is minimal. As the modern world system expands, the frontier of adventure/ecotourism moves. In fact, adventure/ecotourism is a part of this process of expansion, bringing those on the frontier into closer contact with those from the core of the modern world. The moving frontier of this type of tourism occurs as an area is seen to have become too integrated into the larger world and as the inhabitants adapt to the presence of tourists to the point that exotic experiences are no longer felt to be authentic but staged for the tourist market. For example, in Indonesia, Lake Toba and the Toba Batak are increasingly seen as inappropriate for this type of tourism as the number of tourists increases and a more institutionalized, or overly "touristy," tourist industry develops. The frontier for adventure/ecotourists in Indonesia today is to be found in Kalimantan, the Indonesian portion of Borneo, and Irian Jaya.

Although ecotourism may employ local peoples, often little of the wealth goes to them; the bulk goes to outsiders anxious to cash in. Take the case of Sarawak Cavern, the world's largest enclosed space, opened to the public in 1985. The cave is within 52,000 hectare of Mulu National Park, which is largely relatively pristine rain forest. The Royal Mulu Resort has been

Many anthropologists today take an active role in working with a people to produce a desired sociocultural condition. Here Thai anthropologist Napat Sirisambhand interviews T'aiLü members of a weaving cooperative in northern Thailand.

constructed near the cave, with plans to add an 18-hole golf course. The hotel is a joint-venture between a Japanese hotel group and the sister of Sarawak's chief minister. In 1992 there were 12,000 visitors to the cave, up from 950 in 1986. The local Berawan people, who work as tour guides, boat operators, and laborers, are not opposed to the tourist development, but they are not pleased with their share. In particular, they were upset when the resort was built on their customary land, the site of an old longhouse and a burial ground. In August 1993 they went on strike and demanded compensation. "We Berawan want to be part of development and progress," read one of their banners.

Adventure/ecotourism can have a beneficial impact on local populations when handled with sensitivity. It can provide positive experiences for both tourists and those being visited, especially when care is given to prepare the tourists for contact with different cultures. It can be a low-impact form of contact that allows people slowly to adjust to the outside world. However, all too often such care is not shown. One of the worst examples of this is in northern Thailand, where trekkers have arrived in hill tribe villages primarily in search of drugs and sex, thereby contributing to the illegal drug trade, the spread of prostitution, and the introduction of diseases related to both. Whatever the intentions of trekkers, their presence in remote areas of Thailand may lead to such cultural change as the abandonment of native dress (sold to tourists) and adoption of the dress of tourists, changes in consumer patterns as stores appear to sell consumer items to trekkers, and, in some cases, the relocating of a village into an area more accessible to tourists (Dearden 1992: 222–223).

Anthropologists have studied the impact of both types of tourism and, as applied anthropologists, have sought to offer suggestions for avoiding or eliminating problems. They also have a role to play in educating tourists, government officials, and those in the tourist industries about local communities. Such education can not only reduce problems, but also enhance the tourist experience. In addition, some anthropologists are employed directly in the tourist industry. One Dutch anthropologist, for example, who was born in Irian Jaya, works as a guide taking small tour groups to visit peoples in Irian Jaya, such as the Dani and Asmat.

Environmental Destruction

As the world becomes increasingly urbanized and industrialized, we are producing pollutants at an unprecedented rate. Disasters such as those at the Bhopal chemical plant in India in 1984 and the Chernobyl nuclear power plant in the Soviet Union in 1986 have no historical parallel. The range of pollutants discharged into the air, soil, and water today is far greater than at any time in the past. Mexico City suffers from the worst air pollution of any city in the world, with its vast number of industries and three million vehicles, unthinkable in cities of the past. Many of the deserts and treeless landscapes of the world today are testimony to past destruction of the environments by an expanding human population, but now we are destroying our environment at a far more rapid pace. In the past, we were comforted by the thought that there were always more resources to be had and that the atmosphere, oceans, and soil could absorb the pollutants we produced. But today, in the face of unparalleled environmental disaster, we are quickly coming to realize that such assumptions were naive. Four hundred years ago 90 percent of Haiti was forested; today, only five percent of Haiti is covered in forest. The environment is under major stress from air and water pollution, and we are being exposed to increasing levels of dangerous solar radiation as by-products of human technology destroy the atmosphere's protective ozone layer.

One of the most serious ecological problems is the large-scale destruction of tropical rain forests. If the current rate of deforestation continues, tropical rain forests may virtually disappear within the next couple of decades as a result of logging, burning, acid rain, and other factors. The current speed of deforestation is exemplified by the forests of Sumatra, one-third of which disappeared between 1982 and 1990. This possibility is of immediate importance to those living in the forests. Also threatened are many archaeological sites within the rain forests. Acid rain in southern Mexico, partly resulting from oil refineries and tourist buses, is now threatening millions of acres of tropical rain forest as well as pre-Columbian ruins and forest-dwellers such as the Lacandones. Moreover, since the world consists of a single large ecological system, the loss of such a major natural component as the tropical forests has serious global implications.

Clearly, the destruction of rain forests is an extremely complex and important issue. The lives of indigenous peoples are being ruined, and local lands are being eroded into uselessness by excessive logging, improper forest farming, wasteful ranching practices, migration leading to overpopulation, road construction, and other commercial interests such as mining, industrial agriculture, and hydroelectric dams. As the delicate ecological balance of vast regions is being thrown into disarray, many species of plants (including many that are medically useful) and animals are becoming extinct. In recent years, erosion in areas that have been subject to severe deforestation has resulted in flooding that has caused considerable loss of life and damage to property.

Research also has shown that deforestation disturbs both local and global climatic patterns, including rainfall and temperatures. One reason is that the forests return significant amounts of moisture to the atmosphere and play a major role in converting carbon dioxide to oxygen. Many scientists believe that a reduction in this conversion, as well as an increased level of carbon dioxide from burning of the forests, contributes in a major way to the **greenhouse effect**—a warming of the atmosphere caused by air pollutants that trap heated air near the earth's surface. The greenhouse effect could result in drier and warmer weather in extensive portions of the northern temperate zones, including the American and Canadian grain-growing belts. It could also result in rising sea levels because of melting ice at the poles, which would flood many coastal areas and lead to the disappearance of island states such as Kiribati and Tuvalu, in the Central Pacific

Concern with environmental problems poses particular questions for the poorer countries of the world. As they strive to improve the standard of living, such countries are faced with difficult contradictions. How are they to reconcile the imperative of development with their reliance on exports of timber from their forests, food from their fragile soils, and nonrenewable mineral and oil resources? Likewise, if they seek to limit the development of energy sources such as hydroelectric dams, they risk creating even greater pressure on their forests as sources of firewood. Even more than developed countries, the poorer countries also face difficulties in trying to bring about environmental improvements. Cleaning up the waste that already exists and reducing the amount of pollutants produced by vehicles and factories is expensive. Moreover, stricter enforcement of regulations puts greater strain on the already limited resources of governments.

< TOWARD SOLVING THE >
PROBLEMS

Given the immensity of the problems facing people around the world today, it is little wonder that many people seek to ignore them, give up in despair, or retreat into cynicism. Yet thousands of organizations, agencies, and individuals are working toward solutions. That so many problems persist attests not so much to the failures of those seeking solutions as to the scale and complexity of the difficulties we face in searching for an adaptive strategy that provides a more equitable standard of living on a world-wide basis.

From its very inception, sociocultural anthropology has been intimately caught up in the problems associated with underdevelopment and with efforts to find solutions. In particular, this subfield of anthropology has played an important role in improving dialogue and understanding between cultures. For example, the work of developmental planners and administrators has become more attuned to the needs of the poor communities they are seeking to help as sociocultural anthropologists provide them with relevant information concerning the beliefs and feelings of the poor.

Applied Anthropology

While the role of many anthropologists in seeking solutions to human problems is indirect through their teaching and writing, some anthropologists have determined to take a more active role in effecting change. Those who engage in such activities are called applied anthropologists. **Applied anthropology**, as discussed in Chapter 1, refers to research and activities intended to produce a desired sociocultural condition that optimally will improve the lives of the people concerned. This may be simply a matter of keeping them from being exterminated or being reduced to even lower levels of poverty.

The term *applied anthropology* was first employed by British anthropologist Lane Fox Pitt-Rivers in 1881. The subdiscipline originated as "a kind of social work and community development effort for non-white peoples" (James 1973: 41). British anthropologists, for example, helped to train colonial officers and also carried out research on behalf of colonial governments on such topics as indigenous legal systems, land tenure, religious movements, diet and nutrition, and migration. Anthropologists were sometimes commissioned to carry out ethnographic research in crisis-ridden areas to facilitate the establishment of colonial authority.

In the United States in the 1930s anthropologists were hired by the Bureau of Indian Affairs and the Soil Conservation Service to work on problems concerning reserve-dwelling native Americans. During World War II, anthropologists were employed to study and make recommendations about problems associated with the forced removal from the West Coast of Japanese-Americans and Japanese immigrants. After the war, anthropologists worked with the American administration in its new Micronesian colonies in the Pacific.

The destruction of the colonial order following World War II left anthropology, particularly applied anthropologists, open to attack. In many parts of the world, nationalist leaders who had replaced colonial administrators identified anthropologists with the former colonial regimes, viewing anthropologists as agents of colonial repression. Although this attitude in some instances was justifiable, overall it represented a distorted oversimplification. Some anthropologists were active proponents of colonialism, but most sought in limited ways to try to improve conditions for those living under colonial rule.

With applied anthropology in ill repute in the immediate postcolonial period, cultural anthropologists opted to retreat to colleges and universities. Some continued to work for international development agencies, government departments, and industry, but such work was far from the mainstream of anthropological research. Applied anthropology survived the demise of colonialism best in the United States, partly because of the country's relatively large indigenous population and partly because of American global geopolitical activities. The kind of work done by applied anthropologists during this period and their tendency to avoid larger issues in favor of solving smaller problems was much the same as in the colonial era.

The late 1960s and early 1970s was a critical period for applied anthropology in the United States. Of particular concern was the employment of anthropologists by business and government, at the risk of serving the interests of the rich and powerful instead of those supposedly being helped. Debate was especially intense over the role of anthropologists in relation to America's military involvement in Southeast Asia (see Wakin 1992).

While anthropologists continue to debate the ethics of applied work, the number of full-time applied anthropologists and of academics doing part-time applied work has greatly expanded in recent years. Their activities are wide-ranging, including helping to implement culturally sensitive educational programs, studying the social impact of highways and oil pipelines, and helping indigenous peoples with land claims. For the most part, such activities fall within two categories: development planning and advocacy on behalf of cultural groups.

Development Planning

Anthropologists help in both formulating and implementing development plans. Most often, they serve as part of a multidisciplinary team including other experts, such as agronomists, engineers, physicians, economists, and geographers. The anthropologist brings to such a team detailed knowledge of the people in an area and the holistic, integrated perspective that is essential to successful planning.

One of the most valuable roles played by anthropologists in development projects is in bringing about discussion between planners and the local population. Typically, the local population distrusts the planners. Such distrust may be warranted, because planners often lack knowledge of the local culture and the specific needs and goals of the local population. Peter Weil (1980: 315) argued that to bridge the gap between the people and the planners, the anthropologist must (1) identify and explain the local decision-making processes and (2) help both residents and the planners adapt local structures to better meet developmental needs as expressed by the residents. These steps clarify which residents the planners should interview; they also help to ensure that local customs will be preserved as much as possible and that plans reflect the needs of the people.

In making and implementing development plans, anthropologists do not just work with national and international agencies. They may also work with community-based or private local-level groups. Some indigenous groups in Canada, the United States, and Australia employ anthropologists as community advisors to assist the people with local problems and in their dealings with government agencies. Anthropologists have also worked with nongovernmental organizations in developing countries. For example, anthropologists have worked with cooperatives, using their knowledge of both local conditions and the outside world to help meet the developmental goals of primary producers and to educate those who purchase the goods about the people who make them and their problems.

In addition to their work on specific projects, anthropologists also contribute to the development process through studies on the culture of development, in which the planning process is examined in the same way as other sociocultural phenomena are examined. This includes a consideration of the culture and social organization of the planners themselves. Thus, planners are seen as social beings with their own goals, whose actions are influenced by their own environment. For example, to understand the developmental work of an international agency such as the World Bank, it is important to understand the world of those working for the agency (e.g., the political context of their work, their career goals, and how information is received and translated into practice).

Sustainable Development

During the 1980s criticism of traditional approaches to economic development, especially as those concerned with the environment saw development, led to a new approach known as sustainable development. **Sustainable development** refers to the use of natural resources for

Famine area of Sahel, Africa. The program of distributing food to this area was ineffective largely because of policymakers' poor understanding of the people's adaptation.

economic growth in such a way that the use does not deplete them or reduce their renewable usefulness for future generations. In order to achieve sustainable development, certain conditions must be met. These include economic and technological change and efficiency and ecological security. In addition, there must be a consideration of the people affected by development and the protection of their rights.

The concept of sustainable development applies to both industrialized and developing countries. In industrialized countries, the use of natural resources per capita is many times higher than that in nonindustrialized countries. In societies such as ours, therefore, sustainable development will depend greatly on a steady reduction in wasteful energy and resource consumption and changes in patterns of economic consumption. However, while the countries of Asia, for example, consume a smaller amount of the world's energy supply, their use of energy in recent years has increased almost sixty percent,

while that in Western Europe and North America has increased very little (Howard 1993:6). Adding to the growing environmental crisis in many developing countries is the fact that they may show considerably less concern for ecological security than they do for generating and maintaining economic growth.

Rather than simply assuming that new resources can be found or new technology can increase production, both industrialized and developing countries need to seek more efficient ways of using resources that are available. The need is evident in agriculture, for example, where management of resources is increasingly a problem. Although great progress has been made in food production since the 1950s, most agronomists agree that it is going to be more and more difficult to maintain the levels of growth in food production that have been achieved in the past decades. Most increased production has come about by *intensification*—altering methods of food production to increase it—which usually results in an alteration of the ecology. Environmental problems such as contamination, for example, result from the use of pesticides, and the homogenization of crops leads to problems of crop disease. Because intensified agriculture tends to require a greater use of water, largely from irrigation, water resources are also threatened.

Careful management of economic initiatives is also a consideration even when the activity, such as mining, is not sustainable. In the author's study of the impact of the Freeport copper and gold mine in Irian Jaya, with the anthropology department at Cenderawasih University, funded by the Canadian aid agency CIDA, attention is being given not only to the impact of mining on other activities and the need to avoid the usual boom and bust cycle of mining but also to how to employ the wealth generated by mining for some form of development that is sustainable.

Economic efficiency includes technological changes that help minimize energy and natural resource consumption and waste. A number of recent innovations promote greater efficiency. These technological advances include those that allow the paper industry to use resources other than trees, relieving some of the pressure on existing forests, as well as advances in the control of industrial pollutants. A number of efforts have been made in industrialized countries to reduce waste, some at great expense. Efforts have also been made in regions such as Asia to increase efficiency, though often they are small in light of the magnitude of pollution.

Among the problems that face the application of sustainable development programs in non-Western countries are political and economic questions about control of and access to technology, and its effect on people. Transnational corporations from developed Western countries dominate much of the new technology, raising concerns about dependency on the West. In addition, whereas hydroelectricity and nuclear power are potential energy sources that reduce pollution, these sources have been opposed for environmental and social reasons. Opponents of hydroelectricity have argued that the required construction of dams not only causes damage to the environment but also forces rural people to relocate, causing severe social disruption. Building the Tehri dam in northern India, for example, is seen as threatening the fragile Himalayan ecology and the cultures of the local hill-dwelling peoples (Howard 1993:6–8).

For economic and political reasons, ensuring ecological security in many countries has not proven to be an easy task. While many Asian countries, for example, are responding to political pressure to recognize the environmental crisis, problems remain. These include inadequate government programs to clean up the environment and illegal exploitation of the environment, such as illegal logging, sometimes aided by local leaders open to bribes. Another factor is the breakdown of forms of resource management applied by traditional peoples. Also, in some areas, wildlife conservation programs have led to conflict with poor rural farmers, who may be required to give up access to farm land to make way for wildlife refuges.

Other requirements of sustainable development are slow to be realized. Although the impact of economic development on the environment must be assessed, programs of assessment are not always fulfilled. Typical of environmental impact assessment (EIA) studies are the environmental action plans the World Bank requires of nations seeking loans. Unfortunately, however, many environmental impact assessments are done hurriedly, often after a project is underway. A study of environmental action plans in Africa found that most were ineffective because of disagreements among various interests within the countries or because they were ignored (Falloux and Talbot 1993).

Sustainable development requires a multidisciplinary approach, each discipline adding its particular insights (Serageldin 1993). The sociocultural view of anthropology provides its own insights, giving crucial attention to human social organization and culture for achieving viable solutions. In particular, anthropologists draw attention to questions of social cohesion, cultural identity, institutional development, and popular participation.

Anthropologists are especially concerned about environmental management plans that ignore or show little understanding of the role of local populations in managing the environment and do not deal with problems of social equity. This has been the case in Thailand, for example, where anthropologists have been active in promoting the participation of hill tribe communities in watershed management and community forestry.

A plan supported by the World Bank's Global Environment Facility to protect biodiversity in the Thung Yai Naresuan Wildlife Sanctuary in Thailand provides an example of how anthropologists see the problems involved. The plan, drawn up by international consultants, calls for the removal of Karen villagers, who, for at least 200 years, have been living within the boundary of what is now the wildlife sanctuary. The initiative to remove the villagers is based on the notion that all forest-dwellers who practice slash-and-burn cultivation destroy the forest. This belief ignores the important role that the Karen have played over the years in protecting the forest.

The Karen along the Thai-Burmese border are widely recognized as careful managers of forest resources who view themselves as an integral part of the forest ecosystem. As one Karen villager commented, they are now being punished for the careful stewardship of their ancestors rather than being rewarded and encouraged to continue such practices. Even the chief of the sanctuary disagrees with the plan to remove the Karen: "The destruction of the Karens' forest culture will eventually cause the pristine forest to be unsafe" (Traisawasdichai 1994). The chief's view is based not only on respect for the abilities of the Karen, but also on an understanding of the limited abilities of forest officials to protect forest lands from poaching and illegal logging— a task virtually beyond them without the help of the Karen.

Ironically, while removing the Karen from their forests both deprives the people of their rights and threatens sustainable development, ensuring an indigenous people's control over the land may also create serious problems. By 1988 the Kayapo of Brazil, for example, were making more than $30 million a year from royalties on mining and logging. Unfortunately, much of the income has been pocketed by chiefs who "spend it on ranches, cars, and aeroplanes, or in discotheques," while in one village, "a quarter of its people die in infancy" (*Economist* 1993a). Native peoples seeking to generate wealth from land over which they have finally gained some control may also find themselves in conflict with environmentalists who do not approve of the new adaptive strategies involved in generating the wealth. When environmentalists tried to stop the Kayapo from logging on their land, a group of Kayapo went to the capital to protest and forced the government to allow the logging to continue.

Women and Development

Another area of development planning where the work of anthropologists has been particularly useful is the subject of women and development. In recent decades, those in the development field have become increasingly aware of the extent to which women disproportionately suffer from the problems of underdevelopment and of their important role in the development process. An important problem addressed by anthropologists is the extent to which women's economic activities have been ignored. Participant observation studies by anthropologists have identified a much higher degree of economic activity by women and provided a clearer sense of their importance to overall economic performance (Bossen 1984, Leacock and

Safa 1986, Nash and Safa 1986). This research has also highlighted the extent to which social and cultural factors, such as expectations concerning childcare and other domestic activities, interfere with women's economic participation outside the home. The applied side of such research is to promote projects that are more sensitive to gender issues, assist in overcoming the particular problems of women, and build on their economic potential.

Promotion of the development of women involves consciousness-raising in the area of equality and expanding the roles of women beyond the more traditional domestic ones. Applied anthropologists have sought to promote this not only through development projects, but also by way of example. Thus, female anthropologists who go into the field provide an expanded sense of female role models in places where women are traditionally homebound.

Advocacy

Anyone engaged in planning or implementing change is, in a sense, advocating particular goals and a particular way of life. In most applied work, this advocacy role is not made explicit. The applied anthropologist is viewed more or less as a technician utilizing his or her particular skill in pursuit of some neutral goal. But applied anthropologists do not always claim or even try to be neutral. Many feel compelled by the poverty and exploitation of people with whom they work to serve as lobbyists on their behalf, as suggested by Thomas Melville's plea for the embattled Maya of Guatemala:

> Anthropologists have sat at the tables of Guatemalan Indians, eaten their meager food, laughed, smoked, and drunk with them, and made livings writing about their culture. It will be a shame if we leave the stage in silence. [1981: 1]

This advocacy approach by no means implies that local populations are incapable of speaking for themselves. Instead, it recognizes the social responsibility of the anthropologist to lobby on behalf of people in need and to promote values associated with fundamental human rights.

Advocacy on the part of anthropologists has been particularly evident in relation to the rights of indigenous peoples (see "Focus on Anthropologists"). Anthropologists have been involved with a number of groups promoting indigenous rights, including Cultural Survival, Survival International, and the International Work Group for Indigenous Affairs. Such groups seek to publicize the problems faced by indigenous peoples and act as lobbyists on their behalf; they also attempt to provide indigenous peoples with opportunities to make their own voices heard. These groups have been especially active in petitioning governments on behalf of indigenous peoples threatened as a result of the exploitation of natural resources. In 1990, for example, Survival International took part in a campaign to have the government of the Philippines cancel the logging concession given to a company in the southern part of the country after it was discovered that the company was responsible for the torture and murder of local native peoples opposed to its activities.

Anthropologists also have become involved in major political issues concerning domestic and foreign policies in their own countries. They have worked as advocates for those with drug-related problems, for the homeless, for retired people, and for the terminally ill. They have sought both to educate people about the cultures of these groups and to promote policies designed to assist them. In terms of foreign policy, perhaps the most controversial actions by anthropologists have been associated with recent wars. In the United States, anthropologists were prominent among those who organized teach-ins during the Vietnam War in the 1960s and early 1970s. In the 1970s and early 1980s anthropologists were active in trying to stop U.S. assistance to military regimes in Central America. Such activities still generate debate

Survival International, a group concerned with the rights of indigenous peoples, has conducted a campaign against excessive logging in the Philippines (top). Flooding in Thailand results from illegal logging of large stands of forest. This logging has stripped the hillsides, causing mud slides and the destruction of agricultural land, deaths, and homelessness (bottom).

among anthropologists themselves over their roles as scholars and citizens. Such debate illustrates the extent to which anthropologists are active participants in the modern world-system.

One of the questions that comes up with advocacy is at what point the anthropologist should get involved in human causes. The answer is when the lives of people being studied are at risk. All the efforts to document abuses against indigenous people just mentioned come under this principle. One frame of reference is the United Nations covenants against such things as slavery, racism, unfair treatment of women, and genocide. It serves anthropologists from various cultures working all over the globe. In the final analysis, the decision to get involved in peoples' rights is an individual one. But more and more such individual choices are made within the framework of the knowledge of how others have decided.

< ANTHROPOLOGY IN THE > CONTEMPORARY WORLD

Anthropology and all its subdisciplines have changed a great deal since the nineteenth century. Anthropology has grown in its professionalism, in its understanding of human evolution and cultural and biological diversity, and in its methodology. It has not grown in a vacuum. Anthropologists are influenced by their environment as we all are. The state of the discipline today is very much a reflection of the nature of the contemporary world-system. Greater world integration and improved communication, for example, have made possible a discipline consisting of persons from every part of the globe—it is no longer the exclusive domain of a few Europeans and North Americans.

The small-scale societies that were the focus of sociocultural anthropologists for decades remain an important part of anthropological study. Because ways of life associated with these societies are disappearing more rapidly every year,

contemporary anthropologists share the concern of earlier anthropologists in recording these vanishing life-styles. There remain many important lessons to be learned from studying people who live in smaller, nonindustrial societies. These people can tell us much about ourselves, about our past, about medicine and curing, and about how humans relate to the physical environment. Perhaps most important, knowledge about small-scale societies reinforces the notion that humans are highly adaptive. Furthermore, small-scale societies illustrate that many of the characteristics we often assume to be instinctive, or biologically based, such as aggression, are not—they are largely based on cultural adaptation within an environmental context.

Anthropologists' continuing interest in small-scale societies involves a different theoretical approach than in the past. Anthropologists have shifted from looking at smaller societies as isolated entities to examining how they fit into the broader environmental context. No longer do anthropologists merely study these societies. As noted earlier, many anthropologists work as planners and advocates to help overcome the poverty, genocide, and ethnocide that have often characterized integration of small-scale societies into the modern world-system.

Anthropologists, of course, do not study only past and present small-scale societies. Many anthropologists today study people who are fully integrated into large-scale industrial societies. Urbanism is one of the major features of modern life; within a few years over half of the world's population will be living in urban areas. Anthropologists have come to devote considerable effort to understanding all aspects of life in these rapidly growing cities.

The recording of human cultural diversity continues to be one of anthropology's main concerns. It has become commonplace to talk about how everything and everyone is becoming homogenized—wearing the same clothes, eating the same foods, watching the same television programs. But while many aspects of

SCOTT S. ROBINSON

FOCUS ON ANTHROPOLOGISTS

Scott Robinson did his doctoral dissertation research for Cornell University in Ecuador (1968–1969), where he became fascinated with documentary film production. After making three films in that country (with Michael Scott), he decided to devote his career to anthropological film. An opportunity to show his first films took him to Mexico, where he had lived as a child and lives now. Beginning in 1972, he began to apply his self-taught skills, producing documentaries throughout Mexico and Latin America. In addition to filmmaking, he also teaches anthropology at the Universidad Autonoma Metropolitana-Iztapalapa in Mexico City.

∧∧∧∧∧∧∧∧

From Filmmaking To Advocacy

In 1981, a contract documentary obliged me to film the construction of a large hydropower dam south of Mexico City. Federal Power Commission (CFE) executives wanted a documentary about the technical aspects of dam construction, illustrating the geophysical preliminaries, including the preparation of the bedrock on which the dam's curtain (in this case, layers of impermeable clay) would be slowly deposited and packed, and construction of an underground powerhouse. During helicopter flyovers of the dam site and the upstream basin to be flooded, I noticed a series of small villages and a good-sized town, Balsas, Guerrero. When I repeatedly asked my engineer clients what would become of

all the small farmers (*campesinos*) once the reservoir inundated their homes and fertile lands, I always got the same response: "Not to worry, they'll be given new homes in the new towns we're constructing for them." The completed film made no mention of the involuntary resettlement provoked by the dam.

The following year I began teaching social anthropology at the Universidad Autonoma Metropolitana-Iztapalapa campus in Mexico City. The undergraduate degree at the UAM-I requires all students to engage in two field-research trips prior to presenting their theses. It was evident that groups of students, distributed through the dam region's *mestizo* (Spanish-speaking) villages, could effectively gather ethnographic data as well as monitor the changes about to occur in the lives of the 5,500 inhabitants of the reservoir basin. From 1983 to 1986,

at the end of each year's rainy season (October to December), students settled in the modest homes of local residents and began taking notes, making maps, and conducting interviews. During the final fieldtrip, the students and I became caught up in the frantic moving of household goods, pigs, poultry, scarce corral posts, and roof beams above the waterline, once the flooding began. The experience of witnessing others—informants who had become friends—lose their homes, chapels, schools, and cemeteries, not to speak of valuable farmland, made a profound impression on us all.

Each fieldtrip generated a set of student papers describing kinship patterns; maize, bean, squash, and cash-crop farming; diet; fiestas; and village outmigration (primarily to Chicago in the United States). Also detailed in these reports was the factionalism born of ongoing, improvised negotiations with the CFE engineers and representatives of the Guerrero state government, apparently more concerned about the project's smooth management than the well-being of its constituents. Each field report was distributed to the project engineers and members of the state governor's office, as well as to the leadership of the six communities scheduled to be resettled. Our field reports were providing information not to be found elsewhere, given the absence of any comprehensive resettlement plan within the CFE. The legality of other such large-scale resettlements in Mexico; the vociferous international campaign to make multilateral lending institutions accountable for the social impact of their loans; the local information gap; the growing campesino distrust of the CFE, state, and federal authorities; and the haphazard and nonparticipatory nature of the resettlement process inadvertently placed us in the role of advocates for the disenfranchised villagers. What began as a simple student field-research project became a controversial call for respect for human rights and due process, a novelty in the history of involuntary resettlement in Mexico and elsewhere.

As our research generated discussion and resentment among the CFE project engineers, it also became apparent that some research about resettlement precedents and policy

A village empty after resettlement resulting from the construction of a dam.

inside the CFE was in order. I approached my wife's brother, then director of construction for the CFE, and offered to prepare a review paper of the "state of the resettlement art," an issue of growing visibility in what has come to be called development anthropology. He accepted my offer, and my team's consultancy report was circulated among CFE top management. We received almost no feedback, however, and no discussions about how policy changes took place. The traditional pattern of resettlement occurring as a function of the personal concerns and whims of the responsible project engineer was not to be modified so easily. Subsequent events proved that policy changes would be made only when the professional ca-

reers of top-level project engineers were jeopardized by the news of campesino resistance to arbitrary resettlement schemes under their jurisdiction. (Caracol dam project engineers, to whom, by the end of Fieldtrip 3, 1985, we were persona non grata never could discount the possibility that I was an informant to their administrative superior. Thus, the lines between research and action were blurred.)

At the beginning of this endeavor, I had not realized how the social organization of a government or private agency responsible for an infrastructure project with a resettlement component (such as dams, airports, tourist resorts, ports, and urban-renewal projects) could be a priority research objective similar to the culture and economy of the affected communities. Because resettlement was a basic policy issue, and planning was largely nil, its reformulation became a political process as community resistance obliged the CFE bureaucracy to adapt and improvise.

In 1986, the fourth group of student researchers discovered in the archives of the Ministry of Agrarian Reform that all but 33 hectares of the 1,447 hectares of the lands to be flooded had never been legally expropriated before the dam's reservoir was filled. This information was shared with a group of dissident villagers who were unwilling to pick up and move across a then-imaginary body of water, far from their fields and with insufficient space on their assigned urban lots to build small corrals for their livestock. A community for resistors to the planned resettlement evolved and, persuaded by a charismatic leader and able negotiator, decided to literally "move up the hill," refusing to accept their paltry cash indemnification for their soon-to-be-flooded homes—a decision that chagrined the CFE engineers. Thus, although in hindsight this resettlement can be considered a

case study of how not to do it, it taught planners and administrators some valuable lessons. In the final analysis, without some form of local participation, consensus, and accountability, any resettlement process is bound to generate resistance, raising the political costs for all responsible parties.

The outcome of the 1988 Mexican federal elections redefined the way in which many federal programs were planned and administered at the local level. Accountability became a major issue, and the negotiation of the two new loans for a hydropower project financed by the World Bank led to a dramatic turnaround of CFE resettlement planning and policy implementation. The policy of the World Bank went like this: "If you don't comply with our resettlement guidelines, you don't receive the loan disbursements on schedule." Although it is still too soon to evaluate the impact of these recent changes in resettlement planning, it is clear that independent researchers are vital to the monitoring process.

From my experience with involuntary resettlement, several crucial aspects of the process became clear to me. First, all participants must be made

aware of the larger political arena in which the terms and costs are negotiated and the corollary political strategies are defined. Fax machines, laptop computers, and portable video camcorders allow feedback to occur swiftly among village-level leaders, the responsible government agency, and monitoring personnel. Second, it is essential that independent researchers define their ethical and analytical criteria regarding when and how to monitor a project. By providing reliable information about what a government agency may or may not be doing, such researchers *can make a difference.* They can create a common ground or neutral negotiating space for the resettlers and those being resettled. Finally, the local and regional context in which guidelines are implemented must be understood. Those responsible for implementation have families and kin obligations and are continually engaged in adjusting their political relations with neighbors and others beyond the community. Resettlement studies, then, must focus on the political process obtaining at *all* levels of society—a complex task and theoretical challenge, to say the least.

Western industrial society have spread across the globe, considerable diversity remains. The resurgence of pride in ethnic identity attests to the tenacity of many cultural traditions. Moreover, while many of the distinctive "tribes" of the past are gone, they have been replaced by many new forms of tribalism relating to such things as occupation, residence, and religion.

It has always been anthropology's role not only to look at human diversity, but also to analyze it holistically. In an age subject to specialization and simplistic glosses passing for generalized understanding, the holistic perspective remains important, for it is a view that is vital to an informed understanding of both the diversity and the integration of the totality of human experience in the context of the modern world. Moreover, holism provides an inclusive view of the modern world at a time when people appear keen to construct boundaries around themselves to the exclusion of others, whether on the basis of ethnic identity, relative wealth, lifestyle, age, or health. Within our own society those who are homeless, victims of AIDS, refugees, or the elderly poor are being increasingly marginalized and excluded. But for the anthropologist they are an integral part of the wider society, and their problems are problems for the entire society of which they are a part.

S U M M A R Y

The modern world system, integrated and technologically advanced, is nevertheless a source of major human problems, including environmental destruction and widespread poverty, hunger, and disease. With its holistic perspective and focus on adaptation, anthropology deepens our understanding of the problems and helps us find solutions.

Economic inequality in the modern world system is reflected in the difference between those developed countries that have come closest to achieving an adequate social, political, and economic standard of living and those underde-

veloped countries that are further from achieving these goals. The indigenous peoples of colonized or incorporated lands have suffered the most from underdevelopment. Some groups have been the targets of genocide, or extermination, while other indigenous groups have suffered ethnocide, seeing their cultures destroyed.

Among the causes of environmental destruction are pollution, technological disasters, and the large-scale destruction of tropical rainforests. Deforestation has profound consequences. Local and global climates are disrupted, plant and animal species become extinct, and the quality of life of local peoples is severely undermined.

Sociocultural anthropology plays an important role in solving human problems. Applied anthropologists actively promote beneficial changes by providing information, making policy recommendations, and working directly with local populations. Such activities fall largely within two categories: development planning and advocacy. Anthropologists assist in development planning through their detailed knowledge of local populations and their holistic, integrated perspective. Anthropologists are especially concerned about environmental management plans that ignore or show little understanding of the role of local populations in managing the environment and that do not deal with problems of social equity. They seek to promote sustainable development that is sensitive to local conditions and people, including the role of women. Anthropologists have also studied the impact of tourism and as applied workers, have sought to offer suggestions for avoiding or eliminating the problems that often stem from this major industry. Out of a recognition of their social responsibility, many anthropologists have become advocates for the poor and on behalf of national and international issues.

K E Y   T E R M S

Applied anthropology Anthropological research and activities intended to produce a desired sociocultural condition that optimally will improve the lives of the people concerned.

Development   Improvement in the quality of human lives by ensuring an adequate level of nutrition and suitable physical surroundings and by forging social, political, and economic systems that recognize individual potential and promote self-esteem.

Ethnocide   The systematic destruction of a people's culture.

Genocide   The deliberate and systematic destruction of a political or cultural group.

Greenhouse effect   Warming of the atmosphere caused by air pollutants that trap heated air near the earth's surface.

Sustainable development   The use of natural resources for economic growth in such a way that the use does not deplete them or reduce their renewable usefulness for future generations.

Transnational corporation   A corporation that may be headquartered in one country but has divisions in a number of countries.

Underdeveloped country or society   A country with persistent low standards of living that can be linked historically and structurally with the manner of its integration into the world system.

Undeveloped society   A society that is materially poor because it has not developed a complex industrial technology.

SUGGESTED READINGS

Readings on applied anthropology:

Chambers, Erve. 1985. *Applied Anthropology: A Practical Guide.* Englewood Cliffs, NJ: Prentice-Hall.

Eddy, Elizabeth M., and William L. Partridge, editors. 1987. *Applied Anthropology in America.* New York: Columbia University Press.

Franke, Richard W., and Barbara H. Chasin. 1980. *Seeds of Famine: Ecological Destruction and the Development Dilemma in the West African Sahel.* Montclair, NJ: Allenheld, Osmun.

Gibson, Margaret A. 1988. *Accommodation Without Assimilation: Sikh Immigrants in an American High School.* Ithaca: Cornell University Press.

Gill, Lesley. 1987. *Peasants, Entrepreneurs, and Social Change: Frontier Development in Lowland Bolivia.* Boulder, CO: Westview Press.

Green, Edward C., editor. 1986. *Practicing Development Anthropology.* Boulder, CO: Westview Press.

Justice, Judith. 1986. *Policies, Plans and People: Culture and Health Development in Nepal.* Berkeley: University of California Press.

Partridge, William, editor. 1984. *Training Manual in Development Anthropology.* Washington, DC: American Anthropological Association and Society for Applied Anthropology.

Rodman, Margaret. 1989. *Deep Water: Development and Change in Pacific Village Fisheries.* Boulder, CO: Westview Press. [Vanuatu]

Scheper-Hughes, Nancy, editor. 1987. *Child Survival: Anthropological Perspectives on the Treatment and Maltreatment of Children.* Boston: D. Reidel.

Sutherland, Anne. 1986. *Caye Caulker: Economic Success in a Belizean Fishing Village.* Boulder, CO: Westview Press.

Willigen, John van. 1986. *Applied Anthropology: An Introduction.* South Hadley, MA: Bergin & Garvey.

Willigen, John van, Barbara Rylko-Bauer, and Ann McElroy, editors. 1989. *Making Our Research Useful: Case Studies in the Utilization of Anthropological Knowledge.* Boulder, CO: Westview Press.

Wulff, Robert M., and Shirley J. Fiske, editors. 1987. *Anthropological Praxis: Translating Knowledge into Action*. Boulder, CO: Westview Press.

Readings on indigenous peoples:

Berndt, Ronald M., editor. 1982. *Aboriginal Sites, Rights and Resource Development*. Nedlands, WA: University of Western Australia Press.

Bodley, John H., editor. 1988. *Tribal Peoples and Development Issues: A Global Overview*. Mountain View, CA: Mayfield.

———. 1990. *Victims of Progress*. Mountain View, CA: Mayfield.

Cultural Survival. 1987. *Southeast Asian Tribal Groups and Ethnic Minorities*. Cambridge, MA: Cultural Survival.

Furer-Haimendorf, C. von. 1982. *Tribes of India: The Struggle for Survival*. Berkeley: University of California Press.

Goodland, Robert. 1982. *Tribal Peoples and Economic Development: Human Ecological Considerations*. Washington, DC: World Bank.

Hong, Evelyne. 1987. *Natives of Sarawak: Survival in Borneo's Vanishing Forests*. Pulau Pinang, Malaysia: Institut Masyarakat.

Howard, Michael C. 1987. *The Impact of the International Mining Industry on Indigenous Peoples*. Sydney: University of Sydney, Transnational Corporations Research Project.

Manz, Beatriz. 1988. *Refugees of a Hidden War: The Aftermath of Counterinsurgency in Guatemala*. Albany: State University of New York Press.

Tonkinson, Robert, and Michael Howard, editors. 1990. *Going it Alone? Prospects for Aboriginal Autonomy*. Canberra: Aboriginal Studies Press.

Treece, Dave. 1987. *Bound in Misery and Iron: The Impact of the Grande Caraja's Programme on the Indians of Brazil*. London: Survival International.

Publications on indigenous issues are available from these organizations:

International Work Group for Indigenous Affairs
Fiolstraede 10, DK–1171 Copenhagen K, Denmark

Survival International (USA)
2121 Decatur Place NW, Washington DC 20008, USA

Cultural Survival
11 Divinity Avenue, Cambridge, MA 02138 USA

APPENDIX

THE GROWTH OF SOCIOCULTURAL
ANTHROPOLOGY: MODELS OF EXPLANATION

Anthropology is not a static discipline with a fixed conception of what humans are like and why they behave and think as they do. As with all academic disciplines, it is evolving constantly.

In many ways, anthropological ideas at any given time reflect the social climate of anthropologists; as this climate changes, so do anthropologists' views. For example, until recently, many anthropologists ignored or minimized the place of women in society. However, during the past few decades, recognition of the male bias within Western culture has led anthropologists to reevaluate the position of women in other societies and to reexamine older accounts of these societies. Anthropologists now hope to present a more accurate view of women's roles and status and, therefore, a more accurate view of society as a whole.

But anthropology is not merely the product of the whims of a particular age; it is also the product of a gradual accumulation and testing of knowledge and ideas about people. Through the amassing of accurate information about people's behavior and beliefs and through the constant questioning and refining of theories of human culture, anthropology has grown into a more sophisticated discipline and profession.

In this appendix, we look at how sociocultural anthropology changed from being the province of an odd assortment of Eurocentric amateurs concerned with exotic "native" customs to the profession of an international group of highly trained specialists interested in all of humanity. We also look at how the ideas of sociocultural anthropologists grew from rather naive assumptions concerning the sociocultural evolution of humankind to much more sophisticated attempts to explain how we go

about living in the world around us. The story is not complete, of course. The science of humanity remains a continuously developing and ever-expanding process of discovery.

◄ EARLY BEGINNINGS AND ► EVOLUTIONISM

While the roots of sociocultural anthropology can be traced through the history and intellectual traditions of Western culture as far back as ancient Greece, sociocultural anthropology did not begin to take shape as a distinct field of study until the mid-nineteenth century. At this time there were no professional anthropologists, but a growing number of amateurs were interested in the relationships between the various "races" and in comparing the customs of exotic peoples.

Perhaps no one epitomizes the nineteenth-century amateur ethnographer more than the English explorer Richard Burton (1821–1890), who traveled in disguise to Mecca and became embroiled in debates over the source of the Nile. In 1863, Burton, together with James Hunt, founded the Anthropological Society of London (forerunner of the Royal Anthropological Institute of Great Britain and Ireland). Burton saw the society, in part, as an alternative to more prudish scholarly bodies such as the Royal Geographical Society. He and Hunt also founded the Cannibal Club, which held dinners after the society's meetings, and attracted a variety of nonconformists. Writing on Burton's mission to the Kingdom of Dahomey, 1863–1864, biographer Byron Farwell (1990: 226) comments that Burton would have been better suited for the post of "Roving Ambassador to Barbarians" than to the more restricted diplomatic posts available to him at the time. No doubt partly out of a desire to shock prudish Victorians, Burton often championed the "barbaric" customs of other peoples. For example, he defended the Islamic practice of polygamy, arguing that "monogamy, polygamy, and polyandry are an affair of geography" and that polygamy was a sensible adaptation in "hot and enervating climates" (Farwell 1990: 101). Although Burton's ethnographic observations were often of very good quality, his theoretical speculations tended to be far from scientific.

In addition to the London society, anthropological societies were established in several other Western cities in the mid-nineteenth century. The members of these associations shared the conviction that non-European peoples were worthy of study, but they differed about whether all peoples should be considered "truly human" (rather than some form of nonhuman primate) and why people looked and acted differently. According to one popular theory of the day, humans had been created in a state of perfection, but had degenerated after the expulsion from Eden. Those who believed this theory claimed that some peoples (i.e., nonwhites) had "fallen" further than others from the original state of perfection. Another theory held that the Christian God had created the various "races" separately. In this view it was considered no more of a problem to explain the contrast between Africans and Europeans than to show why tigers and monkeys are not alike. The major shortcoming of both theories was that they were based on theological, and not scientific, principles: they were based on Western religious traditions and not on systematic observation.

A more scientific and humanistic approach to the study of humanity developed from another school of thought, which came to be known as *evolutionism*. The evolutionists drew inspiration from evolutionary theories that had been gaining currency in geology (e.g., from Charles Lyell) and biology (e.g., from Jean-Baptiste Lamarck) since the early nineteenth century. The cultural evolutionists asserted that human societies, like animal species, undergo changes over vast periods of time, with "primitive" stages of culture succeeded by more "advanced" stages. Many of these first anthropologists are called *unilineal evolutionists* because they maintained that all cultures pass through essentially the same stages along a single line of development, moving from "savage" to "civilized." Contemporary "savages" were seen as living cultural fossils. This theory was especially important at the time as a justification for the study of non-Western peoples, the idea being that by studying them anthropologists could learn something about the past of their own culture.

The concept of cultural evolution made it possible to begin studying human nature systematically without resorting to theological dogma. In addition, the evolutionists made a clear distinction between biologically inherited characteristics and those acquired socially through learning. The distinction between biology and culture offered a solution to the fundamental paradox in the study of humanity: the question of why we are all so alike, and yet so different. The evolutionists believed in the existence of biological differences as seen in such traits as skin color, eye shape, and hair form. But they stoutly supported the principle of *psychic unity,* according to which all people essentially have the same mental capacities and potentials. They felt that the most important human differences were the result of social environment and not biology.

Through their acceptance of the psychic unity of humanity, evolutionists were willing to acknowledge that nonwhites were the equals of whites in basic capabilities. But they were not willing to accept that the cultures of these people were equal to those of whites. It seemed obvious to the evolutionists that some cultures were more advanced than others. They saw *progress,* rather than simply change, as the most important feature of evolution. To them, evolution was a sequence leading from the simple to the complex, or the primitive to the advanced. This notion sometimes took the extreme form and beliefs of white people were held to be superior to those of nonwhites.

Tylor: The Evolution of Reason

The most prominent of the evolutionists was Edward B. Tylor (1832–1917), an English scholar whom some call "the father of ethnology." Tylor's most important contribution to anthropology was his concept of culture, which he defined as "that complex whole which includes knowledge, belief, art, law, morals, customs, and any other capabilities and habits acquired by man as a member of society" (Tylor 1891: I: 1). Tylor, more than anyone else, established the distinction between biologically inherited characteristics and those characteristics we acquire through learning.

For Tylor, cultural evolution consisted of "the advance of reason." What distinguished the "savage" from the "civilized" was that the civilized person had progressed further in abandoning "superstition" in favor of customs based on more scientific or rational principles. Recognizing that Western cultures continue to exhibit customs that seem irrational, Tylor explained these as being *survivals.* Originating in earlier evolutionary stages, they had lost their original meaning and function, but persisted nevertheless. One of the examples was the custom of saying "God bless you" after a sneeze (Tylor 1891: I: 98). This was a survival of the ancient belief that the soul might leave the body during a sneeze and that uttering the spell "God bless you" would counteract the danger. The concept of survivals was important to Tylor's approach, for he believed that they provided evidence of a

culture's history and could therefore be used to reconstruct cultural evolution.

Morgan: The Evolution of Technology

Another important proponent of evolution was Lewis Henry Morgan (1818–1881). A lawyer by training, Morgan began his anthropological career when he joined a young men's club in New York state called the Grand Order of the Iroquois, which Morgan patterned after the Iroquois confederacy. Besides his contributions to Iroquois and kinship studies Morgan wrote *Ancient Society* (1877), in which he produced an elaborate developmental scheme of cultural evolution, dividing evolutionary progress into a series of stages based primarily on technological innovation. For instance, cultures advanced from "middle savagery," characterized by foragers, or those who hunt and gather to meet their subsistence needs, who gain the capability of fishing and making fire; to "upper savagery," with the introduction of the bow and arrow; and on to "lower barbarism" with the mastery of pottery making; and so on. Morgan felt that such stages and technological innovations were associated with the evolution of cultural patterns. For example, he proposed that the family had evolved through six forms that were linked to his technologically based stages.

Although evolutionists such as Tylor and Morgan made great contributions to the development of anthropology, their works had shortcomings. For example, Morgan's linking of technology with other aspects of culture represented an important contribution, but his scheme suffered from its ethnocentrism. Other cultures were viewed in terms of Western technology and social organization. Moreover, the categories of the evolutionists tended to be overly rigid, and their explanations of how cultures progressed from one stage to the next were not always well developed. In addition, they were hampered by poor data. Their information was obtained from travelers, traders, soldiers, explorers, missionaries, and others. Some of this information was of very good quality, but much of it was unreliable or simply wrong. The increasingly obvious need for more reliable data led to a new stage in the evolution of anthropology.

◄ PROFESSIONALIZATION ►

By the late 1870s anthropology was beginning to emerge as a profession. A major impetus for the growth of anthropology was the expansion of Western colonial powers and their consequent desire to better understand the peoples living under colonial domination. In the United States, for example, especially in the West, the government sought information on Native American peoples who were being subdued and placed on reservations. Similarly, when the United States assumed control of the Philippines from Spain in the late 1890s, it was faced with tribal rebellions. As the tribes were subdued, anthropologists were employed to assist in devising means to administer these people. Britain and other European nations had a similar interest in the peoples of their far-flung empires.

Anthropologists did not simply serve as agents of colonial administrations, however. Both for scientific purposes and out of a sense of humanitarian obligation, many were motivated to record local customs before they disappeared and were forgotten.

Museum Anthropology

Anthropology emerged as a profession primarily in museums. The collection of ethnographic material dates back over the centuries, but modern ethnographic museums date only from the nineteenth century. The Ethnographic Department of the National Museum of Denmark, opened in 1849, was the first modern ethnographic museum—its collection being based on items accumulated in the Royal Cabinet of Art in the seventeenth and eighteenth centuries. Many museums devoted to the study of humankind were founded in Europe, North America, and South America during the last few decades of the nineteenth century. In addition, ethnographic collections came to play a larger role in natural history museums.

Anthropology's link with museums influenced its development throughout the late nineteenth and early twentieth centuries. In the United States and continental Europe this link remains important to some extent even today. Museums affected cultural anthropology in two ways. The first was in the emphasis on material culture, stemming from museums' concern for collecting displayable materials. Second, the museum orientation encouraged anthropologists to classify their data according to natural history typologies (along the same lines as stones or butterflies) rather than focusing on the more dynamic aspects of culture. Human practices and ideas were treated as concrete and static, rather than being in a continual state of flux. Moreover, culture was seen as an assembly of distinct items, not as a system of interrelated ideas and activities.

Academic Anthropology

Professionalization during the latter part of the nineteenth century and the early twentieth century provided great breakthroughs in the quality and quantity of ethnographic research. Beginning in the 1870s, the quality of research began to improve. In the United States, for example, the Bureau of American Ethnology employed a professional anthropologist in 1879 to conduct research among native peoples in the Southwest. Franz Boas, who was to become a leading figure in American anthropology, conducted research among native peoples in Canada in the 1880s and 1890s. In Britain, A.C. Haddon, who was appointed to the first position to be set aside for an anthropologist at Cambridge University in 1893, championed the lasting value of fieldwork over the ephemeral value of speculative theorizing (Haddon and Quiggin 1910:3). At the time a professor of zoology, Haddon had visited the islands of the Torres Straits, between Australia and New Guinea in 1888, where he had become interested in the people living in the area. Between 1898 and 1899, in the meantime having become an anthropologist, he led a major anthropological expedition from Cambridge University to the Torres Straits.

As ethnographic research—that is, the descriptive studies of the fieldworker—was improving, anthropology gradually was being introduced into university curricula. At first the courses were presented by self-taught anthropologists, since formal professional training did not yet exist. Joint appointments at museums and universities were relatively common and ensured a continued link between museum and academic anthropology. After 1900, the number of persons employed as anthropologists in Europe and North America slowly grew. For example, as late as 1940, there were still only a few dozen professional anthropologists in the United States, and even fewer in England. As more of these anthropologists were employed by universities where they came into contact with scholars in other disciplines, the museum influence was reduced.

In the 1920s and 1930s, anthropology departments were founded in countries such as Australia, South Africa, and Brazil. The anthropologists in these countries were trained in the United States and Western Europe. The anthropologists in these new departments focused on the collection of ethnographic data on the indigenous peoples of their respective countries, while leaving theoretical debate largely to anthropologists from the colonial powers.

Diffusionism

As more reliable information was amassed and as the profession of anthropology developed, there was growing dissatisfaction with the theories of the early evolutionists. New schools of thought began to emerge. One of these was *diffusionism,* the view that the main process by which cultures change is through cultural borrowing. Morgan had argued that cultures passed through stages marked by important inventions, such as the wheel, metallurgy, and the alphabet. Diffusionists doubted that these important inventions occurred independently in each culture. They maintained that critical inventions were rare and that most peoples who had, say, the wheel, did not invent it themselves but picked it up from a neighboring society. Since diffusion was seen to depend on "historical accident," the diffusionists saw no need for laws of progress as believed by the evolutionists.

Diffusionism was first developed in Germany during the latter part of the nineteenth century. German scholars studied specific culture "traits" (such as fishhook styles or myths) and sought to explain their distribution. The German diffusionists of the early twentieth century claimed that initially there were a limited number of cultural circles (*Kreise*), and that human culture had evolved through diffusion from these points of origin. They proposed that "higher civilizations" such as those of ancient Mesopotamia and Egypt had evolved in geographically favorable places. The basic inventions characteristic of civilization, diffusionists believed, had occurred in these regions; and changes elsewhere resulted from the diffusion of these inventions through borrowing, migration, and conquest. This view of cultural evolution became known as the *Kulturkreis,* or "culture-circle," theory.

While the grander propositions of the diffusionists were little more than imaginative speculation, some of the more limited studies did point to important linkages among peoples. G. Friederici (1913), for example, carried out research in 1908 on the cultural relationship between the peoples of the eastern Indonesian island of Seram, often referred to in the region as the "mother" island, and peoples farther to the east as far as the Solomon Islands and Vanuatu. The relationship continues to interest anthropologists today. More generally, diffusionism served to place greater emphasis on physical environment and context than had the earlier notions of cultural evolution.

Historical Particularism

Diffusionist ideas were brought to anthropology in North America by Franz Boas (1858–1942). He believed that ethnology should emphasize the detailed study of the geographical distribution of cultural traits. By analyzing these trait distributions, anthropologists could reconstruct historical and psychological processes of cultural change. This approach came to be called *historical particularism.* Instead of seeking to discover universal laws governing culture change as had the evolutionists, Boas called for the investigation of the unique histories of individual cultures. While historical particularism limited its adherents to the view that every culture is unique, within these boundaries it demanded very complete field notes. As a result, Boas and his early followers collected a great deal of factual information about particular cultures which is still of value to researchers today.

Closely associated with Boas' historical particularism were his efforts to promote cultural relativism and to demonstrate the independence of cultural and biological factors. His experience as a Jew in nineteenth-century Germany no doubt shaped the position he took against explaining culture in terms of race. His writings on these topics were important scientifically and also served to counter widespread racist notions in the United States about the inferiority of nonwhite and non-Western peoples.

Many of Boas' followers turned to the study of *culture areas,* or regions where clusterings of shared, diffused cultural traits could be observed. The Great Plains of North America was one such culture area. Great Plains native peoples all hunted buffalo and placed a high value on warfare. Most of their societies incorporated the Sun Dance ceremony and military societies. When anthropologists mapped out such culture areas in North America and South America, they discovered that each was closely correlated with a particular ecological zone, such as the Amazon Basin or the Great Basin.

Franz Boas was one of the first people to emphasize that museum collections should represent cultures and be arranged in some kind of cultural context. However, he continued to view culture itself very much as an accumulation of artifacts and traits rather than as an integrated whole.

‹ CULTURE AS AN INTEGRATED › WHOLE

Throughout the first two decades of the twentieth century, the museum tradition in ethnology prevailed, but changes were afoot. Anthropologists continued to shy away from grand evolutionary "schemes," but there was dissatisfaction with the various diffusionist approaches. Armed with improving ethnographic accounts, anthropologists tried to move beyond the view of society and culture as mixed bags of traits toward a more *integrated* view. Morgan had sought to examine how cultural parts were interrelated, but he was hampered by poor data, and his evolutionary scheme fell into disrepute.

In light of the growing sophistication of ethnographic data, some anthropologists called for better analyses of how the parts of specific societies fit together.

Functionalism

The approach of those looking more carefully at how cultures were integrated wholes was termed *functionalism*. This new school of thought asked questions different from those of the historical particularists. Functionalists believed that what was most important about the Sun Dance ritual of the Dakota, for instance, was not where, how, and when it was invented and diffused, or how it fit into some large pattern of traits in a region, but how this religious ceremony functioned—how it fit in with the rest of Dakota culture.

To understand the complex interrelationships of elements in a total cultural system, anthropologists had to carry out even more intensive fieldwork. A pioneer in the functionalist approach and intensive fieldwork was Bronislaw Malinowski (1884–1942), who conducted research on the Trobriand Islands (eastern Papua New Guinea) between 1915 and 1918. His study of the Trobriand Islanders demonstrated that a long-term, in-depth involvement with an ongoing way of life could lead to far greater understanding of a people's culture than could a speculative reconstruction of a people's cultural past based on random interviews with a handful of informants. When Malinowski first announced that he was going to study the morals and manners of the Trobriand Islanders, he was told that "they don't have any morals and their manners are vile." Yet, in his study of ceremonial trade, he found a complex system that linked myth, magic, economic exchange, and highly developed social rules.

Malinowski's theory of functionalism stressed that all people share requirements for *basic needs* such as food, shelter, and means of defense and reproduction. In addition, there are *derived needs* —such as economics and law—that are ultimately traceable to more basic needs associated with the fundamental requirements for biological survival. Malinowski's argument was that each part of a culture, which he saw as a working whole, functions in one way or another to fulfill these kinds of needs.

Malinowski attempted not only to explain the more obvious aspects of a culture, but also to make sense of those aspects that seemed irrational to many Westerners. For example, he found that Trobriand Islanders made extensive use of magic. Instead of explaining this by

Bronislaw Malinowski talks with a Trobriand sorcerer. Malinowski viewed sorcery as one of the integrative needs, along with knowledge, religion, art, and play; these, like the basic and derived needs, had to be met by all cultures.

reference to the Islanders' being "superstitious savages," or by viewing their magical beliefs as survivals or diffused traits, he reasoned that magic functioned to reduce the tensions and anxieties that resulted from the uncertainties of life. Thus, he found that magic was employed when people fished in the dangerous open sea, but not when they fished in the safer waters of lagoons.

Malinowski deserves a great deal of credit for his advances in fieldwork and his ability to portray the lives of Trobriand Islanders so that Westerners would perceive these people as thinking, rational beings—not mere superstitious savages. However, his theory of functionalism contained some serious flaws. For example, if all people have the same basic needs, then why do not all cultures meet those needs in the same way? Another problem was that by emphasizing how culture functions to meet the needs of individuals, Malinowski failed to adequately take into account those aspects of life that transcend the individual. It is difficult to argue that political revolutions or families merely reflect the fulfillment of individual needs.

Structural-Functionalism

Malinowski's theoretical shortcomings were in part offset by his contemporary A. R. Radcliffe-Brown (1881–1955), somewhat of a rival of Malinowski for the allegiance of students in England. Radcliffe-Brown was strongly influenced by the great French sociologist Emile Durkheim (1858–1917), one of the first scholars to develop the analysis of society as an integrated system of interrelated parts. Durkheim stressed that culture is the product of a community, not of single individuals. He argued that the ultimate reality of human life was sociological and not psychological—that it consisted of the social products of people interacting in groups over generations. The sociological reality (which Durkheim called the "collective consciousness") existed beyond the individual; individual actions and beliefs were simply manifestations of this larger reality.

Radcliffe-Brown likened society to an organism—an integrated whole, dependent on the proper functioning of its constituent parts in order to exist. Moreover, for him, society had a life of its own, obeying laws that transcended the individual. His mission was to investigate the anatomy of society and document the dynamics of its components. Unlike the functionalism of Malinowski, which stressed how culture works to sustain individuals, Radcliffe-Brown's theory of *structural-functionalism* focused on how various elements of social structure (such as a society's major groups and institutions; see Chapter 6) function to maintain social order and equilibrium.

If Malinowski and Radcliffe-Brown had observed the same funeral ceremony, it is likely that they would have analyzed it very differently. Malinowski would have interpreted the lamentations of the bereaved as a custom functioning to alleviate the tensions created in these individuals by the death. Radcliffe-Brown would have looked at the social groups and institutions involved to see how the behavior of the bereaved served to reaffirm the values of the society and promote the solidarity of social groups. In other words, Radcliffe-Brown would have stressed how the funeral rites fulfill the needs of the social system. The two views are not so much mutually exclusive; they differ largely in emphasis. Culture clearly has functions for the individual as well as for society.

The functionalists helped establish the concept of cultural integration, and they refined fieldwork methods considerably. Their ideas emphasized the need to look at the social context within which customs and institutions occur, rather than simply viewing them as isolated components of a society. In addition, they sought to look at contemporary societies as they actually functioned rather than seeking to reconstruct the past.

But the context they recognized was still narrow. For the most part, the sociocultural system they studied was the local community or group, and they treated the group as an isolated unit with no history. This focus often meant ignoring the impact of colonial conquest and rule, an aspect of the more general problem of failing to deal adequately with sociocultural change. By looking at a social system as a set of mutually supporting elements in a state of equilibrium, the functionalists made it hard to explain how change takes place. When pressed, as with the diffusionists before them, they tried to account for change by reference to the outside world, but by and large they ignored the world beyond the tribe or village. Dealing with the impact of the British Empire on African tribes or fitting the tribes they studied into a wider world system was beyond their theoretical grasp. Most of their studies also paid little attention to the physical and biotic environment.

The Comparative Method

One thing in common to the anthropologists mentioned so far is their belief that insights can be gained by comparing different cultures. This approach, known as the comparative method, was first employed by the unilineal evolutionists. As used by them for the study of evolution, apparently similar practices, beliefs, and material items from different cultures are grouped together and compared for the insights they can provide concerning human culture at different states of evolution. Accordingly, ethnographic material in the Pitt Rivers Museum at Oxford University, which opened in 1890, was organized on the basis of problems that have presented themselves to humans and how they have been solved in an evolutionary sequence

rather than by the culture they come from. Thus, weaving implements and textiles are placed together and analyzed from an evolutionary perspective—from barkcloth to cloth woven on simple looms to the use of more complex techniques and technologies.

The comparative method was taken from the fields of anatomy and philology, where it had been employed with considerable success. In these fields, there was considerable agreement about what was to be compared and what inferences could be made. Among anthropologists, however, there was no overall agreement in regard to how to order the data or to interpret it.

While anthropologists subsequently have tended to study data according to culture or period, the comparative method of the evolutionists is not without its uses even today. As one writer on the Pitt Rivers Museum has noted, "the juxtaposition [of items] can be interesting and revealing, and for some visitors [to the museum], such as musicologists or students of textile design, the method is ideal" (Cranstone 1984:1–2).

The structural-functionalists also adopted the comparative method, although they were less concerned with evolutionary questions and focused on case studies of the interrelated institutions of societies. Case studies of societies were employed to allow them to progress toward discovering general laws about society and its institutions. Radcliffe-Brown, for example, viewed the process as one of proceeding systematically from empirical observation to description and then to comparison and, finally, to generalization. While, as noted above, the work of structural functionalists had its faults, and their use of the comparative method did not result in the discovery of any general laws, as Andre Beteille (1992:1866) comments: "The comparative method remains of great value because it forces a certain discipline that does not come naturally to us when we examine the varieties of social life. It forces us to give equal consideration . . . to all societies irrespective of our personal engagements."

Culture and Personality

Structural functionalism developed largely in England, though it had its North American adherents. In the United States, understanding cultural integration became a psychological rather than a sociological pursuit. This new school of thought was labeled *culture and personality*. People were thought to acquire certain personality characteristics in keeping with the dominant themes of their culture. Also important was the so-called nature-versus-nurture debate, concerning the extent to which behavior was learned and the extent to which it was a result of biology.

Franz Boas saw the individual as primarily being shaped by culture (nurture). Studies were carried out by a number of his students, one of whom was Margaret Mead, who became one of the best-known anthropologists among laypeople. Mead (1901–1978) sought to link psychology with the study of culture, focusing specifically on the ways in which children were taught their cultures. In her classic work *Coming of Age in Samoa* (1928) she attempted to demonstrate how certain child-rearing practices produced certain character structures among adults. She argued that the supposedly universal "strain and stress" of adolescence need not occur in societies such as Samoa, which, according to Mead, values peaceful conformity and promotes a tolerant attitude toward sex. Mead's work on Samoa was later criticized by Derek Freeman, who with more modern methods of fieldwork was able to discover some tensions among Samoan adolescents. Nevertheless, Mead remains a pioneer in studies of how people grow up in cultures. At the time she did her work, ethnologists did not have the tools for study that they have today.

Another of Boas' students identified with the culture-and-personality approach is Ruth Benedict (1887–1948), who brought her training in the humanities to anthropology. She argued that a culture developed a range of potential themes into a cultural style, much as an individual develops a personality style. According to Benedict, whole cultures could be categorized according to which of these themes had been adopted. Over time, Benedict believed, aspects of a culture that contradicted this overriding theme were eliminated, until the entire system became consistent with it.

Benedict's best-known work, *Patterns of Culture* (1934), discusses a few of these themes. As an example of the Apollonian type, she cited the Zuni of the American Southwest, which showed a preference for compromise and avoidance of psychological and emotional excesses. Another type, the Dionysian, she assigned to the Kwakiutl of the northwest coast of North America. The Dionysian theme involved seeking out excitement, terror, and danger.

The search for *national character* was an important part of the culture and personality school. This involved establishing traits of the type outlined by Benedict that characterized the psyches of different nationalities. These studies became important around World War II, when the U.S. government used them to assess the psychological characteristics of people involved in the war. Most influential was Benedict's book *The Chrysanthemum and the Sword* (1946), which played a role in justifying the American administration's restoration of the Japanese emperor.

The culture-and-personality approach did not break totally with the museum-derived natural history tradition. It represented a blend of the typological emphasis of natural history with ideas current in psychology. The natural history tendency to look for types simply was moved to the realm of psychology, well removed from the material aspect of culture.

By the 1950s, the culture-and-personality approach was coming under increasing criticism. The categories proposed by Benedict and

Margaret Mead, the first woman to study the native peoples of the Pacific Islands on her own—an endeavor shocking to many in her day—in native costume in Samoa in the 1920s. Mead's work on Samoan adolescence stressed the role of culture in shaping personality.

others were gross oversimplifications and removed cultures from any sense of actual history or other context. For example, Douglas Haring (1949) argued that rather than looking to such things as toilet training to understand the compulsive traits exhibited by the Japanese, they could best be explained as part of the heritage of centuries of living in a police state. Beyond this was the very question of whether there was such a thing as a "psychological type" for an entire society.

◄ SPECIALIZATION: WORLD ► WAR II TO THE PRESENT

By the end of World War II in 1945, the basic methods that characterize anthropology had been developed. Non-Western peoples had become fairly familiar to anthropologists, and their cultures were recognized as integrated and logical. At this time new trends in anthropological theory and areas of specialization began to emerge. These trends were accelerated by a marked increase in the number of professional anthropologists. In the early part of the twenti-

eth century, there were so few anthropologists that most knew one another, and most shared similar cultural and class backgrounds. Following World War II, the profession grew in numbers, and anthropologists were drawn from a much wider range of socioeconomic and cultural backgrounds. Today, there are thousands of anthropologists with diverse backgrounds, interests, and personalities, creating a discipline of many and varied ideas, approaches, and specialties. The era of the ethnographic pioneer discovering unknown peoples is past. Today, some of the most stimulating discoveries lie in the insights anthropologists derive from asking old questions in new ways and from delving into uncharted areas of knowledge.

Contemporary anthropology has been influenced by what goes on outside the discipline itself. After World War II, culture contact rapidly accelerated. People who previously were only marginally affected by the industrial world were rapidly drawn into the global economy and integrated into newly established nations. For many non-Western peoples, the past few decades have been a period of enormous upheaval and change. The Western world has experienced turbulence during this period as well. The energy crisis, environmental pollution, and the restructuring of much of the communist world are among the factors forcing us to reexamine our values and institutions. Not surprisingly, contemporary sociocultural anthropology emphasizes the study of change.

Neoevolutionism

Interest in cultural evolution had subsided in the early twentieth century, and few anthropologists wrote on the subject over the intervening years prior to World War II. American anthropologist Leslie White (1900–1975), however, played an important role in reviving interest in the writings of the nineteenth-century evolutionists and in questions of cultural evolution in general. His version of evolutionism has been labeled *neoevolutionism.*

As with the earlier evolutionists, White was interested in the general evolution of human society rather than the evolution of specific societies. To White, the primary force in social evolution was technological advancement. What distinguishes "advanced" from "primitive" societies, he argued, was the amount of energy at their disposal. In a technologically primitive society, people have only human muscle power as an energy source. Societies evolve as humans find ways to harness new sources of power— domesticating draft animals and inventing means of capturing energy from wind, water, fossil fuels, and so forth. By increasing the amount of energy available, each technological advance makes possible greater social and cultural complexity and facilitates the growth of ever-larger sociocultural systems.

White published his important work *The Evolution of Culture* in 1959, the 100th anniversary of Darwin's *Origin of Species*. In addition to helping reintroduce to anthropology the study of cultural evolution, White also influenced how anthropologists perceived culture. For Boas and his followers, culture was a loose accumula-

tion of elements assumed under the heading of learned behavior. For White this was too sloppy. Instead, he defined culture as a phenomenon "made up of events that are dependent upon a faculty peculiar to the human species, namely, the ability to use symbols" (White 1949: 15). For White, without symbols there could be no culture. He hoped to establish a more scientific study of culture by defining it as a distinct class of phenomena.

Cultural Ecology

Another important figure in the early postwar period was the American Julian Steward (1902–1972). Steward's work laid the basis for the study of *cultural ecology*. This approach investigates how culture functions as a dynamic means of adapting to the physical environment. In sharp contrast to the cultural relativism of Franz Boas, who tended to see all cultural phenomena as equal, Steward argued that certain phenomena caused others. He wrote of "core" features of culture, such as work or power, and "secondary" features, such as magic and religion. His focus was on work and livelihood and especially subsistence, or food-getting, activities, as the most important core features. He emphasized what people do instead of what they believe.

His well-known triumvirate comprised resources, technology, and labor. He saw technology and resources as fundamental. These were brought together through human labor. Such labor was linked to a commonsense view of the world as actually lived by people seeking to make a living within the constraints of their surroundings. He found internal social constraints and external environmental constraints facing all societies. This came out clearly in his early monograph *Basin-Plateau Aboriginal Sociopolitical Groups* (1938), in which he described Shoshone Indian local groups and subsistence activities. His analysis took into account the constraints presented by the environment and the adapta-

Julian Steward emphasized the adaptive relation between culture and environment. Shoshone Indians, studied by Steward, are shown here in summer, when conditions allowed families to come together in larger groups. In winter, they had to disperse again, as resources became scarce.

tion of those living within it. He described Shoshone society as a social structure reduced to its bare essentials, because of its sparse habitat and limited technology. The work was pioneering in theoretical and methodological terms.

Steward did not believe that environmental constraints automatically cause cultural patterns, but that the environment provides part of the *context* that shaped a culture. He believed that most subsistence activities had a degree of flexibility, offering people choices in their adaptive strategies; it was important for the anthropologist, however, to determine the range of these choices. Thus, a simple technology offered fewer choices in relation to one's environment

than did a more complex technology.

Steward also championed the study of complex societies. In this pursuit, he took a different approach from many others of the time. Instead of looking at isolated pieces of a society or making generalizations about national characters, Steward examined "subcultures" as parts of larger regions and nations. In the early 1950s, he organized a team study of Puerto Rico (see Steward et al 1956), with members of the team looking at specific aspects of Puerto Rican society, including coffee-growing and private and government sugar plantations, with a view to seeing the parts as segments of a larger whole.

Much of Steward's work focused on change. He looked for like sequences of cultural development in different times and places, an approach known as *multilinear evolution*. For example, the development of agriculture in both the Near East and Mesoamerica led to similar social and political developments. He did not seek to discover "universal stages," as had the unilineal evolutionists, but rather sought to determine "those limited parallels of form, function, and sequence which have empirical reality" (Steward 1955: 19). Recognizing that particular cultures might have cultural features that were distinct, he nevertheless sought to discover cross-cultural regularities that corresponded to cultural patterns found in distinct adaptive strategies, such as those associated with tribal societies and state-based societies. However, as did the functionalists and many others at the time, Steward continued to see cultures essentially as stable. This meant that change had to be based largely on such external factors as culture contact, technological diffusion, population growth, or changes in the physical environment.

Theories of Conflict

A fundamental shortcoming of the anthropological perspectives discussed up to this point is their failure to deal with conflict. Pre-World War II anthropologists assumed an orderly world, neglecting to include competition and conflict. Motivations behind this omission probably include a desire to present cultures as integrated systems and a desire to present the peoples being studied not as brutal savages but as humans who led orderly and sensible lives. Moreover, colonial conquest of the peoples studied usually had taken place before anthropologists arrived on the scene, leaving them to examine the lives of people existing under an externally imposed order. Employment by colonial administrations may have led anthropologists to ignore aspects of the lives of colonized peoples that might have reflected unfavorably on the colonial governments.

World War II and the postwar struggles for liberation among colonial peoples in Africa, Asia, and elsewhere changed this situation dramatically. Conflict was everywhere, and anthropologists could ignore it no longer. While some chose to view the competition and conflict they witnessed as arising out of unique postwar conditions, perceiving the period to be one of disequilibrium or perhaps a completely new situation, others argued that conflict was a normal part of human culture.

NEOFUNCTIONALISM. One of the first anthropologists to try to reform the functionalist perspective to fit postwar conditions was Max Gluckman (1911–1975), a South African who migrated to England. His approach is known as *neofunctionalism*. Gluckman criticized Malinowski for his failure to treat conflict "as an inherent attribute of social organization" (1949: 8). To Gluckman, feuds, estrangements within families, witchcraft accusations, challenges to authority, and the like were normal parts of social life. He argued that despite (or sometimes because of) conflict, social solidarity was maintained.

In *Custom and Conflict in Africa* (1956), Gluckman argued that the social order is maintained through the checks and balances of overlapping allegiances. People may quarrel in the context of one set of allegiances, but they find themselves restrained by other allegiances. People who become enemies in one situation may become allies in another. For example, cousins who feud with each other in support of two quarreling brothers may join forces in a dispute with another kin group. Through the web of these cross-cutting ties, the social fabric is maintained. Gluckman even viewed rebellions as no threat to the social order. Rebels, following customary norms and procedures with ritual-like precision, serve to reaffirm rather than undermine the traditional order. Their actions are "rituals of rebellion."

Gluckman succeeded in bringing conflict into the normal scheme of things, but he continued to emphasize the fundamentally unchanging social order. In this regard, he failed to deal adequately with the question of structural change—how social orders are transformed or break down. In addition, social order itself still was treated as a given, not as something to be explained.

MARXIST ANTHROPOLOGY. Another group of anthropologists, drawing their inspiration from the writings of Karl Marx (1818–1883), also saw conflict as a normal part of human culture. Unlike Gluckman, *Marxist anthropologists* are concerned specifically with the transformation of social orders and the relationship between conflict and cultural evolution (see Bloch 1983; Leacock 1982; Wessman 1981). Marx himself, in his early writings, and many later Marxist scholars employed a unilineal model of social evolution, beginning with the "primitive community" and subsequently passing through the "classical," "feudal," and bourgeois" stages. In his later writings, however, Marx recognized that change was much more complex; hence, a number of Marxists have recently allowed for variations in the evolutionary path rather than a single, universal line (see Melotti 1977). For Marxist evolutionists, the key to understanding evolution is through attention to changes within societies that lead to growing strains and conflicts as a new form of social and economic organization emerges and eventually becomes dominant.

In explaining the conditions that generated change, Marx emphasized the exploitative rather than, as the functionalists had done, the harmonious nature of social relations. Marxists believe that most societies are characterized by an unequal distribution of resources and power. This imbalance creates a continual potential for conflict between those who are well off and those who are not. While the objective elements between oppressors and oppressed are a necessary condition for a Marxian revolution, they are not enough. The people on the bottom must feel deprived and sense that some drastic measures are needed to change this. Without such arousal, large populations remain enslaved and resigned to their fates. According to the Marxists, cultural evolution is characterized by a reordering of the means of production and distribution. This transformation is rarely smooth (as exemplified in the French Revolution of the late eighteenth century and the Russian Revolution of the early twentieth century), as those who prospered under the old system try to defend their status against those seeking to establish a new order.

Marxist thought entered contemporary anthropology in France in the late 1960s, when such scholars as Maurice Godelier (1977) and Claude Meillassoux (1981) sought to analyze the structure of tribal and peasant societies from a Marxist perspective, with emphasis on the economic basis of social organization in these societies. Within a short time, anthropologists in the English-speaking world also began to employ Marxist concepts, paying greater attention to historical developments and acknowledging the relevance of the world-system for understanding smaller social units.

Studies of Cognitive Structure

Whereas Marxists and neofunctionalists sought to explain the function of conflict in society, other schools of thought that began to emerge in the 1950s and early 1960s focused on the cognitive or mental structures that provide order to culture. Two different approaches to this effort are *structuralism* and *ethnoscience*. Despite their differences, both are heavily influenced by structural linguistics, the attempt to discover the structural principles underlying speech patterns.

STRUCTURALISM. The main proponent of the structural approach to the study of culture is French anthropologist Claude Levi-Strauss (b. 1908). In his view, the origin of the universal principles that order the ways we behave and think about the world is to be found in the structure of human thought. While his ideas have influenced the study of kinship and mythology, their usefulness is limited because they are largely untestable. Furthermore, they view societies as static and do little to explain variations among cultures.

Other structuralists have pursued the less ambitious task of trying to discover the structural operating principles of specific cultural systems. One of the leaders has been another French anthropologist, Louis Dumont (b. 1911). Dumont (1970) explained the caste system in India by reference to three structural principles in that society: separation, hierarchy, and interaction. The first is illustrated by the distinctive ritual statuses of each caste, the second by their being ranked, and the third by their interdependence in the performance of various tasks. Although this approach is useful in pointing out some of the cognitive underpinnings of social behavior, it does not explain why such principles exist, nor does it give a sense of their history. Furthermore, it largely ignores the adaptive dimension of culture because it fails to link underlying structural principles with the physical and social environment. For example, Dumont's study pays insufficient attention to the impact of political and economic competition on different segments of Indian society as well as to the role of British colonialism in transforming the caste system historically.

ETHNOSCIENCE. The search for the structural principles in specific societies has been refined by the largely American school of ethnoscience (sometimes known as *cognitive anthropology*). Ethnoscientists seek to discover the structural principles of specific cultures by analyzing ethnographic data in minute detail. Their main interest is in learning how people view the world—the manner in which members of a society perceive and structure their environment through language categories, and the rules and principles that guide their decision making.

An early example of ethnoscientific analysis is Conklin's (1955) study of the Hanunoo of the island of Mindanao in the Philippines. Conklin, for example, pointing out that not all cultures have the same system of color classification, examined how the Hanunoo perceived the color spectrum. As we saw in Chapter 3, cross-cultural studies of different systems of color categorization have provided insights into the interrelationships among the cultural, environmental, and physiological factors that determine color perception. While noting differences, ethnoscientists' studies of color perception also suggest that certain features of color classification systems are universal.

SYMBOLIC ANTHROPOLOGY. An approach similar to structuralism in its emphasis on the cognitive or ideological rather than material aspects of culture is known as *symbolic anthropology*. In this perspective, culture is viewed as a system of shared symbols and meanings.

A principal advocate of symbolic anthropology is American anthropologist Clifford Geertz (b. 1926). Instead of relying solely on people's statements about their culture, as ethnoscientists do, Geertz argues that the cultural meanings of rituals, myths, kinship, and the like need to be explored in terms of how they are actually used in the context of social life. In his analyses, Geertz focuses on significant cultural events and the cultural themes that he feels they exemplify. He analyzes Balinese cockfighting (1973), for example, as an embodiment of many of the fundamental themes of Balinese culture. He sees the etiquette of people attending the fights and the masculine symbolism of the roosters as public enactments of Balinese culture themes associated with poise, envy, brutality, status, pride, and chance. One striking aspect of

Geertz's view is that he sees culture as "disconnected." He does not view culture as a thoroughly integrated whole but as a collection of often very contradictory emotions, beliefs, and rules.

Anthropology itself is not an integrated whole. Throughout the course of its history, anthropology has been marked by a diversity of opinion and perspective. Given the scope of the undertaking—the study of the human condition, such differences are understandable, perhaps even inevitable. No single approach has a monopoly on the truth. Yet despite anthropologists' differing viewpoints, there is one driving force behind all anthropological thought—a continual striving for objectivity, for a view of the human condition that is as free as possible from ethnocentric bias.

SUGGESTED READINGS

Diamond, Stanley, editor. 1980. *Anthropology: Ancestors and Heirs.* The Hague: Mouton.

Harris, Marvin. 1968. *The Rise of Anthropological Theory.* New York: Crowell.

Hinsley, Curtis M., Jr. 1981. *Savages and Scientists: The Smithsonian Institution and the Development of American Anthropology (1846–1910).* Washington, DC: Smithsonian Institution Press.

Kuper, Adam. 1983. *Anthropologists and Anthropology: The Modern British School.* London: Routledge, Chapman and Hall.

Rosenberry, William. 1989. *Anthropologists and Histories: Essays in Culture, History, and Political Economy.* New Brunswick, NJ: Rutgers University Press.

Stocking, George W., Jr. 1984. *Observers and Observed: Essays on Ethnological Fieldwork.* History of Anthropology Series, Vol. 1. Madison: University of Wisconsin Press.

———. 1984. *Functionalism Historicized: Essays on British Social Anthropology.* History of Anthropology Series, Vol. 2. Madison: University of Wisconsin Press.

———. 1985. *Objects and Others: Essays on Museum and Material Culture.* History of Anthropology Series, Vol. 3. Madison: University of Wisconsin Press.

———. 1986. *Malinowski, Rivers, Benedict and Others: Essays on Culture and Personality.* History of Anthropology Series, Vol. 4. Madison: University of Wisconsin Press.

———. 1990. *Bones, Bodies and Behavior: Essays on Behavioral Anthropology.* History of Anthropology Series, Vol. 5. Madison: University of Wisconsin Press.

Thornton, Robert, and Peter Skalnik. 1993. *The Early Writings of Bronislaw Malinowski.* New York: Cambridge University Press.

Voget, Fred W. 1975. *A History of Ethnology.* New York: Holt, Rinehart and Winston.

Aberle, David F. 1961. "Matrilineal descent in cross-cultural perspective." In D. M. Schneider and K. Gough (editors), *Matrilineal Kinship:* 655–727. Berkeley: University of California Press.

———. 1966. *The Peyote Religion Among the Navaho.* Chicago: Aldine.

Achebe, Chinua. 1960. *No Longer at Ease.* New York: Obolensky.

Adams, Marie J. 1969. *Systems of Meaning in East Sumba Textile Design.* Southeast Asian Studies Cultural Reports No. 16. New Haven: Yale University.

Alam, Sultana. 1985. "Women and poverty in Bangladesh." *Women's Studies International Forum* 8(4): 361–371.

Amadi, Adolphe O. 1981. *African Libraries: Western Tradition and Colonial Brainwashing.* Metuchen, NJ: The Scarecrow Press.

Arnove, Robert F. 1981. "The Nicaraguan National Literacy Crusade of 1980" *Comparative Educational Review* 25 (June): 244–260.

Asad, Talal. 1970. *The Kababish Arabs: Power, Authority and Consent in a Nomadic Tribe.* London: Hurst.

Atchley, Robert C. 1988. *Social Forces and Aging.* Belmont, CA: Wadsworth Publishing Company.

Ayanga, Hazel. 1986. "Polygamy in the '80s." *Connexions* 20 (Spring): 8–10.

Baal, J. van. 1975. *Reciprocity and the Position of Women.* Assen, The Netherlands: Van Gorcum.

Baaran, Theodoor Pieter van. 1968. *Korwars and Korwar Style: Art and Ancestor Worship in North-West New Guinea.* The Hague and Paris: Mouton & Co.

Bailey, Frederick G. 1969. *Stratagems and Spoils: A Social Anthropology of Politics.* Oxford: Blackwell.

Bailey, Robert C., Genevieve Head, Mark Jenike, Bruce Owen, Robert Rechtman, and Elizabeth Zechenter. 1989. "Hunting and Gathering in Tropical Rain Forests: Is It Possible?" *American Anthropologist* 92:59–82.

Banerjee, Sumanta. 1992. "Uses of literacy: Total Literacy Campaign in three West Bengal districts." *Economic and Political Weekly,* 29 February: 445–449.

Bangkok Post. 1992. "Religion as a subject for sociology." *Economic and Political Weekly,* 29 August:1865–1870.

Barber, E.J.W. 1991. *Prehistoric Textiles: The Development of Cloth in the Neolithic and Bronze Ages with Special Reference to the Aegean.* Princeton, NJ: Princeton University Press.

Barker, David K. 1985. *Designs of Bhutan.* Bangkok: White Lotus.

Barnes, Ruth. 1989. *The Ikat Textiles of Lamalera: A Study of an Eastern Indonesian Weaving Tradition.* Leiden: E.J. Brill.

Barnet, Richard J., and John Cavangh. 1994. *Global Dreams: Imperial Corporations and the New World Order.* New York: Simon & Schuster.

Barnett, Homer G. 1953. *Innovation: The Basis of Cultural Change.* New York: McGraw-Hill.

Barrett, Leonard E. 1977. *The Rastafarians: The Dreadlocks of Jamaica.* Kingston: Sangster's/Heinemann.

Barth, Frederick. 1969. "Introduction." In F. Barth (editor), *Ethnic Groups and Boundaries:* 9–38. Bergen/Oslo: Universtetsforlaget/London: George Allen & Unwin.

Basilov, Vladimir N. (editor) 1989. *Nomads of Eurasia.* Los Angeles: Natural History Museum of Los Angeles County/Seattle: University of Washington Press.

Beattie, John. 1964. *Other Cultures: Aims, Methods and Achievements in Social Anthropology.* New York: Free Press.

Belshaw, Cyril S. 1965. *Traditional Exchange and Modern Markets.* Englewood Cliffs, NJ: Prentice-Hall.

Benedict, Ruth. 1934. *Patterns of Culture.* Boston: Houghton Mifflin.

————. 1946. *The Chrysanthemum and the Sword.* Boston: Houghton Mifflin.

Berlin, Brent, and Paul Kay. 1991. *Basic Color Terms: Their Universality and Evolution.* Berkeley: University of California Press.

Bernal, Ignacio. 1968. *3,000 Years of Art and Life in Mexico.* New York: Harry N. Adams.

Berndt, Ronald M. 1951. *Kunapipi.* Melbourne: Chesire.

————. 1965. "Law and order in Aboriginal Australia." In R. M. Berndt and C. H. Berndt (editors), *Aboriginal Man in Australia:* 167–206. Sydney: Angus and Robertson.

————. 1978. *Love Songs of Arnhem Land.* Chicago: University of Chicago Press.

————. and Catherine H. Berndt. 1982. *Aboriginal Australian Art: A Visual Perspective.* Sydney: Methuen Australia.

Berreman, Gerald. 1962. "Pahari polyandry: A comparison." *American Anthropologist* 64: 60–75.

————. 1972. *Hindus of the Himalayas: Ethnography and Change.* Berkeley: University of California Press.

Beteille, Andre. 1992. "Religion as a subject for sociology." *Economic and Political Weekly,* 29 August: 1865–1870.

Bhattacharji, Sukumari. 1991. "Economic rights of ancient Indian women." *Economic and Political Weekly,* 2–9 March: 507–512.

Bhola, Harbans S. 1981. "Why literacy can't wait: issues for the 1980's." *Convergence* 14(1): 6–22.

Bhowmik, Sharit K. 1992. "Caste and class in India." *Economic and Political Weekly,* 13–20 June: 1246–1248.

Bickerton, Derek. 1990. *Language and Species.* Chicago: University of Chicago Press.

Birdwhistell, Ray L. 1960. "Kinesics and communication." In E. Carpenter and M. McLuhan (editors), *Explorations in Communications:* 54–64. Boston: Beacon Press.

Blaug, M. 1966. "Literacy and economic development." *The School Review* 74(4): 393–415.

Bloch, Maurice. 1983. *Marxism and Anthropology.* Oxford: The Clarendon Press.

Bohannon, Laura, and Paul Bohannon. 1953. *The Tiv of Central Nigeria.* London: International African Institute.

Bohannon, Laura. 1966. "Shakespeare in the bush." *Natural History* 75 (Aug.–Sept.): 28–33.

Boissevain, Jeremy. 1974. *Friends of Friends: Networks, Manipulation and Coalitions.* Oxford: Blackwell.

Bolinger, Dwight. 1968. *Aspects of Language.* New York: Harcourt, Brace and World.

Boserup, Ester. 1981. *Population and Technological Change.* Chicago: University of Chicago Press.

Bossen, Laurel. 1984. *The Redivision of Labor: Women and Economic Choice in Your Guatemalan Communities.* Albany: State University of New York Press.

Brady, Ivan (editor). 1983. "Speaking in the name of the real: Freeman and Mead on Samoa." *American Anthropologist* 85(4): 908–947.

Brand, Michael. 1992. "Cultures and crossroads: The context of a collection." In G. Grayston (editor) *Cultures at Crossroads: Southeast Asian Textiles from the Australian National Gallery:* 2–5. Canberra: Australian National Gallery.

Brandl, E.J. 1973. *Australian Aboriginal Paintings in Western and Central Arnhem Land.* Canberra: Australian Institute of Aboriginal Studies.

Braverman, Harry. 1974. *Labor and Monopoly Capital.* New York: Monthly Review Press.

Briggs, Jean. 1970. *Never in Anger: Portrait of an Eskimo Family.* Cambridge: Harvard University Press.

Buchbinder, Georgeda, and Roy A. Rappaport. 1976. "Fertility and death among the Maring." In P. Brown and G. Buchbinder (editors), *Man and Woman in the New Guinea Highlands:* 13–35. Washington, DC: American Anthropological Association.

Burling, Robbins. 1974. *The Passage of Power: Studies in Political Succession.* New York: Academic Press

Burridge, Kenelm. 1969. *New Heaven New Earth: A Study of Millenarian Activities.* Oxford: Blackwell.

Calvin, Martin. 1978. *Keepers of the Game: Indian-Animal Relationships and the Fur Trade.* Berkeley: University of California Press.

Campbell, J. K. 1974. *Honour, Family, and Patronage: A Study of Institutions and Moral Values in a Greek Mountain Community.* New York: Oxford University Press.

Carpenter, Betsy. "The greening of the church." *U.S. News & World Report.* 27 November:1989, pp. 66–67.

Carrier, M. 1992. "Miguel: Sexual life history of a gay Mexican-American." In G. Herdt (editor) *Gay Culture in America*: 202–224. Boston: Beacon.

Carroll, Vern. 1970. "Adoption on Nukuoro." In V. Carroll (editor), *Adoption in Eastern Oceania*: 121–157. Honolulu: University of Hawaii Press.

Carter, J., R. Heath, R. Wilson, S. Sava, P. Sinnock, and D. Gohdes. 1989. "Tribal differences in diabetes: Prevalence among American Indians in New Mexico." *Public Health Report 104* (6):665–669.

Caruna, Wally. 1993. *Aboriginal Art.* New York: Thames and Hudson.

Cawte, John. 1974. *Medicine Is the Law: Studies in Psychiatric Anthropology of Australian Aboriginal Tribal Societies.* Honolulu: University of Hawaii Press.

Chagnon, Napoleon A. 1983. *Yanomamo: The Fierce People.* New York: Holt, Rinehart and Winston.

Chandler, Michele. 1986. "Widows ripped off." *Connexions* 20 (Spring): 14.

Chetley, Andrew. 1989. *Kill or Cure? The Global Pharmaceutical Industry.* Atlantic Highlands, NJ: Zed Press.

Chignell, A. K. 1911. *An Outpost in Papua.* London: Murray.

Chodorow, Nancy. 1974. "Family structure and feminine personality." In M. Rosaldo and L. Lamphere (editors), *Women in Culture and Society*: 45–56. Stanford: Stanford University Press.

Claessen, Henri J. M., and Pieter van de Velde. 1985. "The evolution of sociopolitical organi-zation." In H. J. M. Claessen, P. van de Velde, and M. E. Smith (editors), *Development and Decline: The Evolution of Sociopolitical Organization*: 1–12, 126–140, 196–218. South Hadley, MA: Bergin and Garvey.

———. 1987. "Introduction." In H. J. M. Claessen and P. van de Velde (editors), *Early State Dynamics*: 1–23. Leiden: E. J. Brill.

Clammer, John R. 1976. *Literacy and Social Change.* Leiden: E. J. Brill.

Clark, Margaret. 1970. *Health in the Mexican-American Culture: A Community Study.* Berkeley: University of California Press.

Cohen, Abner. 1969. *Custom and Politics in Urban Africa.* Berkeley: University of California Press.

Cohen, Margot. 1990. "A menu for malnutrition." *Far Eastern Economic Review,* 12 July: 38–39.

Cohen, Mark Nathan. 1989. *Health and the Rise of Civilization.* New Haven: Yale University Press.

Colson, Anthony C., and Karen F. Selby. 1974. "Survey article on medical anthropology." *Annual Review of Anthropology* 3: 245–262.

Conklin, H.C. 1955. "Hanunoo color categories." *Southwestern Journal of Anthropology* 11: 339–344.

Cook, Carolyn. 1988. "Traditional tribal land tenure and the effects of development: A case study of the Amung-me of Irian Jaya, Indonesia." M.A. thesis, Washington State University.

Cooper, Robert L. 1989. *Language Planning and Social Change.* New York: Cambridge University Press.

Cordry, Donald. 1980. *Mexican Masks.* Austin: University of Texas Press.

Covarrubias, Miguel. 1954. *The Eagle, the Jaguar and the Serpent: Indian Art of the Americas.* New York: Alfred A. Knopf.

Crambs, Jean D. 1989. *Women over Forty: Visions and Realities.* New York: Springer Publishing Company.

Crane, Julia, and Michael Angrosino. 1974. *Field Projects in Anthropology: A Student Handbook.* Glenview, IL: Scott, Foresman.

Cranstone, B. A. L. 1984. *The General's Gift: A Celebration of the Pitt Rivers Museum Centenary,* 1884–1984. Oxford: Journal of the Anthropological Society of Oxford.

Crawford, I.M. 1968. *The Art of the Wandjina.* Melbourne: Oxford University Press.

Crosby, Alfred, Jr. 1972. *The Columbian Exchange: Biological and Cultural Consequences of 1492.* Westport, CT: Greenwood Press.

Culbert, Sidney S. (editor). 1991. *The World Almanac and Book of Facts.* New York: Newspaper Enterprise Association.

Curr, E. M. 1886–1887. *The Australian Race.* 4 volumes. Melbourne: Government Printer.

Curtain, Philip D. 1990. *The Rise and Fall of the Plantation Complex: Essays in Atlantic History.* New York: Cambridge University Press.

Dagmar, Hans. 1978. *Aborigines and Poverty: A Study of Interethnic Relations and Culture Conflict in a Western Australian Town.* Nijmegen, Netherlands: Katholieke Universitiet.

Dahl, Gudrum. 1987. "Women in pastoral production: Some theoretical notes on roles and resources." *Ethnos* 52(1–2): 246–279.

Damas, David. 1972. "The Copper Eskimo." In M. G. Bicchieri (editor), *Hunters and Gatherers Today:* 3–50. New York: Holt, Rinehart and Winston.

Datta, V. N. 1988. *Sati: A Historical, Social and Philosophical Enquiry into the Hindu Rite of Widow Burning.* New Delhi: Manohar.

Davis, D. L., and R. G. Whitten. 1987. "The cross-cultural study of human sexuality." *Annual Review of Anthropology* 16: 69–68.

Dearden, Philip. 1992. "Tourism and development in Southeast Asia: Some challenges for the future." In A. Pongsapich, M. Howard, and J. Amyot, *Regional Development and Change in Southeast Asia in the 1990s.* Bangkok, Thailand: Chulalongkorn University Social Research Institute.

DeCamp, David. 1971. "Introduction: the study of pidgin and creole languages." In D. Hymes (editor), *Pidginization and Creolization of Languages:* 13–39. New York: Cambridge University Press.

Degregori, Carlos Ívan. 1990. *El Surgimiento de Sendero Luminosos.* Lima: Instituto de Estudios Peruanas. [1992, Chapel Hill, NC: University of North Carolina Press.]

Dentan, Robert. 1968. *The Semai: A Nonviolent People of Malaya.* New York: Holt, Rinehart and Winston.

Dicken, Peter. 1992. *Global Shift: The Internationalization of Economic Activity,* 2d ed. New York: The Guilford Press.

Dissanayake, Ellen. 1992. *Homo Aestheticus: Where Art Comes From and Why.* New York: The Free Press.

Divale, William, and Marvin Harris. 1976. "Population, warfare and the male supremist complex." *American Anthropologist* 78: 521–538.

Dobbs, Michael. 1987. "In Iraq, one of the world's earliest civilizations is pushed to the brink of extinction." *International Herald Tribune,* 12 December: 5.

Dobzansky, Theodosius. 1974. "Chance and creativity in evolution." In F. J. Ayala and T. Dobzansky (editors), *Studies in the Philosophy of Biology:* 309–339. Berkeley: University of California Press.

Domhoff, G. William. 1974. *The Bohemian Grove and Other Retreats: A Study in Ruling Class Cohesiveness.* New York: Harper and Row.

Draper, P. 1975. "! Kung Women: Contrasts in sexual egalitarianism in foraging and sedentary contexts." In R. Reiter (editor); *Toward an Antropology of Women:* 77–109. New York: Monthly Review Press.

DuBois, Cora. 1960. *The People of Alor: A Social-Psychological Study of an East Indian Island.* New York: Harper & Row.

Dumont, Louis. 1970. *Homo Hierarchicus: The Caste System and Its Implications.* London: Weidenfield and Nicolson.

Dunham, Carroll. 1993. "The Many Husbands of Tsering Zangmo." *Discovery,* January:80–86.

Dunn, Frederick I. 1968. "Epidemiological factors: health and disease in hunter-gatherers." In R. B. Lee and I. DeVore (editors), *Man the Hunter:* 221–228. Chicago: Aldine-Atherton.

Durant, Will. 1939. *The Life of Greece.* New York: Simon and Schuster.

Durkheim, Emile. 1951. *Suicide: A Study in Society.* Glencoe, IL: Free Press.

Duvignaud, Jean. 1970. *Change at Shebika: Report from a North African Village.* New York: Random House.

Economist. 1993–94. "Russia's secret cities." 25 December–7 January: 65–68.

Economist. 1993b. "Trouble on the farm." 7 August: 681–62.

Edwards, Robert. 1979. *Australian Aboriginal Art: The Art of the Alligator Rivers Region, Northern Territory.* Canberra: Australian Institute of Aboriginal Studies.

Eggan, Fred. 1950. *Social Organization of the Western Pueblos.* Chicago: University of Chicago Press.

Eidheim, Harald. 1971. *Aspects of the Lappish Minority Situation.* Bergen/Oslo: Universtetsforlaget.

Elmberg, John-Erik. 1968. *Balance and Circulation: Aspects of Tradition and Change Among the Mejprat of Irian Barat.* Stockholm: Etnografiska Museet.

Elwood, J. M. 1989. "Epidemiology and control of melanoma in white populations and in Japan." *Journal of Investigative Dermatology* 92 (5 Suppl.): 214–221.

Epstein, A. L. 1969. *Matupit: Land, Politics, and Change Among the Tolai of New Britain.* Berkeley: University of California Press. Oxford: Clarendon Press.

Evans-Pritchard, E. E. 1937. *Witchcraft, Oracles and Magic Among the Azande.* Oxford: Oxford University Press.

———. 1940. *The Nuer: A Description of the Modes of Livelihood and Political Institutions of a Nilotic People.* Oxford: Oxford University Press.

———. 1970. "Sexual inversion among the Azande." *American Anthropologist.* 72(6): 1428–34. Oxford: Oxford University Press.

Eysenck, Hans J., and R. Grossarth-Maticek. 1989. "Prevention of cancer and coronary heart disease and the reduction of the cost of the National Health Service." *Journal of Social,* Political and Economic Studies 14 (Spring): 25–47.

Fabrega, Horacio, Jr., and Daniel B. Silver. 1973. *Illness and Shamanistic Curing in Zinacantan.* Stanford: Stanford University Press.

Falloux, Francois, and Lee Talbot. 1993. *Crisis and Opportunity: Environment and Development in Africa.* London: Earthscan.

Farwell, Byron. 1990. *Burton: A Biography of Sir Richard Francis Burton.* New York: Viking Penguin.

Ferguson, Charles. 1959. "Diglossia." *Word* 15: 325–340.

Fernandez, John P. , with Mary Barr. 1993. *The Diversity Advantage: How American Business Can Out-Perform Japanese and European Companies in the Global Marketplace.* New York: Lexington Books.

First, Ruth. 1975. *Libya: The Elusive Revolution.* New York: Holmes and Meier.

Forde, C. Daryll. 1964. *Yakö Studies.* London: Oxford University Press.

Fortes, Meyer. 1958. "Introduction." In J. Goody (editor), *The Developmental Cycle in Domestic Groups.* Cambridge: Cambridge University Press.

Foster, George M. 1965. "Peasant society and the image of the limited good." *American Anthropologist* 67: 293–315.

Foster, George M., and Barbara G. Anderson. 1978. *Medical Anthropology.* New York: John Wiley.

Foster, Phillips. 1992. *The World Food Problem: Tackling the Causes of Undernutrition in the Third World.* Boulder, CO: Lynne Rienner.

Foulks, Edward F. 1985. "The transformation of Arctic hysteria." In R. Simons and C. Hughes (editors), *The Culture-Bound Syndromes:* 307–324. Boston: D. Reidel.

Fouts, Roger, and Richard I. Budd. 1979. "Artificial and human language acquisition in the chimpanzees." In D. A. Hamburg and E. R. McCown (editors), *The Great Apes:* 375–392. Menlo Park, CA: Cummings.

Fowler, Marian. 1993. *In a Gilded Cage: From Heiress to Duchess.* New York: Random House.

Fraenkel, M. 1964. *Tribe and Caste in Monrovia.* London: Oxford University Press.

Fraser, Douglas (editor.). 1966. *The Many Faces of Primitive Art: A Critical Anthology.* Englewood Cliffs, NJ: Prentice-Hall.

Freeman, J. D. 1983. *Margaret Mead in Samoa.* Cambridge: Harvard University Press.

Fried, Jacob. 1959. "Acculturation and mental health among Indian migrants in Peru." In M. K. Opler (editor), *Culture and Mental Health:* 119–137. New York: Macmillan.

Furst, Peter T. (editor). 1972. *Flesh of the Gods: The Ritual Use of Hallucinogens.* London: George Allen and Unwin.

Gajdusek, D. C. 1977. "Unconventional viruses and the origin and disappearance of kuru." *Science* 197: 943–960.

Galbraith, John K. 1977. *The Age of Uncertainty.* Boston: Houghton Mifflin.

Gardner, Robert G., and Karl Heider. 1969. *Gardens of War: Life and Death in the New Guinea Stone Age.* New York: Random House.

Geertz, Clifford. 1973. *The Interpretation of Cultures.* New York: Basic Books.

Geirnaert-Martin, Danielle C. 1992. *The Woven Land of Laboya: Socio-cosmic Ideas and Values in West Sumba, Eastern Indonesia.* CNWS Publications No. 11. Leiden: Centre of Non-Western Studies, Leiden University.

Gelb, Ignace J. 1963. *A Study of Writing,* rev. ed. Chicago: University of Chicago Press.

Gittinger, Mattiebelle. 1972. "A Study of the ship cloths of South Sumatra: Their design and usage." Ph.D. dissertation, Columbia University.

Glasse, R. M. 1969. "Marriage in South Fore." In R. M. Glasse and M. J. Meggit (editors), *Pigs, Pearlshells and Women:* 16–37. Englewood Cliffs, NJ: Prentice-Hall.

Gluckman, Max. 1949. *Malinowski's Sociological Theories.* Rhodes-Livingstone Papers No. 16. Oxford.

———. 1950. "Kinship and marriage among the Lozi of Northern Rhodesia and the Zulu of Natal." In A. R. Radcliffe-Brown and C. D. Forde (editors), *African Systems of Kinship and Marriage:* 166–206. London: Oxford University Press.

———. 1956. *Custom and Conflict in Africa.* Oxford: Blackwell.

———. 1965. *Politics, Law and Ritual in Tribal Society.* Chicago: Aldine.

———. 1973. *The Judicial Process Among the Barotse of Northern Rhodesia (Zambia).* Manchester: Manchester University Press.

Godelier, Maurice. 1977. *Perspectives in Marxist Anthropology.* New York: Cambridge University Press.

Goldstein, Joshua S. 1994. *International Relations.* New York: HarperCollins College Publishers.

Goodale, Jane C. 1971. *Tiwi Wives: A Study of the Women of Melville Island, North Australia.* Seattle: University of Washington Press.

Goodall, Jane. 1964. "Tool using and aimed throwing in a community of free-living chimpanzees." *Nature* 201: 1264–1266.

Goodenough, Ward H. 1949. "Premarital freedom on Truk: theory and practice." *American Anthropologist* 54: 615–620.

Gooding, Kenneth. 1992. "Aids seen as hitting output from African copperbelt." *Financial Times,* 23 January: 27.

Goodland, Robert, and Howard Irwin. 1975. *Amazon Jungle: Green Hell to Red Desert?* New York: Elsevier.

Goody, Jack R. 1959. "The mother's brother and sister's son in West Africa." *Journal of the Royal Anthropological Institute* 89: 61–88.

———. 1968. "Introduction." In J. R. Goody (editor), *Literacy in Traditional Societies:* 1–26. Cambridge: Cambridge University Press.

———. 1970. "Cousin terms." *Southwestern Journal of Anthropology* 26: 125–142.

Graburn, Nelson. 1976. "Introduction." In N. Graburn (editor), *Ethnic and Tourist Arts:* 1–32. Berkeley: University of California Press.

Greub, Suzanne (editor). 1992. *Art of Northwest New Guinea.* New York: Rizzoli

Groger-Wurm, H.M. 1973a. *Australian Aboriginal Bark Paintings and their Mythological Interpretation: Eastern Arnhem Land.* Canberra: Australian Institute of Aboriginal Studies.

Gumerman, George J. (editor). 1988. *The Anasazi in a Changing Environment.* New York: Cambridge University Press.

Gumperz, John. 1962. "Types of linguistic communities." *Anthropological Linguistics* 4: 28–40.

Haddon, A. C. 1937. *The Canoes of Melanesia, Queensland, and New Guinea.* Honolulu: B. P. Bishop Museum.

Haddon, A.C., and A.H. Quiggin. 1910. *History of Anthropology.* London: Watts & Co.

———, and L.E. Start. 1982. *Iban or Sea Dayak Fabrics and Their Patterns.* Carlton, Bedford: Ruth Bean.

Hagesteijn, Renée. 1987. "The Angkor state: rise, fall and in between." In H. J. M. Claessen and P. van de Velde (editors), *Early State Dynamics:* 154–169. Leiden: E. J. Brill.

Hall, Edward T. 1966. *The Hidden Dimension.* Garden City, NY: Doubleday.

Hall, P. and P. Preston 1988. *The Carrier Wave: New Information Technology and the Geography of Innovation, 1946–2003.* London: Unwin Hyman.

Hanks, Lucien M. 1972. *Rice and Man: Agricultural Ecology in Southeast Asia.* Honolulu: University of Hawaii Press.

Harden, Blaine. 1991. *Africa: Dispatches from a Fragile Continent.* New York: HarperCollins.

Haring, Douglas. 1949. *Personal Character and Cultural Milieu.* Syracuse: Syracuse University Press.

Harner, Michael J. (editor). 1973. *Hallucinogens and Shamanism.* New York: Oxford University Press.

Hart, C. W. M., and A. R. Pilling. 1979. *The Tiwi of North Australia.* New York: Holt, Rinehart and Winston.

Heath, G.W., R.H. Wilson, J. Smith, and B.E. Leonard. 1991. "Community-based exercise and weight control: Diabetes risk reduction and glycemic control in Zuni Indians." *American Journal of Clinical Nutrition* 53 (6 Supplement):1642S–1646S.

Heider, Karl. 1970. *The Dugum Dani: A Papuan Culture in the Highlands of West New Guinea.* Chicago: Aldine.

Helms, Mary W. 1976. "Competition, power and succession to office in pre-Columbian Panama." In M. W. Helmds and F. O. Loveland (editors), *Frontier Adaptation in Lower Central America:* 25–36. Philadelphia: Institute for the Study of Human Issues.

Henry, Donald O. 1988. *From Foraging to Agriculture.* Philadelphia: University of Pennsylvania Press.

Henry, Jules. 1963. *Culture Against Man.* New York: Random House.

———. (editor) 1984. *Ritualized Homosexuality in Melanesia.* Berkeley: University of California Press.

Heston, Alan. 1971. "An approach to the sacred cow of India." *Current Anthropology* 12: 191–209.

Hiatt, Les R. (editor). 1975. *Australian Aboriginal Mythology.* Canberra: Australian Institute of Aboriginal Studies.

Hicks, Frederick. 1979. "Flowery war in Aztec history." *American Ethnologist* 6: 87–92.

Hoebel, E. Adamson. 1940. *The Political Organization and Law-ways of the Commanche Indians. Memoir 54.* Menasha, WI: American Anthropological Association.

———. 1978. *The Cheyenne Indians of the Great Plains.* New York: Holt, Rinehart and Winston.

Hogbin, Ian. 1970. *The Island of Menstruating Men: Religion in Wogeo, New Guinea.* Scranton, PA: Chandler.

Holm, John. 1989. *Pidgins and Creoles, Volume II: Reference Survey.* New York: Cambridge University Press.

Holmgren, Robert J., and Anita E. Spertus. 1989. *Early Indonesian Textiles from Three Island Cultures: Sumba, Toraja, Lampung.* New York: The Metropolitan Museum of Art.

Holtved, Erik. 1967. "Eskimo shamanism." In C. M. Edsman (editor), *Studies in Shamanism:* 23–31. Stockholm: Almquist and Wiksell.

Holy, Ladislav. 1991. *Religion and Custom in a Muslim Society: The Berti of Sudan.* New York: Cambridge University Press.

Honigmann, John J. 1970. "Sampling in ethnographic fieldwork." In R. Naroll and R. Cohen (editors), *Handbook of Method in Cultural Anthropology:* 266–281. New York: Columbia University Press.

Hoogerbrugge, Jac. 1977. *The Art of Woodcarving in Irian Jaya.* Rotterdam: Asmat Art Depot.

———. 1992. *Maro Paintings of Lake Sentani and Humboldt Bay.* In S. Greub (editor) Art of Northwest New Guinea: 127–139. New York: Rizzoli.

Horwood, Harold. 1969. *Newfoundland.* Toronto: Macmillan of Canada.

Hough, Richard A. 1972. *Captain Bligh and Mr. Christian: The Men and the Mutiny.* London: Hutchinson.

Howard, Michael C. 1977. *Political Change in a Mayan Village in Southern Belize.* Greeley: Katunob, University of Northern Colorado.

———. 1980. "Ethnicity and economic integration in southern Belize." *Ethnicity* 7: 119–136.

———. 1981. *Aboriginal Politics in Southwestern Australia.* Nedlands: University of Western Australia Press.

———. 1987. *The Impact of the International Mining Industry on Indigenous Peoples.* Sydney: Transnational Corporations Research Project, University of Sydney.

———. 1991a. *Fiji: Race and Politics in an Island State.* Vancouver: University of British Columbia Press.

———. 1991b. *Mining, Politics, and Development in the South Pacific.* Boulder, CO: Westview Press.

———, (editor). 1993. *Asia's Environmental Crisis.* Boulder, CO: Westview Press.

———. 1994a. *Textiles of Southeast Asia: An Annotated and Illustrated Bibliography.* Bangkok: White Lotus.

———. 1994b. "An artist of two worlds." *Asian Art News* 4 (2):64–66.

Hsu, Francis L.K. 1984. *Rugged Individualism Reconsidered.* Knoxville: University of Tennesee Press.

Hughes, Charles C., and John M. Hunter. 1972. "Disease and development in Africa." *Social Science and Medicine* 3: 143–193.

Hume, David. 1748. "Of national characters." In *Essays: Moral, Political, and Literary: Essay 21.* London: A. Millar.

Hunt, Edward E., Jr. 1978. "Ecological frameworks and hypothesis testing in medical anthropology." In M. H. Logan and E. H. Hunt, Jr. (editors), *Health and the Human Condition:* 84–99. North Scituate, MA: Duxbury Press.

Hutheesing, Otome Klein. 1990. *Emerging Sexual Inequality Among the Lisu of Northern Thailand.* Leiden: E.J. Brill.

Hvalkof, Søren, and Peter Aaby (editors). 1981. *Is God an American?* Copenhagen: International Work Group for Indigenous Affairs.

Hymes, Dell. 1972. "Models of the interaction of language and social life." In J. J. Gumperz and D. Hymes (editors), *Directions in Sociolinguistics:* 35–71. New York: Holt, Rinehart and Winston.

Ignatius, Adi. 1990. "Secrets of Bama: in a corner of China, they live to be 100." *Wall Street Journal,* 19 March: A1.

Ishige, Neomichi. 1977. "Roasting dog in earth oven (Ponape)." In J. Kuper (editor), *The Anthropologists' Cookbook:* 203–205. New York: Universe Books.

James, Wendy. 1973. "The anthropologist as reluctant imperialist." In T. Asad (editor), *Anthropology and the Colonial Encounter:* 41–70. London: Ithaca Press.

Jansen, G. 1973. *The Doctor-Patient Relationship in an African Tribal Society.* Assen: Van Gorcum.

Johnson, William. 1993. "Native leaders out of touch with the reality of their people, survey shows." *Vancouver Sun,* 2 July: A4.

Jones, Delmos. 1971. "Social responsibility and the belief in basic research: an example from Thailand." *Current Anthropology* 12: 347–350.

Joseph, Ammu. 1991. "Political parties and 'sati.'" *Economic and Political Weekly,* 20 April: 1025–1026.

Kanato, Manop. 1990. "Becoming 'opportunistic' commercial sex workers: An anthropological-epidemiological study." M.Sc. thesis, McMaster University.

Karp, Jonathan. 1993. "Torting in tongues." *Far Eastern Economic Review,* 8 July: 18.

Kauffmann, Hans Eberhard. 1972. "Some social and religious institutions of the Lawa (Northwest Thailand), Part I." *Journal of the Siam Society* 60:237–306.

Kaut, C. R. 1957. *The Western Apache Clan System: Its Origins and Development.* Albuquerque: University of New Mexico Press.

Kay, Paul, and Chad K. McDaniel. 1978. "The linguistic significance of the meanings of basic color terms." *Language* 54: 610–646.

Kelly, R.C. 1976. "Witchcraft and sexual relations: An exploration in the social and semantic implications of the structure of belief." In *Man and Woman in the New Guinea Highlands,* (editors). P. Brown and G. Buchbinder, 36–53. Special Publication, no. 8. Washington, DC: American Anthropological Association.

Kennedy, E.L., and M.D. Davis. 1993. *Boots of Leather, Slippers of Gold: The History of a Lesbian Community.* New York: Routledge.

Kennedy, Helena. 1992. *Eve Was Framed: Women and British Justice.* London: Chatto and Windus.

Kennedy, John G. 1973. "Cultural psychiatry." In J.J. Honigmann (editor), *Handbook of Social and Cultural Anthropology:* 1119–1120. Chicago: Rand McNally.

Kinross, Louise. 1992. "Inuit vote to change face of the Arctic: Nunavut native first to gain self-government." *The Financial Post,* 17 November: 23.

Kirch, Patrick V. 1989. "Prehistory." In Alan Howard and Robert Borofsky, (editors). *Developments in Polynesian Ethnology.* Honolulu: University of Hawaii Press.

Kolosi, Tamás, and Edmund Wnuk-Lipinski (editors). 1983. *Equality and Inequality Under Socialism: Poland and Hungary Comparison.* Beverly Hills, CA: Sage.

Komin, Suntaree. 1993. "A social analysis of the environmental problems in Thailand." In

Howard, Michael C., (editor), *Asia's Environmental Crisis.* Boulder, CO: Westview Press.

Kooijman, Simon. 1959. *The Art of Lake Sentani.* New York: Museum of Primitive Art.

Kotkin, Joel. 1993. *Tribes: How Race, Religion and Identity Determine Success in the New Global Economy.* New York: Random House.

Krishnaraj, Maithreyi. 1992. "Women craft workers as security for family subsistence." *Economic and Political Weekly,* 25 April: WS17.

Kroeber, Arthur R. 1989. "Half man, half woman." *Far Eastern Economic Review,* 2 March: 76.

Kubota, Gary T. 1994. "Lanai families sinking since pineapple era." *Honolulu Star-Bulletin,* 1 July: A1, A6.

Kuhn, Thomas S. 1970. *The Structure of Scientific Revolutions.* Chicago: University of Chicago Press.

Kunstadter, Peter. 1966. "Residential and social organization of the Lawa of Northern Thailand." *Southwestern Journal of Anthropology* 22:61–84.

Lambert, Wallace E., et al. 1960. "Evaluational reactions to spoken languages." *Journal of Abnormal Psychology* 66: 44–51.

Langness, L. L. 1969. "Marriage in Bena Bena." In R. M. Glasse and M. J. Meggitt (editors), *Pigs, Pearlshells and Women:* 38–55. Englewood Cliffs, NJ: Prentice-Hall.

Lanternari, Vittorio. 1963. *The Religions of the Oppressed: A Study of Modern Messianic Cults.* New York: Alfred A. Knopf.

Laracy, Hugh. 1983. *The Maasina Rule Movement.* Suva: Institute of Pacific Studies, University of the South Pacific.

Layton, Robert. 1991. *The Anthropology of Art.* New York: Cambridge University Press.

Leach, Jerry, and Edmund Leach (editors). 1983. *The Kula: New Perspectives on Massim Exchange.* New York: Cambridge University Press.

Leacock, Eleanor, and Helen Safa (editors). 1986. *Women's Work: Development and the Division of Labor by Gender.* South Hadley, MA: Bergin and Garvey.

Leacock, Eleanor. 1982. "Marxism and anthropology." In B. Ollman and E. Vernoff (editors),

The Left Academy: 242–276. New York: McGraw-Hill.

Lee, Richard. 1969. "Eating Christmas in the Kalahari." *Natural History* 78 (December): 14–22, 60–63.

Levi-Strauss, Claude. 1961. *Triste Tropiques: An Anthropological Study of Primitive Societies in Brazil.* New York: Hutchinson.

———. 1969. *The Elementary Structures of Kinship.* Boston: Beacon Press.

Levine, Nancy E. 1988. *The Dynamics of Polyandry: Kinship Domesticity, and Population on the Tibetan Border.* Chicago: University of Chicago Press.

Lewis, Oscar. 1966. "The culture of poverty." *Scientific American* 215: 19–25.

Lewis, Phillip H. 1969. *The Social Context of Art in Northern New Ireland.* Chicago: Field Museum of Natural History.

Lewis, William. 1993. *Soul Rebels: The Rastafarians.* Prospect Heights, IL: Waveland Press.

Lieban, Richard W. 1962. "Qualifications for folk medicinal practice in Sibulan, Negros Oriental, Philippines." *The Philippine Journal of Science* 91: 511–521.

Lienhardt, Godfrey. 1961. *Divinity and Experience: The Religion of the Dinka.* Oxford: Clarendon Press.

Lieten, G.K. 1992. "Literacy in post-land reform village." *Economic and Political Weekly,* 18 January:103–109.

Linden, Eugene. 1991. "Lost tribes, lost knowledge." *Time,* 23 September: 44–56.

Lindenbaum, Shirley. 1979. *Kuru Sorcery: Disease and Danger in the New Guinea Highlands.* Palo Alto, CA: Mayfield.

Lindenbaum. S. 1972. "Sorcerers, ghosts, and polluting women: An analysis of religious belief and population control." *Ethnology* 11: 241– 253.

Linnaeus, Carolus. 1758–1759. *Systema Naturae per Regna tria Naturae, Secundum Classes, Ordenes, Genera, Species, cum Characteribuus Differentis* . . . 10th ed. Holmiae: L. Salvii.

Little, Kenneth. 1965/66. "The political functions of the Poro." *Africa* 35: 349–365; 36: 62–72.

Lommel, Andres. 1981. *Masks: Their Meaning and Function.* London: Ferndale Editions.

Long, Norman. 1975. "Structural dependency, modes of production and economic brokerage in rural Peru." In I. Oxaal, T. Barnett, and D. Booth (editors), *Beyond the Sociology of Development:* 253–282. London: Routledge and Kegan Paul.

Lyon, David. 1988. *The Information Society: Issues and Illusions.* Cambridge: Polity Press.

Maclean, Una. 1971. *Magical Medicine: A Nigerian Case-Study.* New York: Penguin.

Maddock, Kenneth. 1972. *The Australian Aborigines: A Portrait of Their Society.* London: Allan Lane.

Madsen, William. 1967. "Religious syncretism." In R. Wauchope (editor), *Handbook of Middle American Indians,* vol. 6: 369–391. Austin: University of Texas Press.

Malefijt, Annemarie de Waal. 1968. *Religion and Culture: An Introduction to Anthropology of Religion.* New York: Macmillan.

Malinowski, Bronislaw. 1929. *The Sexual Life of the Savages in Northwestern Melanesia.* London: Routledge and Kegan Paul.

———. 1992. *Argonauts of the Western Pacific.* London: Routledge & Kegan Paul.

Marett, Robert R. 1909. *The Threshold of Religion.* London: Methuen.

Mariner, William. 1827. *An Account of the Natives of the Tonga Islands, in the Pacific Ocean.* 2 volumes. London: Hurst, Chance.

Marshall, Lorna. 1961. "Sharing, talking, and giving: relief of social tensions among !Kung Bushmen." *Africa* 31: 231–249.

Martin, Calvin. 1978. *Keepers of the Game: Indian-Animal Relationships and the Fur Trade.* Berkeley, CA: University of California Press.

Martin, M. K. 1974. *The Foraging Adaptation—— Uniformity or Diversity?* Reading, MA: Addison-Wesley.

Martin, M. Kay, and Barbara Voorhies. 1975. *Female of the Species.* New York: Columbia University Press.

Martinez-Alier, Verena. 1974. *Marriage, Class and Colour in Nineteenth-Century Cuba.* New York: Cambridge University Press.

Maybury-Lewis, David. 1968. *The Savage and the Innocent.* Boston: Beacon Press.

McLean, Scilla, and Stella Efua Graham (editors). 1985. *Female Circumcision, Excision and Infibulation: The Facts and Proposals for Change.* London: Minority Rights Group.

McLuhan, Marshall and Bruce R. Powers 1989. *The Global Village: Transformation in World Life and Media in the 21st Century.* New York: Oxford University Press.

McWilliams, Cary. 1961. *North from Mexico.* Philadelphia: J. B. Lippincott.

Mead, Margaret. 1928. *Coming of Age in Samoa.* New York: Morrow.

———. 1947. "The concept of culture and the psychosomatic approach." *Psychiatry* 10: 57–76.

———. 1967. "Alternatives to war." In M. Fried, M. Harris, and R. Murphy (editors), *War:* 215–228. Garden City, NY: Doubleday.

Meggitt, Mervyn J. 1962. *Desert People: A Study of the Walbiri Aborigines of Central Australia.* Sydney Angus and Robertson.

———. 1977. *Blood Is Their Argument: Warfare Among the Mae Enga Tribesmen of the New Guinea Highlands.* Palo Alto, CA: Mayfield.

Meillassoux, Claude. 1981. *Maidens, Meal and Money.* New York: Cambridge University Press.

Meintel, Deidre. 1973. "Strangers, homecomers, and ordinary men." *Anthropological Quarterly* 46: 47–58.

Melotti, Umberto. 1977. *Marx and the Third World.* London: Macmillan.

Melrose, D. 1982. *Bitter Pills: Medicines and the Third World.* Oxford: Oxfam.

Melville, Thomas. 1981. "Guatemala: The Indian awakening." *ARC Newsletter* 5 (2): 1.

Mengham, Roderick. 1993. *On Language: Descent from the Tower of Babel.* Boston: Little, Brown.

Migdal, Joel S. 1968. *Peasants, Politics, and Revolution: Pressures towards Political and Social Change in the Third World.* Princeton, NJ Princeton University Press.

Millar, Susan Bolyard. 1989. *Bugis Weddings: Rituals of Social Location in Modern Indonesia.* Berkeley: University of California at Berkeley, Center for South and Southeast Asia Studies.

Mink, Barbara. 1989. "How modernization affects women." *Cornell Alumni News,* III (3): 10–11.

Mitchell, J. Clyde. 1969. "The concept and use of social networks." In J. C. Mitchell (editor), *Social Networks in Urban Situations:* 1–50. Manchester: Manchester University Press.

Mörner, Magnus. 1967. *Race Mixture in the History of Latin America.* Boston: Little, Brown.

Mooney, James. 1965. *The Ghost-Dance Religion and the Sioux Outbreak of 1890.* Chicago: University of Chicago Press.

Moorehead, Alan. 1960. *The White Nile.* New York: Harper and Brothers.

Morgan, Lewis H. 1877. *Ancient Society.* New York: Henry Holt.

Morris, Desmond, Peter Collett, Porter Marsh, and Marie O'shaughnessy. 1979. *Gestures, Their Origins and Distribution.* New York: Stein and Day.

Motolinía de Benavente. Toribio. 1950. *Motolinía's History of the Indians of New Spain.* Translated by Elizabeth A. Foster. Berkeley: The Cortés Society.

Mouer, Ross, and Yoshio Sugimoto. 1986. *Images of Japanese Society.* London: KPI.

Muller, M. 1982. *The Health of Nations: A North-South Investigation.* London: Faber and Faber.

Munson, Henry. 1989. *Islam and Revolution in the Middle East.* New Haven: Yale University Press.

Murphy, Yolanda, and Robert F. Murphy. 1974. *Women of the Forest.* New York: Columbia University Press.

Myerhoff, Barbara. 1970. "The deer-maize-peyote symbol complex among the Huichol Indians of Mexico." *Anthropological Quarterly* 39 (2): 60–72.

———. 1974. *Peyote Hunt: The Sacred Journey of the Huichol Indians.* Ithaca: Cornell University Press.

————. 1978. *Number Our Days.* New York: Simon and Schuster.

Myers, Fred R. 1982. "Ideology and experience: the cultural basis of politics in Pintupi life." In M. C. Howard (editor), *Aboriginal Power in Australian Society:* 79–114. Honolulu: University of Hawaii Press.

Nanda, Serena. 1990. *Neither Man nor Woman: The Hijaras of India.* Belmont, CA: Wadsworth Publishing.

Nankivell, Neville. 1992. "Sony chief takes shot at U.S. executives." *Financial Post,* 5 February:7.

Nash, Dennison. 1963. "The ethnologist as stranger." *Southwestern Journal of Anthropology* 19: 149–167.

Nash, June, and Helen Safa (editors). 1986. *Women and Change in Latin America.* South Hadley, MA: Bergin and Garvey.

Nash, Robert Frazier. 1989. *The Rights of Nature: A History of Environmental Ethics.* Madison: University of Wisconsin.

Newman, Philip L. 1965. *Knowing the Gururumba.* New York: Holt, Rinehart and Winston.

Newton, E. 1993. *Cherry Grove, Fire Island: Sixty Years in America's First Gay and Lesbian Town.* Boston: Beacon.

Ng, Cecilia. 1987. "The Weaving of prestige: Village women's representations of the social categories of Minangkabau society." Ph.D. dissertation, Australian National University.

Niessen, Sandra A. 1993. *Batak Cloth and Clothing: A Dynamic Indonesian Tradition.* Kuala Lumpur: Oxford University Press.

Nind, Scott. 1831. "Description of the natives of King George's Sound (Swan River Colony) and adjoining country." *Royal Geographical Society Journal* 1: 21–51.

Ogden, Schubert M. 1981. "The concept of a theology of liberation: Must a Christian theology be so conceived?" In B. Mahan and L. D. Richesin (editors), *The Challenge of Liberation Theology:* 127–140. Maryknoll, NY: Orbis Books.

Olshansky, S. Jay, Mark A. Rudberg, Bruce A. Carnes, Christine K. Cassel, and Jacob A. Brody. 1991. "Trading off longer life for worsening health." *Journal of Aging and Health,* 3 (2): 194–216.

Onwuejeugwu, M. Angulu. 1975. *The Social Anthropology of Africa.* London: Heinemann Educational Books.

Ortiz de Montellano, Bernard R. 1990. *Aztec Medicine, Health, and Nutrition.* New Brunswick: Rutgers University Press.

Paige, J. 1975. *Agrarian Revolution: Social Movements and Export Agriculture in the Underdeveloped World.* London: The Free Press.

Panos Institute 1992. *The Hidden Cost of AIDS: The Challenge of HIV to Development.* London: The Panos Institute.

Panyacheewin, Saowarup. 1990. "Phi Tong Luang: A culture for sale." *Bangkok Post,* 2 August: 31,33.

Parkin, David, and David Nyamwaya, editors. 1988. *Transformation of African Marriage.* Manchester: Manchester University Press.

Patterson, F., and E. Linden. 1981. *The Education of Koko.* New York: Holt, Rinehart and Winston.

Pettengill, John S. 1981. "Firearms and the distribution of income: a neoclassical model." *The Review of Radical Political Economy* 13 (2): 1–10.

Phillips, Herbert P. 1992. *The Integrative Art of Modern Thailand.* Berkeley: Lowie Museum of Anthropology, University of California at Berkeley.

Phongpaichit, P. 1982. *From Peasant Girls to Bangkok Masseusses.* Geneva: International Labour Office.

Pigafetta, Antonio. 1524/1969. *First Voyage Around the World.* Translated by J. A. Robertson. Manila: Filipina Book Guild.

Pookajorn, Surin, ed. 1992. *The Phi Tong Luang (Mlabri): A Hunter-Gatherer Group in Thailand.* Bangkok: Odeon Store.

Poshyananda, Apinan. 1992. *Modern Art in Thailand: Nineteenth and Twentieth Centuries.* Singapore: Oxford University Press.

Pospisil, Leopold. 1958. *Kapauku Papuans and Their Law.* New Haven, CT: Yale University, Publications in Anthropology No. 54.

Potter, Sulamith H. 1980. *Family Life in a Northern Thai Village: A Study of the Structural Significance of Women.* Berkeley: University of California Press.

Premack, D., and A. J. Premack. 1983. *The Mind of an Ape.* New York: W. W. Norton.

Price, Sally. 1989. *Primitive Art in Civilized Places* Chicago: University of Chicago Press.

Prieto, Abel. 1981. "Cuba's national literacy campaign." *Journal of Reading* 25 (3): 215–221.

Rambo, A. Terry. 1985. *Primitive Polluters: Semang Impact on the Malaysian Tropical Ecosystem.* Ann Arbor: University of Michigan.

Rane, Wishwas. 1990. "Dangerous antidiarrhoeals." *Economic and Political Weekly* 1–8 December: 2649.

Rao, Nitya. 1993. "Total literacy campaigns: A field report." *Economic and Political Weekly,* 8 May:914–918.

Rappaport, Roy. 1967. "Ritual regulation of environmental relations among New Guinea people." *Ethnology* 6: 17–30.

Reaves, Dick. 1978. "Never love a Bandido." *Texas Monthly,* May: 100–107, 208–219.

Redfield, Robert. 1952. "The primitive world view." *Proceedings of the American Philosophical Society* 96: 30–36.

Rees, Judith. 1990. *Natural Resources: Allocation, Economics and Policy.* New York: Routledge.

Reichel-Dolmatoff, Gerardo. 1971. *Amazonian Cosmos: The Sexual and Religious Symbolism of the Tukano Indians.* Chicago: University of Chicago Press.

Reid, Anthony. 1988. *Southeast Asia in the Age of Commerce 1450–1680: Volume One, The Lands Below the Winds.* New Haven: Yale University Press.

Ribeiro, Darcy. 1970. *Os Índiosea Civilização.* Rio de Janeiro: Editora Civilização Brasileira.

Riesman, David. 1953. *The Lonely Crowd: A Study of the American Character.* Garden City, NY: Doubleday.

Ritchie, Jane. 1989. "Dying marks of beauty." *New Sunday Times* (Malaysia), 28 May: 22.

Rosengren, Dan 1987. "Hunting and gender complementarity among the Maksigenka of Southeastern Peru." In *Annual Report for 1985/86:* 25–34. Goteborg: Etnografiska Museum.

Rubin, William. 1984a. "Modernist primitivism: An introduction." In W. Rubin (editor) *"Primitivism" in 20th Century Art,* vol. I: 1–81. New York: The Museum of Modern Art.

———. "Picasso." *Ibid.*

Rudé, George. 1980. *Ideology and Popular Protest.* New York: Pantheon.

Ruhlen, Merritt. 1987. *A Guide to the World's Languages.* Stanford: Stanford University Press.

Saberwal, Satish. 1991. "Segmentation and literacy." *Economic and Political Weekly, Annual Number,* March: 723–738.

Sackett, Lee. 1978. "Clinging to the law: Leadership at Wiluna." In M. C. Howard (editor), *Whitefella Business*: 37–48. Philadelphia: Institute for the Study of Human Issues.

Sahlins, Marshall. 1965. "On the sociology of primitive exchange." In M. Banton (editor), *The Relevance of Models for Social Anthropology:* 139–236. London: Tavistock.

Saltman, Michael. 1991. *The Demise of the "Reasonable Man": A Cross-Cultural Study of a Legal Concept.* New Brunswick: Transaction Publishers.

Sanchez Vazquez, Adolfo. 1973. *Art and Society.* New York: Monthly Review Press.

Sanday, P. R. 1974. "Female status in the public domain." In M. Z. Rosaldo and L. Lamphere, (editors), *Women, Culture, and Society:* 189–206. Stanford, CA: Stanford University Press.

Sanggenafa, Naffi. 1990. "Kain Timur and the payment of fines: A preliminary study of the Karondori people of Irian Jaya's Bird's Head region." *Irian: Bulletin of Irian Jaya* 18: 93–101.

Santasombat, Yos. 1992. *Mae Ying Si Khaai Tue (Woman Sell Yourself): The Community and Commercial Sex in Thai Society.* Bangkok: Institute of Local Community Development.

Sapir, Edward. 1929. "The status of linguistics as a science." *Language* 5: 207–214.

Satyarthi, Kailash. 1993. "Indian Crusader Seeks to Halt Child Slavery." *Far Eastern Economic Review,* 8 July: 62.

Schneeberger, W.F. 1979. "Contributions to the ethnology of central northeast Borneo (Parts of Kalimantan, Sarawak and Sabah)." *Studia Ethnologica Berensia* 2. Berne: Institute of Ethnology, University of Berne.

Schneider, Jane. 1971. "Of vigilance and virgins: honor, shame, and access to resources in Mediterranean societies." *Ethnology* 10: 1–24.

Schultes, Richard E. 1963. "Botanical sources of the New World narcotics." *Psychedelic Review* 1: 145–166.

Schultes, Richard E., and A. Hoffmann. 1979. *Plants of the Gods.* New York: McGraw-Hill.

Scott, James. 1976. *The Moral Economy of the Peasant: Rebellion and Subsistence in Southeast Asia.* New Haven: Yale University Press.

Serageldin, Ismail. 1993. "Making development sustainable." *Finance & Development,* December 6–10.

Shankman, Paul. 1983. "Fear and loathing in Samoa." *The Global Reporter* 1 (2): 12.

———. 1991. "Culture contact, cultural ecology, and Dani warfare." *Man* (N.S.) 26: 602–624.

Shannon, Thomas R. 1989. *An Introduction to the World-System Perspective.* Boulder, CO: Westview Press.

Shapiro, Judith. 1968. "Tapirapé kinship." *Boletim do Museu Paraense Emilio Geoldi, Antropologia* 37.

Siegel, Jacob S., and Cynthia M. Taeuber. 1986. "Demographic dimensions of an aging population." In Alan Pifer and Lydia Bronte (editors), *Our Aging Society: Paradox and Promise:* 79–110. New York/London: W. W. Norton and Company.

Silk, Steve. 1993. "Marketing culture: Close encounters of the artificial kind." *Vancouver Sun,* 9 October: C6.

Silverman, Milton, P. R. Lee, and M. Lydecker. 1982. *Prescriptions for Death: The Drugging of the Third World.* Berkeley: University of California Press.

Sinha, D. P. 1972. "The Bihors." In M. G. Bicchieri (editor), *Hunters and Gatherers Today:* 371–403. New York: Holt, Rinehart and Winston.

Siverts, Hennig. 1971. "On politics and leadership in highland Chiapas." In E. Z. Vogt and A. Ruz L. (editors), *Desarrollo Cultural de los Mayas:* 387–408. Mexico: Universidad Nacional Autonoma de Mexico.

Skinner, Willian G. 1975. *Change and Persistence in Thai Society.* Ithaca, NY: Cornell University Press.

Smith, Anthony. 1980. *The Geopolitics of Information: How Western Culture Dominates the World.* London: Faber.

Smith, M. G. 1960. *Government in Zazzau, 1881–1950.* London: Oxford University Press.

Sorensen, Arthur P. 1973. "South American Indian linguistics at the turn of the seventies." In D. R. Gross (editor), *Peoples and Cultures of Native South America:* 312–341. Garden City, NY: Doubleday.

Spencer, Baldwin, and F. J. Gillen. 1899. *The Native Tribes of Central Australia.* London: Macmillan.

Spencer, Robert F. 1959. *The North Alaskan Eskimo: A Study in Ecology and Society.* Bulletin 171. Washington, DC: Bureau of American Ethnology.

Spores, John C. 1988. *Running Amok: An Historical Inquiry.* Athens, OH: Center for International Studies, Ohio University.

Spradley, James P. 1970. *You Owe Yourself a Drunk: An Ethnography of Urban Nomads.* Boston: Little, Brown.

Steadman, L. B., and C. F. Merbs. 1982. "Kuru cannibalism." *American Anthropologist* 84 (3): 611–627.

Steward, Julian H. 1938. *Basin-Plateau Aboriginal Sociopolitical Groups.*

———. 1955. *Theory of Culture Change: The Methodology of Multilinear Evolution.* Urbana: University of Illinois Press.

———, et al. 1956. *The People of Puerto Rico.* Urbana: University of Illinois Press.

Stokes, William. 1952. "Violence as a power factor in Latin American politics. *Western Political Quarterly* 5 (3): 445–468.

Stoll, David. 1982. *Fishers of Men or Founders of Empire?* London: Zed Press.

———. 1990. *Is Latin America Turning Protestant?: The Politics of Evangelical Growth.* Berkeley: University of California Press.

Swadesh, Morris. 1971. *The Origin and Diversification of Language.* Chicago: Aldine/Atherton.

Tanner, D. 1990. *You Just Don't Understand: Women and Men in Conversation.* New York: Wm. Morrow.

Tasker, Rodney, Michael Vatikiotis, and Robert Delfs. 1993. "Asian royalty: Thrones that count." *Far Eastern Economic Review,* 29 April: 16–18.

Tasker, Rodney. 1988. "Manila's bitter pill." *Far Eastern Economic Review,* 8 December: 54–56.

Taylor, J.L. 1993. *Forest Monks and the Nation-State: An Anthropological and Historical Study in Northeastern Thailand.* Singapore: Institute of Southeast Asian Studies.

Taylor, John C. 1977. "Diet, health and economy: Some consequences of planned social change in an Aboriginal community." In R. M. Berndt (editor), *Aborigines and Change:* 147–158. Canberra: Australian Institute of Aboriginal Studies.

Tenney, Jack B. (chairman). 1943. *Report: Joint Fact-finding Committee on Un-American Activities in California.* California Legislature, Senate 55th Session. Sacramento: California State Printing Office.

Thaitawat, Nusera. 1990. "Spirits from a different world." *Bangkok Post,* 19 April:27–28.

Thayer, Nate. 1993. "The grand illusion." *Far Eastern Economic Review,* 25 February:12.

Thesiger, Wilfred. 1985. *Arabian Sands.* New York: Penguin.

Thomason, Sarah Grey, and Terrence Kaufman. 1988. *Language, Contact, Creolization, and Genetic Linguistics.* Berkeley: University of California Press.

Thompson, J. E. S. 1930. *Ethnology of the Mayas of Southern and Central British Honduras.* Publication 274. Chicago: Field Museum of Natural History.

———. 1970. *Maya History and Religion.* Norman: University of Oklahoma Press.

Tiesler, Frank. 1969–70. Die intertribale Beziehungen an der Nordküste Neiguineas im Gebiet du Klainen Schouten-Inseln. *Abhandlungen und Berichte des Staatlichen Museums fur Volkerkunde* (Dresden) 30 (1), 31(2). Berlin: Akadamie Verlag.

Toland, Judith Drick. 1987. "Discrepancies and dissolution: breakdown of the early Inca state." In H. J. M. Claessen and P. van de Velde (editors), *Early State Dynamics:* 1–23. Leiden: E. J. Brill.

Tonkinson, Robert. 1974. *The Jigalong Mob: Aboriginal Victors of the Desert Crusade.* Menlo Park, CA: Cummings.

———. 1978. *The Mardudjara Aborigines: Living the Dream in Australia's Desert.* New York: Holt, Rinehart and Winston.

Tout, Ken. 1989. *Aging in Developing Countries.* Oxford: Oxford University Press, for Helpage International.

Tozzer, Alfred M. 1907. *A Comparative Study of the Mayas and Lacandones.* New York: Macmillan.

Trezise, P.J. 1971. *Rock Art of South-east Cape York.* Canberra: Australian Institute of Aboriginal Studies.

Turton, David. 1980. "The economics of Mursi bridewealth: A comparative perspective." In J. Comaroff (editor), *The Meaning of Marriage Payments.* New York: Academic Press.

Tylor, Edward B. 1891. *Primitive Culture.* 2 volumes. London: John Murray.

Ucko, Peter J. (editor) 1977. *Form in Indigenous Art.* Canberra: Australian Institute of Aboriginal Studies.

UNESCO. 1957. *World Illiteracy at Mid-Century.* Paris: UNESCO.

United Nations Department of Social and Economic Development. 1993. *World Investment*

Report 1993: Transnational Corporations and Integrated International Production. New York: United Nations Publications.

United Nations Development Programme. 1992. *Economic Impact of AIDS in Asia.* New York: United Nations Publications.

Valdman, Albert. 1975. "The language situation in Haiti." In V. Rubn and R. P. Schaedel (editors), *The Haitian Potential:* 61–82. New York: Teachers College Press.

Van Gennep, Arnold. 1960. *The Rites of Passage.* Chicago: University of Chicago Press.

Van Landingham, Mark J., Somboon Suprasert, Werasit Sittitrai, Chayan Vaddhanaphuti, Nancy Grandjean. 1993. "Sexual activity among never-married men in Northern Thailand." *Demography* 30 (3):297–313.

Vance, C.S. 1991. "Anthropology rediscovers sexuality: A theoretical comment." *Social Science and Medicine.* 33:8, 875–84.

Varnedoe, Kirk. 1984. "Gauguin." In W. Rubin (editor), *"Primitivism" in 20th Century Art:* vol. I, 179–209. New York: The Museum of Modern Art.

Vatikiotis, Michael. 1991. "A question of priorities." *Far Eastern Economic Review,* 12 December:28, 30.

Vecsey, Christopher, and Robert W. Venables, editors. 1980. *American Indian Environments: Ecological Issues in Native American History.* Syracuse, NY: Syracuse University Press.

Vivelo, Frank R. 1978. *Cultural Anthropology Handbook.* New York: McGraw-Hill.

Voegelin, Charles F., and F. M. Voegelin. 1977. *Classification and Index of the World's Languages.* New York: Elsevier.

Vogt, Evon Z. 1970. *The Zinacantecos of Mexico: A Modern Maya Way of Life.* New York: Holt, Rinehart and Winston.

Wagley, Charles. 1977. *Welcome of Tears: The Tapirapé Indians of Central Brazil.* New York: Oxford University Press.

Wagstyl, Stephan. 1992. "The child victims of India's slave trade." *Financial Times,* 19–20 December: Weekend FT I.

Wakin, Eric. 1992. *Anthropology Goes to War: Professional Ethics and Counter Insurgency in Thailand.* Madison: Center for Southeast Asian Studies, University of Wisconsin–Madison.

Walker, Anthony R. 1986. *The Toda of South India: A New Look.* Delhi: Hindustan Publishing Corporation.

Walker, Rangiuni. 1989. "Colonisation and development of the Maori people." In M. C. Howard (editor), *Ethnicity and Nation-building in the Pacific:* 152–168. Tokyo: United Nations University.

Wallace, Anthony F. C. 1966. *Religion: An Anthropological View.* New York: Random House.

———. 1970. *Culture and Personality.* New York: Random House.

———. 1972. "Mental illness, biology and culture." In F. L. K. Hsu (editor), *Psychological Anthropology:* 362–402. Cambridge, MA: Schenkman.

Wallerstein, Immanuel. 1979. *The Capitalist World-Economy.* New York: Cambridge University Press.

Walton, J. 1984. *Reluctant Rebels: Comparative Studies of Revolution and Underdevelopment.* New York: Columbia University Press.

Wasson, R. Gordon. 1972. "The divine mushroom of immortality." In P. T. Furst (editor), *Flesh of the Gods:* 185–200. London: George Allen & Unwin.

Watanabe, Teresa. 1992. "A nation of lost childhood." *Vancouver Sun,* 19 September: A14.

Watson, Rubie S. 1985. *Inequality Among Brothers: Class and Kinship in South China.* New York: Cambridge University Press.

Weeks, Jeffrey. 1977. *Coming Out: Homosexual Politics in Britain from the 19th Century to the Present.* London: Quartet Books.

Weil, Peter. 1980. "Mandinko adaptation to colonial rule in the Gambia." *Cultures et Développement* 12 (2): 295–318.

Weiss, Anita. 1988. *Islamic Reassertion in Pakistan.* Syracuse: University of Syracuse Press.

Werner, Dennis. 1979. "A cross-cultural perspective on theory and research on male homosexuality." *Journal of Homosexuality* 4: 345–62.

Wessman, James W. 1981. *Anthropology and Marxism.* Cambridge, MA: Schenkman.

Westlake, Melvyn. 1990. "Money can't buy you wealth." *South* 116: 18–19.

Weston, Kath. 1991. *Families We Choose: Lesbians, Gays, Kinship.* New York: Columbia University Press.

White, Leslie. 1949. *The Science of Culture.* New York: Grove Press.

———. 1959. *Evolution of Culture.* New York: McGraw-Hill.

White, Lynn, Jr. 1967. "The historical roots of our ecologic crisis." *Science.* 10 March: 1203–06.

Wienpahl, Jan. 1984. "Women's roles in livestock production among the Turkana of Kenya." In B. Isaac (editor), *Research in Economic Anthropology.* Greenwich, CT: JAI Press.

Wilkinson, Julia. 1993. "English Street." *Discovery,* July: 48, 50–51.

Williams, Glyn. 1979. "Welsh settlers and native Americans in Patagonia." *Journal of Latin American Studies* 11: 41–66.

Williams, Harvey. 1984. "An uncertain prognosis: some factors that may limit future progress in the Nicaraguan health care system." *Medical Anthropology Quarterly* 15 (3): 72–73.

Williams, Thomas. 1858. *Fiji and the Fijians.* London: A. Heylin.

Williams. Walter L. 1986. *The Spirit and the Flesh: Sexual Diversity in American Indian Culture.* Boston: Beacon Press.

Wilson, Monica. 1963. *Good Company: A Study of Nyakyusa Age-villages.* Boston: Beacon Press.

Wolf, Eric. 1968. *Peasant Wars of the Twentieth Century:* New York. Harper and Row.

———. 1971. *Peasant wars of the Twentieth Century,* London: Faber and Faber.

Wolf, Eric R., and Edward C. Hansen. 1972. *The Human Condition in Latin America.* New York: Oxford University Press.

World Bank. 1993. *The 1993 World Development Report: Investing in Health.* Washington, DC: The World Bank.

Worsley, Peter. 1982. "Non-Western medical systems." *Annual Review of Anthropology* 11: 315–348.

Wright, B.J. 1968. *Rock Art of the Pilbara Region, North-west Australia.* Canberra: Australian Institute of Aboriginal Studies.

Yoffee, Norman, and George L. Cowgill (editors). 1988. *The Collapse of Ancient States and Civilizations.* Tucson: University of Arizona Press.

Young, John. 1994. "Peasants and revolution in Ethiopia: Tigray 1975–1989." Ph.D. dissertation, Simon Fraser University.

Young, M. W. 1971. *Fighting with Food: Leadership, Values and Social Control in a Massim Society.* New York: Cambridge University Press.

———, and E.S. Phillips (editors.) 1973. *The Australian Aboriginal Heritage: An Introduction Through the Arts.* Sydney: Ure Smith.

———. 1963. *Kapauku Papuan Economy.* New Haven: Yale University, Publications in Anthropology No. 67.

———. 1973. "Bark painting." In R.M. Berndt and E.S. Phillips (editors), *The Australian Aboriginal Heritage:* 201–224. Sydney: Ure Smith.

———. 1984b. "Picasso." In W. Rubin (editor) *"Primitivism" in 20th Century Art:* vol. I: 241–343. New York: The Museum of Modern Art.

CREDITS

Color Essay Photo Credits:

1 Naffi Sanggenafa
2 (all) Dr. Michael Howard
3 (all) Dr. Michael Howard
4 (top) Dr. Michael Howard
4 (bottom) John Moore
5 (top) Dr. Michael Howard
5 (bottom) John Moore
6 (all) Dr. Michael Howard
7 (top) Dr. Michael Howard
7 (bottom) P. T. Freeport Indonesia
8 Naffi Sanggenafa

Interior Photo Credits:

Page **2** Loren McIntyre
Page **5** George Steinmetz
Page **7 (left)** Jason Laure; **(right)** Charles Caratin/Sygma
Page **9** Wolfgang Kaehler
Page **11** Des Bartlett/Photo Researchers
Page **12** Drs. Cynthia Beall and Melvyn Goldstein
Page **13** William Franklin McMahon
Page **15 (all)** Dr. Homa Hoodfar
Page **16** Leon Kai-Tai/Woodfin Camp & Associates
Page **20** Anthro-Photo
Page **23** Crawford/Anthro-Photo
Page **25** Dr. Hans Dagmar
Page **29** Anthro-Photo
Page **30** Dr. Michael Howard
Page **34** Anthro-Photo
Page **37** Dr. Michael Howard
Page **42** Marsha Cooper/Peter Arnold, Inc.
Page **45 (top)** Focus On Sports; **(bottom)** Dr. Carol Berman
Page **47 (left)** Jerry Jacka Photography; **(right)** Jean-Claude LeJeune
Page **50** Jerry Cooke/Photo Researchers
Page **55** Leonard McCombe
Page **61** Dr. Joan Gross
Page **68** J.Barker
Page **73** Henning Christopher/Foto Archiv/Black Star
Page **78** Charisse/Gamma-Liaison
Page **82** Anthro-Photo
Page **86** Helene Tremblay/Peter Arnold, Inc.
Page **88** Milt & Joan Mann/Cameramann International, Ltd.
Page **92** Dr. Cynthia Beall and Dr. Melvyn Goldstein
Page **95 (left)** Alan Berner/Seattle Times; **(right)** Milt & Joan Mann/Cameramann International, Ltd.
Page **96** Hiroji Kubota/Magnum Photos
Page **97** Arvind Garg/Gamma-Liaison
Page **102** Sebastiao Salgado/Magnum Photos\
Page **104** Victor Englebert/Photo Researchers
Page **106** William Franklin McMahon
Page **107** Bob Daemmrich

Page **110** **(left)** Stuart Franklin/Magnum Photos; **(right)** Don Smetzer/Tony Stone Images
Page **112** Frans Lanting/Minden Pictures
Page **113** Irven DeVore/Anthro-Photo
Page **117** **(all)** Dr. Sandra Niessen
Page **119** Popperfoto
Page **124** Henry H.Bagish/Anthro-Photo
Page **126** Anthro-Photo
Page **128** Culver Pictures
Page **131** Dr. Diane Wilhelm
Page **134** F.Paolini/Sygma
Page **135** **(left)** Mike Greenlar/The Image Works; **(right)** Loren McIntyre
Page **137** (top) University of Oklahoma; **(bottom)** AP/Wide World
Page **140** Bob Daemmrich
Page **142** Karen Wollins
Page **144** Wolfgang Kaehler
Page **150** **(left)** Peter Arnold/Peter Arnold, Inc.; **(right)** Claude Poulet/Gamma-Liaison
Page **151** Miguel Luis Fairbanks
Page **155** Robert Frerck/Odyssey Productions, Chicago
Page **156** Fredrik Bodin/Stock Boston
Page **159** Dr. James Loucky
Page **162** Alberto Venzago/Magnum Photos
Page **166** Koons/Anthro-Photo
Page **177** Dr. Philip Herbst
Page **179** Courtesy Royal British Columbia Provincial Museum, Victoria, B.C.
Page **181** Dr. Michael Howard
Page **183** Arvind Garg/Photo Researchers
Page **185** David Mardires
Page **190** Gamma-Liaison
Page **193** **(left)** Abbas/Magnum Photos **(right)** Mark Sadan
Page **195** James Schnepf/Gamma-Liaison
Page **199** Loren McIntyre
Page **206** Hulton Deutsch Collection Ltd.
Page **211** Anthro-Photo
Page **215** Dr. Miriam Sharma
Page **218** Dr. J.F.E.Bloss/Anthro-Photo
Page **220** Susan Bolyard Millar
Page **222** Tim Lamon/Anthro-Photo
Page **226** The Kobal Collection
Page **234** Les Stone/Sygma
Page **237** AP/Wide World
Page **238** Jon Jones/Sygma
Page **241** AP/Wide World
Page **247** Arthur Tress
Page **249** Dr. Mark Moberg
Page **251** Dr. Michael Howard
Page **252** George Bellrose/Stock Boston
Page **255** Bettmann Archive
Page **258** AP/Wide World
Page **260** SOVFOTO
Page **264** AP/Wide World
Page **266** Talal Asad from The KABABISH ARABS
Page **268** Jon Levy/Gamma-Liaison
Page **269** Anthro-Photo
Page **271** (top) Anthro-Photo; **(bottom)** Robert F. Kusel/Sygma
Page **275** Jack Weatherford
Page **279** Carolyn Redenius/Monkmeyer Press Photo Service
Page **281** Natl.Institute of Anthropology and History, Mexico
Page **284** AP/Wide World
Page **286** UPI/Bettmann

Page **287** Olivier Douvry/Sygma
Page **288** Tim Graham/Sygma
Page **293** Susan Meiselas/Magnum Photos
Page **298** AP/Wide World
Page **300** Annette Kentie
Page **302** J.Langevin/Sygma
Page **304** Wolfgang Kaehler
Page **306** Peter Simon/Peter Arnold, Inc.
Page **308** Cliche des Musees Nationaux, Paris
Page **311** Bernard Pierre Wolfe/Magnum Photos
Page **313** John Running
Page **315** Jehangir Gazdar/Woodfin Camp & Associates
Page **317** McConnell/Bruce Coleman Inc.
Page **319** Margarita Melville, University of Houston
Page **323** Dr. John Barker
Page **326** Muller/Woodfin Camp & Associates
Page **327** Mohsen Shandiz/Sygma
Page **334** David Austen
Page **337** Neg.39686, Courtesy Department of Library Services/American Museum of Natural History
Page **338** Dr. Michael Howard
Page **339** Dr. Michael Howard
Page **340** **(left)** Robert Frerck/Odyssey Productions, Chicago; **(right)** Dr. Michael Howard
Page **342** Dr. Michael Howard
Page **343** Dr. Michael Howard
Page **346** Musee Picasso, Paris, Reunion des Musees Nationaux/Spadem
Page **348** David Neel/Tony Stone Images
Page **349** Dr. Michael Howard
Page **352** Dr. Michael Howard
Page **355** Dr. Michael Howard
Page **358** FPG
Page **361** Robert M. Glasse
Page **362** Biblioteca Medices Laurenziana, Florence, Italy
Page **363** Betty Press/Woodfin Camp & Associates
Page **367** Dr.Otome Klein Hutheesing
Page **369** James Nachtwey/Magnum Photos
Page **371** Helene Tremblay/Peter Arnold, Inc.
Page **375** Robert Tonkinson, University of Western Australia
Page **380** (top) Jim Anderson/Woodfin Camp & Associates; **(bottom)** Cordelia Dilg
Page **384** Frans Lanting/Minden Pictures
Page **387** Herve Collart-Odinetz/Sygma
Page **389** Bibliotheque Royale, Denmark
Page **391** Jean Gaumy/Magnum Photos
Page **392** Martin Rogers/Tony Stone Images
Page **395** J.L.Atlan/Sygma
Page **396** Dr. Michael Howard
Page **397** Dr. Michael Howard
Page **402** FAO/Courtesy The United Nations
Page **406** (top) Candy Hernandez/SIPA-Press; **(bottom)** Haruhart Prapanya/Gamma-Liaison
Page **409** Dr. Scott Robinson
Page **421** Yale University Library
Page **425** Institute for Intercultural Studies, Inc.